D0153884

Sophocles: Plays
Antigone

TEXAS WOMAN'S UNIVERSITY LIBRARY
BOX 425528
DENTON, TEXAS 76204-5528

R.C. Jebb

SOPHOCLES: PLAYS

Antigone

General editor
P.E. Easterling

Introduction
Ruby Blondell

Bristol Classical Press

This edition first published in 2004 by
Bristol Classical Press
an imprint of
Gerald Duckworth & Co. Ltd.
90-93 Cowcross Street, London EC1M 6BF
Tel: 020 7490 7300
Fax: 020 7490 0080
inquiries@duckworth-publishers.co.uk
www.ducknet.co.uk

General Preface, General Introduction © 2004 by P.E. Easterling
Antigone Introduction © 2004 by Ruby Blondell

The main text is a facsimile reprint of Jebb's 1900 edition of
Antigone, originally published by Cambridge University Press

All rights reserved. No part of this publication
may be reproduced, stored in a retrieval system, or
transmitted, in any form or by any means, electronic,
mechanical, photocopying, recording or otherwise,
without the prior permission of the publisher.

A catalogue record for this book is available
from the British Library

ISBN 1 85399 647 5

Printed and bound in Great Britain by
Biddles Ltd, *www.biddles.co.uk*

Preface

P.E. Easterling

The timing of these new editions of Richard Jebb's commentaries on the tragedies of Sophocles is not accidental. The commentaries have never ceased to be used and quoted as if they were contemporary works, but as library copies have become more fragile and second-hand texts ever scarcer, there has been a widely felt need for a new edition of the whole set. Contemporary interest in Jebb's wider output is reflected, too, in the recent publication of his *Collected Works*, edited in nine volumes by Robert B. Todd (Thoemmes Press, Bristol, 2002).

John Betts was responsible for the idea of re-publishing the Sophocles commentaries, with a general introduction on Jebb himself and separate introductions for each play by different scholars, designed to place Jebb's work in its original context and to look at the plays from the vantage point of Greek studies in the early twenty-first century. This initiative was later followed up by Deborah Blake, and the project has owed a great deal to them both for their skilful editorial guidance. For me personally it has been an exciting way to get closer both to Jebb and to Sophocles, and I am grateful to the contributors for their comments and suggestions and their willingness to share ideas. We have aimed at achieving a broad 'series style', but the introductions, as we expected, are quite varied in their approach both to the plays themselves and to what can be learned from Jebb's work. For help of various kinds in relation to the General Introduction I am grateful to John Easterling, Neil Hopkinson, Ted Kenney, Chris Stray and Bob Todd.

General Introduction

P.E. Easterling

Richard Jebb's commentaries on Sophocles are unique: a series of editions of one of the most intensely studied of all ancient poets, which have never fallen out of regular use since they were first produced (1883-96). No one studying Sophocles and making any serious engagement with the original Greek can afford to neglect them; they are still quoted as often and with as much sense of their current relevance as any modern edition, and 'dated and flawed as in some respects they may be, [they] remain the yardstick by which all subsequent ones are measured' (Dawe 1990: 241).[1] The main point of re-issuing these nineteenth-century commentaries is to contribute to contemporary critical discussion of Sophocles by making them once more available in their original form, but with new introductions which sketch the main lines of later interpretation; the project has a degree of historical interest, too, and in what follows I try to set Jebb's Sophocles in context, starting with some biographical notes and going on to consider what he did that was new and different, or what it was that gave his commentaries their remarkable capacity to go on being useful.

When Richard Claverhouse Jebb died in 1905 at the age of sixty-four, he was the most distinguished British hellenist of his time, well known abroad as well as in Britain. He was also a considerable public figure: he had been MP for the University of Cambridge for fourteen years, was knighted in 1900, and made a member of the Order of Merit, the rarest award attainable in British public life, a few months before his death. His productive career can be divided into three phases: his years at Cambridge as a young Fellow of Trinity (1863-75, the last six of these as Public Orator), the period he spent at Glasgow as Professor of Greek (1875-89), and his tenure of the Regius Chair at Cambridge (1889-1905). He never, in fact, lost familiar contact with Cambridge and his old colleagues, as the Jebbs kept a house in Cambridge and spent the summer vacations there all through the Glasgow years. So the three periods were not sharply distinct in terms of intellectual contacts and influences, although his responsibilities differed a good deal in the three phases of his professional life.

Several threads run throughout his career and the different roles he played in the course of it.

The teacher

Jebb always showed the instincts of a teacher, and among his first publications were school and undergraduate texts: introductory commentaries on two plays of Sophocles, *Electra* in 1867 when he was 26, and *Ajax* the following year. George Eliot must have been referring to one of these when she told him in 1873 that she first came to know Sophocles through what Jebb describes as 'a small book of mine' (*LL* 155-6). The series in which they appeared, called Catena Classicorum, was an innovative response to educational change: public examinations for school pupils were a new phenomenon in the 1860s, opening up wider opportunities than the old system of competition for entrance scholarships to Oxbridge (Roach, 1971). In 1877 Jebb wrote a Macmillan Primer on Greek literature, another introductory book into which he put a great deal of effort: it sold well, and was translated into Italian and Dutch. Then there was the school text *Selections from the Attic Orators* (1880), a companion volume to his big book on the orators (1876),[2] designed, according to the Preface, to 'give in a compact form a series of the most characteristic and interesting passages ... with a commentary adapted to the requirements of students at the Universities or in the higher forms of Public Schools' (vii). Here too Jebb represents the new approach to classical teaching: the orators in his selection were not read in the normal school curriculum of the time.

Even when the series of full-scale commentaries on Sophocles was well launched he still took an interest in abridgements for schools, beginning in 1885 with a shortened *OT* commentary.[3] The most unusual of his student texts, published in 1879 specifically for the Middle Class in Greek at Glasgow – the modern equivalent would be a set of photocopied handouts – was Xenophon's *Anabasis* III, with the ancient Greek on the left-hand page and a modern Greek translation on the right; it was designed, Jebb explains, to 'help the student of Old Greek learn Modern Greek' and to give a sense of the continuity of the Greek language.[4] Interest in contemporary Greece and the modern language was a strong feature of Jebb's hellenism, and evidently it was something he wanted to share with his pupils. The last publication of his Glasgow years was another introductory book, *Homer: an Introduction to the Iliad and the Odyssey* (1887), praised by Walter Leaf in the first issue of the *Classical Review* (1888: 14-16) for its 'quiet and luminous criticism' as well as for Jebb's bold statements of position on contentious subjects, particularly on the 'Homeric Question'. This series of publications for the general reader and the student market clearly has to be taken seriously when we try to understand how Jebb defined his own role.

His widow, Caroline Jebb, records the systematic way in which he organised the large Glasgow Greek classes: 'Professor Jebb followed a method of his own invention as exact as book-keeping, by which he knew the number of each bench, the seat of every student, the number of times each had been examined and how often he was absent. These books are a marvel of neatness and detail. Without thorough method it would have been impossible to keep the class in order, and to make the students benefit by his teaching' (*LL* 203-4). The recollections of his old pupils on his lecturing style are not all equally positive – some evidently found him touchy and pernickety – but there is no doubt that he took the work very seriously and used his initiative in finding ways of tackling it.[5]

This thoroughness comes through in a publication of 1878, which Jebb shared with his old Cambridge colleagues Henry Jackson and W.E. Currey, though he seems to have been the one who did most of the work for it. This is *Translations*, a collection of 'fair copies' to help students prepare for examinations in translation from Greek and Latin into English, and in Greek and Latin prose and verse composition.

Nearly half are by Jebb, and his name appears first on the title page. The Preface fills in the background:

> Some years ago, when it was our duty as lecturers at Trinity College, Cambridge, to set passages from Greek and Latin authors to be translated at sight, we found it convenient to give to our pupils versions of the extracts selected. These versions had not been very long in private circulation before several schoolmasters urged us to publish some of them, telling us that specimens of a style that might be adopted in Examinations would be found useful in classical schools. It is hoped that this volume may in some measure supply what is wanted. Most of the translations which it contains have been actually used in the lecture-room; and in all we have had in view the needs of young students. We have therefore throughout studied accuracy and fidelity, rather than liveliness and effect.

As Public Orator, Jebb had of course been much concerned with composition at a high level of stylistic elegance (the Orator's task was to compose Latin speeches for honorary degree ceremonies in Cambridge and congratulatory addresses or poems for special occasions elsewhere), and throughout his life he continued to compose Greek and Latin verses, many of which were published (the first collection in 1873), but he never lost interest in the pedagogic side of this activity, and he never seems to have thought of it simply as a gentlemanly pastime. There is a revealing perspective on what composing and translating meant to him in the lecture 'On present tendencies in Classical studies'.[6] He begins with a review of the new 'scientific' trends in classical scholarship (which he finds exciting) and then insists on the importance of avoiding an over-technical kind of specialisation which neglects other kinds of skills:

> We gladly recognise that such specialists are doing invaluable service, in their several lines, to the cause of knowledge; but we may also wish that the desire to be scientific was more uniformly tempered by a regard for the nature of the materials with which all scholarship has to deal. Those materials are the creation of the human intellect, whether as seen in the evolution of language, or of literature, or of art. When principles, determined with a scientific precision, have assured the student of language that a kinship is *possible* between two words, one of the elements in the probability which he may have to consider is the precise *usage* of these

words, as attested by literature; and here it is no longer enough to be logically exact; it is necessary to possess also that delicate instinct for expression which is called the literary sense (555).

All this leads up to an elaborately argued plea for ever greater attention in school studies to the practice of Greek and Latin composition (especially verse) which he thought was in danger of being neglected – and he optimistically suggests that as the study of modern languages becomes more integrated in the curriculum the need for composition in the original will be more fully appreciated for the ancient languages, too. The important point, for Jebb, is the practice of *idiomatic* writing (his emphasis), which, for Greek and Latin, where there are no native speakers to consult, can only be approached through literature: 'it requires very careful study – study which tasks not only intellect, but feeling and taste – to seize that subtle reflection of a living personality which in language appears as idiom, and which can still be appre-hended, though sometimes but dimly, and with an inevitable element of uncertainty, in the literary records of the ancient world' (558).

This belief in the importance of studying literature is crucial in all Jebb's work, and his emphasis here on its educational role is of a piece with the methodology of his own scholarship. In the Prefatory Note to his life of Bentley (1882), for example, after giving a detailed list of published sources, he points out the new contributions this biography makes: he has been able to adduce new evidence from his research on the history of the University and of Trinity College in Bentley's time and from a fresh examination of the controversy on the letters of Phalaris, and above all his aim has been to make a new estimate of 'his work, the character of his powers, and his place in scholarship. Here the fundamental materials are Bentley's writings themselves. To these I have given a comparatively large share of the allotted space. My treatment of them has been independent of any predecessor' (vii).[7] The essential claim that Jebb is making, and it provides a significant clue to what he thought important, is that the critic's authority comes from his *ability to read and judge texts for himself*, a doctrine with strong ancient precedent which informs all his work. Perhaps this is why he admired Samuel Johnson; 'All Johnson's criticism', he wrote, has one great merit; it is thoroughly independent. It is also marked, almost everywhere, by strong good sense; and though good sense does not necessarily mean good taste, at any rate there can be no good taste without it' (*EA* 501).

The man of letters

Jebb's deeply held belief in the value of composition and translation seems to have responded to a need for creative expression which was closely bound up with his sense of himself as a man of letters. There was no affectation in this, and it was not untypical of people of his time and place, as the extracts from his diaries and letters reveal. He enjoyed getting to know Tennyson (whose son Hallam was at Trinity in the early 1870s), George Eliot and G.H. Lewes, Robert Browning, Leslie Stephen and other luminaries, and he wrote articles for literary reviews, as well as being a leader-writer for *The Times* for a period in the 1870s. It may be relevant that one of his academic role-models was the great translator Benjamin Jowett (1817-93; Regius Professor of Greek at Oxford and Master of Balliol). The Jebbs knew Jowett well, and went regularly to stay with him in Oxford; Caroline remarks that her husband cherished the memory of his friendship 'as among the best things it had been given to him to know' (*LL* 288). Jebb himself, commenting in a prize-giving address on what he saw as signs of the public's increasing sympathy for classical authors, singled out as a particularly influential factor 'good English translations, in the forefront of which stands that beautiful work ... through which Professor Jowett has made Plato an English classic' (*EA* 615). Jebb's own translations, of Sophocles most of all, evidently aimed in the same direction and (although they seem sometimes absurdly archaic now) won admiration for their stylishness. R.P.G. Williamson recalled the Greek Honours Class at Glasgow stamping their feet in approval (*LL* 191-2); another old pupil[8] is quoted as remarking that 'his renderings of Sophocles, which have since become known to all the world, came on us like a revelation', although their studied elegance could lead hostile (or envious) reviewers to accuse him of 'fine writing'. In paying serious attention to the prose translation of poetry he was reflecting a trend given impetus by Matthew Arnold and represented in his own time by the translations of the *Odyssey* by his friend Samuel Butcher and Andrew Lang (1879) and of the *Iliad* by Lang, Leaf and Myers (1882).[9]

It is typical of Jebb's whole approach that in explaining why he chose to publish his *Selections from the Attic Orators* he should have had in mind the general reader with an interest in English prose style as well as the schoolboy learning to construe the Greek. He quotes with approval (Preface, x) a remark by Henry Nettleship, Professor of Latin at Oxford, that the 'harmonies of prose-rhythm ... as first appreciated and elaborated by the Greeks, must live in the ears of men so long as they continue to speak or write prose with any sense of beauty. There is a more obvious affinity between Demosthenes and Burke than between Aeschylus and Goethe.' This comment is drawn from Nettleship's extraordinarily acute and robust review of *The Attic Orators from Antiphon to Isaeos*;[10] it is more relevant for an understanding of Jebb's originality than the review by J.P. Mahaffy, which accused Jebb of plagiarism and sparked off a furious dispute (Todd, 2002: xix n. 49 gives the references). 'Mr Jebb's aim', writes Nettleship, 'is to produce a book accessible to the general literary public as well as to students of Greek. His attitude is as much that of the modern literary critic as of the professional scholar. And his gifts are such as entirely to justify his adopting this point of view' (41). He praises Jebb's style, his translations ('often brilliant') and his detailed discussions of the selected orators; what he objects to (reasonably enough, to a modern reader) is the long and in parts obscure section in the Introduction in which Jebb discusses the true significance of the term 'sculpturesque' as applied to Greek literature and the orators in particular, enthusiastically defines what he means by 'plastic', and illustrates these ideas by means of a comparison of the three tragedians (from which Sophocles emerges victorious) and an elaboration of the essential differences between Greek and Roman oratory. The vocabulary that Jebb chooses, and his references to Pater and Hegel, make clear that he is applying the insights of aestheticism to his study of the orators, but Nettleship finds it irritatingly woolly: 'He would have been clearer and more coherent had he avoided a somewhat over-rigid application of the formulae of modern criticism. Epithets such as "Greek", "Roman", "modern", "plastic" are, if too hastily or too comprehensively applied, apt to cramp the freedom of criticism and divert the view of the critic from a historical to a formal view of art' (45-6). What Nettleship admires is the 'clearness and elegance with which he can treat the subject of Greek style when he allows himself to write without the trammels of formulae. His native feeling for the beauties of Greek literature is so keen that he never writes better than when he is following its unassisted light' (47). Perhaps Jebb took this criticism to heart; there is certainly less sign of the 'formulae' in the introductions to the Sophocles commentaries (more, perhaps, on *OT* than in later volumes), and with time he found his own voice more consistently.

A revealing feature of *The Attic Orators from Antiphon to Isaeos* is the Pindaric lyric printed as its epigraph, an elegant triad in Jebb's favourite manner. He was noted for his Pindaric odes, which included translations of a long poem, 'The Reign of Youth', by Rann Kennedy, the father of Jebb's predecessor in the Greek chair at Cambridge, and of Browning's 'Abt Vogler' (found more intelligible by some readers than Browning's original), and a composition celebrating the octocentenary of the University of Bologna,[11] but this was something particularly personal. Here is my attempt at a plain translation (in an inevitably 'somewhat antiquated prose', cf. n. 9 above):

As a man travelling abroad gazes at sculpted statues, the work of artists of the past, which through their silent forms convey the minds of the departed to those still living, and is not yet able to grasp what the life was like, and whence came the ideas, of those who had fashioned these things;

but he is charmed by looking at them, and in the end apprehends some all-governing beauty, and all day long he studies the radiant calm that rests on the godlike faces and the delicate strength of their well-proportioned limbs, and he cries out in joy, 'May the long years, O famous ones, never grow tired of honouring you!'

Even so, you speeches ever-remembered, from mouths delightful to Zeus, your power remains, a marvel for men from elsewhere, for us who did not see the flash of Apollo of the golden reins in old Hellas and could not proclaim that ours is the land of Athena. For you, I say, the sun has gone down, yet there is not darkness, but your graces shine forth in the bright light of the Evening Star.[12]

This poem is best read, perhaps, as a kind of parallel to the rather odd section in the Introduction that Nettleship singled out for criticism. Intense imaginative contact with the texts must have been important to Jebb; one way of articulating this was by means of currently influential critical terms of reference, and another was through poetic composition in the medium in which he felt at home. What he was still working out, though he was already well on the way to achieving it, was a more ambitious and less idiosyncratic overall approach, which would integrate his highly personal response with the latest findings of modern scholarship. It was his skill as a Greek lyricist in the manner of Pindar that drew Tennyson's attention: in the dedicatory verses to 'Demeter' he wrote of Jebb, 'Fair things are slow to fade away, / Bear witness you, that yesterday / From out the ghost of Pindar in you / Roll'd an Olympian ...'.[13]

The 'scientific' scholar

Jowett was not the only distinguished predecessor who could serve as a model for Jebb, and there was a side to his activities and aspirations that was quite un-Jowett-like, namely his serious and professional interest in what he called 'scientific' scholarship. He was keenly interested in all the new developments in nineteenth-century research that in any way related to the texts that were the *raison d'être* of his work. Archaeology and topography deeply absorbed him: he made his first visit to Greece in 1878 (and later used his observations to illustrate points in his commentaries), and went to see the Troad in 1882 after Schliemann's excavations had begun to generate controversy; Jebb at once engaged in the debate. The first article in the first issue of *The Journal of Hellenic Studies* (1880: 7-62) is a detailed account by Jebb of the French excavations at Delos, set in the context of a history of the island in antiquity. It begins with a vivid piece of topographical description and ends with a businesslike programme for the newly founded Society for the Promotion of Hellenic Studies, including the establishment of an English institute in Athens (see p. [18] below). One of his plans for the Society was that it should publish photographic reproductions of major manuscripts; he spent time in Florence collating the Laurentian MS of Sophocles and collaborated with Edward Maunde Thompson over the publication of a magnificent facsimile in 1885. His still useful contribution to the Introduction (pp. 12-23), and the detailed notes on L in the apparatus to each of his commentaries, show how thoroughly this work was done, and he was better equipped than many would have been to tackle the Bacchylides papyrus when it arrived at the British Museum in 1896.

The introductions to most of the plays reflect his interest in the evidence from ancient art, particularly vase-paintings:[14] there is a parallel here with the work of his slightly younger contemporary, friend and successor as Public Orator, John Sandys, whose commentary on Euripides' *Bacchae*, first published in 1880, and several times reprinted, presents itself as 'a kind of handbook to the criticism, interpretation and archaeological illustration of the play' (Preface, iii). Sandys draws particular attention to exciting new developments in the study of ancient art. At Cambridge, for example, 'Under the new scheme for the Classical Tripos, one of the special subjects in which students will be able henceforth to obtain distinction, after taking honours in pure scholarship, is Classical Archaeology, including ancient art and mythology, with certain prescribed portions of the wide province of topography and antiquities; and provision is already being made by Professorial and other teaching for the due instruction of students in that department' (v-vi). This was a thrilling departure; in Cambridge as elsewhere the excitement comes through in many different contexts, from the setting up of a cast-gallery to the staging of Greek plays, and Jebb, like Sandys, was eager to be involved.

The lecture 'On present tendencies in Classical studies' (1889) gives a little more of the context of 'scientific' scholarship, stressing the progress made in linguistics, palaeography, epigraphy and archaeology. Most of the work in these areas had of course been done by German scholars, and we need to remember how much of it was new at the time: Gardthausen's fundamental *Griechische Paläographie* had come out in 1879 and Meisterhans' *Grammatik der Attischen Inschriften* in 1885, too late for the first edition of Jebb's *OT* (as he notes in the preface to the second edition, 1887). Dörpfeld's work on the theatre of Dionysus at Athens (1884-8, not published until 1896) was still fresh news: 'For instance, quite lately an archaeological architect has affirmed, as the result of a close inspection, that the Dionysiac Theatre at Athens had no permanent stage before at least the second half of the fourth century BC, and that in the days of the great dramatists the actors stood on the same level with the chorus'.[15]

Closer to home, it may be that the strongest intellectual influence that Jebb absorbed from his seniors was from J.B. Lightfoot, who had been his Tutor at Trinity. Lightfoot had been Senior Classic at Cambridge in 1851 (as Jebb himself was in 1862), and he was giving college lectures from 1854, but by the time Jebb knew him he was already an established New Testament and patristic scholar, and after some years as a university theologian he reluctantly left Cambridge to become Bishop of Durham in 1879. The two were close friends (*LL* 119), and Lightfoot may well have represented for Jebb the ideal of enlightened modern scholarship. His commentaries on the Pauline Epistles became standard (one was reprinted as recently as 1997); Claude Jenkins in the *Dictionary of English Church History* (2nd edn. 1919) described him as 'bringing home to English students the fact that St Paul was not an imperfect writer of a debased form of Greek but a master of a living language'. Lightfoot was the first president of the Hellenic Society (presumably this was Jebb's idea), and he was the dedicatee of *The Attic Orators*. In the essay on present tendencies (*EA* 551) the only British scholars singled out by Jebb (for their chapter on 'Methods of Textual Criticism') are the New Testament scholars Westcott and Hort, with whom Lightfoot was closely associated; this 'scientific' strand in British scholarship may have been important in Jebb's intellectual formation and relevant to understanding his attitude to traditional and less ambitious ways of studying Classics.

Another focus of interest, not discussed in the lecture 'On present tendencies', but already a feature of Jebb's own work, was the history of scholarship and more broadly the Classical tradition: by this time he had published his short book on Bentley, and in 1890 he chose Erasmus for the subject of the Rede Lecture at Cambridge. Soon afterwards he was responsible for causing John Sandys to be invited to write a survey of the History of Scholarship for *Social England* (1896 and 1897), thus sowing the seed which grew into Sandys's monumental three-volume work, published in 1906-8. This self-consciousness about intellectual and literary history helps to explain his own sense of what he was doing when he aimed at integrating a very wide range of material in his large-scale commentaries.

The pioneer

It was natural, given his wide-ranging interests and sympathies, for Jebb to see the importance of creating modern, quasi-professional organisations and institutions. So he was one of the prime movers in establishing the Society for the Promotion of Hellenic Studies, which from the start was designed to have many links with the contemporary Greek world: the Greek chargé d'affaires in London, Joannes Gennadius, was a founder member. Others were the publisher George Macmillan, Charles Newton the archaeologist and Keeper of Greek and Roman Antiquities in the British Museum, and Sidney Colvin, the first Director of the Fitzwilliam Museum in Cambridge. Jebb also campaigned energetically for the founding of a school of archaeology in Athens as a means of facilitating research and for the establishment of cast collections in the UK (more detail in Beard, 1993), and we find him in at the beginning of the Cambridge Philological Society (for the discussion of philology in its broadest sense) and more ambitiously, on a national level, of the British Academy. The models for these institutions were largely German and French; Jebb's way of going about things was not in the least typical of the amateur English gentlemanly approach to the Classics. He found it exciting to discuss the old texts in new ways and situate them in new contexts; it is not surprising to see him and his friends on the first committee set up to manage the Cambridge Greek Play, and he was the one to provide the translation for the first acting edition (*Ajax*, 1882; more detail in Easterling, 1999).

This energetic interest in new developments is matched by his wider educational views – and by his willingness to work on behalf of what he saw as progressive movements, from his early days as a keen supporter of the higher education of women in Cambridge (in 1872 he gave lectures to 'a class of ladies' on Milton's *Areopagitica*) to his public role as spokesman on education: he was a member of royal commissions on secondary education and Irish universities, and put serious effort into promoting all forms of what would now be called 'access': his interest in the University Extension Scheme is a good example (*EA* 581-608). As MP for Cambridge University he sat as a member of the Unionist Party, but he was not a career politician and certainly not a reactionary: he seems to have seen himself as an educational reformer rather than a sustainer of privilege.

The private person

What sort of person, then, was Richard Jebb? A perfectionist, evidently: 'careful and finished to the smallest detail', Verrall's assessment of his commentary on *Oedipus Coloneus* (*CR* 1, 1887: 53-6), could be used to describe how he looked and behaved and presented himself to the world. He was particular about his appearance, easily offended by criticism, and easily mocked, but the private persona was different, and those close to him enjoyed his wit and even playfulness (Bobbitt, 1960: 103-6; Dawe, 1990). He came from an affectionate family and seems despite his reserve to have been eager for warm personal attachments. He had many close friendships, with a range of very different but creative people, from the shy and scholarly Lightfoot to the flamboyant Oscar Browning. Samuel Butcher, John Sandys, Sidney Colvin and Charles Newton the archaeologist, were all closely associated with Classical causes that meant much to him, and he was deeply attached to Henry Sidgwick, the philosopher and educational pioneer who represented late Victorian Cambridge at its most adventurous. He was also a clubman and in his younger days seems to have had a man-about-town image of himself.

His marriage was very important to him; after three years of dogged correspondence he managed, against strong competition, to persuade Caroline Slemmer to accept him. This extremely attractive American widow (there are many descriptions of her 'Titianesque' auburn hair, dark blue eyes and 'velvety' voice) had enraptured the bachelor dons when she visited Cambridge in 1871; and after she and Richard married in 1874 Caroline did a great deal for his confidence. She was tough and shrewd as well as decorative: she took over the practical management of his life, rescuing his chaotic financial affairs and working hard to stop him drinking too heavily.

The Jebbs lived in some style; they kept their fashionably furnished Cambridge house during the Glasgow years and spent a good deal of time in London when Richard was MP. By that time he must have seemed a natural member of the ranks of the Great and the Good, and even from his first year as an undergraduate had been marked out as a future member of the intellectual élite (F.W. Cornish in *LL* 20-1). But he was anxious about his social image; there are revealing passages in Caroline Jebb's frank correspondence with her sister, the main source of Mary Reed Bobbitt's biography of her (1960),[16] which fill some of the gaps left by the selective portrait she created in *Life and Letters*. A letter she wrote from Cambridge in 1874, a few months after their wedding, describes how 'Dick' hated her to do anything unrefined, using the sewing machine, for example.

> He was dreadfully shocked the other day when he found me sitting on the rug before the fire, eating a sweet biscuit for my luncheon and reading the newspaper. He said I seemed to have a natural taste for squalid things ... It amuses me, but I try to shock what he calls his refinement as little as possible ...
>
> His mother and his aunts told me that I must not pay any attention to his criticism, and that in time when he saw how well I got on with other people, he would give up his anxiety. A shy, self-conscious man cannot comprehend the ease and absence of terror another feels who is not self-conscious, and Dick is in consequence as much in terror for me as he used to be for himself.
>
> Mrs Adams says I have made a most favorable impression on everybody, and that, heaven save the mark, Dick is thought to be much improved in manner, because less shy, since his marriage. I told him this and was amused to see how wrathful it made him. We get on very well together, chiefly, I must say, because I have so little sensitive 'amour propre'; but then he has enough for both, and more would overwhelm the family (Bobbitt, 1960: 102).

Other letters give Caroline's analysis of the way her husband's upbringing had prepared him for a more lavish lifestyle than he could afford. His grandfather had been a distinguished judge in Dublin, and his great-uncle a bishop; his father was a barrister who thought himself a failure because he never became a judge, although the family lived elegantly, and his mother had 'her own maid to dress her, a pony carriage, and every comfort ... The consequence was that when Dick and [his sister] Eglantyne were young, they were wretched. They wanted to be richer, they wanted servants in livery, a pair of horses, a title, and everything that would make them of as much consequence as the people they associated with. Dick says these things used to make him very unhappy and envious, until he got some sense' (Bobbitt, 1960: 116-17, 164-5).

The marriage was childless; Caroline had had a son by her first husband, but he had died of diphtheria at the age of five; she had been told by her doctors that she was unable to have any more children (Bobbitt, 1960: 66). Whether Richard ever regretted the lack of children is not discoverable; there was no shortage of contact with his wife's Darwin great-nieces and nephew, who lived almost next door. The children's vantage point is recalled by Gwen Raverat (1952: 103): 'To our childish minds he was a figure of extreme unimportance, a sort of harmless waif, who was kindly allowed to live in a corner of the Library. ... He used to slip furtively in and out, and never recognised us when he met us. ... I suppose he was terrified of children'). He was more at ease with grown-up young relatives: his wife's niece Maud DuPuy found him 'bright and witty' in private, and his own niece Eglantyne (founder, in later life, of the Save the Children Fund) had a long stay with the Jebbs in Cambridge and got to know the countryside from cycling expeditions with him. Jebb was a keen tricyclist, gleefully remembered by his Trinity colleague Alfred Whitehead for having once ridden into the river (Bobbitt, 1960: 103-4; Wilson, 1967: 99-100).

There is plenty of evidence about a good many of the people in Jebb's life, but on his closest friendships the record is disappointingly patchy. It would be interesting, for example, to know more about his discussions with J.B. Lightfoot on their walks in the Lake District, which he describes in a letter to Caroline: 'Alone with Lightfoot there, in that splendid country, talking in our long walks, about things we both really care for, it has been possible sometimes to forget the hard side of life and to live for the time in better things – in a region above the frost-line of perpetual shams and misunderstandings' (February 1872, *LL* 119). How much they talked about religion is hard to guess, and the miscellaneous pieces of evidence we have on Jebb's own religious position are not very illuminating. He came from a clerical family: as well as his great-uncle the bishop there were two uncles in orders, and his younger brother Heneage gave up the law for the church, but Jebb never seems to have thought seriously of getting ordained himself (cf. *LL* 36). Although he spoke on church issues when he was an MP and was elected chairman of the Church Parliamentary Committee, he was not in sympathy with strong doctrinal positions. He defends Anglicanism as having 'afforded the best safeguard of religious freedom', and his speech in Parliament in 1894, opposing the Welsh Church Disestablishment Bill, is well informed about history and respectful of Nonconformist traditions (*LL* 290-300). He had read the sermons of the great Catholic preacher Bossuet with admiration, perhaps as inspiring examples of prose style rather than for their doctrine; there may have been a strong aesthetic element in his approach to religion, and in an early letter to Caroline he shows a preference for the simplicity and plainness of early Christianity (*LL* 104). These hints may help to account for the flexible and sympathetic way in which he writes on ancient Greek religious attitudes.

The classic commentator

If he had not made his great contribution to the study of Sophocles, Jebb would still be remembered, on the strength of *The Attic Orators* and the important Bacchylides commentary which occupied his last years (published in 1905), but he would not have become almost a (scholarly) classic in his own right, an extraordinary achievement for a commentator.

A work of creative literature survives, if it does, because of what can be called its serviceability, or the capacity to yield unlimited fresh meanings to readers of new generations. A commentary has to be ancillary, an adjunct, however penetrating, to the understanding of a primary text, and its chances of having much to say directly to later times are not great, except indirectly through absorption into the work of later scholars. Its style can quickly seem archaic, and its arguments can be overtaken by the discovery of new evidence or new theories. Metricians have long since lost interest in the approach to Greek lyric of J.H.H. Schmidt, approved at the time by good scholars like Gildersleeve and Platt as well as by Jebb himself. Inscriptions, papyri, or artistic evidence may come to light which definitively alter the understanding of a particular word or context. Erudition alone could not guarantee success of the kind that Jebb's commentaries have had; we should look elsewhere for an explanation, and the best starting point is the context in which he was working.

He had begun his scholarly career at a time (the 1860s) when ingenious emendation was more highly valued than any other service an editor might perform for a text, and there was particular prestige to be won from tackling works as familiar and central as the surviving tragedies, many of them still rich in famous cruces. A new text with critical notes was what an editor had typically aimed at producing, and the German tradition also generated large numbers of short dissertations in which conjectural emendation also took pride of place,[17] but more sustained commentary at a higher level than the school text had begun to make an impact: for Sophocles the most widely influential contribution was that of Schneidewin-Nauck.[18] This provided introductions to each play, offering interpretation as well as mythological and literary background, notes that aimed at fairly detailed elucidation of meaning, and a critical appendix discussing textual variants and emendations. In English the most important, and in some ways ground-breaking, contribution had been made by Lewis Campbell, Professor of Greek at St Andrews and an old pupil of Jowett's, with a two-volume edition[19] which must have been a particular stimulus to Jebb: he often engages with Campbell's interpretations, and in the preface to the first edition of *OT* (1883) goes out of his way to make gracious acknowledgement of their importance.

Even so, Jebb was trying to do something ambitiously different from what had gone before; and right from the early days of the school texts for the Catena Classicorum he had been interested in what might be called a holistic approach to a chosen play, although at that stage he was content to use Dindorf's text rather than creating his own. By the time he produced the first commentary in his large-scale series he had worked out most of the detail of his bolder project, for which the two big volumes of *The Attic Orators* were, he explains, a preparatory stage. Work on the small commentaries on *Electra* and *Ajax* had made him more clearly aware of 'the intimate relation which in certain respects exists between Greek tragic dialogue and Greek rhetorical prose, and to feel the desire of studying more closely the whole process by which Greek oratory had been developed' (preface to 1st edn of *OT*, 1883: v). What he was engaged on now after this intensive period of preparation was the production of a complete Sophocles on a much bigger scale, in eight volumes: one for each play, with a final volume covering the fragments, short essays on 'matters of general interest in relation to Sophocles' and an annotated bibliography. In the event he was unable to get far with work on the fragments: his busy life as a public figure, the time needed for intensive work on the new Bacchylides, and his relatively early death, put paid to that plan, but all seven plays had been safely published by 1896.

The other things that Jebb draws attention to in the *OT* preface are first, his aim to show 'fully and exactly how the work of Sophocles is understood by me, both in its larger aspects, and at every particular point', which is where the need is felt to supply a prose translation, to act as an adjunct to the commentary, as an 'indispensable instrument of lucid interpretation: "This rendering, I can see, is not literal" – we may suppose a reader to say. "In what sense, then, and *why*, is it equivalent to the Greek?" Here – supposing the translation to be sound – is the opportunity of the commentary. It comes in to show that there is no flaw in the process by which an advance has been made from a literal rendering to one which, though less literal, is more faithful' (vi-vii). Anyone who uses Jebb's translations regularly will recall instances where he elucidates the meaning of an elusive particle by a faithful rather than a literal translation (cf. Dawe, 1990: 243: '... in a sense they *are* a running commentary').

His second objective is equally interesting. Jebb makes it clear that he is thinking of the general reader as well as the student and scholar (this chimes with both his wider literary aspirations and his interest in making the Classics accessible). Hence his decision to print the translation facing the text, which in the classroom or lecture room was unthinkable (the later adaptations for school use leave out the translation), but might 'induce some persons to read a play of Sophocles as they would a great poem of a modern poet' (vii). This was certainly the spirit in which some of his reviewers welcomed the book: 'In fact', says the *Athenaeum*, 'one might take this edition with him on a journey, and without any other help whatever, acquire with comfort and delight a thorough acquaintance with the noblest production of, perhaps, the most difficult of all Greek poets' (No. 2948, 26.4.84).

Such considerations did not weigh with conservative scholars such as Benjamin Hall Kennedy, Regius Professor of Greek at Cambridge from 1867 to 1889; he had brought out his *Oedipus Tyrannus* a year before Jebb's with a verse translation following the Greek text in which no general reader could have found 'comfort and delight'. Jebb made polite remarks about this edition in the preface to his *OT*, but it did not stop Kennedy from reacting with extraordinary fury to his treatment of the text and devoting many vehement pages to attacking it in his own larger edition (1885). The contrast in manner between the two commentaries throws light on more than a contrast of personalities: it underlines the difference in approach between an elderly grammarian, steeped in the ancient texts, and the ambitious new-style professional who was building on his traditional training but also setting himself broader objectives. Jebb collated thirteen manuscripts for his edition, and made use of Campbell's reports of several others; Kennedy was unconvinced that all this effort was justified if a man made claims about syntax that he could not accept.

Campbell, by contrast, was generously appreciative of Jebb's work, even though it ultimately overshadowed his own, but he was a forward-looking scholar: there are many signs in his Sophocles that he was interested in a broader range of annotation than most previous editors of plays had been. He was resistant to the prevailing passion for conjectural emendation, partly because of his conviction that Sophoclean language was exceptionally bold and idiosyncratic, and the 'Introductory Essay on the Language of Sophocles', which takes up the first 107 pages of vol. 1, was a *tour de force* which has been lastingly influential. His introductions show that he had a particular interest in the 'dramatic force and meaning' of the plays as plays, and he later wrote an engaging introduction to Greek drama for the modern reader.[20]

Jebb was in sympathy with this approach, and particularly with Campbell's resistance to irresponsible conjecture, but he went further in pursuit of the 'thoroughness of interpretation' which he later described as the 'one distinctive aim' of his edition of Sophocles.[21] The introductions are a good place to look for a guide to what he meant by 'thoroughness', though it is the notes themselves that best demonstrate the way it works (sensitively illustrated by Verrall in *LL*). All the introductions follow a broadly similar pattern: they begin with the ancient literary background, setting the myth and the poet's distinctive handling of it in the context of Homeric and cyclic epic, the lyric poets, and the other dramatists; give a detailed analysis of the action of the play; discuss the characters; examine possible historical connections (Jebb generally takes a sceptical view of these); consider the play's reputation in antiquity and its influence on later drama, as a way of pointing more precisely to what is distinctively Sophoclean about it. There is usually a section on the evidence from ancient art, and in plays where it matters, on topography. The literary judgements are liable to seem the most dated parts of the introductions now, because we don't these days write about 'ideal beauty attained by truth to human nature' (preface to *Ant.*, vi), for example, but they were all designed to help the reader make contact with the play as if it were a modern work, and the novel attention that he paid to reception shows how concerned Jebb was to see it in a larger perspective.

The introduction to *Oedipus Tyrannus* discusses Oedipus plays by Seneca, Corneille, Dryden and Voltaire in some detail, using them to make a serious critical comparison with Sophocles, and ends with an enthusiastic section on modern revivals, which is taken further in the Appendix with lavish quotations from a published account of the staging of the play at Harvard in 1881. For Jebb this was a significant development, helping the critic to understand the dynamics of ancient drama, and he explains how strongly he was affected by seeing the *Ajax* performed at Cambridge in 1882 (*OT*, 1st edn: lii).

In each volume the introduction is followed by technical sections:

on manuscripts and editions, and on metre (with full scansion of the lyric passages). As well as providing texts of the hypotheses and other prefatory pieces that appear in the manuscripts, Jebb also supplies them with notes, which is more than most editors have troubled to include, but again this shows his interest in every aspect of the process of reception and transmission.

Not surprisingly, the earliest commentaries (on *OT* and *OC*) are more self-conscious than the later ones about methodology and (on textual criticism) more defensive. For someone so sensitive to criticism and so easily angered in his everyday dealings Jebb shows remarkable care and restraint in the way he phrases his polemics, but he is clearly passionate about the need to resist irresponsible emendation, and there is some fine irony in his paragraph 'The use of conjecture' (*OT* lviii). He is more magisterial, and allows himself more knockabout, in *OC* l-liii: 'The emendations which I propose in the text of this play are few; though I should not have found it difficult to increase their number a hundredfold, if I had conceived that the originality proper to an editor consists in re-writing his author'.

The metrical theories on which Jebb based his analyses were discredited long ago, when scholars came to understand that it was fruitless to use the rhythms of western classical music as a guide to interpreting ancient Greek metrical practice; more interesting for the modern reader is his attempt to describe what he calls 'the relations of lyric form and matter' (*OT*, 1st edn: xcvii-viii), in an attempt to capture the mood and atmosphere of the lyrics, what he calls their 'ethical meaning'. This is an extraordinarily difficult thing to do, and there is no separate section on the subject in the later volumes, but it is interesting to see one of the most recent editors of Sophocles, Mark Griffith, making the same attempt in his commentary on *Antigone* (Cambridge, 1999).

The notes themselves are both full and severely selective; this is where the particular artistry of the commentary is most clearly felt, though one needs more than a few random examples to illustrate its cumulative effect (for a fine discussion see Verrall in *LL*; I try to elaborate some points in Stray, *Owl of Minerva*, forthcoming). As a typical sample of his range and style, as well as his self-discipline, one might look at the notes on *OT* 596, *OC* 1542-55, *Ant.* 1344f., *Phil.* 293f. (with Verrall's comments, *LL* 442-4), *Tr.* 1166ff. (with Appendix), *El.* 1505-7, *Aj.* 650f. (with Appendix; cf. Introduction xxxiii-viii). The impact of the whole owes a good deal to the excellent logistical decision to use an appendix for the detailed discussion of alternative views or specialised evidence. This enables the commentary to sit neatly in double columns below the text and translation, and the layout on the page contributes to the sense that what we are given has been thoroughly thought about and digested. The use of English for the *apparatus criticus* was an innovation of the second edition of *OT* (1887), which Jebb says he has adopted reluctantly (v), but once adopted it evidently contributed to the sense given by these commentaries that nothing is being withheld from the intelligent reader. For anyone who is willing to make a serious effort, everything that scholarship and literary awareness can offer, or as Jebb himself put it in the preface to the first edition of *OT* (vii), 'the vivid exposition of my own mind in relation to Sophocles', is here for the taking.

Abbreviations

EA = *Essays and Addresses by Sir Richard Jebb*, edited by Caroline Jebb (Cambridge, 1907)

LL = *Life and Letters of Sir Richard Claverhouse Jebb O.M., Litt.D.* by his wife Caroline Jebb (Cambridge, 1907) (this includes a chapter on Sir Richard Jebb as Scholar and Critic by Dr A.W. Verrall)

Notes

1. Cf. Lloyd-Jones and Wilson, 1990: 4-5; Goldhill, 1997: 330.

2. *The Attic Orators from Antiphon to Isaeos*, 2 vols (London, 1876); in the 2nd ed. (1893) Isaeus is given his usual spelling.

3. This was produced with the help of M.A. Bayfield; the later ones were made from 1903 onwards by E.S. Shuckburgh (*OC*, *Ant.*, *Phil.*), G.A. Davies (*Tr.*, *El.*), and A.C. Pearson (*Aj.*).

4. In 1885 he produced a text of Books III and IV with a new modern Greek translation.

5. Cf. the detailed account of Jebb's teaching methods at Glasgow by R.P. Williamson, quoted in *LL* 188-92, and by contrast A.S.F. Gow's dismissive

comments on Jebb at a later period in his *Letters from Cambridge* (London, 1945): 240.

6. Given as his inaugural address as President of the Philological Section in the Philosophical Society of Glasgow in 1889 (*EA* 545-59).

7. Brink, 1985, esp. ch. 2, pays Jebb's study of Bentley serious respect, even though he has been influenced by the rather patronising attitude of Housman and Gow to Jebb as a Greek scholar (144-5).

8. James Denney (1856-1917), Principal of the United Free Church College, Glasgow and Professor of New Testament Language Literature and Theology. (Quoted in *LL* 188.)

9. Butcher and Lang persuasively explain their reasons for choosing 'a somewhat antiquated prose', Preface pp. viii-ix.

10. *Macmillan's Magazine* (November 1876): 41-7.

11. All reprinted in R.D. Archer-Hind (ed.) (1907), *Translations into Greek and Latin Verse*, 2nd edn, Cambridge.

12. Jebb no doubt intended the phrase 'the bright beam of Hesperos' in the last line to suggest the West, as the direction in which Greek culture had travelled.

13. *Demeter and Other Poems* (London, 1889), 12-13.

14. In the appendix to *OT* (on v. 508) he uses the evidence of sphinx figures from recent excavations.

15. *EA* 552; cf. W. Dörpfeld and E. Reisch (1896), *Das Griechische Theater*, Athens: 191.

16. See Spalding, 2001, for some additional material.

17. See Lloyd-Jones and Wilson, 1990: 1-6 for a helpful historical survey.

18. F.W. Schneidewin's six-volume original had been published in Berlin between 1849 and 1854; soon after his death in 1856 August Nauck took over the task of revising it, and the last of his revised editions appeared in 1886.

19. Vol. 1 containing *OT, OC, Ant.* appeared in 1871 with a 2nd edn. in 1879, vol. 2 , the four other plays, in 1881.

20. *A Guide to Greek Tragedy for English Readers* (London, 1891).

21. Preface to the 3rd edn. of *OC*, 1900, where it is coupled with some defensive remarks about textual criticism.

Bibliography

Beard, M. (1993) 'Casts and cast-offs', *PCPS* 39: 1-29

Bobbitt, M.R. (1960), *With Dearest Love to All: the life and letters of Lady Jebb*, London

Brink, C.O. (1986), *English Classical Scholarship: historical reflections on Bentley, Porson, and Housman*, Cambridge and New York

Dawe, R.D., 'R.C. Jebb' in W.W. Briggs and W.M. Calder III (eds) (1990)

Classical Scholarship: a biographical encyclopaedia, New York and London: 239-47

Easterling, P.E. (1999) 'The early years of the Cambridge Greek Play: 1882-1912' in Stray, 1999: 27-47

Goldhill, S. (1997), 'Modern critical approaches to Greek tragedy' in P.E. Easterling (ed.) *The Cambridge Companion to Greek Tragedy*, Cambridge: 324-47

Lloyd-Jones, H. and Wilson, N.G. (1990), *Sophoclea*, Oxford

Raverat, G. (1952), *Period Piece*, London

Roach, J.P.C. (1971), *Public Examinations in England 1850-1900*, Cambridge

Sandys, J.E. (1908), *A History of Classical Scholarship*, vol. 3, Cambridge

Spalding, F. (2001), *Gwen Raverat: friends, family, and affections*, London

Stray, C. (1999), *Classics in 19th and 20th Century Cambridge: curriculum, culture and community*, Cambridge Philological Society, suppl. vol. 24

Stray, C.A. (forthhcoming), 'Mr Jebb and his friends (and enemies): the making of a reputation' in Stray (ed.), *The Owl of Minerva: the Cambridge Praelections of 1906*, Cambridge Philological Society, suppl. vol.

Todd, R.B. (2002), *Collected Works of Richard Claverhouse Jebb*, vol. I, Bristol, including a bibliography of his publications and an appendix on archival material

Wilson, F.M. (1967), *Rebel Daughter of a Country House: the life of Eglantyne Jebb*, London

Antigone: Introduction

Ruby Blondell

Antigone has always dominated interpretation of her eponymous drama.[1] The degree to which she does so in Jebb's edition is exhibited in the Preface, where he tacitly equates 'the figure of Antigone' as an 'embodiment of woman's heroism' with 'a work of Greek art', and then with 'the play, as a work of art' (v-vi). This ambiguous entity – Antigone or *Antigone*? – is distinguished by its artistic 'singleness of motive' and 'self-restraint', qualities that mark an idealising view of classical Greek culture typical of Jebb's time. This kind of idealism has always found Sophocles especially congenial.[2] Even among this dramatist's works, however, *Antigone* has a special sublimity in Jebb's eyes: 'There could be no better example of ideal beauty attained by truth to human nature' (vi). It is also uniquely timeless, since its central theme, alone among all Greek plays, 'might be discussed on similar grounds in any age and in any country of the world' (xx). This aesthetic idealism, universalism, and unproblematic faith in human nature evoke an intellectual world untouched by the anxieties not only of post-modernism, but even of modernism.

'Singleness of motive' informs Jebb's own outlook along with his heroine's. He rarely displays the kind of concern with consistency that is the hobgoblin of small minds, and is critical of the application of 'rigid rules' (see nn. on 576, 804f. and cf. e.g. n. on ἀποστάζει in 959). But an overarching concern with Antigone's unity of motive, which evidently underwrites for him the unity of the play, informs his judgement at every turn. For Jebb, she is unproblematically analogous to a Christian saint, more specifically, a martyr in the Roman arena (xxv; cf. also xxxiii-ix). His preoccupation with the religious aspects of her motivation accords with attitudes expressed in his own life, especially his religious aestheticism and respect for religious freedom (see General Introduction, p. [22]), as well as with his larger view of Sophocles as a 'pious' poet (cf. n. on 1337). At the same time, his Antigone is the essence of Victorian womanhood. Her most fundamental quality, besides 'enthusiasm ... for the performance of her duty', is an 'intense tenderness, purity, and depth of domestic affection' (xxvii). These two features, the 'religious duty' and womanly 'tenderness' that he views as the driving forces of Antigone's character, are leitmotifs of Jebb's commentary. He sees no tension between them, since both strive towards the fulfilment of a 'peculiarly sacred and tender duty' (n. on 872; cf. n. on 517).

This harmonious marriage of religious devotion and proper femininity may be seen in the use Jebb makes of Edwin Long's painting, 'Diana or Christ?', which was painted (in two almost identical versions) just before the publication of the first of his Sophocles commentaries. Jebb sees in it an analogue for Sophocles' portrayal of Antigone, Haemon and Creon (xxv). 'Antigone' is a Christian martyr under the Romans, refusing to sacrifice even a grain of incense to Diana. She stares out of the painting in the direction of the viewer, eyes rolled up towards heaven, the virginal pallor of her costume setting her apart from the dark-clad figures behind her. She ignores 'Creon' – a muscular Roman in charge of the proceedings – and brushes away 'Haemon', a young man evidently urging her to compromise her beliefs. Her psychological isolation, like that of Antigone, is well conveyed. But her radiant expression, with its slight but beatific smile, conveying an absolute confidence in her own future bliss, is a far cry from the angry, confrontational tone of Sophocles' indignant heroine. She does not insultingly avoid eye contact with 'Creon' by staring at the ground before his feet, as Antigone does (*Ant.* 441), but turns her back on any human interaction to gaze tranquilly up at heaven. The eyes of almost all the bystanders are upon her, as those of Sophocles' dramatis personae – not to mention his critics – rest literally or figuratively upon Antigone until her final exit. But the divine sanction claimed by the young martyr's upturned eyes is not one that calls for validation by the vast crowd of pagans and apostates that frames her, in contrast to Antigone's concern, in Sophocles' play, with *timê* or status, glory and reputation, resentment towards those who have failed to support her, and final calls for public validation (cf. 5, 86-7, 509, 839-49, 904, 937-43).

It is hardly surprising, then, that Jebb underplays these features of Antigone's character. Her 'tenderness', upon which he insists from the Preface onwards, requires more active special pleading. A certain defensiveness may be detected in his insistence that she is 'no virago, but a true woman, most tender-hearted' (xxxiv), and the repeated repudiation of any suggestion that she is harsh, sullen, scornful or bitter, especially towards Ismene (xii, xxix; cf. also nn. on 411, 441, 495f., 941). It is hard, however, to see lines 69-70 as prompted by 'tenderness', as Jebb would have it (xxviii), or 32 as profoundly 'pathetic' (n. ad loc.). He allows her 'bitterness' only in 470 – where a recent editor speaks more convincingly of sarcasm and rudeness (Griffith 1999) – and translates ὠμός in 471 as 'passionate', though he glosses it as 'fierce'. The latter is a revealing instance of the way Jebb allowed his translation to be coloured by his interpretive assumptions, thus allowing it to serve – quite consciously – as a further mode of commentary (see General Introduction, p. [24]).

Little wonder, then, that Jebb attributes to Antigone the notorious line in which Ismene, according to the MSS, expresses her affection for 'dearest Haemon' (572). The attribution to Antigone provides a badly needed shred of credence for her vaunted 'tenderness', especially in Jebb's translation, fortified as it is with romantic punctuation as well as diction: 'Haemon, beloved! How thy father wrongs thee!' As Jebb's note on the line makes clear, a crucial aspect of Antigone's 'womanly tenderness' is her supposed romantic attachment to her fiancé. The need to supply evidence for such an attachment is permitted to trump both Jebb's usual conservatism on speaker attribution (e.g. nn. on 576, 935-6), and his concern with coherence of character.[3] The same concern colours his translation of 570 ('There can never be such love as bound him to her'), though again, the literal meaning of ἡρμοσμένα and its associations are elucidated in the note.

Jebb's conception of Antigone's character, with its purported tenderness and strong focus on 'religion', transparently influences his interpretation of the play. It is this that leads him to excise the notorious lines 904-20 – lines for which, as Knox remarked, 'our authority ... is better than what we have for most of the rest of the play' (1964: 104) – despite his usual caution as a textual critic and repudiation of all other suggested interpolations in this text (liii). He does express some linguistic concerns about the passage, which make its composition allegedly 'unworthy of Sophocles' (ad loc.). But these are neither numerous nor weighty. His other two main reasons for rejecting the passage both depend on the fact that it places restrictions on the supposed 'general validity of the divine law, as asserted in 450-460' (ad loc.). He expands on the issue in his Appendix. The bulk of the Appendix is devoted to learned philological detail on various textual cruces, but the lengthy treatment of this passage stands apart as, quite consciously, an essay on dramatic character and literary taste. The passage is rejected for undermining the essential unity of Antigone's character and motivation, as grounded in the 'immovable basis of her action – the universal and unqualified validity of the divine law' (p. 259). Any such violation is unthinkable in a 'great poet' (p. 260). Jebb is well aware that the central issue is one of 'modern taste' vs. 'ancient modes of thought' (p. 259). But despite the acknowledged ancient predilection for the kind of 'quaint subtleties' employed by Antigone in her speech (p. 260), the deciding factor is whether this violation of 'modern' taste is also a violation of universal canons of artistic merit applicable to any time and place. The passage is rejected because it does indeed violate such canons in a way that is impossible for Sophocles (a 'great poet' if ever there was one).

More recent critics who continue to reject 904-20 have little to add to Jebb's 'characteristically fair and lucid statement of the problem' (Winnington-Ingram 1980: 145 n.). In the course of the last century, however, the overwhelming trend has been increasingly towards acceptance of the lines.[4] This is associated, in part, with a stripping from Antigone's character of Jebb's sentimental veneer. The Antigone who, as Perrotta witheringly expressed it, had been 'sugar-coated' ('inzuccherata') in the guise of a Christian martyr (1935: 114), has yielded the field to the 'savage daughter of a savage father' (471-2) more readily apparent to modern eyes.[5] No longer does Antigone's heroism demand the moral purity or absolute clarity of vision with which Jebb endowed her (xxxii). She may be seen as the embodiment of her family curse, or as expressing a death-wish or a subconscious incestuous urge, or simply as self-absorbed and irrational. This passionate figure is not beyond defending her action irrationally, as she does, in the view of many scholars, in the notorious passage in question.[6]

This changing picture of Antigone is related to the strong twentieth-century interest in defining the nature of the 'Sophoclean hero'. For Jebb, 'heroism' as a category appears to have required no critical examination (cf. xxxii). But the dominance of most of Sophocles' plays by a single powerful character prompted a number of detailed studies of these figures,[7] culminating in Knox's influential book, *The Heroic Temper* (1964). This now classic composite portrait of the 'Sophoclean hero' cuts a very different figure from Jebb's Christian saint, marked as it is by, among other things, anger, resentment, intransigence, vengefulness, and an acute sensitivity to personal insult. *Antigone* takes pride of place in this book, playing a role in the first two of its six chapters and serving as the primary subject of two more. And Antigone herself embodies the essence of Knox's 'heroic temper' (1964: 67). His treatment did not, however, put an end to the preoccupation of scholars with Antigone *qua* 'Sophoclean hero' (see e.g. Rohdich, 1980).

Shifting conceptions of Greek social and personal relationships have also facilitated the stripping of sentimental accretions from Antigone's character. A majority of scholars would now agree that the devotion she shows towards her dead brother is primarily a fierce loyalty towards the family of her birth, as opposed to a personal affection for Polyneices in particular. The *philia* that drives Antigone is informed by specifically Athenian constructions of personal and social relations within the institution of the democratic *polis* (Goldhill, 1986: ch. 4). Moreover there are other parallels for the notorious argument in 904-20 besides the well-known passage of Herodotus. Twentieth-century scholars were able to make cultural sense of the lines by placing them into a broader anthropological context, especially regarding the conflict of loyalties for women between their natal and marital families.[8]

Jebb was well aware that one's attitude towards 904-20 'profoundly affect[s] our conception of the great drama as a whole' (263). Most modern critics would place more emphasis on the other side of this coin: that our conception of the drama as a whole – and of Greek tragedy generally – will undoubtedly affect our decision whether or not to exclude these lines. Jebb would doubtless have acknowledged this too, especially given the disarming pronouncement that he is offering, in his commentaries, an exposition of *his own mind* in relation to Sophocles (General Introduction, p. [28]). A contemporary scholar, however, would be less likely to exclude a passage on the grounds that the author of the text is a 'great poet'. Textual criticism inevitably requires an element of aesthetic judgment, and this remains the deciding factor for most scholars who still excise these lines.[9] But the tendency towards accepting them reflects the fact that modern critics have become much less inclined to cut the fabric of the text to fit preconceived notions of how a poet should have written or what a drama should look like. This, of course, reflects their own conception of Sophocles' text, not as a presumptive work of transcendent 'greatness', but as an alien artifact, which the critic should attempt to comprehend on its own terms by locating it in a larger web of social meanings. Modern criticism for the most part embraces an ideology of the alien which prefers to err on the side of inclusiveness.

This kind of cultural recontextualisation has involved changes in our understanding of Greek religion and ritual. Jebb felt no need to explain his own conceptual categories, such as 'duty', 'sin', and 'conscience' – all words that have no direct Greek equivalent – or to justify their application to Sophocles. It was in part because such categories and terms were unproblematic and unexamined that he could view this play as unique, even among Greek tragedies, for its timelessness (xx). The challenging of such conceptual structures led to a reconsideration of Jebb's 'classicising' picture of Sophocles as a 'pious' poet – a view typical of his own time, which was echoed repeatedly, in various forms, during the first half of the twentieth century (see e.g. Bowra 1944). Criticism of this view received its most extreme expression in Whitman, who used Jebb as the starting point for his opinionated but bracing survey of 'classicizing' scholarship (1951: ch. 2).[10] Whitman's brand of romantic humanism now seems as quaint as Jebb's (his *Antigone* chapter is entitled 'Man the Measure'); but since he wrote

Sophocles' piety has largely lost its Christian gloss.[11] Kitto, for example, emphasised the relative detachment of the Greek gods from 'morality' (1958: ch. 3), while Knox posited a Sophocles especially devoted to the peculiarly Greek cult of heroes (1964: 53-8). Recent critics are less likely to speculate on Sophocles' personal religious views, but the interest provoked by the role of the gods in his works remains perennial (see e.g. Parker, 1999).

Jebb was very interested in the concrete details of Greek ritual and cult (see e.g. nn. on 429, 431), but his understanding of such practices was heavily conditioned by conceptual frameworks derived from the Christianity of his time. Modern scholars, while inheriting and developing his interest in such specifics, are primarily concerned with elucidating their socio-cultural functions (see e.g. Parker, 1983; Seaford, 1994). 'Religion' in classical Athens has come, increasingly, to be seen less as a distinct sphere of human activity – Jebb's 'acknowledged province' (xxxvi) – than as a complicated set of practices and stories woven into all aspects of the fabric of human life, specifically the life of the *polis*. As a result, religious cult and associated rituals are now commonly seen as materials for tragedy in a way that departs from Jebb's positivist perspective. Thus Bushnell uses the theme of prophecy to explore fate and heroism in the Theban Plays, employing perspectives derived from history, culture and politics as opposed to 'metaphysics' (1988: xi). For *Antigone*, the most important rituals are those surrounding marriage and death, which in the heroine's own case are notoriously equated. Jebb provides parallels from epitaphs for the notion of 'marriage to death' (n. on 804f.), together with much pertinent information on Athenian marriage (n. on 813ff.). (Somewhat surprisingly, he fails to note the allusion to marriage ritual in 569, but he does give poetic parallels.) He thus supplies, albeit without comment, the starting point for exploration of an idea whose cultural significance has been spun out in rich and enlightening detail in recent years.[12]

Jebb's assumptions about unity of character and motivation have also fallen victim to subsequent critical approaches. Just a few years after his death, Tycho von Wilamowitz's posthumously published dissertation argued, following Aristotle, that characterisation in Greek tragedy is secondary to plot. Moreover consistency of character – and other forms of consistency – could be, and often were, sacrificed by Sophocles to more immediate forms of dramatic effect (Wilamowitz, 1917). This mode of argument frees the dramatic critic from the obsessive concern with consistency reflected in such matters as that critical chestnut, the 'double burial'. From Jebb's perspective, if the ritual of burial was properly completed the first time, then Antigone had done her 'duty' and had no reason to endanger her life by doing it again. He was apparently the first to perceive this as a problem (n. on 429), but he thought the 'modern reader' would 'naturally' notice it (xiv), and its critical afterlife has been voluminous. (If we seek specific instances of his influence on the scholarly interpretation of *Antigone*, we need look no further.) Yet the alleged problem is rarely noticed by the 'modern reader' of my own experience. Why, then, was it a problem for Jebb? Because of his preoccupation with the religious basis of Antigone's action, and the coherence of her character around this core. The solution he offers ad loc. satisfies both of these concerns (cf. also p. xiv). On other plausible readings of her character, the 'double burial' can easily be accommodated (see Bradshaw, 1962). But Wilamowitz provided a new way altogether of looking at such 'inconsistencies', not by explaining them away naturalistically, but by emphasising their dramatic usefulness for other purposes, and pointing out that a 'unity' consisting in precise coherence of detail is not an overriding dramatic value.[13]

Another case in point is a plot detail condemned by Jebb – and others – as a structural fault, namely Creon's decision to bury Polynices before rescuing Antigone (xvii-xx). 'Fault' is a critical term rarely seen in modern discussions of ancient plays, where more and more works previously deemed inferior are being recuperated and their virtues recognised. Indeed, criticising any text for its 'faults' has started to smack of culture-blindness, since just about any alleged fault can be explained by the rhetorical strategies of the text or the different cultural expectations of the original audience, and so on. Jebb himself, though he does not back away from the word 'fault', explains this feature of the play in a remarkably modern fashion, by acknowledging the ancient taste for rhetoric and the lesser importance of consistency for events that occur, in Aristotle's phrase, 'outside the drama'. Most strikingly, he views the resulting 'blemish' as a locus to assist our understanding of the particular character of Greek tragedy or of Sophocles' tragic art (xx).

Wilamowitz's book exerted an enormous influence on subsequent Sophoclean scholarship by focussing attention away from minute psychological analyses of character and towards other aspects of dramatic technique. It also shook up conventional assumptions about the ways in which dramatic characters can – and should – be read, by challenging the importance of naturalism. Waldock (1951) argued influentially against the reading of Sophocles' characters as 'real' people. And A.M. Dale, in a brief but oft-quoted comment, argued that the speeches of characters in tragedy 'can rarely be interpreted as primarily or consistently expressive of their natures', since character often takes second place to 'the trend of the action and the rhetoric of the situation' (1954: xxv). John Jones decentred character by employing Aristotelian categories to argue both that Greek conceptions of character (*êthos*) are quite different from more recent notions focussing on idiosyncrasy and 'inwardness', and that in Greek drama character takes second place to plot (Jones, 1962). Without mentioning Jebb by name, he criticised the Romantic reading of *Antigone* that goes back to Goethe, whereby 'Antigone's action ... should be impelled by the single heroic motive of duty to her dead brother' (1962: 193). He went on to argue that lines 904-20 become unproblematic if one adopts 'a new flexibility in contemplating Sophocles' version of the human self' (1962: 198).

'Human nature' tout court as an explanatory category now seems naive. Conceptions of coherence, and of the nature and functions – dramatic, rhetorical, or cultural – of perceived inconsistencies in plot and/or character, have become much more flexible than they were for Jebb. The relationship between fictional characters and 'real life' is now widely understood to be far more complex than much of earlier scholarship had allowed (Gould, 1978; Goldhill, 1990). Yet Jebb's humanism lives on, albeit defensively at times (Vickers, 1973: ch. 2). The backlash against 'Tychoism' was not long in arriving (Schadewaldt, 1929), and neither naturalism nor coherence of character has disappeared as a yardstick for dramatic criticism. Greek tragedy in

Ruby Blondell

general does, after all, routinely invite us to assess its characters' states of mind and construct their motives, and *Antigone* notoriously so (Easterling, 1990: 93-9). Ever since Hegel, this play has remained the poster-child for tragedy as a site for philosophical reflection, contributing, through the actions and arguments of its characters, to serious ethical debate.[14] The play invites this treatment for several reasons: it explores fundamental conceptual antinomies; it features two substantial central characters with dramatically opposed moral, religious, social and political perspectives; it is loaded – even by the standards of Greek tragedy – with language of deliberation and 'right-thinking'.[15]

These aspects of the play seduce the reader – almost irresistibly, it seems – to view it as an antithetical drama of right and wrong. This antithesis was once mapped onto a further question as to which character was 'the' hero of the play. In recent years, with the fading of the demand for a single 'tragic hero' in any Greek drama, 'this pseudo-problem has evaporated' (Griffith, 1999: 26). Nevertheless, most critics still seem to feel obliged to comment on the relative 'rightness' of Antigone and Creon, if only to assert that the question is a wrong-headed one. Jebb expounded his view on this subject trenchantly, in opposition to Hegel's then-recent, and still notorious, interpretation of the play (xxi-xxii). The Hegelian view lives on, however, in more contemporary dress (see e.g. Nussbaum, 1986: ch. 3; Blundell, 1989). A majority of critics over the last century have shared Jebb's stout preference for Antigone over Creon.[16] But few would now express it so categorically, acknowledging at a minimum that an Athenian audience would find her blindness towards the *polis* problematic (e.g. Knox, 1964: 114-16). The occasional defence of Creon may also be found.[17]

Scholars who continue to explore the moral positions of dramatic characters now do so in a way that tries self-consciously to avoid the accretions of thousands of years of philosophy and religion, as far as that is possible. In an important contribution to the reaction against 'classicism' E.R. Dodds, under the influence of twentieth-century anthropology, stimulated a far-reaching scholarly fascination with Greek psychology, related ethical, metaphysical and religious concepts, and the language used to express them (1951). After Dodds, no commentator, could gloss αἰσχρόν the way Jebb does (on *Ant.* 5), as 'shocking the moral sense'. All such terminology must now be contextualised, scrutinised and glossed with great care, in an attempt to understand Greek psychology and ethics on their own terms.[18] Attention to the irrational aspects of character and motivation, and the ways they are imbricated with traditional religious views regarding fate, *atê*, and so on, continues to be central to the study of tragedy generally, and *Antigone* in particular.[19] The application of modern Freudian and post-Freudian psychological categories to Greek drama has been less significant for the interpretation of *Antigone* than for some other plays (but see Griffith, 1998; Johnson, 1997). Nevertheless, the play continues to provide grist to the mill of post-Freudian philosophers and theorists (Lacan, 1992 [1973]; Butler, 2000).

What much of the best contemporary criticism adds to the old view of the play as a drama of right vs. wrong is an alertness to the complexity, ambivalence, and ironic undercurrents in the linguistic texture of the play, which complicate the seductive binaries with which it presents us. This is in large part the legacy of French structuralism, embodied most notably in the work of Jean-Paul Vernant, Pierre Vidal-Naquet, and their students, which drew upon early twentieth-century developments in linguistics, anthropology, sociology and psychology. Structuralism problematised such notions as 'the state' and 'the family' by conceptualising them as ideological categories enmeshed with others in a system of antinomies. Like words in a linguistic system, these antinomies create meaning through opposition, providing structuralist critics with a grammar of ideas for the interpretation of particular texts. The influence of structuralism on the interpretation of Greek literature and myth, and especially tragedy, can scarcely be overstated. Its most important practitioner in English, and the most important for Sophocles, was Charles Segal (1981, 1995). *Antigone* offers a fertile field for this approach, and Vernant used it to exemplify the tensions he saw built into legal, religious, social and psychological terms in tragedy (1988 [1972]: 41-2). The play has received much analysis of this kind, including an exhaustive study that displays some of the strengths and weakesses of this approach (Oudemans and Lardinois, 1987).

Complexity and ambivalence are structuralism's stock in trade, as the title of Vernant's seminal article implies (1988 [1972]). The ambiguous, allusive language of choral lyric therefore makes this aspect of the drama particularly susceptible to such analysis. Jebb's notes on the first stasimon of *Antigone*, for example, betray no indication of the ironic undercurrents in its praise of 'man'; but Charles Segal, in an influential article, used structuralist methodology to elucidate its internal tensions and ironies (1964; see also 1981: ch. 6).[20] Structuralism was also sensitive to the tensions within the persona of the chorus, which both participates in the dramatic action as a character and comments on it through lyric song and dance (cf. Vernant, 1988 [1972]: 33-4). Jebb's remarks on the persona of the chorus are sensible, but perfunctory (xxvi-xxvii). Since his time, however, much thought has been devoted to their problematic status, particularly the tensions between their social role as a character and their authoritative voice as choral performers.[21] The chorus of *Antigone* is exceptionally elusive qua character, and the lyrics of the play, though famous for their beauty, are notoriously difficult to interpret within the context of the drama as a whole.[22] Jebb's metrical analyses of these lyrics – the most outdated part of his commentaries – have been superseded by the modern study of metre.[23] But he would certainly have been interested in the attempts of recent scholars to understand the ways that music and lyric metre contribute to the larger meanings of the drama.[24]

One of the central binaries of structuralism is that of *polis* vs. *oikos* – an antinomy obviously central to *Antigone*, which is almost obsessively preoccupied with the *polis*, its concerns and its challenges. For this reason the play has always attracted attention as a meditation on Athenian politics or, more grandly, a contribution to political thought.[25] Jebb speaks of politics, like religion, in terms that are quite abstract, though at the same time redolent of his own time and place. He often speaks of 'the State', where most modern scholars would use 'the *polis*' or an uncapitalised 'city-state'. Creon, as king, rules by 'divine grace' (n. on 745), the relationship of citizen to king is expressed in terms of 'loyalty',[26] and Antigone is a 'rebel' (nn. on 730 and 732). As one would expect of someone who views Sophocles' works as timeless and universal, he is not hospitable to the practice of perceiving concrete political or historical allusions in the text (see e.g. n. on 699). Yet he remains aware of larger cultural resonances, for an Athenian audience, in Sophocles' themes and language.[27] In this respect he foreshadows the late twentieth-century emphasis on tragedy as a peculiarly Athenian phenomenon, produced in a specific social and political context, with resonances for its original audience reflecting on the *polis* of which they were citizens, especially on democratic political culture and its sometimes uneasy relationship to its aristocratic past.[28]

Structuralism has also been important for feminist scholarship, since gender in Greek texts is so heavily intertwined with other conceptual antinomies, such as *polis* and *oikos*, public and private, nature and culture. The rise of feminist theory and criticism, in its several waves, was one of the most pervasively influential aspects of later twentieth-century scholarship. As a result, questions about gender have complicated such central matters as conceptions of Greek heroism – whether Sophoclean or otherwise. Jebb drew attention to the gendered dynamic between Antigone and Creon (e.g. nn. on 248, 376, 679f.; cf. also xxvii). But his account of 'the heroic nature', as exemplified in Antigone, remained ungendered (xxxii). For Knox too, Antigone embodied a heroic essence that transcends gender (1964: 9). But such interpretations are no longer possible. The Athenian ideology of gender creates what may be called the problem of female heroism. Antigone, as Knox argued, shares many qualities with the great Sophoclean male heroes, and also with Achilles. (Ismene is clearly introduced in part to underline the 'unfemininity' of her behaviour.) How, then, is her heroism to be understood in the context of a culture that differentiates so markedly between proper male and female spheres of action and character? Above all, if silence, self-restraint, and seclusion within the house are the proper virtues of women, how are we to construe the volubility and assertiveness that she shares with so many other tragic heroines? In the case of 'wicked women' like Clytemnestra and Medea, this is less problematic – or at least problematic in a different way. But Antigone employs her 'masculine' qualities for purposes that are ultimately shown to win both divine and human approval. If assertive female speech and action are 'unfeminine' per se, how would the original, predominantly male, audience have reacted to her? This adds a new layer of nuance to the old question regarding the relative 'rightness' of Antigone and Creon.

The modern discussion of this kind of problem goes back to Gomme (1925), and has been the subject of much recent criticism (e.g. McClure, 1999). Among works of special importance for *Antigone*, Foley (2001) stands out for the original use she makes of various strands of twentieth-century theory and criticism, rearticulating feminist concerns in the light of developments in anthropology and moral psychology. Other feminist scholars have paid close attention to the way women's identity is structured through marriage. Thus Ormand argues for the centrality of the ideology of marriage to the meaning of *Antigone*, specifically as a way of complicating the superficial dichotomy between family and *polis* that is so often seen to drive the play (1999: ch. 4).

The rise of feminist theory and criticism clearly distinguishes our own critical culture from Jebb's. Yet Jebb did live in the early days of modern feminism, and took a 'progressive' interests in all kinds of intellectual and social movements of his day, many of which we inherit. Not only did he support such issues as women's higher education (General Introduction, p. [18]), but he was aware of feminism as a nascent intellectual trend. Attention to such currents, as well as to the contemporary reception of ancient texts, is illustrated in his fascinating footnote (xii) on William Francis Barry's novel *The New Antigone* (Barry 1887) – an intriguing nineteenth-century appropriation of Antigone as a 'feminist' hero. (This work is not for the faint-hearted, weighing in at nearly nine hundred pages of florid prose.) For Jebb – as presumably for most fifth-century Athenians – Ismene is 'the average woman', but he observes that her reaction would have been made not just by 'most women', but 'perhaps by a still larger percentage of men' (xxviii). In his note on 570 he speaks of the seclusion of women as an aspect of 'the Attic notions of feminine propriety' – a phrase that, while not untrue, vastly understates the case from a modern feminist perspective. The same note, however, provides enough parallels to start the reader on an exploration of Athenian gender roles. Despite the absence of theoretical structures and assumptions that inform modern treatments, then, one might do worse than begin with Jebb as a source of cultural information surrounding the status of women and ideology of gender.

The same may be said, to varying degrees, of other critical concerns that have developed since his time, such as his interest in what is now known as 'reception'. In the century since his death, Jebb's Christian martyr has been repeatedly recanonised as the patron saint of civil disobedience and free speech and a martyr to state oppression.[29] *Antigone* has served as a receptacle for such preoccupations in countless works realised in many different media, as well as hundreds of re-stagings of Sophocles' play, in versions more or less close to the original.[30] This proliferation – which shows no sign of abating – is now seen as evidence of a slightly different kind of 'universality' from that intended by Jebb. The current emphasis is less on transcendence than on the text's extraordinary availability for appropriation by a wide range of other cultures.[31] Each such appropriation is a translation into a different cultural language, as specific as that of Sophocles, and can only be properly understood as such. In Jebb's day, it was *The New Antigone* that appropriated Sophocles' play as a vehicle for the exploration of contemporary concerns. A century later, it is works like Liliana Cavani's film *I Cannibali*, released in 1970 in the aftermath of the European student uprisings of May 1968. In this reimagining of Sophocles' story, Antigone buries not just her brother but heaps of corpses of rebels against a fascist regime, assisted by a Tiresias who represents 'a particular kind of middle-class rebel youth sub-culture' (MacKinnon, 1986: 107). These appropriations in turn affect our reading of Sophocles' play, in so far as 'judgements and uses of Antigone, from Aristotle to Lacan, will form some part of [one's] own experience of the work' (Steiner, 1984: 296).

A related scholarly development that has blossomed since Jebb's time is the interpretation of ancient plays not merely as texts to be read, but as scripts for dramatic performance. His interest in the circumstances of ancient theatre production was reflected in his involvement with the Cambridge Greek play (General Introduction, p. [18]), and there are traces of it in his notes (e.g. nn. on 467, 1172f., 1294). This kind of study took a giant step forward with the landmark work of Pickard-Cambridge (1946, 1953). Csapo and Slater's more recent book (1995) makes this kind of information available to non-specialists – a move of which Jebb would certainly have approved (General Introduction, pp. [24-5]). Performance criticism has by now become an enormously important aspect of dramatic scholarship. Its application to Greek tragedy was initiated, for practical purposes, by Taplin (1977), and it has been flourishing ever since, becoming ever more sophisticated in the process.[32] Other new work has explored the material and institutional aspects of Attic theatre with a view to its social and political functions within the Athenian democracy (Wilson 2000). Metatheatrical analysis, another related theoretical trend, focuses on the self-consciousness of drama about its own performativity (e.g. Ringer 1998). A further dimension has been added by feminist attention to the fact that the performers – as well as the playwrights – were all male. This calls into question their capacity to represent the subjectivity of a 'woman' like Antigone at all, not to mention their agenda – conscious or otherwise – in doing so (see esp. Zeitlin, 1985; Griffith, 2001).

Such issues were, of course, of no concern to Jebb, with his transcendent view of 'human nature'. Needless to say, he serves as a more fruitful ancestor for some scholarly trends than others. Yet despite the quaintness, to twenty-first century eyes, of his language and many of his theoretical assumptions, other qualities have saved him from fossilisation. His awe-inspiring wealth of citations and detailed exposition of alternative interpretations, coupled with his intellectual honesty (cf. e.g. n. on 907), allow for, and indeed make possible, informed disagreement on the part of his reader. (It is not uncommon to see his own evidence used against him by later scholars.) His copious learning, and thorough observation of the text and its implications, make his notes essential reading for anyone who relies on close readings of the text, acknowledging, as Jebb did, the interpenetration of detailed linguistic study and larger interpretive gestures – something he saw as particularly essential to a proper reading of *Antigone* (vi). This applies, for example, to the kind of analysis popularised in the mid-twentieth century by the New Criticism, which was characterised, among other things, by close and detailed attention to nuances of language. This is well exemplified for *Antigone* by Goheen's study of the play's imagery (1951), whose notes are riddled with references to Jebb.

The same is true of detailed structuralist analyses of the text, and of many more recent trends in cultural studies. Despite Jebb's own admiration for *Antigone's* timelessness, his commentary remains indispensable to modern scholarly efforts to unravel the specific cultural meanings of words, images, and concepts, and to understand the play as the product of its particular time and place.[33] His fascination with all aspects of the ancient world, and the lavishness with which this fascination is expressed in his notes, have made his commentaries a gold mine for generations of scholars, no matter how widely their theoretical approaches and interests may diverge from his. This huge wealth of material has been recycled selectively in later commentaries, but never in its entirety, making him fundamental for the effective use of any methodology that values both text and cultural context. It is this extraordinary 'capacity to go on being useful' (General Introduction, p. [7]) that makes his commentaries meta-classics, in so far as they facilitate Sophocles' own enduring availability to all flavours of critic.

One final concern of Jebb's that anticipates modern critical trends is his engagement with the history of scholarship (General Introduction, p. [17]). Though classical scholarship has always kept one eye cast back at its own development, that eye has in recent years focussed more sharply on the ways in which scholarship itself is culture-bound. Greater attention is now being paid not just to the ways in which past scholars have enhanced our understanding of the ancient world, but to the conditions that made them the kind of scholars and interpreters that they were. This volume is an expression of such attention, in that it does not merely reprint Jebb's work (thus attesting to an unproblematic 'timelessness'), but seeks, in a modest way, to contextualise his *Antigone* historically and culturally, using some of the same intellectual tools that have been applied, in the course of the intervening century, to Sophocles' *Antigone*. By incorporating Jebb into this trend, and thus challenging the 'timelessness' of his Sophocles, the introductions to these reissues challenge Jebb's own 'timelessness' in the very act of celebrating it. This 'timelessness', like that of Sophocles, is grounded in the particularity of Jebb's own time and place (which saw the start of many currently flourishing scholarly trends), and also in his particular personality, with the imprint that it leaves (of thoroughness, of generosity) in his texts. By showing us '[his] own mind in relation to Sophocles' he resonates with Sophocles both by means of and in spite of that particularity.

*

I would like to thank John Betts, Pat Easterling, Helene Foley, Michael Halleran, and Kirk Ormand for helpful comments on an earlier draft of this Introduction.

Notes

1. There have been important exceptions, however, such as H.D.F. Kitto, who surmised that 'modern minds make more of Antigone than was intended' (1961: 127).

2. It can be traced back to the 'good-tempered' and respected Sophocles of Aristophanes' *Frogs* (76-82, 786-94, 1515-19), who is largely immune from the engagement with Athenian culture implied by comic lampooning (Dover, 1972: 181). Traces remain in modern criticism (cf. Ormand, 1999: 6).

3. The words cohere better, on the face of it, with Ismene's more affectionate character. Formal considerations also support Ismene's retention of the line (see Griffith, 1999 and Lloyd-Jones/Wilson, 1990 ad loc.).

4. A concise and judicious statement of the predominant modern view, on this feature of the play as on many others, may be found in Griffith, 1999 (ad loc.).

5. Cf. e.g. Whitman, 1951: 85; Knox, 1964: 65; Winnington-Ingram, 1980: 128-38.

6. See e.g. Knox, 1964: 106-7; Kitto, 1964: 170-1.

7. E.g. Reinhardt, 1979 [1933], Whitman, 1951; Kirkwood, 1958: 169-80.

8. E.g. Perrotta, 1935: 120; Murnaghan, 1986; Neuburg, 1990.

9. 'In the end I cannot believe that Soph. wrote this rubbish' (Brown, 1987: 200); cf. also Winnington-Ingram, 1980: 145.

10. Ironically, Whitman has more in common with Jebb than may appear at first glance, though his 'humanism' has a very different flavour. E.g. for his Antigone, like Jebb's, 'love and duty were one' (84); his conception of heroism is essentialist and ungendered (cf. below, p. [43]); and lines 904-20 are rejected as 'disillusioning' (92).

11. Méautis, 1957, was an already anachronistic exception.

12. See esp. Rehm, 1994: ch. 4; Seaford, 1987 and 1994 passim; Ormand, 1999.

13. For application of this kind of approach to *Antigone*, and especially to the 'double burial', see Kitto, 1964: ch. 5. Cf. also Kitto, 1961.

14. For a contrary view, however, see Hester, 1971.

15. Coray, 1993, provides a recent exhaustive study of intellectual language in Sophocles. See also Sullivan, 1999.

16. Cf. e.g. Whitman, 1951; Müller, 1967; Reinhardt, 1979.

17. E.g. Calder, 1968; Sourvinou-Inwood, 1989. For useful surveys of opinion see Hester, 1971; Oudemans and Lardinois, 1987: ch. 5.

18. Important recent studies include Williams, 1993 and Gill, 1996.

19. See Else, 1976; Winnington-Ingram, 1980; Lloyd-Jones, 1983: ch. 5; Padel, 1995.

20. Goheen had previously commented on the ode's 'paradoxical' quality, focussing similarly on linguistic ambiguity, albeit starting from a different theoretical position (1951: 53-6; see also pp. [46-7]).

21. See especially the exchange between Gould and Goldhill in Silk, 1996.

22. Recent studies include Burton, 1980; Gardiner, 1987.

23. Dale, 1968, 1971, 1981, 1983; West, 1982; Griffith, 1999.

24. Ditmars, 1992; Scott, 1996; Griffith, 1999. For Jebb's interest see General Introduction, p. [27].

25. The play has also served as a foundational text for jurisprudence. Douzinas and Warrington claim that '*Antigone* is as important for the explorations of the origins and force of the law as Freud believed that *Oedipus* was for the understanding of the psyche' (1994: 28).

26. E.g. in the gloss on δικαίως at 292 and the translation of ἀπιστοῦσαν in 381; cf. also nn. on 517 and 781-800.

27. Cf. nn. on σύγκλητον in 160, ἄγουσι in 382, παραστάτην in 670, Ἰταλίαν in 1119.

28. For tragedy generally see esp. Winkler and Zeitlin, 1990; Sommerstein et al., 1990; Meier, 1993 [1988]; Wilson, 2000; for Sophocles, esp. *Antigone*, see Ehrenberg, 1954; Foley, 1995; Griffith, 1998; Tyrrell and Bennett, 1998.

29. Nelson Mandela played the part of Creon in a performance of the play on Robben Island while he was imprisoned there (Mandela, 1994: 456). For numerous examples of politically charged productions see Steiner, 1984; Hardwick, 2000; Wetmore, 2002; McDonald and Walton, 2002.

30. *Antigone* is the third most frequently performed Greek tragedy (following *Medea* and *Agamemnon*), with 484 productions worldwide since the Renaissance. This figure, derived from Oxford University's Archive of Performances of Greek and Roman Drama (www.classics.ox.ac.uk/apgrd), is current as of October 2002, but is constantly increasing as new evidence is discovered.

31. Wetmore calls it the 'most transculturable' tragedy (2002: 170), but also argues that its themes give it a special pertinence to the twentieth and twenty-first centuries (ibid., 171).

32. Two striking recent contribution are Wiles, 1997 and Rehm, 2002.

33. See, for example, his notes on καλχαίνουσα (20), on chariot-racing (140), on μύδρους (264) and trial by fire (265ff.), on different kinds of nets (345f.), on Zeus ἑρκεῖος (487), on κόπις (601f. and pp. 253-4), on augury and related matters (999-1013), on doors (1186f.), on σαίνει (1213f.), and on swords (1233f.).

Editions

Dawe, R.D. (1996), *Sophoclis Tragoediae*, 3rd ed., Stuttgart and Leipzig

Lloyd-Jones, H. and Wilson, N.G. (1990; corr. edn 1992), *Sophoclis Fabulae*, Oxford

Commentaries

Brown, A. (1987), *Sophocles: Antigone*, Warminster (with facing translation)

Griffith, M. (1999), *Sophocles: Antigone*, Cambridge

Kamerbeek, J.C. (1978), *Antigone* (*The Plays of Sophocles: Commentaries*, Part III), Leiden

Müller, G. (1967), *Sophokles Antigone*, Heidelberg

Translations

Blondell, R. (2002) Sophocles: *The Theban Plays. Antigone, King Oidipous, Oidipous at Colonus*, Focus Classical Library, Newburyport, MA

Ewans, M. (ed.) (1999), *Sophocles: Four Dramas of Maturity. Aias, Antigone, Young Women of Trachis, Oidipous the King*, trans. Michael Ewans, Graham Ley and Gregory McCart, Everyman edition, London and Vermont

Fagles, R. (1982), *Sophocles: The Three Theban Plays*, Introduction and notes by Bernard Knox, London

Gibbons, R. (2003), *Sophocles: Antigone*, Introduction and notes by Charles Segal, Oxford

Kitto, H.D.F. (1994), *Sophocles: Antigone, Oedipus the King, Electra*, edited with Introduction and notes by Edith Hall, Oxford

Lloyd-Jones, H. (1994), *Sophocles II*, Loeb Classical Library vol. 21, Cambridge and London

Bibliography

Barry, W.F. (1887), *The New Antigone*, New York; reprinted New York 1976

Blundell, M.W. (1989), *Helping Friends and Harming Enemies: a study in Sophocles and Greek ethics*, Cambridge

Bowra, C.M. (1944), *Sophoclean Tragedy*, Oxford

Bradshaw, A.T. von S. (1962), 'The watchman scenes in the *Antigone*', *CQ* 12: 200-11

Burton, R.W.B. (1980), *The Chorus in Sophocles' Tragedies*, Oxford

Bushnell, R.W. (1988), *Prophesying Tragedy: sign and voice in Sophocles' Theban plays*, Ithaca, NY

Butler, J. (2000), *Antigone's Claim: kinship between life and death*, New York 2000)

Calder, W.M. III. (1968), 'Sophokles' political tragedy: *Antigone*', *GRBS* 9: 389-407

Coray, M. (1993), *Wissen und Erkennen bei Sophokles*, Basel

Csapo, E. and Slater, W.J. (1995), *The Context of Ancient Drama*, Ann Arbor

Dale, A.M. (ed.) (1954), *Euripides: Alcestis*. Oxford

Dale, A.M. (1968), *The Lyric Meters of Greek Drama*, 2nd ed., Cambridge

Dale, A.M. (1971), 'Metrical analyses of tragic choruses', *BICS* Supp. 21.1

Dale, A.M. (1981), 'Metrical analyses of tragic choruses', *BICS* Supp. 21.2

Dale, A.M. (1983), 'Metrical analyses of tragic choruses', *BICS* Supp. 21.3

Ditmars, E. van Nes (1992), *Sophocles' Antigone: Lyric Shape and Meaning*, Pisa

Dodds, E.R. (1951), *The Greeks and the Irrational*, Berkeley and Los Angeles

Douzinas, C. and Warrington, R. (1994), *Justice Miscarried: ethics, aesthetics and the law*, New York

Dover, K.J. (1972), *Aristophanic Comedy*, Berkeley and Los Angeles

Easterling, P.E. (1990), 'Constructing character in Greek tragedy', in Pelling, 1990: 83-99

Ehrenberg, V. (1954), *Sophocles and Pericles*, Oxford

Else, G.F. (1976), *The Madness of Antigone*, Heidelberg

Foley, H. (1995), 'Tragedy and democratic ideology', in *History, Tragedy, Theory*, ed. B. Goff, Austin, TX: 131-50

Foley, H. (2001), *Female Acts in Greek Tragedy*, Princeton

Gardiner, C.P. (1987), *The Sophoclean Chorus: a study of character and function*. Iowa City

Gill, C. (1996), *Personality in Greek Epic, Tragedy and Philosophy: the self in dialogue*, Oxford

Goheen, R.F. (1951), *The Imagery of Sophocles' Antigone*, Princeton

Goldhill, S. (1986), *Reading Greek Tragedy*, Cambridge

Goldhill, S. (1990), 'Character and action, representation and reading: Greek tragedy and its critics', in Pelling, 1990: 100-27

Gomme, A.W. (1925), 'The position of women in Athens in the fifth and fourth centuries', *CP* 20: 1-25.

Gould, J. (1978), 'Dramatic character and "human intelligibility" in Greek tragedy', *PCPS* 24: 43-67; reprinted in *Myth, Ritual, Memory, and Exchange: essays in Greek literature and culture*, Oxford, 2001: 78-111

Griffith, M. (1998), 'The king and eye: the rule of the father in Greek tragedy', *PCPS* 44: 20-84

Griffith, M. (2001), 'Antigone and her sister(s): embodying women in Greek tragedy', in A. Lardinois and L. McClure (eds), *Making Silence Speak*, Princeton: 117-36

Hardwick, L. (2000), *Translating Words, Translating Cultures*, London

Hester, D.A. (1971), 'Sophocles the unphilosophical', *Mnemosyne* 24: 11-59

Johnson, P.J. (1997), 'Woman's third face: a psycho-social reconsideration of Sophocles' *Antigone*', *Arethusa* 30: 369-98

Jones, J. (1962), *On Aristotle and Greek Tragedy*, London

Kirkwood, G.M. (1958), *A Study of Sophoclean Drama*, Ithaca NY

Kitto, H.D.F. (1958), *Sophocles: dramatist and philosopher*, London

Kitto, H.D.F. (1961), *Greek Tragedy*, 3rd ed., London

Kitto, H.D.F. (1964), *Form and Meaning in Drama*, 2nd ed., London

Knox, B.M.W. (1964), *The Heroic Temper*, Berkeley

Lacan, J. (1992 [1973]), *The Ethics of Psychoanalysis, 1959-1960: the seminar of Jacques Lacan book VII*, ed. J.A. Miller, Eng. trans., New York

Lloyd-Jones, H. and Wilson, N.G. (1990), *Sophoclea: studies on the text of Sophocles*, Oxford

MacKinnon, K. (1986), *Greek Tragedy into Film*, Cranbury, NJ

McClure, L. (1999), *Spoken like a Woman: speech and gender in Athenian drama*, Princeton

McDonald, M. and Walton, J.M. (eds) (2002), *Amid Our Troubles: Irish versions of Greek tragedy*, London

Mandela, N. (1994), *Long Walk to Freedom: the autobiography of Nelson Mandela*, Boston

Méautis, G. (1957), *Sophocle: essai sur le héros tragique*, 2nd ed., Paris

Meier, C. (1993 [1988]), *The Political Art of Greek Tragedy*, Eng. trans., Baltimore, MD

Müller, G.M. (ed.) (1967), *Sophokles: Antigone*, Heidelberg

Murnaghan, S. (1986), '*Antigone* 904-920 and the institution of marriage', *American Journal of Philology* 107: 192-207

Neuburg, M. (1990), 'How like a woman: Antigone's "inconsistency" ', *CQ* 40: 54-76

Nussbaum, M.C. (1986), *The Fragility of Goodness*, Cambridge

Ormand, K. (1999), *Exchange and the Maiden: marriage in Sophoclean tragedy*, Austin, TX

Oudemans, Th.C.W. and Lardinois, A.P.M.H. (1987), *Tragic Ambiguity: anthropology, philosophy and Sophocles' Antigone*, Leiden

Padel, R. (1995), *Whom Gods Destroy: elements of Greek and tragic madness*, Princeton

Parker, R. (1983), *Miasma: pollution and purification in early Greek religion*, Oxford

Parker, R. (1999), 'Through a glass darkly: Sophocles and the divine', in J. Griffin (ed.) *Sophocles Revisited: essays presented to Sir Hugh Lloyd-Jones*, Oxford

Pelling, C.B.R. (ed.) (1990), *Characterization and Individuality in Greek Literature*, Oxford

Perrotta, G. (1935), *Sofocle*, Messina-Florence

Pickard-Cambridge, A.W. (1946), *The Theatre of Dionysus in Athens*, Oxford

Pickard-Cambridge, A.W. (1953), *The Dramatic Festivals of Athens*, Oxford; revised by J. Gould and D.M. Lewis, 1968; reissued with a new supplement, 1988

Rehm, R. (1994), *Marriage to Death: the conflation of wedding and funeral rituals in Greek tragedy*, Princeton

Rehm, R. (2002), *The Play of Space: spatial transformation in Greek tragedy*, Princeton

Reinhardt, K. (1979 [1933]), *Sophocles*, English trans., Oxford

Ringer, M. (1998), *Electra and the Empty Urn: metatheater and role playing in Sophocles*, Chapel Hill

Rohdich, H. (1980), *Antigone: Beitrag zu einer Theorie des sophokleischen Helden* (Heidelberg)

Schadewaldt, W. (1929), 'Sophokles, Aias und Antigone', *Neue Wege zur Antike* 8: 61-109

Scott, William C. (1996), *Musical Design in Sophoclean Theater*, Hanover, NH

Seaford, R. (1987), 'The tragic wedding', *JHS* 107: 106-30

Seaford, R. (1994), *Reciprocity and Ritual: Homer and tragedy in the developing city-state*, Oxford

Segal, C.P. (1964), 'Sophocles' praise of man and the conflicts of the *Antigone*', *Arion* 3: 46-66

Segal, C.P. (1981), *Tragedy and Civilization: an interpretation of Sophocles*, Cambridge, MA

Segal, C.P. (1995), *Sophocles' Tragic World: divinity, nature, society*, Cambridge, MA

Silk, M.S. (ed.) (1996), *Tragedy and the Tragic: Greek theatre and beyond*, Oxford

Sommerstein, A.H., Halliwell, S., Henderson, J. and Zimmermann, B. (eds) (1993), *Tragedy, Comedy and the Polis: papers from the Greek drama conference, Nottingham, 18-20 July 1990*, Bari

Sourvinou-Inwood, C. (1989), 'Assumptions and the creation of meaning: reading Sophocles' *Antigone*', *JHS* 109: 134-48

Steiner, G. (1984), *Antigones: how the Antigone legend has endured in western literature, art, and thought*, Oxford

Sullivan, S.D. (1999), *Sophocles' Use of Psychological Terminology: old and new*, Ottawa

Taplin, O. (1977), *The Stagecraft of Aeschylus*, Oxford

Tyrrell, W.B and Bennett, L.J. (1998), *Recapturing Sophocles' Antigone*, Lanham, MD

Vernant, J.-P. (1988 [1972]), 'Tensions and ambiguities in Greek tragedy', in J.-P. Vernant and P. Vidal-Naquet, *Myth and Tragedy in Ancient Greece*, Eng. trans., New York: 29-48

Vickers, B. (1973), *Towards Greek Tragedy*, London

Waldock, A.J.A. (1951), *Sophocles the Dramatist*, Cambridge

West, M.L. (1982), *Greek Metre*, Oxford

Wetmore, K.J. (2002), *The Athenian Sun in an African Sky: modern African adaptations of classical Greek tragedy*, Jefferson NC

Whitman, C.H. (1951), *Sophocles: a study in heroic humanism*, Cambridge, MA

Wilamowitz, T. von. (1917), *Die dramatische Technik des Sophokles*, Berlin

Wiles, D. (1997), *Tragedy in Athens: performance space and theatrical meaning*, Cambridge

Williams, B. (1993), *Shame and Necessity*, Berkeley and Los Angeles

Wilson, P. (2000), *The Athenian Instutition of the Khoregia: the chorus, the city and the stage*, Cambridge

Winkler, J.J. and Zeitlin, F.I. (eds), *Nothing to Do with Dionysos?*, Princeton

Winnington-Ingram, R.P. (1980), *Sophocles: an interpretation*, Cambridge

Zeitlin, F.I. (1985), 'Playing the Other: theater, theatricality, and the feminine in Greek drama', *Representations* 11: 63-94; reprinted in Winkler and Zeitlin, 1990: 63-96, and in Zeitlin, *Playing the Other: gender and society in classical Greek literature*, Chicago, 1996: 341-74

SOPHOCLES

THE PLAYS AND FRAGMENTS

WITH CRITICAL NOTES, COMMENTARY, AND
TRANSLATION IN ENGLISH PROSE,

BY

Sir RICHARD JEBB, Litt.D.,

HON. D.C.L. OXFORD: HON. LL.D. EDINBURGH, HARVARD, DUBLIN,
AND GLASGOW: HON. DOCT. PHILOS., BOLOGNA.

PART III.

THE ANTIGONE.

PREFACE.

THE *Antigone*, one of the earliest of its author's extant plays,—the *Ajax* alone having a rival claim in this respect,—belongs by time, as by spirit, to the very centre of the age of Pericles. At the probable date of its composition, the Parthenon was slowly rising on the Acropolis, but was still some years from completion; Pheidias, a few years older than Sophocles, and then about sixty, was in the zenith of his powers. The traditional, and best, reading of a verse in the ode to Dionysus (v. 1119) suggests the fresh interest in Southern Italy which Athenians had lately acquired by the foundation of Thurii[1], and recalls the days, then recent, when one of the new colonists, Herodotus, had been in the society of Sophocles. The figure of Antigone, as drawn by the poet, bears the genuine impress of this glorious moment in the life of Athens. It is not without reason that moderns have recognised that figure as the noblest, and the most profoundly tender, embodiment of woman's heroism which ancient literature can show; but it is also distinctively a work of Greek art at the highest. It is marked by the singleness of motive, and the

---

[1] In his able work, *The Age of Pericles* (vol. II. p. 132), Mr Watkiss Lloyd makes an interesting remark with reference to the *Antigone*. Thurii stood near the old site of Sybaris. Têlys was despot of Sybaris when it was destroyed by Croton (*circ.* 510 B.C.). Shortly before that event, he had put some Crotoniat envoys to death, and exposed their unburied bodies before the walls, according to the historian Phylarchus (*circ.* 220 B.C.) in Athen. p. 521 D. Callias, the soothsayer of Têlys, afterwards forsook him,—alarmed by the omens (Her. 5. 44). This story may well have been brought into notoriety at Athens by the keen interest felt just then in Thurii. Creon's part would thus suggest a striking reminiscence.

self-restraint, which belonged to such art; it deserves to be studied sympathetically, and as a whole; for there could be no better example of ideal beauty attained by truth to human nature.

Such a study of the play, as a work of art, stands here in a more than usually intimate relation with that study of language and of detail which it is the secondary office of an interpreter to assist. The poetical texture of the work is, even for Sophocles, remarkably close and fine; it is singularly rich in delicate traits which might easily escape our observation, but which are nevertheless of vital consequence to a just appreciation of the drama in larger aspects. The *Antigone* is thus a peculiarly exacting subject for a commentator. In estimating the shortcomings of an attempt to illustrate it, it may at least be hoped that the critic will not altogether forget the difficulties of the task.

A reference to the works chiefly consulted will be found at p. liv. The editor has been indebted to Mr W. F. R. Shilleto, formerly Scholar of Christ's College, for his valuable assistance in reading the proof-sheets; and must also renew his acknowledgments to the staff of the Cambridge University Press.

The present edition has been carefully revised.

R. C. JEBB.

CAMBRIDGE, *April,* 1900.

CONTENTS.

INTRODUCTION.

§ 1. THE *Oedipus Tyrannus* is concerned with the fall of the Theban king; the *Coloneus*, with the close of his life; and the *Antigone*, with a later episode in the fortunes of his children. But the order of composition was, *Antigone, Tyrannus, Coloneus;* and the first was separated from the last by perhaps more than thirty years of the poet's life. The priority of the *Antigone* admits of a probable explanation, which is not without interest. There is some ground for thinking that the subject—though not the treatment—was suggested by Aeschylus.

The sisters Antigone and Ismene are not mentioned by Homer, Hesiod, or Pindar[1]. Antigone's heroism presupposes a legend that burial had been refused to Polyneices. Pindar knows nothing of such a refusal. He speaks of the seven funeral-pyres provided at Thebes for the seven divisions of the Argive army[2]. Similarly Pausanias records a Theban legend that the corpse of Polyneices was burned on the same pyre with that of Eteocles, and that the very flames refused to mingle[3]. The refusal of burial was evidently an Attic addition to the story.

Earliest trace of the story.

---

[1] Salustius, in his Argument to this play (p. 5), notices that the fortunes of the sisters were differently related by other writers. Mimnermus (*c.* 620 B.C.) spoke of Ismene having been slain at Thebes by Tydeus, one of the Argive chiefs. Ion of Chios (*c.* 450 B.C.) said that both sisters were burned in the Theban temple of Hera by Laodamas, son of Eteocles, when Thebes was taken in the later war of the Epigoni. Here, then, we have an Ionian contemporary of Sophocles who did not know the legend of Antigone's deed,—another indication that the legend was of Attic growth.

[2] Pind. *Ol.* 6. 15; *Nem.* 9. 24.

[3] Paus. 9. 18. 3.

It served to contrast Theban vindictiveness with Athenian humanity; for it was Theseus who ultimately buried the Argives at Eleusis. If Creon's edict, then, was an Attic invention, it may be conjectured that Antigone's resolve to defy the edict was also the conception of an Attic poet. Aeschylus is the earliest author who refers to the edict against burial, and he is also the first who tells of Antigone's resolve. His Theban trilogy consisted of the *Laïus*, the *Oedipus*, and the *Seven against Thebes*[1]. At the end of the last play a herald proclaims an edict just published by the Council of Thebes; sepulture shall be given to Eteocles, but denied to Polyneices. Antigone at once declares her resolve; she will bury Polyneices. The Theban maidens who form the Chorus are divided. One half of their number goes to attend the funeral of Eteocles; the other half accompanies Antigone to her task. There the play ends.

The Aeschylean situation— contrast with the Sophoclean. § 2.   The situation, as it is thus left by the *Seven against Thebes*, is essentially different from that in the play of Sophocles. The Antigone of Aeschylus is not isolated in her action, but is escorted by a band of maidens who publicly avow their sympathy. Though the herald enters a formal protest, and hints that the rulers are likely to be 'severe,' yet he does not say that death is to be the price of disobedience, nor, indeed, does he specify any penalty. The Chorus represents average civic opinion; and one half of the Chorus openly defies the decree. A plot which began thus could scarcely end in the Council taking the heroine's life. It rather foreshadows a final solution which shall be favourable to her; and we might surmise that, in loosing the knot, Aeschylus would have resorted to a divine mandate or intervention. But the Antigone of Sophocles stands alone; the penalty of a dreadful death is definitely set before her; and, whatever the Thebans may think of Creon's edict, no one dares to utter a word of disapproval. Taking the two primary facts—the veto, and Antigone's resolve— Sophocles has worked in a manner which is characteristically his own.

---

[1] With regard to this trilogy, see Introd. to the *Oedipus Tyrannus*, p. xvi.

§ 3.　Let us first trace the outline of the action.

The scene is laid before the palace of Creon,—once that of
Oedipus,—at Thebes. The city has just been delivered from a great peril. It had been besieged by an Argive army, the allies of the exile Polyneices, whom his brother Eteocles had driven out of Thebes, that he himself might be sole king. But on the day before that with which the play begins, the two brothers had slain each other in single fight. Besides Polyneices, six other leaders of the besiegers had been killed by as many Theban chiefs. Thus deprived of its commanders, the besieging host had fled, panic-stricken, in the night.

It is the moment of dawn. Antigone has asked her sister Ismene to come forth with her from the house, in order that they may converse alone. Creon, their uncle, is now king. He has put forth an edict,—that Eteocles, the champion of Thebes, shall be honourably buried; but the body of Polyneices, the country's foe, shall be left on the plain outside the walls of Thebes, for dogs and birds to mangle at their will. If any citizen dares to disobey, he shall be stoned to death. Antigone tells her sister that she is resolved to defy this edict, and to bury their brother Polyneices. Ismene vainly seeks to dissuade her; and Antigone goes forth, alone, to do the deed.

The Chorus of fifteen Theban elders now enters. Creon has summoned them to meet him,—they do not yet know wherefore. They greet the rising sun, and, in a splendid ode, describe the danger from which Thebes has been saved. The dramatic effect of the ode is to make us feel how grievous, from a Theban point of view, has been the act of Polyneices.

Creon comes forth. Declaring his resolve that patriotism and treason shall never miss their due rewards, he acquaints the Chorus with the purport of his edict,—that Eteocles shall be honoured, and Polyneices dishonoured. The elders receive the decision with unquestioning respect; though their words are more suggestive of acquiescence than of approval.

A guard arrives, with the startling news that unknown hands have already paid burial rites to Polyneices, by the symbolical act of sprinkling dust on the corpse. Creon dismisses the man with threats of a terrible death, which the other guards shall share, if they fail to discover the men who have thus broken the edict.

First stasimon: 332—375. Anapaests, 376—383.

The choral ode which follows is a beautiful treatment of a theme which this mysterious deed suggests,—human inventiveness,—its audacity and its almost infinite resource, save for the limits set by fate. As these strains cease, anapaests spoken by the leader of the Chorus express sudden amazement and pain.—Antigone, the royal maiden, the niece of the king, is led in, a prisoner, in the hands of the guard.

III. Second episode: 384—581.

Questioned by Creon, Antigone replies that she knew the edict, but nevertheless paid funeral rites to her brother because she held that no human law could supersede the higher law of the gods. She is ready to die.

Creon, still more incensed by her demeanour, vows that she shall indeed perish by a shameful death. He suspects Ismene also; and she is presently brought in. Agonised by grief for her sister's impending doom, Ismene entreats that she may be considered as sharing the responsibility of the deed; she wishes to die with her sister. Antigone firmly and even sternly, though not bitterly, rejects this claim, which 'justice will not allow'; the deed has been hers only. Ismene vainly seeks to move Creon; he is not touched by her despair, or by the thought—to which Ismene also appeals—that his son Haemon is betrothed to Antigone. He orders that both sisters shall be taken into the house, and closely guarded; for his present purpose is that both shall die.

Second stasimon: 582—625. Anapaests, 626—630.

Moved by the sentence which has just been passed, the Chorus speaks of the destiny which has pursued the royal line of Thebes: 'When a house hath once been shaken from heaven, there the curse fails nevermore.' The sisters were the last hope of the race; and now they too must perish. The ode closes with a strain of general reflection on the power of Zeus and the impotence of human self-will. There is no conscious reference to Creon; but, for the spectators, the words are suggestive and ominous.

IV. Third episode: 631—780.

Haemon enters. He has come to plead with his father for the life of his betrothed Antigone. This scene is one of the finest in the play. A lesser dramatist would have been apt to depict Haemon as passionately agitated. The Haemon of Sophocles maintains an entire calm and self-control so long as a ray of hope remains; his pleading is faultless in tone and in tact; he knows Creon, and he does not intercede with him as a lover for his betrothed; he speaks as a son solicitous for his father's reputation, and as a subject concerned for the authority of his king; he keeps his temper under stinging taunts; it is only when Creon is found to be inexorable that the pent-up fire at last flashes out. Then, when Haemon rushes forth,—resolved, as his latest words hint, not to survive his beloved,—he leaves with the spectators a profound sense of the supreme effort which he has made in a cause dearer to him than life, and has made without success.

Haemon having quitted the scene, Creon announces, in reply to a question of the Chorus, the mode of death which he designs for Antigone. As for Ismene, he will spare her; her entire innocence has been proved, to his calmer thoughts, by the words which passed between the sisters in his presence. Antigone is to be immured in a sepulchral chamber,—one of the rock-tombs in the low hills that fringe the plain of Thebes,—and there she is to be left, with only the formal dole of food which religion prescribes, in order to avert the pollution which the State would otherwise incur through the infliction of death by starvation.

A choral song celebrates the power of Love,—as seen in Haemon, who has not feared to confront a father's anger in pleading for one who has broken the law. While implying that Haemon has acted amiss, the ode also palliates his action by suggesting that the deity who swayed him is irresistible. At the same time this reference to Haemon's passion serves to deepen the pathos of Antigone's fate. *Third stasimon 781—80c Anapaes 801—80;*

She is now brought out of the house by Creon's servants, who are to conduct her to her living tomb. At that sight, the Theban elders cry that pity constrains them, even as love constrained Haemon, to deplore the sentence. Antigone speaks to them of her fate, and they answer not unkindly; yet they say plainly that the blame for her doom rests with herself alone; the king could not grant impunity to a breach of his edict. Creon enters, and reproves the guards for their delay. In her *V. Fout episode: 806—94;*

latest words, Antigone expresses her confidence in the love which awaits her beyond the grave; and also the trouble which overclouds her trust in the gods, who knew her deed, and yet have permitted her to suffer this doom. Then she is led forth, and is seen no more.

Fourth
stasimon:
944—987. The rocky tomb to which she is passing suggests the theme of a choral ode, commemorating three other sufferers of a cruel imprisonment,—Danaë, Lycurgus, and Cleopatra.

VI. Fifth
episode:
988—
1114. As the choral strains cease, the blind and aged prophet Teiresias is led in by a boy. He comes with an urgent warning for the king. The gods are wroth with Thebes; they will no longer give their prophet any sign by the voice of birds, or through the omens of sacrifice. The king is himself the cause, by his edict. Carrion-creatures have defiled the altars of Thebes with the taint of the unburied dead. Let burial rites be at once paid to Polyneices. He speaks for Creon's own good.

Here we pause for a moment to answer a question which naturally occurs to the modern reader. Why is Polyneices said to be still unburied? Has not Antigone already rendered burial rites to him; is it not precisely for that action that she is dying? Antigone had, indeed, given symbolical sepulture to Polyneices by sprinkling dust upon the corpse, and pouring libations. The performance of that act discharged her personal duty towards the dead and the gods below; it also saved her dead brother from the dishonour (which would else have been a reproach to him in the other world) of having been neglected by his nearest kinsfolk on earth. But Antigone's act did not clear Creon. Creon's duty to the dead and to the gods below was still unperformed. So far as Creon was concerned, Polyneices was still unburied. And Creon's obligation could not be discharged, as Antigone's had been, merely by the symbolical act, which religion accepted only when a person was unavoidably hindered from performing regular rites. There was nothing to hinder Creon from performing such rites. These were still claimed from him. After Antigone's tribute had been rendered, birds and dogs had been busy with the corpse. Creon's duty to the dead and to the gods below was now also a duty towards the polluted State, from which his impiety had alienated the gods above.

In reply to the friendly and earnest warning of Teiresias, Creon angrily accuses the seer of mercenary complicity in a disloyal plot; malcontent Thebans wish to gain a triumph over their king by frightening him into a surrender. Never will he grant burial rites to Polyneices.

Teiresias, angered in his turn, then declares the penalty which the gods reserve for such obduracy. With the life of his own son shall Creon atone for his twofold sin,—the detention of the dead among the living, and the imprisonment of the living in the abode of the dead. The seer then departs.

Creon is deeply moved. In the course of long and eventful years he has learned a lesson which is present also to the minds of the Theban elders. The word of Teiresias has never failed to come true.

After a hurried consultation with the Chorus, Creon's resolve is taken. He will yield. He immediately starts, with his servants, for the upper part of the Theban plain, where the body of Polyneices is still lying,—not very far, it would seem, from the place of Antigone's prison.

At this point an objection might suggest itself to the spectator. Is there not something a little improbable in the celerity with which Creon,—hitherto inflexible,—is converted by the threats of a seer whom he has just been denouncing as a venal impostor? Granting that experience had attested the seer's infallibility when speaking in the name of the gods, has not Creon professed to believe that, in this instance, Teiresias is merely the mouthpiece of disloyal Thebans? The answer will be found by attentively observing the state of mind which, up to this point, has been portrayed in Creon. He has, indeed, been inflexible; he has even been vehement in asserting his inflexibility. But, under this vehemence, we have been permitted to see occasional glimpses of an uneasy conscience. One such glimpse is at vv. 889 f., where he protests that *his* hands are clean in regard to Antigone;—he had given her full warning, and he has not shed her blood,—'but at any rate' (δ' οὖν,—*i.e.*, wherever the guilt rests)—'she shall die.' Another such trait occurs at v. 1040, where he says that he will not bury Polyneices, though the throne of Zeus in heaven should be defiled,—quickly adding, 'for I know that no mortal can pollute the gods.'[1] It may further be remarked that a latent self-mistrust is suggested by the very violence of his rejoinder to the Chorus, when they venture, with timid respect, to hint the possibility that some divine agency may have been at work in the mysterious tribute paid to Polyneices (278 f.). A like remark applies to the fury which breaks out at moments in his interviews with Haemon and with Teiresias. The delicacy of the dramatic tact which forbids these touches to be obtrusive is such as Sophocles, alone of the Attic masters, knew how to use. But they suffice to indicate the secret trembling of the balance behind those protestations of an unconquerable resolve; the terrible prophecy of Teiresias only turns the scale.

Hypor-cheme (taking the place of the fifth stasimon): 1115—1154.

The Chorus is now gladdened by the hope that Creon's re-pentance, late though it is, may avail to avert the doom threatened by Teiresias. This feeling is expressed in a short and joyous ode, which invokes the bright presence of Dionysus. May the joyous god come with healing virtue to his favourite Thebes! The substitution of this lively dance-song ('hyporcheme') for a choral ode of a graver cast here serves the same purpose of contrast as in the *Oedipus Tyrannus*, the *Ajax*, and the *Trachiniae*. The catastrophe is approaching[2].

VII. Exo-dos: 1155—1352.

A Messenger now enters,—one of the servants who had accompanied Creon to the plain. The words in which he briefly intimates the nature of his tidings (v. 1173) are overheard, within the house, by Eurydicè, then in the act of going forth with offerings to Pallas; and she swoons. On recovering consciousness, she comes forth, and hears the full account from the Messenger. He says that, when they reached the plain, Creon's first care was for the funeral rites due to Polyneices. After prayer to Pluto and Hecatè, the remains—lacerated by birds and dogs—were washed, and solemnly burned; a high funeral-mound was then raised on the spot. Creon and his followers then repaired to the tomb of Antigone. They found her already dead; she

---

[1] See note on v. 1044.   [2] See note on v. 1115.

had used her veil to hang herself. Haemon, in a frenzied state,
was embracing her corpse. He drew his sword upon his father,
who fled. Then, in a swift agony of remorse, the son slew
himself.

Having heard this news, Eurydicè silently retires into the
house.

She has hardly withdrawn, when Creon enters, with attendants, carrying Haemon's shrouded corpse[1] upon a bier. He
bewails his own folly as the cause of his son's death. Amid his
laments, a Messenger from the house announces that Eurydicè
has stabbed herself at the household altar, with imprecations on
the husband. Wholly desolate and wretched, Creon prays for
death; nor has the Chorus any gentler comfort for him than
the stern precept of resignation,—'Pray thou no more; mortals
have no escape from destined woe.' As he is conducted into
the house, the closing words of the drama are spoken by the
leader of the Chorus: 'Wisdom is the supreme part of happiness,
and reverence towards the gods must be inviolate. Great words
of prideful men are ever punished with great blows, and in old
age teach the chastened to be wise.'

§ 4. This sketch may serve to illustrate the powerful unity *Unity of*
of the play. The issue defined in the opening scene,—the *motive.*
conflict of divine with human law,—remains the central interest
throughout. The action, so simple in plan, is varied by masterly
character-drawing, both in the two principal figures, and in those
lesser persons who contribute gradations of light and shade to
the picture. There is no halting in the march of the drama; at
each successive step we become more and more keenly interested
to see how this great conflict is to end; and when the tragic
climax is reached, it is worthy of such a progress. It would not, *The mode*
however, be warrantable to describe the construction of the play *of the*
as faultless. No one who seeks fully to comprehend and enjoy *strophe.*
this great work of art can be content to ignore certain questions
which are suggested by one part of it,—the part from v. 998 to
1243, which introduces and developes the catastrophe.

---

[1] *i.e.*, an effigy. The deuteragonist, who had acted Haemon, had been on the
stage, as Messenger, up to v. 1256, and had still to come on as Second Messenger
at v. 1278.

Teiresias, as we saw, came with the benevolent purpose of warning Creon that he must bury Polyneices. Creon was stubborn, and Teiresias then said that the gods would punish him. Haemon would die, because his father had been guilty of two sins,—burying Antigone alive[1], and dishonouring the corpse of Polyneices. This prophecy assumed that Creon would remain obdurate. But, in the event, he immediately yielded; he buried Polyneices, and attempted, though too late, to release Antigone. Now suppose that he had been in time to save Antigone. He would then have cancelled both his offences. And then, we must infer, the divine punishment predicted by Teiresias would have been averted; since the prediction does not rest on any statement that a specific term of grace had expired. Otherwise we should have to suppose that the seer did not know the true mind of the gods when he represented that Creon might still be saved by repentance (1025 ff.). But the dramatic function of Teiresias obviously requires us to assume that he was infallible whenever he spoke from 'the signs of his art'; indeed, the play tells us that he was so (1094).

Everything depended, then, on Creon being in time to save Antigone. Only a very short interval can be imagined between the moment at which she is led away to her tomb and that at which Creon resolves to release her; in the play it is measured by 186 verses (928—1114). The Chorus puts Creon's duties in the natural order; 'free the maiden from her rocky chamber, and make a tomb for the unburied dead' (1100); and Creon seems to feel that the release, as the more urgent task, ought to have precedence. Nevertheless, when he and his men arrive on the ground, his first care is given to Polyneices. After the rites have been performed, a high mound is raised. Only then does he proceed to Antigone's prison,—and then it is too late. We are not given any reason for the burial being taken in hand before

---

[1] In his first, or friendly, speech to Creon (998—1032) Teiresias says not a word concerning Antigone. Possibly he may be conceived as thinking that the burial of Polyneices would imply, as a consequence, the release of Antigone; though it is obvious that, from Creon's point of view, such an inference would be illogical: Antigone was punished because she had broken the edict; not because the burying of Polyneices was intrinsically wrong.

the release. The dramatic fault here has nothing to do with any estimate of the chances that Creon might actually have saved Antigone's life, if he had gone to her first. The poet might have chosen to imagine her as destroying herself immediately after she had been left alone in her cell. In any case, the margin for Creon must have been a narrow one. The dramatic fault is that, while we, the spectators, are anxious that Antigone should be saved, and while every moment is precious, we are left to conjecture why Creon should be spending so many of these moments in burial rites which could have been rendered equally well after Antigone had been rescued: nay, when the rites have been finished, he remains to build a mound. The source of pathos contained in the words 'too late' is available for Tragedy, but evidently there is one condition which must be observed. A fatal delay must not seem to be the result merely of negligence or of caprice. As Bellermann has justly said, modern drama has obeyed this rule with a heedfulness not always shown by the ancients. Shakespeare took care that there should be a good reason for the delay of Lorenzo to resuscitate Juliet ; nor has Schiller, in the 'Death of Wallenstein,' left it obscure why Octavio arrived only after Buttler's deed had been done. Euripides, on the other hand, is content that the prolixity of a Messenger's speech should detain Iocasta until the sons whom she longed to reconcile had killed each other.

The dramatic blemish.

§ 5. With regard to Creon's delay in the *Antigone*, I venture to suggest that the true explanation is a simple one. If it seems inadequate when tried by the gauge of modern drama, it will not do so (I think) to those who remember two characteristics of old Greek drama,—first, the great importance of the rhetorical element, more particularly as represented by the speeches of messengers ; secondly, the occasional neglect of clearness, and even of consistency, in regard to matters which either precede the action of the drama (τὰ ἔξω τῆς τραγῳδίας), or, though belonging to the drama itself, occur off the stage. The speech of the first Messenger in the *Antigone* (1192—1243) relates the catastrophe with which the tragedy culminates. Its effect was therefore of the highest importance. Now, if this

A suggested explanation.

speech had first related the terrible scene in Antigone's tomb, and had then passed on to the quiet obsequies of Polyneices, its rhetorical impressiveness would have been destroyed. It was indispensable that the latter part of the recital should correspond with the climax of tragic interest. This, I believe, was the motive present to the poet's mind when, after indicating in the dialogue that the release was to precede the burial, he reversed that order in composing the Messenger's speech. He knew that his Athenian audience would be keenly susceptible to the oratorical quality of that speech, while they would be either inattentive, or very indulgent, to the defect in point of dramatic consistency. The result is a real blemish, though not a serious one; indeed, it may be said to compensate the modern reader for its existence by exemplifying some tendencies of the art which admitted it.

§ 6. The simplicity of the plot is due,—as the foregoing sketch has shown,—to the clearness with which two principles are opposed to each other. Creon represents the duty of obeying the State's laws; Antigone, the duty of listening to the private conscience. The definiteness and the power with which the play puts the case on each side are conclusive proofs that the question had assumed a distinct shape before the poet's mind. It is the only instance in which a Greek play has for its central theme a practical problem of conduct, involving issues, moral and political, which might be discussed on similar grounds in any age and in any country of the world. Greek Tragedy, owing partly to the limitations which it placed on detail, was better suited than modern drama to raise such a question in a general form. The *Antigone*, indeed, raises the question in a form as nearly abstract as is compatible with the nature of drama. The case of Antigone is a thoroughly typical one for the private conscience, because the particular thing which she believes that she ought to do was, in itself, a thing which every Greek of that age recognised as a most sacred duty,— viz., to render burial rites to kinsfolk. This advantage was not devised by Sophocles; it came to him as part of the story which he was to dramatise; but it forms an additional reason for thinking that, when he dramatised that story in the precise

The question raised by the play.

manner which he has chosen, he had a consciously dialectical purpose[1]. Such a purpose was wholly consistent, in this instance, with the artist's first aim,—to produce a work of art. It is because Creon and Antigone are so human that the controversy which they represent becomes so vivid.

§ 7. But how did Sophocles intend us to view the result? What is the drift of the words at the end, which say that 'wisdom is the supreme part of happiness'? If this wisdom, or prudence ($\tau\grave{o}$ $\phi\rho o\nu\epsilon\hat{\iota}\nu$), means, generally, the observance of due limit, may not the suggested moral be that both the parties to the conflict were censurable? As Creon overstepped the due limit when, by his edict, he infringed the divine law, so Antigone also overstepped it when she defied the edict. The drama would thus be a conflict between two persons, each of whom defends an intrinsically sound principle, but defends it in a mistaken way; and both persons are therefore punished. This view, of which Boeckh is the chief representative, has found several supporters. Among them is Hegel:—'In the view of the Eternal Justice, both were wrong, because they were one-sided; but at the same time both were right[2].'

Or does the poet rather intend us to feel that Antigone is wholly in the right,—*i.e.*, that nothing of which the human lawgiver could complain in her was of a moment's account beside the supreme duty which she was fulfilling;—and that Creon was wholly in the wrong,—*i.e.*, that the intrinsically sound maxims of government on which he relies lose all validity when opposed to the higher law which he was breaking? If that was the poet's meaning, then the 'wisdom' taught by the issue

[1] This point might be illustrated by contrast with an able romance, of which the title is borrowed from this play of Sophocles. 'The New Antigone' declined the sanction of marriage, because she had been educated by a father who had taught her to regard that institution as wrongful. Such a case was not well suited to do dramatically what the *Antigone* of Sophocles does,—to raise the question of human law against private conscience in a general form,—because the institution concerned claims to be more than a human ordinance, and because, on the other hand, the New Antigone's opinion was essentially an accident of perverted conscience. The author of the work was fully alive to this, and has said (*Spectator*, Nov. 5, 1887) that his choice of a title conveyed 'a certain degree of irony.'

[2] *Religionsphilosophie*, II. 114.

of the drama means the sense which duly subordinates human to divine law,—teaching that, if the two come into conflict, human law must yield.

This question is one which cannot be put aside by merely suggesting that Sophocles had no didactic purpose at all, but left us to take whichever view we please. For, obviously, according as we adopt one or other of the views, our estimate of the play as a work of art must be vitally affected. The punishments meted out to Creon and Antigone respectively require us to consider the grounds on which they rest. A difference will be made, too, in our conception of Antigone's character, and therefore in our judgment as to the measure of skill with which the poet has portrayed her.

A careful study of the play itself will suffice (I think) to show that the second of the two views above mentioned is the true one. Sophocles has allowed Creon to put his case ably, and (in a measure from which an inferior artist might have shrunk) he has been content to make Antigone merely a nobly heroic woman, not a being exempt from human passion and human weakness; but none the less does he mean us to feel that, in this controversy, the right is wholly with her, and the wrong wholly with her judge.

§ 8. In the first place it is necessary to appreciate the nature of Creon's edict against burying Polyneices. Some modern estimates of the play have seemed to assume that such refusal of sepulture, though a harsh measure, was yet one which the Greek usage of the poet's age recognised as fairly applicable to public enemies, and that, therefore, Creon's fault lay merely in the degree of his severity. It is true that the legends of the heroic age afford some instances in which a dead enemy is left unburied, as a special mark of abhorrence. This dishonour brands the exceptionally base crime of Aegisthus[1]. Yet these same legends also show that, from a very early period, Hellenic feeling was shocked at the thought of carrying enmity beyond the grave, and withholding those rites on which the welfare of the departed spirit was believed to depend. The antiquity of

The character of Creon's edict.

---

[1] Soph. *El.* 1487 ff.

the maxim that, after a battle, the conquerors were bound to allow the vanquished to bury their dead, is proved by the fact that it was ascribed either to Theseus[1] or to Heracles[2]. Achilles maltreated the dead Hector. Yet, even there, the *Iliad* expresses the Greek feeling by the beautiful and touching fable that the gods themselves miraculously preserved the corpse from all defacement and from all corruption, until at last the due obsequies were rendered to it in Troy[3]. The Atreidae refused burial to Ajax; but Odysseus successfully pleaded against the sentence, and Ajax was ultimately buried with all honour[4]. In giving that issue to his play, Sophocles was doing what the general feeling of his own age would strongly demand. Greeks of the fifth century B.C. observed the duty towards the dead even when warfare was bitterest, and when the foe was barbarian. The Athenians buried the Persians slain at Marathon, as the Persians buried the Lacedaemonians slain at Thermopylae. A notable exception may, indeed, be cited; but it is one of those exceptions which forcibly illustrate the rule. The Spartan Lysander omitted to bury the Athenians who fell at Aegospotami; and that omission was remembered, centuries later, as an indelible stigma upon his name[5].

Thus the audience for which Sophocles composed the *Antigone* would regard Creon's edict as something very different from a measure of exceptional, but still legitimate, severity. They would regard it as a shocking breach of that common piety which even the most exasperated belligerents regularly respected.

§ 9. The next point to be considered is, In what sense, and how far, does Creon, in this edict, represent the State? He is the lawful king of Thebes. His royal power is conceived as having no definite limit. The words of the Chorus testify that he is acting within the letter of his right; 'thou hast power, I ween, to take what order thou wilt, both for the dead, and for all us who live' (211 f.). On the other hand, he is acting

The edict in its political aspect.

---

[1] Plut. *Thes.* 29.   [2] Aelian *Var. Hist.* 12. 27.
[3] *Il.* 24. 411 ff.   [4] Soph. *Ai.* 1332 ff.
[5] Paus. 9. 32. 6.

against the unanimous, though silent, sense of Thebes, which, as his son Haemon tells him, held that Antigone had done a glorious deed (695). Creon replies: 'Shall Thebes prescribe to me how I shall rule?' His son rejoins: 'That is no city (πόλις), which belongs to one man' (737). Where the unanimous opinion of the community was ignored, the Athenians of the poet's day would feel that, as Haemon says, there was no 'city' at all. Indeed, when Creon summoned 'the conference of elders,' that summons was itself an admission that he was morally bound to take account of other judgments besides his own. We may often notice in the Attic drama that the constitutional monarchy of the legendary heroic age is made to act in the spirit, and speak in the tone, of the unconstitutional *tyrannis*, as the historical age knew it. This was most natural; it gave an opening for points sure to tell with a 'tyrant-hating' Athenian audience, and it was perfectly safe from objection on the ground of anachronism,—an objection which was about the last that Athenian spectators were likely to raise, if we may judge by the practice of the dramatists. Now, the Creon of the *Antigone*, though nominally a monarch of the heroic age, has been created by the Attic poet in the essential image of the historical *tyrannus*. The Attic audience would mentally compare him, not to an Agamemnon or an Alcinous, but to a Hippias or a Periander. He resembles the ruler whose absolutism, imposed on the citizens by force, is devoid of any properly political sanction. Antigone can certainly be described, with technical correctness, as acting 'in despite of the State,' since Creon is the State, so far as a State exists. But the Greeks for whom Sophocles wrote would not regard Creon's edict as having a constitutional character, in the sense in which that character belonged to laws sanctioned (for instance) by the Athenian Ecclesia. They would liken it rather to some of the arbitrary and violent acts done by Hippias in the later period of his 'tyranny.' To take a modern illustration, they would view it in a quite different light from that in which we should regard the disobedience of a Russian subject to a ukase of the Czar.

If, then, we endeavour to interpret Creon's action by the

standards which the poet's contemporaries would apply, we find, first, that he is doing a monstrous act; secondly, that, in doing it, he cannot, indeed, be said to exceed his prerogative, since this is indefinite; but he is exceeding his moral right in such a manner that he becomes the counterpart of the *tyrannus* who makes a cruel use of an unconstitutional power.

§ 10. Antigone, on the other hand, is fulfilling one of the most Antigone's sacred and the most imperative duties known to Greek religion; position. and it is a duty which could not be delegated. She and her sister are the nearest kinsfolk of the dead. It is not to be expected that any stranger should brave the edict for the dead man's sake. As the Chorus says, 'no man is so foolish that he is enamoured of death' (220). Creon is furious when the Chorus suggests that the rites so mysteriously paid to the corpse may have been due to the agency of the gods (278 f.). That very suggestion of the Chorus shows how impossible it seemed to the Theban mind that Polyneices could receive the ministration of any human hand. A modern critic, taking the view that Antigone was wrong, has observed (not ironically) that she ought to have left the gods to provide the burial. It would have been ill for the world if all who have done heroic deeds had preferred to await miracles. As to another suggestion,—that Antigone ought to have tried persuasion with Creon,—the poet has supplied the answer in his portraiture of Creon's character,—a character known to Antigone from long experience. The situation in which Antigone was placed by Creon's edict was analogous to that of a Christian martyr under the Roman Empire. It was as impossible for Antigone to withhold those rites, which no other human being could now render, as it was impossible for the Christian maiden to avoid the torments of the arena by laying a grain of incense on the altar of Diana[1]. From both alike those laws which each believed to be 'the unfailing statutes of Heaven' claimed an allegiance which no human law could cancel, and it was by the human

---

[1] Mr Long's beautiful picture, 'Diana or Christ,' will be remembered by many,— and the more fitly, since it presents a counterpart, not only for Antigone, but also for Creon and for Haemon.

ruler, not by his victim, that the conflict of loyalties had been made inevitable.

The attitude of the Chorus.

§ 11. One of the main arguments used to show that Sophocles conceived Antigone as partly censurable has been drawn from the utterances of the Chorus. It is therefore important to determine, if we can, what the attitude of these Theban Elders really is. Their first ode (the Parodos) shows how strongly they condemn Polyneices, as having led a hostile army against his country. We might have expected, then, that, when Creon acquainted them with his edict, they would have greeted it with some mark of approval. On the contrary, their words are confined to a brief utterance of submission : ‘Such is thy pleasure, Creon, son of Menoeceus, touching this city’s foe, and its friend ; and thou hast power, I ween, to take what order thou wilt, both for the dead, and for all us who live’ (211 ff.). We can see that they are startled by such a doom, even for a man whom they hold deeply guilty. Their words suggest a misgiving. Just afterwards, they significantly excuse themselves from taking any part in the enforcement of the edict (216). But it is otherwise when the edict, having been published, is broken. Then they range themselves on Creon’s side. They refer to the disobedience as a daring offence (371). When Antigone is brought in, they speak of her folly (383). Nevertheless, Antigone is convinced that, in their hearts, they sympathise with her (504). And, indeed, it is plain that they do so, to this extent,—that they consider the edict to have been a mistake ; though they also hold that it was wrong to break the edict. Hence they speak of Antigone’s act as one prompted by ‘frenzy at the heart’ (603). The clearest summary of their whole view—up to this point of the drama—is given in verses 872—875, and amounts to this :—Antigone’s act was, in itself, a pious one ; but Creon, as a ruler, was bound to vindicate his edict. Her ‘self-willed temper’ has brought her to death.

So far, then, the view taken by the Chorus is very much Boeckh’s :—the merits are divided ; Creon is both right and wrong ; so, too, is Antigone. But then Teiresias comes (v. 988), and convinces the Chorus that Creon has been wholly wrong ; wrong in refusing burial to Polyneices ; wrong in punishing

Antigone. It is at the urgent advice of the Chorus that Creon yields. And when, a little later, Creon blames himself as the cause of all the woe, the Chorus replies that now at last he sees the truth (v. 1270). Thus the Theban Elders entertain two different opinions in succession. Their first opinion is overthrown by Teiresias. Their second opinion—which they hold from verse 1091 onwards—is that which the poet intends to be recognised as the true one.

§ 12. After thus tracing the mind of the Chorus, we can see more clearly why it is composed of Theban elders. When the chief person of a Greek tragedy is a woman, the Chorus usually consists of women, whose attitude towards the heroine is more or less sympathetic. Such is the case in the *Electra* and the *Trachiniae,* and in seven plays of Euripides,—the *Andromache, Electra, Hecuba, Helena,* both *Iphigeneias,* and *Medea.* The Chorus of the *Alcestis,* indeed, consists of Pheraean elders: but then Alcestis is withdrawn from the scene at an early moment, and restored to it only at the end: during the rest of the play, the interest is centred in Admetus. In the *Antigone,* Sophocles had a double reason for constituting the Chorus as he did. First, the isolation of the heroine would have been less striking if she had been supported by a group of sympathetic women. Secondly, the natural predisposition of the Theban nobles to support their king heightens the dramatic effect of their ultimate conversion.

Why the Chorus is so constituted.

§ 13. The character of Antigone is a separate question from the merit of the cause in which she is engaged. She might be doing right, and yet the poet might have represented her as doing it in such a manner as to render her heroism unattractive. We may now turn to this question, and consider what manner of woman she is.

Character of Antigone.

Two qualities are at the basis of her character. One is an enthusiasm, at once steadfast and passionate, for the right, as she sees it,—for the performance of her duty. The other is intense tenderness, purity, and depth of domestic affection ; manifested here in the love of sister for brother, a love which death has not weakened, but only consecrated ; as in the *Oedipus Coloneus*—where the portraiture of her is entirely in unison with that given here—it is manifested in the tender anxiety to reconcile her living brothers, and in the fearless, completely selfless devotion—through painful wanderings, through all misery and all reproach—to the old age of her blind and homeless father. In the opening scene of the play, we find her possessed by a burning indignation at the outrage done to her dead brother; the deep love which she feels for him is braced by a clear sense of the religious duty which this edict lays upon her, and by an unfaltering resolve to do it; it never occurs to her for an instant that, as a true sister, she could act otherwise; rather it seems wonderful to her that the author of the edict should even have expected it to prove deterrent—for *her* (ver. 32).

Her relation to Ismene. With her whole heart and soul dominated by these feelings, she turns to her sister Ismene, and asks for her aid; not as if the response could be doubtful—she cannot imagine its being doubtful; it does not enter her mind that one whom she has just addressed by so dear a name, and with whom her tie of sisterhood is made closer still by the destiny which has placed them apart, can be anything but joyful and proud to risk life in the discharge of a duty so plain, so tender, and so sacred. And how does Ismene meet her? Ismene reminds her that other members of their house have perished miserably, and that, if Antigone acts thus, Antigone and she will die more miserably still: they are women, and must not strive with men; they are subjects, and must not strive with rulers: Ismene will ask the dead to excuse her, since she is constrained, and will obey the living: 'for it is witless *to be over-busy*' (περισσὰ πράσσειν, v. 68). Ismene is amiable enough; she cannot be called exceptionally weak or timid; she is merely the average woman; her answer here is such as would have been made by most women—and perhaps by a still larger proportion of men, as the Chorus afterwards forcibly reminds us. But, given the character and the present mood of Antigone, what must be the effect of such a reply to such an appeal? It is the tenderness, quite as much as the strength, of Antigone's spirit that speaks in her answer:—'I will not urge thee,—no, nor, if thou yet shouldst have the mind, wouldst thou be welcome as a worker with me.' And the calmest reason thoroughly approves that answer; for the very terms in which Ismene had repulsed her sister proved a nature which could never rise to the height of such a task, and which would be more dangerous as an ally than as a neutral.

When the sisters next meet, it is in Creon's presence, and the situation is this:—Antigone has done the deed, unaided; and Creon has said that both sisters shall die—for he suspects Ismene of complicity. Ismene's real affection is now quickened by a feverish remorse, and by an impulse towards self-immolation,—an impulse of a sentimental and almost hysterical kind: she will say that she helped Antigone; she will die with her; she will yet make amends to the dead. Was Antigone to indulge Ismene's impulse, and to allow Ismene's words to confirm Creon's suspicions? Surely Antigone was bound to do what she does,—namely, to speak out the truth: 'Nay, Justice will not suffer thee to do that; thou didst *not* consent to the deed, neither did I give thee part in it.' But it will be said that her tone towards Ismene is too stern and hard. The sternness is only that of truth; the hardness is only that of reality: for, among the tragic circumstances which surround Antigone, this is precisely one of the most tragic, that Ismene's earlier conduct, at the testing-point of action, *has* made a spiritual division which no emotional after-impulse can cancel. One more point may be raised: when Ismene says, 'What life is dear to me, bereft of thee?'—Antigone replies, 'Ask Creon—all thy care is for him' (v. 549): is not this, it may be asked, a needless taunt? The answer is found in Antigone's wish to save Ismene's life. Thus far in the dialogue, Ismene has persisted—even after Antigone's denial—in claiming a share in the deed (vv. 536—547). Creon might well think that, after all, the fact was as he suspected. It was necessary for Antigone to make him see—by some trenchant utterance—that she regarded Ismene as distinctly ranged on his side. And she succeeded. Later in the play, where Creon acknowledges Ismene's innocence, he describes it in the very phrase which Antigone had impressed upon his memory; he speaks of Ismene as one '*who has not touched*' the deed (v. 771: cp. v. 546). It is with pain (v. 551), it is not with scorn or with bitterness, that Antigone remains firm. Her attitude is prescribed equally by regard for truth and right, and by duty towards her sister.

**Her rela-
tion to
Haemon.**

Antigone is betrothed to Haemon; the closeness of the
affection between them is significantly marked by the words of
Ismene (v. 570); it is expressed in the words, the deeds, and the
death, of Haemon. If verse 572 is rightly assigned to Antigone
(as, in my opinion, it is), that brief utterance tells much : but let
us suppose that it belongs to Ismene, and that Antigone never
once refers directly to Haemon : we say, 'directly,' because more
than once she alludes to sweet hopes which life had still to offer
her. It is evident that, if Sophocles had given greater prominence to Antigone's love for Haemon, he could have had
only one aim, consistently with the plan of this play,—viz., to
strengthen our sense of the ties which bound her to life,
and, therefore, of her heroism in resigning it. But it is also
evident that he could have done this, with any effect, only at
the cost of depicting a mind divided between the desire of
earthly happiness and the resolve to perform a sacred duty.
Sophocles has preferred to portray Antigone as raised above
every selfish thought, even the dearest, by the absorbing and
inspiring sense of her duty to the dead, and to the gods; silent,
not through apathy, concerning a love which could never be hers,
and turning for comfort to the faith that, beyond the grave, the
purest form of human affection would reunite her to those whom
she had lost. It is no blame to later dramatists that they
found it necessary to make more of the love-motive; but, if our
standard is to be the noblest tragic art, it is a confession of their
inferiority to Sophocles. There is a beautiful verse in the play
which might suggest how little he can have feared that his
heroine would ever be charged with a cold insensibility. Creon
has urged that the honour which she has shown to Polyneices
will be resented by the spirit of Eteocles. Antigone answers,
'It is not my nature to join in hating, but in loving.' As she
had sought to reconcile them while they lived, so now she will
have no part in their feud—if feud there be where they have
gone,—but will love each, as he loves her.

**The re-
action in
Antigone's
mind.**

So long as her task lies before Antigone, she is sustained
by the necessity for action. Nor does she falter for a moment,
even after the deed has been done, so long as she is in the
presence of Creon. For though she has no longer the stimulus

of action, there is still another challenge to her fortitude; she, who is loyal to the divine law, cannot tremble before the man who is its embodied negation. It is otherwise when Creon is gone, and when there are only the Theban elders to see and hear her, as she is led to death. The strain on her mind is relaxed; the end is near; she now feels the longing for some word of pity as she passes to the grave,—for some token of human kindness. But, while she craves such sympathy, the Theban nobles merely console her with the thought of post-humous fame. She compares her doom to Niobe's; and they reply that it is a glory for her to be as Niobe, a daughter of the Tantalidae,—

> the seed of gods,
> Men near to Zeus; for whom on Ida burns,
> High in clear air, the altar of their Sire,
> Nor hath their race yet lost the blood divine[1].

Few things in tragedy are more pathetic than this yearning of hers, on the brink of death, for some human kindness of farewell, thus 'mocked'[2], as she feels it to be, by a cold assurance of renown. She turns from men to invoke 'the fount of Dircè and the holy ground of Thebes'; these, at least, will be her witnesses. In her last words, she is thinking of the dead, and of the gods; she feels sure of love in the world of the dead; but she cannot lift her face to the gods, and feel sure that they are with her. If they are so, why have they allowed her to perish for obeying them? Yet, again, they *may* be with her; she will know beyond the grave. If she has sinned, she will learn it there; but if she is innocent, the gods will vindicate when she is gone. How infinitely touching is this supreme trouble which clouds her soul at the last,—this doubt and per-plexity concerning the gods! For it is not a misgiving as to the paramount obligation of the 'unwritten laws' which she has obeyed: it is only an anguish of wonder and uncertainty as to the mysterious ways of the powers which have laid this

---

[1] From the *Niobe* of Aeschylus (fr. 157): οἱ θεῶν ἀγχίσποροι, | οἱ Ζηνὸς ἐγγύς· οἷς κατ' Ἰδαῖον πάγον | Διὸς πατρῴου βωμός ἐστ' ἐν αἰθέρι, | κοὔπω νιν ἐξίτηλον αἷμα δαιμόνων.

[2] v. 839.

obligation on mortals,—a surmise that, as gods and men seem alike without pity for her, there has perhaps been something wrong in her way of doing the duty which was so clear and so binding.

Distinctive merit of the por- traiture. § 14. The psychology of Sophocles is so excellent in the case of Antigone because he has felt that in a truly heroic nature there is the permanent strength of deep convictions, but there is also room for what superficial observers might think a moral anticlimax. So long as such a nature has to meet antagonism in word or deed, its permanent strength is heightened by a further support which is necessarily transient, —the strength of exaltation. But a mind capable of heroism is such as can see duties in their true proportions, and can sacrifice everything to the discharge of the highest: and it is such a mind, too, which, in looking back on a duty done, is most liable—through very largeness of vision, and sense of human limitations—to misgivings like those which vex the last moments of Antigone. The strength of exaltation has passed away; her clear intelligence cannot refuse to acknow- ledge that the actual results of doing right are in seeming conflict with the faith which was the sanction of the deed. It is worthy of notice that only at one moment of the drama does Antigone speak lightly of the penalty which she has deliberately incurred. That is at the moment when, face to face with Creon, she is asserting the superiority of the divine law. Nor does she, even then, speak lightly of death in itself; she only says that it is better than a life like hers; for at that moment she feels the whole burden of the sorrows which have fallen upon her race,—standing, as she does, before the man who has added the last woe. The tension of her mind is at the highest. But nowhere else does she speak as one who had sought death because weary of life; on the contrary, we can see that that life was dear to her, who must die young, 'without a portion in the chant that brings the bride.' It is a perfectly sane mind which has chosen death, and has chosen it only because the alternative was to neglect a sacred duty.

A comparison with other dramatists may serve to illustrate what Sophocles has gained by thus allowing the temporary strength of excitement to pass off before the end, leaving the permanent strength of the character to wrestle with this pain and doubt. In Alfieri's play of the same name, Antigone shows no touch of human weakness; as death approaches, she seems more and more impatiently eager for it; she says to Creon's guards, who are leading her to her doom,—

> Let us make better speed; so slow a step
> Ill becomes her who has at length just reach'd
> The goal so long desired... Perhaps ye, O guards,
> May feel compassion for my fate?... Proceed.
> Oh terrible Death, I look thee in the face,
> And yet I tremble not[1].

In Massinger's *Virgin Martyr*, again, consider the strain in which Dorothea addresses Theophilus, the persecutor of the Christians, who has doomed her to torture and death:—

> Thou fool!
> That gloriest in having power to ravish
> A trifle from me I am weary of,
> What is this life to me? Not worth a thought;
> Or, if it be esteem'd, 'tis that I lose it
> To win a better: even thy malice serves
> To me but as a ladder to mount up
> To such a height of happiness, where I shall
> Look down with scorn on thee and on the world.

The dramatic effect of such a tone, both in Alfieri's Antigone and in Massinger's Dorothea, is to make their fate not more, but less, pathetic; we should feel for them more if they, on their part, seemed to feel a little 'what 'tis to die, and to die young,'— as Theophilus says to Dorothea. On the other hand, M. Casimir Delavigne, in his *Messéniennes*, is Sophoclean where he describes the last moments of Joan of Arc:

> Du Christ, avec l'ardeur, Jeanne baisait l'image;
> Ses longs cheveux épars flottaient au gré des vents:
> Au pied de l'échafaud, sans changer de visage,
> Elle s'avançait à pas lents.

---

[1] C. Taylor's translation.

Tranquille elle y monta ; quand, debout sur le faîte,
Elle vit ce bûcher, qui l'allait dévorer,
Les bourreaux en suspens, la flamme déja prête,
Sentant son cœur faillir, elle baissa la tête,
Et se prit à pleurer[1].

So it is that the Antigone of Sophocles, in the last scene of her life, feels her heart fail, bows her head, and weeps ; but the first verse of the passage just quoted suggests a difference which makes the Greek maiden the more tragic figure of the two : when Antigone looked to heaven, she could find no certain comfort.

Thus has Sophocles created a true heroine ; no fanatic enamoured of martyrdom, no virago, but a true woman, most tender-hearted, most courageous and steadfast ; whose sense of duty sustains her in doing a deed for which she knows that she must die ;—when it has been done, and death is at hand, then, indeed, there is a brief cry of anguish from that brave and loving spirit ; it is bitter to die thus : but human sympathy is denied to her, and even the gods seem to have hidden their faces. Nowhere else has the poetry of the ancient world embodied so lofty or so beautiful an ideal of woman's love and devotion. The Macaria of Euripides resigns her life to save the race of the Heracleidae ; his Iphigeneia, to prosper the course of the Greek fleet ; his Alcestis, to save the life of her husband. In each of these cases, a divine voice had declared that some one must die ; in each, the heroism required was purely passive ; and in each a definite gain was promised,—for it was at least a pious opinion in the wife of Admetus (when all his other friends had declined his request that some of them would oblige him by dying for him[2]) to think that his survival would be a gain. Not one of these Euripidean heroines, pathetic though they be, can for a moment be ranked with Fedalma in George Eliot's *Spanish Gypsy*, when

---

[1] Quoted by M. Patin in his *Études sur les Tragiques grecs*, vol. II., p. 271.

[2] Has the total absence of the sense of humour, in its disastrous effect upon tragic pathos, ever been more wonderfully illustrated than by Euripides in those lines of the *Alcestis?*—πάντας δ' ἐλέγξας καὶ διεξελθὼν φίλους, | πατέρα, γεραιάν θ' ἥ σφ' ἔτικτε μητέρα, | οὐχ ηὗρε πλὴν γυναικὸς ὅστις ἤθελε | θανεῖν πρὸ κείνου μηδ' ἔτ' εἰσορᾶν φάος. (vv. 15 ff.)

she accepts what seems worse than death for the sake of benefits to her race which are altogether doubtful ;—

'my soul is faint—
Will these sharp pains buy any certain good?'

But Antigone is greater than Fedalma.   There was no father, no Zarca, at Antigone's side, urgently claiming the sacrifice,— on the contrary, there was a sister protesting against it ; Antigone's choice was wholly free ; the heroism which it imposed was one of doing as well as suffering ; and the sole reward was to be in the action itself.

§ 15.   The character of Creon, as Sophocles draws it in this Creon. play, may be regarded in somewhat different lights.   It is interesting, then, to inquire how the poet meant it to be read. According to one view, Creon is animated by a personal spite against both Polyneices and Antigone ; his maxims of state-policy are mere pretexts.   This theory seems mistaken.   There is, indeed, one phrase which might suggest previous dissensions between Creon and Antigone (v. 562).   It is also true that Creon is supposed to have sided with Eteocles when Polyneices was driven into exile.   But Sophocles was too good a dramatist to lay stress on such motives in such a situation.   Rather, surely, Creon is to be conceived as entirely sincere and profoundly earnest when he sets forth the public grounds of his action. They are briefly these.   Anarchy is the worst evil that can befall a State : the first duty of a ruler is therefore to enforce law and maintain order.   The safety of the individual depends on that of the State, and therefore every citizen has a direct interest in obedience.   This obedience must be absolute and unquestioning.   The ruler must be obeyed 'in little things and great, in just things *and unjust*' (v. 667).   That is, the subject must never presume to decide for himself what commands may be neglected or resisted.   By rewarding the loyal and punishing the disloyal, a ruler will promote such obedience.

Creon puts his case with lucidity and force.   We are reminded Comparison of that dialogue in which Plato represents Socrates, on the eve with Plato's of execution, as visited in prison by his aged friend Crito, who *Crito*. comes to tell him that the means of escape have been provided, and to urge that he should use them. Socrates imagines the Laws of Athens remonstrating with him : ' Do you imagine that a State can subsist, in which the decisions of law are set aside by individuals?' And to the plea that 'unjust' decisions may be disobeyed, the Laws rejoin,—' Was *that* our agreement with you? Or were you to abide by the sentence of the State?' When Antigone appeals to the laws of Hades (v. 451), might not Creon's laws, then, say to her what the laws of Athens say with regard to the hypothetical flight of Socrates :—' We shall be angry with you while you live, and our brethren, the Laws in the world below, will receive you as an enemy ; for they will know that you have done your best to destroy us'?

Plato, it has been truly said, never intended to answer the question of casuistry, as to when, if ever, it is right to break the city's law. But at least there is one broad difference between the cases supposed in the *Crito* and the *Antigone*. Antigone had a positive religious duty, about which there was no doubt at all, and with which Creon's law conflicted. For Socrates to break prison might be justifiable, but could not be described as a positive religious duty ; since, however much good he might feel confident of effecting by preserving his life, he was at least morally entitled to think that such good would be less than the evil of the example. Creon is doing what, in the case of Socrates, Athens did not do,—he is invading the acknowledged province of religion. Not that he forgets the existence of the gods : he reveres them in what he believes to be the orthodox way[1]. But he assumes that under no imaginable circumstances can the gods disapprove of penalties inflicted on a disloyal citizen. Meanwhile his characteristic tendency 'to do everything too much' has led him into a step which renders this assumption disastrous. He punishes Polyneices in a manner which violates religion.

Creon's attitude towards Antigone. In Antigone, again, he sees anarchy personified, since, having disobeyed, she seems to glory therein (v. 482). Her defence is unmeaning to him, for her thoughts move in a different region from his own. Sophocles has brought this out with admirable

---

[1] See especially the note on 1044.

skill in a short dialogue between Creon and Antigone (508—525): we see that he cannot get beyond his principle of State rewards and punishments ; she is speaking foolishness to him—as, indeed, from the first she had felt the hopelessness of their understanding each other (469 f., 499 f.). As this dialogue serves to show Creon's unconsciousness of the frontier between divine and human law, so his scene with Haemon brings out his incapacity to appreciate the other great motive of Antigone's conduct,—sisterly piety. Creon regards the Family almost exclusively in one aspect ; for him it is an institution related to the State as the gymnasium to the stadium ; it is a little State, in which a man may prove that he is fit to govern a larger one.

Creon's temper is hasty and vehement. He vows that Haemon 'shall not save those two girls from their doom' ; but, when the Chorus pleads for Ismene, he quickly adds that he will spare *her*,—'thou sayest well' (770 f.). We also notice his love of hyperbole (1039 ff.). But he is not malevolent. He represents the rigour of human law,—neither restricted by the sense of a higher law, nor intensified by a personal desire to hurt. He has the ill-regulated enthusiasm of a somewhat narrow understanding for the only principle which it has firmly grasped.

§ 16. Such, then, are the general characteristics which mark the treatment of this subject by Sophocles. In a drama of rare poetical beauty, and of especially fine psychology, he has raised the question as to the limit of the State's authority over the individual conscience. It belongs to the essence of the tragic pathos that this question is one which can never be answered by a set formula. Enough for Antigone that she finds herself in a situation where conscience leaves her no choice but to break one of two laws, and to die.

These distinctive qualities of the play may be illustrated by a glance at the work of some other poets. The *Antigone* of Euripides is now represented only by a few small fragments, Euripides. and its plot is uncertain. It would seem, however, that, when Antigone was caught in the act of burial, Haemon was assisting her, and that the play ended, not with her death, but with her marriage[1]. Some of the fragments confirm the belief that the love-motive was prominent[2]. The Roman poet Attius (*c.* 140 B.C.) also wrote an *Antigone*. The few remaining verses—some of which have lived only because Vergil imitated them—indicate

---

[1] All that we know as to the plot is contained in the first Argument to this play (see p. 3 below, and notes on p. 4): 'The story has been used also by Euripides in his *Antigone*; only there she is detected with Haemon, and is given in marriage, and bears a son Maion.' In the scholia at the end of L we also read, 'this play differs from the *Antigone* of Euripides in the fact that, there, she was detected through the love of Haemon, and was given in marriage; while here the issue is the contrary' (*i.e.* her death). That this is the right rendering of the scholiast's words—φωραθεῖσα ἐκείνη διὰ τὸν Αἴμονος ἔρωτα ἐξεδόθη πρὸς γάμον—seems probable from a comparison with the statement in the Argument; though others have understood, 'she was detected, and, owing to the love of Haemon, given in marriage.' She was detected, not, as in the play of Sophocles, directly by Creon's guards, but (in some way not specified) through the fact that Haemon's love for her had drawn him to her side.

Welcker (*Griech. Trag.* II. pp. 563 ff.) has sought to identify the *Antigone* of Euripides with the plot sketched by Hyginus in *Fab.* 72. Antigone having been detected, Haemon had been commissioned by Creon to slay her, but had saved her, conveying her to a shepherd's home. When Maion, the son of their secret marriage, had grown to man's estate, he visited Thebes at a festival. This was the moment (Welcker thinks) at which the *Antigone* of Euripides began. Creon noted in Maion a certain mark which all the offspring of the dragon's seed (σπαρτοί) bore on their bodies. Haemon's disobedience was thus revealed; Heracles vainly interceded with Creon; Haemon slew his wife Antigone and then himself.

But surely both the author of the Argument and the scholiast clearly imply that the marriage of Antigone was contained in the play of Euripides, and formed its conclusion. I therefore agree with Heydemann (*Ueber eine nacheuripideische Antigone*, Berlin, 1868) that Hyginus was epitomising some otherwise unknown play.

M. Patin (*Études sur les Tragiques grecs*, vol. II. p. 277) remarks that there is nothing to show whether the play of Euripides was produced before or after that of Sophocles. But he has overlooked a curious and decisive piece of evidence. Among the scanty fragments of the Euripidean *Antigone* are these lines (Eur. fr. 165, Nauck); —ἄκουσον· οὐ γὰρ οἱ κακῶς πεπραγότες | σὺν ταῖς τύχαισι τοὺς λόγους ἀπώλεσαν. This evidently glances at the *Antigone* of Sophocles, vv. 563 f., where Ismene says, οὐδ' ὃς ἂν βλάστῃ μένει | νοῦς τοῖς κακῶς πράσσουσιν, ἀλλ' ἐξίσταται. (For similar instances of covert criticism, see n. on *O. C.* 1116.)

[2] Eur. fr. 160, 161, 162 (Nauck). The most significant is fr. 161, probably spoken by Haemon:—ἥρων· τὸ μαίνεσθαι δ' ἄρ' ἦν ἔρως βροτοῖς.—Another very suggestive fragment is no. 176, where the speaker is evidently remonstrating with Creon:— 'Who shall pain a rock by thrusting at it with a spear? And who can pain the dead by dishonour, if we grant that they have no sense of suffering?' This is characteristic of the difference between the poets. Sophocles never urges the *futility* of Creon's vengeance, though he does touch upon its ignobleness (v. 1030).

eloquence and spirit, but give no clue to the plot[1]. Statius, in Statius. his epic *Thebaid*, departs widely from the Attic version of the story. Argeia, the widow of Polyneices, meets Antigone by night at the corpse. Each, unknown to the other, has come to do the same task; both are put to death by Creon,—'ambae hilares et mortis amore superbae[2].' This rapturous welcoming of death is, as we have seen, quite in the manner of Massinger and Alfieri, but not at all in that of Sophocles.

Alfieri's *Antigone* (published in 1783) follows Statius in asso- Alfieri. ciating Argeia with Antigone; besides whom there are only two other actors, Creon and Haemon. The Italian poet has not improved upon the Greek. There are here two heroines, with very similar parts, in performing which they naturally utter very similar sentiments. Then Alfieri's Creon is not merely a perverse despot of narrow vision, but a monster of wickedness, who, by a thought worthy of Count Cenci, has published the edict for the express purpose of enticing Antigone into a breach of it. Having doomed her to die, he then offers to pardon her, if she will marry his son (and so unite the royal line with his own); but Antigone, though she esteems Haemon, declines to marry the son of such a parent. So she is put to death, while Argeia is sent back to Argos; and Haemon kills himself. It is not altogether unprofitable to be reminded, by such examples, what the theme of Sophocles could become in other hands.

§ 17. A word may be added regarding treatments of the Vase-subject in works of art, which are not without some points of paintings. literary interest. Baumeister reproduces two vase-paintings, both curious[3]. The first[4] represents a group of three figures,—the

---

[1] Only six fragments remain, forming, in all, ten (partly incomplete) lines: Ribbeck, *Trag. Rom. Frag.* p. 153 (1871). The Ismene of Attius said to her sister (fr. 2), *quanto magis te isti modi esse intellego,* | *Tanto, Antigona, magis me par est tibi consulere et parcere:* with which Macrobius (*Sat.* 6. 2. 17) compares Verg. *Aen.* 12. 19 *quantum ipse feroci* | *Virtute exsuperas, tanto me impensius aecum est* | *Consulere atque omnes metuentem expendere casus.* Again, he notes (*Sat.* 6. 1. 59) fr. 5, *iam iam neque di regunt* | *Néque profecto deúm supremus réx* [*res*] *curat hominibus,* as having an echo in *Aen.* 4. 371 *iamiam nec maxima Iuno* | *Nec Saturnius haec oculis pater aspicit aequis.* This latter fragment of Attius is well compared by Ribbeck with Soph. *Ant.* 921 ff.: the words were doubtless Antigone's.

[2] Stat. *Theb.* 12. 679.

[3] *Denkmäler*, pp. 83 f.   [4] From Gerhard, *Ant. Bildw.* Taf. 73.

central figure being an old man who has just doffed the mask
of a young maiden,—while a guard, spear in hand, seizes him by
the neck. This is explained as a comic parody of Antigone's
story; she has sent an old servant to perform the task in her
stead, and he, when confronted with Creon, drops his disguise.
The other vase-painting[1],—of perhaps *c.* 380—300 B.C.,—represents Heracles interceding with Creon, who is on the hero's right
hand, while Antigone and Haemon are on his left. Eurydicè,
Ismene, and a youth (perhaps Maion, the offspring of Antigone's
marriage with Haemon) are also present. Klügmann[2] refers
this picture to the lost play of Euripides. Heydemann[3] (with
more probability, I think) supposes it to represent a scene from
an otherwise unknown drama, of which he recognises the plot in
Hyginus (*Fab.* 72). It is briefly this:—Haemon has disobeyed
Creon by saving Antigone's life; Heracles intercedes with Creon
for Haemon, but in vain; and the two lovers commit suicide.
Professor Rhousopoulos, of Athens, in a letter to the French
Academy[4] (1885), describes a small fragment of a ceramic vase
or cup, which he believes to have been painted in Attica, about
400—350 B.C., by (or after) a good artist. The fragment shows
the beautiful face of a maiden,—the eyes bent earnestly on some
object which lies before her. This object has perished with
the rest of the vase. But the letters ΕΙΚΗΣ remain; and it is
certain that the body of Polyneices was the sight on which the
maiden was gazing. As Prof. Rhousopoulos ingeniously shows,
the body must have been depicted as resting on sloping ground,—
the lowest slope, we may suppose, of the hill upon which the
guards sat (v. 411). The moment imagined by the artist may have
been that at which Antigone returned, to find that the body had
been again stripped of dust (v. 426). The women of ancient
Thebes are said to have been distinguished for stature no less
than beauty; and the artist of the vase appears to have given
Antigone both characteristics.

---

[1] *Mon. Inst.* X. 27.

[2] *Ann. Inst.* 176, 1876.

[3] See footnote above, p. xxxviii, note 1 (3rd paragraph).

[4] Περὶ εἰκόνος Ἀντιγόνης κατὰ ἀρχαῖον ὄστρακον, μετὰ ἀπεικονίσματος. I am indebted to the kindness of Professor D'Ooge, late Director of the American School at
Athens, for an opportunity of seeing this letter.

§ 18. It is not, however, in the form of painting or of sculpture that Art has furnished the *Antigone* with its most famous and most delightful illustration. Two generations have now been so accustomed to associate this play with the music of Mendelssohn that at least a passing notice is due to the circumstances under which that music was composed; Mendels-
sohn. circumstances which, at a distance of nearly half a century, possess a peculiar interest of their own for these later days of classical revivals. After Frederick William IV. had come to the Prussian throne in June, 1840, one of his first acts was to found at Berlin the Academy of Arts for Painting, Sculpture, Architecture, and Music; Mendelssohn, who was then thirty-two, became the first Director of the department of Music, in the spring of 1841. The King had conceived the wish to revive some of the masterpieces of Greek Tragedy,— a project which the versatile poet Tieck, then on the confines of old age, encouraged warmly; none the less so, it would seem, because his own youth had been so vigorously identified with the protests of the Romantic school against classical restraint. Donner had recently published his German translation of Sophocles, 'in the metres of the original,' and the *Antigone* was chosen for the experiment. Mendelssohn accepted with enthusiasm the task of writing the music. The rapidity with which he worked may be estimated from the fact that Sept. 9, 1841, seems to have been about the date at which Tieck first broached the idea to him, and that the first full stage rehearsal took place some six weeks later,—on October 22nd. The success of the music in Germany seems to have been immediate and great; rather more than could be said of the first performance in London, when the *Antigone*, with the new music, was brought out at Covent Garden, on Jan. 2, 1845. The orchestra on that occasion, indeed, had a conductor no less able than the late Sir G. Macfarren; but the Chorus was put on the stage in a manner of which a graphic memorial has been preserved to us[1]. It may be added that the Covent

---

[1] On March 25, 1845, Mendelssohn wrote to his sister:—'See if you cannot find *Punch* for Jan. 18 [1845]. It contains an account of Antigone at Covent Garden, with illustrations,—especially a view of the Chorus which has made me laugh for

Garden stage-manager improved the opportunity of the joyous 'dance-song' to Dionysus (vv. 1115—1154) by introducing a regular ballet.

To most lovers of music Mendelssohn's *Antigone* is too familiar to permit any word of comment here; but it may perhaps be less superfluous to remark a fact which has been brought under the writer's notice by an accomplished scholar[1]. For the most part, the music admits of having the Greek words set to it in a way which shows that Mendelssohn, while writing for Donner's words, must have been guided by something more than Donner's imitation of the Greek metres; he must also have been attentive, as a general rule, to the Greek text.

Date of the play.

§ 19. The question as to the date of the *Antigone* has a biographical no less than a literary interest. It is probable that the play was first produced at the Great Dionysia towards the end of March, 441 B.C. This precise date is, indeed, by no means certain; but all the evidence indicates that, at any rate, the years 442 and 441 B.C. give the probable limits. According to the author of the first Argument to the play[2], the success of the *Antigone* had led to Sophocles obtaining the office of general, which he held in an expedition against Samos. Athens sent two expeditions to Samos in 440 B.C. (1) The occasion of the first expedition was as follows. Samos and Miletus had been at war for the possession of Prienè, a place on the mainland not far from Miletus. The Milesians, having been worsted, denounced the Samians to the Athenians; who required that both parties should submit their case at Athens. This the Samians refused to do. The Athenians then sent forty ships to Samos,—put down the oligarchy there,—and established a democracy in its place[3]. (2) The second expedi-

---

three days.' In his excellent article on Mendelssohn in the *Dictionary of Music*, Sir G. Grove has justly deemed this picture worthy of reproduction.

[1] Mr George Wotherspoon, who has practically demonstrated the point by setting the Greek words to the music for the Parodos (vv. 100—161). It is only in the last antistrophe, he observes, that the 'phrasing' becomes distinctly modern, and less attentive to the Greek rhythms than to harmonic effects.

[2] See below, p. 3.

[3] The Greek life of Sophocles says that he served as general 'in the war against the Anaeans' (ἀναίους). Anaea was a place on the mainland, near Prienè. Boeckh

tion had to deal with Samos in open rebellion. The Samian oligarchs had come back,—overthrown the new democracy,—and proclaimed a revolt from Athens, in which Byzantium joined. Pericles was one of the ten generals for the year. He sailed at once to Samos, with sixty ships. All his nine colleagues went with him. When they reached Samos, sixteen of the sixty ships were detached on special service,—partly to watch the Carian coast, partly to summon aid from the two great islands to the north, Chios and Lesbos. Sophocles, who was one of the ten generals, was sent on the mission to these islands.

The strate-gia of Sophocles.

'I met Sophocles, the poet, at Chios, when he was sailing as general to Lesbos.' These are the words of Ion, the poet and prose-writer—who was only some twelve years younger than Sophocles—in a fragment preserved by Athenaeus[1]. The occasion of the meeting was a dinner given to Sophocles at Chios by Hermesilaus, a friend of his who acted as Athenian 'proxenus' there. Now, there is not the smallest real ground for questioning the genuineness of this fragment[2]. And its genuineness is confirmed by internal evidence. Sophocles said at the dinner-party,—alluding to a playful *ruse* by which he had amused the company,—that he was practising generalship, as Pericles had said that he was a better poet than general. The diplomatic mission to Chios and Lesbos was a service in which

supposes that the first expedition was known as 'the Anaean war,' and that Sophocles took part in it as well as in the second expedition. To me, I confess, there seems to be far more probability in the simple supposition that ἀναίους is a corruption of σαμίους.

[1] p. 603 E. Müller, *Frag. Hist.* II. 46.

[2] Arguments against the genuineness have been brought, indeed, by Fr. Ritter (*Vorgebliche Strategie d. Sophokles gegen Samos:* Rhein. Mus., 1843, pp. 187 ff.). (1) Ion represents Sophocles as saying,—Περικλῆς ποιεῖν με ἔφη, στρατηγεῖν δ' οὐκ ἐπίστασθαι. Sophocles (Ritter argues) would have said φησί, not ἔφη, if Pericles had been alive. The forger of the fragment intended it to refer to the revolt of Lesbos in 428 B.C.,—forgetting that Sophocles would then be 78. But we reply:—The tense, ἔφη, can obviously refer to the particular occasion on which the remark was made: 'Pericles *said* so [when I was appointed, or when we were at Samos together].' (2) Ion says of Sophocles, οὐ ῥεκτήριος ἦν. This (says Ritter) implies that Sophocles was dead; who, however, long survived Ion. [Ion was dead in 421 B.C., Ar. *Pax* 835.] But here, again, the tense merely refers to the time at which the writer received the impression. We could say of a living person, 'he was an agreeable man'—meaning that we found him so when we met him.

Pericles might very naturally utilize the abilities of his gifted, though unmilitary colleague. There is another trait which has not (to my knowledge) been noticed, but which seems worth remarking, as the coincidence is one which is not likely to have been contrived by a forger. It is casually mentioned that, at this dinner-party, an attendant was standing 'near the fire,' and the couch of Sophocles, the chief guest, was also near it. The warm season, then, had not begun. Now we know that Pericles sailed for Samos early in 440 B.C., before the regular season for navigation had yet opened[1].

If the fragment of Ion is authentic, then it is certain that Sophocles held the strategia, and certain also that he held it in 440 B.C.: for Ion's mention of Lesbos cannot possibly be referred to the revolt of that island from Athens in 428 B.C. Apart from the fragment of Ion, however, there is good Attic authority for the tradition. Androtion, whose *Atthis* was written about 280 B.C., gave the names of the ten generals at Samos on this occasion. His list[2] includes Pericles, and 'Sophocles, the poet, of Colonus.'

---

[1] See Curtius, *Hist. Gr.* II. 472 (Eng. tr.).

[2] This fragment of Androtion has been preserved by the schol. on Aristeides, vol. 3, p. 485 (Dind.). Müller, *Frag. Hist.* IV. 645. The names of two of the ten generals are wanting in the printed texts, but have since been restored, from the MS., by Wilamowitz, *De Rhesi Scholiis*, p. 13 (Greifswald, 1877).

I have observed a remarkable fact in regard to Androtion's list, which ought to be mentioned, because it might be urged against the authenticity of the list, though (in my opinion) such an inference from it would be unfair.

Androtion gives (1) the names, (2) the demes of the Generals, but *not* their tribes. The regular order of precedence for the ten Cleisthenean tribes was this:— 1. Erectheis. 2. Aegeis. 3. Pandionis. 4. Leontis. 5. Acamantis. 6. Oeneis. 7. Cecropis. 8. Hippothontis. 9. Aeantis. 10. Antiochis. Now take the demes named by Androtion. His list will be found to follow this order of the ten tribes,— with one exception, and it is in the case of Sophocles. His deme, Colonus, belonged to the Antiochis, and therefore his name ought to have come last. But Androtion puts it second. The explanation is simple. When the ten tribes were increased to twelve, by the addition of the Antigonis and Demetrias (in or about 307 B.C.), some of the demes were transferred from one tribe to another. Among these was the deme of Colonus. It was transferred from the Antiochis, the tenth on the roll, to the Aegeis, the second on the roll. Hence Androtion's order is correct for his own time (*c.* 280 B.C.), but not correct for 440 B.C. It is quite unnecessary, however, to infer that he invented or doctored the list. It is enough to suppose that he re-adjusted the order, so as to make it consistent in the eyes of his contemporaries.

Later writers refer to the poet's strategia as if it were a generally accepted fact[1].

§ 20. We have next to ask,—What ground is there for connecting this strategia of Sophocles with the production of his *Antigone?* The authority for such a connection is the first Argument to the play. This is ascribed to Aristophanes of Byzantium (*c.* 200 B.C.), but is more probably of later origin (see p. 3). It says;—'They say (φασί) that Sophocles was appointed to the strategia which he held at Samos, because he had distinguished himself by the production of the *Antigone.*' Here, as so often elsewhere, the phrase, 'they say,' is not an expression of doubt, but an indication that the story was found in several writers. We know the names of at least two writers in whose works such a tradition would have been likely to occur. One of them is Satyrus (*c.* 200 B.C.), whose collection of biographies was used by the author of the Life of Sophocles[2]; the other—also quoted in the Life—is Carystius of Pergamum, who lived about 110 B.C., and wrote a book, Περὶ διδασκαλιῶν—'Chronicles of the Stage'—which Athenaeus cites. At the time when these works —and there were others of a similar kind—were compiled, old and authentic lists of Athenian plays, with their dates, appear to have been extant in such libraries as those of Alexandria and Pergamum. When, therefore, we meet with a tradition,—dating at least from the second century B.C.,—which affirms that the strategia of Sophocles was due to his *Antigone,* one inference, at least, is fairly secure. We may believe that the *Antigone* was known to have been produced earlier than the summer of 441 B.C. For, if Sophocles was strategus in the early spring of 440 B.C., he must have been elected in May, 441 B.C. The election of the

Had the play any bearing upon the poet's appointment?

---

[1] The Argument to this play, and the Βίος Σοφοκλέους, have already been cited. See also (1) Strabo 14. p. 638 Ἀθηναῖοι δὲ...πέμψαντες στρατηγὸν Περικλέα καὶ σὺν αὐτῷ Σοφοκλέα τὸν ποιητὴν κακῶς διέθηκαν ἀπειθοῦντας τοὺς Σαμίους. (2) Schol. on Ar. *Pax* 696 λέγεται δὲ ὅτι ἐκ τῆς στρατηγίας τῆς ἐν Σάμῳ ἠγυρίσατο (ὁ Σοφοκλῆς). (3) Suidas *s.v.* Μέλητος [but referring to the Samian Μέλισσος: cp. Diog. L. 9. 24] ὑπὲρ Σαμίων στρατηγήσας ἐναυμάχησε πρὸς Σοφοκλῆν τὸν τραγικόν, ὀλυμπιάδι πδ´ (Ol. 84=444—441 B.C.).—The theory that Sophocles the poet was confused with Sophocles son of Sostratides, strategus in 425 B.C. (Thuc. 3. 115), is quite incompatible with the ancient evidence.

[2] See Introduction to the *Oed. Col.*, § 18, p. xli.

ten strategi was held annually, at the same time as the other
official elections (ἀρχαιρεσίαι), in the month of Thargelion, at
the beginning of the ninth prytany of the civic year.[1] Further,
we may conclude that the *Antigone* had not been produced at
any long interval before May, 441 B.C. Otherwise the tradition
that the play had influenced the election—whether it really did
so or not—would not have seemed probable.

Assuming, then, that the *Antigone* was brought out not long
before Sophocles obtained the strategia, we have still to consider whether there is any likelihood in the story that his election
was influenced by the success of the play. At first sight, a
modern reader is apt to be reminded of the man of letters who,
in the opinion of his admirer, would have been competent, at
the shortest notice, to assume command of the Channel Fleet.
It may appear grotesque that an important State should have
rewarded poetical genius by a similar appointment. But here, as
in other cases, we must endeavour to place ourselves at the old
Athenian point of view. The word 'general,' by which we
render 'strategus,' suggests functions purely military, requiring,
for their proper discharge, an elaborate professional training.
Such a conception of the Athenian strategia would not, however,
be accurate. The ten strategi, chosen annually, formed a board
of which the duties were primarily military, but also, in part,
civil. And, for the majority of the ten, the military duties were
usually restricted to the exercise of control and supervision at
Athens. They resembled officials at the War Office, with some
added functions from the province of the Home Office. The
number of strategi sent out with an army or a fleet was, at this
period, seldom more than three. It was only in grave emerg-
encies that all the ten strategi went on active service together.
In May, 441 B.C.,—the time, as it seems, when Sophocles was
elected,—no one could have foreseen the great crisis at Samos.
In an ordinary year Sophocles, as one of the strategi, would not

---

[1] According to [Arist.] Ἀθ. Πολ. 44 § 4 the elections were held after the sixth
prytany and might therefore have been over a month before the Great Dionysia.
Either the story of Sophocles' election must be false or the elections in Sophocles'
time or in that particular year were held later, *e.g.* on account of unfavourable omens
(see Sandys' note, p. 165, on the passage).

necessarily have been required to leave Athens. Among his nine colleagues there were doubtless, besides Pericles, one or two more possessed of military aptitudes, who would have sufficed to perform any ordinary service in the field. Demosthenes—in whose day only one of the ten strategi was ordinarily commissioned for war—describes the other nine as occupied, among other things, with arranging the processions for the great religious festivals at Athens[1]. He deplores, indeed, that they should be so employed; but it is certain that it had long been one duty of these high officials to help in organising the great ceremonies. We are reminded how suitable such a sphere of duty would have been for Sophocles,—who is said to have led in his boyhood the Chorus that celebrated the victory of Salamis,—and we seem to win a new light on the meaning of his appointment to the strategia. In so far as a strategus had to do with public ceremonies and festivals, a man with the personal gifts of Sophocles could hardly have strengthened his claim better than by a brilliant success at the Dionysia. The mode of election was favourable to such a man. It was by show of hands in the Ecclesia. If the *Antigone* was produced at the Great Dionysia, late in March, 441 B.C., it is perfectly intelligible that the poet's splendid dramatic triumph should have contributed to his election in the following May. It is needless to suppose that his special fitness for the office was suggested to his fellow-citizens by the special maxims of administration which he ascribes to Creon,—a notion which would give an air of unreality,—verging, indeed, on comedy,—to a result which appears entirely natural when it is considered in a larger way[2].

---

[1] Dem. or. 4 § 26.

[2] One of Aelian's anecdotes (*Var. Hist.* 3. 8) is entitled, ὅτι ὁ Φρύνιχος διά τι ποίημα στρατηγὸς ᾑρέθη. Phrynichus, he says, 'having composed suitable songs for the performers of the war-dance (πυρριχισταῖς) in a tragedy, so captivated and enraptured the (Athenian) spectators, that they immediately elected him to a military command.' Nothing else is known concerning this alleged strategia. It is possible that Phrynichus, the tragic poet of *c.* 500 B.C., was confounded by some later anecdote-monger with the son of Stratonides, general in 412 B.C. (Thuc. 8. 25), and that the story was suggested by the authentic strategia of Sophocles. At any rate, the vague and dubious testimony of Aelian certainly does not warrant us in using the case of Phrynichus as an illustration.

Internal
evidence
for an
early date.

§ 21. The internal evidence of the *Antigone* confirms the belief that it is the earliest of the extant seven. Certain traits of composition distinguish it. (1) The division of an iambic trimeter between two or more speakers—technically called ἀντι-λαβή—is avoided, as it is by Aeschylus. It is admitted in the other six plays. (2) An anapaest nowhere holds the first place of the trimeter. It may further be noticed that the resolution of any foot of the trimeter is comparatively rare in the *Antigone.* Including the proper names, there are less than 40 instances. A considerably higher proportion is found in later plays. (3) The use made of anapaestic verse is archaistic in three points. (*a*) The Parodos contains regular anapaestic systems (see p. 27, note on vv. 100—161). (*b*) The Chorus uses anapaests in announcing the entrance of Creon, Antigone, Ismene, Haemon. In the case of Ismene, these anapaests do not follow the stasimon, but occur in the midst of the epeisodion (see vv. 526—530). (*c*) Anapaests are also admitted, for purposes of dialogue, within an epeisodion (vv. 929—943, where the Chorus, Creon, and Antigone are the speakers). Aeschylus allowed this; but elsewhere it occurs only in the *Ajax* of Sophocles (another comparatively early play), and in the *Medea* of Euripides (431 B.C.).

Place of
the play in
the series of
the poet's
works.

§ 22. The first Argument (p. 3) ends by saying that the play 'has been reckoned as the thirty-second[1].' This statement was doubtless taken from authentic διδασκαλίαι—lists of performances, with their dates—which had come down from the 5th century B.C. to the Alexandrian age. The notice has a larger biographical interest than can often be claimed for such details.

---

[1] λέλεκται δὲ τὸ δρᾶμα τοῦτο τριακοστὸν δεύτερον. Bergk (*Hist. Gr. Lit.* III. p. 414) proposes to read, δεδίδακται δὲ τὸ δρᾶμα τοῦτο τριακοστόν· δεύτερος ἦν. He assumes that Sophocles gained the second prize, because, according to the Parian Chronicle (60), the first prize was gained by Euripides in the archonship of Diphilus (442—1 B.C.). He adds that the word εὐδοκιμήσαντα, applied to Sophocles in the Argument, would suit the winner of the second prize,—as Aristophanes says of his own Δαιταλεῖς, which gained the second prize, ἄριστ' ἠκουσάτην (*Nub.* 529). But two things are wanting to the probability of Bergk's conjecture, viz., (1) some independent reason for thinking that the *Antigone* was the 30th, rather than the 32nd, of its author's works; and (2) some better ground for assuming that it gained the second prize.

In 441 B.C. Sophocles was fifty-five: he died in 40⅚ B.C., at ninety or ninety-one. More than 100 lost plays of his are known by name: the total number of his works might be roughly estimated at 110. It appears warrantable to assume that Sophocles had produced his works by tetralogies,—*i.e.*, three tragedies and one satyric drama on each occasion. If the number 32 includes the satyric dramas, then the *Antigone* was the fourth play of the eighth tetralogy, and Sophocles would have competed on seven occasions before 441 B.C. He is recorded to have gained the first prize at his first appearance, in 468 B.C., when he was twenty-eight. The production of 28 plays in the next 27 years would certainly argue a fair measure of poetical activity. If, on the other hand, this 32 is exclusive of satyric dramas, then the *Antigone* was the second play of the eleventh trilogy, and the whole number of plays written by the poet from 468 to 441 B.C. (both years included) was 44.

On either view, then, we have this interesting result,—that the years of the poet's life from fifty-five to ninety were decidedly more productive than the years from twenty-eight to fifty-five. And if we suppose that the number 32 includes the satyric dramas—which seems the more natural view—then the ratio of increased fertility after the age of fifty-five becomes still more remarkable. We have excellent reason, moreover, for believing that this increase in amount of production was not attended by any deterioration of quality. The *Philoctetes* and the *Coloneus* are probably among the latest works of all. These facts entitle Sophocles to be reckoned among the most memorable instances of poetical genius prolonging its fullest vigour to extreme old age, and—what is perhaps rarer still—actually increasing its activity after middle life had been left behind.

§ 23. Nothing is known as to the plays which Sophocles may have produced along with the *Antigone*. Two forms of trilogy were in concurrent use down at least to the end of the fifth century,—that in which the three tragedies were parts of one story,—and that in which no such link existed. The former was usually (though doubtless not always) employed by Aeschylus; the latter was preferred by his younger rival. Thus it is

The Theban plays—not a connected trilogy.

possible,—nay, probable,—that the two tragedies which accompanied the *Antigone* were unrelated to it in subject. Even when the Theban plays of Sophocles are read in the order of the fable, they do not form a linked trilogy in the Aeschylean sense. This is not due merely to discrepancy of detail or incompleteness of juncture. The perversely rigorous Creon of the *Antigone* is, indeed, an essentially distinct character from the ruthless villain of the *Coloneus;* the *Coloneus* describes the end of Oedipus in a manner irreconcileable with the allusion in the *Antigone* (v. 50). But, if such differences existed between the *Choephori* and the *Eumenides,* they would not affect the solidarity of the 'Oresteia.' On the other hand, it does not suffice to make the triad a compact trilogy that the *Tyrannus* is, in certain aspects, supplemented by the *Coloneus*[1], and that the latter is connected with the *Antigone* by finely-wrought links of allusion[2]. In nothing is the art of Sophocles more characteristically seen than in the fact that each of these three masterpieces—with their common thread of fable, and with all their particular affinities—is still, dramatically and morally, an independent whole.

[1] See Introd. to *Oed. Col.* p. xxi. § 3.
[2] See *Oed. Col.* 1405—1413, and 1770—1772.

Manuscripts. Editions and Commentaries.

§ 1. In this play, as in the others, the editor has used the Autotype Facsimile of L (published by the London Hellenic Society in 1885); and, with its aid, has endeavoured to render the report of that manuscript as complete and exact as possible. In some instances, where discrepancies existed between previous collations, the facsimile has served to resolve the doubt; in a few other cases, it has availed to correct errors which had obtained general currency: the critical notes on 311, 375, 770, 1098, 1280 will supply examples.

The Laurentian MS (L).

The MSS., besides L, to which reference is made, are:—A (13th cent.), E (ascribed to 13th cent., but perhaps of the 14th), T (15th cent.), V (late 13th or early 14th), V² (probably 14th), with the following 14th century MSS.,—V³, V⁴, Vat., Vat. b, L², R. Some account of these has been given in the Introduction to the *Oedipus Tyrannus*; cp. also the Introd. to the *Oed. Col.* p. xlix. A few references are also made to an Augsburg MS. (Aug. b, 14th cent.), to Dresd. a (cod. 183, 14th cent.), and to M⁴ (Milan, Ambrosian Library, cod. C. 24 sup., 15th cent.). The symbol 'r' is occasionally used in the critical notes to denote 'one or more of the MSS. other than L'. The advantages of such a symbol are twofold: (1) the note can often be made shorter and simpler; (2) the paramount importance of L is thus more clearly marked, and, so far, the relative values of the documents are presented to the reader in a truer perspective. But this symbol has been employed only in those cases where no reason existed for a more particular statement.

Other MSS.

§ 2. The *Antigone* furnishes three instances in which the older scholia do what they rarely do for the text of Sophocles,—give a certain clue to a true reading which all the MSS. have lost. One is ʼφάπτουσα in v. 40; another, φονώσαισιν in v. 117; the third, δεδραγμένος in v. 235.

Readings due to the Scholia.

Points
bearing on
the rela-
tion of L
to the
other
MSS.

§ 3. Again, this play presents some points of curious interest in regard to the much-discussed question whether L is the source from which all other known MSS. of Sophocles have been derived.

(1) There are two places in which an apparently true reading has been preserved by some of the later MSS., while L has an apparently false one. The first example is in v. 386, where L has εἰς μέσον, while A and others have εἰς δέον. Some editors, indeed, prefer εἰς μέσον: but A's reading seems far preferable (see comment.). The other example is clearer. In v. 831 L has τάκει, a manifest error, occasioned by τακομέναν shortly before. The true reading, τέγγει, is in A and other of the MSS. later than L.

(2) Verse 1167, ζῆν τοῦτον, ἀλλ' ἔμψυχον ἡγοῦμαι νεκρόν, is in none of the MSS. It is supplied by Athenaeus 7. 280 C, who quotes vv. 1165—1171. The earliest printed edition which contains it is that of Turnebus (Paris, 1553 A.D.). Now Eustathius (p. 957. 17) quotes v. 1165 (partly) and v. 1166,—remarking that, after v. 1166, 'the careful copies' (τὰ ἀκριβῆ ἀντίγραφα) give the verse ζῆν τοῦτον, ἀλλ' ἔμψυχον ἡγοῦμαι νεκρόν. Eustathius wrote in the second half of the 12th century: L was written in the first half of the eleventh century. It would be a very forced explanation to suppose that Eustathius, in speaking of τὰ ἀκριβῆ ἀντίγραφα, meant those MSS. of Sophocles on which Athenaeus, some 1000 years before, had relied for his quotation; or, again, those MSS. of Athenaeus in which Eustathius found it. According to the natural (or rather, the necessary) sense of the words, Eustathius is referring to MSS. of Sophocles extant in his own time. But did his memory deceive him, leading him to ascribe to MSS. of Sophocles what he had seen in Athenaeus? This, again, would be a very bold assumption. His statement has a *prima facie* claim to acceptance in its plain sense. And if his statement is accepted, it follows that, when L was written (in the first half of the eleventh century), two classes of MSS. of Sophocles could be distinguished by the presence or absence of verse 1167. But that verse is absent from every MS. of Sophocles now known. If, therefore, L was not the common parent of the rest, at any rate that parent (or parents) agreed with L in this striking defect, which (according to Eustathius) could have been corrected from other MSS. known in the twelfth century. There is no other instance in which a fault, now universal in the MSS. of Sophocles, is thus alleged to have been absent from a MS. or MSS. extant after the date at which L was written. Whatever construction may be placed on the statement of Eustathius, it is certain that it deserves to be carefully noted.

§ 4. Another noteworthy fact is the unusually large number of The MSS. *versus* ancient citations. passages in which the MSS. of the *Antigone* vary from the quotations made by ancient writers. In every one of these instances (I think) our MSS. are right, and the ancient citation is wrong: though there are some cases in which modern scholars have thought otherwise. See the critical notes on vv. 186, 203, 223 (with commentary), 241, 292 (with note in Appendix), 324, 456, 457, 563, 564, 678, 742, 911 f., 1037, 1167.

§ 5. Among the interpolations which modern criticism has suspected, Interpolation. there is one which is distinguished from the rest alike by extent and by importance. This is the passage, founded on Herodotus 3. 119, in Antigone's last speech. I concur in the opinion of those who think that this passage,—*i.e.*, vv. 904—920,—cannot have stood in the text as Sophocles left it. The point is one of vital moment for our whole conception of the play. Much has been written upon it; indeed, it has a small literature of its own; but I am not acquainted with any discussion of it which appears to me satisfactory. In a note in the Appendix I have attempted to state clearly the reasons for my belief, and to show how the arguments on the other side can be answered.

This is the only passage of the play which seems to afford solid ground for the hypothesis of interpolation. It is right, however, to subjoin a list of the verses which have been suspected by the critics whose names are attached to them severally. Many of these cases receive discussion in the notes; but there are others which did not require it, because the suspicion is so manifestly baseless. It will be seen that, if effect were given to all these indictments, the *Antigone* would suffer a loss of nearly 80 verses.

Verses 4—6 rejected by Paley.—5 Bergk.—6 Nauck.—24 Wunder.—30 Nauck.— 46 Benedict.—203 Herwerden.—212 Kvíčala.—234 Göttling.—287 f. Nauck.—313 f. Bergk.—393 f., to be made into one verse, Nauck.—452 Wunder.—465–468 Kvíčala and Wecklein.—495 f. Zippmann.—506 f. Jacob.—570 and 573, with a rearrangement of 569–574, Nauck.—652–654, to be made into two verses, Nauck.—671 f., to be made into one verse, Heiland.—679 f. Heimreich.—680 Meineke and Bergk.—687 Heimreich, with δή for μή in 685.—691 Nauck.—838 Dindorf.—851 Hermann.— 1045–1047, 1053–1056, 1060 f., Morstadt.—1080–1083 Jacob.—1092–1094 and 1096 f. Morstadt.—1111–1114 Bergk.—1159 Nauck.—1167 Hartung.—1176 f. Jacob.—1225 Dindorf.—1232 Nauck.—1242 f. Jacob.—1250 Meineke.—1256 Nauck.—1279 Bothe. —1280 Wex.—1281 Heiland.—1301 Dindorf.—1347–1353 F. Ritter.

§ 6. In v. 125 f., where the MSS. have ἀντιπάλῳ...δράκοντι (with Emendations. indications of correction to ἀντιπάλου...δράκοντος), I propose with some confidence the simple emendation ἀντιπάλῳ...δράκοντος. In v. 606 I give πάντ᾽ ἀγρεύων for παντογήρως. In 966, πελάγει for L's πελάγεων (*sic*). In 1102, δοκεῖ for δοκεῖς. In 1124, ῥεῖθρόν τ᾽ for ῥέεθρον. In v. 23 f. I had conjectured δίκης | χρήσει as a correction of δίκῃ | χρησθείς before learning that Gerh. H. Müller had already suggested the same. He had not, however, forestalled my arguments for it. If the admission of it into the text is deemed too bold, it may be submitted that the barbarous character of the traditional reading, and the absence of any emendation which can claim a distinctly higher probability, render the passage one of those in which it is excusable to adopt a provisional remedy.

With regard to οὐκ ἄτης ἄτερ in v. 4, I would venture to invite the attention of scholars to the note in the Appendix. My first object has been to bring out what seems the essential point,—viz., that the real difficulty is the palaeographical one,—and to help in defining the conditions which a solution must satisfy before it can claim more than the value of guess-work. By the kind aid of Mr E. M. Thompson, I have been enabled to give a transcript of the words οὐκ ἄτης ἄτερ as they would have been written in an Egyptian papyrus of *circ.* 250 —200 B.C.

Editions, etc.

§ 7. Besides the various complete editions of Sophocles (*Oed. Tyr.*, p. lxi), these separate editions of the *Antigone* have been consulted.—Aug. Boeckh. With a German translation, and two Dissertations. (Berlin, 1st ed. 1843; new ed. 1884.)—John William Donaldson. With English verse translation, and commentary. (London, 1848.)—Aug. Meineke. (Berlin, 1861.)—Moriz Seyffert. (Berlin, 1865.)—Martin L. D'Ooge. On the basis of Wolff's edition. (Boston, U.S.A., 1884.)—A. Pallis. With critical notes in Modern Greek. (Athens, 1885.)—D. C. Semitelos. With introduction, critical notes, and commentary, in Modern Greek. (Athens, 1887.)—Selected passages of this play are discussed by Hermann Schütz, in the first part of his *Sophokleische Studien*, which deals with the *Antigone* only (Gotha, 1886, pp. 62). Many other critics are cited in connection with particular points of the play which they have treated. Lastly, reference may be made to the list of subsidia, available for Sophoclean study generally, which has been given in the Introduction to the *Oedipus Tyrannus*, p. lxii.

METRICAL ANALYSIS.

THE unit of measure in Greek verse is the short syllable, ◡, of which the musical equivalent is the quaver, ♪. The long syllable, –, has twice the value of ◡, being musically equal to ♩.

Besides ◡ and –, the only signs used here are the following.

(1) ◡̄ for –, when the value of – is increased by *one half*, so that it is equal to ◡◡◡, –◡, or ◡–.

(2) >, to mark an 'irrational syllable' ($\sigma\upsilon\lambda\lambda\alpha\beta\grave{\eta}$ ἄλογος), *i.e.*, bearing a metrical value to which its proper time-value does not entitle it; viz. ◡ for –, or – for ◡. Thus ἐργῶν means that the word serves as a choree, –◡, not as a spondee, – –.

(3) ◡̄◡◡, instead of –◡◡, in logaoedic verses. This means that the dactyl has not its full time-value, but only that of – ◡. This loss is divided between the long syllable, which loses $\frac{1}{4}$th of its value, and the first short, which loses $\frac{1}{2}$. Thus, while the normal dactyl is equivalent to ♩♫, this more rapid dactyl is equivalent to ♪·♫. Such a dactyl is called 'cyclic.'

(4) –ω, instead of –◡◡, in choreic verses. Here, again, the dactyl has the value only of – ◡. But in the cyclic dactyl, as we have seen, the loss of ◡ was divided between the long syllable and the first short. Here, in the choreic dactyl, the long syllable keeps its full value; but each of the two short syllables loses half its value. That is, the choreic dactyl is equivalent to ♩ ♪♫.

The choreic dactyl is used in two passages of this play: (1) First Stasimon, 1st Strophe, period III., vv. 1, 2 (vv. 339 f.), ἄφθιτον...ἔτος εἰς ἔτος: and *ib.* 2nd Strophe, per. I., vv. 1, 2 (vv. 354 f.) καὶ φθέγμα...καὶ ἐδιδάξατο. (2) First Kommos (No. V. in this Analysis), Epode, per. II., v. 1 (v. 879) οὐκέτι μοι τόδε λαμπάδος. Here, as elsewhere, the effect of such a dactyl is to give vivacity, relieving the somewhat monotonous repose of a choreic series. Other examples will be found in Schmidt's *Rhythmic and Metric*, p. 49, § 15. 3.

The last syllable of a verse is common (ἀδιάφορος, *anceps*). It is here marked ⏑ or − according to the metre: *e.g.*, ἐργῶν, if the word represents a choree, or ἐργᾱ, if a spondee.

Pauses. At the end of a verse, ⋀ marks a pause equal to ⏑, ⋀̄ a pause equal to −, and ⊥̸ a pause equal to − ⏑.

The *anacrusis* of a verse (the part preliminary to its regular metre) is marked off by three dots placed vertically, ⋮ If the anacrusis consists of two short syllables with the value of only one, ω is written over them. In v. 1115 the first two syllables of πολυώνυμε form such an anacrusis. (Analysis, No. VII., first v.)

Metres used in this play. The lyric elements of the *Antigone* are simple. Except the dochmiacs at the end (1261—1347), all the lyric parts are composed of logaoedic and choreic verses, in different combinations.

1. *Logaoedic*, or *prose-verse* (λογαοιδικός),—so called by ancient metrists because, owing to its apparent irregularity, it seemed something intermediate between verse and prose,—is a measure based on the choree, − ⏑, and the cyclic dactyl, metrically equivalent to a choree, − ⏑ ⏑. The following forms of it occur in the *Antigone*.

(*a*) The logaoedic verse of four feet, or tetrapody. This is called a Glyconic verse, from the lyric poet Glycon. It consists of one cyclic dactyl and three chorees. According as the dactyl comes first, second, or third, the verse is a First, Second, or Third, Glyconic. Thus the first line of the First Stasimon (v. 332) consists of a First Glyconic

followed by a Second Glyconic: πολλα τα | δεινα | κουδεν | ανθρ ‖ ωπου |

δεινοτερ | ον πελ | ει ⋀. Glyconic verses are usually shortened at the end ('catalectic'), as in this example.

(*b*) The logaoedic verse of three feet, or tripody,—called 'Pherecratic,' from the poet of the Old Comedy. It is simply the Glyconic verse with one choree taken away, and is called 'First' or 'Second' according as the dactyl comes first or second. Thus the fourth line of the Third Stasimon (vv. 788 f.) consists of a Second, followed by a First, Pherecratic: − > ⏑ ⏑ ⊥ ⏑ ⏑ ⊥ −

και σ ουτ | αθανατ | ων ‖ φυξιμος | ουδ | εις ⋀ .

(*c*) Logaoedic verses of six feet (hexapodies) are also frequent in this play. Such is the first line of the second Strophe of the Parodos

‿‿ ‿ | ‿ ‿ ‿ | ‿ ‿ | L̲ _

(v. 134), αντιτυπ | ος δ επι | γᾳ πεσε | τανταλ | ωθ | εις ∧.

(*d*) The logaoedic verse of two feet (dipody) occurs once in this

‿‿ ‿ _ ‿

play, as an ἐπῳδός, or postlude, to a choral strophe, v. 140 δεξιο | σειρος (= 154 Βάκχιος | ἄρχοι); Parodos, Second Strophe, period III. This is the '*versus Adonius*,' which closes the Sapphic stanza.

2. *Choreic* measures are those based simply on the choree (or 'trochee'), _ ‿. They usually consist either of four or of six feet. In this play we have both tetrapodies and hexapodies. Thus in vv. 847 ff. a choreic hexapody is followed by a choreic tetrapody: see Analysis, No. V., Second Strophe, period III., vv. 1, 2 οἷα φίλων ἄκλαυτος...τάφου ποταινίου. As the Analysis will show, choreic measures are often combined with logaoedic in the same strophe. The first Strophe of the First Stasimon affords an instance.

3. *Dochmiacs* occur in the closing kommos (1261—1347, No. VIII. in the Analysis). A dochmiac has two elements, viz. a bacchius, _ _ ‿ (= 5 short syllables), and a shortened choree, _, (= 2 short syllables). Thus odd and even were combined in it. The name δόχμιος, 'slanting,' expressed the resulting effect by a metaphor. The rhythm seemed to diverge side-ways from a straight course.

The regular type of dochmiac dimeter (with anacrusis) is ‿ : _ _ ‿ | _, ‿ ‖. The comma marks the ordinary caesura. As Dr Schmidt has noticed, the dochmiacs of the *Antigone* are remarkable for frequent neglect of the regular caesura. The dochmiac measure may be remembered by this line, in which '*serfs*' and '*wrongs*' must receive as much stress as the second syllable of '*rebel*' and of '*resent*':

> *Rebél!   Sérfs, rebél!   Resént wróngs so díre.*

This is a dochmiac dimeter, with anacrusis, written ‿ : _ _ ‿ | _, ‿ ‖ _ _ ‿ | _ ∧ ‖.

The diagrams added to the metrical schemes are simply short ways of showing how the verses are put together in rhythmical wholes. Thus the first diagram (No. I., First Str., per. 1.) is merely a symbol of the following statement. 'There are here two verses. Each contains three rhythmical groups or 'sentences' (κῶλα); and each 'sentence' contains four feet. The first verse, as a whole, corresponds with the second, as a whole. And the three parts of the first verse correspond consecutively

Rhythm.
—The
diagrams.

with the three parts of the second verse. These two verses together form a rhythmical structure complete in itself,—a rhythmical 'period' (περίοδος).' Some simple English illustrations have been given in the *Oed. Coloneus* (p. lx).

I. Parodos, vv. 100—154.

FIRST STROPHE.—Logaoedic. The second Glyconic is the main theme.

I., II., denote the *First* and *Second Rhythmical Periods*. The sign ‖ marks the end of a *Rhythmical Sentence;* ⫼ marks that of a *Period*.

I. 1. ακτις | αελι | ου το | καλλ ‖ ιστον | επταπυλ | ῳ φαν | εν ‖
στας δ υπ | ερ μελαθρ | ων φον | ωσ ‖ αισιν | αμφιχαν | ων κυκλ | ῳ ‖

θηβα | των προτερ | ων φα | ος Λ ‖
λογχαις | επτα πυλ | ον στομ | α

2. ε : φανθ | ης ποτ | ω χρυσε | ας ‖ αμερ | ας βλεφαρ | ον Διρκ | αι ‖
ε : βα | πριν ποθ | αμετερ | ων ‖ αιματ | ων γεννσ | ιν πλησθ | ην ‖

ων υπ | ερ ρεεθρ | ων μολ | ουσα ⫼
αι τε | και στεφαν | ωμα | πυργων

II. 1. τον λευκ | ασπιν | αργοθεν | εκ ‖ βαντα | φωτα | πανσαγι | ᾳ Λ ‖
πευκα | ενθ ηφ | αιστον ελ | ειν ‖ τοιος | αμφι | νωτ εταθ | η

2. φυγαδα | προδρομον | οξυτερ | ῳ ‖ κινησ | ασα χαλ | ιν | ῳ Λ ⫸
παταγος | αρεος | αντιπαλ | ῳ ‖ δυσχειρ | ωμα δρακ | οντ | ος

I.   II.

$$\begin{cases} 4 \\ 4 \\ 4 \\ 4 \\ 4 \\ 4 \end{cases} \quad\quad \begin{cases} 4 \\ 4 \\ 4 \\ 4 \end{cases}$$

After the first Strophe follows the first system of Anapaests (110 ὅς...116 κορύθεσσι): after the first Antistrophe, the second system (127 Ζεὺς...133 ἀλαλάξαι).

SECOND STROPHE.—Logaoedic, in sentences of varying lengths, viz.:
—I. two hexapodies: II. two tetrapodies, with one tripody between
them: III. two tetrapodies, followed by a *versus Adonius* ($-\smile\smile \mid -\smile$)
as epode.

$$\smile\smile \qquad \smile\smile \qquad \smile\smile \qquad -\smile \qquad \llcorner \quad -$$

I. 1. αντιτυπ | ᾳ δ επι | γᾳ πεσε | τανταλ | ωθ | εις ∧ ‖
        αλλα γαρ | α μεγαλ | ωνυμος | ηλθε | νικ | α

$$\smile\smile \qquad \smile\smile \qquad \smile\smile \qquad -\smile \qquad \llcorner \quad -$$

2. πυρφορος | ος τοτε | μαινομεν | ᾳ ξυν | ορμ | ᾳ ∧ ⟧
    τᾳ πολυ | αρματῳ | αντιχαρ | εισα | θηβ | ᾳ

$$- > \qquad \smile\smile \qquad - > \qquad \llcorner \quad - > \qquad \smile\smile \quad -$$

II. 1. βακχευ | ων επεπν | ει ριπ | αις ‖ εχθιστ | ων ανεμ | ων ∧ ‖
         εκ μεν | δη πολεμ | ων των | νυν ‖ θεσθαι | λησμοσυν | αν

$$- \smile \qquad \llcorner \qquad - \smile \qquad -$$

2. ειχε δ | αλλ | ᾳ τα | μεν ∧ ⟧
    θεων δε | να | ους χορ | οις

$$\smile\smile \quad \llcorner \qquad \smile\smile \quad \llcorner \qquad \smile \quad \smile \quad \llcorner \qquad \smile\smile \quad -> \qquad \smile\smile \quad -\smile$$

III. αλλα δ επ|αλλ| οις επε |νωμ‖α στυφελ| ιζ | ων μεγας| αρης ‖δεξιο|σειρος⟧
      παννυχι | οις |παντας επ| ελθ ‖ ωμεν ο |θηβ| ας δ ελελ |ιχθων‖βακχιος| αρχοι

I.	II.	III.
$\left.\begin{array}{c} \dot{6} \\ \dot{6} \end{array}\right)$	$\left.\begin{array}{c} \dot{4} \\ \dot{3} \\ \dot{4} \end{array}\right)$	$\left.\begin{array}{c} \dot{4} \\ \dot{4} \end{array}\right)$ $\dot{2} = \dot{\epsilon}\pi.$

After the second Strophe follows the third system of Anapaests (141 ἑπτά...147
ἄμφω): after the second Antistrophe, the fourth system (155 ἀλλ᾽ ὅδε...161 πέμψας).

II. First Stasimon, vv. 332—375.

FIRST STROPHE.—Period I. is logaoedic. It consists of one First
Glyconic verse, followed by three Second Glyconics. Periods II. and
III. are choreic. But the first verse of Period II. is logaoedic (a Second
Glyconic), and thus smooths the transition from logaoedic to choreic
measures.

I. 1. πολλα τα | δεινα | κουδεν | ανθρ ‖ ωπου | δεινοτερ | ον πελ | ει ⋏ ‖

κουφονο | ων τε | φυλον | ορν ‖ ιθων | αμφιβαλ | ων αγ | ει

2. τουτο | και πολι | ου περ | αν ‖ ποντου | χειμερι | ῳ νοτ | ῳ ⋏ ⟧

και θηρ | ων αγρι | ων εθν | η ‖ ποντου τ | ειναλι | αν φυσ | ιν

II. 1. χωρ ⋮ ει περ | ιβρυχι | οισ | ιν ⋏ ‖

σπειρ ⋮ αισι | δικτυο | κλωστ | οις

2. περ ⋮ ων υπ | οιδμασ | ιν ⋏ ‖

περ ⋮ ι φραδ | ης αν | ηρ

3. θε ⋮ ων τε | ταν υπ | ερτατ | αν γαν ⟧

κρατ ⋮ ει δε | μηχαν | αις αγρ | αυλου

III. 1. αφθιτον | ακαματ | αν απο | τρυεται ‖

θηρος ορ | εσσιβατ | α λασι | αυχενα θ

2. ιλλομεν | ων αροτρ | ων ετος | εις ετος ‖

ιππον οχμ | αζεται | αμφι λοφ | ον ζυγων

3. ιππ | ει | ῳ γεν | ει πολ | ευ | ων ⋏ ⟧

ουρ | ει | ον τ α | κμητα | ταυρ | ον

I.
$\left\{ \begin{matrix} 4 \\ 4 \\ 4 \\ 4 \end{matrix} \right)$

II.
$\left. \begin{matrix} 4 \\ 3 \\ 4 \end{matrix} \right)$

III.
$\left. \begin{matrix} 4 \\ 4 \\ 6 \end{matrix} \right) = ἐπῳδός$

SECOND STROPHE.—Choreic.

I. 1. και ⋮ φθεγμα και | ανεμο | εν ⋏ ‖

σοφ ⋮ ον τι το | μηχανο | εν

2. φρον ⋮ ημα και | αστυνομ | ους οργ | ας εδι ‖ δαξατο | και δυσ | αυλ | ων ⋏ ‖

τεχν ⋮ ας υπερ | ελπιδ εχ | ων τοτε | μεν κακον ‖ αλλοτ επ | εσθλον | ερπ | ει

II. 1.   παγ ⋮ ων εν | αιθρ | εια | και δυσ ‖ ομβρα | φευγ | ειν βελ | η Λ ‖
     νομ ⋮ ους γερ | αιρ | ων χθον | ος θε ‖ ων τ εν | ορκ | ον δικ | αν

2.   παντο | πορος α | πορος επ | ουδεν | ερχετ | αι Λ ‖
     υψι | πολις α | πολις ο | τῳ το | μη καλ | ον

3.   το ⋮ μελλον | αιδ | α μον | ον ‖ φευξιν | ουκ επ | αξετ | αι Λ ‖
     ξυν ⋮ εστι | τολμ | ας χαρ | ιν ‖ μητ εμ | οι παρ | εστι | ος

4.   νοσ ⋮ ων δ α | μηχαν | ων φυγ | ας | ξυμπε | φρασται ⟧
     γεν ⋮ οιτο | μητ ισ | ον φρον | ων | ος ταδ | ερδει

Note.—In Period III. of the first Strophe, and in Period I. of the
second, the apparent dactyls (marked – **ω**) are choreic dactyls; *i.e.*, the
two short syllables, ⏑⏑, have the time-value of one short, ⏑. This is
proved by the caesura after ὀργάς in verse 2 of the second Strophe.
The choreic dactyl is usually found, as here, in a transition from (or into)
logaoedic verse. Cp. Schmidt, *Rhythmic and Metric,* § 15. 3.

I. $\overset{\cdot}{3} = προῳδίς.$
    $\left.\begin{matrix} 4 \\ 4 \end{matrix}\right)$

II. $\begin{cases} \overset{\cdot}{4} \\ 4 \\ 6 \end{cases}$
$\begin{cases} \overset{\cdot}{4} \\ 4 \\ \underset{\cdot}{6} \end{cases}$

III. Second Stasimon, vv. 582—625.

FIRST STROPHE.—Period I. is logaoedic (two hexapodies). Periods
II. and III. are choreic. Just as in the first strophe of the first Stasimon,
the first verse of Period II. is logaoedic, forming a transition. The
remaining verses are choreic tetrapodies.

I. 1.   ευ ⋮ δαιμονες | οισι κακ | ων α | γευστος | αι | ων Λ ‖
     αρχ ⋮ αια τα | λαβδακιδ | αν οικ | ων ορ | ωμ | αι

2.   οις γαρ | αν σεισ | θη θεο | θεν δομος | ατ | ας Λ ⟧
     πημματ | α φθιτ | ων επι | πημασι | πιπτ | οντ

    J. S. III.[3]   *f*

II. 1. ‒ ◡   ‒ ◡ ‒ >   ◡‿◡   ◡‿◡   ‒ ◡   ‒ ◡
     ουδεν | ελλειπ | ει γενε | ας επι | πληθος | ερπον ‖
     ουδ απ | αλλασσ | ει γενε | αν γενος | αλλ ερ | ειπει

2.   ◡   ‒◡ ‒   ‒ ◡   ‒ ◡   └   ‒ ◡ ‒   ‒ ◡   ‒
   ομ ⋮ οιον | ωστε | ποντι | αις ‖ οιδμα | δυσπνο | οις οτ | αν Λ ‖
   θε ⋮ ων τις | ουδ εχ | ει λυσ | ιν ‖ νυν γαρ | εσχατ | ας υπ | ερ

3.   >   ‒ ◡   ◡◡◡   ◡◡◡   ⏜◡   ‒ ◡
   θρησσ ⋮ αισιν | ερεβος | υφαλον | επιδραμ | η πνο | αις Λ ⟧
   ριξ ⋮ ας ο | τετατο | φαος εν | οιδιπ | ου δομ | οις

III. 1.   ◡   └   └   ‒ ◡   ‒ ◡   └   └   ‒ ◡   ‒
    κυλ ⋮ ινδ | ει | βυσσο | θεν κελ ‖ αιν | αν | θινα | και Λ ‖
    κατ ⋮ αυ | νιν | φοινι | α θε ‖ ων | των | νερτερ | ων

2.   ◡   ‒ ◡   ◡ ◡   ‒ ◡   ‒ ◡   ‒ ◡   └   ‒
  δυσ ⋮ ανεμ | οι στον | ῳ βρεμ | ουσιν ‖ αντι | πληγες | ακτ | αι Λ ⟧
  αμ ⋮ α κοπ | ις λογ | ου τ α | νοια ‖ και φρεν | ων ερ | ιν | υς

    I.   6⎞   II.   6⎞   III.   ⎧4⎞
       6⎠   4   ⎪4⎟
                4   ⎨4⎬
                6   ⎩4⎠

SECOND STROPHE.—Logaoedic.—In Period III., the first and third verses are choreic.

I. 1.   ⌐   └   ◡‿◡   ‒ ◡   └   ‒ >   ◡‿◡   ‒ ◡   ‒ ◡
   τε ⋮ αν | ζευ δυνασ | ιν τις | ανδρ ‖ ων υπ | ερβασι | α κατ | ασχοι ‖
   α ⋮ γαρ | δη πολυ | πλαγκτος | ελπ ‖ ις πολλ | οις μεν ον | ασις | ανδρων

2.   >   ◡‿◡   └   ◡‿◡   ‒ ◡   └   ‒
  ταν ⋮ ουθ υπνος | αιρ | ει ποθ ο | παντ αγρ | ευ | ων Λ ⟧
  πολλ ⋮ οις δ απατ | α | κουφονο | ων ερ | ωτ | ων

II. 1.   ◡‿◡ θε | ων α | └   └   ◡‿◡   └
   ουτε θε | ων α | κματ | οι ‖ μηνες α | γηρ | ως δε χρον | ῳ Λ ‖
   ειδοτι δ | ουδεν | ερπ | ει ‖ πριν πυρι | θερμ | ῳ ποδα | τις

2.   ◡   └   ◡‿◡   ‒ ◡   ‒ >   ◡‿◡   ‒ ◡   └   ‒
  δυν ⋮ αστ | ας κατεχ | εις ολ | υμπου ‖ μαρμαρο | εσσαν | αιγλ | αν Λ ⟧
  προσ ⋮ αυσ | η σοφι | ᾳ γαρ | εκ του ‖ κλεινον επ | ος πε | φαν | ται

$$\omega \qquad - \cup \qquad - \cup \qquad \llcorner \quad -$$

III. 1. το τ επ : ειτα | και το | μελλ | ον ∧ ‖
  το κακ : ον δοκ | ειν ποτ | εσθλ | ον

$$> \qquad \smile \cup \quad \cup \qquad - \cup \qquad -$$

 2. και : το πριν επ | αρκεσ | ει ∧ ‖
  τῳδ : εμμεν ο | τῳ φρεν | ας

$$\cup \cup \cup \qquad - \cup \qquad \llcorner \qquad -$$

 3. νομος οδ | ουδεν | ερπ | ει ∧ ‖
  θεος αγ | ει προς | ατ | αν

$$> \qquad \smile \cup \quad \llcorner \qquad \smile \cup \quad \cup \qquad - \cup \quad \llcorner \quad -$$

 4. θνατ : ων βιοτ | ῳ | παμπολυ γ | εκτος | ατ | ας ∧ ⟧
  πρασσ : ει δ ολιγ | ιστ | ον χρονον | εκτος | ατ | ας

I.	II.	III.
.	.	.
4	⎧ 4	.
4	⎪ 4 ⟩	4 ⟩
.	⎨ .	3
6 = ἐπῳδός.	⎪ 4	4
	⎩ 4	.
	.	6 = ἐπ.

IV. Third Stasimon, vv. 781—800.

STROPHE.—Logaoedic.—(Period I., Glyconic verses: II., Glyconics varied by Pherecratic verses.)

$$\cup \qquad - \cup \quad \llcorner \quad \llcorner \qquad \smile \cup \qquad - \cup \quad \llcorner \qquad \smile \cup \qquad - \cup$$

I. 1. ερ : ως α | νικ | ατε μαχ | αν ερ ‖ ως ος | εν | κτημασι | πιπτεις ‖
  συ : και δικ | αι | ων αδικ | ους φρεν ‖ ας παρ | α | σπᾳς επι | λωβᾳ

$$\cup \qquad \smile \cup \quad \cup \qquad - \cup \qquad \llcorner \qquad - \cup \qquad \smile \cup \qquad - \cup \quad \llcorner \quad -$$

 2. ος : εν μαλακ | αις παρ | ει | αις νε ‖ ανιδος | εννυχ | ευ | εις ∧ ⟧
  συ : και τοδε | νεικος | ανδρ | ων ξυν ‖ αιμον εχ | εις ταρ | αξ | ας

$$> \qquad \smile \cup \quad \llcorner \qquad \llcorner \qquad \llcorner \quad \llcorner \quad -$$

II. 1. φοιτ : ᾳς δ υπ | ερ | ποντιος | εν τ ‖ αγρονομ | οις | αυλ | αις ∧ ‖
  νικ : ᾳ δ εν | αργ | ης βλεφαρ | ων ‖ ιμερος | ευ | λεκ | τρου

$$- \quad > \qquad \smile \cup \quad \llcorner \qquad \underset{\smile\smile}{\smile\smile} \quad \llcorner \quad -$$

 2. και σ ουτ | αθανατ | ων ‖ φυξιμος | ουδ | εις ∧ ‖
  νυμφας | των μεγαλ | ων ‖ παρεδρος εν | αρχ | αις

$$> \qquad \smile \cup \quad \llcorner \qquad \llcorner \qquad \smile \cup \quad \llcorner \quad -$$

 3. ουθ : αμερι | ων σε γ | ανθρ | ωπ ‖ ων ο δ εχ | ων με | μην | εν ∧ ⟧
  θεσμ : ων αμαχ | ος γαρ | εμ | παιζ ‖ ει θεος | α φροδ | ιτ | α

In Period II., v. 2, φύξιμος = πάρεδρος ἐν : but the words πάρεδρος ἐν ἀρχαῖς are of doubtful soundness. As the text stands, πάρεδρος requires us to suppose that the arsis of the logaoedic dactyl is resolved into ◡◡. See Appendix on v. 797 f. Prof. D'Ooge writes ⌣ ω : *i.e.*, φύξιμος is a choreic dactyl, in which ◡◡ has the time-value only of ◡. This suits the resolution of πάρεδρος, for it means that the syllables -δρος ἐν are uttered very rapidly. On the other hand, in this otherwise purely logaoedic strophe we hardly look for a choreic dactyl.

I.
$$\begin{cases} 4 \\ 4 \end{cases}$$
$$\begin{cases} 4 \\ 4 \end{cases}$$

II.
$$\begin{cases} 4 \\ 4 \end{cases}$$
$$\begin{pmatrix} 3 \\ 3 \end{pmatrix}$$
$$\begin{cases} 4 \\ 4 \end{cases}$$

V. Kommos, vv. 806—882.

First Strophe.—Logaoedic (Glyconics).

I. 1. ορ : ατ εμ | ω | γας πατρι | ας πολ ‖ ιται | ταν νεατ | αν οδ | ον Λ ‖
       ηκ : ουσα | δη | λυγροτατ | αν ολ ‖ εσθαι | ταν φρυγι | αν ξεν | αν

   2. στειχουσ | αν νεατ | ον δε | φεγγος ‖ λευσσ | ουσαν | αελι | ου Λ ‖
       τανταλ | ου σιπυλ | ῳ προς | ακρῳ ‖ ταν | κισσος | ως ατεν | ης

   3. κουποτ | αυθις | αλλα μ ο | παγ ‖ κοιτας | αιδας | ζωσαν αγ | ει Λ ‖
       πετραι | α βλαστ | α δαμασ | εν ‖ και νιν | ομβροι | τακομεν | αν

   4. ταν αχερ | οντος]]
       ως φατις | ανδρων

II. 1. ακτ : αν | ουθ υμεν | αιων | εγ ‖ κληρον | ουτ επι | νυμφει | ος Λ ‖
        χι : ων τ | ου δαμα | λειπει | τεγγ ‖ ει δ υπ | οφρυσι | παγκλαυτ | οις

    2. πω με τις | υμνος | υμν | ησεν ‖ αλλ αχερ | οντι | νυμφευσ | ω Λ]]
        δειραδας | ᾳ με | δαιμ | ων ομ ‖ οιοτατ | αν κατ | ευναξ | ει

The First Strophe is followed by the first system of Anapaests (vv. 817—822); the first Antistrophe, by the second system (vv. 834—838).

2 = ἐπῳδός.

SECOND STROPHE.—Period I. is logaoedic. Period II., while mainly logaoedic, introduces choreics (v. 1), which are continued in III.

I. 1. οιμ ⁞ οι γελ | ωμ | αι τι με | προς θε | ων πατρ | ῳων ‖
      ε ⁞ ψαυσας | αλγ | εινοτατ | ας εμ | οι μερ | ιμνας

   2. ουκ ⁞ οιχομεν | αν υβρ | ιζεις | αλλ επι | φαντ | ον ∧ ‖
      πατρ ⁞ ος τριπολ | ιστον | οικτον | του τε προ | παντ | ος

   3. ω πολις | ω πολ | εως πολ | υ | κτημονες | ανδρες ⟧
      αμετερ ⁞ ου ποτμ | ου κλειν | οις | λαβδακιδ | αισιν

II. 1. ι ⁞ ω διρκ | αιαι | κρην | αι ∧ ‖
       ι ⁞ ω ματρ | ῳαι | λεκτρ | ων

    2. θηβ ⁞ ας τ ευ | αρματου | αλσος | εμ ‖ πας ξυμ | μαρτυρας | υμμ επ | ι |
       ατ ⁞ αι κοιμ | ηματα τ | αυτο | γενν ‖ ητ εμ | ω πατρι | δυσμορ | ου |

                                                    κτωμ | αι ∧ ⟧
                                                    ματρ | ος

III. 1. οι ⁞ α φιλ | ων α | κλαυτος | οι | οις νομ | οις ∧ ‖
        οι ⁞ ων εγ | ω ποθ | α ταλ | αι | φρων ε | φυν

2. προς : εργμα | τυμβο | χωστον | ερχομ ‖ αι ταφ | ου ποτ | αινι | ου ∧ ‖
    προς : ους αρ | αιος | αγαμος | αδ εγ ‖ ω μετ | οικος | ερχομ | αι

3. ι : ω | δυσταν | ος βροτ | οις ‖ ουτε νεκρ | οις κυρ | ουσ | α ∧ ‖
    ι : ω | δυσποτμ | ων κασ | ι ‖ γνητε γαμ | ων κυρ | ησ | ας

4. μετ : οικος | ου | ζωσιν | ου θαν | ουσ | ιν ∧]]
    θαν : ων ετ | ουσ | αν κατ | ηναρ | ες | με

I.   6̇)
   6̇)
   6̇

II.   4̇)
    4̇)
    6̇ = ἐπ.

III.

THIRD STROPHE.—A single period. Choreic.

1. προ : βασ επ | εσχατ | ον θρασ | ους ∧ ‖
    σεβ : ειν μεν | ευσεβ | εια | τις

2. υψ : ηλον | ες δικ | ας βαθρ | ον ∧ ‖
    κρατ : ος δ ο | τω κρατ | ος μελ | ει

3. προσ : επεσες | ω τεκν | ον πολ | υ ∧ ‖
    παρ : αβατον | ουδαμ | ᾳ πελ | ει

4. πατρ : ῳ | ον δ | εκτιν | εις τιν | αθλ | ον ∧]]
    σε δ : αυτ | ο | γνωτος | ωλεσ | οργ | α

        4̇)
        4̇)
        4̇)
        6̇ = ἐπ.

EPODE (vv. 876—882).—Choreic.   The choreic dactyls (– ω) serve to vary and enliven the movement.

$$\smile \quad\quad -\smile \quad \smile\smile\smile \quad \smile\smile\smile \quad \llcorner \quad -\quad\smile \quad \llcorner \quad\quad -\quad \omega \quad -$$

I. 1.   α : κλαυτος | αφιλος | ανυμεν | αι ‖ ος ταλ | αι | φρων αγομ | αι ⋀ ‖

$$-\quad\smile \quad -\smile \quad -\quad\smile$$

2.   τανδ ετ | οιμ | αν οδ | ον ⋀ ⟧

$$-\quad \omega \quad -\quad \omega \quad -\quad \omega \quad -\smile$$

II. 1.   ουκετι | μοι τοδε | λαμπαδος | ιρον ‖

$$-\quad\smile \quad -\quad\smile \quad -\quad\smile$$

2.   ομμα | θεμις ορ | αν ταλ | αινα ‖

$$-\quad\smile \quad -\quad\smile \quad \smile\smile\smile \quad -\smile$$

3.   τον δ εμ | ον ποτμ | ον αδακρ | υτον ‖

$$> \quad\quad -\quad\smile \quad -\quad\smile \quad -$$

4.   ουδ : εις φιλ | ων στεν | αζ | ει ⋀ ⟧

I. and II. metrical schemes with mesode notation.

VI.   Fourth Stasimon, vv. 944—987.

FIRST STROPHE.—Periods I. and II. are logaoedic (Pherecratic verses in I., and Pherecratic and Glyconic in II.).   Period III. is choreic.

$$-\quad > \quad\quad \smile\smile \quad\smile \quad \llcorner \quad -\smile \quad\smile \quad \llcorner \quad -$$

I. 1.   ετλα | και δανα | ας ‖ ουρανι | ον | φως ⋀ ‖

ζευχθη δ | οξυχολ | ος ‖ παις ο δρυ | αντ | ος

$$-\quad > \quad\quad \smile\smile \quad\smile \quad \llcorner \quad -\quad\smile \quad -\quad > \quad -$$

2.   αλλαξ | αι δεμας | εν ‖ χαλκοδετ | οις αυλ | αις ⋀ ⟧

ηδων | ων βασιλ | ευς ‖ κερτομι | οις οργ | αις

$$\smile\smile \quad\smile \quad -\quad > \quad\quad -\quad > \quad\quad \smile\smile \quad\smile \quad -\quad\smile \quad -\quad > \quad -$$

II. 1.   κρυπτομεν | α δ εν | τυμβηρ ‖ ει θαλαμ | φ κατ | εζευχθ | η ⋀ ‖

εκ διο | νυσου | πετρωδ ‖ ει κατα | φαρκτος | εν δεσμ | φ

2. $-\ >\ \ \ \smile\smile\ \smile\ \llcorner\ \ \smile\smile\ \ -\ >\ \ \ -$

καιτοι | και γενε | ᾳ ‖ τιμιος | ω παι | παι ∧ ‖
ουτω | τας μανι | ας ‖ δεινον απ | ο σταζ | ει

3. $-\ >\ \ \ \smile\smile\ \smile\ \llcorner\ \ \smile\smile\ \llcorner\ \ \smile\smile\ -$

και ζην | ος ταμι | ευ ‖ εσκε γον | ας | χρυσορυτ | ους ∧ ‖
ανθηρ | ον τε μεν | ος ‖ κεινος επ | εγν | ω μανι | αις

4. $-\ >\ \ \ \smile\smile\ \smile\ \llcorner\ \ \smile\smile\ \ -\ >\ \ \ -$

αλλ α | μοιριδι | α ‖ τις δυνασ | ις δειν | α ∧ ⟧
ψαυων | τον θεον | εν ‖ κερτομι | οις γλωσσ | αις

III. 1. $>\ -\ \smile\ \smile\ -\ \smile\smile\ -\ \smile\ -\ \breve{\smile}\ -\ \smile\ -\ \smile\ \smile\ -\ \smile\ -$

ουτ ∶ αν νιν | ολβος | ουτ αρ | ης ου ‖ πυργος | ουχ αλ | ικτυπ | οι ∧ ‖
παυ ∶ εσκε | μεν γαρ | ενθε | ους γυν ‖ αικας | ευ | ι | ον τε | πυρ

2. $\smile\ \llcorner\ \ \llcorner\ \ -\smile\ -\ \smile\ \llcorner\ -$

κελ ∶ αιν | αι | ναες | εκφυγ | οι | εν ∧ ⟧
φιλ ∶ αυλ | ους τ | ηρεθ | ιζε | μου | σας

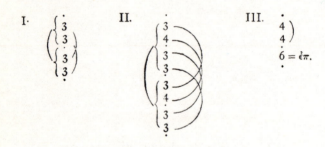

I. $\left\{\begin{matrix} 3 \\ 3 \\ 3 \\ 3 \end{matrix}\right\}$ II. $\left\{\begin{matrix} 3 \\ 4 \\ 3 \\ 3 \\ 3 \\ 4 \\ 3 \\ 3 \end{matrix}\right.$ III. $\left.\begin{matrix} 4 \\ 4 \\ 6 \end{matrix}\right)$ $= \dot{\epsilon}\pi.$

SECOND STROPHE.—Periods I. and II. are logaoedic : III. is choreic.

I. 1. $\smile\smile\ \smile\ \ \smile\smile\ \smile\ \ \smile\smile\ \smile\ \ -\smile\ -\ \ -\ \smile\ \ -$

παρα δε | κυανε | αν πελαγ | ει διδυμ | ας αλ | ος ∧ ‖
κατα δε | τακομεν | οι μελε | οι μελε | αν παθ | αν

2. $-\ >\ \ \ \smile\ \ \smile\ \ \smile\smile\ \ -\ >\ \ \ -\smile\ -$

ακται | βοσπορι | αι ιδ ο | θρηκων | αξεν | ος ∧ ⟧
κλαιον | ματρος εχ | οντες α | νυμφευτ | ον γον | αν

[I. 1. $\quad\underline{}\smile\quad\smile\smile\quad\llcorner\quad\overset{\smile\smile}{\frown}\smile\smile\quad-$

σαλμυδ | ησσος ιν | αγχ ‖ ιπολις αρ | ης ⋀ ‖
α δε | σπερμα μεν | αρχ ‖ αιογον | ων

2. $\quad\gt\quad-\smile\quad\overset{\smile\smile}{\frown}\smile\quad-$

δισσ : οισι | φινεϊδ | αις ⋀ ‖
αντ : ασ ερ | εχθεϊ δ | αν

3. $\quad\smile\smile\quad-\smile\quad\llcorner\quad-$

ειδεν αρ | ατον | ελκ | ος ⋀ ⟧
τηλεπορ | οις δ εν | αντρ | οις

[I. 1. $\quad\smile\quad-\smile\quad\llcorner\quad-\smile\quad-\smile\quad\llcorner\quad-$

τυφλ : ωθεν | εξ | αγρι | ας δαμ | αρτ | ος ⋀ ‖
τραφ : η θυ | ελλ | αισιν | εν πατρ | φ | αις

2. $\quad\smile\quad\smile\smile\smile\quad-\smile\quad-\smile\quad\overset{\smile\smile}{\frown}\smile\quad-$

α : λαον α | λαστορ | οισιν | ομματ | ων κυκλ | οις ⋀ ‖
βορ : εας αμ | ιππος | ορθο | ποδος υπ | ερ παγ | ου

3. $\quad\smile\quad\llcorner\quad\llcorner\quad-\smile\quad-\smile\quad\llcorner\quad-$

αρ : αχθ | εν | των υφ | αιματ | ηρ | αις ⋀ ‖
θε : ων | παις | αλλα | καπ εκ | ειν | ᾳ

4. $\quad\gt\quad-\smile\quad\llcorner\quad-\smile\quad-$

χειρ : εσσι | και | κερκιδ | ων ακμ | αισ | ιν ⋀ ⟧
μοιρ : αι μακρ | αι | ωνες | εσχον | ω | παι

I. $\left.\begin{array}{c}\dot{6}\\[2pt]\dot{6}\\[2pt]\cdot\end{array}\right)$
II. $\left.\begin{array}{c}\dot{3}\\[2pt]\dot{2}\ m.\\[2pt]\dot{3}\\[2pt]\dot{4}=\dot{\epsilon}\pi.\end{array}\right)$ [*m.* = mesode.]
III. $\left.\begin{array}{c}\dot{6}\\[2pt]\dot{6}\\[2pt]\dot{6}\\[2pt]\dot{6}\end{array}\right)$

VII. Hyporcheme (taking the place of a Fifth Stasimon),
vv. 1115—1154.

First Strophe.—Period I. is logaoedic, except that vv. 3 and 6 have a choreic character. Per. II. is logaoedic (Pherecratics). Per. III. consists of one logaoedic and one choreic tetrapody.

I. 1. $\quad\overset{\omega}{}\quad\smile\smile\quad-\overset{\gt}{}\quad-\overset{\gt}{}\quad-\smile\quad\llcorner\quad-$

πολυ : ωνυμε | καδμει | ας νυμφ | ας αγ | αλμ | α ⋀ ‖
σε δ υπ : ερ διλοφ | ου πετρ | ας στερ | οψ οπ | ωπ | ε

$$- \; \cup \; - \; \cup \; - \; \cup \; \cup \; -$$

2. και δι | ος βαρ | υβρεμετ | α ⋀ ‖
    λιγνυς | ενθα | κωρυκι | αι

$$\overset{>}{} \; - \; \cup \; - \; \overset{>}{} \; - \; \cup \; -$$

3. γεν : ος κλυτ | αν ος | αμφεπ | εις ⋀ ‖
    στειχ : ουσι | νυμφαι | βακχιδ | ες

$$- \cup \cup \; - \; \cup \; \underline{} \; -$$

4. ιταλι | αν μεδ | εις | δε ⋀ ‖
    κασταλι | ας τε | ναμ | α

$$- \; \overset{>}{} \; - \; \cup \; - \cup \cup \; -$$

5. παγκοιν | οις ελ | ευσινι | ας* ⋀ ‖
    και σε | νυσαι | ων ορε | ων

$$> \; \underline{} \; \underline{} \; - \; > \; - \; > \; \underline{} \; -$$

6. δη : ους | εν | κολποις | βακχευ | βακχ | αν ⋀ ⟧
    κισσ : ηρ | εις | οχθαι | χλωρα τ | ακτ | α

$$\cup \; - \cup \cup \; - \; >$$

II. 1. ο : ματροπολ | ιν θηβ | αν ⋀ ‖
        πολ : υσταφυλ | ος πεμπ | ει

$$- \cup \; - \cup \cup \; - \; \cup \; -$$

2. ναιετ | ων παρ υγρ | ον ⋀ ⟧
    αμβροτ | ων επε | ων

$$- \; > \; - \; > \; - \cup \cup \; - \; - \; - \; \cup \; \underline{} \; -$$

III. ισμην | ου ρειθρ | ον τ αγρι | ου τ επ ‖ ι σπορ | ᾳ δρακ | οντ | ος ⋀ ⟧
      εναζ | οντων | θηβαϊ | ας επ ‖ ισκοπ | ουντ αγ | υι | ας

I.   II.   III.
  · 6   · 3   · 4
  · 4   · 3   · 4
  · 4
  · 4
  · 4
  · 6

---

* The first ι of Ἐλευσινίας is here shortened, as in *Hom. hymn. Cer.* 105 Ἐλευσινίδαο θύγατρες, *ib.* 266 παῖδες Ἐλευσινίων. The metre forbids us to suppose that the ι is long, and that **ιας** form one syll. by synizesis. Vergil avoids the *ῑ* by using the form *Eleusinus* (*G.* I. 163).

SECOND STROPHE (forming a single period).—Logaoedic and Choreic.

1. ταν : εκ | πασ | αν | τιμ ‖ ας υπ | ερτατ | αν πολε | ων ∧ ‖
    ι : ω | πυρ | πνει | οντ ‖ ων χορ | αγ αστρ | ων νυχι | ων

2. ματρι | συν κερ | αυνι | ᾳ ∧ ‖
    φθεγματ | ων επ | ισκοπ | ε

3. και νυν | ως βιαι | ας εχετ | αι ∧ ‖
    παι δι | ος γενεθλ | ον προφαν | ηθ

4. πανδαμ | ος πολις | επι νοσ | ου ∧ ‖
    ωναξ | σαις αμα | περιπολ | οις

5. μολ : ειν καθ | αρσι | ῳ ποδι | παρν ‖ ασι | αν υπ | ερ κλιτ | υν ∧ ‖
    θυι : αισιν | αι σε | μαινομεν | αι ‖ παννυχ | οι χορ | ενουσ | ι

6. η στονο | εντα | πορθμ | ον ∧]]
    τον ταμι | αν ι | ακχ | ον

[The brackets on the left side show that the group formed by verses 1 and 2 corresponds with the group formed by vv. 5 and 6, while v. 3 corresponds with v. 4. Parts of vv. 1 and 2 correspond with parts of 5 and 6, as shown by the curves on the right.]

VIII. Kommos, vv. 1261—1347.

FIRST STROPHE.—Dochmiac.

1. ιω
    ιω

2. φρεν ⋮ ων δυσφρον | ων αμ ‖ αρτηματ | α ⋏ ‖
     ι ⋮ ω δυσκαθ | αρτος ‖ αιδου λιμ | ην

3. στερ ⋮ εα θανατο | εντ ⋏ ‖
     τι μ ⋮ αρα τι μ ολεκ | εις

4. ω κτανοντ | ας τε και ‖
     ω κακαγγ | ελτα μοι

5. θαν ⋮ οντας βλεπ | οντες ‖ εμφυλι | ους ⋏ ⟧
     προ ⋮ πεμψας αχ | η τιν ‖ α θροεις λογ | ον

II. 1. ω ⋮ μοι εμων αν | ολβα ‖ βουλευματ | ων ⋏ ‖
     αι ⋮ αι ολωλοτ | ανδρ επ ‖ εξειργασ | ω

2. ι ⋮ ω παι νε | ος νε ‖ ῳ ξυν μορ | ῳ ⋏ ⟧
     τι ⋮ φης ω παι* | τινα λεγ ‖ εις μοι νε | ον

3. αιαι αιαι
     αιαι αιαι

III. 1. ε ⋮ θανες απελυθ | ης ⋏ ‖
     σφαγ ⋮ ιον επ ολεθρ | ῳ

2. εμ ⋮ αις ουδε | σαισι ‖ δυσβουλι | αις ⋏ ⟧
     γυν ⋮ αικειον | αμφι ‖ κεισθαι μορ | ον

---

* παῖ is here an 'irrational' long syllable, substituted for the normal short, as was sometimes allowed in this place of the dochmiac: cp. Fourth Strophe, v. 3: Aesch. *Eum.* 266 φὲρ ⋮ δῐμᾶν βοσκ | ᾱν, and see Schmidt's *Rhythmic and Metric*, p. 77. Here, some read conjecturally, τί φής, ὦ τίν' αὖ λέγεις μοι νέον. See cr. n. on 1289.

I.

{dochm.
{dochm.
  2 bacchii
  2 paeons
{dochm.
{dochm.

The exclamation ἰώ, at the beginning, is marked (for clearness sake) as verse 1, but is outside of the rhythmical structure, as οἴμοι in the Second Strophe, and αἰαῖ αἰαῖ in the Third (see also Period II., v. 3). Verse 2, a dochmiac dimeter, answers to verse 5. Verse 3 answers to v. 4. Hence, as Schmidt points out (*Rhyth. and Metr.*, p. 190), verse 3 must be regarded as a bacchic dipodia (the bacchius = ⏑ – –), shortened at the end (or 'catalectic'). The symbol ∧ denotes a pause equal in time-value to – ⏑. Verse 4 consists of two paeons of the 'cretic' form (cp. *Rhythm. and Metric*, p. 27).

II.

{dochm.
{dochm.
{dochm.
{dochm.

III.

dochm.
dochm. *m.*   [*m.* = mesode.]
dochm.

SECOND STROPHE (forming a single period).—Dochmiac, varied by iambic trimeters.

1. οιμοι
   οιμοι

2. εχ : ω μαθων δειλ | αιος εν δ εμ | ῳ καρᾳ ∧ ‖
   κακ : ον τοδ αλλο | δευτερον βλεπ | ω ταλας

3. θε : ος τοτ αρα | τοτε μεγ ‖ α βαρος μ εχ | ων ∧ ‖
   τις : αρα τις με | ποτμος ‖ ετι περιμεν | ει

4. ε : παισεν εν δ ε | σεισεν αγρι | αις οδοις ∧ ‖
   εχ : ω μεν εν χειρ | εσσιν αρτι | ως τεκνον

5. οιμ : οι | λακπατ | ητον | αντρεπ | ων χαρ | αν ∧ ‖
   ταλ : ας | τον δ εν | αντα | προσβλεπ | ω νεκρ | ον

6. φευ : φευ ω πον | οι βροτ ‖ ων δυσπον | οι ∧ ⟧
   φευ : φευ ματερ | αθλι ‖ α φευ τεκν | ον

Schmidt observes that verse 5 cannot be regarded as a dochmius followed by a choreic tripody, *i.e.*, > ᝮ : – – ᨺ | – ᨺ ‖ – ᨺ | – ᨺ | – ∧ ‖. Such a verse would be wholly unrhythmical. Nor, again, can it be a dochmiac dimeter, since the second dochmius (ἀντρέπων χαράν) would be of an unexampled form, ᨺ – ᨺ | – ∧ ‖. He considers it, then, to be simply an iambic trimeter, with one lyric feature introduced, viz., the pause (equiv. to – ᨺ) on the second syllable of οἴμοι. This 'melic iambic trimeter' forms a mesode, while the dochmiac dimeters (vv. 3 and 6) correspond. The two regular iambic trimeters (vv. 2 and 4) do not belong to the lyric structure.

THIRD STROPHE.—Dochmiac.

I. 1. αιαι αιαι
    ιτω ιτω

    ᨺ   –   –   ᨺ   –   ᨺ   –   –   ᝮ   –

2. αν ⋮ επταν φοβ | ῳ τι μ ‖ ουκ ανται | αν ∧ ‖
   φαν ⋮ ητω μορ | ων ο ⋮ καλλιστ εχ | ων

    ᨺ   –   –   ᨺ   –   ᨺ   –   –   ᨺ   –

3. ε ⋮ παισεν τις | αμφι ‖ θηκτῳ ξιφ | ει ∧ ⟧
  εμ ⋮ οι τερμι | αν αγ ‖ ων αμερ | αν

      >   ᨺᨺ ᨺ ᨺ ᨺ   –

II. 1. δειλ ⋮ αιος εγω αι | αι ∧ ‖
    υπ   ⋮ ατος ιτω ιτ | ω

     >   – – ᨺ   – ᨺ   – – ᨺ   –

2. δειλ ⋮ αιᾳ δε | συγκε ‖ κραμαι δυ | ᾳ ∧ ⟧
   οπ   ⋮ ως μηκετ | αμαρ ‖ αλλ εισιδ | ω

FOURTH STROPHE.—A single period.   Dochmiac.

1. ω ⋮ μοι μοι ταδ | ουκ επ ‖ αλλον βροτ | ων Λ ‖
   αγ ⋮ οιτ αν ματ | αιον ‖ ανδρ εκποδ | ων

2. ε ⋮ μας αρμοσ | ει ποτ ‖ εξ αιτι | ας Λ ‖
   ος ⋮ ω παι σε τ | ουχ εκ ‖ ων κατεκαν | ον

3. εγ ⋮ ω γαρ σ εγ | ω ε ‖ κανον ω μελ | εος Λ ‖
   σε τ ⋮ αυ τανδ ω* | μοι μελ ‖ εος ουδ εχ | ω

4. εγ ⋮ ω φαμ ετ | υμον ι ‖ ω προσπολ | οι Λ ‖
   προς ⋮ ποτερον ιδω* | πα κλιθ ‖ ω παντα | γαρ

5. αγ ⋮ ετε μ οτι ταχ | ιστ αγ ‖ ετε μ εκποδ | ων Λ ‖
   λεχρ ⋮ ια ταν χερ | οιν τα δ ‖ επι κρατι | μοι

6. τον ⋮ ουκ οντα | μαλλον ‖ η μηδεν | α Λ ⟧
   ποτμ ⋮ ος δυσκομ | ιστος ‖ εισηλατ | ο

Thus each of the six verses is a dochmiac dimeter.   In each verse
the first and second dochmius answer respectively to the first and
second dochmius of the next verse.

· * Cp. n. on παί in First Strophe, Per. II., v. 2.

ΣΟΦΟΚΛΕΟΥΣ

ΑΝΤΙΓΟΝΗ

ΣΟΦΟΚΛΕΟΥΣ

ΑΝΤΙΓΟΝΗ

I.

ΑΡΙΣΤΟΦΑΝΟΥΣ ΓΡΑΜΜΑΤΙΚΟΥ ΥΠΟΘΕΣΙΣ.

Ἀντιγόνη παρὰ τὴν πρόσταξιν τῆς πόλεως θάψασα τὸν Πολυνείκην ἐφωράθη, καὶ εἰς μνημεῖον κατάγειον ἐντεθεῖσα παρὰ τοῦ Κρέοντος ἀνή- ρηται· ἐφ' ᾗ καὶ Αἵμων δυσπαθήσας διὰ τὸν εἰς αὐτὴν ἔρωτα ξίφει ἑαυτὸν διεχειρίσατο. ἐπὶ δὲ τῷ τούτου θανάτῳ καὶ ἡ μήτηρ Εὐρυδίκη ἑαυτὴν ἀνεῖλε.   5

κεῖται ἡ μυθοποιΐα καὶ παρὰ Εὐριπίδῃ ἐν Ἀντιγόνῃ· πλὴν ἐκεῖ φωρα- θεῖσα μετὰ τοῦ Αἵμονος δίδοται πρὸς γάμου κοινωνίαν καὶ τέκνον τίκτει τὸν Μαίονα.

ἡ μὲν σκηνὴ τοῦ δράματος ὑπόκειται ἐν Θήβαις ταῖς Βοιωτικαῖς. ὁ δὲ χορὸς συνέστηκεν ἐξ ἐπιχωρίων γερόντων. προλογίζει ἡ Ἀντιγόνη· ὑπό- 10 κειται δὲ τὰ πράγματα ἐπὶ τῶν Κρέοντος βασιλείων. τὸ δὲ κεφάλαιόν ἐστι τάφος Πολυνείκους, Ἀντιγόνης ἀναίρεσις, θάνατος Αἵμονος καὶ μόρος Εὐρυδίκης τῆς Αἵμονος μητρός. φασὶ δὲ τὸν Σοφοκλέα ἠξιῶσθαι τῆς ἐν Σάμῳ στρατηγίας εὐδοκιμήσαντα ἐν τῇ διδασκαλίᾳ τῆς Ἀντιγόνης. λέλεκται δὲ τὸ δρᾶμα τοῦτο τριακοστὸν δεύτερον.   15

2 ἀνήρηται] An aorist, not a perfect, is required : ἐφωράθη precedes, διεχειρίσατο follows. Nauck conjectures ἀνηρέθη, Wecklein ἀνήρτησεν ἑαυτήν, which Bellermann approves. But ἀνήρηται, though a solecism, may nevertheless be genuine, if the ascription of this Argument to Aristophanes is erroneous, as is now generally held to be the case with regard to some other ὑποθέσεις which bear his name. The use of the perfect in place of the aorist is not rare in scholia of the later age. Thus on Thuc. 3. 68, τὴν δὲ γῆν δημοσιώσαντες ἀπεμίσθωσαν, the schol. has ἐπὶ μισθῷ δεδώκασιν. As here we have ἐφωράθη—ἀνήρηται—διεχειρίσατο, so on Thuc. 1. 20 the schol. gives ἐλίμωξέ ποτε ἡ Ἀττική, καὶ λύσις ἦν τῶν δεινῶν, παίδων σφαγή. Λεὼς οὖν τις τὰς ἑαυτοῦ κόρας ἐπιδέδωκε καὶ ἀπήλλαξε τοῦ λιμοῦ τὴν πόλιν. So, too, on Thuc. 2. 95 the schol. has ὡς δὲ οὐδὲν ἀποδέδωκε πρὸς αὐτὸν ὁ Περδίκκας ἅπερ ὑπέσχετο, ἐστράτευσε κατ' αὐτοῦ. More on this subject may be seen in my

Appendix to Vincent and Dickson's *Handbook of Modern Greek*, 2nd ed., p. 328 (Macmillan, 1881). 4 διεχειρίσατο L, and so most recent edd.: διαχειρίζεσθαι is thus used by Polybius, Plutarch, and others. The commoner reading here was διεχρήσατο, as in the Argument to the *Ajax* διαχρήσασθαι (where now διαχειρίσασθαι is usually read); and in the same Argument ἑαυτὸν διαχρῆται (*v.l.* διαχειρίζεται) is still generally retained. 7 μετὰ τοῦ Αἵμονος L: τῷ Αἵμονι cod. Dresd. D. 183, which may be a corruption of μετὰ τοῦτο Αἵμονι, as Bellermann thinks. 8 Μαίονα Nauck, comparing *Il.* 4. 394 Μαίων Αἱμονίδης.—αἵμονα L, and so Dindorf, who says that L has μαίδον^a in the margin; but it seems rather to be μαίμον^a.

ΑΡΙΣΤΟΦΑΝΟΥΣ ΓΡΑΜΜΑΤΙΚΟΥ] Aristophanes of Byzantium, librarian at Alexandria (flor. 200 B.C.), to whom the metrical argument for the *Oedipus Tyrannus* is also ascribed in the MSS., but incorrectly: see *Oed. Tyr.* p. 4. Though the genuineness of this prose ὑπόθεσις has not such a *prima facie* case against it as exists against that of all the metrical arguments ascribed to Aristophanes, it must at least be regarded as very doubtful. If the perfect ἀνῄρηται in line 2 is sound, it is an indication of much later age, as has been shown in the critical note above. Another such indication, I think, is the phrase εἰς μνημεῖον κατάγειον ἐντεθεῖσα παρὰ (instead of ὑπὸ) τοῦ Κρέοντος (l. 2),—a later (and modern) use of the prep. which does not surprise us in Salustius (Arg. II. l. 11 παρὰ τοῦ Κρέοντος κωλύεται), but which would be strange in the Alexandrian scholar of *circ.* 200 B.C. In the Laurentian MS. this Argument precedes, while the other two follow, the play. 6 ἐν 'Αντιγόνῃ] Only some 21 small fragments remain (about 80 verses in all), and these throw no light on the details of the plot. 8 τὸν Μαίονα. This reading is made almost certain by the mention of ' Maion, son of Haemon' in *Il.* 4. 394, coupled with the fact that L has Μαίμονα in the margin (see cr. n.). But the reading μετὰ τοῦ Αἵμονος just before is doubtful. If it is sound, then we must understand: 'having been discovered in company with Haemon, she was given in marriage (to him).' But I am strongly inclined to think that the conjecture μετὰ τοῦτο τῷ Αἵμονι (which would explain the *v.l.* τῷ Αἵμονι) is right. Dindorf differs from other interpreters in supposing that it was not Haemon, but someone else—perhaps a nameless αὐτουργός, as in the case of the Euripidean Electra—to whom Euripides married Antigone: and he reads τίκτει τὸν Αἵμονα. We have then to suppose that Antigone marked her affection for her lost lover by giving his name to her son by the αὐτουργός. At the end of the scholia in L we find these words:—Ὅτι διαφέρει τῆς Εὐριπίδου 'Αντιγόνης αὕτη, ὅτι φωραθεῖσα ἐκείνη διὰ τὸν Αἵμονος ἔρωτα ἐξεδόθη πρὸς γάμον· ἐνταῦθα δὲ τοὐναντίον. The contrast meant is between her marriage in Euripides and her death in Sophocles: but the words obviously leave it doubtful whether the person to whom Euripides married her was Haemon or not. 13 τῆς ἐν Σάμῳ στρατηγίας] The traditional στρατηγία of Sophocles, and its relation to the production of the *Antigone*, are discussed in the Introduction. 15 τριακοστὸν δεύτερον] Written λβ in L. The statement seems to have been taken from Alexandrian διδασκαλίαι which gave the plays in chronological order. Sophocles is said to have exhibited for the first time in 468 B.C., *aet.* 28. See Introd.

II.

ΣΑΛΟΥΣΤΙΟΥ ΥΠΟΘΕΣΙΣ.

Τὸ μὲν δρᾶμα τῶν καλλίστων Σοφοκλέους. στασιάζεται δὲ τὰ περὶ
τὴν ἡρωίδα ἱστορούμενα καὶ τὴν ἀδελφὴν αὐτῆς Ἰσμήνην· ὁ μὲν γὰρ Ἴων
ἐν τοῖς διθυράμβοις καταπρησθῆναί φησιν ἀμφοτέρας ἐν τῷ ἱερῷ τῆς Ἥρας
ὑπὸ Λαοδάμαντος τοῦ Ἐτεοκλέους· Μίμνερμος δέ φησι τὴν μὲν Ἰσμήνην
προσομιλοῦσαν Θεοκλυμένῳ ὑπὸ Τυδέως κατὰ Ἀθηνᾶς ἐγκέλευσιν τελευτῆσαι. 5
ταῦτα μὲν οὖν ἐστι τὰ ξένως περὶ τῶν ἡρωίδων ἱστορούμενα. ἡ μέντοι
κοινὴ δόξα σπουδαίας αὐτὰς ὑπείληφεν καὶ φιλαδέλφους δαιμονίως, ᾗ καὶ οἱ
τῆς τραγῳδίας ποιηταὶ ἐπόμενοι τὰ περὶ αὐτὰς διατέθεινται. τὸ δὲ δρᾶμα
τὴν ὀνομασίαν ἔσχεν ἀπὸ τῆς παρεχούσης τὴν ὑπόθεσιν Ἀντιγόνης. ὑπόκειται δὲ ἄταφον τὸ σῶμα Πολυνείκους, καὶ Ἀντιγόνη θάπτειν αὐτὸ πειρω- 10
μένη παρὰ τοῦ Κρέοντος κωλύεται. φωραθεῖσα δὲ αὐτὴ θάπτουσα ἀπόλλυται. Αἵμων τε ὁ Κρέοντος ἐρῶν αὐτῆς καὶ ἀφορήτως ἔχων ἐπὶ τῇ τοιαύτῃ
συμφορᾷ αὐτὸν διαχειρίζεται· ἐφ' ᾧ καὶ ἡ μήτηρ Εὐρυδίκη τελευτᾷ τὸν
βίον ἀγχόνῃ.

4 Λαοδάμαντος Brunck (cp. Apollod. 3. 7. 3): Λαομέδοντος MSS.

9 τὴν ὀνομασίαν L: τὴν ἐπιγραφὴν cod. Paris.   π̅χούσης L (i.e. περιεχούσης):
παρεχούσης Par.

ΣΑΛΟΥΣΤΙΟΥ] A rhetorician of the 5th cent. A.D.: see on *Oed. Col.*, p. 6.—
In the Laurentian MS., which alone records him as the writer, this Argument stands
at the end of the play, immediately after the anonymous Argument (our III.).

1 στασιάζεται, pass., 'are made subjects of dispute,' *i.e.* are told in conflicting
ways, are 'discrepant': a late use of the word, which cannot be deduced from the
older, though rare, active use of στασιάζω (τὴν πόλιν, etc.) as 'to involve in party
strife.'   2 Ἴων] Of Chios, the poet and prose-writer, flor. *circ.* 450 B.C.
His dithyrambs are occasionally mentioned (schol. on Ar. *Pax* 835 and on Apollon.
Rhod. 1. 1165): it is probably from them that Athenaeus quotes (35 E): but only
a few words remain.   4 Μίμνερμος] Of Smyrna, the elegiac poet, flor. *circ.*
620 B.C.   5 Θεοκλυμένῳ] The only persons of this name in Greek mythology
seem to be the soothsayer in the *Odyssey* (*Od.* 15. 256 etc.), and a son of Proteus
(Eur. *Helen.* 9): Wecklein suggests Ἐτεόκλῳ, an Argive who was one of the seven
leaders against Thebes (*O. C.* 1316 n.).   6 ξένως] *i.e.* in a way foreign to
the version followed by Sophocles.   14 ἀγχόνῃ] Eurydice kills herself with
a sword (1301). Possibly ἀγχόνῃ should follow ἀπόλλυται in l. 11 (cp. Arg. III.
l. 10 ἀπολομένη ἀγχόνῃ): but more probably it is due to a slip of memory, or to a
confusion with the case of Iocasta in the *Oed. Tyr.*

III.

Ἀποθανόντα Πολυνείκη ἐν τῷ πρὸς τὸν ἀδελφὸν μονομαχίῳ Κρέων
ἄταφον ἐκβαλὼν κηρύττει μηδένα αὐτὸν θάπτειν, θάνατον τὴν ζημίαν ἀπει-
λήσας. τοῦτον Ἀντιγόνη ἡ ἀδελφὴ θάπτειν πειρᾶται. καὶ δὴ λαθοῦσα
τοὺς φύλακας ἐπιβάλλει χῶμα· οἷς ἐπαπειλεῖ θάνατον ὁ Κρέων, εἰ μὴ τὸν
5 τοῦτο δράσαντα ἐξεύροιεν. οὗτοι τὴν κόνιν τὴν ἐπιβεβλημένην καθάραντες
οὐδὲν ἧττον ἐφρούρουν. ἐπελθοῦσα δὲ ἡ Ἀντιγόνη καὶ γυμνὸν εὑροῦσα
τὸν νεκρὸν ἀνοιμώξασα ἑαυτὴν εἰσαγγέλλει. ταύτην ὑπὸ τῶν φυλάκων παρα-
δεδομένην Κρέων καταδικάζει καὶ ζῶσαν εἰς τύμβον καθεῖρξεν. ἐπὶ τούτοις
Αἵμων, ὁ Κρέοντος υἱός, ὃς ἐμνᾶτο αὐτήν, ἀγανακτήσας ἑαυτὸν προσεπισφάζει
10 τῇ κόρῃ ἀπολομένῃ ἀγχόνῃ, Τειρεσίου ταῦτα προθεσπίσαντος· ἐφ' ᾧ λυπη-
θεῖσα Εὐρυδίκη, ἡ τοῦ Κρέοντος γαμετή, ἑαυτὴν ἀποσφάζει. καὶ τέλος
θρηνεῖ Κρέων τὸν τοῦ παιδὸς καὶ τῆς γαμετῆς θάνατον.

1 τῷ...μονομαχίῳ L: τῇ...μονομαχίᾳ vulg.

5 καθάραντες vulg., καθαίροντες L, and so most recent edd. But the present
partic. cannot stand here; the removal of the dust was not a continued or repeated
act (cp. v. 409). The form ἐκάθαρα has earlier epigraphic evidence (347 B.C.) than
ἐκάθηρα: see Meisterhans, Gramm. Att. Inschr. p. 86.   9 προσεπισφάζει L:
ἐπισφάζει vulg.   11 ἀποσφάζει L: κατασφάζει vulg.

4 ἐπιβάλλει χῶμα, because the strewing of dust on the corpse was a symbolical
sepulture: see v. 256, and n. on 10. The phrase is strange, but no emendation
seems probable.   7 ἑαυτὴν εἰσαγγέλλει, 'denounces herself': see v. 435.
10 προθεσπίσαντος: alluding to vv. 1064 ff.

ΤΑ ΤΟΥ ΔΡΑΜΑΤΟΣ ΠΡΟΣΩΠΑ.

ΑΝΤΙΓΟΝΗ.	ΑΙΜΩΝ.
ΙΣΜΗΝΗ.	ΤΕΙΡΕΣΙΑΣ.
ΧΟΡΟΣ ΘΗΒΑΙΩΝ ΓΕΡΟΝΤΩΝ.	ΑΓΓΕΛΟΣ.
ΚΡΕΩΝ.	ΕΥΡΥΔΙΚΗ.
ΦΥΛΑΞ.	ΕΞΑΓΓΕΛΟΣ.

The parts may have been cast as follows:

1. *Protagonist.* Antigone. Teiresias. Eurydice.

2. *Deuteragonist.* Ismene. Watcher. Haemon. Messenger. Second Messenger.

3. *Tritagonist.* Creon.

Schneidewin gives Eurydice to the second actor, and the two Messengers to the first actor. But, as the part of Eurydice is much lighter than the combined parts of the Messengers, it is more naturally assigned to the first actor, who already bears the heaviest burden. From Demosthenes *De Falsa Legat.* § 247 it is known that the third actor played Creon.

It is a general rule of Greek Tragedy that, when the protagonist represents a woman, the Chorus represent women. The dramatic motive for the exception in this play is noticed in the Introduction.

STRUCTURE OF THE PLAY.

1. πρόλογος, verses 1—99.
2. πάροδος, 100—161.

---

3. ἐπεισόδιον πρῶτον, 162—331.
4. στάσιμον πρῶτον, 332—375. Anapaests, 376—383.

---

5. ἐπεισόδιον δεύτερον, 384—581.
6. στάσιμον δεύτερον, 582—625. Anapaests, 626—630.

---

7. ἐπεισόδιον τρίτον, 631—780.
8. στάσιμον τρίτον, 781—800. Anapaests, 801—805.

---

9. ἐπεισόδιον τέταρτον, 806—943, beginning with a κομμός, 806—882.
10. στάσιμον τέταρτον, 944—987.

---

11. ἐπεισόδιον πέμπτον, 988—1114.
12. ὑπόρχημα, 1115—1154, taking the place of a fifth stasimon.

---

13. ἔξοδος, 1155—1352, including a κομμός, 1261—1347.

ΑΝΤΙΓΟΝΗ.

῏Ω ΚΟΙΝΟΝ αὐτάδελφον Ἰσμήνης κάρα,
ἆρ᾽ οἶσθ᾽ ὅ τι Ζεὺς τῶν ἀπ᾽ Οἰδίπου κακῶν
ὁποῖον οὐχὶ νῷν ἔτι ζώσαιν τελεῖ;
οὐδὲν γὰρ οὔτ᾽ ἀλγεινὸν οὔτ᾽ ἄτης ἄτερ
οὔτ᾽ αἰσχρὸν οὔτ᾽ ἄτιμόν ἐσθ᾽, ὁποῖον οὐ 5
τῶν σῶν τε κἀμῶν οὐκ ὄπωπ᾽ ἐγὼ κακῶν.

L = cod. Laur. 32. 9 (first half of eleventh century). r = one or more of the later MSS. This symbol is used where a more particular statement is unnecessary. 'MSS.,' after a reading, means that it is in all the MSS. known to the editor.

1 κοινὸν] κλεινὸν Wecklein *Ars Soph. em.* 52: μοῦνον M. Schmidt.
2 ἆρ᾽ οἶσθ᾽ ὅ, τι L. For the emendations proposed here and in v. 3, see Appendix.

Scene:—*The same as in the* Oedipus Tyrannus,—*viz., an open space before the royal palace (once that of Oedipus) at Thebes. The back-scene represents the front of the palace, with three doors, of which the central and largest (the βασίλειος θύρα) is that which in v.* 18 *is called* αὔλειοι πύλαι, *as being the principal entrance to the* αὐλή *of the house.*

1—99 Prologue. At daybreak (v. 100) on the morning after the fall of the two brothers and the flight of the Argives, Antigone calls Ismene forth from the house, in order to speak with her apart. She tells her that Creon has forbidden the burial of Polyneices, and declares her resolve to perform it herself. Ismene declines to assist, and endeavours to dissuade her. Antigone then goes alone to the task.

1 The words **κοινὸν** (kindred) **αὐτάδελφον** (very sister) form a single emphatic expression ('my sister, mine own sister'), not a climax ('kinswoman, and sister')—κοινόν strengthening αὐτάδελφον much as in *O. C.* 535 κοιναί γε πατρὸς ἀδελφεαί ('yea, very sisters of their sire'). κοινόν refers simply to birth from the same parents (cp. 202): it will not bear the added moral sense, 'having common interests and feelings': that is only implied, in so far as it may be a result of kinship. αὐτάδελφος (subst. below, 503, 696) is merely a poetical strengthening of ἀδελφός, and does not necessarily imply (as it might here) what prose expresses by ἀδελφὸς ὁμοπάτριος καὶ ὁμομήτριος (Lys. or. 42 § 4): thus Apollo, son of Zeus and Leto, can address Hermes, son of Zeus and Maia, as αὐτάδελφον αἷμα καὶ κοινοῦ

πατρός (Aesch. *Eum.* 89).—**κάρα**: the periphrasis (as with κεφαλή) usu. implies respect, affection, or both (cp. Horace's *tam cari capitis*).—The pathetic emphasis of this first line gives the key-note of the drama. The origin which connects the sisters also isolates them. If Ismene is not with her, Antigone stands alone.

2 f. **ἆρ᾽ οἶσθ᾽...τελεῖ**; For the various interpretations and emendations, see Appendix. The soundness of the text is doubtful, but no proposed correction is probable. I read ὅ τι, pron., not ὅτι, conjunction, and supply ἐστί. In the direct question, τί ὁποῖον οὐ τελεῖ; we understand ἐστί with τί. In the indirect form, it is simplest to say οὐκ οἶδ᾽ ὅ τι οὐ τελεῖ: and we certainly could not say, οὐκ οἶδ᾽ ὅ τι [ἐστὶν] ὁποῖον οὐ τελεῖ, if ὅ τι came immediately before ὁποῖον. Here, however, the separation of ὅ τι from ὁποῖον by Ζεὺς τῶν ἀπ᾽ Οἰδίπου κακῶν makes a vital difference. The sentence begins as if it were to be, ἆρ᾽ οἶσθ᾽ ὅ τι Ζεὺς οὐ τελεῖ; But when, after an interval, ὁποῖον comes in, the Greek hearer would think of the direct form, τί ὁποῖον οὐ τελεῖ; and so his ear would not be offended. This, too, suggests the answer to the objection that Ζεύς ought to follow ὁποῖον. Certainly Eur. *I. A.* 525, οὐκ ἔστ᾽ Ὀδυσσεὺς ὅ τι σὲ κἀμὲ πημανεῖ, would be parallel only if here we had ἆρ᾽ οἶσθα, Ζεύς (without ὅ τι). Nor could we have (e.g.) ἆρ᾽ οἶσθ᾽ ἥτις Ζεὺς τῶν νόσων ὁποίαν οὐ τελεῖ; But, since ὅ τι might be acc., Ζεύς seems to follow it naturally; and, when, afterwards, the sentence takes a shape which makes ὅ τι nom., the ear does not return on Ζεύς as on a misplaced

ANTIGONE.

ISMENE, my sister, mine own dear sister, knowest thou what ill there is, of all bequeathed by Oedipus, that Zeus fulfils not for us twain while we live? Nothing painful is there, nothing fraught with ruin, no shame, no dishonour, that I have not seen in thy woes and mine.

4 ff. οὔτ' ἄτης ἄτερ MSS. For the proposed emendations, see Appendix.—Paley regards vv. 4—6 as interpolated: v. 6 is suspected by Nauck.—οὐκ ὄπωπ'] εἰσόπωπ' B. Todt. The 1st hand in L wrote οὐχὶ (thinking of v. 3), but the letters

---

word, because the whole is felt as = τί Ζεὺς ὁποῖον οὐ τελεῖ;—The main objection to reading ὅτι, and taking ὁποῖον as substituted for the direct ποῖον ('that he fulfils—what not?') is the shortness of the sentence.

τῶν ἀπ' Οἰδ. κακῶν, the ills derived from Oed. (cp. *Ph.* 1088 λύπας τὰς ἀπ' ἐμοῦ): *i.e.* the curse upon the Labdacidae (594) which he had inherited, and which he bequeathed to his children in a form intensified by his own acts,—the parricide, the incest, the imprecation upon his sons. That imprecation finds a further fulfilment in Creon's edict. ἔτι ζώσαιν does not mean, 'living wearily on,' but simply, 'still living' (not yet dead), so that ἔτι is almost pleonastic, as in 750 ἔτι ζώσαν, and so *Tr.* 305. Sometimes, indeed, the use of ἔτι with ζῆν is more emphatic, as in *Ai.* 990 ἔτι ζῶν...ἐφίετο (while *yet* alive), Eur. *Bacch.* 8 πυρὸς ἔτι ζῶσαν φλόγα (*still* smouldering).

4—6 Paley (*Journ. Ph.* 10. 16) regards these three verses as interpolated, because (1) Antigone, like Ismene, should have only seven verses: (2) the words only repeat vv. 2, 3: (3) the double negative offends. But we have no warrant for requiring such a correspondence; and this is not repetition, but development. On (3), see below.

4 οὔτ' ἄτης ἄτερ. I translate as if οὔτ' ἄτην ἄγον (or the like) stood in the text, since there can be no doubt that such was the general sense; but I leave the traditional words, οὔτ' ἄτης ἄτερ, thinking no emendation sufficiently probable to be admitted. A discussion will be found in the Appendix. Here, the following points may be noted. (1) This seems to have been the only reading known to Didymus of Alexandria, *circ.* 30 B.C. (2) It certainly does not yield any tolerable sense. (3) But the phrase

ἄτης ἄτερ is not, in itself, at all suspicious: cp. *Tr.* 48 πημονῆς ἄτερ: Aesch. *Suppl.* 377 βλάβης ἄτερ, 703 ἄτερ πημάτων: *Ag.* 1148 κλαυμάτων ἄτερ: *Th.* 683 αἰσχύνης ἄτερ: *Ch.* 338 τί δ' ἄτερ κακῶν; Eur. *Her.* 841 οὐκ ἄτερ πόνων. (4) The gentlest remedy would be οὐδ' for the second οὔτ': 'nothing painful and not-free from calamity' (= nothing painful and calamitous). The mental pain was accompanied by ruin to their fortunes. I think this possible, but not quite satisfactory. (5) One word, instead of ἄτης ἄτερ, might seem desirable: I had thought of ἀτηφόρον (cp. δικηφόρος). (6) Donaldson's ἄτην ἄγον can be supported by fr. 325 ὅτῳ δ' ὄλεθρον δεινὸν ἀλήθει' ἄγει, and fr. 856. 5 ἐν κείνῃ τὸ πᾶν, | σπουδαῖον, ἡσυχαῖον, ἐς βίαν ἄγον. (7) But no emendation has yet been made which, while giving a fit sense, also accounts palaeographically for ἄτης ἄτερ being so old. We cannot assume marginal glosses (as ἀτηρ') in MSS. of 30 B.C.

5 f. αἰσχρόν, shocking the moral sense: ἄτιμον, attended by outward marks of dishonour,—as Oedipus imagines his daughters exposed to slights at the public festivals (*O. T.* 1489 ff.). Thus αἰσχρόν in a manner balances the subjective ἀλγεινόν, as the external ἀτιμία corresponds with the ἄτη. Cp. *O. T.* 1283 ff.—ὁποῖον οὐ...οὐκ ὄπωπα. The repetition of the negative is warranted by the emphasis: cp. *Ph.* 416 οὐχ ὁ Τυδέως γόνος, | οὐδ' οὑμπολητὸς Σισύφου Λαερτίῳ, | οὐ μὴ θάνωσι: *Tr.* 1014 οὐ πῦρ, οὐκ ἔγχος τις ὀνήσιμον οὐκ ἐπιτρέψει; Aesch. *Ag.* 1634 ὃς οὐκ, ἐπειδὴ τῷδ' ἐβούλευσας μόρον, | δρᾶσαι τόδ' ἔργον οὐκ ἔτλης αὐτοκτόνως: and so oft. after οὐ μά, as *El.* 626. We need not, then, change οὐ (in v. 5) to ὄν, with Blaydes, nor οὐκ ὄπωπ' to εἰσόπωπ' with B. Todt.—τῶν...κακῶν, sc. ὄν, possessive (or 'partitive') gen. with

καὶ νῦν τί τοῦτ᾽ αὖ φασὶ πανδήμῳ πόλει
κήρυγμα θεῖναι τὸν στρατηγὸν ἀρτίως;
ἔχεις τι κεἰσήκουσας; ἤ σε λανθάνει
πρὸς τοὺς φίλους στείχοντα τῶν ἐχθρῶν κακά; 10

ΙΣΜΗΝΗ.

ἐμοὶ μὲν οὐδεὶς μῦθος, Ἀντιγόνη, φίλων
οὔθ᾽ ἡδὺς οὔτ᾽ ἀλγεινὸς ἵκετ᾽, ἐξ ὅτου
δυοῖν ἀδελφοῖν ἐστερήθημεν δύο,
μιᾷ θανόντοιν ἡμέρᾳ διπλῇ χερί·
ἐπεὶ δὲ φροῦδός ἐστιν Ἀργείων στρατὸς 15
ἐν νυκτὶ τῇ νῦν, οὐδὲν οἶδ᾽ ὑπέρτερον,
οὔτ᾽ εὐτυχοῦσα μᾶλλον οὔτ᾽ ἀτωμένη.

χι were afterwards erased.—For οὐ, Blaydes conject. ὄν.   10 τῶν] τάξ Blaydes.

ὄπωπα,—'which I have not seen as belonging to, being in the number of,' our woes. For the omission of ὄν cp. O. C. 694 ἔστιν δ᾽ οἷον ἐγὼ γᾶς Ἀσίας οὐκ ἐπακούω.

7 αὖ is oft. thus joined with the interrogative τίς ('what new thing?'): cp. 1172, 1281: O. C. 357 νῦν δ᾽ αὖ τίν᾽ ἥκεις μῦθον... | φέρουσα...; ib. 1507 τί δ᾽ ἐστίν ...νέορτον αὖ;—**πανδήμῳ πόλει**, the whole body of the citizens: so 1141, El. 982: πανδήμου στρατοῦ Ai. 844. For the adj. compounded with a noun cognate in sense to the subst., cp. βίος μακραίων (O. T. 518), εὐήρετμος πλάτα (O. C. 716 n.).

8 θεῖναι, not θέσθαι. τίθημι νόμον denotes simply the legislative act as such; hence it is fitting when the lawgiver is supreme or absolute; as Athena says, θεσμὸν...θήσω (Aesch. Eum. 484). τίθεμαι νόμον further implies the legislator's personal concern in the law; hence it is said of legislative assemblies (Ar. Pol. 4. 1. 9): but it can be said also of the despot, if his interest is implied: Plat. Rep. 338 E τίθεται δέ γε τοὺς νόμους ἑκάστη ἡ ἀρχὴ πρὸς τὸ αὑτῇ ξυμφέρον, δημοκρατία μὲν δημοκρατικούς, τυραννὶς δὲ τυραννικούς. **τὸν στρατηγόν.** Creon is already βασιλεὺς χώρας (155), having become so by the fact of Eteocles falling (173). She calls him στρατηγός because that was the special capacity in which, as king, he had first to act; but the title serves also to suggest rigour. The poets sometimes speak of the δῆμος as στρατός (Pind. P. 2. 87, Aesch. Eum. 566).

9 ἔχεις, cognitum habes: Tr. 318 οὐδ᾽ ὄνομα πρός του τῶν ξυνεμπόρων ἔχεις;—**κεἰσήκουσας**, simply 'heard' (not, 'given heed to'), as O. C. 1645, Ai. 318, Tr. 351, 424.

10 τῶν ἐχθρῶν κακά, 'that evils belonging to (proper for) our enemies are coming upon our friends'; i.e. that our brother Polyneices is to share the doom of the Argive dead, by being left unburied. As appears from vv. 1081 ff., Soph. supposes that burial was denied to the slain foemen generally, and not to Polyneices alone. No legend was more familiar at Athens than that of Theseus recovering the Argive corpses from Creon (Eur. Suppl.). Cp. 1162, where, as here, ἐχθρῶν are the Argives,—the πολέμιοι in their relation to individuals. Ismene, too, seems to understand the Argives; in her reply verses 11—14 refer to φίλους, and vv. 15—17 to ἐχθρῶν. It is rare that ἐχθρῶν should have the art., while κακά has none; but cp. 365: O. T. 1530 τέρμα τοῦ βίου.—We might take τῶν ἐχθρῶν κακά as 'evils planned by our foes' (i.e. by Creon): cp. Ph. 422 τά γε | κείνων κάκ᾽ ἐξήρυκε: ib. 512 τὸ κείνων κακόν. So schol., τὰ τῶν ἐχθρῶν μηχανήματα ἐπὶ τοὺς φίλους ἰόντα. But (a) the authorship of the decree having been already named, we now expect a hint of its purport: and (b) ἐχθροί being the natural persons to hurt φίλοι, the antithesis loses point. Some join στείχοντα τῶν ἐχθρῶν, 'coming from foes'; which is open to the objec-

And now what new edict is this of which they tell, that
our Captain hath just published to all Thebes? Knowest thou
aught? Hast thou heard? Or is it hidden from thee that our
friends are threatened with the doom of our foes?

ISMENE.

No word of friends, Antigone, gladsome or painful, hath
come to me, since we two sisters were bereft of brothers twain,
killed in one day by a twofold blow; and since in this last
night the Argive host hath fled, I know no more, whether my
fortune be brighter, or more grievous.

13 δύο has been made from δύω in L, o being also written above. **14** θανόντοιν

tions just mentioned, and also to this,
that, after such a verb as στείχειν, the
simple gen. ought to denote place (*O. T.*
152 Πυθῶνος ἔβας), not agent.

11 f. μέν does not answer to the
δέ in 15, but merely gives a slight emphasis to ἐμοί; cp. Xen. *Cyr.* 1. 4. 12
ἐγὼ μὲν οὐκ οἶδα (though others may
know).—'Ἀντιγόνη, placed as in *O. C.*
1 n., 1415; while once (*O. C.* 507) the
anapaest is in the 4th place.—φίλων,
objective gen. with μῦθος, tidings *about*
them: cp. *Ai.* 221 ἀνδρὸς αἴθονος ἀγγε-
λίαν: *ib.* 998 ὀξεῖα γάρ σου βάξις. In
O. C. 1161 f. σοῦ...μῦθον (where the gen.
is objective) = 'speech *with* thee.'—ἐξ
ὅτου, referring to a definite time, as
1092, *O. C.* 345, *Tr.* 326, *Ph.* 493, like
ἐξ οὗ (*O. T.* 1201, *Tr.* 38, *Ai.* 661,
1337). It refers to an indefinite time
below, 457. The brothers had fallen on
the preceding day.

13 δυοῖν...δύο. The addition of δύο
would have more point if two pairs were
in question, each consisting of one brother
and one sister (as, *e.g.*, one might say,
'the two husbands were taken from the
two wives'): yet it is not pointless, since
it helps to suggest the isolation of the
sisters. As Greek (esp. tragic) idiom loves
to mark reciprocity by a repeated word
(73 φίλη...φίλον, *Ai.* 267 κοινὸς ἐν κοινοῖσι),
so it also loves to mark coincidence or
contrast of number, whether this is, or is
not, especially relevant (cp. 14, 55, 141).

14 θανόντοιν is clearly required here,
though our MSS. have θανόντων. So in *El.*
1297, where νῷν ἐπελθόντοιν is certainly
right, L has ἐπελθόντων (with οι written
over ω as a correction). A plur. noun
can stand with δύο (*Od.* 12. 73), and in

Il. 16. 428 we have αἰγυπιοὶ γαμψώνυχες
...κλάζοντε. But I have been able to
find only one proper parallel for such a
combination as δυοῖν ἀδελφοῖν θανόντων,
viz., a verse of an unknown poet, fr.
adesp. 153 in Nauck *Trag. Frag.* p. 679
Αἴαντε δ' ὁρμήσαντες ἐκ συνωρίδος: and
this has survived because Herodian
cited it as a solecism (*Anecd. Boiss.* 3.
244): ἔδει γὰρ ἐπενεχθῆναι δυϊκῷ δυϊκόν.
In that verse, too, the license had an
obvious metrical motive, which did not
exist here. Cp. 55 f. ἀδελφὼ δύο...αὐτο-
κτονοῦντε; 58 λελειμμένα; 62 μαχουμένα.—
διπλῇ χερί, *i.e.* each by the other's right
hand (as in *O. C.* 1425 θάνατον ἐξ ἀμφοῖν
= ἐξ ἀλλήλοιν): so 170 διπλῆς μοίρας, a
doom given by each to the other. Cp.
El. 206 θανάτους...διδύμαιν χειροῖν, a murder done by two right hands (that of
Clytaemnestra and that of Aegisthus).
Distinguish the use of the plur. διπλοῖ
for δύο, as 51, 1233.

15 ff. ἐπεί, temporal, 'since' (like ἐξ
οὗ), as oft. in Her. and the poets. So
also ὅτε (Thuc. 1. 13 ἔτη δ' ἐστί...τρια-
κόσια...ὅτε...ἦλθε).—ἐν νυκτὶ τῇ νῦν, last
night: so νυκτὸς τῆσδε *Ai.* 21 (cp. *ib.*
209): νυκτὶ τῇδε *El.* 644: while 'to-
night' is τῆς ἐπιούσης νυκτός (Plat. *Crito*
46 A). The Argives, having on the preceding day lost all their leaders except
Adrastus, fled shortly before dawn (cp.
100).—ὑπέρτερον here simply = πλέον (cp.
nihil supra).—As οἶδ' εὐτυχοῦσα = οἶδ' ὅτι
εὐτυχῶ, so the participles **εὐτυχοῦσα** and
ἀτωμένη are epexegetic of οὐδὲν ὑπέρτερον, = οὔθ' ὅτι εὐτυχῶ οὔθ' ὅτι ἀτῶμαι.
Of ἀτᾶσθαι we find only this pres. part.
(below, 314, *Ai.* 384, Eur. *Suppl.* 182)
and ἀτώμεσθα *Ai.* 269.

ΑΝ. ἤδη καλῶς, καί σ᾽ ἐκτὸς αὐλείων πυλῶν
τοῦδ᾽ οὕνεκ᾽ ἐξέπεμπον, ὡς μόνη κλύοις.

ΙΣ. τί δ᾽ ἔστι; δηλοῖς γάρ τι καλχαίνουσ᾽ ἔπος.　　　20

ΑΝ. οὐ γὰρ τάφου νῷν τὼ κασιγνήτω Κρέων
τὸν μὲν προτίσας τὸν δ᾽ ἀτιμάσας ἔχει;
Ἐτεοκλέα μέν, ὡς λέγουσι, σὺν δίκης
*χρήσει δικαίᾳ καὶ νόμου, κατὰ χθονὸς
ἔκρυψε, τοῖς ἔνερθεν ἔντιμον νεκροῖς·　　　25

Blaydes: θανόντων MSS.　　　**18** ἤδειν L: ἤδη Pierson. Schol., ἀντὶ τοῦ ᾔδεα;
he therefore read ἤδη in the text, though in his own note he writes, καὶ ἤδειν σε

---

18 ff. ἤδη: see on *O. T.* 1525.
κᾱλῶς has a slightly ironical tone (*O. T.*
1008), glancing at Ismene's apathy.
—αὐλείων πυλῶν, the outer door (or gate)
of the court-yard, the αὔλειοι (or αὐλῆς)
θύραι of the Homeric house (*Od.* 18. 239),
in distinction from the θύραι μεγάρου, or
inner door from the court into the men's
hall. This was the αὔλειος θύρα, or front
door, of the later Greek house, in distinction from the μέταυλος θύρα leading
from the court to the inner part. The
tragedians commonly use the more stately
word πύλαι, rather than θύραι, for these
outer doors of the palace: cp. Eur. *Helen.*
431 πύλας τε σεμνὰς ἀνδρὸς ὀλβίου τινὸς |
προσῆλθον: *ib.* 438 πρὸς αὐλείοισιν ἐστη-
κὼς πύλαις. ἐξέπεμπον, 'sought to bring
thee forth': the act., since she had herself fetched or called Ismene; the midd.
meaning to summon by a messenger,
O. T. 951 τί μ᾽ ἐξεπέμψω δεῦρο τῶνδε
δωμάτων; cp. on 161, 165. The imperf.,
because she speaks of the motive present
to her mind while the act was being done:
cp. *O. C.* 770 τότ᾽ ἐξεώθεις κἀξέβαλλες, n.
20 τί δ᾽ ἔστι; marking surprise (*O. T.*
319 n.). δηλοῖς is not intransitive, the
thing shown being expressed by the
partic. in the nomin., just as below, 242
(cp. on 471), Thuc. I. 21 ὁ πόλεμος οὗτος
...δηλώσει...μείζων γεγενημένος. There
is a really intransitive use of δηλόω in
[Andoc.] or. 4 § 12 δηλώσει δὲ ἡ τῶν
συμμάχων ἔχθρα πρῶτον, etc., unless δηλώσεται should be read there; but the
speech is a work of the later rhetoric (see
Attic Orators, I. 137). Not one of the
few instances adduced from classical
Greek requires δηλόω to be intransitive:
Her. 2. 117 (subject τόδε): 5. 78 (ἡ

ἰσηγορίη): Plat. *Gorg.* 483 D (ἡ φύσις).
In Her. 9. 68 δηλοῖ τέ μοι ὅτι πάντα...
ἤρτητο..., εἰ καὶ τότε...ἔφευγον, the real
subject is the clause with εἰ (the fact of
their flight shows me).
καλχαίνουσ᾽ ἔπος τι (for the enclitic
τις placed before its noun, see on *O. C.*
280 f.), 'that thou art troubled by some
tidings.' The verb is intrans., ἔπος being
the 'internal,' or cognate, accus. (*Ph.*
1326 νοσεῖς τόδ᾽ ἄλγος): for its sense cp.
O. C. 302 τίς δ᾽ ἔσθ᾽ ὁ κείνῳ τοῦτο τοὔπος
ἀγγελῶν; From κάλχη, the purple limpet
(perh. connected with κόχλος, κόγχη),
comes καλχαίνω, to make, or to be,
purple: then fig., to be darkly troubled
in mind: Eur. *Her.* 40 ἀμφὶ τοῖσδε καλ-
χαίνων τέκνοις. Hence perh. Κάλχας,
the seer who darkly broods on the future.
The descent of this metaphor is curious.
φυρ, the root of πορ-φύρ-ω, signified 'to
be agitated,'—like heaving water, for
instance (Skt. *bhur*, Lat. *ferv-ere*, Curt.
§ 415). In *Il.* 14. 16 ff. a man's troubled
hesitation is likened to the trouble of the
sea just *before* a storm, while as yet the
waves are not driven either way: ὡς δ᾽
ὅτε πορφύρῃ πέλαγος μέγα κύματι κωφῷ
(not yet breaking in foam)...ὣς ὁ γέρων
ὥρμαινε δαϊζόμενος κατὰ θυμόν. The Homeric image is thus subtler than that of a
storm in the soul (*Volvere curarum tristes
in pectore fluctus*, Lucr. 6. 34). (2) Then
πορφύρω is said of the mind itself: *Il.* 21.
551 ἔστη, πολλὰ δέ οἱ κραδίη πόρφυρε
μένοντι, 'was troubled.' (3) From πορφύρω, as='to be turbid,' came πορφύρα
as=simply '*the dark*' (purple-fish and
dye): and then in later Greek the verb
took on the specific sense, 'to be *purple*.'
(4) κάλχη=πορφύρα: and hence καλχαίνω

ANTIGONH13

AN. I knew it well, and therefore sought to bring thee
beyond the gates of the court, that thou mightest hear alone.

IS. What is it? 'Tis plain that thou art brooding on some
dark tidings.

AN. What, hath not Creon destined our brothers, the one
to honoured burial, the other to unburied shame? Eteocles,
they say, with due observance of right and custom, he hath
laid in the earth, for his honour among the dead below.

καλῶς κ.τ.λ. **23 f.** σὺν δίκῃ | χρησθεὶς δικαίᾳ καὶ νόμῳ MSS. (δίκαια for
δικαίᾳ R). In the margin of L the first corrector has written δικαία (sic) κρίσει
χρησάμενος.—The emendation σὺν δίκης χρήσει, printed in my 1st ed. (1888), was
made by me before I learned that it had already been proposed by Gerh.
Heinrich Müller (*Emend. et interpr. Sophocleae*, p. 51, Berlin, 1878). For other

is figuratively used like the Homeric πορφύρω. In πορφύρω the idea of trouble
precedes that of colour: in καλχαίνω, *vice
versa*.

21 f. οὐ γάρ, 'what, has not,' etc.,
introducing an indignant question, as *Ai.*
1348, *Ph.* 249. τὼ κασιγνήτω...τὸν μὲν
...τὸν δέ, partitive apposition (σχῆμα καθ'
ὅλον καὶ μέρος), the whole, which should
be in the genitive, being put in the same
case as the part,—a constr. freq. in nom.,
but rare in accus.: cp. 561: Thuc. 2. 92
δύο ὑποσχέσεις τὴν μὲν βουλόμενος ἀνα-
πρᾶξαι, τὴν δὲ αὐτὸς ἀποδοῦναι.—The
place of **τάφου** before τὼ κασιγνήτω
shows the first thought to have been,—
'*of a tomb*, he has deemed our two
brothers, the one *worthy*, the other
unworthy': but **προτίσας**, which has
taken the place of a word in the sense of
ἀξιώσας, substitutes the idea of preferring
one brother to the other. Thus **τάφου** is
left belonging, in strict grammar, to
ἀτιμάσας only; for the genit. with
which, cp. *O. C.* 49.—**ἀτιμάσας ἔχει** = a
perfect, *O. T.* 577.

23 f. σὺν δίκῃ | χρησθεὶς δικαίᾳ καὶ
νόμῳ, the reading of our MSS., was a
clumsy attempt to mend a corrupt text,
in the sense: 'having treated (him) in
accordance with righteous judgment and
usage.' The lateness of the corruption
is shown by **χρησθεὶς** as = χρησάμενος,
since in classical Greek χρησθῆναι is
always pass., Her. 7. 144 (the ships) οὐκ
ἐχρήσθησαν, Dem. or. 21 § 16 ἕως ἂν χρησθῇ
(ἡ ἐσθής); of oracles being delivered,
O. T. 604, *O. C.* 355: in Polyb. 2. 32
ἐβούλοντο συγχρήσθαι ταῖς...δυνάμεσι, συγ-
χρησθῆναι is found, indeed, in some MSS.,
but is manifestly corrupt. Several conjectures are discussed in the Appendix.
It is most improbable that vv. 23, 24

have grown out of one verse, either by
the interpolation of v. 24, or by the
expansion of v. 23. For it is evidently
essential to the contrast with vv. 26—30
that the honours paid to Eteocles should
be described with emphasis. Were v. 23
immediately followed by v. 25, the
effect would be too bald and curt. I
read σὺν δίκης | χρήσει δικαίᾳ καὶ
νόμου, 'with righteous observance of justice and usage' [νόμῳ could be retained,
but would be harsh; and the corruption
of δίκης would have caused that of νόμου].
δίκης, following σύν, was changed to
δίκη, and then χρήσει became χρησθείς,
in an attempt to mend the sense. σὺν
χρήσει δικαίᾳ δίκης καὶ νόμου = δίκη καὶ
νόμῳ δικαίως χρώμενος. For the latter,
cp. Antiphon or. 5 § 87 χρῆσθαι τῇ δίκῃ καὶ
τῷ νόμῳ. Eur. *I. A.* 316 οὐδὲν τῇ δίκῃ
χρῆσθαι θέλει. The substantival periphrasis (σὺν χρήσει τινὸς for χρώμενός τινι)
is of a common kind; *e.g.* Thuc. 2. 39
διὰ...τὴν ἐν τῇ γῇ ἐπὶ πολλὰ ἡμῶν αὐτῶν
ἐπίπεμψιν: 5. 8 ἄνευ προόψεως...αὐτῶν
(= εἰ μὴ προΐδοιεν αὐτούς).—Schütz (1876,
Jahr. f. kl. Phil. p. 176) proposed
χρῆσθαι δικαιῶν, 'deeming it right to treat
(him) in accordance with justice,' etc.:
where, however, to supply αὐτῷ is most
awkward: I should prefer τῷ (instead of
καὶ) νόμῳ. *O. T.* 1526 is an instance in
which καὶ seems to have supplanted an
article (ταῖς) after the sense had become
obscured. But χρῆσθαι δικαιῶν τῷ νόμῳ
appears somewhat too prosaic and cold,
and, in so lucid a phrase, would δικαιῶν
have been likely to become δικαίᾳ?—
νόμου, of funeral rites, cp. 519: so νόμιμα
(Thuc. 3. 58), τὰ νομιζόμενα ποιεῖν (*iusta
facere*): Plut. *Sull.* 38 κηδείας τῆς νενομισ-
μένης, the usual obsequies.

25 τοῖς ἔνερθεν ἔντιμον νεκροῖς, ethic

τὸν δ᾽ ἀθλίως θανόντα Πολυνείκους νέκυν
ἀστοῖσί φασιν ἐκκεκηρῦχθαι τὸ μὴ
τάφῳ καλύψαι μηδὲ κωκῦσαί τινα,
ἐᾶν δ᾽ ἄκλαυτον, ἄταφον, οἰωνοῖς γλυκὺν
θησαυρὸν εἰσορῶσι πρὸς χάριν βορᾶς.   30
τοιαῦτά φασι τὸν ἀγαθὸν Κρέοντα σοὶ
κἀμοί, λέγω γὰρ κἀμέ, κηρύξαντ᾽ ἔχειν,
καὶ δεῦρο νεῖσθαι ταῦτα τοῖσι μὴ εἰδόσιν
σαφῆ προκηρύξοντα, καὶ τὸ πρᾶγμ᾽ ἄγειν

---

conjectures see comment. and Appendix.   **27** φασὶν made from φησὶν
L.   **29** ἄταφον ἄκλαυτον (which a late hand sought to change into ἄκλαυστον) L: ἄκλαυστον ἄταφον r.   **30** θησαυρὸν] ἕρμαιον Heimreich, from
schol. (*Beitr.* p. 9).—εἰσορῶσι] εἰσορμῶσι is an anonymous conject. mentioned
by Burton. ὡς φέρωσι Semitelos. Nauck would omit the verse.   **33** τοῖς

---

dat., in their sight (*O. T.* 8 πᾶσι κλεινός,
cp. *O. C.* 1446). The dead repelled the
spirit of the unburied from their converse:
Il. 23. 71 (the shade of the unburied
Patroclus to Achilles) θάπτε με ὅττι
τάχιστα, πύλας Ἀΐδαο περήσω. | τῆλέ με
εἴργουσι ψυχαί, εἴδωλα καμόντων, | οὐδέ μέ
πω μίσγεσθαι ὑπὲρ ποταμοῖο ἐῶσιν.

26 θανόντα … Πολυνείκους νέκυν,
by enallage for θανόντος, but also with
a reminiscence of the Homeric νεκύων
κατατεθνηώτων: cp. 515 ὁ κατθανὼν
νέκυς.

27 f. ἐκκεκηρῦχθαι = προκεκηρῦχθαι,
as in 203. The compound with ἐκ usu.
='to banish by proclamation' (*O. C.*
430 n.).—τὸ μή…καλύψαι, instead of the
ordinary μὴ καλύψαι: cp. 443: *O. C.*
1739 ἀπέφυγε… | …τὸ μὴ πίτνειν κακῶς.
Though τὸ μὴ καλύψαι might be viewed
as subject to ἐκκεκηρῦχθαι, the latter was
probably felt as an impersonal pass.
The addition of the art. to the infin.
is freq. in drama: cp. 78, and *O. C.*
47 n.

29 ἐᾶν δ᾽. Since τινά can mean
πάντα τινά, it is not necessary to supply
πάντας as subject for ἐᾶν, though in *O. T.*
238 ff. we have μήτ᾽ ἐσδέχεσθαι μήτε
προσφωνεῖν τινα,…ὠθεῖν δ᾽ ἀπ᾽ οἴκων
πάντας.—L has ἄταφον ἄκλαυτον. For
this order it may be said, that a tribrach
contained in one word forms the second
foot in *Ph.* 1235 πότερα, *ib.* 1314 πατέρα,
Aesch. *Ch.* 1 χθόνιε. Also, ἄταφον thus
gains a certain abrupt force, and the order
corresponds with καλύψαι…κωκῦσαι. But
against it we may urge:—(1) The other
order was the usual one: *Il.* 22. 386

κεῖται πὰρ νήεσσι νέκυς ἄκλαυτος ἄθαπτος:
Eur. *Hec.* 30 | ἄκλαυτος, ἄταφος. (2) On
such a question of order no great weight
belongs to L, in which wrong transposi-
tions of words certainly occur; *e.g. Ph.*
156, 1332: *O. C.* 1088. Here some
MSS. give ἄκλαυστον ἄταφον. There is
no ground for distinguishing ἄκλαυστος,
as 'not to be wept,' from ἄκλαυτος, 'not
wept' (see *O. T.* 361 note in Appendix
on γνωτός and γνωστός). L gives the
form without sigma here, as below, 847,
876, and in *O. C.* 1708; but the sigmatic
form in *El.* 912.

30 θησαυρόν: schol. ἕρμαιον, εὕρημα,
taking it as merely 'treasure *trove*'; but
here 'treasure' evidently implies 'store'
(cp. *Ph.* 37 θησαύρισμα); the carrion-
birds can return again and again to their
feast.—εἰσορῶσι, when they look down
upon it from the air. There is no ground
for saying that εἰσορᾶν was specially 'to
eye *with desire*': in Xen. *Cyr.* 5. 1. 15
οὔτε πυρὸς ἅπτομαι οὔτε τοὺς καλοὺς εἰσορῶ,
it is simply 'look at.' The conjecture
εἰσορμῶσι, to be taken with πρὸς χάριν
βορᾶς, 'swooping *to* the joy of the feast,'
is not only needless, but bad. Far finer
is the picture of the birds pausing in their
flight at the moment when they first
descry the corpse below.

Take πρὸς χάριν βορᾶς with γλυκὺν
θησαυρόν, not with εἰσορῶσι: lit., a
welcome store to the birds, when they
look upon it, *with a view to pleasure in
feeding.* For the sensual use of χάρις cp.
Plat. *Phaedr.* 254 A τῆς τῶν ἀφροδισίων
χάριτος. πρὸς χάριν is used either
adverbially or with a genitive. (1) As

But the hapless corpse of Polyneices—as rumour saith, it hath been published to the town that none shall entomb him or mourn, but leave unwept, unsepulchred, a welcome store for the birds, as they espy him, to feast on at will.

Such, 'tis said, is the edict that the good Creon hath set forth for thee and for me,—yes, for *me*,—and is coming hither to proclaim it clearly to those who know it not ; nor counts the matter

MSS.: τοῖσι Heath. **34** προκηρύξαντα L, made from προκηρύσσοντα : the first of the two σσ almost erased. προκηρύξοντα r.—ἄγειν] ἔχειν r, probably a mere oversight.

---

an adverb, it means literally, 'with a view to gratification': hence (*a*) when the χάρις is one's own, '*at pleasure*,' as Philoctetes calls the birds (*Ph.* 1156) κορέσαι στόμα πρὸς χάριν, to glut their beaks on him 'as they will': (*b*) when the χάρις is another's, 'so as to *give* pleasure,' '*graciously*,' as *O. T.* 1152 σὺ πρὸς χάριν μὲν οὐκ ἐρεῖς. (2) A genitive after πρὸς χάριν can denote (*a*) that *in which* the χάρις consists, as βορᾶς here : or (*b*) the person or thing *whose* the χάρις is, as below, 908, τίνος νόμου...πρὸς χάριν ; 'in deference to what law?' Eur. *Med.* 538 νόμοις τε χρῆσθαι μὴ πρὸς ἰσχύος χάριν, 'not at the pleasure of force,'— *i.e.* not so that force can do what it pleases. Here, **πρὸς χάριν** βορᾶς differs from a simple χάριν βορᾶς by implying the same notion as the adverbial πρὸς χάριν in *Ph.* 1156 quoted above: 'to feast on *at their pleasure*.'—Eustathius on *Il.* 8. 379 (p. 719. 9) defines carrion-birds as τοῖς πρὸς χάριν ὁρῶσι βορᾶς τῆς ἀπὸ τῶν σαρκῶν. It cannot be doubted that he was thinking of our passage, and that his text, like ours, had εἰσορῶσι : but, using the simple ὁρῶσι, he has made a new phrase, '*looking to* pleasure in food,' and his words afford no argument for joining πρὸς χάριν with εἰσορῶσι here.

31 f. σοί, like **κἀμοί**, depends on **κηρύξαντ' ἔχειν** (for which see 22). Creon's edict, addressed to all Thebans, touches the sisters first, since, as the nearest relatives of the dead, they were most concerned to see that he received burial. Antigone speaks with burning indignation. She says, in effect:—'Thus hath Creon forbidden thee and me to render the last offices to our brother.' The parenthesis λέγω γὰρ κἀμέ is prompted by the intense consciousness of a resolve.

To her, who knows her own heart, it seems wonderful that Creon should even have imagined her capable of obeying such an edict. It is a fine psychological touch, and one of the most pathetic in the play.—**τὸν ἀγαθόν**, ironical, as *O. T.* 385 Κρέων ὁ πιστός, *Ph.* 873 ἀγαθοὶ στρατηλάται.—**λέγω γὰρ κἀμέ** (instead of κἀμοί), a constr. most freq. when the acc. is a proper name, as Dem. or. 24 § 6 προσέκρουσ' ἀνθρώπῳ πονηρῷ...Ἀνδροτίωνα λέγω. So *Tr.* 9, *Ph.* 1261, Aesch. *Th.* 609, Eur. *Her.* 642. On the other hand cp. Dem. or. 8 § 24 παρ' ὧν ἂν ἕκαστοι δύνωνται, τούτων τῶν τὴν Ἀσίαν ἐνοικούντων λέγω, χρήματα λαμβάνουσιν: Aesch. fr. 169 ἀλλ' Ἀντικλείας ἆσσον ἦλθε Σίσυφος, | τῆς σῆς λέγω τοι μητρός. In *Ai.* 569 where L has Ἐριβοίᾳ (*sic*) λέγω, most edd. now give the dat.

Two other explanations may be noticed. Both make **σοι** enclitic. (1) Taking **σοι** as ethic dat. with **τοιαῦτα**: 'There is the good Creon's proclamation for you,—aye, and for *me* too, for I count myself also amongst those forbidden' (Campbell). Thus **κἀμοί** is not, like **σοι**, a mere ethic dat., but rather a dat. of interest. Such a transition seems hardly possible. (2) Taking **σοι** as ethic dat. with **ἀγαθόν**: 'your good Creon, aye and mine, for I own I too thought him so' (Kennedy). But Antigone is too much occupied with the edict itself to dwell with such emphasis at such a moment on the disappointment which she has experienced as to Creon's amiability.

33 νεῖσθαι pres. (*Od.* 15. 88): Eur. has νεῖσθε (*Alc.* 737) and νεόμενος (in lyr. *El.* 723): otherwise the word is not tragic.—**τοῖσι μὴ εἰδόσιν**, synizesis, as 263, 535, *O. C.* 1155 ὡς μὴ εἰδότ' αὐτόν, *Tr.* 321 καὶ ξυμφορά τοι μὴ εἰδέναι.

οὐχ ὡς παρ' οὐδέν, ἀλλ' ὃς ἂν τούτων τι δρᾷ, 35
φόνον προκεῖσθαι δημόλευστον ἐν πόλει.
οὕτως ἔχει σοι ταῦτα, καὶ δείξεις τάχα
εἴτ' εὐγενὴς πέφυκας εἴτ' ἐσθλῶν κακή.

ΙΣ. τί δ', ὦ ταλαῖφρον, εἰ τάδ' ἐν τούτοις, ἐγὼ
λύουσ' ἂν ἢ 'φάπτουσα προσθείμην πλέον; 40

ΑΝ. εἰ ξυμπονήσεις καὶ ξυνεργάσει σκόπει.

ΙΣ. ποῖόν τι κινδύνευμα; ποῦ γνώμης ποτ' εἶ;

ΑΝ. εἰ τὸν νεκρὸν ξὺν τῇδε κουφιεῖς χερί.

ΙΣ. ἦ γὰρ νοεῖς θάπτειν σφ', ἀπόρρητον πόλει;

---

40 ἦ θάπτουσα MSS. The true ἦ 'φάπτουσα is indicated by the schol. in L, who first explains the vulgate, λύουσα τὸν νόμον καὶ θάπτουσα τὸν ἀδελφόν : and then proceeds, εἰ δὲ γρ. ἦ θάπτουσα (the θ in an erasure), ἀντὶ τοῦ, λύουσα τὸν νόμον ἢ ἐπιβεβαιοῦσα αὐτόν. Brunck restored ἦ 'φάπτουσα.—λύουσ' ἂν εἴθ'

---

35 παρ' οὐδέν : cp. 466 : *O. T.* 983 ταῦθ' ὅτῳ | παρ' οὐδέν ἐστι. The addition of ὡς serves to mark Creon's point of view more strongly : cp. *O. C.* 732 ἥκω γὰρ οὐχ ὡς δρᾶν τι βουληθείς, n.—ὃς ἂν... δρᾷ, the antecedent τούτῳ being suppressed, = a dat., τῷ δρῶντι : cp. Isocr. or. 18 § 37 προσήκει βοηθεῖν ὑμᾶς οὐχ οἵτινες ἂν δυστυχεστάτους σφᾶς αὐτοὺς ἀποδείξωσιν ἀλλ' οἵτινες ἂν δικαιότερα λέγοντες φαίνωνται. That such a relative clause was felt as practically equivalent to a noun-case may be seen from Thuc. 2. 62, where it is co-ordinated with a dative : αὔχημα μὲν...καὶ δειλῷ τινὶ ἐγγίγνεται, καταφρόνησις δέ, ὃς ἂν καὶ γνώμῃ πιστεύῃ. Thuc. uses this constr. esp. in definitions, as 6. 14, τὸ καλῶς ἄρξαι τοῦτ' εἶναι, ὃς ἂν τὴν πατρίδα ὠφελήσῃ.

36 προκεῖσθαι : cp. 481 : *O. T.* 865 νόμοι πρόκεινται.—**δημόλευστον** = λευσθέντα ὑπὸ τοῦ δήμου, the epith. of the victim being transferred to the doom : *Tr.* 357 ὁ ῥιπτὸς Ἰφίτου μόρος. Cp. Aesch. *Ag.* 1616 δημορριφεῖς...λευσίμους ἀράς. Death by public stoning would mean that the transgressor was execrated as a traitor to the commonweal : see n. on *O. C.* 435.

37 f. σοι ethic dat. : so *O. C.* 62 and *El.* 761 τοιαῦτά σοι ταῦτ' ἐστίν.—**ἐσθλῶν,** gen. of origin with πέφυκας, from a good stock : *O. T.* 1062 ἐὰν τρίτης ἐγὼ | μητρὸς φανῶ τρίδουλος n. Cp. fr. 601 (race cannot be relied upon, since often) πέλεται |

οὔτ' ἀπ' εὐγενέων ἐσθλὸς οὔτ' ἀχρείων | τὸ λίαν κακός.

39 ὦ ταλαῖφρον, 'my poor sister' : cp. ἄνολβος (1026), δύσποτμος (*O. T.* 888), μέλεος, etc.—**εἰ τάδ' ἐν τούτοις :** cp. *O. C.* 1443 ταῦτα... | ...τῇδε φῦναι. The plur. **ἐν τούτοις** means either (1) 'in these circumstances,' as here, and Plat. *Phaed.* 101 C : or (2) 'meanwhile,' *inter haec,* as Plat. *Symp.* 220 B. The sing. ἐν τούτῳ usually = 'meanwhile' ; more rarely 'in this case' (Thuc. 1. 37), or 'at this point' (id. 2. 8).

40 λύουσ'...ἢ 'φάπτουσα, 'by seeking to loose or to tighten the knot,'—a phrase, perhaps proverbial, for 'meddling in any way.' She can do no good by touching the tangled skein. The Greek love of antithesis naturally tended to expressions like our 'by hook or by crook,' 'by fair means or foul,' 'for love or money,' 'good or bad,' etc. Cp. 1109 οἵ τ' ὄντες οἵ τ' ἀπόντες (n.) : Eur. *Bacch.* 800 ἀπόρῳ γε τῷδε συμπεπλέγμεθα ξένῳ, | ὃς οὔτε πάσχων οὔτε δρῶν σιγήσεται, which is plainly colloquial,—meaning 'who will not hold his peace on any terms' ; for though πάσχων suits the recent *imprisonment* of Dionysus, δρῶν could not mean definitely, 'as a free agent.' Similarly we may suppose that some such phrase as οὔτε λύων οὔτε ἅπτων (Plat. *Crat.* 417 E τὸ δὲ ἅπτειν καὶ δεῖν ταὐτόν ἐστι) was familiar as = 'by no possible means.' If **ἐφάπτουσα** is sound,

light, but, whoso disobeys in aught, his doom is death by
stoning before all the folk. Thou knowest it now; and thou
wilt soon show whether thou art nobly bred, or the base
daughter of a noble line.

Is. Poor sister,—and if things stand thus, what could I help
to do or undo?

An. Consider if thou wilt share the toil and the deed.

Is. In what venture? What can be thy meaning?

An. Wilt thou aid this hand to lift the dead?

Is. Thou wouldst bury him,—when 'tis forbidden to Thebes?

ἅπτουσα Porson.   **42** ποῖ L: ποῦ r.   **43** χερί] ἄθρει or ὅρα Meineke.
44 ἤ] εἰ L, which an early hand sought to change into ἤ: η is also written above.

---

the poet has refined a colloquialism by
modifying ἄπτουσα into ἐφάπτουσα, just
as τί δρῶν ἢ τί λέγων (cp. Aesch. *P. V.*
660) appears in *O. T.* 71 as ὅ τι | δρῶν ἢ
τί φωνῶν. Some find a reference to
weaving;—'by loosening the web, or
fastening a new thread'; but, though the
phrase may have been first suggested by
the loom, it was probably used without
any such conscious allusion. Quite different from our passage is *Ai.* 1317 εἰ μὴ
ξυνάψων ἀλλὰ συλλύσων πάρει, 'not to
embroil the feud, but to help in solving
it': cp. Eur. *Hipp.* 670 τίνας νῦν τέχνας
ἔχομεν ἢ λόγους | σφαλεῖσαι κάθαμμα λύειν
λόγου; 'to loose the knot of controversy.'
—Another view makes the phrase refer
to Creon's edict: 'seeking to undo it, or
to tighten it,'—*i.e.* to break it, or to make
it more stringent than it already is (schol.
λύουσα τὸν νόμον, ἢ βεβαιοῦσα αὐτόν).
But, though Antigone has not yet revealed her purpose, too great callousness
is ascribed to Ismene if she is supposed
to doubt whether her sympathy is invited
against or *for* such an edict.—The *act.*
ἐφάπτειν is rare: *Tr.* 933 τοὔργον ὡς
ἐφάψειεν, that he had imposed the deed
on her (by his fierce reproaches): Pind.
O. 9. 60 μὴ καθέλοι νιν αἰὼν πότμον
ἐφάψαις | ὀρφανὸν γενεᾶς. Was Porson
right in conjecturing εἴθ' ἅπτουσα? For
it, we may observe:—(1) An opposition
of the simple λύειν and ἅπτειν suits a
proverbial phrase: (2) ἤ and εἰ are elsewhere confused, as *O. C.* 80 (n.): (3) the
single εἴτε is found in *O. T.* 517 λόγοισιν
εἴτ' ἔργοισιν, *Tr.* 236 πατρῴας εἴτε βαρ-
βάρου; Against the conjecture is the fact
that εἴθ' ἅπτουσα would have been much
less likely to generate the ἢ θάπτουσα

of our mss., since the intermediate εἰ
θάπτουσα, being obviously unmeaning,
would have been likely to cure itself.—
προσθείμην: cp. *O. C.* 767 προσθέσθαι
χάριν, n.—**πλέον**, 'for thine advantage':
O. T. 37 οὐδὲν ἐξειδὼς πλέον, n.

41 f. ξυμπονήσεις is the more general word,—'co-operate'; ξυνεργάσει, the
more explicit,—'help to accomplish the
deed.'—**ποῖόν τι κ.**, cognate acc. to the
verbs in 41: cp. *O. C.* 344 κακὰ | ὑπερ-
πονεῖτον, n.—Read **ποῦ** γνώμης...εἶ (from
εἶναι): cp. *El.* 390 ποῦ ποτ' εἶ φρενῶν.
The question between **ποῦ** and **ποῖ** here
is one of sense, not of idiom. **ποῖ** γνώμης
...εἶ (from ἰέναι) would mean, 'to what
thought will you have recourse?' Cp.
O. C. 170 ποῖ τις φροντίδος ἔλθῃ; (n.),
Tr. 705 οὐκ ἔχω...ποῖ γνώμης πέσω. But
the meaning here is, 'what can you be
thinking of?'

43 f. εἰ *sc.* σκόπει.—Join ξὺν τῇδε
χερί: she lifts her hand.—**κουφιεῖς**, take
up for burial: cp. *Ai.* 1410 πλευρὰς σὺν
ἐμοὶ | τάσδ' ἐπικούφιζ' (the dead Ajax):
and the common phrase ἀναιρεῖσθαι νεκρούς.—**ἢ γάρ** marks surprise (*O. C.* 64).
The absence of caesura in the first three
feet allows each of the two important
words (νοεῖς θάπτειν) to fall slowly from the
astonished speaker's lips.—**σφε** = αὐτόν,
as 516, 1226. σφε can be s. or pl., m.
or f.: νιν, s. or pl., m., f. or n.—**ἀπόρρητον**, acc. neut. in appos. with θάπτειν
σφε: Plat. *Gorg.* 507 E ἐπιθυμίας...πλη-
ροῦν, ἀνήνυτον κακόν.—**πόλει**, 'to' or 'for'
(dat. of interest), not 'by' (dat. of agent),
though the latter might be supported by
Eur. *Phoen.* 1657 ἐγώ σφε θάψω, κἂν
ἀπεννέπῃ πόλις.

ΑΝ. τὸν γοῦν ἐμόν, καὶ τὸν σόν, ἢν σὺ μὴ θέλῃς,　　45
　　ἀδελφόν· οὐ γὰρ δὴ προδοῦσ᾽ ἁλώσομαι.
ΙΣ. ὦ σχετλία, Κρέοντος ἀντειρηκότος;
ΑΝ. ἀλλ᾽ οὐδὲν αὐτῷ τῶν ἐμῶν μ᾽ εἴργειν μέτα.
ΙΣ. οἴμοι· φρόνησον, ὦ κασιγνήτη, πατὴρ
　　ὡς νῷν ἀπεχθὴς δυσκλεής τ᾽ ἀπώλετο,　　50
　　πρὸς αὐτοφώρων ἀμπλακημάτων διπλᾶς
　　ὄψεις ἀράξας αὐτὸς αὐτουργῷ χερί·
　　ἔπειτα μήτηρ καὶ γυνή, διπλοῦν ἔπος,
　　πλεκταῖσιν ἀρτάναισι λωβᾶται βίον·
　　τρίτον δ᾽ ἀδελφὼ δύο μίαν καθ᾽ ἡμέραν　　55

45 f. L points thus: τὸν γοῦν ἐμὸν καὶ τὸν σόν· ἢν σὺ μὴ θέλῃς ἀδελφὸν, etc.—
Benedict (*Observ. in Soph.*, Leipsic, 1820, p. 104) is followed by several edd. in
rejecting v. 46, which was already suspected in antiquity: see comment. In v. 45

45 f. τὸν γοῦν ἐμὸν κ.τ.λ. To the
question—'Do you really mean to bury
him?'—the simple answer would have
been, τὸν γοῦν ἐμὸν ἀδελφόν, 'I certainly
mean to bury my own brother.' But the
word ἐμόν—reminding her that he is
equally *Ismene's* brother—prompts the
insertion of the reproachful clause, καὶ
τὸν σόν, ἢν σὺ μὴ θέλῃς. Thus the
contrast between τὸν ἐμόν and τὸν σόν
anticipates the emphasis on the word
ἀδελφόν. The whole thought is,—'I will
certainly do *my* duty,—and *thine*, if thou
wilt not,—to a *brother*.' Since ὁ ἐμός is
the same person as ὁ σός, this thought
can be poetically expressed by saying,
'I will certainly bury *my* brother,—and
thine, if thou wilt not': for the tribute
rendered to him by one sister represents
the tribute *due* from both. Remark
that γοῦν often emphasises a pers. or
possessive pron. (as here ἐμόν): 565 σοὶ
γοῦν: *Ai.* 527 πρὸς γοῦν ἐμοῦ: *O. T.* 626
τὸ γοῦν ἐμόν: *El.* 1499 τὰ γοῦν σ᾽.—
Two other versions are possible, but less
good. (1) Taking τὸν...ἐμὸν καὶ τὸν
σόν as='him who is my brother and
thine,' and ἢν as='*even* if.' But for this
we should expect τὸν γοῦν ἐμόν τε καὶ
σόν, and κἄν. (2) Taking καὶ with ἤν,
'I will bury my brother, even if thou wilt
not bury thine.' But (i) the separation
of καί from ἤν is abnormal: (ii) the mode
of expression would be scarcely natural
unless ὁ ἐμός and ὁ σός were different
persons.

ἀδελφὸν...ἁλώσομαι. Didymus (*circ.*
30 B.C.) said this verse was condemned
as spurious 'by the commentators' (ὑπὸ
τῶν ὑπομνηματιστῶν). I believe it to be
undoubtedly genuine. One modern argument against it is that Antigone should
here speak only one verse. But these
two verses express the resolve on which
the action of the play turns: it is an
important moment in the dialogue. And,
at such a moment, Soph. often allows
a stichomuthia to be broken by two or
more verses for the same speaker. See
the stichomuthia in 401—406, broken
by 404 f.: *O. T.* 356—369, broken by
366 f.: *ib.* 1000—1046, broken by 1002 f.
and 1005 f.: *O. C.* 579—606, broken by
583 f. and 599 ff. Further, verse 46 is
Sophoclean in three traits: (*a*) ἀδελφόν
emphasised by position as first word,
with a pause after it: cp. 72, 525: *O. T.*
278 δεῖξαι: *O. C.* 1628 χωρεῖν. (*b*) οὐ
γὰρ δή in rejecting an alternative: *O. T.*
576 ἐκμάνθαν᾽· οὐ γὰρ δὴ φονεὺς ἁλώσομαι. Cp. *O. C.* 110 n. (*c*) The phrase
with the aor. part.: *Ai.* 1267 χάρις
διαρρεῖ καὶ προδοῦσ᾽ ἁλίσκεται. Lastly,
v. 45, if alone, would be too bald and
curt.

47 ὦ σχετλία, 'over-bold.' The
word primarily means 'enduring' (√σχε,
σχεθεῖν). Hence: (1) Of *persons*, (*a*) 'un-
flinching,' in audacity or cruelty,—the
usu. Homeric sense, as *Od.* 9. 494 σχέτλιε,
τίπτ᾽ ἐθέλεις ἐρεθιζέμεν ἄγριον ἄνδρα; So
Ph. 369, 930 ὦ σχέτλιε, Eur. *Alc.* 741

AN. I will do my part,—and thine, if thou wilt not,—to a brother. False to him will I never be found.

Is. Ah, over-bold! when Creon hath forbidden?

AN. Nay, he hath no right to keep me from mine own.

Is. Ah me! think, sister, how our father perished, amid hate and scorn, when sins bared by his own search had moved him to strike both eyes with self-blinding hand; then the mother wife, two names in one, with twisted noose did despite unto her life; and last, our two brothers in one day,—

Dindorf conject. κοὐ τὸν σόν: M. Schmidt, τὸν καὶ σόν: Nauck, ἔγωγε τὸν ἐμόν, τὸν σόν.   48 μ' was added by Brunck, from the schol., εἴργειν με ἀπὸ τῶν ἐμῶν.
53 ἔπος] πάθος was a variant. L has ἔπος in the text, with πάθος written above by the first corrector (S). Other MSS. (as A) read πάθος in the text, with γρ. ἔπος.

σχετλία τόλμης. (b) 'Suffering,'=τλή-μων, as Aesch. P. V. 644 (of Io), Eur. Hec. 783. Neither Homer nor Soph. has this use. (2) Of things, 'cruel,' 'wretched,'—a use common to all the poets: so Ai. 887 σχέτλια γάρ ('tis cruel'), Tr. 879.

48 οὐδέν, adv.: μέτα=μέτεστι: τῶν ἐμῶν (masc.) with εἴργειν only: cp. El. 536 ἀλλ' οὐ μετῆν αὐτοῖσι τήν γ' ἐμὴν κτανεῖν. Plat. Apol. 19 C ἐμοὶ τούτων... οὐδὲν μέτεστι. For the plur. cp. O. T. 1448 ὀρθῶς τῶν γε σῶν τελεῖς ὕπερ ('thou wilt merely render the last rites to thine own,'—Iocasta).

50 νῷν ethic dat. with ἀπώλετο (cp. O. C. 81 βέβηκεν ἡμίν). ἀπεχθής, hateful to mankind for his involuntary crimes. ἀπώλετο, 'died,' not merely 'was disgraced' (cp. 59 ὀλούμεθ') : she is speaking of the deaths which had left them alone. But ἔπειτα in 53 is merely 'then,' 'in the next place,' and need not mean that Oedipus died before Iocasta. Here Soph. follows the outline of the epic version, acc. to which Oed. died at Thebes: see Introd. to Oed. Tyr. pp. xvi ff. The poet of the Odyssey (11. 275) makes him survive his consort's suicide, and no version appears to have assumed the contrary. The Antigone knows nothing of his exile from Thebes, or of the sacred honour which surrounded the close of his life, as the story is told in the later Oedipus at Colonus.

51 ff. πρὸς...ἀμπλακημάτων...ἀράξας, 'impelled by them to strike his eyes': cp. O. T. 1236 (τέθνηκε) πρὸς τίνος ποτ' αἰτίας;—αὐτοφώρων=ἃ αὐτὸς ἐφώρασεν (cp. fr. 768 τὰ πλεῖστα φωρῶν αἰσχρὰ

φωράσεις βροτῶν), detected by himself, when he insisted on investigating the murder of Laïus (cp. O. T. 1065). Elsewhere αὐτόφωρος=φωραθεὶς ἐπ' αὐτῷ τῷ ἔργῳ, 'taken in the act': Thuc. 6. 38 κολάζων, μὴ μόνον αὐτοφώρους (χαλεπὸν γὰρ ἐπιτυγχάνειν), ἀλλὰ καὶ ὧν βούλονται μέν, δύνανται δ' οὔ: and so in the adv. ἐπ' αὐτοφώρῳ λαμβάνειν etc.—ἀράξας, with the golden brooches (περόναι): O. T. 1276 ἤρασσ' ἐπαίρων βλέφαρα.—αὐτὸς αὐτουργῷ χειρί, emphatic, like αὐτὸς πρὸς αὑτοῦ (1177), but not strictly pleonastic, since αὐτός='by his own act,' i.e. 'of his free will,' while αὐτ. χειρί refers to the instrument, 'with hand turned against himself.' Cp. on 56.

53 f. διπλοῦν ἔπος, a two-fold name (for the same person): as conversely Aesch. P. V. 209 ἐμοὶ δὲ μήτηρ...Θέμις καὶ Γαῖα, πολλῶν ὀνομάτων μορφὴ μία. Valckenär on Eur. Phoen. p. 153 cites Heracleitus Alleg. Hom. 21 (of Hera) διπλοῦν ὄνομα φύσεως καὶ συμβιώσεως, 'a name signifying at once birth and marriage' (since she was coniunx Iovis et soror). Seneca Oed. Tyr. 389 mixtumque nomen coniugis, nati, patris. (The feeble v. l. πάθος for ἔπος meant, 'a double calamity,' since both mother and wife perished.)—ἀρτάναισι: cp. O. T. 1264 πλεκταῖσιν αἰώραισιν ἐμπεπλεγμένην.

55 f. δύο...μίαν: see on 13.—αὐτο-κτονοῦντε is not literally, 'slaying themselves,' or 'slaying each other,' but, 'slaying with their own hands': the context explains that the person whom each so slew was his own brother. So either (1) suicide, or (2) slaying of kinsfolk, can be expressed by αὐθέντης, αὐτοκτόνος, αὐ-

αὐτοκτονοῦντε τὼ ταλαιπώρω μόρον
κοινὸν κατειργάσαντ᾽ ἐπαλλήλοιν χεροῖν.
νῦν δ᾽ αὖ μόνα δὴ νὼ λελειμμένα σκόπει
ὅσῳ κάκιστ᾽ ὀλούμεθ᾽, εἰ νόμου βίᾳ
ψῆφον τυράννων ἢ κράτη παρέξιμεν.   60
ἀλλ᾽ ἐννοεῖν χρὴ τοῦτο μὲν γυναῖχ᾽ ὅτι
ἔφυμεν, ὡς πρὸς ἄνδρας οὐ μαχουμένα·
ἔπειτα δ᾽ οὕνεκ᾽ ἀρχόμεσθ᾽ ἐκ κρεισσόνων,
καὶ ταῦτ᾽ ἀκούειν κἄτι τῶνδ᾽ ἀλγίονα.
ἐγὼ μὲν οὖν αἰτοῦσα τοὺς ὑπὸ χθονὸς   65
ξύγγνοιαν ἴσχειν, ὡς βιάζομαι τάδε,

56 αὐτοκτενοῦντε L, αὐτοκτενοῦντες r: αὐτοκτονοῦντε (sic) Coraës ad Heliod. vol. 2,
p. 7.   57 ἐπ᾽ ἀλλήλοιν MSS.: ἐπαλλήλοιν Hermann. In L the ᾽ after ἐπ᾽ and the
breathing on ἁ are either from the first hand or from S.—Nauck conject. δαΐοιν:

τοσφαγής, αὐτοφόνος, etc. The compound
merely expresses that the deed is done
with one's own hand, implying that such
a use of one's own hand is unnatural.
The object of the deed may be one's
own life, or another's. This ambiguity
of the compound is illustrated by 1175 f.
αὐτόχειρ δ᾽ αἱμάσσεται.—XO. πότερα
πατρῴας ἢ πρὸς οἰκείας χερός; ‘by his
father's hand, or by his own?’
57 κατειργάσαντ᾽, plur. verb with
dual subject, as oft., even when another
verb with the same subject is dual, as
Xen. Cyr. 6. 1. 47 ὡς εἰδέτην...ἠσπάσαν-
το: Plat. Euthyd. 294 E ὅτε παιδία ἤστην
...ἠπίστασθε: see O. C. 343 n.—ἐπαλλήλοιν χεροῖν, ‘with mutual hands,’—each
brother lifting his hands against the other.
It is hard to believe that Soph. would
here have written ἐπ᾽ ἀλλήλοιν, ‘against
each other,’ when χεροῖν would seem a
weak addition, and the double οιν would
be brought into harsh relief by the inde-
pendence of the two words. The verse is
in every way better if we can read ἐπαλλήλοιν as an epithet of χεροῖν. Now we
know that the word ἐπάλληλος was in
common use at least as early as the 2nd
century B.C. In the extant literature it
seems always to correspond with ἐπ᾽ ἀλλήλοις as = ‘one on top of another’ (Od.
23. 47 κεῖατ᾽ ἐπ᾽ ἀλλήλοισι), being used
to mean, ‘in close order’ or ‘in rapid
sequence’ (as Polyb. 11. 11 ἐν ἐπαλλήλοις
τάξεσι, in close ranks: Alciphro Epp.
3. 6 τὰς ἐπαλλήλους πληγάς, the showers

of blows). An exception might, indeed,
be supposed in Philo Judaeus De Mose
3, p. 692, where he is saying that the
continuity of human record has been
broken διὰ τὰς ἐν ὕδασι καὶ πυρὶ γενομένας
συνεχεῖς καὶ ἐπαλλήλους φθοράς:
which Adrian Turnebus rendered, ‘prop-
ter illas eluvionum et exustionum conti-
nuas et alternas (‘mutual’) interneciones.’
But Philo was evidently (I think) using
ἐπάλληλος in its ordinary sense, and
meant merely, ‘owing to the continuous
and rapid succession of calamities by flood
and fire.’ It by no means follows, however, that a poet of the 5th cent. B.C.
could not have used ἐπάλληλος in a sense
corresponding with ἐπ᾽ ἀλλήλοις as =
‘against each other,’—the more frequent
and familiar sense of the words, as in
the Homeric ἐπ᾽ ἀλλήλοισιν ἰόντες, ἐπ᾽
ἀλλήλοισι φέρον πολύδακρυν Ἄρηα (Il. 3.
132): cp. Ar. Lys. 50 ἐπ᾽ ἀλλήλοισιν
αἱρεσθαι δόρυ. The use of ἐπάλληλος
here may have been partly prompted
by a reminiscence of Aesch. Theb. 931
ἐτελεύ|τασαν ὑπ᾽ ἀλλαλοφόνοις χερσὶν ὁμο-
σπόροισιν (cp. Xen. Hier. 3. 8 ἀδελφοὺς...
ἀλληλοφόνους).
58 νῦν δ᾽ αὖ. Though in L δ᾽ has
been inserted by a later hand, it is found
in A, and its omission by the first hand
in L (which has made other such over-
sights) cannot weigh much against it.
Some of the recent edd. omit it: but the
effect of νῦν αὖ without it would here
be intolerably abrupt. For αὖ (‘in our

each shedding, hapless one, a kinsman's blood,—wrought out with mutual hands their common doom. And now *we* in turn—we two left all alone—think how we shall perish, more miserably than all the rest, if, in defiance of the law, we brave a king's decree or his powers. Nay, we must remember, first, that we were born women, as who should not strive with men; next, that we are ruled of the stronger, so that we must obey in these things, and in things yet sorer. I, therefore, asking the Spirits Infernal to pardon, seeing that force is put on me herein,

Semitelos, πολεμίαιν. **58** In L the first hand wrote νῦν αὖ: a later inserted δ': νῦν δ' αὖ r. **60** ἢ κράτη] καὶ κράτη Axt. **63** ἔπειτα δ' οὔνεκ'] ἔπειθ' ὁθούνεκ' Wecklein.—κρειττόνων L, with σσ written above by an early hand.

---

turn') cp. **7.—μόνα δή**, '*all* alone': *Tr.* 1063 μόνη με δὴ καθεῖλε: *Ai.* 992 ἁπάντων δή: so esp. with superlatives, *ib.* 858 πανύστατον δή: Thuc. 1. 50 μεγίστη δή.

60 ψῆφον, the pebble used in voting, then, the vote; here (as below, 632) applied to the resolve or decree of an absolute monarch. Cp. *O. T.* 606 μή μ' ἁπλῇ κτάνῃς | ψήφῳ, διπλῇ δέ, *i.e.* not by thine own royal voice alone, but by mine also.—**τυράννων**, *i.e.* Creon: allusive plur., as 67: *O. T.* 366 n.—**κράτη**, the *powers* of the king, as 173 (cp. *O. C.* 392 n.). The disjunctive ἢ (for which Axt proposed καί) means: 'if we offend against this edict, or (in any way) against the royal powers.' It could not mean: 'if we infringe his *edict*, or (by persistence after warning) come into conflict with his *power*.'

61 f. τοῦτο μὲν is not governed by ἐννοεῖν, but is adv., 'on the one hand,' answered by ἔπειτα δ' (63) instead of τοῦτο δέ, as elsewhere by τοῦτ' αὖθις (167), τοῦτ' ἄλλο (*O. T.* 605), εἶτα (*Ph.* 1346), or δέ (*O. C.* 441).—**ὡς**, with **οὐ μαχουμένα**, marks the intention of nature as expressed in sex,—'showing that we were not meant to strive with men.' This might be illustrated by Arist.'s phrase, βούλεται ἡ φύσις ποιεῖν τι, in regard to nature's intention or tendency (*De Anim. Gen.* 4. 10, etc.).

63 f. οὔνεκ', 'that' (as *O. T.* 708, *O. C.* 1395, and oft.): *not*, 'because,' as some take it, supplying χρή with ἀκούειν.—**ἐκ**, as from the head and fount of authority; so *El.* 264 κἀκ τῶνδ' ἄρχομαι: cp. *O. C.* 67 n.—**ἀκούειν**, infin. expressing consequence ('so that we should hearken'), without ὥστε, as 1076

ληφθῆναι. We find ἀκούω τινός, 'to obey a person,' but not ἀκούω τι, as 'to hear (and obey) a command.' Here **ταῦτα** and **ἀλγίονα** are accusatives of respect, 'in regard to these things,' as πάντα in *El.* 340, τῶν κρατούντων ἐστὶ πάντ' ἀκουστέα, 'I must obey the rulers in all things.' If the accusatives were objective, the sense would be, 'to hear these taunts' (or, 'to be called these names'): cp. *Ph.* 607, *Ai.* 1235.

65 f. ἐγὼ μὲν οὖν. μέν (with no answering δέ) emphasises ἐγώ (see on 11), while οὖν has its separate force, 'therefore,' as in *O. T.* 483, *O. C.* 664. The composite μὲν οὖν ('nay rather') would be unfitting here.—**τοὺς ὑπὸ χθονός**, the gods below (451), and also the departed spirit of Polyneices,—which, like the spirit of the unburied Patroclus (*Il.* 23. 65), can have no rest till sepulture has been given to the corpse. Cp. *O. C.* 1775 τῷ κατὰ γῆς (Oedipus): for the allusive plur., *El.* 1419 ζῶσιν οἱ γᾶς ὑπαὶ κείμενοι (Agamemnon). In ref. to the nether world, Attic writers regularly join ὑπό with *gen.*, not dat.: *El.* 841 ὑπὸ γαίας... ἀνάσσει: *Tr.* 1097 τόν θ' ὑπὸ χθονὸς | Ἅιδου...σκύλακα: Plat. *Phaedr.* 249 Α τὰ ὑπὸ γῆς δικαστήρια. Indeed ὑπό with *dat.* is altogether rare in Attic prose, except as meaning (*a*) under an authority, as ὑπὸ νόμοις, or (*b*) under a class, as Plat. *Symp.* 205 Β αἱ ὑπὸ πάσαις ταῖς τέχναις ἐργασίαι. In poetry, Attic and other, it is freq. also in the local sense: cp. 337 ὑπ' οἰδμασιν.—**βιάζομαι τάδε**, pass. with cogn. acc., as 1073 βιάζονται τάδε. Cp. *Ph.* 1366 κἄμ' ἀναγκάζεις τάδε; and below, 219.

τοῖς ἐν τέλει βεβῶσι πείσομαι· τὸ γὰρ
περισσὰ πράσσειν οὐκ ἔχει νοῦν οὐδένα.

ΑΝ. οὔτ' ἂν κελεύσαιμ', οὔτ' ἄν, εἰ θέλοις ἔτι
πράσσειν, ἐμοῦ γ' ἂν ἡδέως δρῴης μέτα.   70
ἀλλ' ἴσθ' ὁποία σοι δοκεῖ· κεῖνον δ' ἐγὼ
θάψω· καλόν μοι τοῦτο ποιούσῃ θανεῖν.
φίλη μετ' αὐτοῦ κείσομαι, φίλου μέτα,
ὅσια πανουργήσασ'· ἐπεὶ πλείων χρόνος
ὃν δεῖ μ' ἀρέσκειν τοῖς κάτω τῶν ἐνθάδε.   75
ἐκεῖ γὰρ ἀεὶ κείσομαι· σοὶ δ' εἰ δοκεῖ,

---

68 f. In L the first hand wrote τὸ γὰρ | περισσὰ πράσσειν ἐμοῦ γ' ἂν ἡδέως δρῴης μέτα. He then effaced περισσά, and added one of the omitted verses (68) in the margin, and the other (69) in the text, between 67 and 70.   **70** ἐμοῦ γ'] ἐμοὶ γ' Meineke. —ἡδέως] ἀσμένης Lehrs.—δρῴης] δρώσης Mekler, understanding πράσσοις.   **71** ὁποῖά σοι δοκεῖ L: ὁποῖα r. The Schol. knew both readings: γίγνωσκε ὁποῖα σὺ θέλεις, τὸ

---

67 f. τοῖς ἐν τέλει βεβῶσι=τυράννων in 60, i.e. Creon. **βεβῶσι,** as El. 1094 μοίρᾳ μὲν οὐκ ἐν ἐσθλᾷ | βεβῶσαν: O. C. 1358 ἐν πόνῳ | ταὐτῷ βεβηκώς. Elsewhere Soph. has the simple phrase: Ai. 1352 κλύειν...τῶν ἐν τέλει, and so Ph. 385, 925. οἱ ἐν τέλει are 'those in authority,' —τέλος meaning 'final or decisive power,' as Thuc. 4. 118 τέλος ἔχοντες ἰόντων, 'let the envoys go as plenipotentiaries.' Pindar's τέλος δωδεκάμηνον ('an office held for a year'), N. 11. 10, is perh. poetical. As synonyms for οἱ ἐν τέλει we find (1) οἱ τὰ τέλη ἔχοντες, Thuc. 5. 47, and (2) τὰ τέλη simply,—'the authorities,' sometimes with masc. part., as Thuc. 4. 15 ἔδοξεν αὐτοῖς...τὰ τέλη καταβάντας βουλεύειν. Xen. Hellen. 6. 5 has τὰ μέγιστα τέλη, 'the highest magistrates' (like Thuc. 1. 10 ἔξω τῶν βασιλέων καὶ τῶν μάλιστα ἐν τέλει: cp. 2. 10).—**τὸ γὰρ** | ...**πράσσειν:** for the art. in the 6th place, with its noun in the next v., cp. 78: O. T. 231: O. C. 265, 351: Ph. 674.—**περισσὰ πρ.:** cp. 780: so Tr. 617 περισσὰ δρᾶν,=πολλὰ πράττειν, πολυπραγμονεῖν.—**οὐκ ἔχει νοῦν οὐδ.**= ἀνόητόν ἐστι: prop. of persons, as Tr. 553 γυναῖκα νοῦν ἔχουσαν.

69 f. ἔτι, 'yet,'—at some future time: so El. 66 (κἄμ' ἐπαυχῶ) ἄστρον ὡς λάμψειν ἔτι: Tr. 257 δουλώσειν ἔτι (he vowed that he would yet enslave him).—**πράσσειν...δρῴης** (instead of πράσσοις): for such substitution of a synonym cp. O. T. 54 ἄρξεις...κρατεῖς (n.): O. C. 1501 σαφὴς

...ἐμφανής. With **δρῴης** we have a double **ἄν,** the first after the negative, the second after the emphatic **ἐμοῦ γ':** cp. O. T. 339 n.—Objection has been made to **ἡδέως** on the ground that it ought to mean, 'with pleasure to yourself.' Wecklein, indeed, takes that to be the sense, supposing γε to be misplaced; i.e. the proper order would have been, **ἡδέως γε ἂν ἐμοῦ** κ.τ.λ.: but the position of **ἐμοῦ** in the verse sufficiently shows that γε must go with it. **ἐμοὶ γ'** (Meineke) would leave **μέτα** awkward: and **ἀσμένης** (Lehrs) would not have been displaced by **ἡδέως,** which the old scholia confirm. All the difficulty has arisen from failing to distinguish between (1) οὐκ ἂν ἡδέως δρῴης, and (2) οὐκ ἂν μετὰ ἐμοῦ ἡδέως δρῴης. In (1) ἡδέως could mean only, 'agreeably to yourself.' But in (2) it is ambiguous; for the statement is equivalent to saying, 'your co-operation with me would not be agreeable'; i.e. to you, or to me, or to either of us,—as the context may imply. Here, as the emphatic **ἐμοῦ γε** indicates, she means ἡδέως ἐμοί. Cp. Plat. Rep. 426 c δς...ἂν σφᾶς...ἥδιστα θεραπεύῃ, i.e. 'whoever serves them most acceptably' (not, 'most gladly'). Ar. Nub. 79 πῶς δῆτ' ἂν ἥδιστ' αὐτὸν ἐπεγείραιμι; (i.e. most pleasantly for him).

71 ἴσθ' from εἰμί: 'be such as thou wilt,'—show what character thou wilt. Cp. Ph. 1049 οὐ γὰρ τοιούτων δεῖ, τοιοῦτός εἰμ' ἐγώ: ib. 1271 τοιοῦτος ἦσθα τοῖς λόγοισι: El. 1024 ἄσκει τοιαύτη νοῦν δι' αἰῶνος μέ-

will hearken to our rulers; for 'tis witless to be over-busy.
AN. I will not urge thee,—no, nor, if thou yet shouldst
have the mind, wouldst thou be welcome as a worker with *me*.
Nay, be what thou wilt; but I will bury him: well for me to
die in doing that. I shall rest, a loved one with him whom I
have loved, sinless in my crime; for I owe a longer allegiance
to the dead than to the living: in that world I shall abide for
ever. But if *thou* wilt,

πείθεσθαι τοῖς τυράννοις· ἢ τοιαύτη γενοῦ ὁποῖα βούλει. **76** αἰεί L, as in iambics
O. C. 1530, 1532, *Tr.* 16, *El.* 305 (but made from ἀεί), 650, 917: in anapaests *Ph.*
148. But L has ἀεί (ᾱ) in iambics *O. T.* 786, 1513, *O. C.* 1584, in anapaests *El.* 218,
in lyrics six times (*El.* 1242, *Ph.* 172, 717, *O. T.* 481, *O. C.* 682, *Ai.* 599).—σοὶ δ']
σὺ δ' Elms., Dindorf, Hartung.

νειν: *O.T.* 435 ἡμεῖς τοιοίδ' ἔφυμεν.—**ὁποῖα**
σοι δοκεῖ = (τοιαύτη) ὁποίᾳ (or ὁποίαν) εἶναι
δοκεῖ σοι, the relative being attracted into
the case of the suppressed antecedent.
This was the more natural since ὁποῖα
σοι δοκεῖ, 'of any kind you please,' was
felt as almost one word, ὁποιαδήποτε;
just so ὃς βούλει (*quivis*), instead of
οὗτος ὃν βούλει, Plat. *Gorg.* 517 A μή-
ποτέ τις τῶν νῦν ἔργα τοιαῦτα ἐργάσηται
οἷα τούτων ὃς βούλει εἴργασται: *Crat.* 432
A ὥσπερ αὐτὰ τὰ δέκα ἢ ὅστις βούλει
ἄλλος ἀριθμός.—Those who read **ἴσθ'**
(from οἶδα) **ὁποῖά σοι δοκεῖ** compare *El.*
1055 ἀλλ' εἰ σεαυτῇ τυγχάνεις δοκοῦσά
τι | φρονεῖν, φρόνει τοιαῦτα. But εἰδέναι
is not φρονεῖν. In Attic, ἴσθ' ὁποῖά σοι
δοκεῖ could mean nothing but 'know
such things as seem good to thee.' It
could not mean (*a*) 'Have such sentiments as seem good to thee': nor (*b*) 'Be
wise in thine own wisdom.' The Homeric phrases, πεπνυμένα εἰδώς ('wise of
heart'), ἀθεμίστια εἰδώς, ἤπια οἶδε ('he
has kindly feelings,' *Od.* '13. 405), etc.,
have no counterpart in the Attic usage of
εἰδέναι. In 301 δυσσέβειαν εἰδέναι, and
in *Ph.* 960 δοκοῦντος οὐδὲν εἰδέναι κακόν,
the verb means simply 'to know.'
72 f. θάψω, emphatic by place and
pause: see on 46 ἀδελφόν.—**φίλη...φίλου**,
loved by him, as he is loved by her: *Ai.*
267 κοινὸς ἐν κοινοῖσι: *ib.* 620 ἄφιλα παρ'
ἀφίλοις.—**μετ' αὐτοῦ κείσομαι**, *i.e.* in the
same world of the dead (76). The repetition of μετά serves to bring out the reciprocity of love more strongly: φίλη μετ'
αὐτοῦ κείσομαι, μετὰ φίλου (κειμένη),—
instead of the simpler φίλη μετὰ φίλου
κείσομαι.
74 f. ὅσια πανουργήσασ': having

broken a human law in a manner which
the gods permit,—viz., in order to observe a divine law. Creon uses the
word πανουργίας below, 300. **ὅσια** is
peculiarly appropriate since the word was
familiar where duty to heaven was distinguished from duty to man: cp. Polyb.
23. 10 παραβῆναι καὶ τὰ πρὸς τοὺς ἀνθρώπους δίκαια καὶ τὰ πρὸς τοὺς θεοὺς ὅσια. The
phrase is an ὀξύμωρον (a paradox with a
point), like 'splendide mendax'; *i.e.* the
qualification (ὅσια) seems contrary to the
essence of the thing qualified. Cp. Milton
(*Tetrachordon*), 'Men of the most renown-
ed virtue have sometimes by transgressing
most truly kept the law'; which is not
an oxymoron, because the words, 'most
truly,' suggest an explanation by showing
that 'kept' is not used in its ordinary
sense.—ἐπεὶ κ.τ.λ.: (I will obey gods
rather than men), *for* the other world is
more to me than this.—τῶν ἐνθάδε = ἢ τοῖς
ἐνθάδε: *O. C.* 567 τῆς ἐς αὔριον | οὐδὲν
πλέον μοι σοῦ (= ἢ σοί) μέτεστιν ἡμέρας (n.).
76 f. κείσομαι, though we have had
the word in 73. For other examples of
such repetition, see n. on *O. C.* 554, and
cp. below 163 ὥρθωσαν, 167 ὄρθου: 207
ἐκ γ' ἐμοῦ, 210 ἐξ ἐμοῦ: 613, 618 (ἕρπει):
614, 625 (ἐκτὸς ἄτας).—**σοὶ δ'** is better
than Elmsley's σὺ δ', since the primary
contrast is between their points of view:
'if it seems right *to thee*, dishonour the
dead,' rather than, 'do *thou*, if it seems
right, dishonour the dead.' Remark, too,
that the *simple* εἰ δοκεῖ (without def. of
pron.) is usually a polite formula, 'if it is
pleasing to you (as well as to me)': *Ph.*
526 ἀλλ' εἰ δοκεῖ, πλέωμεν: *ib.* 645 ἀλλ' εἰ
δοκεῖ, χωρῶμεν: *ib.* 1402 εἰ δοκεῖ, στείχω-
μεν.—**τὰ τῶν θεῶν ἔντιμα**, the honoured

24 ΣΟΦΟΚΛΕΟΥΣ

τὰ τῶν θεῶν ἔντιμ' ἀτιμάσασ' ἔχε.
ΙΣ. ἐγὼ μὲν οὐκ ἄτιμα ποιοῦμαι, τὸ δὲ
βίᾳ πολιτῶν δρᾶν ἔφυν ἀμήχανος.
ΑΝ. σὺ μὲν τάδ' ἂν προύχοι'· ἐγὼ δὲ δὴ τάφον   80
χώσουσ' ἀδελφῷ φιλτάτῳ πορεύσομαι.
ΙΣ. οἴμοι ταλαίνης, ὡς ὑπερδέδοικά σου.
ΑΝ. μὴ 'μοῦ προτάρβει· τὸν σὸν ἐξόρθου πότμον.
ΙΣ. ἀλλ' οὖν προμηνύσῃς γε τοῦτο μηδενὶ
τοὔργον, κρυφῇ δὲ κεῦθε, σὺν δ' αὔτως ἐγώ.   85
ΑΝ. οἴμοι, καταύδα· πολλὸν ἐχθίων ἔσει
σιγῶσ', ἐὰν μὴ πᾶσι κηρύξῃς τάδε.
ΙΣ. θερμὴν ἐπὶ ψυχροῖσι καρδίαν ἔχεις.
ΑΝ. ἀλλ' οἶδ' ἀρέσκουσ' οἷς μάλισθ' ἁδεῖν με χρή.

78 Between μὲν and οὐκ L has an erasure of some letters (οὖν?).   **83** μή
μου προτάρβει MSS.   μὴ 'μοῦ Schaefer, Donaldson, M. Seyffert : μὴ ἐμοῦ
Nauck, Wecklein.—πότμον] In L, S has written γρ. βίον above ; some of

---

things of the gods; the laws which are
theirs (454 θεῶν νόμιμα), held in honour
(by them and by men). τὰ τοῖς θεοῖς
ἔντιμα (25, *El.* 239 ἔντιμος τούτοις) would
have presented the gods only as *observers*,
not also as *authors*, of the laws.—**ἀτιμάσασ' ἔχε** (cp. 22), 'be guilty of dishonouring': cp. *Ai.* 588 μὴ προδοὺς ἡμᾶς
γένῃ, and n. on *O. T.* 957.

78 f. ἐγὼ is slightly emphasised by
μέν (see on 11), which goes closely with
it, and does not here answer to the following **δέ.**—ἄτιμα ποιοῦμαι=ἀτιμάζω: cp.
O.C. 584 δι' οὐδενὸς ποιεῖ.—**τὸ δὲ | ...δρᾶν:**
see on 67 τὸ γὰρ | ...πράσσειν. The inf.
with art. is strictly an acc. of respect ('as
for the acting..., I am incapable of it'),
but is practically equiv. to the simple inf.,
ἀμήχανος δρᾶν: see n. on *O. C.* 47 οὐδ'
ἐμοὶ...τοὐξανιστάναι... | ...ἐστὶ θάρσος.

80 f. τάδ' ἂν προύχοιο, 'thou canst
make these excuses' (*sc.* εἰ βούλοιο): Aesch.
Ag. 1394 χαίροιτ' ἄν, εἰ χαίροιτ'· ἐγὼ δ'
ἐπεύχομαι. For προέχεσθαι as=προφασί-
ζεσθαι cp. Thuc. 1. 140 ὅπερ μάλιστα προὔ-
χονται. So πρόσχημα=πρόφασις (*El.* 525).
—**δή,** 'now,' as the next thing to be done:
cp. 173.—**τάφον χώσουσ',** prop. to raise
a mound on the spot where the remains
of the dead had been burned: *Il.* 7. 336
τύμβον δ' ἀμφὶ πυρὴν ἕνα χεύομεν. So *Il.*
24. 799 σῆμ' ἔχεαν,—after placing the
bones in an urn (λάρναξ), and depositing

this in a grave (κάπετος). She speaks as
if she hoped to give him regular sepulture.
This is ultimately done by Creon's command (1203 τύμβον...χώσαντες), though
the rites which Antigone herself is able to
perform are only symbolical (255, 429).

82 f. Join οἴμοι ταλαίνης, 'alas for
thee, unhappy one': *O. C.* 1399 οἴμοι κε-
λεύθου τῆς τ' ἐμῆς δυσπραξίας, | οἴμοι δ'
ἑταίρων: but the *nom.* when the ref. is to
the speaker, as *El.* 1143 οἴμοι τάλαινα
τῆς ἐμῆς πάλαι τροφῆς.—**μὴ 'μοῦ προτάρβει** (or, as some write it, μὴ ἐμοῦ) is clearly
right. If we read **μή μου προτάρβει,** then
the emphasis is solely on the verbal notion.
'I fear for thee.'—'*Fear* not so: make
thine own fate prosperous.' But the stress
on **τὸν σόν** renders it certain that the poet
intended a corresponding stress on the
preceding pronoun: 'Fear not for *me*—
make *thine own* fate prosperous.' And
μὴ 'μοῦ is no more objectionable than μὴ
'γώ in *El.* 472. **προτάρβει,** as *Tr.* 89
(with gen. πατρός). Distinguish προδείσας,
'afraid beforehand,' *O. T.* 90 (n.).—**ἐξόρθου** here='straighten out,' *i.e.* guide in a
straight or prosperous course: cp. 167
ὤρθου πόλιν, 675 ὀρθουμένων. Elsewhere
ἐξορθόω is usu. 'to correct, amend' (Plat.
Tim. 90 D); more rarely, like ἀνορθόω
(*O. T.* 51), 'to set upright' (τὸ πεσόν,
Plat. *Legg.* 862 C). In the figurative uses
of ὀρθός and its derivatives the context

be guilty of dishonouring laws which the gods have stablished in honour.

Is. I do them no dishonour; but to defy the State,—I have no strength for that.

An. Such be thy plea:—I, then, will go to heap the earth above the brother whom I love.

Is. Alas, unhappy one! How I fear for thee!

An. Fear not for me: guide thine own fate aright.

Is. At least, then, disclose this plan to none, but hide it closely,—and so, too, will I.

An. Oh, denounce it! Thou wilt be far more hateful for thy silence, if thou proclaim not these things to all.

Is. Thou hast a hot heart for chilling deeds.

An. I know that I please where I am most bound to please.

---

the later MSS. read βίον.　　**85** αὕτως MSS.: αὔτως Hermann, Bergk,
Ellendt, and others; see on *O. T.* 931.　　**86** πολλὸν] μᾶλλον Porson, and

---

must always guide our choice between the notion of 'upright' and that of 'straight.'

84 f. ἀλλ' οὖν...γε. In this combination ἀλλά is like our 'well'; οὖν = 'at any rate' (*i.e.* if you *must* do it); and γε emphasises the word which it follows. Cp. *El.* 233 ἀλλ' οὖν εὐνοίᾳ γ' αὐδῶ, 'well, at any rate (*i.e.* though you will not listen to me) it is with *good-will* that I speak.' *Ph.* 1305.—**κρυφῇ δέ**: here δέ = ἀλλά: Thuc. 4. 86 οὐκ ἐπὶ κακῷ, ἐπ' ἐλευθερώσει δέ.—σὺν δ', adv., *sc.* κεύσω: cp. *Ai.* 1288 ὅδ' ἦν ὁ πράσσων ταῦτα, σὺν δ' ἐγὼ παρών. —**αὕτως** (adv. of αὐτός, see on *O. T.* 931), in just that way—'likewise': *Tr.* 1040 ὧδ' αὔτως ὥς μ' ὤλεσε.

86 f. καταύδα, *sc.* τὸ ἔργον, 'denounce it.' The word occurs only here, the pres. used in this sense being καταγορεύω (Thuc. 4. 68 καταγορεύει τις ξυνειδὼς τοῖς ἑτέροις τὸ ἐπιβούλευμα): aor. κατεῖπον.— **πολλόν**: this Ionic form occurs also *Tr.* 1196 πολλὸν δ' ἄρσεν ἐκτεμόνθ' ὁμοῦ | ἄγριον ἔλαιον, though in no other places of tragedy. And Soph. also used the epic form πουλύπους in a trimeter, fr. 286 νόει πρὸς ἀνδρί, σῶμα πουλύπους ὅπως | πέτρᾳ, κ.τ.λ. Porson on Eur. *Hec.* 618 wished to read in our verse either πλεῖον (which is inadmissible, as Nauck observes, *Eur. Stud.* 2. 27), or μᾶλλον, which some edd. receive. But **πολλὸν** is manifestly better than μᾶλλον.—σιγῶσ' is explained by ἐὰν...τάδε, while the thought is strengthened by πᾶσι: she is to tell the news *to all.*

88 θερμὴν ἐπὶ ψυχροῖσι κ.τ.λ.: 'thou hast a hot heart for chilling deeds'; *i.e.* in thy rash enthusiasm thou art undertaking deeds which might well chill thy soul with a presage of death. ἐπί with dat. here = 'with a view to' (Xen. *An.* 3. 5. 18 ἐπὶ τούτοις ἐθύσαντο): not 'in,' like ἐπ' ἔργοις πᾶσι *O. C.* 1268 (n.). Cp. 157. θερμήν has suggested ψυχρά, and the thought of the *dead* has helped (cp. *O. C.* 621 νέκυς ψυχρός). In Aesch. *P. V.* 693 δείματα are said ἀμφάκει κέντρῳ ψύχειν ψυχάν (to chill,—where Meineke's ψήχειν, 'to wear,' is improbable). Cp. Ar. *Ach.* 1191 στυγερὰ τάδε κρυερὰ πάθεα: Eur. fr. 908 κρυερὰ Διόθεν | θανάτου πεμφθεῖσα τελευτή. For the verbal contrast, Schütz cp. *Ad Herenn.* 4. 15. 21 *in re frigidissima cales, in ferventissima friges,* and Hor. *A. P.* 465 *ardentem frigidus Aetnam Insiluit.* He thinks that Ismene (hurt by vv. 86 f.) implies, 'and a cold heart for thy living sister,' to which Ant. rejoins by v. 89. But θερμήν is not 'affectionate,' and Ant. seems to mean simply, 'love and piety banish fear.'— Some understand, 'with a view to *joyless* things' (cp. on 650): but this would be weak.

89 f. ἀδεῖν, an aor. inf. used in *Il.* 3. 173, as also by Solon (fr. 7 ἔργμασιν ἐν μεγάλοις πᾶσιν ἀδεῖν χαλεπόν), Her., and Pind. This is the only place in classical Attic where any part of the aor. ἔαδον occurs.

ΙΣ. εἰ καὶ δυνήσει γ'· ἀλλ' ἀμηχάνων ἐρᾷς.   90
ΑΝ. οὐκοῦν, ὅταν δὴ μὴ σθένω, πεπαύσομαι.
ΙΣ. ἀρχὴν δὲ θηρᾶν οὐ πρέπει τἀμήχανα.
ΑΝ. εἰ ταῦτα λέξεις, ἐχθαρεῖ μὲν ἐξ ἐμοῦ,
ἐχθρὰ δὲ τῷ θανόντι προσκείσει δίκη.
ἀλλ' ἔα με καὶ τὴν ἐξ ἐμοῦ δυσβουλίαν   95
παθεῖν τὸ δεινὸν τοῦτο· πείσομαι γὰρ οὐ
τοσοῦτον οὐδὲν ὥστε μὴ οὐ καλῶς θανεῖν.
ΙΣ. ἀλλ' εἰ δοκεῖ σοι, στεῖχε· τοῦτο δ' ἴσθ', ὅτι
ἄνους μὲν ἔρχει, τοῖς φίλοις δ' ὀρθῶς φίλη.

so Nauck, Wecklein: see comment.   **91** In L the first h. omitted μή: S added
it.   **93** ἐχθαρεῖ] ἐχθρανῆι L, with γρ. ἐχθαρῇ from a later hand in marg.

---

90 εἰ καὶ δυνήσει γ', yes, if (besides having the wish to please them) you shall *also* have the power. καί goes closely with δυνήσει: cp. *O. T.* 283 εἰ καὶ τρίτ' ἐστί. Such cases must be carefully distinguished from those in which εἰ καί form a single expression; see *O. T.* p. 296.

91 Since οὐκοῦν ('well, then') precedes, δή is best taken as giving precision to ὅταν,—'so soon as.'—πεπαύσομαι, 'I will cease *forthwith*': so *Tr.* 587. Cp. the perf., *Ph.* 1279 εἰ δὲ μή τι πρὸς καιρὸν λέγων | κυρῶ, πέπαυμαι, 'I have done.'

92 ἀρχήν, adv., 'to begin with,' 'at all,'—in *negative* sentences; often placed, as here, before the negative word; *El.* 439 ἀρχὴν δ' ἂν...οὐκ ἂν...ἐπέστρεφε: *Ph.* 1239 ἀρχὴν κλύειν ἂν οὐδ' ἅπαξ ἐβουλόμην: Her. 3. 39 ἔφη χαριεῖσθαι μᾶλλον ἀποδιδοὺς τὰ ἔλαβε ἢ ἀρχὴν μηδὲ λαβών. In *affirmative* sentences the art. is usually added: Andoc. or. 3 § 20 ἐξῆν γὰρ αὐτοῖς καὶ τὴν ἀρχὴν ἐῶσιν Ὀρχομενίους αὐτονόμους εἰρήνην ἄγειν: so Isocr. or. 15 § 272.

93 ἐχθαρεῖ, pass.: so, from liquid stems, 230 ἀλγυνεῖ: *O.T.* 272 φθερεῖσθαι: *Ai.* 1155 πημανούμενος. The 'midd.' fut. in σ affords numerous examples, as below, 210, 637, 726: see n. on *O. T.* 672 and *O. C.* 1185.—ἐξ ἐμοῦ, 'on my part' (cp. 95), rather than simply 'by me' (cp. 63).

94 ἐχθρά...τῷ θανόντι προσκείσει δίκη, 'thou wilt be subject to the lasting enmity of the dead.' The word προσκείσει means literally, '*wilt be attached to*...,' i.e., '*wilt be brought into a lasting relation with*'; and ἐχθρά defines the nature of

that relation. The sense is thus virtually the same as if we had, ὁ θανὼν ἐχθρός σοι προσκείσεται, 'the enmity of the dead will cleave to thee.' The convertible use of προσκεῖσθαι is illustrated by 1243 ἀνδρὶ πρόσκειται κακόν, as compared with *El.* 1040 ᾧ σὺ πρόσκεισαι κακῷ, and *ib.* 240 εἴ τῳ πρόσκειμαι χρηστῷ. Here, προσκείσει expresses merely the establishment of the permanent relation between the two persons. It does not mean, 'you will be brought, as his foe, *into dependence* on him' (*i.e.* under the power of his curse); as in Eur. *Tro.* 185 τῷ πρόσκειμαι δούλα τλάμων; 'to whom have I been assigned as a slave?' (*i.e.* by the casting of lots:—the answer is, ἐγγύς που κεῖσαι κλήρου). Nor, again, 'you will *press upon* the dead as his foe,' *i.e.* be hostile and grievous to him: for, as δίκη shows, the punishment is to be hers, not his. The idea might have been expressed in a converse form by τὸν θανόντα ἐχθρὸν προσθήσει (cf. Xen. *Cyr.* 2. 4. 12).

Lehrs proposed Δίκη, *i.e.* 'you will fall under the chastisement of justice.' Donaldson, following Emper, reads ἐχθρά... δίκη, as *iure inimicorum apud mortuum eris: i.e.* on the part of the dead you will be deemed to have only the rights of a foe. This is impossible. The ordinary reading is sound.

95 ff. ἔα, one syll. by synizesis, as *O. T.* 1451 (n.).—τὴν ἐξ ἐμοῦ δυσβ., the folly proceeding from me, the folly *on my part*, for which I bear the sole blame: *El.* 619 ἀλλ' ἡ γὰρ ἐκ σοῦ δυσμένεια καὶ τὰ σὰ | ἔργ' ἐξαναγκάζει με, 'it is the enmity on thy part,' etc. *Tr.* 631 μὴ

Is. Aye, if thou canst; but thou wouldst what thou canst not.

An. Why, then, when my strength fails, I shall have done.

Is. A hopeless quest should not be made at all.

An. If thus thou speakest, thou wilt have hatred from me, and wilt justly be subject to the lasting hatred of the dead. But leave me, and the folly that is mine alone, to suffer this dread thing; for I shall not suffer aught so dreadful as an ignoble death.

Is. Go, then, if thou must; and of this be sure,—that, though thine errand is foolish, to thy dear ones thou art truly dear.

[*Exit* ANTIGONE *on the spectators' left.* ISMENE *retires into the palace by one of the two side-doors.*]

---

94 ἐχθρά] ἐχθρᾷ Emper, Donaldson. ἔχθρᾳ Kvičala.—δίκῃ] Δίκη Lehrs: κάσει Dindorf: κάτω L. Dindorf. πρὸς δίκης ἔσει Herwerden (*Stud. crit.* p. 9). **96** οὐ] οὖν Elms. on Eur. *Med.* 804, M. Seyffert, Dindorf.

πρῳ λέγοις ἂν τὸν πόθον τὸν ἐξ ἐμοῦ, | πρὶν εἰδέναι τἀκεῖθεν εἰ ποθούμεθα. Cp. *O. C.* 453 n.—**τὸ δεινὸν τοῦτο**, ironical: cp. *El.* 376 (Electra in answer to her sister's warnings) φέρ' εἰπὲ δὴ τὸ δεινόν.— **πείσομαι γὰρ οὐ**: for the position of the negative (which belongs to the verb, not to τοσοῦτον), cp. 223, *O. C.* 125 προσέβα γὰρ οὐκ ἄν. We still write οὐ here, not οὔ, because the sentence runs on without pause: but 255 τυμβήρης μὲν οὔ, *Ai.* 545 ταρβήσει γὰρ οὔ, since in each case a comma can follow the negative.—**μὴ οὐ**, not μή, because the principal verb πείσομαι is negatived: *O. T.* 283 n. She means, 'even if I have to die, at least I shall not suffer the worst of evils; which is not death, but an ignoble death.' Cp. frag. adesp. 61 οὐ κατθανεῖν γὰρ δεινόν, ἀλλ' αἰσχρῶς θανεῖν.

99 τοῖς φίλοις δ' ὀρθῶς φίλη, 'but truly dear to thy friends,'—*i.e.* both to the dead brother and to the living sister. The words are especially a parting assurance (ἴσθι) that *Ismene's* love is undiminished. ὀρθῶς = ἀληθῶς, as Diphilus frag. incert. 20 τὸν ὀρθῶς εὐγενῆ. Others make φίλη active,—'a true friend to thy friends' (*i.e.* to Polyneices): which is certainly the fittest sense in Eur. *I. T.* 609 ὡς ἀπ' εὐγενοῦς τινος | ῥίζης πέφυκας, τοῖς φίλοις τ' ὀρθῶς φίλος (Orestes, when he devotes his life to save his friend's). But here the other view is decidedly preferable.

100—161 Parodos. For the metres

see Metrical Analysis. The framework is as follows. (1) *1st strophe*, 100 ἀκτίς to 109 χαλινῷ = *1st antistrophe*, 117 στὰς to 133 ἀλαλάξαι. (2) *2nd strophe*, 134 ἀντιτύπᾳ to 140 δεξιόσειρος = *2nd antistrophe*, 148 ἀλλὰ γὰρ to 154 ἄρχοι. Each strophe and each antistrophe is followed by an anapaestic system (σύστημα) of seven verses, recited by the Coryphaeus alone, in the pauses of the choral dance. The fourth and last of these systems, following the second antistrophe, announces the approach of Creon.

The *Ajax* is the only play of Sophocles which has a Parodos beginning, in the older style, with a regular anapaestic march. But something of the same character is given to this ode by the regularity of the anapaestic systems. In the Parodos of the *O. C.*, on the other hand, though anapaests similarly divide each strophe from each antistrophe, the systems are of unequal lengths, and the general character is wholly different, being rather that of a κομμός: see n. on *O. C.* 117.

The fifteen Theban elders who form the Chorus have been summoned to the palace by Creon,—they know not, as yet, for what purpose (158). They greet the newly-risen sun, and exult in the flight of the Argives.

The ode vividly portrays the enormous sin of Polyneices against his country, and the appalling nature of the peril which Thebes has just escaped. We already

ΧΟΡΟΣ.

στρ. α΄. ἀκτὶς ἀελίου, τὸ κάλλιστον ἑπταπύλῳ φανὲν   100
2 Θήβᾳ τῶν προτέρων φάος,
3 ἐφάνθης ποτ᾿, ὦ χρυσέας
4 ἁμέρας βλέφαρον, Διρκαίων ὑπὲρ ῥεέθρων μολοῦσα,
5 τὸν λεύκασπιν Ἀργόθεν *ἐκβάντα φῶτα πανσαγίᾳ   106
6 φυγάδα πρόδρομον ὀξυτέρῳ κινήσασα χαλινῷ·

---

100 ἀελίοιο L. The first hand wrote ἀελίου, which is also in the lemma of the scholium. An early hand then changed υ into ιο. Hence Bothe, ἀελίοιο κάλλιστον (omitting τό). **102** τῶν προτέρων L: τῶν πρότερον A, Brunck, Blaydes. **104** βλεφαρίς Nauck. **106** ἀργόθεν | φῶτα βάντα MSS. A syllable is wanting (cp. 123). For Ἀργόθεν, Erfurdt

---

know Antigone's motive. This is a dramatic prelude to the announcement of Creon's.

100 f. ἀελίου, Dor. for the epic ἠελίου, with ᾱ as usu. (808, *O. C.* 1245), though it is sometimes used with ᾰ, as *Tr.* 835, Eur. *Med.* 1252.—**τὸ κάλλιστον ...φάος.** Two constructions are possible; I prefer the first. (1) Θήβᾳ φανὲν τὸ κάλλιστον φάος, the art. going with the superlative, which it emphasises,—'the very fairest,'—a common use, as Plat. *Hipp.* 289 B οὐχ ἡ καλλίστη παρθένος αἰσχρὰ φανεῖται; *Od.* 17. 415 οὐ μέν μοι δοκέεις ὁ κάκιστος Ἀχαιῶν. (2) τὸ Θήβᾳ φανὲν κάλλιστον φάος, the art. going with φανέν. This seems awkward. When a voc. is followed by a noun or partic. with art., this is normally in direct agreement with the voc., as ὦ ἄνδρες...οἱ παρόντες (Plat. *Prot.* 337 C), as if here we had ἡ φανεῖσα. The Schol., who prefers this constr., shirks the difficulty by his paraphrase, ὦ τῆς ἀκτῖνος τοῦ ἡλίου φῶς, τὸ φανὲν κ.τ.λ.—**ἑπταπύλῳ**: epithet of Θήβη in *Od.* 11. 263, Hes. *Op.* 161, as ἑκατόμπυλοι in *Il.* 9. 383 of Θῆβαι Αἰγύπτιαι.—**τῶν προτέρων**: cp. 1212 f.: Thuc. 1. 10 στρατείαν...μεγίστην...τῶν πρὸ αὑτῆς. Tacitus *Hist.* 1. 50 *solus omnium ante se principum.* Milton *P. L.* 4. 322 *Adam, the goodliest man of men since born, His sons, the fairest of her daughters Eve.* Goethe *Hermann und Dorothea* 5. 101 *Von ihren Schwestern die beste.*

103 f. ἐφάνθης with an echo of φανέν (παρήχησις): cp. *O.C.* 794 στόμα | ...στόμωσιν.—χρυσέας, with ῠ as *O.T.* 157, 188. So Pind. *Pyth.* 4. 4 ἔνθα ποτὲ χρυσέων Διὸς αἰητῶν πάρεδρος. The ῠ was admitted by the lyrists, and from them borrowed by the dramatists, though only in lyrics,

and even there only occasionally. Homer never shortens the υ: for, as χρυσέῳ ἀνὰ σκήπτρῳ (*Il.* 1. 15) shows, the Homeric χρυσέης (etc.) must be treated as disyll. by synizesis.—**βλέφαρον** = ὄμμα : Eur. *Ph.* 543 νυκτὸς τ᾿ ἀφεγγὲς βλέφαρον (the moon). Cp. Job iii. 9 (Revised Version), 'neither let it behold the eyelids of the morning.'—**Διρκαίων.** The Dircè was on the w. of Thebes, the Ismenus on the E.: between them flowed the less famous Strophia : Callim. *Hymn Del.* 76 Δίρκη τε Στροφίη τε μελαμψηφῖδος ἔχουσαι | Ἰσμηνοῦ χέρα πατρός (alluding to their common source s. of the town). Though the Ismenus, as the eastern stream, would have been more appropriately named here, the Dircè is preferred, as the representative river of Thebes : so Pindar, 'the Dircaean swan,' expresses 'at Thebes and at Sparta' by ῥεέθροισί τε Δίρκας...καὶ παρ᾿ Εὐρώτᾳ (*Isthm.* 1. 29). Cp. 844.

106 τὸν λεύκασπιν...φῶτα, in a collective sense : so ὁ Πέρσης, the Persian army, Her. 8. 108, etc. Cp. Aesch. *Theb.* 90 ὁ λεύκασπις λεώς (Dind. λευκοπρεπής) : Eur. *Phoen.* 1099 λεύκασπιν εἰσορῶμεν Ἀργείων στρατόν. The round shield, painted white, which the Argive soldier carried on his left arm, is the λευκῆς χιόνος πτέρυξ of 114. The choice of *white* as the Argive colour may have been prompted by a popular association of Ἄργος with ἀργός.

The words τὸν λεύκασπιν Ἀργόθεν answer metrically to 123 πευκάενθ᾿ Ἥφαιστον ἑλεῖν. Instead of Ἀργόθεν (‒ ⏑ ‒) we therefore require ‒ ⏑ ⏑ ‒. The short final of λεύκασπιν is legitimate, the metre being Glyconic (see Metr. Analysis). In the antistrophic verse, the Η of Ἥφαιστον is 'irrational,' *i.e.* is a long syllable doing

CHORUS.

Beam of the sun, fairest light that ever dawned on Thebè 1st
of the seven gates, thou hast shone forth at last, eye of golden strophe.
day, arisen above Dircè's streams! The warrior of the white
shield, who came from Argos in his panoply, hath been stirred
by thee to headlong flight, in swifter career;

conject. ἀπ' Ἀργόθεν: Ahrens, Ἀπιόθεν: Boeckh, Ἀργεῖον: Wolff, Ἀργογενῆ:
Blaydes, Ἀργολίδος or Ἀργολικόν: Wecklein, γᾶς Πέλοπος: Mekler, Ἰναχόθεν:
Hermann, Ἀργόθεν ἐκ φῶτα βάντα: Feussner and Schütz, Ἀργόθεν ἐκβάντα φῶτα.
108 ὀξυτόρωι L (with ὀξεῖ written above): ὀξυτέρῳ r, and Schol. Blaydes conject.

duty for a short: and Nauck is incorrect
in saying that the metre 'requires' (though
it admits) a choriambus beginning with a
consonant. The simplest remedy is to
read **Ἀργόθεν ἐκ|βάντα φῶτα**, and to
suppose that, after the loss of ἐκ, βάντα
and φῶτα were accidentally transposed.
Cp. *O. C.* 1088 where σθένει 'πινικείῳ is
certainly the right order, but the MSS.
reverse it. (See also above on v. 29.)
Dindorf reads ἐκ φῶτα βάντα, assuming
tmesis: but tmesis of ἐκ in Soph. occurs
elsewhere only before μέν (*Tr.* 1053) or
δέ, and there was no motive here for
interposing φῶτα. Hermann reads Ἀργόθεν ἐκ as = ἐξ Ἀργόθεν: but elsewhere
ἐκ comes before, not after, such forms
(ἐξ Αἰσύμηθεν, *Il.* 8. 304: ἐξ ἀλόθεν, ἐξ οὐ-
ρανόθεν, etc.). If Ἀργόθεν is not genuine,
then it was probably a gloss on some
other form in -θεν. Had γᾶς Πέλοπος
(or Δαναοῦ) been in the text, a scholiast
would have been more apt to paraphrase
with ἀπ' or ἐξ Ἄργους. This is against
such conjectures as Ἀργεῖον, Ἀργογενῆ,
Ἀργολικόν, Ἰναχίδαν, Ἰνάχιον, as is also
the fact that βάντα suggests a mention of
'the place whence.' Ἀπιόθεν (Ahrens)
would mean 'from Ἄπιος,' but we require
'from Ἀπία' sc. (γῆ, the Peloponnesus,
O. C. 1303 n.), *i.e.* Ἀπίαθεν: cp. Ὀλυμ-
πίαθεν. I had thought of **Ἰναχόθεν**,
which Mekler, too, has suggested, though
he has not supported it by argument. The points in its favour are:
(*a*) the order φῶτα βάντα can be kept:
(*b*) after 'Dircè's streams' in v. 105 a
reference to the Argive river would be
appropriate: (*c*) ἀργόθεν might have come
in either as a gloss, or a corruption of the
letters αχόθεν, if ιν had dropped out after
λεύκασπιν. But I hesitate to displace
Ἀργόθεν, esp. when a direct mention of
Argos here so naturally corresponds with
the direct mention of Thebes in v. 101.

107 ff. πανσαγίᾳ (only here) = παν-
οπλίᾳ, modal dat. σάγη (for accent, cp.
Chandler § 72) = 'what one carries,' and
so, generally, 'equipment' (Aesch. *Cho.*
560 ξένῳ γὰρ εἰκώς, παντελῆ σάγην ἔχων),
or, specially, *body-armour:* Aesch. *Pers.*
240 ἔγχη σταδαῖα καὶ φεράσπιδες σάγαι
(opp. to the *light* equipment of the
τοξότης).—**φυγάδα πρ.**, proleptic, with
κινήσασα, 'having stirred to flight,'
etc. cp. *O. C.* 1292 ἐξελήλαμαι φυγάς.
πρόδρομον, 'running *forward,' i.e.* 'in
headlong haste': Aesch. *Th.* 211 ἐπὶ
δαιμόνων πρόδρομος ἦλθον ἀρ|χαῖα βρέτη.
In prose, always of *precursors* (as heralds,
or an advanced guard).—**ὀξυτέρῳ...χα-
λινῷ**, 'in swifter career,' dat. of manner
with φυγάδα πρόδρομον. Cp. *O. C.* 1067
(where the Attic horsemen are described
rushing in pursuit of the Thebans), πᾶς
γὰρ ἀστράπτει χαλινός, 'the steel of
every bridle flashes,'—as they gallop on
with slack reins. So here, the χαλινός,
which glitters as the horse rushes along,
is poetically identified with the career
itself, and thus is fitly joined with
ὀξύτερος. The phrase seems happy in
this context. The Argives began their
retreat in the darkness (16): when the
sun rises, the flashing steel of their bridles
shows them in headlong flight.—**ὀξυτέρῳ**
does not mean (1) 'in flight swifter than
their former approach'; nor (2) that the
reins are shaken ever faster on the
horses' necks. ὀξυτόρῳ (L) was a mere
blunder: it could only mean 'piercing'
(the horse's mouth), not, 'giving a sharp
sound,' when the reins are shaken.—Cp.
Aesch. *Th.* 122 (describing the Argive
besiegers) διάδετοι δέ τοι γενῦν ἱππιᾶν |
κινύρονται (μινύρονται L. Dind.) φόνον
χαλινοί. *Ib.* 152 ὄτοβον ἁρμάτων ἀμφὶ
πόλιν κλύω. Our passage suggests horsemen rather than drivers of war-chariots:
perh. the poet imagined both, as in *O. C.*
1062 πώλοισιν ἢ ῥιμφαρμάτοις | φεύγοντες
ἀμίλλαις.

σύστ. α΄. *ὃς ἐφ᾽ ἡμετέρᾳ γᾷ *Πολυνείκους   110
ἀρθεὶς νεικέων ἐξ ἀμφιλόγων
ὀξέα κλάζων
αἰετὸς εἰς γᾶν ὣς ὑπερέπτα,
λευκῆς χιόνος πτέρυγι στεγανός,
πολλῶν μεθ᾽ ὅπλων   115
ξύν θ᾽ ἱπποκόμοις κορύθεσσι.

ἀντ. α΄. στὰς δ᾽ ὑπὲρ μελάθρων, *φονώσαισιν ἀμφιχανὼν κύκλῳ
2 λόγχαις ἑπτάπυλον στόμα,

ὀξυτόνῳ or ὀξυντόμῳ: Nauck, ὀξυκρότῳ. **110 ff.** L has ὃν ἐφ᾽ ἡμετέρα (the first hand wrote ἡμερα, but added τέ above) γᾶι πολυνεικησ | ἀρθεὶσ νεικέων ἐξ ἀμφιλόγων | ὀξέα κλάζων αἰετὸσ εἰσ γᾶν | ὣσ (sic) ὑπερέπτα. All MSS. have accus. ὃν and nom. Πολυνείκης. Scaliger conject. ὃς...Πολυνείκους.—Dindorf gives γᾷ, γᾶν, ὑπερέπτη instead of the Doric forms. **112** Before ὀξέα κλάζων, Erfurdt conjecturally supplies ἐπόρευσε· θοῶς δ᾽: J. F. Martin, ὦρσεν· κεῖνος δ᾽: Pallis, ἤλασ᾽ ὁ δ᾽: Nauck, ἤγαγεν· ἐχθρὸς δ᾽,

110 f. The MSS. have ὃν...Πολυνείκης. If this were sound, it would be necessary to suppose that after ἀμφιλόγων a dipodia has been lost, such as Nauck supplies by <ἤγαγεν· ἐχθρὸς δ᾽> ὀξέα κλάζων. For (1) a verb is wanted to govern ὃν, and (2) the description of the eagle, beginning with ὀξέα κλάζων, clearly refers to the Argive host, not to Polyneices only. But if, with Scaliger, we read ὃς ...Πολυνείκους, no such loss need be assumed. The correspondence between anapaestic systems is not always strict, and the monometer ὀξέα κλάζων could stand here, though the anti-system has a dimeter in the same place (129). The MS. reading ὃν ...Πολυνείκης probably arose from a misunderstanding of the scholium:—ὅντινα στρατὸν Ἀργείων, ἐξ ἀμφιλόγων νεικέων ἀρθείς, ἤγαγεν ὁ Πολυνείκης, οἷον ἀμφιλογίᾳ χρησάμενος πρὸς τὸν ἀδελφόν· διὰ βραχέων δὲ εἶπεν αὐτό, ὡς γνωρίμου οὔσης τῆς ὑποθέσεως. The Schol. wrote ἀρθείς, to agree with Πολυνείκης, and not ἀρθέντα, to agree with στρατόν, because it suited the form of his paraphrase, οἷον ἀμφιλογίᾳ χρησάμενος πρὸς τὸν ἀδελφόν. By διὰ βραχέων δὲ εἶπεν αὐτό, the Schol. meant not merely the indefiniteness of νεικέων ἐξ ἀμφιλόγων, but also the compactness of Πολυνείκους | ἀρθεὶς ἐκ νεικέων for ὅντινα στρατὸν ἤγαγεν ὁ Πολυνείκης. But a transcriber, noticing that the Schol. joined ἀρθείς with Πολυνείκης, might easily infer that ὃν...Πολυνείκης ought to stand in the text, and might take διὰ βραχέων

as meaning that the verb ἤγαγε could be understood.—L has the Doric γᾷ, and presently γᾶν, ὑπερέπτα, which I keep: see Appendix.

Πολυνείκους...νεικέων, playing on the name, like Aesch. (*Th.* 577, 658, 829): as elsewhere on that of Ajax (*Ai.* 432 αἰάζειν), and of Odysseus (fr. 877, πολλοὶ γὰρ ὠδύσαντο δυσμενεῖς ἐμοί, have been bitter).—**ἀρθείς,** 'having set forth': so Her. 1. 165 ἀερθέντες ἐκ τῶν Οἰνουσσέων ἔπλεον· 9. 52 (of a land-force) ἀερθέντες ...ἀπαλλάσσοντο. Attic prose similarly uses the act. ἄρας, either absolutely, or with dat. (ταῖς ναυσί, τῷ στρατῷ), or, more rarely, with acc. (τὰς ναῦς Thuc. 1. 52). Here the choice of the word suits the image of an eagle soaring.—νεικ. ἐξ ἀμφιλόγων, lit. in consequence of contentious quarrels, *i.e.* his claims to the Theban throne, against his brother Eteocles. Eur. *Med.* 636 ἀμφιλόγους ὀργὰς (contentious moods) ἀκόρεστά τε νείκη: *Ph.* 500 ἀμφίλεκτος...ἔρις. The prep. as *O. C.* 620 ἐκ σμικροῦ λόγου.

112 f. ὀξέα κλάζων: Homeric, *Il.* 17. 88 (of Hector) ὀξέα κεκληγώς: *Il.* 16. 429 μεγάλα κλάζοντε (of vultures fighting): so Aesch. *Ag.* 48 (the Atreidae) μέγαν ἐκ θυμοῦ κλάζοντες "Ἄρη.—αἰετὸς εἰς γᾶν ὣς ὑπερέπτα seems clearly right. If ὣς is omitted, we have a metaphor instead of a simile, with harsh effect. If we read αἰετὸς ὣς, and omit εἰς, γᾶν ὑπερέπτα could mean only, 'flew over the land,' not, 'flew over the border into the land.' Further, it is better that the flow of these

OEDIPUS

— PA 4414.07 Y68

1991

MEDEA PA 3973.M4

1938

— ANTIGONA
PA 4414.A7 T6

1962

03/27/2019

who set forth against our land by reason of the vexed claims of
Polyneices; and, like shrill-screaming eagle, he flew over into
our land, in snow-white pinion sheathed, with an armèd throng,
and with plumage of helms.

1st anapaestic system.

He paused above our dwellings; he ravened around our
sevenfold portals with spears athirst for blood;

1st antistrophe.

---

or ἤγαγε· κεῖνος δ'. **113** εἰς γᾶν ὥς] ὥς is omitted by Hermann : εἰς by Blaydes,
who places ὥς before γᾶν. **117** στὰς] πτὰς K. L. Struve, Nauck (referring to
Lobeck *Phryn.* p. 255).—φονίαισιν MSS. : Schol. ταῖς τῶν φόνων ἐρώσαις λόγχαις,
whence Bothe and Boeckh restored φονώσαισιν. In such a MS. as L, where φονί|αισιν
is thus divided between two verses, the corruption would have been easy. **119** λόγ-
χαις] χηλαῖς Blaydes.—ἐπτάπυλον] ἑπταπύλῳ Semitelos.—στόμα] πόλισμ' Nauck.

---

descriptive verses should not be broken
by a paroemiac before v. 116. No argument either way can be founded on
v. 130 (where see n.), since, even if it
were a paroemiac, that would not require
a paroemiac here.—ὑπερέπτα. The act.
strong aor. ἔπτην (as if from ἵπτημι) occurs
simple only in the *Batrachomyomachia*
(210, if sound) and the Anthol.: compounded, only in the tragic lyrics and in
late prose. Cp. 1307.
114 ff. λευκῆς χιόνος πτ., 'a wing
white as snow' (the white shield, see on
106); genitive of quality (or material),
equiv. to an epithet : cp. *O. T.* 533 τόλμης
πρόσωπον (a bold front); *El.* 19 ἄστρων
εὐφρόνη (starry night): Eur. *Ph.* 1491
στολίδα...τρυφᾶς (a luxurious robe): *ib.*
1526 γάλακτος...μαστοῖς (milky breasts).
—στεγανός, pass. here, 'covered'; but
act. in Aesch. *Ag.* 358 στεγανὸν δίκτυον :
cp. Xen. *Cyr.* 7. 1. 33 αἱ ἀσπίδες...στεγά-
ζουσι τὰ σώματα.—ὅπλων...κορύθεσσι.
The image of the eagle with white wings,
which suited the Argive *descent* on Thebes,
here passes into direct description of an
invader who comes with many ὅπλα and
κόρυθες,—the shield, spear, and helmet
of heavy-armed troops. For the dat. in
-εσσι cp. 976 χείρεσσι. ἱπποκόμοις, 'with
horse-hair crest' (*Il.* 13. 132 ἱ. κόρυθες).
For ξύν denoting what one wears or
carries, cp. *O. T.* 207, *O. C.* 1258, *Ai.* 30
πηδῶντα πεδία ξὺν νεορράντῳ ξίφει. There
is no real difference here between μετά
and ξύν : Donaldson refines too much in
suggesting that μετά means merely 'by
their sides,' while ξύν 'denotes a closer
union' (*i.e.* 'on their heads').
117 ff. In στὰς δ' ὑπὲρ μελάθρων
there is a momentary return to the image
of the flying eagle,—'having stayed his

flight above my dwellings,'—before swooping. The words do not mean that the
Argive army was posted on hills around
Thebes : the only hills available were to
the N. of the town. The Ἰσμήνιος λόφος
(Paus. 9. 10. 2), on which Donaldson
places the Argives, was merely a low
eminence close to one of the city gates.
Thebes stood on a low spur of ground
projecting southward, and overlooking the
plain. Sophocles has elsewhere described
the Argive besiegers, with topographical
correctness, as having 'set their leaguer
round the plain of Thebes' (*O. C.* 1312 τὸ
Θήβης πεδίον ἀμφεστᾶσι πᾶν). Struve's
πτάς (a participle not found elsewhere
except in composition with a preposi-
tion) seems improbable, and also less
forcible.
The words φονώσαισιν ἀμφιχανὼν...
λόγχαις once more merge the image of
the eagle,—as at v. 115,—in literal description of a besieging army, save in so
far as the figurative ἀμφιχανὼν suggests
a monster opening its jaws. The word
was perh. suggested by *Il.* 23. 79 ἐμὲ
μὲν κὴρ | ἀμφέχανε στυγερή (hath gaped
for me—*i.e.* 'devoured me'). These
transitions from clear imagery to language in which the figure is blurred by
the thought of the object for which it
stands, are thoroughly Sophoclean : cp. n.
on *O. T.* 866.—φονώσαισιν : the word is
not rare in later writers, but in classical
Greek occurs only here and *Ph.* 1209
φονᾷ, φονᾷ νόος ἤδη. Cp. τομάω (*Ai.* 582).
—ἑπτάπυλον στόμα, prop. the access
afforded by seven gates : fr. 701 Θήβας
λέγεις μοι τὰς πύλας ἑπταστόμους (seven-
mouthed as to its gates). Nauck changes
στόμα to πόλισμ' to avoid hiatus : but cp.
O. T. 1202 βασιλεὺς καλεῖ | ἐμός, n.

3 ἔβα, πρίν ποθ' ἁμετέρων   120
4 αἱμάτων γένυσιν πλησθῆναί τε καὶ στεφάνωμα πύργων
5 πευκάενθ' Ἥφαιστον ἑλεῖν. τοῖος ἀμφὶ νῶτ' ἐτάθη
6 πάταγος Ἄρεος, ἀντιπάλῳ δυσχείρωμα δράκοντος. 126

σύστ. β'. Ζεὺς γὰρ μεγάλης γλώσσης κόμπους
ὑπερεχθαίρει, καί σφας ἐσιδὼν
πολλῷ ῥεύματι προσνισσομένους,
χρυσοῦ καναχῆς *ὑεροπλίαις,   130

122 πλησθῆναι καὶ MSS. A short syllable is wanting before καί, since the corresponding strophic words are Διρκαίων ὑπὲρ (v. 105). For καί, Triclinius gives τε καί: Blaydes νιν ἢ (suggesting also σφε καί, γε or τι καί, and τό τε). Supposing the syllable to be common, Wolff writes καὶ πρίν: while, keeping the simple καί, Boeckh changes πλησθῆναι to ἐμπλησθῆναι, and Semitelos to πληρωθῆναι. Naber's γένυιν (for γένυσιν) ἐμπλησθῆναι καί still leaves a syllable wanting. 125 f. ἀντιπάλωι—δράκοντι L, with ου written above ωι, and οσ above ι, by an early hand. I read ἀντιπάλῳ—δράκοντος. One of the later MSS. (V, 13th or 14th cent.) has ἀντιπάλω—δράκοντος, but prob. by accident: the rest agree with L, some (as A) having the correction, ου—οσ, written above.—δυσχεί-

120 ff. ἔβα, emphatic by place: cp. 46.—πρὶν ποθ', 'or ever,' as Tr. 17.—αἱμάτων, streams of blood, as Aesch. Ag. 1293 αἱμάτων εὐθηνσίμων | ἀπορρυέντων (with ref. to one person). Soph. has the plur. only here: Aesch. and Eur. use it several times each, either in this sense, or as = 'deeds of bloodshed' (once as = 'slain persons,' αἵματα σύγγονα, Eur. Ph. 1503).—γένυσιν might be locative dat., 'in'; but seems rather instrumental, 'with.' After πλησθῆναι the missing short syllable is best supplied by τε (Triclinius). The constr. is, πρὶν (αὐτός) τε πλησθῆναι, καὶ Ἥφαιστον στεφάνωμα πύργων ἑλεῖν. For τε irregularly placed, cp. O. T. 258 n.—στεφάνωμα: Hec. 910 (of Troy) ἀπὸ δὲ στεφάναν κέκαρσαι | πύργων: cp. n. on O. C. 15.—πευκάενθ' Ἥφαιστον, the flame of pine-wood torches (Verg. Aen. 11. 786 pineus ardor). Cp. 1007, Il. 2. 426 σπλάγχνα δ' ἄρ' ἀμπείραντες ὑπείρεχον Ἡφαίστοιο.

124 ff. τοῖος, introducing the reason; O. C. 947 n.—ἐτάθη, lit. 'was made intense,' here suggesting both loud sound and keen strife. Cp. Il. 12. 436 ἐπὶ ἶσα μάχη τέτατο πτόλεμός τε: 23. 375 ἵπποισι τάθη δρόμος: Aesch. Pers. 574 τείνε δὲ δυσβάϋκτον | βοᾶτιν τάλαιναν αὐδάν.—πάταγος, clatter of arms (a word expressive of the sound), as distinguished from βοή, a human cry; cp. Her. 7. 211 οἱ δὲ βάρβαροι ὀρέοντες φεύγοντας βοῇ τε καὶ πατάγῳ ἐπήϊσαν. The Argives began to

retreat in the night: at dawn, the Thebans made a sally in pursuit of them, and turned the retreat into a rout.

ἀντιπάλῳ δυσχείρωμα δράκοντος, a thing hard to vanquish for him who was struggling against the (Theban) dragon, —i.e. for the Argive eagle. The two readings between which the MSS. fluctuate, viz., ἀντιπάλῳ ... δράκοντι and ἀντιπάλου...δράκοντος, arose, I feel sure, from ἀντιπάλῳ...δράκοντος (V has ἀντιπάλω...δράκοντος). For the gen. after this adj., cp. Pind. O. 8. 94 μένος γήραος ἀντίπαλον, a spirit that wrestles with old age: Eur. Alc. 922 ὑμεναίων γόος ἀντίπαλος, wails contending with marriage-songs.

The interpretation of the passage turns primarily on two points.

(1) The δράκων certainly means the Thebans,—the σπαρτοί (O. C. 1534) sprung from the dragon's teeth sown by Cadmus, and thence called δρακοντογενεῖς (schol.), Ovid's anguigenae (Met. 3. 531): cp. 1125 ἐπὶ σπορᾷ δράκοντος. Poetry often represented a struggle between an eagle and a dragon or snake (δράκων could mean either, the 'dragon' being conceived as a sort of huge python); as Il. 12. 201, Hor. Od. 4. 4. 11.

(2) The δυσ in δυσχείρωμα must refer to difficulty experienced by the vanquished Argives, not by the victorious Thebans. The word must mean, then, 'a thing hard to overcome,' not, 'a victory won with diffi-

but he went hence, or ever his jaws were glutted with our gore,
or the Fire-god's pine-fed flame had seized our crown of towers.
So fierce was the noise of battle raised behind him, a thing too
hard for him to conquer, as he wrestled with his dragon foe.

For Zeus utterly abhors the boasts of a proud tongue; and
when he beheld them coming on in a great stream, in the haughty
pride of clanging gold, *2nd ana- paestic system.*

ρωμα] Keeping ἀντιπάλῳ—δράκοντι, Blaydes conject. δυσχείρωτα: M. Schmidt, δοὺς
χείρωμα. Reading ἀντιπάλου . . δράκοντος, Herwerden conject. συσπείραμα, Gleditsch
τε σπείραμα. **128** εἰσιδὼν L, ἐσιδὼν Γ: ἐπιδὼν conject. Nauck. **129** πολλῷ
ῥεύματι] ῥεύματι πολλῷ Blaydes.—προσνισσομένους L (the fut. part., cp. Eusth. 1288.
56): προσνισσομένους Γ. **130** χρυσοῦ καναχῆσ ὑπεροπτίασ L (with ὑπερόπτας
written above by an early hand): ὑπεροπτείας and ὑπερόπτα Γ. Dorville conject. ὑπερο-
πλίας: Vauvilliers, ὑπεροπλίαις, which is now received by several edd.—Other conjectures are: Emper, καναχῇ θ᾽ ὑπερόπτας (others, καναχῆς with ὑπερόπτας or -ης, or
ὑπέροπτα as adv.): Donaldson, καναχῇ θ᾽ ὑπερόπλους: Boeckh, καναχῆς ὑπεροπτείαις:

culty.' So δυσχείρωτος is 'hard to subdue'
(Her. 7. 9), as ἀχείρωτος is 'unsubdued'
(Thuc. 6. 10), and εὐχείρωτος 'easy to subdue' (Xen. *Hellen.* 5. 3. 4). Cp. δυσπάλαι-
στος, δυσπάλαμος, δύσμαχος, etc., used with
poetical irony to express the irresistible.
In *O. T.* 560 θανάσιμον χείρωμα is a deed
of deadly violence: in Aesch. *Th.* 1022
τυμβοχόα χειρώματα are works of the
hand in mound-making. In itself, δυσχείρωμα might mean 'a thing achieved
with difficulty'; but here the irony is
clearly pointed against the routed Argives:
the poet does not mean that the Thebans
won with difficulty. Thus δυσχείρωμα is
here the opposite of what Aesch. calls
εὐμαρὲς χείρωμα, a thing easily subdued: *Ag.* 1326 δούλης θανούσης, εὐμα-
ροῦς χειρώματος. The Theban πάταγος
Ἄρεος was a thing which the Argives
could not overcome.

Those who read ἀντιπάλῳ...δράκοντι
explain either (*a*) 'a hard-won victory for
the dragon foe': but this gives a wrong
sense to δυσχείρωμα: or (*b*) join the dat.
with ἐτάθη: 'a din was raised by the
dragon foe (cp. *Il.* 22. 55 Ἀχιλῆϊ δαμασ-
θείς), a thing hard (*for the Argive*) to
subdue.' But δυσχείρωμα, placed as it
is, cannot be thus dissociated from the
dat. ἀντιπ. δράκοντι and mentally referred to another dat. which is left to be
understood.

Those who read ἀντιπάλου...δράκοντος
understand (*a*) a thing *on the part of*
the dragon foe which was hard (for the
Argive) to overcome; *i.e.* 'an irresistible
onset of the dragon foe.' But such a

construction of δυσχείρωμα with the gen.
seems impossible, esp. when there is no
dat. to help it out. Or (*b*) 'a hard-won
victory of the dragon foe'; which gives
a wrong sense to δυσχείρωμα.—The form
of the word is in one respect unique.
Every similar neuter noun compounded
with δυσ is from a verb so compounded:
as δυσέργημα, δυσημέρημα, δυσπράγημα,
δυσσέβημα, δυστύχημα, δυσφήμημα, δυσ-
χέρασμα, δυσχρήστημα, δυσώπημα. But
there is no such verb as δυσχειρόω, 'to
subdue with difficulty.' The noun has
been boldly coined to express δυσχείρωτον
πρᾶγμα.

127 ff. μεγάλης: 1350 μεγάλοι...
λόγοι: Plato *Phaed.* 95 B μὴ μέγα λέγε:
Verg. *Aen.* 10. 547 *Dixerat ille aliquid
magnum.*—ῥεύματι: Aesch. *Pers.* 88
μεγάλῳ ῥεύματι φωτῶν (so *ib.* 412 ῥεῦμα
Περσικοῦ στρατοῦ). Eur. *I. T.* 1437 παύ-
σαι διώκων ῥεῦμά τ᾽ ἐξορμῶν στρατοῦ. The
transposition ῥεύματι πολλῷ is unnecessary. In the same dipodia an anapaest
must not precede a dactyl, nor a dactyl
an anapaest; but a spondee can be followed by a dactyl, as *O. C.* 146 δηλῶ δ᾽.
οὐ γὰρ ἂν ᾠδ᾽ ἀλλοτρίοις.

130 χρυσοῦ καναχῆς ὑπεροπλίαις, 'in
the haughty pride of clanging gold.'
ὑπεροπλίαις seems a certain correction of
ὑπεροπτίας (see cr. n.), and has justly
won its way with recent edd. The word
is fitting, since ὑπεροπλία is prop. 'overweening confidence in arms'; and Soph.
has used the epic plur. with the epic ῑ,
Il. 1. 205 ἧς ὑπεροπλίῃσι: so too Theocr.
ῑ, 25. 138 σθένεϊ ᾧ | ἠδ᾽ ὑπεροπλίῃ Φαέθων

παλτῷ ῥιπτεῖ πυρὶ βαλβίδων
ἐπ' ἄκρων ἤδη
νίκην ὁρμῶντ' ἀλαλάξαι.

στρ. β'. ἀντιτύπᾳ δ' ἐπὶ γᾷ πέσε τανταλωθεὶς
2 πυρφόρος, ὃς τότε μαινομένᾳ ξὺν ὁρμᾷ   135
3 βακχεύων ἐπέπνει
4 ῥιπαῖς ἐχθίστων ἀνέμων.
5 εἶχε δ' ἄλλα τὰ μέν,
6 ἄλλα δ' ἐπ' ἄλλοις ἐπενώμα στυφελίζων μέγας Ἄρης

Hartung, καναχῆς ὑπερηφανίαις. **134** ἀντίτυπα L, which a later hand wished to make into ἀντιτύπως (not ἀντίτυπος, as the accent shows). The later MSS. read with L, except those which have the conject. of Triclinius, ἀντίτυπος. Porson restored ἀντιτύπᾳ. Bergk and Wieseler conject. ἀντιτυπὰς (cp. ἐντυπὰς). **138** εἶχε δ' ἄλλαι τὰ μὲν ἄλλαι τὰ δ' ἐπ' ἄλλοισ | L. The first hand wrote ἄλλα—ἄλλα: the first corrector added ι to each. The word μὲν is represented by μ in an erasure, with < above it.

μέγας. In post-Homeric poetry ὑπέρ-οπλος is a freq. epith. of overweening strength (ἠνορέη, βίη, ἥβη, etc.).—Other readings are:—(1) χρυσοῦ καναχῇ θ' ὑπερόπτας, 'and haughty in the clang of gold.' This involves an improbable change; the subst. ὑπερόπτης, too, is unsuitable here, and cannot be defended by Theocr. 22. 58 πρὸς πάντα παλίγκοτος ἠδ' ὑπερόπτης. Wecklein, reading ὑπερόπτας, keeps καναχῆς in the sense, 'hoffärtig auf': but a genit. after ὑπερόπτης could not denote that in which one takes pride. (2) χρυσοῦ καναχῆς ὑπερόπτης, or -όπτα, i.e., 'Zeus, a despiser of the clang of gold.' (3) χρυσοῦ καναχῆς ὑπερόπτα, adv. neut. plur. (as O. T. 883), 'advancing haughtily in a great stream of clanging gold.' But the adv. comes weakly at the end, and χρυσοῦ κ. is harshly joined with π. ῥεύματι.—Aesch., too, gives prominence to gold in picturing the Argive chiefs: Capaneus has golden letters on his shield (Th. 434), Polyneices has the image of a warrior in golden armour, with a golden legend (644, 660).—**κανα-χῆς**, of metal, as Il. 16. 105 πήληξ βαλλομένη καναχὴν ἔχε.

131 ff. παλτῷ πυρί, i.e. with the thunderbolt which Zeus brandishes in his hand before hurling it: Ar. Av. 1714 πάλ-λων κεραυνόν, πτεροφόρον Διὸς βέλος.—**βαλβῖδων ἐπ' ἄκρων**, at his topmost goal, i.e. at his goal on the top of our walls. ἄκρων might mean merely 'uttermost,' but is rather associated in the poet's mind with the object meant by

βαλβῖδων. In Eur. Ph. 1180 Capaneus is struck by Zeus at the moment that he is surmounting the γεῖσα τειχέων, the coping of the walls. The βαλβῖδες were the posts, to which a rope was attached, marking the point from which runners in the double foot-race (δίαυλος) set out, and to which they returned: hence both starting-point and goal.—**ὁρμῶντα**: for the partic. as subst., without either art. or τις, cp. El. 697 δύναιτ' ἂν οὐδ' ἂν ἰσχύων φυγεῖν: Plat. Gorg. 498 A ΚΑΛ. εἶδον. ΣΩ. τί δέ; νοῦν ἔχοντα λυπούμενον καὶ χαίροντα; The name of Capaneus could be left unmentioned, since the story was so famous. No leader of the Argive host, except Polyneices, is named in this play. The attack of Capaneus was said to have been made at the Ἠλέκτραι πύλαι on the s. side of Thebes (Aesch. Th. 423, Paus. 9. 9. 8). His fall from the scaling-ladder, as the lightning struck him, was often represented in art.—**νίκην**, cogn. acc. with **ἀλαλάξαι**, to raise the cry ἀλαλαί for victory: Ar. Av. 1763 ἀλαλαί, ἰὴ παιήων, | τήνελλα καλλίνικος.

134 ἀντιτύπᾳ, restored by Porson (Adv. p. 169) for ἀντίτυπα, is certainly right. Adjectives in os, compounded with a prep., are oft. of three terminations in epic poetry, as ἀμφιέλισσα, ἀμφιρύτη, ἀντιθέη (Od. 13. 378), ἀμφιβρότη (Il. 2. 389), ὑποδεξίη (Il. 9. 73), etc. The dramatists could admit some such forms, esp. in lyrics; thus they have ἡ ἐναλία as well as ἡ ἐνάλιος, ἡ ἐννυχία as well as ἡ ἐννύχιος.

he smote with brandished fire one who was now hasting to shout victory at his goal upon our ramparts.

Swung down, he fell on the earth with a crash, torch in hand, he who so lately, in the frenzy of the mad onset, was raging against us with the blasts of his tempestuous hate. But those threats fared not as he hoped; and to other foes the mighty War-god dispensed their several dooms, dealing havoc around, *2nd strophe.*

The scribe had written τὰ δ' ἄλλα (his eye running on to τὰ δ' ἄλλοις): then, on perceiving the error, he deleted δ', but, in the narrow space between τὰ and ἄλλα, could not write μὲν at full length. With regard to the last word of the v., Campbell thinks that the first hand wrote ἄλλουσ, and that the corrector made this into ἄλλοισ: but I doubt whether the ι was ever υ.—The only noteworthy variation in the later MSS. is that, instead of L's second ἄλλαι, V has δεινὰ, prob. a grammarian's conjecture.—For

---

As regards the sense, ἀντίτυπος was regularly used of hard surfaces, which, as it were, *repel* that which strikes them (for the accent ἀντίτυπος, not ἀντιτύπος, though the sense is act., see on *O. T.* 460). Arist. *Probl.* 5. 40 οἱ...ἐν ἀντιτύποις περίπατοι. Lucian *Amor.* 13 τὴν ἀντίτυπον οὕτω καὶ καρτερὰν τοῦ λίθου φύσιν. So, fig., Plat. *Crat.* 420 D τὸ...ἀναγκαῖον καὶ ἀντίτυπον, what is necessary, and what *resists* us.— **τανταλωθείς**, 'swung,' that is, sent flying through the air from the edge of the wall on which he was just setting foot. The word expresses the force with which the thunderbolt struck him, just as ἀντιτύπᾳ expresses the crash when he struck earth. This form of the verb occurs only here. Arist. uses both ταλαντεύομαι (pass.) and ταλαντεύω (act. intr.) as 'to sway to and fro.' The Schol., explaining by διασεισθείς (i.e. 'with a rude shock,' which is substantially right) quotes Anacreon 78 [ἐν] μελαμφύλλῳ δάφνᾳ χλωρᾷ τ' ἐλαίᾳ τανταλίζει (where the subject was perh. a god, or the wind).

135 ff. πυρφόρος, 'torch in hand': so of Prometheus (*O. C.* 55, where see n.) and Artemis (*O. T.* 207). Aesch. *Th.* 433 φλέγει δὲ λαμπὰς διὰ χερῶν ὡπλισμένη | χρυσοῖς δὲ φωνεῖ γράμμασιν, πρήσω πόλιν.—**βακχεύων**: so oft. Eur. as *H. F.* 898 Λύσσα βακχεύσει: but this is the only place where Soph. connects *evil* frenzy with the name of a god whom this same Ode invokes (154). — **ῥιπαῖς...ἀνέμων.** Capaneus, breathing fury and slaughter, is likened to a deadly tempest. For ῥιπαί, 'blasts,' cp. 929 and *O. C.* 1248 n. So Aesch. *Th.* 63 πρὶν καταιγίσαι πνοὰς | Ἄρεως.

138 ff. εἶχε δ' ἄλλᾳ τὰ μέν, 'but

those things indeed' (the threats of Capaneus) 'went otherwise' (than he had expected): ἄλλα δ' ἐπ' ἄλλοις μέγας Ἄρης ἐπενώμα, 'while to others great Ares assigned various dooms,' etc. The poet has described how *Zeus* smote the most formidable foe. As to the other Argive chiefs, he briefly adds that *Ares* struck them down by various deaths: *i.e.* they perished, not by a stroke from heaven, but in the course of battle. In L's reading, εἶχε δ' ἄλλαι τὰ μὲν ἄλλαι τὰ δ' ἐπ' ἄλλοις, one cause of corruption has evidently been a confusion between alternative modes of expressing 'some' and 'other,' viz. (1) by doubled ἄλλος, (2) by τὰ μέν, τὰ δέ. It is in favour of our reading (Erfurdt's) that it helps to account for it, since it supposes that τὰ μέν was answered by ἄλλα δέ. Cp. *O. C.* 1671 οὐ τὸ μέν, ἄλλο δὲ μή: *Il.* 6. 147 τὰ μέν τ' ἄνεμος χαμάδις χέει, ἄλλα δέ θ' ὕλη | τηλεθόωσα φύει. It is immaterial that, here, τὰ μέν means, not, '*some* things,' but, '*those* things'; since the latter is its first sense also where we render it by 'some.' Further, with regard to ἄλλᾳ, remark that this form of adverb is used elsewhere also in ref. to the course ordained by *gods or fate:* *O. C.* 1443 ταῦτα δ' ἐν τῷ δαίμονι, | καὶ τῇδε φῦναι χἀτέρᾳ: Aesch. *P. V.* 511 οὐ ταῦτα ταύτῃ μοῖρά πω τελεσφόρος | κρᾶναι πέπρωται. For other proposed readings, see Appendix. — **ἐπενώμα:** Aesch. *Eum.* 310 λάχη τὰ κατ' ἀνθρώπους | ὡς ἐπινωμᾷ στάσις ἁμά, apportions.— **στυφελίζων** (στύφελός, 'firm,' στύφω, to compress), 'striking heavily': *Il.* 1. 581 ἐξ ἑδέων στυφελίξαι.

3—2

7 δεξιόσειρος.　　　　　　　　　　　　　140

συστ. γ'. ἑπτὰ λοχαγοὶ γὰρ ἐφ' ἑπτὰ πύλαις
ταχθέντες ἴσοι πρὸς ἴσους ἔλιπον
Ζηνὶ τροπαίῳ πάγχαλκα τέλη,
πλὴν τοῖν στυγεροῖν, ὣ πατρὸς ἑνὸς
μητρός τε μιᾶς φύντε καθ' αὑτοῖν　　　　　　145
δικρατεῖς λόγχας στήσαντ' ἔχετον
κοινοῦ θανάτου μέρος ἄμφω.

ἀντ. β'. ἀλλὰ γὰρ ἁ μεγαλώνυμος ἦλθε Νίκα

emendations, see Appendix.　　**140** In L the first σ of δεξιόσειροσ has been altered
from χ either by the first hand itself or by the first corrector.　The latter has written
in the right-hand margin, ὁ γενναῖος· οἱ γὰρ ἰσχυροὶ ἵπποι εἰς τὴν δεξιὰν σειρὰν ζεύγνυνται

δεξιόσειρος, 'right-hand trace-horse,'
here means a vigorous ally, who does
more than his own share of the work.
Ares has brought the Theban chariot vic-
toriously through the crisis of the race
against its Argive rival.　In the four-
horse chariot-race the four horses were
harnessed abreast: the two in the middle
were under the yoke (ζύγιοι), being called
ὁ μέσος δεξιός and ὁ μέσος ἀριστερός (schol.
Ar. *Nub.* 122): the two outside horses
drew in traces (σειραῖοι).　The chariot
went down the right-hand side of the
course, turned sharply from right to left
at the distance-post (καμπτήρ, νύσσα), and
came back down the left side.　Hence,
at the turning-point, the right-hand trace-
horse had most work to do; and the best
horse was put in that place.　Cp. *El.*
721 (at the turning-post) δεξιὸν τ' ἀνεὶς |
σειραῖον ἵππον εἶργε τὸν προσκείμενον.
Xen. *Symp.* 4. 6 ἁρματηλατοῦντα δεῖ ἐγγὺς
μὲν τῆς στήλης κάμψαι, quoting from *Il.*
23. 336 the precept τὸν δεξιὸν ἵππον |
κένσαι ὁμοκλήσαντ', εἶξαί τέ οἱ ἡνία χερσίν.
Cp. Aesch. *Ag.* 842 ζευχθεὶς ἕτοιμος ἦν
ἐμοὶ σειραφόρος (said by Agam. of Odysseus): and cp. *ib.* 1640.—The old *v. l.*
δεξιόχειρος, explained by the schol. γεν-
ναῖος καὶ παραδέξιος, is read by Musgrave,
Hartung, and A. Pallis.　Hartung renders it 'der Starke,'—understanding it as
'the strong and deft striker.'　Neither
δεξιόχειρος nor δεξιόχειρ seems to occur,
though ἀριστερόχειρ (left-handed) is found
in late Greek.
　141 ff. ἑπτὰ λοχαγοί. In *O. C.* 1313
ff. the list agrees with that of Aesch.,—

Amphiaraus, Tydeus, Eteoclus, Hippo-
medon, Capaneus, Parthenopaeus, Polyneices.　(Adrastus, who escaped, is not
counted as one of the seven.)　Capaneus,
though not slain by human hand, is included, since he was vanquished.　Amphiaraus, according to the legend which
Soph. recognises in *El.* 837, was swallowed up by the earth, but seems here to be
reckoned among those who fell in fight
(cp. n. on *O. C.* 1313).—**ἴσοι πρὸς ἴσους,**
instead of saying simply πρὸς ἑπτά,—a
common idiom: Eur. *Ph.* 750 ἴσους ἴσοισι
πολεμίοισιν ἀντιθείς: Her. 1. 2 ἴσα πρὸς
ἴσα: 9. 48 ἴσοι πρὸς ἴσους: Plat. *Legg.* 774C
ἴσα ἀντὶ ἴσων.
　Ζηνὶ τροπαίῳ, to Zeus who makes a
τροπή, or rout, of enemies.　Eur. *El.*
671 ὣ Ζεῦ πατρῷε καὶ τροπαῖ' ἐχθρῶν
ἐμῶν.　So he is invoked after a victory, *Her.* 867.　(In *Tr.* 303 ὣ Ζεῦ
τροπαῖε is usu. taken as = ἀποτρόπαιε,
'averting.')　In his relation to war, Zeus
was worshipped also as Ἀγήτωρ (esp. at
Sparta), Ἄρειος (at Olympia, etc.), Στρά-
τιος, Χρυσάωρ (in Caria), Στήσιος or Ἐπι-
στάσιος (the Roman *stator,* stayer of
flight).—**πάγχαλκα τέλη,** 'tributes of
panoplies,' as *Tr.* 238 Heracles dedicates
βωμοὺς τέλη τ' ἔγκαρπα Κηναίῳ Διΐ, i.e.
'dues of fruits,'—alluding to the τέμενος
of which the produce was given to the
god (*ib.* 754).　Not, (1) 'complete suits
of armour': nor (2) ὁπλιτικὰ τάγματα,
'troops of warriors,' as Eustath. took it
(p. 686. 16), led perh. by Aesch. *Pers.*
47 δίρρυμά τε καὶ τρίρρυμα τέλη.—It was
the ordinary practice to set up a τρό-

a mighty helper at our need.

For seven captains at seven gates, matched against seven, left the tribute of their panoplies to Zeus who turns the battle; save those two of cruel fate, who, born of one sire and one mother, set against each other their twain conquering spears, and are sharers in a common death. 3rd ana-
paestic
system.

But since Victory of glorious name hath come to us, 2nd
anti-
strophe.

τοῦ ἅρματος. Another schol., in the left-hand marg., has δεξιόχειρος in its lemma, and explains both readings. The later MSS. have δεξιόσειρος. Blaydes conject. δεξιόγυιος.

παιον (old Att. τροπαῖον) after a victory, on the spot where it had been won, or, in the case of a sea-fight, on the nearest land (Thuc. 2. 92). Such a trophy ordinarily consisted of shields, helmets, and weapons, conspicuously displayed on wooden supports, and dedicated, with an inscription, to a deity. Cp. Eur. *Ph.* 1473 (of the Thebans after the victory) οἱ μὲν Διὸς τροπαῖον ἵστασαν βρέτας (*i.e.* a wooden image of Zeus Τροπαῖος), | οἱ δ' ἀσπίδας συλῶντες Ἀργείων νεκρῶν | σκυλεύματ' εἴσω τειχέων ἐπέμπομεν. Part of the armour would be affixed to the walls of Theban temples (cp. Aesch. *Ag.* 577, *Th.* 276).

144 ff. πλὴν τ. στυγεροῖν, 'wretched' (as *Ph.* 166): not, 'hateful,' nor, 'filled with hate.' Of the seven Argive leaders, Polyneices was the only one who could not properly be said to have been vanquished, since he was not more vanquished than victorious. But, in excepting him, the poet associates him with the brother who was his victim as well as his conqueror. Thus ἑπτὰ...ἔλιπον..., πλὴν τοῖν στυγεροῖν, is a lax way of saying, 'defeat befell each of the seven Argive leaders, except *in the case of* the two brothers,'—in which an Argive leader and a Theban leader slew *each other.*— πατρός, etc., gen. of origin (38).—καθ' αὑτοῖν=κατ' ἀλλήλοιν. Cp. Dem. or. 40 § 29 ὧν ἂν ἐν αὐτοῖς διενεχθῶσι γυνὴ καὶ ἀνήρ. Plat. *Prot.* 347 D λέγοντάς τε καὶ ἀκούοντας ἐν μέρει ἑαυτῶν.—δικρατεῖς λόγχας, two spears, each of which was victorious over the wielder of the other. So *Ai.* 251 δικρατεῖς Ἀτρεῖδαι, two Atreidae, each of whom is a king. That is, δικρατεῖς is equiv. to two distinct epithets (δύο and κρατοῦσαι): cp. *O. C.* 1055 δι-

στόλους...ἀδελφάς, two journeying sisters: *ib.* 17 πυκνόπτεροι=many, and feathered (n.): see *O. T.* 846 n.—στήσαντε, having set in position, *levelled*, against each other. The Homeric δόρυ was chiefly a missile; here the λόγχη is used for thrusting.

148 f. ἀλλὰ γάρ, like ἀλλ' οὐ γάρ (*O. C.* 988 n.), can be used with or without an ellipse. Here there is no ellipse, since ἐπέλθωμεν follows (153), and γάρ, introducing the reason given by ἦλθε, = '*since.*' Below, 155, there is an ellipse, —'But (let us cease), for Creon comes'; where γάρ might be rendered '*indeed.*' —μεγαλώνυμος: schol. ἡ μεγάλην περιποιοῦσα δόξαν: the personified Nikè is 'of great name,' because victory is glorious.—πολυαρμάτῳ implies warlike renown, as well as wealth and splendour (cp. 845). Already in *Il.* 4. 391 the Cadmeans are 'urgers of horses' (κέντορες ἵππων): so *Scut. Herc.* 24 Βοιωτοὶ πλήξιπποι: Pindar *Ol.* 6. 85 has πλάξιππον...Θήβαν, *Isthm.* 7. 20 φιλαρμάτου πόλιος (as elsewhere χρυσάρματος, εὐάρματος). Critias, speaking of the inventions for which various cities were famous, says (fr. 1. 10) Θήβη δ' ἁρματόεντα δίφρον συνεπήξατο πρώτη.—ἀντιχαρεῖσα, with gladness responsive to that of Thebè. The goddess Nikè has come to meet the victors, and their joy is reflected in her radiant smile. (We can imagine her descending towards them from the sky, like the winged Nikè of Paeonius found at Olympia.) The doubts which have been felt as to ἀντιχαρεῖσα disappear if it is observed that χαρεῖσα here refers to the *outward manifestation* of joy, not merely to the feeling in the mind. Thus ἀντί expresses the *answer* of smile to

2 τᾷ πολυαρμάτῳ ἀντιχαρεῖσα Θήβᾳ,
3 ἐκ μὲν δὴ πολέμων   150
4 τῶν νῦν θέσθαι λησμοσύναν,
5 θεῶν δὲ ναοὺς χοροῖς
6 παννυχίοις πάντας ἐπέλθωμεν, ὁ Θήβας δ' ἐλελίχθων
7 Βάκχιος ἄρχοι.

ἀλλ' ὅδε γὰρ δὴ βασιλεὺς χώρας,   155
Κρέων ὁ Μενοικέως, ▭ – νεοχμὸς
νεαραῖσι θεῶν ἐπὶ συντυχίαις
χωρεῖ, τίνα δὴ μῆτιν ἐρέσσων,
ὅτι σύγκλητον τήνδε γερόντων   160
προύθετο λέσχην,

---

149 ἀντιχαρεῖσα] M. Schmidt conject. ἄρτι φανεῖσα, which Nauck adopts. Blaydes, ἄρτι χαρεῖσα. **151** θέσθε L. The second ε has been made either from ω (as Dübner thinks), or from αι (as Campbell). Almost all the later MSS. (including A) have θέσθε: but one (V) has θέσθαι, with ε written above. Hense conject. πᾶς νῦν θέσθω: Nauck, χρὴ νῦν θέσθαι.—λησμοσύνην L, -αν Brunck. **153** παννύχοισ L: παννυχίοις r.—

---

smile, as in ἀντιλάμπω of light to light, or in ἀντιφθέγγομαι of sound to sound. I do not take ἀντί here to mean *merely* 'over against,' as when Pind. *Ol.* 3. 19 says ἤδη γὰρ αὐτῷ... | ...ὀφθαλμὸν ἀντέφλεξε Μήνα, the (mid-month) moon showed the light of her eye over against him. —Not (1) ἴσον αὐτῇ χαρεῖσα (schol.), i.e. merely, 'rejoicing as Thebes does,' which extenuates ἀντιχαρεῖσα into συγχαρεῖσα. Nor (2) ἀντὶ τῶν κακῶν χαρεῖσα, i.e. rejoicing in requital of past troubles. **150 ff.** ἐκ...πολέμων τῶν νῦν, 'after the recent wars.' For ἐκ, cp. *Ph.* 271 ἐκ πολλοῦ σάλου | εὕδοντ', sleeping, after long tossing on the sea. For νῦν referring to the recent past (='just now'), cp. Dem. or. 18 § 13 ἡλίκα νῦν ἐτραγῴδει καὶ διεξῄει: Xen. *An.* 7. 1. 26 ἀναμνησθέντας τὰ νῦν ἤδη γεγενημένα (i.e. the events of the Peloponnesian war, which had ended four years before).—θέσθαι (L), as infin. for imperative (*O. C.* 481 n.), has a certain solemnity which seems to make it better here than θέσθε, though the latter is not excluded by ἐπέλθωμεν. The last syll. of θέσθαι answers to the second of ἐχθίστων in 137; each is an 'irrational' syllable (– for ⏑): see Metr. Anal.—θεῶν, monosyll. by synizesis (*O. C.* 964 n.).— παννυχίοις, since a παννυχίς was esp. grateful to the city's tutelar god Dionysus (1147), whose rites are νύκτωρ τὰ πολλά

(Eur. *Bacch.* 486).—ὁ Θήβας (gen. sing.) ἐλελίχθων, = ὁ τὴν Θήβης χθόνα ἐλελίζων, shaking the ground of Thebes (with his dances): for the objective gen., cp. *O. C.* 333 λόγων αὐτάγγελος.—Βάκχιος = Βάκχος, as Eur. *Bacch.* 225 τὴν δ' Ἀφροδίτην πρόσθ' ἄγειν τοῦ Βακχίου, and oft.—ἄρχοι sc. τῆς χορείας (schol.). Cp. 1146. **155 ff.** ἀλλά...γάρ: see on 148.— Κρέων, monosyll. by synizesis, as πλέων *Od.* 1. 183; in Aesch. *Ag.* 1493 ἐκπνέων is a spondee. Cp. *O. C.* 1073 Ῥέας, a monosyll.—Μενοικέως, = ⏑–⏑–, as *O. C.* 1003 Θησέως (––), and so oft.—νεοχμὸς νεαραῖσι. Neither adj. is suspicious; *new* events have made a *new* ruler; and the doubled adj. is quite in the poet's manner. Cp. 1266 νέος νέῳ ξὺν μόρῳ: *Ai.* 735 νέας | βουλὰς νέοισιν ἐγκαταζεύξας τρόποις: *O. C.* 475 οἰός...νεαρᾶς νεοπόκῳ μαλλῷ: *ib.* 1259 γέρων γέροντι συγκατῴκηκεν πίνος: *Tr.* 613 καινῷ καινὸν ἐν πεπλώματι, etc. Though νεαρός usu. = 'young,' it occurs also in the sense of 'novel,' as in Pindar's νεαρὰ ἐξευρεῖν (*N.* 8. 20). Three views of the metre have been taken. (1) That v. 156 should be enlarged to a dimeter by supplying one anapaest or its equivalent. (2) That v. 156 should be reduced to a monometer by omitting νεοχμὸς or Μενοικέως. (3) That both v. 156 and v. 160 should be made dimeters by supplying three anapaests or

ΑΝΤΙΓΟΝΗ

with joy responsive to the joy of Thebè whose chariots are many,
let us enjoy forgetfulness after the late wars, and visit all the
temples of the gods with night-long dance and song; and may
Bacchus be our leader, whose dancing shakes the land of Thebè.

But lo, the king of the land comes yonder, Creon, son of
Menoeceus, our new ruler by the new fortunes that the gods
have given; what counsel is he pondering, that he hath proposed this special conference of elders,

ἐλελίζων L, with γρ. ἐλελίχθων written above by S: ἐλελίχθων r. The Aldine has
ἐλελίζων, which Heath, Vauvilliers, and Brunck preferred: but nearly all later edd.
read ἐλελίχθων. Musgrave conject. ἐλελιχθείς (as='invoked with cries').
154 βακχεῖος MSS.: Βάκχιος Bothe.　　　**156 f.** κρέων ὁ μενοικέως νεοχμὸς | νεα-
ραῖσι θεῶν ἐπὶ συντυχίαις | MSS.　　**159** ἐρέσσων] ἐλίσσων Johnson.

---

their equivalents. See Appendix. I
prefer the first of these views. An
anapaest or spondee, meaning 'ruler,'
has probably dropped out before **νεοχμός**.
Seyffert's **κρείων** is at first sight attractive,
as accounting for its own disappearance;
but, since it is the same word as Κρέων—
which had an epic form Κρείων, as conversely Pind. and Aesch. use κρέων—this
would be rather a feeble pun than a
strong παρήχησις. Either ἄρχων or ταγός
is possible.—θεῶν...συντυχίαις, fortunes
sent by the gods,—the possessive gen. denoting the authors, just as it can denote the
parents: cp. *Ph.* 1116 πότμος...δαιμόνων:
Eur. *Aeol.* fr. 37 τὰς δὲ δαιμόνων τύχας |
ὅστις φέρει κάλλιστ', ἀνὴρ οὗτος σοφός.
(In *O. T.* 34 δαιμόνων συναλλαγαῖς is different.) ἐπὶ συντυχίαις means that the
fortunes are the *conditions* which have
made Creon king: this ἐπὶ with dat. of
attendant circumstance sometimes=our
'in,' as *O. C.* 1268 ἐπ' ἔργοις πᾶσι (n.),
sometimes 'for,' as Ar. *Eq.* 406 πῖν' ἐπὶ
συμφοραῖς (*i.e.* to celebrate them), cp.
El. 1230 : here we could say, '*under* the
new dispensations of the gods.' (Distinguish 88 ἐπὶ ψυχροῖσι as ='for' in the
sense 'with a view to.')
158 ff. μῆτιν ἐρέσσων, *consilium
animo volutans*, 'turning it over' busily
in the mind. ἐρέσσειν, to ply the oar, is fig.
said of putting a thing in lively motion,
as Eur. *I. A.* 139 ἐρέσσων σὸν πόδα.
Then also of activity in speech, as *Ai.*
251 ἐρέσσουσιν ἀπειλάς, 'they *ply* threats'
(utter them repeatedly and loudly) : or,
as here, in thought. Cp. 231.—(*Not*,
'speeding his counsel hitherward,' *i.e.*
coming to disclose it: '*advolvens, i.e.*

patefacturus,' Ellendt.)—σύγκλητον, specially convoked ;—implying that there
were other and regularly appointed seasons at which the king met the γέροντες
in council. At Athens four meetings
of the ἐκκλησία were regularly held in
each πρυτανεία (a period of 35 or 36
days): these were κύριαι (though the
term may once have been restricted to
the *first* of them), or νόμιμοι. An extraordinary meeting was σύγκλητος or κατά-
κλητος. Pollux 8. 116 σύγκλητος ἐκκλησία ἦν ἐξαίφνης ἐποίουν μείζονος
χρείας ἐπιλαβούσης· ἐκαλεῖτο δὲ καὶ κατα-
κλησία, ὅτι καὶ τοὺς ἐκ τῶν ἀγρῶν κατεκά-
λουν (*down* to the ἄστυ). Arist. *Pol.* 3.
1. 10 ἐνίαις γὰρ οὐκ ἔστι δῆμος, οὐδ' ἐκκλησίαν νομίζουσιν ἀλλὰ συγκλήτους: 'in
some States there is no popular body,
and they have no regular assembly, but
only *meetings on special occasions.*' σύγκλητος is one of those words which,
though a technical term at Athens,
could still be used by Attic poets without
any prosaic local allusion being felt,—
just as they used πρύτανις, ἐπιστάτης,
ἄρχων, ψήφισμα, etc.—προὔθετο is another example. The presidents of the
ecclesia were said γνώμας προθεῖναι
when they invited a discussion. Thuc. 6.
14 ὦ πρύτανι...γνώμας προτίθει αὖθις
Ἀθηναίοις, 'lay the question again before
the assembly.' *Id.* 3. 42 τοὺς προθέντας
τὴν διαγνώμην. Cp. Xen. *Mem.* 4. 2. 3
τῆς πόλεως λόγον περί τινος προτιθείσης.
Lucian *Menipp.* 19 has προὔθεσαν οἱ
πρυτάνεις ἐκκλησίαν, 'gave notice of':
but for this the usual phrase was that of
Aeschin. or. 2 § 60 προγράψαι τοὺς πρυτάνεις ἐκκλησίας δύο. Here, λέσχην is

κοινῷ κηρύγματι πέμψας;

ΚΡΕΩΝ.

ἄνδρες, τὰ μὲν δὴ πόλεος ἀσφαλῶς θεοὶ
πολλῷ σάλῳ σείσαντες ὤρθωσαν πάλιν·
ὑμᾶς δ᾽ ἐγὼ πομποῖσιν ἐκ πάντων δίχα
ἔστειλ᾽ ἱκέσθαι, τοῦτο μὲν τὰ Λαΐου   165
σέβοντας εἰδὼς εὖ θρόνων ἀεὶ κράτη,
τοῦτ᾽ αὖθις, ἡνίκ᾽ Οἰδίπους ὤρθου πόλιν,
κἀπεὶ διώλετ᾽, ἀμφὶ τοὺς κείνων ἔτι
παῖδας μένοντας ἐμπέδοις φρονήμασιν.

162 πόλεωσ L (it was never πόλεοσ): πόλεος r.   **167** τοῦτ᾽] εἶτ᾽ Reisig.
Wecklein suspects the loss of a verse after 167, such as τούτῳ βεβαίους ὄντας

not the meeting, but the discussion which is to take place there : thus the poet's phrase, true to Attic usage, corresponds with γνώμας προθεῖναι rather than with ἐκκλησίαν προθεῖναι. Herod. uses λέσχη of a public discussion (9. 71): cp. *O. C.* 167. The midd. **προύθετο** suggests Creon's personal interest in the question : the active would denote the mere act (see on 8 θεῖναι). Cp. 1249. προτίθεσθαι more oft. denotes what one proposes *to* oneself.—**κοινῷ κ. πέμψας,** lit. having sent (notice of the meeting) by means of a summons addressed to each of us. The κήρυγμα is the mandate which κήρυκες carried to each of the fifteen elders,—not, of course, a public proclamation: cp. 164. For the absolute πέμπω, cp. Thuc. 5. 43 πέμπει εὐθὺς ἐς Ἄργος ἰδίᾳ: and so oft. (Not, 'having sent for us,' μεταπεμψάμενος: cp. on 19.)

162—331 First ἐπεισόδιον. Creon, the new king, enters from the central door of the palace. Recognising the loyalty which the elders had shown to his predecessors, he expresses his own conception of the duty which a king owes to the State. He then announces the edict which, in accordance with that conception, he has published concerning the two brothers. The Chorus submissively acknowledge his right to do so, but express no approval. A guard now arrives (223), and announces that the king's edict has already been violated by an unknown hand, which has strewn dust upon the corpse of Polyneices. Creon dis-

misses him with threats of a dreadful death for him and for his fellows, if they fail to discover and produce the offender.

162—210 There is a general dramatic analogy between this speech and that of Oedipus in *O. T.* 216—275. In each case a Theban king addresses Theban elders, announcing a stern decree, adopted in reliance on his own wisdom, and promulgated with haughty consciousness of power ; the elders receive the decree with a submissive deference under which we can perceive traces of misgiving ; and as the drama proceeds, the elders become spectators of calamities occasioned by the decree, while its author turns to them for comfort.

162 ff. τὰ μὲν δὴ πόλεος . . ὑμᾶς δ᾽. The perils of the war are now over ; the affairs of civil government claim my next care ; and I have therefore sent for you, the nearest supporters of my throne.—**πόλεος** occurs only here in Soph., but twice in the trimeters of Aesch. (*Th.* 218, *Suppl.* 344), and thrice in those of Eur. (*Or.* 897, *El.* 412, *Ion* 595). Eur. has also in trimeters ὄφεος (*Bacch.* 1027, 1331, *Suppl.* 703), and κόνεος (*Cycl.* 641). In Comedy we find ὕβρεος (Ar. *Th.* 465, *Plut.* 1044), and φύσεος (*Vesp.* 1282, 1458). Such forms, which metrical convenience recommended to Attic poets, must not be confounded with the Ionic genitives in ι, such as πόλιος. The gen. πόλευς, contracted from πόλεος, is used by Theogn. 776 etc.— **πολλῷ σάλῳ σείσαντες.** Cp. *O. T.* 22.

summoned by his general mandate?

Enter CREON, *from the central doors of the palace, in the garb of king; with two attendants.*

CR. Sirs, the vessel of our State, after being tossed on wild waves, hath once more been safely steadied by the gods: and ye, out of all the folk, have been called apart by my summons, because I knew, first of all, how true and constant was your reverence for the royal power of Laïus; how, again, when Oedipus was ruler of our land, and when he had perished, your steadfast loyalty still upheld their children.

αὖ παραστάτας (*Ars Soph. em.* 40).   **169** ἐμπέδοις] ἐμπέδους Reiske.

The image of the State as a ship dates in Greek literature from Alcaeus (whom Horace copied, *Carm.* I. 14), fr. 18. The ship of Alcaeus is labouring in the trough of a wild sea,—water is coming in,—the sail is torn,—the anchor will not hold: ναΐ φορήμεθα σὺν μελαίνᾳ | χείμωνι μοχθεῦντες μεγάλῳ μάλα, κ.τ.λ. It is only through Heracleides *Alleg. Homer.* 5 that we know the meaning of Alcaeus to have been figurative and political. Aesch. often uses the image (*Th.* 2, 62, 208 etc.). Creon returns to it at 189. It is peculiarly well suited to his point,—the unity of the public interest.—**ὤρθωσαν**, made *upright*, 'righted': but below 167, ὤρθου=was keeping *straight*: cp. on 83.

164 f. ἐκ **πάντων**, (chosen) out of all, **δίχα** *adv.* (with ἱκέσθαι) apart from them: cp. 656 πόλεως .. ἐκ πάσης μόνην, 1137 τὰν ἐκ πασᾶν τιμᾷς: *El.* 1351 ὅν ποτ' ἐκ πολλῶν ἐγὼ | μόνον προσηῦρον πιστόν. In other places, where δίχα is *prep.* with gen., we find it similarly connected with another expression of like purport, as *Ai.* 749 ἐκ...κύκλου | .. μεταστὰς οἷος Ἀτρειδῶν δίχα.—**ἔστειλ'** ἱκέσθαι: lit., by means of messengers I *caused* you *to set forth*, so that you should come (epexeg. inf.): *Ph.* 60 οἵ σ' ἐν λιταῖς στείλαντες ἐξ οἴκων μολεῖν. But στέλλεσθαι (midd.) 'to summon *to oneself*' (*O. T.* 434): cp. n. *O. T.* 860.— **τοῦτο μέν**, answered by τοῦτ' αὖθις: see 61 n.—**σέβοντας**, like μένοντας (169), part. of the imperf., = ὅτι ἐσέβετε: so 1192: *O. T.* 835 τοῦ παρόντος (n.): and cp. on *O. C.* 1565 f.—**θρόνων** .. **κράτη**, powers belonging to the throne: cp. 60, 173.

167 ff. ἡνίκ' Οἰδίπους κ.τ.λ. The only obscurity arises from the use of the plur. **κείνων** in 168. **κείνων παῖδας** ought to mean, 'the descendants of Laïus and Oedipus,' viz. Eteocles and Polyneices. But, as the sentence stands, it must mean, 'the offspring of Laïus and of Oedipus *respectively*'; viz. Oedipus, the son of Laïus; Eteocles and Polyneices, the sons of Oedipus. The relative clause, ἡνίκ' .. ὤρθου πόλιν, induced the poet to add immediately the other relative clause to which the same person is subject, viz. ἐπεὶ διώλετο, instead of inserting, after ὤρθου πόλιν, words expressing their loyalty to Oedipus. We might, indeed, suppose that, after ὤρθου πόλιν, we were intended to supply mentally, καὶ τὰ ἐκείνου θρόνων κράτη σέβοντας. But against this is the fact that, after **τοῦτο μέν.. τοῦτ' αὖθις,**—'in the first place' .. 'in the second place,'—**καὶ** (in κἀπεὶ) would scarcely have been thus used to introduce a distinct third clause. Evidently **καὶ** links ἡνίκα ὤρθου to ἐπεὶ διώλετο.—**ἐμπέδοις φρονήμασιν**, with steadfast sentiments (of loyalty), modal dat., as oft. προθυμία, εὐνοίᾳ, φρονήματι (Thuc. 2. 62), etc. Hartung, whom some recent editors follow, adopts **ἐμπέδους** on the strange ground that Soph. must otherwise have written ἐμμένοντας. But **μένοντας** ἀμφὶ τοὺς κείνων παῖδας='remaining around them,' and the modal dat. is added no less legitimately than the causal dat. in Eur. *Her.* 701 δειλίᾳ μένειν, 'to remain through cowardice.' Soph. could have said ἐμπέδους φρονήμασιν, as he has said συντρόφοις | ὀργαῖς ἔμπεδος (*Ai.* 639): but **ἐμπέδοις** is better here, both (*a*) be-

ὅτ᾽ οὖν ἐκεῖνοι πρὸς διπλῆς μοίρας μίαν   170
καθ᾽ ἡμέραν ὤλοντο παίσαντές τε καὶ
πληγέντες αὐτόχειρι σὺν μιάσματι,
ἐγὼ κράτη δὴ πάντα καὶ θρόνους ἔχω
γένους κατ᾽ ἀγχιστεῖα τῶν ὀλωλότων.
ἀμήχανον δὲ παντὸς ἀνδρὸς ἐκμαθεῖν   175
ψυχήν τε καὶ φρόνημα καὶ γνώμην, πρὶν ἂν
ἀρχαῖς τε καὶ νόμοισιν ἐντριβὴς φανῇ.
ἐμοὶ γὰρ ὅστις πᾶσαν εὐθύνων πόλιν
μὴ τῶν ἀρίστων ἅπτεται βουλευμάτων,

171 παίσαντες] In L the letters αισ are small and cramped, having been substituted by the first corrector (S) for two erased letters. I suppose that the first hand

---

cause a series of accusatives has preceded, and (*b*) because, as μένοντας has already marked their constancy, we now want an epithet for their φρονήματα.

170 ff. ὅτε causal, *O. T.* 918 n.—πρὸς διπλῆς μ.: cp. 14 n.: for πρός, 51 n.: for διπλῆς .. μίαν, 13 n.—παίσαντες .. πληγέντες. In Attic prose the verb 'to strike' usu. had as pres. τύπτω (or παίω), fut. τυπτήσω (or πατάξω), aor. ἐπάταξα, aor. pass. ἐπλήγην. The aor. of παίω is mainly a poetical word, used in tragedy, more rarely in comedy, and by Xen. In Attic prose ἔπαισα is usu. the aor. of παίζω. Meineke proposed πλήξαντες here, but that aor. (except in comp. with a prep.) is almost unknown to classical Attic. παισθέντες, again, though that aor. pass. occurs twice in Aesch., is very rare. —αὐτόχειρι .. μιάσματι, the stain of a kinsman's murder (see on 52, and cp. 1176): cp. Aesch. *Th.* 849 κακὰ | αὐτόφονα. σύν, as 1266 νέῳ ξὺν μόρῳ: *O. C.* 1663, σὺν νόσοις: Pind. *O.* 2. 42 σὺν ἀλλαλοφονίᾳ.

173 f. ἐγὼ .. δή, I *now*: where δή nearly=ἤδη, *O. T.* 968 n. Aesch. *Eum.* 3 (after Gaia came Themis) ἡ δὴ τὸ μητρὸς δευτέρα τόδ᾽ ἕζετο | μαντεῖον.—κράτη: cp. 166.—γένους κατ᾽ ἀγχιστεῖα τῶν ὀλ., by nearness of kinship to the dead, γένους ἀγχιστεῖα forming one notion, on which the genit. τῶν ὀλ. depends, as on words meaning 'near.' The neut. plur. ἀγχιστεῖα (only here) would most properly mean 'rights' or 'privileges' of such nearness (cp. ἀριστεῖα, πρωτεῖα, etc.), but seems here to be merely a poetical equiv. for the abstract ἀγχιστεία. In Attic law ἀγχιστεία was any degree of

relationship on which a claim to an inheritance could be founded in the absence of a will otherwise disposing of it. To claim an inheritance under a will was ἀμφισβητεῖν κατὰ διαθήκην: to claim on the ground of relationship, ἀμφισβητεῖν κατ᾽ ἀγχιστείαν. συγγένεια, consanguinity, might, or might not, constitute ἀγχιστεία: *e.g.* Isaeus says of the relationship of mother to son that it is συγγενέστατον μὲν τῇ φύσει πάντων, ἐν δὲ ταῖς ἀγχιστείαις ὁμολογουμένως οὐκ ἔστιν (or. 11 § 17), since a mother could not inherit from her son. (See *Selections from the Attic Orators*, pp. 331, 344.) Creon succeeds as the nearest male relative. Aesch., Soph., and Eur. ignore the Boeotian legend which gave a son, Laodamas, to Eteocles (Her. 5. 61), and a son, Thersander, to Polyneices (id. 4. 147, etc.). The sisters represent the ἐσχάτη ῥίζα (599).

175 ἀμήχανον δέ. 'You were loyal to the kings whose successor I am. Now (δέ) a man cannot be really known until he has been tried in office. (I do not, therefore, ask you to pledge your loyalty to me until I have been so tested.) I will, however, tell you the principles which I intend to observe.' Thus δέ merely marks the transition to a new topic. It is not directly adversative, as if he meant: 'You were loyal to my predecessors, *but* I do not yet ask you to be loyal to me.' On that view, however, the general connection of thoughts would remain the same.

Demosthenes, in his speech on the Embassy (343 B.C.), quotes this passage (vv. 175—190) as illustrating maxims

Since, then, his sons have fallen in one day by a twofold doom,
—each smitten by the other, each stained with a brother's blood,
—I now possess the throne and all its powers, by nearness of
kinship to the dead.

No man can be fully known, in soul and spirit and mind, until he hath been seen versed in rule and law-giving. For if any,
being supreme guide of the State, cleaves not to the best counsels,

had by a mere oversight written πφσαντες (πείσαντες). The erasure of the original
σ was necessary in order to make room for αι.　　**178** πᾶσαν] Nauck con-

---

which Aeschines had violated, though,
accustomed as he had been to play
tritagonists' parts, he ought to have
known them by heart (or. 19 § 247).

176 ψυχήν, 'soul,' the man's moral
nature generally: **φρόνημα**, the 'spirit'
of his dealing in public affairs, according as his aims are lofty or mean,
his policy bold or timid (cp. 207 τοιόνδ'
ἐμὸν φρόνημα): **γνώμην**, the intellectual aspect of the man, his ability and
judgment. In Her. 5. 124 ψυχὴν οὐκ
ἄκρος, 3. 14 διεπειρᾶτο αὐτοῦ τῆς ψυχῆς,
the word = 'fortitude.' But the usage of
Soph. favours the more general sense here:
cp. 227, 929, Ai. 1361 σκληρὰν...ψυχήν,
El. 219 σᾷ δυσθύμῳ τίκτουσ' ἀεὶ | ψυχᾷ
πολέμους. Plato has the phrase τῆς ψυχῆς
τὴν γνώμην for 'the intellect' (Legg.
672 B).

177 ἀρχαῖς, duties of administration.
It might be explained as a generic plur.
of ἀρχή, in the sense of 'sovereignties,'
as Isocr. or. 3 § 15 αἱ μοναρχίαι, § 16 τὰς
τυραννίδας, etc.: but it seems truer to say
that the Athenian poet was thinking of
public offices or magistracies. νόμοισιν
has a general sense: the king is concerned
with νόμοι both as νομοφύλαξ and as νο-
μοθέτης: but, as the context suggests, it is
of law-giving that Creon is more particularly thinking. **φανῇ** 'be found,'
without ὤν, as Pind. P. 5. 107 πέφανταί
θ' ἁρματηλάτας σοφός: Thuc. 1. 8 Κᾶρες
ἐφάνησαν (were found to be). Not: 'be
revealed, by being conversant.' Cp.
Arist. Eth. N. 5. 3 πολλοὶ γὰρ ἐν μὲν
τοῖς οἰκείοις τῇ ἀρετῇ δύνανται χρῆσθαι, ἐν δὲ τοῖς πρὸς ἕτερον ἀδυνατοῦ-

σιν. καὶ διὰ τοῦτο εὖ δοκεῖ ἔχειν τὸ τοῦ
Βίαντος, ὅτι ἀρχὴ ἄνδρα δείξει· πρὸς
ἕτερον γὰρ καὶ ἐν κοινωνίᾳ ἤδη ὁ ἄρχων.
Besides Bias of Priene, others of the
ἑπτὰ σοφισταί,—as Chilon, Pittacus, Solon,—had this saying ascribed to them.
Plut. Sull. 30 (Sulla) εἰκότως προσετρίψατο
ταῖς μεγάλαις ἐξουσίαις διαβολὴν ὡς τὰ ἤθη
μένειν οὐκ ἐώσαις ἐπὶ τῶν ἐξ ἀρχῆς
τρόπων (as not allowing characters to
be constant under the influence of habits
formed in office), ἀλλ' ἔμπληκτα καὶ χαῦνα
καὶ ἀπάνθρωπα ποιούσαις. Shaksp. Jul.
Caes. ii. 1. 12 He would be crown'd:—
How that might change his nature, there's
the question....The abuse of greatness is,
when it disjoins | Remorse from power.

178 ff. ἐμοὶ γάρ. A ground for the
preceding statement is introduced by γάρ,
though the compression of the thought
slightly obscures the connection. 'A man
cannot be known until he has been tested
in power. For (γὰρ) a man in power
may easily be deterred, by fear of unpo-
pularity, from pursuing the counsels best
for the State: and if he is so deterred,
I think him worthless.' **πᾶσαν...πόλιν**,
the whole city, as 656 πόλεως ... ἐκ
πάσης, 776 πᾶσα...πόλις, Ai. 851 ἐν
πάσῃ πόλει (in the hearing of all the
city). In prose the art. would have
been added (cp. Thuc. 7. 29 τῇ πόλει
πάσῃ, 4. 87 ξυμπάσῃ τῇ πόλει, 2. 65 ἡ
ξύμπασα πόλις); but its omission in
poetry being so common, it is strange
that πᾶσαν should have been suspected
here.—μὴ...ἅπτεται, not οὐ, since the
relative clause is general ('such an one as
does not...,' Lat. qui with subjunct.): cp.
O. C. 1175 ἃ μὴ | χρήζεις. Instead of
ὅστις μὴ ἅπτεται we should more often
find ὅστις ἂν μὴ ἅπτηται: yet the instances of the indic. after ὅστις in general
statement are not rare even in prose; cp.
Thuc. 2. 64 οἵτινες...ἥκιστα λυποῦνται,

ἀλλ' ἐκ φόβου του γλῶσσαν ἐγκλήσας ἔχει,   180
κάκιστος εἶναι νῦν τε καὶ πάλαι δοκεῖ·
καὶ μείζον' ὅστις ἀντὶ τῆς αὑτοῦ πάτρας
φίλον νομίζει, τοῦτον οὐδαμοῦ λέγω.
ἐγὼ γάρ, ἴστω Ζεὺς ὁ πάνθ' ὁρῶν ἀεί,
οὔτ' ἂν σιωπήσαιμι τὴν ἄτην ὁρῶν   185
στείχουσαν ἀστοῖς ἀντὶ τῆς σωτηρίας,
οὔτ' ἂν φίλον ποτ' ἄνδρα δυσμενῆ χθονὸς
θείμην ἐμαυτῷ, τοῦτο γιγνώσκων ὅτι
ἥδ' ἐστὶν ἡ σῴζουσα, καὶ ταύτης ἔπι
πλέοντες ὀρθῆς τοὺς φίλους ποιούμεθα.   190

---

ject. ταγὸς: Blaydes, πρύμναν . . πόλεως.   **180** ἐγκλείσασ L: ἐγκλήσας Elmsley.
Cp. on *O. T.* 1388.   **182** μείζον'] In L the first hand wrote μεῖον: another hand
added ' after ν, indicating μείζον', but left the circumflex unchanged. μεῖζον, which
Wakefield conjectured, is read by Nauck and others.—αὑτοῦ] αὐτοῦ L.   **184** ἴστω]
Nauck conject. ἴστωρ.   **186** ἀστοῖς] ἆσσον is conjectured by Dobree (*Adv.* I. 436)

ἔργῳ δὲ μάλιστα ἀντέχουσιν: *ib.* ὅστις
λαμβάνει.—**ἐκ φ. του**: cp. 111 νεικέων ἐξ
ἀμφιλόγων.—**ἐγκλήσας ἔχει** (cp. 22),=a
perf., in the sense 'has shut once for all,'
'keeps shut.' Distinguish the prose idiom,
Dem. or. 9 § 12 Φερὰς...ἔχει καταλαβών,
has seized, and keeps.—**νῦν τε καὶ πάλαι,**
an emphatic formula ('seems, and has
always seemed'), *El.* 676, *Ph.* 966: cp.
El. 1049 πάλαι δέδοκται ταῦτα κοὐ νεωστί
μοι: *Il.* 9. 105 οἷον ἐγὼ νοέω, ἠμὲν πάλαι
ἠδ' ἔτι καὶ νῦν.

182 f. μείζον': whoever recognises
a friend *more important* than his country,
—*i.e.* with stronger claims upon him:
ἀντὶ τῆς...πάτρας instead of the simple
gen., or ἤ with accus., as *Tr.* 576 ὥστε
μήτιν' εἰσιδὼν | στέρξει γυναῖκα κεῖνος
ἀντὶ σοῦ πλέον. Cp. 638 (γάμος) μείζων
φέρεσθαι, more important to win: *O. T.*
772 τῷ γὰρ ἂν καὶ μείζονι | λέξαιμ' ἂν ἢ
σοί..., 'to whom more important,' *i.e.*
with a better claim on my confidence,—
nearer and dearer. **μεῖζον** (which was
written by the first hand in L) is specious,
—'a more important thing,' a greater
good: cp. Eur. *Or.* 784 μέγα γὰρ ηὐγέ-
νειά σου, Andr. 209 ἡ Λάκαινα μὲν πό-
λις | μέγ' ἐστί. But Demosthenes, at
least, seems to have read **μείζον'**: for,
in applying the verses to Aeschines,
he paraphrases thus (or. 19 § 248):
τούτων οὐδὲν Αἰσχίνης εἶπε πρὸς αὐτὸν
ἐν τῇ πρεσβείᾳ, ἀλλ' ἀντὶ μὲν τῆς πόλεως
τὴν Φιλίππου ξενίαν καὶ φιλίαν πολλῷ

μείζονα ἡγήσατο αὐτῷ καὶ λυσιτε-
λεστέραν, ἐρρῶσθαι πολλὰ φράσας τῷ
σοφῷ Σοφοκλεῖ.—**οὐδαμοῦ λέγω**: Aesch.
Pers. 497 θεοὺς δέ τις | τὸ πρὶν νομίζων
οὐδαμοῦ, τότ' ηὔχετο. Eur. *Andr.* 210
Σκῦρον οὐδαμοῦ τίθης (*nullo in numero
habes*). Xen. *Mem.* 1. 2. 52 ὥστε μηδα-
μοῦ παρ' αὐτοῖς τοὺς ἄλλους εἶναι πρὸς
αὐτόν, 'so that the rest *were nowhere* with
them in comparison to him.' So οὐδενὸς
λόγου (or ἐν οὐδενὶ λόγῳ) ποιεῖσθαι, ἐν οὐ-
δεμιᾷ μοίρᾳ ἄγειν, etc.

184 ἐγὼ γάρ. Here, as in ἐμοὶ γάρ
above (178), **γάρ** introduces a reason;
but here, again, the connection is obscured by the form of the sentence. The
reason is contained in **τοῦτο γιγνώσκων**
κ.τ.λ. (188). 'I have no esteem for a
man who prefers popularity or private
friendship to the good of the State (178—
183); *for* (184) I well know that all private welfare depends on the welfare of
the State; and so I should never commit
the faults which I have just condemned
in others.'—**ἴστω** is confirmed against the
conjecture ἴστωρ (or ἴστω) by those passages in which it is joined with an accus.,
as *Il.* 7. 411 ὅρκια δὲ Ζεὺς ἴστω, 15. 36
ἴστω νῦν τόδε Γαῖα, etc.

185 οὔτ' ἂν σιωπήσαιμι. Applied
to the actual case, Creon's words mean,
'I should never be deterred by fear of
popular murmurs (cp. 692 ff.) from pub-
lishing such an edict as this against
burying Polyneices, when I clearly saw

but, through some fear, keeps his lips locked, I hold, and
have ever held, him most base; and if any makes a friend of
more account than his fatherland, that man hath no place in
my regard. For I—be Zeus my witness, who sees all things
always—would not be silent if I saw ruin, instead of safety,
coming to the citizens; nor would I ever deem the country's foe
a friend to myself; remembering this, that our country is the
ship that bears us safe, and that only while she prospers in our
voyage can we make true friends.

and Shilleto (Dem. *De Falsa Legat.* p. 146): but see comment.   **187** χθονὸς] L
has πόλεως written above by S (not by the first hand).   It was prob. a mere conjecture
suggested by the schol., οὐκ ἂν κτησαίμην φίλον τῆς ἐμῆς πόλεως δυσμενῆ: Nauck,
however, places πόλεως in the text.—Lugebil conject. οὔτ' ἄν ποτ' ἄνδρα δυσμενῆ πόλει
φίλον.   **190** τοὺς φίλους] Gomperz suspects these words: Mekler conject. πλοῦς

---

that otherwise a disastrous precedent
would be set. And though Polyneices
was my nephew, I should never allow
myself to recognise as friend or kinsman
a man who had borne arms against the
country.'
186 στείχουσαν ἀστοῖς. Demosthenes paraphrases this by στείχουσαν
ὁμοῦ (or. 19 § 248); whence Dobree
and Shilleto surmised that he read ἆσσον
(cp. *O. C.* 312 στείχουσαν ἡμῶν ἆσσον).
Now I think that I can explain why
Demosthenes so paraphrased. He is
applying the verses to Aeschines (see
above, n. on 182): τὴν δὲ ἄτην ὁρῶν στείχουσαν ὁμοῦ, τὴν ἐπὶ Φωκέας στρατείαν, οὐ προεῖπεν οὐδὲ προεξήγγειλεν.
The ἄτη which Aeschines saw approaching was the interference of Philip in the
Sacred War,—his action against the
Phocians. If Demosthenes had said στείχουσαν ἀστοῖς, this must have seemed to
refer to the fellow-citizens of Aeschines,
—the Athenians. The orator therefore
modified the poet's phrase by substituting
ὁμοῦ,—a word vague enough to suggest
the concern of other Greek states besides
Phocis in the peril.—ἀντὶ τῆς σωτηρίας,
added for emphasis; 'ruin, *and not*
welfare, which a king is bound to promote.' (The art. τῆς is merely generic, as
in τὴν ἄτην.) So *Tr.* 267 φανεὶς δὲ
δοῦλος ἀνδρὸς ἀντ' ἐλευθέρου, a slave, and
not a free man (as he ought to be): *O. T.*
1490 κεκλαυμέναι | πρὸς οἶκον ἵξεσθ' ἀντὶ
τῆς θεωρίας.
187 f. ἄνδρα δυσμενῆ χθονός; cp.
Plat. *Lysis* 213 B τὸ φίλον ἂν εἴη φίλον τοῦ
φιλουμένου...τὸ μισοῦν ἄρα πάλιν ἐχθρὸν

τοῦ μισουμένου. Andoc. or. 1 § 96 (in
a νόμος) πολέμιος ἔστω Ἀθηναίων.—ἐμαυτῷ with φίλον. Some MSS. of Dem. (or.
19 § 247) give ἐμαυτοῦ in the quotation,
but here the dat. is clearly better. θείμην
'hold' (rather than 'make'): cp. Tyrt.
12. 1 οὔτ' ἂν μνησαίμην οὔτ' ἐν λόγῳ ἄνδρα
τιθείμην.
189 f. ἡ σῴζουσα, 'who bears us
safe.' σῴζειν was esp. said of a ship or
its captain: cp. Plat. *Gorg.* 511 D ἐὰν..
ἐξ Αἰγίνης δεῦρο σώσῃ, if she (ἡ κυβερνη-
τική) has carried us safely from Aegina
to Athens.—ταύτης κ.τ.λ. It is only
while she remains upright, as we sail
on board of her, that we can make
real friends. ὀρθῆς (like ὤρθωσαν in
163) refers to the ship maintaining a
safe stability, as opposed to capsizing:
the contrast is given by ὑπτίοις .. σέλμασιν .. ναυτίλλεται in 716 (where see
n.). So Cic. *Ep. ad Fam.* 12. 25. 5
ut rectam teneamus (navem). — τοὺς
φίλους ποιούμεθα, we make the friends
(whom we really make): since friends
made at the cost of endangering or
wrecking the ship of the State cannot
properly be considered friends at all: they
are φίλοι ἄφιλοι. For the use of the art.,
cp. Thuc. 2. 40 οὐ .. πάσχοντες εὖ ἀλλὰ
δρῶντες κτώμεθα τοὺς φίλους. The
thought is like that ascribed to Pericles
by Thuc. 2. 60, ἐγὼ γὰρ ἡγοῦμαι πόλιν
πλείω ξύμπασαν ὀρθουμένην ὠφελεῖν
τοὺς ἰδιώτας ἢ καθ' ἕκαστον τῶν πολιτῶν
εὐπραγοῦσαν ἀθρόαν δὲ σφαλλομένην. καλῶς μὲν γὰρ φερόμενος ἀνὴρ τὸ καθ' ἑαυτὸν διαφθειρομένης τῆς πατρίδος οὐδὲν
ἦσσον ξυναπόλλυται, κακοτυχῶν δὲ ἐν

τοιοῖσδ' ἐγὼ νόμοισι τήνδ' αὔξω πόλιν·
καὶ νῦν ἀδελφὰ τῶνδε κηρύξας ἔχω
ἀστοῖσι παίδων τῶν ἀπ' Οἰδίπου πέρι·
Ἐτεοκλέα μέν, ὃς πόλεως ὑπερμαχῶν
ὄλωλε τῆσδε, πάντ' ἀριστεύσας δορί,   195
τάφῳ τε κρύψαι καὶ τὰ πάντ' ἐφαγνίσαι
ἃ τοῖς ἀρίστοις ἔρχεται κάτω νεκροῖς·
τὸν δ' αὖ ξύναιμον τοῦδε, Πολυνείκην λέγω,
ὃς γῆν πατρῴαν καὶ θεοὺς τοὺς ἐγγενεῖς
φυγὰς κατελθὼν ἠθέλησε μὲν πυρὶ   200
πρῆσαι κατ' ἄκρας, ἠθέλησε δ' αἵματος
κοινοῦ πάσασθαι, τοὺς δὲ δουλώσας ἄγειν,

καλούς. **191** αὔξω] Schneidewin conj. ἄξω, or τῆσδ' ἄρξω πόλεως.   **193** τῶν ϝ,
τῶνδ' L.   **195** δορὶ L, with χε (*i.e.* χερὶ) written above by S.   **196** ἐφαγνίσαι

εὐτυχούσῃ πολλῷ μᾶλλον διασῴζεται.
'Pericles Thucydidis II. 60 Sophoclem
videtur respexisse, vel eum Sophocles,' is
Dobree's remark (*Adv.* 2. 37); but there
is no adequate ground for such a view.
The verbal coincidence of ὀρθῆς with ὀρθουμένην may well have been accidental.
What is really common to poet and historian is the general sentiment of Peri-
clean Athens. For another example of
this, cp. *O. C.* 116 n.

191 νόμοισι, here, rules of conduct,
principles, as *El.* 1043; cp. *O. C.* 907.—
αὔξω, pres. (used also in Attic prose):
the Attic fut. was αὐξήσω. The pres.
here expresses purpose ('I intend to
make Thebes prosperous'). Cp. Plat.
Legg. 731 A φιλονεικείτω δὲ ἡμῖν πᾶς
πρὸς ἀρετήν· ὁ γὰρ τοιοῦτος αὔξει τὰς
πόλεις.

192 f. ἀδελφὰ τῶνδε, the more usu.
constr.: but *O. C.* 1262 ἀδελφὰ τούτοισιν
(n.). This use of the word is freq. in
Attic prose, as Plat. *Phaedr.* 276 D ὅσα
τούτων ἀδελφά.—τῶν ἀπ' Οἰδίπου. In
regard to origin, ἐκ is properly said of
parents, ἀπό of ancestors: Isocr. or. 12
§ 81 τοὺς μὲν ἀπὸ θεῶν τοὺς δ' ἐξ αὐτῶν
τῶν θεῶν γεγονότας. Cp. 466, 471, 1066;
Ph. 260 παῖ πατρὸς ἐξ Ἀχιλλέως. *Ai.*
202 χθονίων ἀπ' Ἐρεχθειδᾶν. But poetry
oft. has ἀπό of the parent, as *O. C.* 571
κἀφ' ὅτου πατρὸς γεγώς: while, again, ἐκ
oft. denotes merely the stock (including
progenitors above the parent): cp. 1056:

so ἀγαθοὶ καὶ ἐξ ἀγαθῶν (Plat. *Phaedr.*
246 A), etc.   The poetical indifference on
this point is well seen in fr. 104, where
τοὺς μὲν δυσσεβεῖς κακῶν τ' ἄπο | βλα-
στόντας is opposed to τοὺς δ' ὄντας ἐσ-
θλοὺς ἔκ τε γενναίων ἅμα | γεγῶτας.

195 f. δορί was the ordinary Attic
form, occurring in prose (as Thuc. 1. 128,
4. 98), and was prob. used by Soph. as
well as δόρει, which metre requires in *O.
C.* 620 (n.), 1314, 1386: cp. n. on *O. C.*
1304.—τὰ πάντ' ἐφαγνίσαι, to perform
all due rites over the grave; *i.e.* to make
the proper offerings to the dead (ἐναγί-
σματα, *O. C.* 402 n.), esp. libations, χοαί.
For ἐπί in the compound cp. *El.* 440
χοὰς | οὐκ ἄν ποθ', ὅν γ' ἔκτεινε, τῷδ' ἐπέ-
στεφε: *O. C.* 484 τάσδ' ἐπεύχεσθαι λι-
τάς, *i.e.* 'over' the rite. ἐφαγνίσαι is
the reading of L; the force of the
prep. is rightly given in the glosses, ἐπὶ
τῷ τάφῳ ἁγνίσαι τὰ πάντα, and ἐπὶ τῷ
τάφῳ ὅσια ποιῆσαι. Though ἐφαγνίζειν
is not elsewhere extant, there seems no
reason to question it. ἀφαγνίσαι has
been preferred by some, merely because
that compound is recognised by the old
grammarians (Suid., Hesych., Phrynichus in Bekk. *Anecd.* 26). But ἀφαγνίζειν meant esp. to purify from guilt (*expi-
are*): Paus. 2. 31. 8 (of Orestes at Troe-
zen) ἐκάθαιρον καὶ εἱστίων, ἐς ὃ ἀφήγνι-
σαν, 'until they had purged him.' Similarly in midd., Eur. *Alc.* 1145 πρὶν ἄν
θεοῖσι τοῖσι νερτέροις | ἀφαγνίσηται, until

Such are the rules by which I guard this city's greatness. And in accord with them is the edict which I have now published to the folk touching the sons of Oedipus;—that Eteocles, who hath fallen fighting for our city, in all renown of arms, shall be entombed, and crowned with every rite that follows the noblest dead to their rest. But for his brother, Polyneices,—who came back from exile, and sought to consume utterly with fire the city of his fathers and the shrines of his fathers' gods,—sought to taste of kindred blood, and to lead the remnant into slavery;

L, ἀφαγνίσαι r.   **197** ἔρχεται] Ludw. Dindorf conject. ἔρδεται.   **201** πρῆσαι]

---

she has made expiatory offerings to them. So ἀφαγνεύω in Plut. *Mor.* 943 C (the souls of the good are to suffer only so long) ὅσον ἀφαγνεῦσαι καὶ ἀποπνεῦσαι τοὺς ἀπὸ τοῦ σώματος .. μιασμούς ('to purge away': perh. we should read ἀφαγνίσαι). The force of ἀπό is thus the same as in ἀφοσιοῦσθαι, and in ἀφιερώμεθα as used by Aesch. *Eum.* 451 ('I have been hallowed,' *i.e.* purified). The case of κἀφαγιστεύσας below (247) is different from that of ἐφαγνίσαι here: it is, I think, for καὶ ἀφαγιστεύσας.

197 τοῖς ἀρίστοις, implying that, in his case, the αὐτόχειρ μίασμα (172) is to make no difference. Cp. *Ai.* 1379, where Odysseus offers to join in funeral honours to Ajax (notwithstanding his offence), μηδὲν ἐλλείπειν, ὅσον | χρὴ τοῖς ἀρίστοις ἀνδράσιν πονεῖν βροτούς.—ἔρχεται κάτω: the χοαί were supposed to pass through the earth, and to be drunk by the spirits of the dead: Aesch. *Ch.* 164 ἔχει μὲν ἤδη γαπότους χοὰς πατήρ: cp. *Od.* 10. 94, Eur. *Hec.* 535 ff. The dat., as *O. T.* 711 χρησμὸς .. ἦλθε Λαΐῳ.

198 L has Πολυνείκην here, but Πολυνείκη in *O. C.* 375. Both forms are sound. From about 400 B.C. the Attic tendency of proper names in -ης was to pass from the 3rd to the 1st declension. Attic inscriptions of *circ.* 410—350 B.C. give the acc. in -ην more often than that in -η. From *c.* 350 to 30 B.C. the gen. in -ου is far more frequent than that in -ους. Even proper names in -κλέης, which kept the acc. in -κλέα to *c.* 300 B.C., afterwards formed it in -κλῆν. (No Attic inscript. gives -κλῆ.)—λέγω: see n. on 32 λέγω γὰρ κἀμέ.

199 ff. γῆν πατρῴαν .. καὶ θεοὺς .. πρῆσαι: cp. Aesch. *Th.* 582 (of Polynei-

ces) πόλιν πατρῴαν καὶ θεοὺς τοὺς ἐγγενεῖς | πορθεῖν, στράτευμ' ἐπακτὸν ἐμβεβληκότα. But πέρσαι, for πρῆσαι, would be a needless change here. 'To burn his country' means 'to burn his native city': so *O. C.* 1421 πάτραν κατασκάψαντι, when thou hast laid thy native city in ruins. θεοὺς πρῆσαι is to burn the gods' temples and the ancient wooden images (βρέτη) therein: cp. Her. 8. 109 ἐμπιμπράς τε καὶ καταβάλλων τῶν θεῶν τὰ ἀγάλματα. Aesch. *Pers.* 809 οὐ θεῶν βρέτη | ᾐδοῦντο συλᾶν οὐδὲ πιμπράναι νεώς.—θ. τοὺς ἐγγενεῖς, of the *race*, here in a large sense, of the Cadmean stock: while θεοὶ πατρῷοι are usu. rather the gods of one's own *family* (*O. C.* 756 n.). Cp. *El.* 428 πρός νυν θεῶν σε λίσσομαι τῶν ἐγγενῶν.—κατελθών, not καταχθεὶς ὑπὸ τῆς πόλεως: on the shield of Polyneices, Dikè was portrayed saying, κατάξω δ' ἄνδρα τόνδε (Aesch. *Th.* 647).—ἠθέλησε μέν .. ἠθέλ. δέ, rhetor. epanaphora (*O. C.* 610 φθίνει μέν .. φθίνει δέ). Since πάσασθαι cannot govern γῆν . καὶ θεούς, ἠθέλησε μὲν should in strictness have preceded γῆν. — πρῆσαι. Prose would have used ἐμπρῆσαι, though Thuc. has the pres. part. of the simple form (6. 94 πίμπραντες).—κατ' ἄκρας, here in its proper sense, of a town being sacked 'from top to bottom' (*Il.* 13. 772): cp. *O. C.* 1241 n.—αἵματος κ. πάσασθαι (πατέομαι), denoting the extreme of savage hatred; *Il.* 4. 35 ὠμὸν βεβρώθοις Πρίαμον: 24. 212 τοῦ ἐγὼ μέσον ἧπαρ ἔχοιμι | ἐσθέμεναι: Theogn. 349 τῶν εἴη μέλαν αἷμα πιεῖν.—τοὺς δὲ .. ἄγειν, as if τῶν μέν had preceded αἵματος. *O. T.* 1228 ὅσα | κεύθει, τὰ δ' αὐτίκ' εἰς τὸ φῶς φανεῖ. *Tr.* 117 στρέφει, τὸ δ' αὔξει. *Il.* 22. 157 παραδραμέτην, φεύγων, ὁ δ' ὄπισθε διώκων.

τοῦτον πόλει τῇδ᾽ * ἐκκεκήρυκται τάφῳ
μήτε κτερίζειν μήτε κωκῦσαί τινα,
ἐᾶν δ᾽ ἄθαπτον, καὶ πρὸς οἰωνῶν δέμας   205
καὶ πρὸς κυνῶν ἐδεστὸν αἰκισθέντ᾽ ἰδεῖν.
τοιόνδ᾽ ἐμὸν φρόνημα, κοὔποτ᾽ ἔκ γ᾽ ἐμοῦ
*τιμῇ προέξουσ᾽ οἱ κακοὶ τῶν ἐνδίκων·
ἀλλ᾽ ὅστις εὔνους τῇδε τῇ πόλει, θανὼν
καὶ ζῶν ὁμοίως ἐξ ἐμοῦ τιμήσεται.   210
ΧΟ. σοὶ ταῦτ᾽ ἀρέσκει, παῖ Μενοικέως Κρέον,

Musgrave conject. πέρσαι. **203** ἐκκεκηρύχθαι (sic) τάφῳ MSS., and so Wolff, understanding λέγω. Musgrave's ἐκκεκήρυκται τάφῳ has been received by most later edd.
But Nauck gives ἐκκεκηρῦχθαι λέγω from the parody by Carneades in Diog. L. 4. 64,
τοῦτον σχολῆς τῆσδ᾽ ἐκκεκηρῦχθαι λέγω, and so Wecklein. **206** αἰ κι σθέν τ° L,
where the final α has been added by S, lest αἰκισθέν τ᾽ should be read. The spaces
left by the scribe (as often) between other letters in the word show that the space

203 f. The traditional ἐκκεκηρῦχθαι
τάφῳ can be explained only by supplying λέγω or the like. But in 196
κρύψαι and ἐφαγνίσαι depended on κηρύξας ἔχω in 192 (I have proclaimed to
the people). It would be intolerably
awkward to communicate the second
part of the proclamation in an oblique
form with the principal verb unexpressed:
—'(I tell you that) it has been proclaimed.' The choice lies between (1) Musgrave's ἐκκεκήρυκται τάφῳ, and (2)
Nauck's ἐκκεκηρῦχθαι λέγω. In favour
of (1) remark:—(a) τάφῳ is not, indeed, necessary with κτερίζειν, which
can be used absolutely; as Il. 11. 455
αὐτὰρ ἐπεί κε θάνω, κτεριοῦσί με δῖοι
Ἀχαιοί, 'will give me funeral honours':
but, as the main point is that a τάφος is
given to one brother and refused to the
other, the addition of τάφῳ to the more
general term κτερίζειν is plainly desirable
here. (b) The misplacement of μήτε is
due to the thought of κωκῦσαι having
come only after τάφῳ had been uttered
(μήτε κτερίζειν μήτε having been preferred to μὴ κτερίζειν μηδέ), and is not
bolder than (e.g.) the misplacement of τε
in Ph. 1411 f. αὐδὴν τὴν Ἡρακλέους | ἀκοῇ
τε κλύειν λεύσσειν τ᾽ ὄψιν. (c) The MS.
error may have arisen from a reminiscence
of ἐκκεκηρῦχθαι in 27. The line of Carneades (Diog. L. 4. 64), τοῦτον σχολῆς
τῆσδ᾽ ἐκκεκηρῦχθαι λέγω, is no argument
for λέγω in the text of Sophocles. What

could the parodist have made of τάφῳ?
The tragic solemnity of the decree was the
point of the parody, which uses ἐκκεκ. in
a different sense from the poet's ('I proclaim that he is banished from this
school': see on 27).

205 ff. ἐὰν δ᾽: see on 29. Construe, ἄθαπτον, αἰκισθέντ᾽ ἰδεῖν, mangled for all to see, δέμας καὶ πρὸς οἰωνῶν καὶ πρὸς κυνῶν ἐδεστόν, in the
body (acc. of respect) which birds and
dogs devour. L favours αἰκισθέντ᾽: but
this is a point on which our MSS. have
little weight. Reading αἰκισθέντ᾽, it
would be also possible to take ἐδεστόν
as masc., with a slight pause after it; but
this seems less good. With αἰκισθέν τ᾽,
δέμας is accus. in appos.: leave him unburied, a body eaten (etc.), and mangled.
Some recent edd. prefer this.—δέμας of a
corpse, as 903, El. 756, Eur. Or. 40 etc.:
in Hom. always of the living, who has
σῶμα only of the dead: in Attic σῶμα is
said of either.—ἰδεῖν: the aor. inf., as in
the epic θαῦμα ἰδέσθαι, since the aor.
suggests the moment at which the startling
sight catches the eye, whereas the pres.
inf. would suggest continued gazing.

207 f. φρόνημα: on 176.—ἔκ γ᾽ ἐμοῦ,
by an act of mine (cp. 63, 93), while ἔν
γ᾽ ἐμοί in a negative sentence = (not) if I
can help it (O. C. 153).

208 The MSS. have τιμὴν προέξουσ᾽
.. τῶν ἐνδ., shall have honour before the
just, schol. ἕξουσι πρὸ τῶν δικαίων. Such

—touching this man, it hath been proclaimed to our people that none shall grace him with sepulture or lament, but leave him unburied, a corpse for birds and dogs to eat, a ghastly sight of shame.

Such the spirit of my dealing; and never, by deed of mine, shall the wicked stand in honour before the just; but whoso hath good will to Thebes, he shall be honoured of me, in his life and in his death.

CH. Such is thy pleasure, Creon, son of Menoeceus,

---

between ν and τ is consistent with his having meant αἰκισθέντ'.—αἰκισθέν τ' τ. **207** ἐκ γ' ἐμοῦ L, with γρ. ἐξ ἐμοῦ written in the marg. by S. **208** τιμὴν MSS.: τιμῇ Pallis. **211** Κρέον] L has κρέον, but the ο has been made from ω by erasure. Cp. on *O. T.* 637. For Κρέον, Seyffert conject. κυρεῖν: Martin, ποιεῖν: Bellermann, τὸ δρᾶν. Keeping Κρέον, Nauck would alter σοὶ ταῦτ' ἀρέσκει to σὺ ταῦτα δράσεις: Hartung would write σοὶ ταῦτ' ἀρέσκει δρᾶν, Μενοικέως παῖ Κρέον (and so Blaydes, with ταῦτ'

---

a constr. of προέχω occurs nowhere else. But the objection to rendering, 'shall have the advantage of the just in honour' (τιμήν as acc. of respect) is that, after προέχειν in this sense, the *point* of advantage was regularly expressed by the *dat.*: see examples on *O. C.* 1007. τιμῇ (A. Pallis) is most probable, since either ΤΙΜΗΙ or τιμηι might easily have become the accus. before the verb. Hermann read **προσέξουσ'** (which I do not understand) because of the hiatus (but cp. *O. T.* 351 προείπας, *ib.* 107 αὐτοέντας); and because the honours claimed for Polyneices are only equal, not superior. But Creon's meaning is explained by vv. 514 ff.: the honour is greater for a public foe than for a patriot.

210 τιμήσεται: cp. on 93.

211 f. I print Dindorf's **κᾆς** for καὶ in v. 212, not as thinking it certain, but because, with the least change, it gives a satisfactory construction. Soph. has this crasis in fr. 428 φίλων τε μέμψιν κεῖς θεοὺς ἁμαρτάνειν. Cp. Plat. *Rep.* 538 B παράνομόν τι δρᾶσαι ἢ εἰπεῖν εἰς αὐτούς ('with regard to them'). For the place of the prep., cp. 367, *O. T.* 734 Δελφῶν κἀπὸ Δαυλίας. With the MS. reading, the accusatives in v. 212 must be governed by **σοὶ ταῦτ' ἀρέσκει** as = σὺ ταῦτα δρᾶσαι διανοεῖ. Greek was bold in constructions κατὰ σύνεσιν, and might possibly have tolerated this: but it seems improbable. In the apparently similar instances the periphrasis for the transitive verb always contains a noun di-

rectly suggestive of that verb: as Eur. *Ion* 572 τοῦτο κἄμ' ἔχει πόθος = τοῦτο κἀγὼ ποθῶ: Aesch. *Ag.* 814 φθορὰς... ψήφους ἔθεντο: *Suppl.* 533 γένος...νέωσον αἶνον: *Theb.* 289 ζωπυροῦσι τάρβος ...λεών: Dem. or. 19 § 81 τεθνάναι τῷ φόβῳ...ξένους. Nor can the accusatives in v. 212 be explained as mere accus. 'of respect'; nor as if, by a euphemism, παθεῖν were understood.—There is much in favour of the view that **Κρέον** in v. 211 has displaced an infin., such as παθεῖν, λαβεῖν, λαχεῖν, ποιεῖν, or τὸ δρᾶν. In v. 1098 L has εὐβουλίας δεῖ, παῖ Μενοικέως, λαβεῖν, where later MSS. have Κρέον in place of λαβεῖν: see n. there. If Κρέον is not genuine in v. 211, then it is much more likely to have been a mere gloss on παῖ Μενοικέως than a corruption of a similar word. The conjecture κυρεῖν, then, merits no preference; though the acc. ταῦτα could stand with it (Aesch. *Ch.* 714 κυρούντων...τὰ πρόσφορα, Eur. *Hec.* 699 ἐπ' ἀκταῖς νιν κυρῶ).—Brunck wrote **ταῦτ'**, understanding ἀρέσκει (με) ταὐτὰ σοί, 'my view is the same as yours.' But **ταῦτ'** is right. The Chorus say—'Such is my lord's pleasure. And, of course, he can do as seems him good.' Their tone is sufficiently interpreted by vv. 216, 220, 278. Cp. Her. I. 119 (Harpagus to Astyages) ἔφη... ἀρεστὸν εἶναι πᾶν τὸ ἂν βασιλεὺς ἔρδῃ. The Chorus do not oppose Creon; but they feel a secret misgiving; they wish at least to remain passive.

τὸν τῇδε δύσνουν *κἀς τὸν εὐμενῆ πόλει·
νόμῳ δὲ χρῆσθαι παντὶ πού γ' ἔνεστί σοι
καὶ τῶν θανόντων χὡπόσοι ζῶμεν πέρι.

ΚΡ. ὡς ἂν σκοποί νυν ἦτε τῶν εἰρημένων.   215
ΧΟ. νεωτέρῳ τῳ τοῦτο βαστάζειν πρόθες.
ΚΡ. ἀλλ' εἰσ' ἕτοιμοι τοῦ νεκροῦ γ' ἐπίσκοποι.
ΧΟ. τί δῆτ' ἂν ἄλλο τοῦτ' ἐπεντέλλοις ἔτι;
ΚΡ. τὸ μὴ 'πιχωρεῖν τοῖς ἀπιστοῦσιν τάδε.
ΧΟ. οὐκ ἔστιν οὕτω μῶρος ὃς θανεῖν ἐρᾷ.   220
ΚΡ. καὶ μὴν ὁ μισθός γ' οὗτος· ἀλλ' ὑπ' ἐλπίδων
ἄνδρας τὸ κέρδος πολλάκις διώλεσεν.

ΦΥΛΑΞ.

ἄναξ, ἐρῶ μὲν οὐχ ὅπως τάχους ὕπο

---

for ταῦτ'). **212** Leaving v. 211 unchanged, M. Schmidt and Todt conject. δρᾶν τόν τε δύσνουν: Wecklein, ἐς τόν τε δύσνουν. Dindorf would merely change καὶ to κἀς. **213** παντί πουτ (sic) ἔνεστί σοι L. The later MSS. have πού τ' or ποτ' ἔνεστί σοι. Erfurdt conject. πού γ': C. Winckelmann, σοί γ' ἔνεστί που: Dindorf, formerly που μέτεστί σοι, then που πάρεστί σοι. **215** ὡς ἂν σκοποὶ νῦν ἦτε MSS. Schneidewin conject. ὡς οὖν . . ἦτε: Dindorf, πῶς ἂν . . εἶτε: Todt, ὅπως σκοποὶ δ' ἔσεσθε: Nauck, καλῶς· σκοποὶ νῦν ἔστε: Semitelos, ὡς οὖν σκοποὶ μενεῖτε. **217** νεκροῦτ' L: the τ' is somewhat like Γ, but the first hand certainly did not mean γ', as may be seen by comparing 207 (ἐκ γ'), and 221 (μισθός γ'). The error is like πουτ' in 213.—νεκροῦ γ'

---

213 f. In παντί πού γ' the enclitic που closely adheres to παντί, and γε emphasises the whole expression; as in *El.* 1506, ὅστις πέρα πράσσειν γε τῶν νόμων θέλει, the γε emphasises the whole phrase πέρα πράσσειν. The transposition σοί γ'...που is open to the objection that παντί, not σοί, claims the chief emphasis. παντί που πάρεστι has also been proposed. But ἔνεστι is slightly more suitable to this context, because more suggestive of *tacit disapproval*. 'It is *possible* for you' ('but we doubt whether it is expedient'). πάρεστί σοι is generally said rather when the speaker means, 'it is easy for you,' or 'it is open to you,'—in seconding a wish of the other person, or in making an offer to him. *Ph.* 364 τἆλλα μὲν πάρεστί σοι | πατρῷ' ἑλέσθαι. Cp. *O. T.* 766.—παντί που μέτεστί σοι, which some prefer, is still less suitable here. It would imply a right shared by the King with some other man or men (cp. on 48).—Though the antecedent (ἡμῶν) to χὡπόσοι ζῶμεν is understood, πέρι can stand at the end of the verse, since such a relative clause was felt al-most as a noun-case: see on 35. Cp. Eur. *Ion* 560 ἢ θίγω δῆθ' οἵ μ' ἔφυσαν; (=τῶν φυσάντων).

215 ὡς ἄν...ἦτε can be explained only by an ellipse of ἐπιμελεῖσθε or the like. After verbs of 'taking care,' the usu. constr. is ὅπως with fut. indic.; but ὡς ἄν with subj. is sometimes found, as Xen. *Hipparch.* 9. 2 ἐπιμελεῖσθαι ὡς ἂν πραχθῇ...ἢν μή τις ἐπιμελῆται ὡς ἂν ταῦτα περαίνηται. In elliptical phrases, where a precept or charge is given (ὅρα, etc., being understood), the regular constr. is ὅπως with fut. ind., as Lys. or. 1. 21 ὅπως τοίνυν ταῦτα μηδεὶς ἀνθρώπων πεύσεται. The elliptical ὅπως μή with subjunct. is different,—'take care *lest*,' —a deferential way of hinting an objection (Plat. *Crat.* 430 D), like the simple elliptical μή with subjunct. *O. C.* 1180. Since, however, ἐπιμελεῖσθαι could be followed by ὡς ἄν with subjunct., it is conceivable that Soph. should write ὡς ἄν σκοποὶ ἦτε instead of the usual ὅπως σκοποὶ ἔσεσθε. I cannot think, with Wecklein, that the sentence is broken off, as though Creon said,—'*In order that* ye

touching this city's foe, and its friend; and thou hast power,
I ween, to take what order thou wilt, both for the dead, and for
all us who live.

CR. See, then, that ye be guardians of the mandate.

CH. Lay the burden of this task on some younger man.

CR. Nay, watchers of the corpse have been found.

CH. What, then, is this further charge that thou wouldst
give?

CR. That ye side not with the breakers of these commands.

CH. No man is so foolish that he is enamoured of death.

CR. In sooth, that is the meed; yet lucre hath oft ruined
men through their hopes.

Enter GUARD.

My liege, I will not say that I come breathless from

Brunck. **218** ἄλλωι L, with o written over ω by the first hand. ἄλλω and ἄλλο r.
Brunck conject. ἄλλο τοῦδ': Pallis, ἀλλ' ἐκ τοῦδ' (or ἐκ τῶνδ'). **219** 'πιχωρεῖν L first
hand, but an early hand has changed ω to ει. Schol., μὴ ἐπιτρέπειν μηδὲ συγχωρεῖν
τοῖς ἀπειθοῦσιν,—showing that he, too, read 'πιχωρεῖν, which almost all the later MSS.
have. L² has ἐπιχειρεῖν, but with the gloss ἐπιτρέπειν (see Campbell). **223 ΦΥΛΑΞ**]
In L the designation of the speaker is ἄγγ, with ε written above (ἄγγελος): below, at
v. 384, it is αγ, but with φύλαξ in the margin. In L's list of the Dramatis Personae
(prefixed to the play) it is φύλαξ ἄγγελος. τάχους MSS.: σπουδῆς Arist. *Rhet.* 3. 14

may be watchers of my mandate,'—being
about to add, μὴ ἐπιχωρεῖτε.—Dindorf's
πῶς ἄν...εἶτε is supported by usage, as
O. T. 765 πῶς ἂν μόλοι δῆθ' ἡμὶν ἐν
τάχει πάλιν; Nauck (*Cur. Eur.* II. 79)
refuses εἶμεν and εἶτε to tragedy, but is
not convincing. In *O. T.* 1046 εἰδεῖν'
(for εἰδείητε) is certain: and εἶτε for εἴητε
is strictly parallel. εἶτε occurs in *Od.* 21.
195 ποῖοί κ' εἶτ' Ὀδυσῆι ἀμυνέμεν, εἴ ποθεν
ἔλθοι; In Eur. *Alc.* 921 ἦμεν might replace εἶμεν: though in *Hipp.* 349, at least,
the opt. εἶμεν seems required. But πῶς
ἂν εἶτε is here less fitting than ὡς ἂν
ἦτε, because a request is less suitable
than an injunction.—**σκοποί**, φύλακες,
who watch to see that no one breaks the
edict.—**νυν** is better than **νῦν**.—**τῶν εἰρ.**,
the commands: cp. Aesch. *Ag.* 1620 σω-
φρονεῖν εἰρημένον, Her. 7. 26 εἴρητο συλ-
λέγεσθαι...στρατόν.

216 f. πρόθες τοῦτο, set him this as a
task (cp. 1249), **βαστάζειν**, for him to
take in hand (*suscipiendum*); the act. inf.
as *O. C.* 231 πόνον...ἀντιδίδωσιν ἔχειν.
For the lit. sense of the verb cp. *Ai.* 827
ὥς με βαστάσῃ | πεπτῶτα (raise me).—
τοῦ νεκροῦ γ': but ἐπίσκοποι τῶν ἀστῶν
are still needed.

218 f. τί δῆτ' ἄν...ἐπεντέλλοις=τί
δῆτ' ἂν εἴη...ὃ ἐπεντέλλεις; cp. *O. C.* 647
μέγ' ἂν λέγοις δώρημα: *Ph.* 26.—The reading **ἄλλῳ** is a bad one, for the contrast is
between commands, not persons; and an
awkward ambiguity would arise, since
τοῦτο might then seem to mean the
watching of the corpse.—**ἐπιχωρεῖν**, *ac-
cedere*, to join their side: Thuc. 4. 107
δεξάμενος τοὺς ἐθελήσαντας ἐπιχωρῆσαι...
κατὰ τὰς σπονδάς. Arist. *Mirab.* 133
τούτῳ τῷ ἐπιγράμματι ἐπεχώρησε καὶ ὁ
τόπος ἐκεῖνος (corroborated it).—**ἀπιστοῦσιν**=ἀπειθοῦσιν: 381, 656.—**τάδε**,
cogn. acc.: cp. 66.

220 ff. ὃς (instead of ὥστε) **ἐρᾷ**, a
constr. most freq. in negative sentences,
usu. with ὅστις (Dem. or. 1 § 15 τίς οὕτως
εὐήθης ἐστὶν...ὅστις ἀγνοεῖ), or ὃς ἄν and
opt. (Plat. *Rep.* 360 B οὐδεὶς ἂν γένοιτο
οὕτως ἀδαμάντινος, ὃς ἂν μείνειεν). But it
occurs also in affirmative sentences, as
Eur. *Andr.* 170 ἐς τοῦτο δ' ἥκεις ἀμαθίας
...ἢ...τολμᾷς. Cp. Her. 4. 52.—**καὶ μὴν**
(lit., 'and verily') here confirms the last
speaker's remark by adding an assurance
that disobedience does indeed mean
death; while **γε** after **μισθός** emphasises
that word. 'And I can tell you that the

δύσπνους ἱκάνω, κοῦφον ἐξάρας πόδα·
πολλὰς γὰρ ἔσχον φροντίδων ἐπιστάσεις,   225
ὁδοῖς κυκλῶν ἐμαυτὸν εἰς ἀναστροφήν·
ψυχὴ γὰρ ηὔδα πολλά μοι μυθουμένη·
τάλας, τί χωρεῖς οἷ μολὼν δώσεις δίκην;
τλήμων, μένεις αὖ; κεἰ τάδ᾽ εἴσεται Κρέων
ἄλλου παρ᾽ ἀνδρός, πῶς σὺ δῆτ᾽ οὐκ ἀλγυνεῖ;   230
τοιαῦθ᾽ ἑλίσσων ἤνυτον σχολῇ βραδύς,
χοὔτως ὁδὸς βραχεῖα γίγνεται μακρά.
τέλος γε μέντοι δεῦρ᾽ ἐνίκησεν μολεῖν

§ 10, and so Dindorf, Hartung, Nauck, Wecklein.   **225** ἔσχον L: εὗρον r.—φρον-
τίδων] Nauck conj. δεῦρ᾽ ἰών.   **229** μένεις αὖ;] In L the first hand seems to have
written μὲν εἰ σαῦ (μὲν εἰς αὖ): a corrector has wished to make this into μενεῖς αὖ, the
reading of most of the later MSS. (including A), but has left the accent on μὲν (cp. n.

---

requital of disobedience is that.' For καὶ μήν so used, cp. *O. T.* 836, 1004 f., *El.* 556.—τὸ κέρδος, 'gain,' *i.e.*, as ἐλπί-δων shows, the prospect of gain, with the generic art. (cp. 1242): so fr. 749 τὸ κέρδος ἡδύ, κἂν ἀπὸ ψευδῶν ἴῃ.—διώλεσεν, gnomic aor.

223 ἐρῶ μὲν οὐχ: cp. on 96.—ὅπως =ὅτι, as *O. T.* 548: cp. *El.* 963 μηκέτ᾽ ἐλπίσῃς ὅπως | τεύξει. This use is rare in Attic prose (for after θαυμάζω, etc., ὅπως ='how'), though freq. in Her., as 2. 49 οὐδὲ φήσω ὅκως...ἔλαβον. Yet cp. Plat. *Euthyd.* 296 E οὐκ ἔχω ὑμῖν πῶς ἀμφισβη-τοίην...ὅπως οὐ πάντα ἐγὼ ἐπίσταμαι.—τάχους ὕπο is the reading of the MSS. Aristotle quotes this verse as an example of a προοίμιον used by the speaker to avert a danger from himself, and gives it thus:—ἄναξ, ἐρῶ μὲν οὐχ ὅπως σπουδῆς ὕπο (*Rhet.* 3. 14 § 10). Hence some edd. adopt σπουδῆς, as coming from a source older than our MSS. But, since τάχους is free from objection, such a change is unwarrantable. Aristotle's quotations seem to have been usually made from memory, and his memory was not in-fallible. To take only three examples cited by Bellermann, we find: (1) *El.* 256 ἀλλ᾽ ἡ βία γὰρ ταῦτ᾽ ἀναγκάζει με δρᾶν, quoted *Metaphys.* 4. 5 ἀλλ᾽ ἡ βία με ταῦτ᾽ ἀναγκάζει ποιεῖν: (2) *O. T.* 774 ἐμοὶ πατὴρ μὲν Πόλυβος ἦν, quoted *Rhet.* 3. 14 § 6 ἐμοὶ πατὴρ ἦν Πόλυβος: (3) *Ant.* 911 μητρὸς δ᾽ ἐν Ἅιδου καὶ πατρὸς κεκευθό-τοιν, quoted *Rhet.* 3. 16 § 9 with βεβηκό-των as last word. So *Il.* 9. 592 κήδε᾽ ὅσ᾽ ἀνθρώποισι πέλει τῶν ἄστυ ἁλώῃ |

ἄνδρας μὲν κτείνουσι, is quoted *Rhet.* 1. 7 § 31 with ὅσσα κάκ᾽ substituted for the first two words, and λαοὶ μὲν φθινύθουσι for the last three.

224 ff. ἐξάρας (ᾰ), aor. part., not pres., because, as ἐξ- shows, the notion is, 'having set in nimble movement' (at starting). Cp. Eur. *Tro.* 342 μὴ κοῦφον αἴρῃ βῆμ᾽ ἐς Ἀργείων στρατόν.—φροντί-δων, possessive gen. with ἐπιστάσεις, halts belonging to thoughts, *i.e.* caused by them. Others understand, 'halts *for* thought' (made in order to reflect),—which is less simple. Cp. Arist. *De Anim.* 1. 3 (p. 407ª 32) ἡ νόησις ἔοικεν ἠρεμήσει τινὶ καὶ ἐπιστάσει (halt) μᾶλλον ἢ κινήσει.—ὁδοῖς, locative dat.; cp. *O. C.* 553 ὁδοῖς | ἐν ταῖσδ᾽, 'in this my coming.'—κυκλῶν = περιστρέφων.

227 ψυχὴ γὰρ ηὔδα κ.τ.λ. The naïveté consists in the direct quotation of what his ψυχή said, rather than in the statement that it spoke; thus Hor. *Sat.* 1. 2. 68 (quoted by Schneid.) is really simi-lar,—*Huic si...Diceret haec animus.* Take πολλά with μυθουμένη only. I do not think that ηὔδα...μυθουμένη was meant to mark garrulity; the language is not homely enough: rather it is simply,—'found a voice, speaking many things,' ἔφη λέγων is not similar (*Ai.* 757).—Cp. Launcelot Gobbo in Shaksp. *Merch.* 2. 2: *Certainly my conscience will serve me to run from this Jew my master. The fiend is at mine elbow and tempts me...My conscience says, 'Launcelot, budge not.' 'Budge,' says the fiend. 'Budge not,' says my conscience.*

speed, or that I have plied a nimble foot; for often did my thoughts make me pause, and wheel round in my path, to return. My mind was holding large discourse with me; 'Fool, why goest thou to thy certain doom?' 'Wretch, tarrying again? And if Creon hears this from another, must not thou smart for it?' So debating, I went on my way with lagging steps, and thus a short road was made long. At last, however, it carried the day that I should come hither—to

on 182). This accent suggests that the scribe of L had μένεις in his archetype.—κεῖ L, but by correction, prob. from καί, which some of the later MSS. (as A) have, while others have εἶ. **231** σχολῇ βραδὺς MSS.: schol. in marg. of L, γρ. ταχύς. Seyffert

228 ff. τάλας...τλήμων, nom., not voc., because each is rather a comment ('hapless that thou art!') than properly an address: so *O. C.* 185 ὦ τλάμων, *ib.* 753 ὦ τάλας ἐγώ, Eur. *Med.* 61 ὦ μῶρος. —μένεις is better than μενεῖς, since, '*are you* tarrying again?' (his halts having been frequent, 225) is more graphic than, '*will you* tarry again?'—αὖ cannot mean here, 'on the contrary' (*i.e.* instead of going on).—πῶς...οὐκ, as *O. T.* 937, 976, etc.—ἀλγυνεῖ, pass.: cp. on 93 ἐχθαρεῖ.

231 ἑλίσσων, turning over and over in the mind: cp. on 158 ἐρέσσων.—ἤνυτον (*sc.* τὴν ὁδόν), gradually made my way (impf.); whereas ἤνυσα would have suited a quick journey. Cp. this impf. in Plat. *Symp.* 127 C οὐδαμῇ ταύτῃ ἤνυτον, 'they could make no progress by that means.' Soph. has this tense also in *Tr.* 319 (ἔργον ἤνυτον): cp. below, 805. In Dem. or. 21 § 104 our MSS. give οὐδὲν ἤνυε. For the use of the verb in ref. to journeys, cp. Thuc. 2. 97 (ὁδὸς) ἡμερῶν ἀνδρὶ εὐζώνῳ τριῶν καὶ δέκα ἀνύσαι. The Attic *pres.* seems to have been ἀνύτω as='to accomplish,' or 'to make way,' but ἀνύειν as='to hasten.' Ar. *Plut.* 413 μὴ νυν διάτριβ' ἀλλ' ἄνυε: *Ran.* 606 ἀνύετον: though in *Plut.* 606 οὐ μέλλειν | χρή σ', ἀλλ' ἀνύειν, some MSS. have ἀνύτειν (see Pors. on *Phoen.* 463). This is the distinction meant by the grammarian in Bekk. *Anecd.* 411. 28 ἀνύττειν (*sic*) οἱ Ἀττικοὶ ὅπερ ἡμεῖς, ἀνύειν δὲ τὸ σπεύδειν. (The aspirated forms lack good evidence.) Cp. ἀρύω, Attic ἀρύτω.

σχολῇ βραδύς, reluctantly and slowly; the opposite of σὺν σπουδῇ ταχύς (*Ph.* 1223), with eagerness and speed. σχολῇ oft.='at a slow pace' (πορεύεσθαι, Xen. *An.* 4. 1. 16; ὑποχωρεῖν, Thuc. 3. 78).

As βραδύς could mean 'sluggish' (*O. C.* 306), we might here refer σχολῇ to pace, and βραδύς to reluctance; but, though the common use of σχολῇ in regard to pace helps to make it suitable here, it is better, in this context, to give σχολῇ the moral and βραδύς the physical sense. For σχολῇ combined with another word in such an expression, cp. Polyb. 8. 30 σχολῇ καὶ βάδην ποιεῖσθαι τὴν πορείαν. There is no lack of point. Such a messenger ought to have come σπουδῇ ταχύς.—The conjecture **σπουδῇ βραδύς** is (I think) not only wrong but bad. It would mean, 'slow in my haste'; eager to arrive, yet moving slowly. σπεῦδε βραδέως, to which it is supposed to allude, meant, 'never remit your efforts, but advance circumspectly towards your aim': *festina lente* (on which see Erasmus in the *Adagia*); *Eile mit Weile;* Goethe's *Ohne Hast, ohne Rast.* (σπεῦδε βραδέως was a favourite maxim of Augustus, Suet. *Aug.* 25; Gellius 10. 11 § 5, on whom, as often, Macrobius has drawn, *Sat.* 6. 8. 9.) The frightened and irresolute φύλαξ, —sent, sorely against his will, on a hateful errand,—had no more σπουδή than Mr Facing-both-ways. Wecklein, keeping σχολῇ, supposes the Guard to mean, 'this was a case of σχολῇ βραδύς, not σπουδῇ βραδύς,'—an improbably obscure and feeble jest at such a critical moment. The variant given by the schol., σχολῇ **ταχύς**, would be an oxymoron, designedly comic; 'I took my time about hurrying,' ''twas but a laggard haste that I made.' A cheerful epigram of this sort would better suit a mind more at ease.

233 τέλος γε μέντοι, *at last*, however; γε emphasising the word before it: *O. T.* 442 n.—ἐνίκησεν, impers., as Thuc. 2. 54 ἐνίκησε δὲ...λοιμὸν εἰρῆσθαι (the opinion prevailed that...): Her. 6. 101 ἐνίκα μὴ

σοί· κεἰ τὸ μηδὲν ἐξερῶ, φράσω δ᾽ ὅμως.
τῆς ἐλπίδος γὰρ ἔρχομαι δεδραγμένος,   235
τὸ μὴ παθεῖν ἂν ἄλλο πλὴν τὸ μόρσιμον.
ΚΡ. τί δ᾽ ἐστὶν ἀνθ᾽ οὗ τήνδ᾽ ἔχεις ἀθυμίαν;
ΦΥ. φράσαι θέλω σοι πρῶτα τἀμαυτοῦ· τὸ γὰρ
πρᾶγμ᾽ οὔτ᾽ ἔδρασ᾽ οὔτ᾽ εἶδον ὅστις ἦν ὁ δρῶν,
οὐδ᾽ ἂν δικαίως ἐς κακὸν πέσοιμί τι.   240
ΚΡ. εὖ γε στοχάζει κἀποφράγνυσαι κύκλῳ
τὸ πρᾶγμα· δηλοῖς δ᾽ ὥς τι σημανῶν νέον.

conject. σπουδῇ βραδύς. **234** σοὶ κ᾽ εἰ L (the apostrophe after κ from a later hand). Erfurdt, κεῖ σοι: Hartung, σοὶ δ᾽ οὖν.—φράσω δ᾽] φράσαι δ᾽ Wunder; φράσων (without δ᾽) Wecklein. **235** πεπραγμένος L, with schol. ὑπὸ γὰρ τῆς ἐλπίδος νενικημένος ἐλήλυθα. ἢ οὕτως· ἀντειλημμένος τῆς ἐλπίδος ἐλήλυθα. We have here two commentators: the first was attempting to explain πεπραγμένος: the second read δεδραγμένος, which is in E (with φαρ written above) and V³: while in Aug. b and V⁴ is the gl., γρ. δὲ καὶ δεδραγμένος. The rest of the later MSS. have either πεπραγμένος (as A, L²), or πεφραγμένος (as Aug. b, Vat., V⁴).—Dindorf wrote πεφαργμένος.—Semitelos conject.

ἐκλιπεῖν τὴν πόλιν. That μολεῖν should not be regarded as the subject to ἐνίκησε, is shown by such an example as Her. 8. 9 ἐνίκα τὴν ἡμέρην ἐκείνην αὐτοῦ μείναντάς τε καὶ αὐλισθέντας μετέπειτα νύκτα μέσην παρέντας πορεύεσθαι, where the length of the interval excludes such a view. The personal constr. occurs below, 274; cp. Thuc. 2. 12 ἦν...Περικλέους γνώμη...νενικηκυῖα.

234 σοί with μολεῖν. In Attic prose a dat. of the person after ἔρχομαι is freq., and oft. can be rendered (as here) only by 'to,' though it is properly rather a dat. of interest. Thus Thuc. 1. 13 Ἀμεινοκλῆς Σάμιος ἦλθε='A. came to the Samians,' though the primary notion is, 'the Samians enjoyed the advantage of A.'s coming' (to build triremes for them). So id. 1. 27 ὡς αὐτοῖς...ἦλθον ἄγγελοι: Plat. Prot. 321 C ἀποροῦντι δὲ αὐτῷ ἔρχεται Προμηθεύς. In poetry this dat. is freely used after verbs of motion, but the idea of interest is always traceable; cp. 186 n. Aesch. P. V. 358 ἀλλ᾽ ἦλθεν αὐτῷ Ζηνὸς ἄγρυπνον βέλος. So here, μολεῖν σοί is not strictly a mere equiv. for μολεῖν πρὸς σέ, but implies Creon's interest in the news. The notion is, 'to come and place myself at your disposal.' For the emphatic place of σοί, cp. 273 (and 46 n.): for the pause after the first syllable of the verse, 250, 464.—κεῖ, 'and if': not, 'even if.' If καί were taken

as='even,' there would be a very harsh asyndeton, whether the stop were at σοί, or (as Nauck places it) after μολεῖν. It is true that καί could mean 'even,' without causing an asyndeton, if we adopted Wecklein's tempting φράσων for φράσω δ᾽: but the latter is confirmed by O. T. 302 εἰ καὶ μὴ βλέπεις, φρονεῖς δ᾽ ὅμως (where see n.),—δέ introducing the apodosis after a concessive protasis. For κεῖ as='and if,' cp. Ai. 447, 1057. The transposition κεῖ σοι is improbable, as destroying the significant emphasis and pause on σοί.—τὸ μηδέν, what is as nought,—a tale of simple discomfiture: since he can only report the deed, without giving any clue to the doer. Cp. Tr. 1107 κἂν τὸ μηδὲν ὦ: Ai. 1275 ἤδη τὸ μηδὲν ὄντας ἐν τροπῇ δορός.

235 f. τῆς ἐλπίδος, not 'hope,' but 'the hope'—defined in next v.—δεδραγμένος is certain. Il. 13. 393 κόνιος δεδραγμένος (and 16. 486). Diod. 12. 67 δράξασθαι καιροῦ. (Cp. Shaks. Per. 1. 1. 49 Gripe not at earthly joys.) Here the phrase is meant to be homely. The v.l. πεφραγμένος was simply an attempt to mend L's πεπραγμένος. We should require the dat. with it. The gen. cannot be justified by instances in which poetry uses a gen. of the agent without ὑπό, after pass. part., as Ai. 807 φωτὸς ἠπατημένη, Eur. Or. 497 πληγεὶς θυγατρός, etc.—τὸ μὴ παθεῖν ἄν=ὅτι οὐ thee ; and, though my tale be nought, yet will I tell it ; for I come with a good grip on one hope,—that I can suffer nothing but what is my fate.

CR. And what is it that disquiets thee thus ?

GU. I wish to tell thee first about myself—I did not do the deed—I did not see the doer—it were not right that I should come to any harm.

CR. Thou hast a shrewd eye for thy mark ; well dost thou fence thyself round against the blame :—clearly thou hast some strange thing to tell.

δεδραμένοις ('on account of my deeds'). **238** πρῶτα L: πάντα r. **241** στοχάζει MSS. : Hartung conject. στιχάζει (others, στιχίζει): Emper, σκεπάζει: F. Jacobs, στεγάζει.—From Arist. *Rhet.* 3. 14. 11 Bergk and others adopt τί φροιμιάζει; Wecklein suggests εὖ φροιμιάζει.—κἀποφράγνυσαι MSS.: κἀποφάργνυσαι Dindorf. **242** σημαίνων L: σημανῶν r. Didymus (*circ.* 30 B.C.) read the latter, as appears from the schol. on *Ai.* 1225 Δίδυμος· καὶ δῆλός ἐστιν ὥς τι σημανῶν νέον, a verse composed by a slip of memory, as Dindorf saw, from this verse and *Ai.* 326 καὶ δῆλός ἐστιν ὥς τι

πάθοιμι ἄν, depending on ἐλπίδος...δεδρ. as = ἐλπίζων : for the art. with infin., cp. 78 n.—τὸ μόρσιμον: *i.e.* if you do kill me, then it was my destiny to be killed.

237 f. ἀνθ' οὗ, on account of which: *O. T.* 264 ἀνθ' ὧν : *El.* 585 ἀνθ' ὅτου.— τὸ γὰρ | πρᾶγμ': cp. on 67. γάρ prefaces the statement: *O. T.* 277 n.: cp. below, 478, 999.

241 f. εὖ γε στοχάζει κ.τ.λ.: 'yes, you take your aim well, and seek to fence yourself round against the charge.' The mark at which the man aims is his own safety; and this is explained by the next phrase. Commentators have made difficulties by assuming that the metaphors of στοχάζει and ἀποφράγνυσαι must be harmonised into a single picture,—as of an archer shooting from covert. But in fact there is a rapid transition from one to the other; the second interprets the first; and all that is common to them is their military source. στοχάζομαι was familiar in a sense akin to that which it has here: cp. Plat. *Lach.* 178 B στοχαζόμενοι τοῦ συμβουλευομένου ἀλλὰ λέγουσι παρὰ τὴν αὑτῶν δόξαν (trying to hit the thought of the person who consults them): Polyb. 6. 16 ὀφείλουσι δὲ ἀεὶ ποιεῖν οἱ δήμαρχοι τὸ δοκοῦν τῷ δήμῳ καὶ μάλιστα στοχάζεσθαι τῆς τούτου βουλήσεως. So here the verb suggests a designing person, whose elaborate preamble covers a secret aim. Creon is quick to suspect bribery (221). Cp.

1033 ὥστε τοξόται σκοποῦ | τοξεύετ' ἀνδρὸς τοῦδε. Schneidewin thought that στοχάζει might here be a term of hunting or war, with ref. to the erecting of nets on poles, or of palisades. στοιχίζειν was so used, of nets in hunting (Xen. *Cyneg.* 6. 8). But στοῖχος is from rt στιχ, while στόχος is from a probably distinct rt σταχ (στάχυς), στεχ (perhaps lengthened from στα). In Ar. *Rhet.* 3. 14 § 10 the citation of v. 223 is immediately followed by the words τί φροιμιάζῃ; which Nauck (with Bergk) substitutes for εὖ γε στοχάζει here. But, though the schol. there says that Creon spoke them, they evidently belonged to some other passage, which Arist. cites as a second example: perh. to Eur. *I. T.* 1162 τί φροιμιάζει νεοχμόν; ἐξαύδα σαφῶς. A schol. on Arist. *l. c.* says, τὸ δὲ τί φροιμιάζῃ ἐν τισὶ τῶν ἀντιγράφων οὐ κεῖται (*i.e.* in some MSS. of Arist.); which looks as if the words had been deleted, in such copies, by readers who could not find them in Soph. —κἀποφράγνυσαι. Inscriptions of the 5th cent. B.C. show φράξαι (not φράξαι) to have been the old Attic aor. (Meisterhans p. 89), and so ναύφαρκτος, etc.: but the analogy of the pres. φράττω recommends φράγνυμι rather than φάργνυμι. For the constr., cp. Thuc. 8. 104 ἐβούλοντο ἀποφάρξασθαι αὐτοὺς οἱ ἐναντίοι (to shut them off).—τὸ πρᾶγμα, so soon after 239: cp. on 76.

242 δηλοῖς δ' ὥς τι σ.: see on 20.

ΦΥ. τὰ δεινὰ γάρ τοι προστίθησ᾽ ὄκνον πολύν.

ΚΡ. οὔκουν ἐρεῖς ποτ᾽, εἶτ᾽ ἀπαλλαχθεὶς ἄπει;

ΦΥ. καὶ δὴ λέγω σοι. τὸν νεκρόν τις ἀρτίως   245
θάψας βέβηκε κἀπὶ χρωτὶ διψίαν
κόνιν παλύνας κἀφαγιστεύσας ἃ χρή.

ΚΡ. τί φής; τίς ἀνδρῶν ἦν ὁ τολμήσας τάδε;

ΦΥ. οὐκ οἶδ᾽· ἐκεῖ γὰρ οὔτε του γενῇδος ἦν
πλῆγμ᾽, οὐ δικέλλης ἐκβολή· στύφλος δὲ γῆ   250
καὶ χέρσος, ἀρρὼξ οὐδ᾽ ἐπημαξευμένη
τροχοῖσιν, ἀλλ᾽ ἄσημος οὑργάτης τις ἦν.
ὅπως δ᾽ ὁ πρῶτος ἡμὶν ἡμεροσκόπος
δείκνυσι, πᾶσι θαῦμα δυσχερὲς παρῆν.
ὁ μὲν γὰρ ἠφάνιστο, τυμβήρης μὲν οὔ,   255
λεπτὴ δ᾽ ἄγος φεύγοντος ὡς ἐπῆν κόνις.

ἔρασείων κακόν.   **249** In L του has been made from που by an early hand (perh.

---

243 f. τὰ δεινά, dangers,—*i.e.* the κακὰ ἔπη (277) which he brings: **γάρ** (yes, I am cautious) for, etc.—**ποτ᾽,** *tandem aliquando, O. T.* 335 n.—**ἀπαλλαχθείς,** 'having been removed,' *i.e.* 'having taken yourself off'; cp. Ar. *Vesp.* 484 ἆρ᾽ ἄν, ὦ πρὸς τῶν θεῶν, ὑμεῖς ἀπαλλαχθεῖτέ μου;
245 ff. καὶ δή, without more ado: *O. C.* 31 n.—**θάψας,** because the essential rite was the throwing of earth on the body: cp. on 80, and below, 256.—The καί in **κἀπί** is 'and' (rather than 'both,' answering to καί in 247); it introduces an explanation of θάψας.—**διψίαν,** as Aesch. *Ag.* 495 πηλοῦ ξύνουρος διψία κόνις: Lucr. 2. 376 *bibula...arena.*—**κἀφαγιστεύσας** (καὶ ἁ.) **ἃ χρή,** *i.e.* having made the due offerings. perh. flowers (*El.* 896), or στέφη of wool. We may doubt whether the poet thought of any χοαί as having been poured by Antigone at this first visit; see n. on 429.—ἀφαγιστεύσας and ἐφαγιστεύσας are equally possible; but I prefer the former, because here, as v. 256 suggests, the idea is that of ἀφοσιωσάμενος,—having avoided an ἄγος by satisfying religion: see on 196 ἐφαγνίσαι.
248 ff. ἀνδρῶν: he does not think of women.—**οὔτε του γενῇδος...οὐ δικέλλης.** For the enclitic του so placed, cp. 20 n.: for οὔτε...οὐ, *O. C.* 972 n. γενῇῖς, **γενῇς** (only here), is prop. an adj., an

implement with a **γένυς** (jaw), or blade: *El.* 485 ἀμφάκης γένυς, the two-edged blade (of a bronze axe). Hesych. γενῇδα· ἀξίνην, πέλεκυν (referring, as the acc. shows, to some other passage): and here the **γενῇς** is prob. the same as the ἀξίνη below (1109), which was to be used in raising the mound (1203). We may render 'pickaxe,' since this properly has a blade as well as a point. The **γενῇς** would break the hard surface. Then the earth would be thrown up (**ἐκβολή**) with the **δίκελλα,** which was a sort of heavy two-pronged hoe, used, like the Roman *ligo* or *bidens*, in hoeing up soil: the μάκελλα (μία, κέλλω to drive forward) being a like tool with one prong. The σμινύη was like the δίκελλα, a two-pronged hoe. 'Mattock' is the nearest word for it. 'Spade' would better suit ἄμη (or the Homeric λίστρον), though this was prop. rather a shovel. For the combination cp. Shaks. *Tit. Andr.* 5. 3. 11 *'Tis you must dig with mattock and with spade.*—**δικ. ἐκβολή,** throwing up of earth by mattock (possessive gen. denoting the subject, γῆ ἦν ἡ δ. ἐκβάλλει): **ἐκβ.,** abstract for concrete, like τροφή for θρέμμα (*O. T.* 1 n.). In Mod. Greek ἐκβολάδες is a mining term, 'out-put.'—The epithets **στύφλος** ('hard,' cp. 139), and **χέρσος** 'dry,' tell something which the preceding words, and the following **ἀρρώξ,** would not alone have told; viz.

GU.   Aye, truly ; dread news makes one pause long.

CR.   Then tell it, wilt thou, and so get thee gone ?

GU.   Well, this is it.—The corpse—some one hath just given it burial, and gone away,—after sprinkling thirsty dust on the flesh, and such other rites as piety enjoins.

CR.   What sayest thou ? What living man hath dared this deed ?

GU.   I know not ; no stroke of pickaxe was seen there, no earth thrown up by mattock ; the ground was hard and dry, unbroken, without track of wheels ; the doer was one who had left no trace. And when the first day-watchman showed it to us, sore wonder fell on all. The dead man was veiled from us ; not shut within a tomb, but lightly strewn with dust, as by the hand of one who shunned a curse.

---

by S).   **251** ἀρὼξ L : ἀρρὼξ r.   **254** θαῦμα] Nauck conject. φάσμα.

---

why no foot-prints were traceable.—ἐπη-μαξευμένη, lit. ʻtraversed (*i.e.* furrowed) by a carriage' with its (four) wheels, =τροχοῖς ἀμάξης κεχαραγμένη: ἐπ-, ἐφ-, since as Eusth. says (on *Il.* 18. 485) τό...ἄμαξα οἱ μὲν παλαιοὶ ψιλοῦσι, οἱ μέντοι νεώτεροι ᾿Αττικοὶ ἐδάσυναν. (Cp. n. on ἀπήνη, *O. T.* 753.)—ἀλλ᾿ ὁ ἐργάτης ἄσημός τις ἦν : for τις added to the predicate, where the subject has the art., cp. *O. T.* 618, Aesch. *Theb.* 491 ὁ σημα-τουργὸς δ᾿ οὔ τις εὐτελὴς ἄρ᾿ ἦν : Ar. *Pl.* 726 ὡς φιλόπολίς τίς ἐσθ᾿ ὁ δαίμων καὶ σοφός. Not: ὁ ἐργάτης τις (the doer, whoever he is) ἄσημος ἦν, like ὁ κύριός τις (*O. C.* 288 n.).

253 f. It is still the early morning of the day on which the drama opens. The Argives having fled in the night, Creon had published his edict shortly before dawn. Antigone had done her deed in the short interval between the publication of the edict and the beginning of the watch over the corpse. ὁ πρῶτος ἡμεροσκόπος, the man who took the first watch of this day, was the first who had watched at all. If a sentinel had been near the body, Ant. must have been seen. The other men were somewhere near. (Afterwards, they all watched, 413.) ἡμεροσκ., in prose ἡμεροφύλαξ (Xen. *H.* 7. 2. 6), as opp. to νυκτοφύλαξ (id. *An.* 7. 2. 18).—δείκνυσι...παρῆν : historic pres. combined with past tense ; cp. Lys. or. 1 § 6 ἐπειδὴ δέ μοι παιδίον γίγνεται, ἐπίστευον ἤδη καὶ πάντα τὰ ἐμαυτοῦ ἐκείνῃ παρέδωκα.—δυσχερές,

not merely ʻperplexing,' but ʻdistressing' (*Ai.* 1395), since they foreboded punishment. So δυσχέρεια, *molestia* (*Ph.* 473).

255 f. ὁ μὲν answered by σημεῖα δ᾿ (257).—τυμβήρης μὲν οὔ (cp. on 96), not entombed : *i.e.* there was no τύμβος, indicating that the ashes had been buried beneath it (1203): the body itself lay there, though covered over with dust. τυμβ., prop., ʻprovided with a mound,' but below, 946, merely = ʻtomb-like'; and so in Ar. *Th.* 889 Euripides says τυμβήρεις ἕδρας, ʻseat on a tomb.'—λεπτὴ δ᾿...ἐπῆν, instead of λέπτῃ δὲ κόνει κε-καλυμμένος (as in *Ph.* 545 δοξάζων μὲν οὔ, | τύχῃ δὲ...ὁρμισθείς): for this introduction of a new finite verb, where a participial clause was expected, cp. 813 ff.—ἄγος φεύγοντος ὥς sc. τινος (*O. T.* 629 οὗτοι κακῶς γ᾿ ἄρχοντος, n.) : the gen. is not absol., but possessive, denoting the author: ʻas of (*i.e.* from) one avoiding.' ἄγος, the guilt incurred by one who passed by an unburied corpse without throwing earth on it : οἱ γὰρ νεκρὸν ὁρῶντες ἄταφον, καὶ μὴ ἐπαμησά-μενοι κόνιν, ἐναγεῖς εἶναι ἐδόκουν. Aelian *Var. Hist.* 5. 14 νόμος καὶ οὗτος ᾿Αττικός, ὃς ἂν ἀτάφῳ περιτύχῃ σώματι ἀνθρώπου πάντως ἐπιβάλλειν αὐτῷ γῆν· θάπ-τειν δὲ πρὸς δυσμὰς βλέποντας. So, too, Aelian says of the hawk, *Hist. Anim.* 2. 49, νεκρὸν δὲ ἄνθρωπον ἰδὼν ἱέραξ, ὡς λόγος, πάντως ἐπιβάλλει γῆν τῷ ἀτάφῳ· καὶ τοῦτο μὲν αὐτῷ οὐ κελεύει Σόλων, ὡς ᾿Αθηναίους ἐπαίδευσε δρᾶν (though our schol. ascribes the precept to a prehistoric

σημεῖα δ᾽ οὔτε θηρὸς οὔτε του κυνῶν
ἐλθόντος, οὐ σπάσαντος ἐξεφαίνετο.
λόγοι δ᾽ ἐν ἀλλήλοισιν ἐρρόθουν κακοί,
φύλαξ ἐλέγχων φύλακα· κἂν ἐγίγνετο   260
πληγὴ τελευτῶσ᾽, οὐδ᾽ ὁ κωλύσων παρῆν.
εἷς γάρ τις ἦν ἕκαστος οὑξειργασμένος,
κοὐδεὶς ἐναργής, ἀλλ᾽ ἔφευγε μὴ εἰδέναι.
ἦμεν δ᾽ ἕτοιμοι καὶ μύδρους αἴρειν χεροῖν,

258 ἐλθόντος] Naber conject. ἕλκοντος.   **263** ἔφευγε τὸ μὴ εἰδέναι MSS.: Erfurdt
deleted τό.   Blaydes reads πᾶς δ᾽ ἔφευγε μὴ εἰδέναι: Dindorf, ἀλλ᾽ ἔφευγε πᾶς τὸ μή:

Βουζύγης): and of the elephant, *H. A.*
5. 49 τὸν ἐλέφαντα θεασάμενος ἐλέφας
νεκρὸν οὐκ ἂν παρέλθοι, μὴ τῇ προβοσκίδι
γῆν ἀρυσάμενος καὶ ἐπιβαλών, ὁσίαν τινὰ
ἀπόρρητον ὑπὲρ τῆς κοινῆς φύσεως
τελῶν ('fulfilling some mysterious law of
piety imposed by Nature'), καὶ φεύγων
ἄγος· εἶναι γὰρ τὸ μὴ δρᾶσαι τοῦτο
ἐναγές. It was remembered as a disgrace
to Lysander that, having put to death
some prisoners of war, οὐδὲ ἀποθανοῦσιν
ἐπήνεγκε γῆν (Paus. 9. 32. 6). Cp. id.
1. 32. 5 πάντως ὅσιον ἀνθρώπου νεκρὸν γῇ
κρύψαι. Hor. *Carm.* 1. 28. 33 *precibus
non linquar inultis, Teque piacula nulla
resolvent...licebit Iniecto ter pulvere curras.*
257 f. θηρός, here a wild beast, as
dist. from domesticated animals (cp.
1081): more often the term excludes only
birds and fishes.—του with θηρός also:
Eur. *Hec.* 370 οὔτ᾽ ἐλπίδος γὰρ οὔτε του
δόξης ὁρῶ | θάρσος παρ᾽ ἡμῖν.—οὐ σπά-
σαντος. The negatives in 257 affect
ἐλθόντος: and οὐ stands with σπάσαντος
as if we had simply οὐκ ἐλθόντος, οὐ
σπάσαντος, σημεῖα ἦν. οὐ is not here an
irregular substitute for οὔτε, as in 250:
this would be so only if we had οὔτ᾽
ἐλθόντος. Either οὐδὲ σπ. or οὔτε σπ.
would be correct, but the latter would
suppose an οὔτε understood before ἐλθόντος. For σπάσαντος of rending, cp.
1003. It could not mean, 'having cast
up earth' over the body (as Triclinius
took it). The point is that the body
must have been covered before the beasts
had had time to come. The poet has
preferred this order to σπάσαντος οὐδ᾽
ἐλθόντος (*i.e.* 'or even having come'),
because, εἰ ἦλθον, καὶ ἔσπασαν ἄν.
259 ff. λόγοι δ᾽...φύλακα. The regular
form would be, λόγοις κακοῖς ἐρρωθοῦμεν

ἐν ἀλλήλοις, ἐλέγχοντες φύλαξ φύλακα
(or ἄλλος ἄλλον), φύλαξ being the part
in apposition with the whole (ἡμεῖς).
The irregularity of the form in the text
is threefold. (1) For λόγοις κακοῖς ἐρρο-
θοῦμεν we have an equiv. in sense, though
not in grammar, λόγοι κακοὶ ἐρρόθουν.
(2) In spite of this, ἐν ἀλλήλοισιν is retained,
whereas ἐν ἡμῖν is now needed.   (3) As
a *plur.* part. would have been awkward
after λόγοι, we have φύλαξ ἐλέγχων φύλακα, which thus is virtually equiv. to a
gen. absol., φύλακος ἐλέγχοντος φύλακα.
Remark that, even in regular examples
of partitive apposition, a participle, describing what all do, is sometimes thus
made singular; Xen. *An.* 7. 3. 47 οἱ
ἱππεῖς οἴχονται μοι ἄλλος ἄλλη διώκων
(instead of διώκοντες). It is only the first
of these three points that this passage
has in common with others to which
it has been compared. 'They disputed,
some saying this, some that,' often appears in Greek as '*there was a dispute*,'
etc., without causing οἱ μὲν...οἱ δέ to be
changed into the gen. absol. Her. 8. 74
πολλὰ ἐλέγετο,...οἱ μὲν ὡς...χρεὸν εἴη
ἀποπλέειν, Ἀθηναῖοι δέ etc.   Thuc. 4. 23
ὑπ᾽ ἀμφοτέρων...ἐπολεμεῖτο, Ἀθηναῖοι
μὲν περιπλέοντες..., Πελοποννήσιοι δὲ etc.
Aesch. *P. V.* 200 στάσις τ᾽ ἐν ἀλλήλοισιν
ὡροθύνετο, | οἱ μὲν θέλοντες...οἱ δέ etc.
(This illustrates the use of ἐν ἀλλήλ. here,
but is less bold, since the noun is sing.)
Eur. *Ph.* 1462 ἦν δ᾽ ἔρις στρατηλάταις, |
οἱ μὲν πατάξαι...οἱ δέ etc.   *Bacch.* 1131
ἦν δὲ πᾶσ᾽ ὁμοῦ βοή, | ὁ μὲν στενάζων...
αἱ δέ etc. For ἐρρόθουν, of a confused
noise of angry tongues, cp. 290. ῥόθος
(onomatop.) is said of a rushing noise
of waves, or of oars dashed into them,
etc.: then, fig., Aesch. *Pers.* 406 Περσίδος

And no sign met the eye as though any beast of prey or any dog had come nigh to him, or torn him.

Then evil words flew fast and loud among us, guard accusing guard ; and it would e'en have come to blows at last, nor was there any to hinder. Every man was the culprit, and no one was convicted, but all disclaimed knowledge of the deed. And we were ready to take red-hot iron in our hands;—

Seyffert, ἀλλ' ἔφη τὸ μὴ εἰδέναι.   **264** αἱρειν] ἔχειν L, with γρ. αἱρειν written above

γλώσσης ῥόθος, of an unintelligible jargon. —ἐλέγχων, questioning (434, O. T. 333, 783: El. 1353), here, in the sense of 'accusing.'—κἂν ἐγίγνετο : and blows would have come at last,—had not the matter been settled by the proposal mentioned at 268. (Not, 'blows would come,' i.e. were often exchanged, as Nauck takes it.)—τελευτῶσ', 'at last,' the adverbial use, found even with another partic., as Thuc. 6. 53 τυραννίδα χαλεπὴν τελευτῶσαν γενομένην.—ὁ κωλύσων: cp. O. T. 297.

262 f. ἦν...οὔξειργ., was the doer (in the belief of his comrades).—ἐναργής, manifestus facti: O. T. 535 λῃστής τ' ἐναργής.—ἀλλ' (ἕκαστος), evolved from οὐδείς: fr. 327 ἐμοὶ δ' οὐδεὶς δοκεῖ | εἶναι, πένης ὤν, ἄνοσος, ἀλλ' ἀεὶ νοσεῖν. Dem. or. 20 § 74 μηδεὶς φθόνῳ τὸ μέλλον ἀκούσῃ, ἀλλ', ἂν ἀληθὲς ᾖ, σκοπείτω.— ἔφευγε μὴ εἰδέναι, 'pleaded in defence that he knew nothing of it.' For this pregnant use of φεύγειν cp. Aesch. Suppl. 390, where the Argive king says to the Danaides, whose cousins threaten to seize them under Egyptian law, δεῖ τοι σὲ φεύγειν κατὰ νόμους τοὺς οἴκοθεν | ὡς οὐκ ἔχουσι κῦρος οὐδὲν ἀμφὶ σοῦ: you must plead, in accordance with Egyptian law, that they have no right over you. So defendere, Cic. In Pison. 10. 5 si triumphum non cupiebas, cuius tandem rei te cupiditate arsisse defendes? ('will you plead?') Note that this use (like the absol. legal sense, 'to be a defendant,' from which it comes) was necessarily restricted to pres. and impf. Hence we must not cite, with Donaldson, Dem. or. 27 § 1 οὗτος τοὺς μὲν σαφῶς εἰδότας τὰ ἡμέτερα ἔφυγε μηδὲν διαγνῶναι περὶ αὐτῶν, εἰς δ' ὑμᾶς τοὺς οὐδὲν τῶν ἡμετέρων ἀκριβῶς ἐπισταμένους ἐλήλυθεν (which means: 'he has avoided any decision on the case being given by

those who knew our affairs thoroughly, but has come to you,' etc.): nor, with Paley, Xen. Hellen. 1. 3. 19 ὑπαγόμενος θανάτου...ἀπέφυγεν, ὅτι οὐ προδοίη τὴν πόλιν ἀλλὰ σώσαι, i.e. 'being put on trial for his life, he was acquitted, (on the plea) that he had not betrayed the city,' etc.—μὴ (not οὐκ) εἰδέναι, as after verbs of denying, Ar. Eq. 572 ἠρνοῦντο μὴ πεπτωκέναι.—Only one other version is tenable, viz., 'shrunk from knowing it'; but this could hardly be said in the sense, 'shrunk from confessing that he knew it.'—Others understand τοὺς ἄλλους as subject to εἰδέναι, 'shrunk from (the others) knowing it' ('entzog sich dem Wissen der anderen'), which is impossible. So also is Campb.'s version, 'always escaped, so that we could not know him,' which would, in the first place, require ἔφυγε.

264 μύδρους, lumps of red-hot iron. μύδρος = a molten mass, from rt μυδ, whence μύδος, 'moisture,' μυδάω, etc. Cyril Adv. Iulian. 359 quotes this verse, after referring to a Chaldean custom of making an oath more solemn by causing those who took it to pass between the severed portions of a victim (διὰ μέσων... διχοτομημάτων). It is probably the oldest trace in Greek of ordeals analogous to the medieval 'judgments of God.' The word μύδρος occurs elsewhere in connection with a solemn sanction for an oath. In Her. 1. 165 the Phocaeans μύδρον σιδήρεον κατεπόντωσαν, swearing not to return till it should float. Plut. Aristid. 25 ὁ δ' Ἀριστείδης ὤρκισε μὲν τοὺς Ἕλληνας καὶ ὤμοσεν ὑπὲρ τῶν Ἀθηναίων (to observe the defensive league against Persia, 479 B.C., Grote 5. 257), μύδρους ἐμβαλὼν ἐπὶ ταῖς ἀραῖς (in sanction of the curses on traitors) εἰς τὴν θάλατταν. I conceive that in these passages, as elsewhere, μύδρος has its proper sense,

καὶ πῦρ διέρπειν, καὶ θεοὺς ὀρκωμοτεῖν   265
τὸ μήτε δρᾶσαι μήτε τῳ ξυνειδέναι
τὸ πρᾶγμα βουλεύσαντι μήτ᾽ εἰργασμένῳ.
τέλος δ᾽, ὅτ᾽ οὐδὲν ἦν ἐρευνῶσιν πλέον,
λέγει τις εἷς, ὃς πάντας ἐς πέδον κάρα
νεῦσαι φόβῳ προύτρεψεν· οὐ γὰρ εἴχομεν   270
οὔτ᾽ ἀντιφωνεῖν οὔθ᾽ ὅπως δρῶντες καλῶς
πράξαιμεν. ἦν δ᾽ ὁ μῦθος ὡς ἀνοιστέον
σοὶ τοὔργον εἴη τοῦτο κοὐχὶ κρυπτέον.
καὶ ταῦτ᾽ ἐνίκα, κἀμὲ τὸν δυσδαίμονα
πάλος καθαιρεῖ τοῦτο τἀγαθὸν λαβεῖν.   275
πάρειμι δ᾽ ἄκων οὐχ ἑκοῦσιν, οἶδ᾽ ὅτι·
στέργει γὰρ οὐδεὶς ἄγγελον κακῶν ἐπῶν.
ΧΟ. ἄναξ, ἐμοί τοι, μή τι καὶ θεήλατον

by S: αἴρειν r.   **267** μήτ᾽] μηδ᾽ Blaydes.   **269** εἷς, ὅς] εἷς ὅ Nauck.   Blaydes

---

a *red-hot mass* of metal, and that the custom was symbolical of an older use of the μύδρος in ordeals by fire. This would explain how the Alexandrian poets of the 3rd cent. B.C. (Lycophron, Callimachus) came to use the word μύδρος, in defiance of its etymology, as simply 'a lump' (or even 'a stone'). They supposed that the μύδροι had been cold masses.

265 ff. πῦρ διέρπειν must here refer to a definite ordeal, by walking through a fire. The idea, at least, of such an ordeal appears in the familiar Attic phrase διὰ πυρὸς ἰέναι ('to go through fire and water'); Xen. *Symp.* 4. 16 ἔγωγ᾽ οὖν μετὰ Κλεινίου κἂν διὰ πυρὸς ἰοίην, Ar. *Lys.* 133 διὰ τοῦ πυρὸς | ἐθέλω βαδίζειν. But it is doubtful whether the actual use of any such ordeal in the historical age can be inferred from Dem. or. 54 § 40 ἀξιοπιστότερος τοῦ κατὰ τῶν παίδων (by the lives of one's children, cp. or. 29 § 26) ὀμνύοντος καὶ διὰ τοῦ πυρός, *i.e.* swearing that one is ready to undergo the test by fire. It has been suggested that ἰόντος has fallen out after πυρός, which seems improbable. But the phrase may be rhetorical. Cp. Verg. *Aen.* 11. 787 (the Hirpi): *medium freti pietate per ignem Cultores multa premimus vestigia pruna.*—Becker *Char.* 183 notices some other ordeals. There was a temple in Achaia, the priestess of which, before election, was proved by drinking bull's

blood; if impure, she died (Paus. 7. 25. 13). Perjury, and some other crimes, were assayed by the accused mounting the steps of an altar for burnt sacrifice (ἐσχάρα): if he was guilty, flames appeared (Heliod. *Aeth.* 10. 8). Incontinence was tried by the test of entering a grotto of Pan at Ephesus (Achilles Tatius 8. 6).—θεοὺς ὀρκ., to swear by the gods; the acc. is cognate (the god being identified with the oath), like ὅρκον ὀμνύναι: Xen. *Cyr.* 5. 4. 31 ταῦτα...ὀμνυμί σοι θεούς.—τὸ μήτε δρ.: for the art., cp. 236.—μήτ᾽ εἰργασμένῳ: the conjecture μηδ᾽ is needless, since μήτε can be understood before βουλεύσαντι: see *O. T.* 239 n.

268 f. πλέον: cp. 40.—λέγει, between two past tenses: cp. 254.—τις εἷς. It is at first sight tempting to write τις, εἷς ὃς πάντας. But such emphasis on the idea of 'one against all' seems hardly appropriate here. And τις εἷς sometimes = εἷς τις: Thuc. 6. 61 καί τινα μίαν νύκτα καὶ κατέδαρθον: Plat. *Soph.* 235 B (οὐκέτ᾽ ἐκφεύξεται) τὸ μὴ οὐ τοῦ γένους εἶναι τοῦ τῶν θαυματοποιῶν τις εἷς: *Parm.* 145 D ἐν τινι γὰρ ἑνὶ μὴ ὂν οὐκ ἂν ἔτι που δύναιτο ἕν γε ἅπασιν εἶναι.

270 ff. προύτρεψεν, impelled, here = ἠνάγκασε: cp. *O. T.* 358 n.—οὐ γὰρ εἴχομεν κ.τ.λ.: 'for we did not know how to gainsay him, nor how, *if we did the thing* (advised by him), we could prosper.'

to walk through fire;—to make oath by the gods that we had
not done the deed,—that we were not privy to the planning or
the doing.

At last, when all our searching was fruitless, one spake,
who made us all bend our faces on the earth in fear; for we
saw not how we could gainsay him, or escape mischance if we
obeyed. His counsel was that this deed must be reported to
thee, and not hidden. And this seemed best; and the lot
doomed my hapless self to win this prize. So here I stand,—
as unwelcome as unwilling, well I wot; for no man delights
in the bearer of bad news.

CH. O King, my thoughts have long been whispering, can

---

conject. ἔπος ὅ.   **278** XO.] L omits this indication, which Triclinius added.

As ἀντιφωνεῖν means *opposing* his suggestion, so δρῶντες means acting on it.
Others join ὅπως δρῶντες, 'by what
course of action.' Since, however, a
definite proposal was before them—viz.,
reference to Creon—we must then understand, 'by what *other* course' (than the
proposed one). But the sense is, 'We
could not refute him, and, on the other
hand, we dreaded your anger if we
followed his advice.' εἴχομεν has the
same sense in both clauses. ἔχω, as = '*to
know how*,' takes (1) an infin., or (2) a
relat. clause with subjunct., as 1342, *Tr.*
705 οὐκ ἔχω...ποῖ γνώμης πέσω. This is
merely an indirect form of the deliberative subjunct., ποῖ γνώμης πέσω; So
here, πράξαιμεν would be πράξωμεν if the
principal verb were in a primary tense.
The direct question would be, πῶς καλῶς
πράξωμεν; Carefully distinguish ὅπως (or
πῶς) ἄν with optat. after this οὐκ ἔχω, as
Tr. 991 οὐ γὰρ ἔχω πῶς ἄν | στέρξαιμι, I
know not how I *could*. The two constructions are combined again in *Ai.* 428
οὔτοι σ᾽ ἀπείργειν οὐδ᾽ ὅπως ἐῶ λέγειν |
ἔχω.

273 ff. σοί (cp. 234), rare for εἰς σέ.
After ἀναφέρω τι the pers. is usu. expressed
by εἴς τινα (less oft. by ἐπί or παρά τινα).
But Lysias has the dat. in or. 12. 84 οἷς
τὰς ἀπολογίας ἀνοίσει, 'to whom he will
carry back his defensive pleas': (*i.e.* 'on
whom he will lay the blame,' and so,
again, in or. 7 § 17): yet *ib.* § 64 τὰς...
ἀπολογίας εἰς ἐκεῖνον ἀναφερομένας. In
Mod. Greek ἀναφορά is used of an official
'report.'—ταῦτ᾽ ἕνεκα: see on 233: the
impf. differs from the aor. only as ἐδόκει

('seemed good') from ἔδοξε ('was resolved').—πάλος, perh. taken by shaking
lots in a helmet (cp. 396, *Ai.* 1285):
καθαιρεῖ, reduces, *i.e.* 'condemns': Lys.
or. 13 § 37 τὴν...ψῆφον...τὴν...καθαιροῦ-
σαν, the vote of condemnation.—τἀγαθόν,
iron., whereas his second errand is a true
ἕρμαιον (397).—ἄκων οὐχ ἑκοῦσιν: cp.
Tr. 198 (the herald detained against his
will by a throng of questioners) οὐχ ἑκὼν
ἑκοῦσι δὲ | ξύνεστιν.—οἶδ᾽ ὅτι, adverbial
('doubtless'), like δῆλον ὅτι, cp. 758 : so
used even in a parenthetic clause,
as Dem. or. 9 § 1 πάντων, οἶδ᾽ ὅτι, φη-
σάντων γ᾽ ἄν ('when all, I know, would
certainly admit,' etc.).

278 f. ἐμοί, ethic dat., 'for me,'
rather than dat. with βουλεύει as = 'ad-
vises'; the latter dat. is rare (Aesch.
Eum. 697 ἀστοῖς...βουλεύω σέβειν); in
Tr. 807, *Ai.* 1055 the dat. with βουλεύω
is a dat. of interest (to plot *against* one).
In poetry the act. can mean, not only
'to form a plan' (*O. T.* 619), or to *give
counsel* (*ib.* 1417), but also, like the
midd., to deliberate.—With μή supply
ἐστί; cp. 1253; Plat. *Theaet.* 145 C ὅρα
μὴ παίζων ἔλεγεν, look *whether he did not
speak* (*i.e.* I suspect that he spoke) in
jest. To supply ἦ is also possible (cp.
O. C. 1180), but less fitting here.—τι,
adv., 'perchance': *O. T.* 969.—θεήλατον,
sent by gods (*O. T.* 992 θεήλατον μάν-
τευμα), *i.e. wrought* by them (cp. 285),
since there was no trace of human agency
(249): not, imposed upon a human agent
by a divine commission (as *O. T.* 255
πρᾶγμα θεήλατον). So in *Il.* 16. 667
Zeus provides supernaturally for the

τοὔργον τόδ᾽, ἡ ξύννοια βουλεύει πάλαι.

ΚΡ. παῦσαι, πρὶν ὀργῆς καί με μεστῶσαι λέγων, 280
μὴ 'φευρεθῇς ἄνους τε καὶ γέρων ἅμα.
λέγεις γὰρ οὐκ ἀνεκτά, δαίμονας λέγων
πρόνοιαν ἴσχειν τοῦδε τοῦ νεκροῦ πέρι.
πότερον ὑπερτιμῶντες ὡς εὐεργέτην
ἔκρυπτον αὐτόν, ὅστις ἀμφικίονας 285
ναοὺς πυρώσων ἦλθε κἀναθήματα
καὶ γῆν ἐκείνων, καὶ νόμους διασκεδῶν;
ἢ τοὺς κακοὺς τιμῶντας εἰσορᾷς θεούς;
οὐκ ἔστιν. ἀλλὰ ταῦτα καὶ πάλαι πόλεως
ἄνδρες μόλις φέροντες ἐρρόθουν ἐμοί, 290
κρυφῇ κάρα σείοντες, οὐδ᾽ ὑπὸ ζυγῷ
λόφον δικαίως εἶχον, ὡς στέργειν ἐμέ.

---

279 τόδ᾽, ἡ ξύννοια] Nauck has now withdrawn his former conjecture, τόδ᾽ ᾗ, ξύννοια.
280 καί με] καμὲ (sic) L.   284 ὑπερτιμῶντας L, ὑπερτιμῶντες r.   Nauck would
delete vv. 287 f., and re-write thus :—πότερον ὑπερτιμῶντας ὡς εὐεργέτην, | ναοὺς
ἐκείνων ὅστις ἀμφικίονας | καὶ γῆν πυρώσων ἦλθε κἀναθήματα; | οὐκ ἔστιν κ.τ.λ.
287 καὶ γῆν] Schneidewin conject. δίκην : Pallis, τιμάς.—ἐκείνων L: ἐκείνην r.

---

burial of Sarpedon. Cp. *O. C.* p. xxxv.
—ἡ ξύννοια, the art. being equiv. to a
possessive pron., as 1089 f. τὴν γλῶσσαν,
τὸν νοῦν. Cp. Plat. *Rep.* 571 E εἰς
σύννοιαν αὐτὸς αὑτῷ ἀφικόμενος.—πάλαι,
i.e. ever since the φύλαξ spoke (249).
Cp. 289.

280 πρὶν ὀργῆς καί με μεστῶσαι,
'before thou hast actually filled me with
anger': καί has nothing to do with πρίν,
but belongs solely to μεστῶσαι, a strong
word, the stress on which makes it easier
for the force of καί to pass over the
enclitic με. Cp. *O. T.* 772 τῷ γὰρ ἂν
καὶ μείζονι | λέξαιμ᾽ ἄν: *ib.* 989 ποίας
δὲ καὶ γυναικὸς ἐκφοβεῖσθ᾽ ὕπερ; where
in each case καί goes with the verb.
We must distinguish the ordinary combination πρὶν καί, 'before even,' which
would be in place here only if Creon
meant, 'Cease, before you have *so much
as* angered me': cp. *Tr.* 396 ἅσσεις, πρὶν
ἡμᾶς κἀννεώσασθαι λόγους (before we have
even renewed our talk): Ar. *Av.* 1033
πέμπουσιν ἤδη 'πισκόπους | ἐς τὴν πόλιν,
πρὶν καὶ τεθύσθαι τοῖς θεοῖς: Plat. *Gorg.*
458 ἐν πάλαι..., πρὶν καὶ ὑμᾶς ἐλθεῖν,...
ἐπεδειξάμην.—κἀμέ would be unmeaning:
no one else is angry.—μεστῶσαι: Plat.
Rep. 330 E ὑποψίας...καὶ δείματος μεστός,

and so often.

284 ff. πότερον κ.τ.λ. Did they
think him *good*? Or, thinking him *bad*,
did they yet honour him?—ἔκρυπτον (sc.
γῇ)=ἔθαπτον : the word is specially suitable here to the covering with dust (256).
Cp. *O. C.* 621 κεκρυμμένος νέκυς: *El.*
838 κρυφθέντα (of Amphiaraus swallowed
up by the earth). Bellermann cites an
inscr. from Smyrna (*Rhein. Mus.* 1872,
27 p. 465) παίδων σε φίλαι χέρες, ὡς θέμις
ἐστί, | κρύψαν. The impf. ('were for bury-
ing') refers to the motive present to the
agent's mind when the act was under-
taken: cp. 19 ἐξέπεμπον n.—ἀμφικίονας
ναούς, temples surrounded by columns,
an epith. marking their stateliness and
splendour, as Eur. *Andr.* 1099 ἐν περι-
στύλοις δόμοις (of a temple), *I. T.* 406
περικίονας ναούς. The ναὸς περίστυλος
or περίπτερος (so called because the
ceiling of the colonnade projected like a
wing, from the cella) had a colonnade on
each of its four sides: the ναὸς ἀμφι-
πρόστυλος, only on two (front and back):
but, though the latter would satisfy the
word ἀμφικίονας, the poet doubtless meant
the former.—κἀναθήματα, votive offerings, such as gold and silver vessels of all
kinds; statues; bronze tripods, etc. (Cp.

this deed, perchance, be e'en the work of gods?

CR. Cease, ere thy words fill me utterly with wrath, lest thou be found at once an old man and foolish. For thou sayest what is not to be borne, in saying that the gods have care for this corpse. Was it for high reward of trusty service that they sought to hide his nakedness, who came to burn their pillared shrines and sacred treasures, to burn their land, and scatter its laws to the winds? Or dost thou behold the gods honouring the wicked? It cannot be. No! From the first there were certain in the town that muttered against me, chafing at this edict, wagging their heads in secret; and kept not their necks duly under the yoke, like men contented with my sway.

M. Schmidt conject. κενώσων.—νόμους] Herwerden conject. δόμους.   **291** κρυφῇ] σιγῇ Meineke, from Plut. *Mor.* 170 E : see comment.   **292** For λόφον δικαίως εἶχον, Hartung writes νῶτ᾽ εὐλόφως ἔχοντες: for ὡς στέργειν ἐμέ, Nauck, εὐλόφως φέρειν: see comment.—ὡς] In L the σ has been added by S : but the scribe's oversight obviously arose through the next word beginning with σ, and in no way warrants

---

Her. 1. 50; Thuc. 6. 46; Isae. or. 7 § 41.) The wealth of Delphi in ἀναθήματα is already proverbial in *Il.* 9. 404: at Thebes the 'Ισμήνιον (*O. T.* 21) also seems to have been rich in them. After ἀνάθημα the gen. denotes either ὁ ἀναθείς (as more oft.), or, as here, the divine owner.—γῆν ἐκείνων (depending on πυρώσων), *i.e.* the territory of Thebes (cp. on 199), since the land belongs to the θεοὶ ἐγχώριοι and πολιοῦχοι: not merely the τεμένη attached to their shrines.—νόμους διασκεδῶν, to scatter the laws abroad, *i.e.* to shatter the fabric of civil order: cp. Tennyson, *Red ruin, and the breaking up of laws.* Cic. *Agr.* 2. 37 *disturbare... legem.* So διασκεδ. of breaking up a treaty (*O. C.* 620), or a king's power (*ib.* 1341).—διασκεδῶν would suit ἀναθήματα, but could not possibly be joined with γῆν (as if the latter meant 'State'): hence it must be taken with νόμους only.

288 τοὺς κακοὺς τιμῶντας...θεούς; owing to the natural emphasis on τοὺς κακούς, the ambiguity is only grammatical. Cp. Her. 7. 150 ἐπεὶ δέ σφεας παραλαμβάνειν τοὺς Ἕλληνας, oblique for ἐπεὶ δέ σφεας παρελάμβανον οἱ Ἕλληνες.

289 f. ταῦτα, the edict, depending on μόλις φέροντες (*aegre ferentes*): καὶ πάλαι, even from the moment when it was proclaimed; cp. 279, where πάλαι only refers back to 249.—πόλεως ἄνδρες, like γῆς τῆσδέ τις (*O. T.* 236 n.).—ἐρρόθουν, muttered: 259 n.—ἐμοί, against me, dat. of object, as after χαλεπαίνω, μέμ-

φομαι, etc.—κάρα σείοντες, 'tossing the head,' in defiant menace (so *caput quassans*, Verg. *Aen.* 12. 894), instead of going quietly under the yoke. Plut. *Mor.* 170 E τοὺς τυράννους ἀσπάζονται, ...ἀλλὰ μισοῦσι σιγῇ κάρα σείοντες (alluding to this v.). So, acc. to Suidas, *s.v.*, Soph. used ἀναχαιτίζειν (prop. said of a horse *throwing the mane back*, rearing) as = ἀπειθεῖν καὶ ἀντιτείνειν, 'to be restive.'—ὑπὸ ζυγῷ. Cp. Aesch. *Ag.* 1639 ζεύξω βαρείαις (ζεύγλαις).—λόφον, the back of the neck, a word used of draught-animals (of the *human* nape, perh. only once, *Il.* 10. 573): hence, fig., Eur. fr. 175 ὅστις δὲ πρὸς τὸ πῖπτον εὐλόφως φέρει | τὸν δαίμον᾽, οὗτος ἧσσόν ἐστ᾽ ἀνόλβιος. id. *Tro.* 302 κάρτα τοι τοὐλεύθερον | ἐν τοῖς τοιούτοις δυσλόφως φέρει κακά, 'impatiently.' (Shaksp. *Henry VI.* Pt. III. 3. 1. 16 *yield not thy neck To fortune's yoke.*)—Nauck writes the verse thus, νῶτον δικαίως εἶχον εὐλόφως φέρειν, because Eustathius, in alluding to it, once represents it by νῶτον εὐλόφως εἶχον (on *Od.* 5. 285), and twice by νῶτον εὐλόφως φέρειν (on *Il.* 10. 573, *Od.* 10. 169). But Eustath. was quoting, or rather paraphrasing, from memory, and confused our verse with Eur. fr. 175 (quoted above); also, perhaps, with Lycophron 776 εὐλόφῳ νώτῳ φέρειν. His references to Sophocles are often loose and inexact. See Appendix.—δικαίως, loyally. Donaldson had a too ingenious view that the word here meant, 'with

ἐκ τῶνδε τούτους ἐξεπίσταμαι καλῶς
παρηγμένους μισθοῖσιν εἰργάσθαι τάδε.
οὐδὲν γὰρ ἀνθρώποισιν οἷον ἄργυρος   295
κακὸν νόμισμ᾿ ἔβλαστε. τοῦτο καὶ πόλεις
πορθεῖ, τόδ᾿ ἄνδρας ἐξανίστησιν δόμων·
τόδ᾿ ἐκδιδάσκει καὶ παραλλάσσει φρένας
χρηστὰς πρὸς αἰσχρὰ πράγμαθ᾿ ἵστασθαι βροτῶν·
πανουργίας δ᾿ ἔδειξεν ἀνθρώποις ἔχειν   300
καὶ παντὸς ἔργου δυσσέβειαν εἰδέναι.
ὅσοι δὲ μισθαρνοῦντες ἤνυσαν τάδε,
χρόνῳ ποτ᾿ ἐξέπραξαν ὡς δοῦναι δίκην.
ἀλλ᾿ εἴπερ ἴσχει Ζεὺς ἔτ᾿ ἐξ ἐμοῦ σέβας,
εὖ τοῦτ᾿ ἐπίστασ᾿, ὅρκιος δέ σοι λέγω,   305
εἰ μὴ τὸν αὐτόχειρα τοῦδε τοῦ τάφου

Mekler's theory that L's archetype had εἴχον...ωσφέρειν, and that the letters εὔλοφ had
become illegible.   **296** κακὸν νόμισμ᾿] Nauck conject. κακῶν ἔναυσμ᾿ ('incitement'):

equal poise' (*New Crat.* 371).—ὡς = ὥστε
(*O. T.* 84): **στέργειν**, *tolerare*: *Tr.* 486
(Lichas advising Deianeira with regard to
Iolè) στέργε τὴν γυναῖκα, *be patient of her.*
293 f. τῶνδε, masc., the malcon-
tents (for **ἐκ**, cp. 63).—**τούτους**, the
watchers of the corpse: the pronouns
joined as in 39 (n.).—**εἰργάσθαι** is best
taken with **ἐξεπίσταμαι**: cp. 1092 ἐπιστάμεσθα...αὐτὸν...λακεῖν. The inf., instead of the partic., with ἐπίσταμαι, seems
unknown in Attic prose, except, of course,
where the sense is 'to know how.'
Cp. 472. The inf. might, indeed, depend
on **παρηγμένους**, as ἐπάγω (to induce) oft.
takes an inf.: but (*a*) as a matter of fact,
an infin. seems not to occur after παράγω
in this sense: and (*b*) it may be noticed
that Attic idiom often prefers the form,
'induced by them, he did it,' to, 'he
was induced by them to do it': *e.g.* Xen.
Mem. 4. 8. 5 πολλοὺς...λόγῳ παραχθέντες
ἀπέκτειναν: Dem. or. 5 § 10 οἷς ἐπα-
χθέντες ὑμεῖς...προεῖσθε Φωκέας. For this
participial expression of the leading idea,
see n. on *O. C.* 1038.
296 f. νόμισμ᾿, *institutum*. This
primary and general sense of the word
was almost confined to poetry (Aesch.
Th. 269 Ἑλληνικὸν νόμισμα θυστάδος
βοῆς), the special sense, 'current coin,'
being the ordinary one. For the other
sense, the usual word was νόμιμον (or
νόμος). Hence in Ar. *Nub.* 247, when So-

crates says, θεοὶ | ἡμῖν νόμισμ᾿ οὐκ ἔστι,
Strepsiades rejoins, τῷ γὰρ ὄμνυτ᾿; ἢ |
σιδαρέοισιν, ὥσπερ ἐν Βυζαντίῳ (*i.e.* if
gods are not *current* with you, do you
swear by iron coin?): where the schol.
remarks that νόμισμα meant ποτὲ μὲν
τὸ νόμιμον ἔθος, ποτὲ δὲ τὸ κόμμα τοῦ
τετυπωμένου χαλκοῦ.—**ἔβλαστε**: cp. *O. C.*
611 βλαστάνει δ᾿ ἀπιστία.—**πορθεῖ**, 'sacks'
(not merely, in a general sense, 'ruins'):
money invites attack, and often purchases
betrayal: cp. Hor. *Carm.* 3. 16. 13 *diffidit
urbium Portas vir Macedo et subruit
aemulos Reges muneribus.*—**τόδ᾿** (after
τοῦτο: cp. 39) **ἄνδρας**, individual citizens, as distinguished from **πόλεις**. **ἐξ-
ανίστ. δόμων**, drives them from their
cities by corrupt intrigue,—for which the
στάσεις of democrat and oligarch in
Greek cities gave many openings. The
phrase is strikingly illustrated by the
verses in which Timocreon of Rhodes,
when an exile, assailed Themistocles
(Plut. *Them.* 21), as τοὺς μὲν κατάγων
ἀδίκως, τοὺς δ᾿ ἐκδιώκων, τοὺς δὲ καί-
νων, | ἀργυρίων ὑπόπλεως.
298 f. τόδ᾿ ἐκδ. καὶ παραλλάσσει,
this trains and perverts good minds of
men, **ἵστασθαι πρὸς αἰσχρ. πράγμ.**, to
address themselves to base deeds. παραλλάσσει = 'alters sideways'; *i.e.* causes
to turn out of a straight course into an
oblique course; hence, like παράγει,
παραστρέφει, perverts. Cp. Arist. *Pol.* 8.

'Tis by them, well I know, that these have been beguiled and bribed to do this deed. Nothing so evil as money ever grew to be current among men. This lays cities low, this drives men from their homes, this trains and warps honest souls till they set themselves to works of shame; this still teaches folk to practise villanies, and to know every godless deed.

But all the men who wrought this thing for hire have made it sure that, soon or late, they shall pay the price. Now, as Zeus still hath my reverence, know this—I tell it thee on my oath:—If ye find not the very author of this burial,

---

Pallis, κακὸν νόσημ'. **299** βροτουσ L (accentless) with ων written above.
300 ἔχειν] Wecklein conject. ἄγειν: Pallis, τέχνην (or -as).

---

7 § 7 αἱ ψυχαὶ παρεστραμμέναι τῆς κατὰ φύσιν ἕξεως (their minds being warped from their natural condition). Since παραλλάσσει implies a bad *training*, it can be followed, like ἐθίζει and like words, by an infin.: it is unnecessary, then, to make ἵστασθαι, in its relation to παραλλάσσει, merely epexegetic ('so that they set themselves'); though it might, of course, be so. Wecklein takes **καὶ παραλλάσσει** as parenthetic =παραλλάσσουσα: but this, too, is needless, nor is it supported by 537 (where see n.).—ἵστασθαι **πρός τι** means here, 'to *set* oneself facing it,' so 'to turn to it, address oneself to it,' just like τρέπεσθαι πρός τι: cp. Plat. *Rep.* 452 E πρὸς ἄλλον τινὰ σκοπὸν στησάμενος ἢ τὸν τοῦ ἀγαθοῦ, 'having set himself to some other aim,' etc. Distinguish some other phrases with ἵστασθαι and πρός which are not really similar: Thuc. 3. 11 πρὸς ὅ τι χρὴ στῆναι (a power to which they could rally): 4. 56 πρὸς τὴν ἐκείνων γνώμην ἀεὶ ἔστασαν (they had always sided with the Athenian policy): 6. 34 πρὸς τὰ λεγόμενα καὶ αἱ γνῶμαι ἵστανται (men's minds adapt their attitudes to what is said).

300 f. πανουργίας...ἔχειν: showed men how to practise villanies. For ἔχειν of the moral habit, cp. *Od.* 1. 368 μνηστῆρες ὑπέρβιον ὕβριν ἔχοντες: *Il.* 9. 305 λύσσαν ἔχων ὀλοήν. The inf. might be epexegetic, but really depends on ἔδειξεν as implying 'taught': cp. Eur. *Med.* 195 οὐδεὶς λύπας | ηὕρετο... | ᾠδαῖς παύειν (has found out *how to*...). δείκνυμι of *invention*, as *Ai.* 1195 ὃς στυγερῶν ἔδειξεν ὅπλων | Ἕλλασι κοινὸν Ἄρη: fr. 396. 6 στρατοῦ φρυκτωρίαν | ἔδειξε, κἀνέφηνεν οὐ δεδειγμένα (Palamedes).—**εἰδέναι**, 'to know,' *i.e.* to be conversant with (cp.

on 71) **παντὸς ἔργου δυσσέβ.**, impiety of (shown in) *any* deed,=πᾶν δυσσεβὲς ἔργον (cp. 603 λόγου τ' ἄνοια): for **πᾶς**, cp. *O. C.* 761 n. Note **παντὸς ἔργ.** after **πανουργίας**: the familiar use of πανουργία extenuates the force to which etymology entitles it, while in πᾶν ἔργον that whole force is felt: so πᾶν ποιεῖν is stronger than πανουργεῖν, and πᾶν λέγειν than παρρησιάζεσθαι (Plat. *Apol.* 39 A ἐάν τις τολμᾷ πᾶν ποιεῖν καὶ λέγειν). Cp. *Ph.* 407 παντὸς ἂν λόγου κακοῦ | γλώσσῃ θιγόντα καὶ πανουργίας, where πάσης must be supplied, showing how πανουργία could be used without direct reference to its derivation.

302 f. ἤνυσαν: cp. 231.—**χρόνῳ ποτέ**, at some time or other: *i.e.* they will be caught sooner or later. With δοῦναι **δίκην**: *Ph.* 1041 τίσασθε, τίσασθ' ἀλλὰ τῷ χρόνῳ ποτέ.—**ἐξέπραξαν ὡς** (=ὥστε, 292), as Aesch. *Pers.* 723 καὶ τόδ' ἐξέπραξεν, ὥστε Βόσπορον κλῇσαι μέγαν; The verb is here ironical; cp. Plat. *Gorg.* 479 A τὸ αὐτὸ διαπεπραγμένοι εἰσὶν ὥσπερ ἂν εἴ τις τοῖς μεγίστοις νοσήμασι συνισχόμενος διαπράξαιτο μὴ διδόναι δίκην .. τοῖς ἰατροῖς, μηδὲ ἰατρεύεσθαι.

304 ff. Ζεύς, in his quality of Βασιλεύς (Xen. *An.* 3. 1. 12), is fitly invoked by a king who vows that he will uphold the royal authority. Cp. 487.—**ὅρκιος**, adverbial: *O. C.* 1637 κατήνεσεν τάδ' ὅρκιος (n.). Cp. 823 (λυγροτάταν).—**τὸν αὐτόχειρα**, the very man (248) whose hand strewed the dust, said with an emphasis corresponding to that with which the Guard had insisted on the absence of any clue (249). For αὐτο-, cp. 56, 172. **τάφου**=ταφῆς, as 490, 534, *O. T.* 1447: in a symbolical sense like that of θάψας (246).

εὑρόντες ἐκφανεῖτ᾽ ἐς ὀφθαλμοὺς ἐμούς,
οὐχ ὑμῖν Ἅιδης μοῦνος ἀρκέσει, πρὶν ἂν
ζῶντες κρεμαστοὶ τήνδε δηλώσηθ᾽ ὕβριν,   310
ἵν᾽ εἰδότες τὸ κέρδος ἔνθεν οἰστέον
τὸ λοιπὸν ἁρπάζητε, καὶ μάθηθ᾽ ὅτι
οὐκ ἐξ ἅπαντος δεῖ τὸ κερδαίνειν φιλεῖν.
ἐκ τῶν γὰρ αἰσχρῶν λημμάτων τοὺς πλείονας
ἀτωμένους ἴδοις ἂν ἢ σεσωσμένους.

ΦΥ. εἰπεῖν τι δώσεις, ἢ στραφεὶς οὕτως ἴω;   315
ΚΡ. οὐκ οἶσθα καὶ νῦν ὡς ἀνιαρῶς λέγεις;
ΦΥ. ἐν τοῖσιν ὠσὶν ἢ ᾽πὶ τῇ ψυχῇ δάκνει;
ΚΡ. τί δὲ ῥυθμίζεις τὴν ἐμὴν λύπην ὅπου;
ΦΥ. ὁ δρῶν σ᾽ ἀνιᾷ τὰς φρένας, τὰ δ᾽ ὦτ᾽ ἐγώ.
ΚΡ. οἴμ᾽ ὡς λάλημα δῆλον ἐκπεφυκὸς εἶ.   320

---

311 L has ἁρπάζητε, not (as has been stated) ἁρπάξητε. The mistake was easy, because the ζ begins low down, being a continuation of the down stroke of the a. But the difference between αζ and αξ, as the scribe of L writes them, can be seen by comparing this word with ἐξέπραξαν in 303, or (e.g.) ἄξω in O. C. 819 with θαύμαζε ib. 1119. **313 f.** ἐκ τῶν . . σεσωσμένους. Bergk rejects these two verses; M. Schmidt would spare them, but place them after v. 326.—Wecklein writes σεσωμένους (Curae epigraph. p. 60). **315** τι δώσεις] δεδώσεις L (no accent on δε): δὲ δώσεις r. Over δε an early hand in L (the first, as Dübner thinks) has written ·τι· **317** ἐν τοῖ σιν

---

308 f. μοῦνος: cp. O. T. 304 n.— 'Death alone shall not suffice for you,' already implies a threat of torture. To make this threat explicit, **πρὶν ἂν . . δηλώσητε** is added, as if merely οὐ θανεῖσθε had preceded. '(You shall not die,) until you have first been hung up alive, and have revealed (the authorship of) this outrage.' They are to be suspended by the hands or arms, and flogged. Cp. Ai. 106 θανεῖν γὰρ αὐτὸν οὔ τί πω θέλω . . πρὶν ἂν δεθεὶς πρὸς κίον᾽ ἑρκείου στέγης . . μάστιγι πρῶτον νῶτα φοινιχθεὶς θάνῃ. Ter. Phorm. I. 4. 43 ego plectar pendens. In Plat. Legg. 872 B a slave who has slain a free man is to be flogged, and then (if he does not die under the lash, ἐάνπερ βιῷ παιόμενος) put to death by other means. Other views of **κρεμαστοί** refer it to (1) mere suspension, as a torture, like that of Melanthius in Od. 22. 175: (2) stretching on a cross-like frame; cp. Alexis ap. Athen. 134 A ἥδιστ᾽ ἀναπήξαιμ᾽ αὐτὸν ἐπὶ ξύλου λαβών. Impalement (ἀνασταυρόω, ἀνασκολοπίζω) is certainly not meant.— **ζῶντες κρεμαστοί,** 'suspended alive,' as

ζῶν is oft. joined with another partic.: Xen. An. 2. 6. 29 οὐχ ὥσπερ οἱ ἄλλοι . . ἀποτμηθέντες τὰς κεφαλάς, ὥσπερ τάχιστος θάνατος δοκεῖ εἶναι, ἀλλὰ ζῶν αἰκισθεὶς ἐνιαυτόν.—**δηλώσηθ᾽:** as to the belief that torture was sure to wring the truth from slaves, cp. Isae. or. 8. 12 ὁπόταν δοῦλοι καὶ ἐλεύθεροι παραγένωνται, . . οὐ χρῆσθε ταῖς τῶν ἐλευθέρων μαρτυρίαις, ἀλλὰ τοὺς δούλους βασανίζοντες οὕτω ζητεῖτε εὑρεῖν τὴν ἀλήθειαν τῶν γενομένων. (Cp. Selections from the Attic Orators, p. 358 n.)—**ὕβριν,** in concrete sense (O. C. 1029).

310 ff. ἵν᾽ . . ἁρπάζητε, with grim irony, since they are to die before they can apply the lesson. So O. C. 1377 (Oed. calls down destruction upon his sons) ἵν᾽ ἀξιῶτον τοὺς φυτεύσαντας σέβειν, where see n. Cp. below, 716.—**τὸ κέρδος,** accus. (cp. 1242): **ἔνθεν οἰστέον** (ἐστί).— **μάθηθ᾽,** aor., learn once for all: but ἁρπάζητε, pres., go on stealing.—**ἐξ ἅπαντος,** from every source, with **τὸ κερδαίνειν:** Xen. Mem. 2. 9. 4 οὐ γὰρ ἦν οἷος ἀπὸ παντὸς κερδαίνειν: Ar. Th. 735 ὦ ποτίσταται | κἀκ παντὸς ὑμεῖς μηχανώμεναι

and produce him before mine eyes, death alone shall not be
enough for you, till first, hung up alive, ye have revealed this
outrage,—that henceforth ye may thieve with better knowledge
whence lucre should be won, and learn that it is not well to
love gain from every source. For thou wilt find that ill-gotten
pelf brings more men to ruin than to weal.

GU. May I speak? Or shall I just turn and go?
CR. Knowest thou not that even now thy voice offends?
GU. Is thy smart in the ears, or in the soul?
CR. And why wouldst thou define the seat of my pain?
GU. The doer vexes thy mind, but I, thine ears.
CR. Ah, thou art a born babbler, 'tis well seen.

ὡσίν L, with an erasure of three or four letters after τοῖ, in which ι has been made
from ν: i.e. the scribe had first written ἐν τούτοισ. **318** δαὶ L, δὲ r. **320** οἴμ'
ὡς λάλημα δῆλον] L has λάλη`μα, with an α erased before it: either, then, the scribe
wrote ἀλάλημα, or he had begun to write ἄλημα, but perceived the error before he
had written η. The later MSS. have λάλημα. The schol. has λάλημα in the lemma,
but interprets ἄλημα,—τὸ περίτριμμα τῆς ἀγορᾶς, οἷον πανοῦργος.—M. Schmidt writes
οἴμοι, λάλημ' ὡς: Gleditsch, ἴσθ' ὡς λάλημα: for δῆλον, Burges δεινόν.

πιεῖν. In O. C. 807 ἐξ ἅπαντος εὖ λέγει
=speaks well on any theme (starting from
anything).

315 f. τι suits a timid appeal: cp.
O. C. 1414 ἱκετεύω σε πεισθῆναί τί μοι.
δέ (Boeckh), though favoured by L, could
not be justified as an expostulatory 'now.'
δώσεις: O. C. 1287 διδοὺς ἐμοὶ | λέξαι.—
οὕτως, 'without more ado,' ὥσπερ ἔχω:
Ph. 1066 οὐδὲ σοῦ φωνῆς ἔτι | γενήσομαι
προσφθεγκτός, ἀλλ' οὕτως ἄπει; Plat.
Phaedr. 237 C νῦν μὲν οὕτως οὐκ ἔχω εἰπεῖν ('off-hand').—ἴω, delib. subjunct.,
somewhat rare in pres. (O. T. 651).—καὶ
νῦν ὡς=ὡς καὶ νῦν: for the hyperbaton of
ὡς, cp. Ai. 590, El. 949, 1243, etc.—
ἀνιαρῶς, with ῑ: but Eur., like Ar., has
ἀνιᾱρός (Or. 230 etc.): Aesch. does not
use the adj., though he has ἄνῑος. ἀνία (ῑ)
is used by Soph., but not by Aesch. or
Eur.

317 ἐν with ὡσίν, through association with such phrases as Aesch. Pers.
605 βοᾷ δ' ἐν ὠσὶ κέλαδος.—ἐπί with τῇ
ψυχῇ denotes the seat, and, equally with
ἐν, here=our 'in': cp. Il. 1. 55 τῷ γὰρ
ἐπὶ φρεσὶ θῆκε θεά.

318 τί δὲ is right, not τί δαὶ (L): see
Appendix.—ῥυθμίζεις, bring under ῥυθμός,
i.e. reduce to a clear form, define, ὅπου
(ἐστί), with respect to its seat (i.e. whether
it is in the ears or in the mind). Cp.
Arist. Metaphys. 11. 10 ἐὰν μὴ ῥυθμίσῃ

τις, unless one reduce (the opinions) to a
clear form, or method. So he oft. associates ῥυθμός with σχῆμα, as Phys. Ausc.
8. 3 τὸ σχηματιζόμενον καὶ ῥυθμιζόμενον,
what is being reduced to form and system.
For the epexegetic ὅπου cp. Ai. 103 ἤ
τοὐπίτριπτον κίναδος ἐξήρου μ' ὅπου; ib.
890 ἄνδρα μὴ λεύσσειν ὅπου.—Cp. Shaksp.
Troil. 4. 5. 244 That I may give the local
wound a name, And make distinct the
very breach whereout Hector's great spirit
flew.

319 f. τὰς φρένας...τὰ δ' ὦτ', acc.
defining σε: Ph. 1301 μέθες με χεῖρα:
cp. on O. C. 113.—οἴμ' ὡς, impatient, as
Ar. Ach. 590 οἴμ' ὡς τεθνήξεις: elsewhere
in Soph. it expresses pity or grief (1270,
Ai. 354, 587).—λάλημα suits Creon's
contemptuous impatience. The schol.
(see crit. n.) prob. read ἄλημα ('a knave,'
lit., 'fine meal,' from ἀλέω): cp. Ar. Av.
430 παιπάλημ' ὅλον. But if Creon used
that word, he would seem to give the
man credit for real subtlety: he would be
taking him too seriously. Thus ἄλημα
is the word applied by Ajax to his
mortal foe, Odysseus (Ai. 381, 389), who
is similarly called πάνσοφον κρότημα in
fr. 827: cp. Ph. 927 πανουργίας | δεινῆς
τέχνημ' ἔχθιστον (Neoptolemus). Cp.
756 δούλευμα: O. T. 85 κήδευμα (n.).—
δῆλον, like ἐναργές (cp. on 263).

ΦΥ. οὔκουν τό γ' ἔργον τοῦτο ποιήσας ποτέ.

ΚΡ. καὶ ταῦτ' ἐπ' ἀργύρῳ γε τὴν ψυχὴν προδούς.

ΦΥ. φεῦ.
ἦ δεινόν, ᾧ δοκεῖ γε, καὶ ψευδῆ δοκεῖν.

ΚΡ. κόμψευέ νυν τὴν δόξαν· εἰ δὲ ταῦτα μὴ
φανεῖτέ μοι τοὺς δρῶντας, ἐξερεῖθ' ὅτι   325
τὰ δειλὰ κέρδη πημονὰς ἐργάζεται.

ΦΥ. ἀλλ' εὑρεθείη μὲν μάλιστ'· ἐὰν δέ τοι
ληφθῇ τε καὶ μή, τοῦτο γὰρ τύχη κρινεῖ,
οὐκ ἔσθ' ὅπως ὄψει σὺ δεῦρ' ἐλθόντα με·
καὶ νῦν γὰρ ἐκτὸς ἐλπίδος γνώμης τ' ἐμῆς   330
σωθεὶς ὀφείλω τοῖς θεοῖς πολλὴν χάριν.

στρ. α'. ΧΟ. πολλὰ τὰ δεινὰ κοὐδὲν ἀνθρώπου δεινότερον πέλει·

---

321 τό γ' Reiske: τόδ' mss.   323 φεῦ in the verse L.—ῆ] ἤ L.—ᾧ δοκεῖ] L has ἦν and η written above ὦ and εῖ, by the first hand. ἦν δοκῇ r (including A).—δοκεῖν] δοκεῖ L.—Vauvilliers conject. ἦν δοκῇ γε καὶ ψευδῆ, δοκεῖν: Kvičala, ἦν δοκῇ γε, κεῖ ψευδῆ δοκεῖ: Hartung, ᾧ δόκησις ῇ, ψευδῆ δοκεῖν: Anonym. in Class. Journ. xvii. 57 ᾧ δοκεῖ γε, τὸ ψευδῆ δοκεῖν: Pallis, ὃς δοκεῖ γε καὶ ψευδῆ δοκεῖν ('that a man of repute should have false opinions').   324 νυν] νῦν L.—For τὴν δόξαν, one late ms. (Aug. b, 14th

---

321 'At any rate (οὖν—babbler or not) I certainly have not done this deed.' εἰμί is supplied with ποιήσας. For οὔκουν . . γε cp. 993, Ph. 907 ΝΕ. αἰσχρὸς φανοῦμαι . . ΦΙ. οὔκουν ἐν οἷς γε δρᾷς· ἐν οἷς δ' αὐδᾷς, ὀκνῶ: and so oft., as O. T. 565, 1357, O. C. 848.
322 'Yes, (you have done it,) and that, too, at the cost of betraying,' etc. The particle γε implies the contradiction, ἐποίησας: καὶ ταῦτα goes with the participle (προδούς): cp. O.T. 37, El. 614 τὴν τεκοῦσαν ὕβρισεν, | καὶ ταῦτα τηλικοῦτος. So Lat., hominem . . studiis optimis deditum, idque a puero (Cic. Fam. 13. 16).
323 ἦ δεινόν. Creon has pronounced the Guard guilty on mere δόξα, without proof. The Guard says, 'It is grievous that, when a man does harbour suspicions (ᾧ δοκεῖ γε), those suspicions should at the same time (καὶ) be false.' γε means that, in such a matter, hasty δόξα should be avoided altogether. It is always bad to assume a man guilty without proof; it is worse when the rash assumption is also erroneous. Cp. δόκησις ἀγνώς, 'a blind suspicion' (O. T. 681), and ib. 608 γνώμη δ' ἀδήλῳ μή με χωρὶς αἰτιῶ. Eur. Bacch. 311 μηδ' ἦν δοκῇς μέν, (ἡ δὲ δόξα σου νοσεῖ,) | φρονεῖν δόκει τι.—Nauck supposes a play on two senses of δοκεῖν, ᾧ δοκεῖ (or, as he reads,

δοκῇ) having been suggested by ἔδοξε τῷ δήμῳ, etc.: ''Tis monstrous that he who decides should have false views.' But, even if the absolute ᾧ δοκεῖ could be thus used, the colloquial frequency of δοκεῖ (μοι ποιεῖν τι) in Aristophanes suffices to show that ᾧ δοκεῖ could not, to an Athenian ear, have suggested 'the ruler' or 'the judge': it would have seemed to mean merely one who 'proposes,' not 'disposes.'—Schütz makes δοκεῖν depend on δοκεῖ: ''Tis grievous when a man is resolved to believe even what is false' (if only he wishes to believe it). A bold speech for the Guard to Creon; nor does it satisfy either γε or καί.
324 κόμψευε . . τὴν δόξαν, make neat sayings about it,—referring to the rhetorical form of the last verse, with its παρήχησις, δοκεῖ...δοκεῖν. Not necessarily, 'quibble upon it,'—as if δοκεῖν had been used in two different senses,—a view of κόμψευε which has been brought to support the interpretations of v. 323 mentioned above. The verb is usually midd., often with acc., as Eur. I. A. 333 εὖ κεκόμψευσαι πονηρά ('thou hast given subtle form to wicked pleas'): Plat. Lach. 197 D πρέπει...σοφιστῇ τὰ τοιαῦτα μᾶλλον κομψεύεσθαι.—τὴν δόξαν, that δόξα of yours: cp. 96: El. 1110 οὐκ οἶδα τὴν σὴν

GU.   May be, but never the doer of this deed.

CR.   Yea, and more,—the seller of thy life for silver.

GU.   Alas! 'Tis sad, truly, that he who judges should misjudge.

CR.   Let thy fancy play with 'judgment' as it will;—but, if ye show me not the doers of these things, ye shall avow that dastardly gains work sorrows.   [*Exit.*

GU.   Well, may he be found! so 'twere best. But, be he caught or be he not—fortune must settle that—truly thou wilt not see me here again. Saved, even now, beyond hope and thought, I owe the gods great thanks.   [*Exit.*

CHORUS.

Wonders are many, and none is more wonderful than man ; 1st
                                                                    strophe.

cent.) has τὸ δόξαν.—Moschopulus περὶ σχεδῶν p. 20 reads κόμψευε τὴν δόκησιν : prob., as Dindorf says, by a confusion with the schol. here, σεμνολόγει· τὴν δόκησιν περιλάλει. **326** δειλὰ] δεινὰ L, which Seyffert and others prefer : schol. γρ. τὰ δειλά· ἀντὶ τοῦ κακά· ἀπὸ τοῦ τοὺς δειλοὺς εἶναι ἀχρείους. Wecklein conject. τἄδηλα.   **327** τοι] σοι L, with τ above from first hand.   **328** καὶ] Blaydes conject. κἂν.   **332** πολλὰ τὰ] Neue conject. πολλά τε.

κληδόν' (the κληδών of which you speak), not merely, 'the word δόξα.' If the *v. l.* τὸ δόξαν (see cr. n.) was intended to mean the latter, it should have been τὸ δόξα.—νυν ('very well,' like οὖν) is better than νῦν, which would mean 'for the present' (as opposed to the near future).— ταῦτα...τοὺς δρῶντας=τοὺς ταῦτα δρῶν- τας: cp. 384: the pron. gains emphasis by its place.

326 δειλά, as involving mean treachery towards king and city. Theognis 835 ἀλλ' ἀνδρῶν τε βίῃ καὶ κέρδεα δειλὰ καὶ ὕβρις | πολλῶν ἐξ ἀγαθῶν ἐς κακότητ' ἔβαλεν (*sc.* ἡμᾶς).—δεινά (L) is defended by Seyffert as='flagitious,' by Whitelaw as='clever' (iron.), 'your wondrous winnings.' In some forms of minuscule writing λ and ν could easily be confused : cp. *O. T.* 1130 ξυναλλάξας, where the first λ has been made from ν : and *O. C.* 1164, where μόνον has been restored from μολόντ'.

327 f. ἀλλ' prefacing the wish (*O. C.* 421): εὑρεθείη *sc.* ὁ δρῶν (319): **μάλιστ'**, denoting the best thing that could happen (*O. T.* 926 n.).—κἂν for καὶ is needless. We find καὶ ἐάν...καὶ ἐάν : ἐάν τε...ἐάν τε : but, as a rule, ἐάν (or ἐάν τε)...καὶ [not καὶ ἐὰν] μή : e.g. Eur. *Hec.* 751 κἂν τύχω κἂν μὴ τύχω : Plat. *Legg.* 660 E ἐάν τε μέγας.. ἐάν τε σμικρὸς...ῇ, καὶ ('and') ἐὰν πλουτῇ καὶ μή.   For the conjunctive

form in stating alternatives, cp. *O. C.* 488 n.

330 καὶ with νῦν, not with γάρ.— γνώμης, of reasonable forecast, cp. *O. T.* 1087.

332—375 First στάσιμον. 1st strophe (332—342)=1st antistrophe (343—353): 2nd strophe (354—364)=2nd antistr. (365 —375). For the metres see Metrical Analysis.

The Chorus had not thought it possible that any one should brave death to bury the corpse (220). But the deed has been done, and without leaving a trace (252). And Creon has silenced the suggestion that gods did it (278). The train of thought is continued in this ode. Its theme is man's daring,—his inventiveness, and the result to his happiness.

Man is master of sea and land ; he sub- dues all other creatures ; he has equipped his life with all resources, except a remedy against death. His skill brings him to prosperity, when he observes divine and human laws, but to ruin when he breaks them.—At that moment Antigone is led in, and the coryphaeus speaks the closing anapaests (376—383).

332 πολλα...κοὐδέν.   Schol. ἐν σχή- ματι εἶπεν, ἀντὶ τοῦ, πολλῶν ὄντων τῶν δεινῶν, οὐδέν ἐστιν ἀνθρώπου δεινότερον. The σχῆμα is the rhetorical parataxis,

70   ΣΟΦΟΚΛΕΟΥΣ

2 τοῦτο καὶ πολιοῦ πέραν πόντου χειμερίῳ νότῳ   335
3 χωρεῖ, περιβρυχίοισιν
4 περῶν ὑπ' οἴδμασιν·
5 θεῶν τε τὰν ὑπερτάταν, Γᾶν
6 ἄφθιτον, ἀκαμάταν ἀποτρύεται,
7 ἰλλομένων ἀρότρων ἔτος εἰς ἔτος,   340
8 ἱππείῳ γένει πολεύων.

335 πόντου made from πόντωι by the first hand in L. **338** θεῶν τε] τ has
been corrected from θ (or δ) by an early hand in L. After τᾶν a point has been
erased. **339 f.** ἀκαμάταν] ἀκαμάτων Semitelos (as Triclinius read), joining it
with ἀρότων, which he substitutes for ἀρότρων.—ἀποτρύετ' ἀπλομένων L, the ο after
λ made from ω: schol. in marg., γρ. ἀποτρύεται ἰλλομένων. A mis-writing of the
latter, with λ for λλ, caused the error, ΑΠΟΤΡΥΕΤΑΠΛΟΜΕΝΩΝ (Π for Π). The

καί being equiv. to 'and yet': cp. Tr.
1046 ὢ πολλὰ δὴ καὶ θερμὰ κού λόγῳ
κακά | ...μοχθήσας ἐγώ | κοῦπω τοιοῦτον
οὔτ' ἄκοιτις ἡ Διὸς | προῦθηκεν κ.τ.λ. It
is stronger to say, 'they are great; and
he is greater': than, 'though they are
great, he is greater.'—τὰ δεινά, not 'dread,'
nor 'able,' but 'wonderful.' There is a
certain resemblance to Aesch. Ch. 585 ff.
πολλὰ μὲν γᾶ τρέφει | δεινὰ δειμάτων
ἄχη...ἀλλ' ὑπέρτολμον ἀνδρὸς φρόνημα τίς
λέγοι; but there δεινά='dread,' and the
scope is limited to the violence of human
passion.

334 τοῦτο, sc. τὸ δεινόν, this wondrous power, man. The schol. quotes
Theocr. 15. 83 σοφόν τοι χρῆμ' ἄνθρωπος.
Not adverbial with χωρεῖ, 'so' (in a
way corresponding with his δεινότης), as
Bellermann takes it, comparing O. T.
1005 (τοῦτ' ἀφικόμην), where see n.—
πέραν, properly, 'to the further side of'
(trans). The point here is that man
dares to cross the sea. πέρα (ultra),
which Blaydes prefers, would imply wanderings (not merely over, but) beyond
sea. A European visitor to New York
goes πέραν πόντου: to San Francisco,
πέρα. Cp. O. C. 885 and p. 279.

335 χειμερίῳ νότῳ with χωρεῖ, goes
(driven) by it: cp. Od. 14. 253 ἐπλέομεν
Βορέῃ ἀνέμῳ, and ib. 299 (of the ship) ἡ
δ' ἔθεεν Βορέῃ ἀνέμῳ. The dat. might be
merely 'with' (dat. of circumstance), but
is better taken as instrumental. Cp. 588
πνοαῖς. Some make χειμερίῳ νότῳ a temporal dat., like ὥρᾳ χειμῶνος, which it
can hardly be.—Soph. is thinking of the
Aegean, where the prevailing winds were
from the N. or N.W. in spring and

summer, while stormy south winds were
associated with winter: Hesiod warns a
man with a voyage before him not to
await χειμῶν' ἐπιόντα νότοιό τε δεινὰς
ἀήτας, | ὅς τ' ὤρινε θάλασσαν ὁμαρτήσας
Διὸς ὄμβρῳ | πολλῷ ὀπωρινῷ, χαλεπὸν δέ
τε πόντον ἔθηκεν. The epithet χειμερίῳ
aptly distinguishes this wintry νότος from
that gentle south breeze (now called
the 'embates') which regularly sets in at
sunset in the fair season (cp. Curt. Hist.
Gr. 1. 14).

336 f. περιβρ...ὑπ' οἴδμασιν, passing
under swelling waters which open depths
around: i.e. he is in the trough of a
heavy sea, while on each side the waves
rise above his ship, threatening to engulf it. Verg. Aen. 1. 106 his unda
dehiscens Terram inter fluctus aperit.
βρύχιος, 'of the depths' (βρυχία...ἠχὼ
βροντᾶς, Aesch. P. V. 1082), is formed
as if from βρύξ, of which Oppian uses
acc. βρύχα ('depth of the sea', Hal. 2.
588). ὑποβρύχιος='under water,' and
so neut. pl. adv. ὑπόβρυχα (Od. 5. 319
etc.). περιβρύχιος occurs only here. For
the ι before βρ cp. 348, 1104, 1117.
The schol.'s ἠχώδεσι means that περιβρύχιος was taken as 'roaring around'
(βρυχάομαι), where the υ would be long,
against metre (cp. 347). The Homeric
ἀμφὶ δὲ κῦμα | βέβρυχεν ῥόθιον (Od. 5.
411) might suggest this view.

338 ὑπερτάταν, highest, as eldest,
παμμήτωρ (Aesch. P. V. 90), and παμ-
βῶτις (Ph. 392): Plat. Tim. 40 C γῆν...
πρώτην καὶ πρεσβυτάτην θεῶν ὅσοι ἐντὸς
οὐρανοῦ γεγόνασι.

339 ἀκαμάταν: this form of the fem.
occurs only here, unless ἀκαμάτῃσι (and

the power that crosses the white sea, driven by the stormy
south-wind, making a path under surges that threaten to
engulf him ; and Earth, the eldest of the gods, the immortal,
the unwearied, doth he wear, turning the soil with the offspring
of horses, as the ploughs go to and fro from year to year.

later MSS. have ἀπλωμένων (as V), εἰλομένων (as Vat.), or παλλομένων (as A).—ἔτοσ
εἰσ ἔτοσ L. Some later MSS. have ἔτους εἰς ἔτος. Musgrave conject. ἔτος ἐξ ἔτους,
from the schol., περικυκλούντων τῶν ἀρότρων ἔτος ἐξ ἔτους.   **341** πολεῦον (corrected
from πόλευον) L: πολεύων ι.

---

not ἀκαμάτοισι) χέρεσσιν be right in
Hes. *Th.* 747, but is warranted by similar
epic forms in tragedy, as ἀθανάτας (gen.)
Aesch. *Ch.* 619, Eur. *Ph.* 235 : ἀδ-
μήταν Soph. *El.* 1238 (and -ης in dial.
O. C. 1321). For the initial ᾱ, cp. the
epic ἀθάνατος, ἀγοράασθε, etc. (and see
Introd. to Homer, Appendix, note 5, p.
195) : but in *El.* 164 we find 'ἀκάματα.—
ἀποτρύεται, prop., wears away for his
own purposes (midd.),—*fatigat*, vexes
(with constant ploughing). Earth is
'immortal,' and not to be exhausted ; but
man's patient toil subdues it to his use.
Cp. *Tr.* 124 ἀποτρύειν ἐλπίδα, to wear it
out.—Not, 'wearies himself by tilling' the
soil.
340 ἰλλομένων ἀρότρων, as the
ploughs go backwards and forwards,—
turning at the end of one furrow, and
going down the next. Cp. Nicander
Ther. 478 φεῦγε δ' ἀεὶ σκολιήν τε καὶ οὐ
μίαν ἀτραπὸν ἴλλων, 'in flying (from the
snake), always *make your course wind*
(ἴλλων) from side to side, instead of keeping it straight.' Xen. *Cyn.* 6. 15 κύνες
ἐξιλλοῦσαι τὰ ἴχνη, 'puzzling out the
tracks,' *i.e.* going backwards and forwards
till they have found a clue. As to the
spelling ἴλλω *versus* εἴλλω, see Appendix.
It is needless to write ἀρότων, 'ploughing-
seasons' (*Tr.* 825), and to take ἰλλομένων
as = περιτελλομένων. The picture of the
ploughs at work is more vivid ; and, with
ἀρότων, ἔτος εἰς ἔτος would be feebly redundant.—**ἔτος εἰς ἔτος**, an adverbial
phrase, like 'year in, year out' : for the
use of the simple acc. in temporal adverbs
(like ἀωρίαν) see *O. T.* 1138 n.; for εἰς,
Od. 9. 134 μάλα κεν βαθὺ λήϊον αἰεὶ | εἰς
ὥρας ἀμῷεν ('as each year comes round'):
Theocr. 18. 15 κῆς ἔτος ἐξ ἔτεος : so εἰς
νέωτα (next year), and the Mod. Gk

χρόνο σὲ (= εἰς) χρόνο, 'year after year.'
341 ἱππείῳ γένει, the 'offspring of
horses,' meaning 'mules'; which are 'far
better than oxen to drag the jointed
plough through the deep fallow' (*Il.* 10.
352). Arist. *Rhet.* 3. 2 § 14 ὁ Σιμωνίδης,
ὅτε μὲν ἐδίδου μισθὸν ὀλίγον αὐτῷ ὁ νικήσας
τοῖς ὀρεῦσιν, οὐκ ἤθελε ποιεῖν ὡς δυσχε-
ραίνων εἰς ἡμιόνους ποιεῖν· ἐπεὶ δ' ἱκανὸν
ἔδωκεν, ἐποίησε, χαίρετ', ἀελλοπόδων
θύγατρες ἵππων. As this story suggests, the very fact that the ordinary Attic
word for 'mule' was ἡμίονος (adj. ὀρικός)
might lead an Attic poet to prefer such a
periphrasis as ἵππειον γένος. The objections to taking ἱππείῳ γένει as simply
= ἵπποις are, that (1) Greek ploughmen used
oxen or mules more than horses, and (2)
the achievement of taming the horse (350)
is thus anticipated. Some understand
both horses and mules, giving γένει a double sense—rather awkwardly, I think.—
πολεύων, κατὰ σύνεσιν after **τοῦτο.** Cp.
Od. 11. 90 ἦλθε δ' ἐπὶ ψυχὴ Θηβαίου Τειρε-
σίαο, | χρύσεον σκῆπτρον ἔχων : 16. 476
μείδησεν δ' ἱερὴ ἲς Τηλεμάχοιο, | ἐς πατέρ'
ὀφθαλμοῖσιν ἰδών : *Il.* 11. 690 ἐλθὼν γὰρ
ἐκάκωσε βίη Ἡρακληείη. But as Soph.
would write ΠΟΛΕΤΟΝ, it was the easier
to read πόλευον.
343—353 Man's conquests over the
animal world are here taken in two
groups. First, those of which the primary aim is to kill or to capture. Here
the means is netting (ἀμφιβαλὼν σπείραισι
δικτυοκλώστοις), in its threefold sporting
use, as applied to fowling (ὀρνίθων), hunting (θηρῶν), and fishing (πόντου φύσιν).
Secondly, those conquests which aim at
reducing wild animals to man's service.
These are effected by μηχαναί (349),—
arts of taming and training. And their
result is aptly expressed by the word

ἀντ. α'. κουφονόων τε φῦλον ὀρνίθων ἀμφιβαλὼν ἄγει   343
　　　2 καὶ θηρῶν ἀγρίων ἔθνη πόντου τ' εἰναλίαν φύσιν   345
　　　3 σπείραισι δικτυοκλώστοις,
　　　4 περιφραδὴς ἀνήρ·
　　　5 κρατεῖ δὲ μηχαναῖς ἀγραύλου
　　　6 θηρὸς ὀρεσσιβάτα, λασιαύχενά θ'   350
　　　7 ἵππον *ὀχμάζεται *ἀμφὶ λόφον ζυγῶν,
　　　8 οὔρειόν τ' ἀκμῆτα ταῦρον.

στρ. β'. καὶ φθέγμα καὶ ἀνεμόεν   354

342 κουφονέωντε L, the ω from ο. The first hand seems to have written κοῦφον ἐόντε. κουφονέων τε or κουφονέον τε ɪ : κουφονόων τε Brunck.　**344** ἀμφιβαλὼν L, with ο above ω from the first hand (for the sake of consistency with πολεῦον in 341).—The first hand in L wrote ἔχει ἄγει: another early hand erased the second word, and changed the first into ἄγει.　**345** εἰναλίαν] ἐναλίαν L.　**350** ὀρεσσιβάτᾱ L: a letter erased

---

κρατεῖ: here, man is not merely the slayer or captor; he becomes the master of docile toilers. The horse and the bull are types.

Thus, in this ode, the scale of achievement ever ascends: man (1) conquers inanimate nature : (2) makes animals his captives: (3) trains them to be his servants : (4) develops his own social and intellectual life.

343 κουφονόων is merely a general epithet, 'light-hearted,' 'blithe and careless'; Theognis 580 σμικρῆς ὄρνιθος κοῦφον ἔχουσα νόον: cp. the proverbial phraseology of Athens, ἄνθρωπος ὄρνις, ἀστάθμητος, πετόμενος, | ἀτέκμαρτος, οὐδὲν οὐδέποτ' ἐν ταὐτῷ μένων (Ar. Av. 169). The epithet is given to ἔρωτες below (617), and to εὐηθία in Aesch. P. V. 383.— Not, 'quick-witted' (and therefore harder to catch).—ἀμφιβαλὼν with σπείραισι δ.: it can precede the dat. by so much, because its meaning is already clear, and the dat. is merely a poet. amplification.

345 f. πόντου...εἰναλίαν φύσιν, a brood living in the waters of the sea, the tautology being only of the same order as in πόντος ἁλός, ἁλὸς ἐν πελάγεσσιν, πέλαγος θαλάσσης, etc.—σπείραισι δικτυοκλ., instr. dat. with ἀμφιβαλὼν, in the coils of woven nets : for the adj. compounded with a subst. (δίκτυον) cognate in sense to σπεῖρα, see n. on O. C. 716 εὐήρετμος πλάτα.—Ar. Av. 528 mentions ἔρκη, νεφέλας, δίκτυα, πηκτάς as nets used by the fowler (ὀρνιθευτής). In hunting the lion, bear, boar, deer, hare, etc., various

nets were used ; the δίκτυον, to enclose large spaces ; the ἐνόδιον, to close passages; the ἄρκυς (cassis) or tunnel-net. The chief fishing-nets were the ἀμφίβληστρον (casting-net), and the σαγήνη (drag-net, whence seine, sean).

348 περιφραδής. Eustath. p. 135, 25 φραδής...ὅθεν σύνθετον ὁ παρὰ Σοφοκλεῖ ἀριφραδὴς ἀνήρ. This was evidently a mere slip of memory. Neither Soph. nor Eur. uses any compound with ἀρι or ἐρι, though Aesch. has ἀρίδακρυς, ἐρίδματος, ἐρικύμων.

349 f. μηχαναῖς. μαχαναῖς in Ai. 181 and μαχανᾷ in Aesch. Th. 133 are the only instances in which Tragedy gives a Doric form to words from this stem.— ἀγραύλου, having his αὐλή, or dwelling, in the open country, as opposed to a domesticated animal : Eur. Bacch. 1187 πρέπει γ' ὥστε θὴρ ἄγραυλος φόβῃ. For the combination with ὀρεσσιβάτα cp. Plat. Crat. 394 E τὸ θηριῶδες τῆς φύσεως καὶ τὸ ἄγριον αὐτοῦ καὶ τὸ ὀρεινόν.

350 λασιαύχενά θ'. The elision at the end of the verse (ἐπισυναλοιφή) is comparatively rare in lyrics, as in dialogue (1031) ; but cp. 595 πίπτοντ', 864 αὐτογέννητ'.

351 ὀχμάζεται, he tames, ἀμφὶ λόφον ζυγῶν, putting the yoke about its neck. ὀχμάζω (prop., 'to get a firm hold upon') was esp. used of breaking horses : Eur. El. 816 (Thessalians honour a man) ὅστις ταῦρον ἀρταμεῖ (cuts to pieces) καλῶς, | ἵππους τ' ὀχμάζει.　Schol. on Apollon.

And the light-hearted race of birds, and the tribes of savage 1st anti-
beasts, and the sea-brood of the deep, he snares in the meshes strophe.
of his woven toils, he leads captive, man excellent in wit.
And he masters by his arts the beast whose lair is in the wilds,
who roams the hills; he tames the horse of shaggy mane, he
puts the yoke upon its neck, he tames the tireless mountain
bull.

And speech, and wind-swift 2nd
strophe.

---

after ᾱ, perhaps ν. **351** λασιαύχενά θ' ἵππον ἕξεται ἀμ|φίλοφον ζυγόν L. Schol.
in marg. (on 352) ἀπὸ κοινοῦ τὸ ὑπὸ ζυγὸν ἕξεται, with ᾱ written over ἕ. The later MSS.
have ἄξεται (A), ἄξετ', ἕξεται, ἕξετ'. See comment. and Appendix. **352** ἀκμῆτα
L, ἀδμῆτα r.

Rhod. 1. 743 κυρίως ἐστὶν ὀχμάσαι τὸ
ἵππον ὑπὸ χαλινὸν ἀγαγεῖν ἢ ὑπὸ ζυγόν.
The midd. voice does not occur elsewhere; but this cannot be regarded as an
objection, when we remember how many
rare middle forms occur in the dramatists.
Thus προσορωμένα in *O. C.* 244 is a solitary example of that verb in the midd.,
and if the license could be taken with so
common a word, much more might it be
allowed with a comparatively rare one.
Blaydes writes ὀχμάζει ὑπ' ἀμφίλοφον
ζυγόν: but the MS. ἕξεται indicates that
the verb, whatever it was, was of the
midd. form. ὀχμάζεται was published
by G. Schöne in 1833, and by Franz in
1846: they appear to have made the conjecture independently. Donaldson (1848)
printed ὀχμάζεται ἀμφὶ λόφον ζυγῶν, and
seems to ascribe ζυγῶν (or ζυγῷ) to Franz and
Schöne; though Franz, at least, proposed
ἀμφὶ λόφον ζυγῷ. ζυγῶν has been re-
vived (seemingly without knowledge of
a predecessor) by H. Schütz (1886). Sophocles would write ΑΜΦΙΛΟΦΟΝΖΥΓΟΝ,
and thus ζυγῶν changes no letter. Aesch.
used the fut. ζυγώσω (fr. 110), and Soph.
has the verbal ζυγωτόν (*El.* 702). To
ἀμφιλόφῳ ζυγῷ it may be objected that,
being clear, it was not likely to become
-ον -όν: but, when ἀμφίλοφον had once
been written, ζυγῶν (or ζυγῷ) would
easily become ζυγόν. As to the schol. on
ἀμφίλοφον,—ἀντὶ τοῦ, περιβαλὼν αὐτῷ
ζυγὸν περὶ τὸν λόφον, ὑπάγει,—it cannot
fairly be urged for ζυγῶν (or for any
partic.), since it may be merely a paraphrase of ἀμφίλοφον.—Schütz's **ἐφέξεται**
is attractive; for the acc. he cp. Aesch.
Eum. 409 βρέτας...ἐφημένῳ, Eur. *Helen.*

1493 Εὐρώταν ἐφεζόμεναι. Add Aesch.
Ag. 664 ναῦν θέλουσ' ἐφέξετο. The sense
would be, 'seats himself behind the horse'
(in a chariot): cp. *Il.* 5. 46 ἵππων ἐπιβη-
σόμενον, etc. But, though oxen were used
for draught, ἐφέξεται suits ταῦρον less well.
The sense, '*tames*,' is clearly that which
we require. See Appendix.

354 φθέγμα κ.τ.λ. The phrase, 'man
has taught himself speech,' should not be
pressed as if the poet was thinking of a
theory on the origin of language. It was
the Eleatic view that language came θέσει,
not φύσει, and Soph. may have known
that; but by his ἐδιδάξατο he meant
simply, 'developed for his own benefit,
by his own effort.' So Isocrates (or. 3 § 6)
conceives primitive man as living in a
brutal state, and emerging from it by the
development of speech and thought,—
λόγος being one of the human faculties
(τῶν ἐνόντων ἐν τῇ τῶν ἀνθρώπων φύσει),
and the distinctive one:—ἐγγενομένου δ'
ἡμῖν τοῦ πείθειν ἀλλήλους καὶ δηλοῦν πρὸς
ἡμᾶς αὐτοὺς περὶ ὧν ἂν βουληθῶμεν, οὐ
μόνον τοῦ θηριωδῶς ζῆν ἀπηλλάγη-
μεν, ἀλλὰ καὶ συνελθόντες πόλεις ᾠκί-
σαμεν καὶ νόμους ἐθέμεθα καὶ τέχνας
εὕρομεν. Cp. Hor. *Sat.* 1. 3. 103 (men
fought,) *Donec verba, quibus voces sen-
susque notarent, Nominaque invenere:
dehinc absistere bello, Oppida coeperunt
munire et ponere leges.* The Aeschylean
Prometheus (*P. V.* 444) claims to have
made men ἔννους...καὶ φρενῶν ἐπηβόλους,
but not (like Shelley's Prometheus) to
have also given them language. Cp.
Peile's chapter 'On the Nature of Language' (*Primer of Philology*), p. 156: 'In
this way then we may conceive of the

2 φρόνημα καὶ ἀστυνόμους ὀργὰς ἐδιδάξατο καὶ δυσ-
    αύλων

3 πάγων ἐναίθρεια καὶ δύσομβρα φεύγειν βέλη,

4 παντοπόρος· ἄπορος ἐπ' οὐδὲν ἔρχεται   360

5 τὸ μέλλον· Ἄιδα μόνον φεῦξιν οὐκ ἐπάξεται·

355 φρόνημα] φώνημα Scaliger (so, too, Valckenaer and Bergk). φρούρημα Semitelos.
ἀμερόφρον νόημα Schneidewin.—ὀργὰς] One of the later MSS., V (13th cent.), has
ὁρμὰς, prob. a late conjecture, if not a mere error. Valckenaer conject. ἀρχὰς:
Musgrave, ὀρχμὰς ('bounds,' Hesych., ὀρχμαί· φραγμοί): Mekler and Semitelos,
ἀγοράς: Gleditsch, ἀρετὰς (and ἀστυνόμον σοφίαν). **356** ἐδαδάξατο L, with ι
over the first α from the first hand. **357** αἴθρια MSS. (marg. gloss in L,
ψυχρά). ἐναίθρεια Helmke: ὑπαίθρεια Boeckh. Musgrave had already proposed
αἴθρεια, which, however, does not satisfy the metre (cp. 368). Blaydes would
prefer ὑπαίθρῖα or δυσαιθρῖα. **359** παντ' ὁποροσ L first hand (πάντ' ἄπορος?):
a later hand has accented the second ο. L has a point after βέλη, and none after
παντοπόρος. **361** ἄιδα L, with ι over the second α from the first hand: the dots

---

beginnings of speech...Speech is the development, through imitation, of a capacity of man—the capacity of making a
noise.' This is quite compatible with ἐδιδάξατο.—ἀνεμόεν φρόνημα: cp. *Il.* 15. 80
ὡς δ' ὅτ' ἂν ἀΐξῃ νόος ἀνέρος...| ὣς κραιπνῶς
μεμανῖα διέπτατο: *Od.* 7. 36 τῶν νέες
ὠκεῖαι ὡσεὶ πτερὸν ἠὲ νόημα: *O. C.* 1081
ἀελλαία ταχύρρωστος πελειάς: fr. 621 ἀελ-
λάδες φωναί. Not 'lofty,' in which sense
ἀνεμόεν could be said only of a high place.
Cp. Shelley, *Prometheus:* 'He gave man
speech, and speech created thought, Which
is the measure of the universe.' Soph.
does not imply that speech created
thought; he is rather thinking of them as
developed (in their riper forms) together.

355 ἀστυνόμους ὀργάς, 'such disposi-
tions as regulate cities'; *i.e.* those feelings
which lead men to organise social life,
and to uphold the social order by their
loyalty. For ὀργάς, cp. *Ai.* 639 συντρό-
φοις | ὀργαῖς, the dispositions that have
grown with his growth: Eur. *Tro.* 53
ἐπήνεσ' ὀργὰς ἠπίους. The relation of
φθέγμα to ἀστυνόμοι ὀργαί is illustrated by
Arist. *Pol.* I. 2 § 12, where he is showing
that man, more than any other ἀγελαῖον
ζῷον, is πολιτικόν: 'Speech is intended
to explain what is expedient and what is
hurtful,—and so also what is just and
unjust. It is characteristic of man, as
compared with other animals, that he
alone has a sense of good and evil, just
and unjust; and it is the association of
beings with this sense that make a Family
and a State.'

356 ἐδιδάξατο here = simply αὐτὸς
ἑαυτὸν ἐδίδαξε. The notion, 'men taught

each other,' 'learned by mutual converse,'
cannot be extracted from it. The passive
διδάσκομαι as = μανθάνειν is freq., but I
can find no parallel for the use of the aor.
midd. here. For the ordinary use, cp.
Plat. *Meno* p. 93 D τὸν υἱὸν ἱππέα...ἐδι-
δάξατο (*had* his son *taught* to ride): so
Plat. *Rep.* 467 E (διδαξαμένους, 'when we
have had them taught'); [Plat.] *Theag.*
122 E, *De Virt.* 377 B; Xen. *Cyr.* 1. 6. 2,
Mem. 4. 4. 5; Ar. *Nub.* 1338. Once or
twice ἐδιδαξάμην is merely ἐδίδαξα with
the idea of the teacher's interest super-
added: Pind. *O.* 8. 59 τὸ διδάξασθαι |
εἰδότι ῥᾴτερον: so Simonides fr. 145
(of himself) διδαξάμενος χορόν (unless he
meant, 'caused to be trained'). In Ar.
Nub. 783 διδάξαιμ' ἂν (Elmsley) should
prob. be read. It is rare for any midd.
form, without a reflexive pron., to denote
that the subject acts *on* (and not for) himself: thus, 'he kills himself' is not ἀποκτεί-
νεται, but ἀποκτείνει ἑαυτόν (Plat. *Phaed.*
61 E). The exceptions are chiefly words of
the toilet, as λούομαι. The dative of the
reflexive can be more easily understood,
as Thuc. 6. 40 πόλις...οὐκ...αὐθαίρετον
δουλείαν ἐπιβαλεῖται, *sibi imponet.*

358 πάγων κ.τ.λ. Construe: καὶ (ἐδιδάξατο) φεύγειν ἐναίθρεια βέλη δυσαύλων
πάγων, καὶ δύσομβρα βέλη. He learned
to build houses, to shelter himself from
frost and rain. πάγοι δύσαυλοι = frosts
which make it unpleasant to bivouack in
the open: cp. Aesch. *Ag.* 555 δυσαυλίας.
ἐναίθρεια = under a clear (frosty) sky: cp.
fr. 154 ὅταν πάγου φανέντος αἰθρίου
('a clear frost') χεροῖν | κρύσταλλον ἁρπά-
σωσι. Nauck takes δυσαύλων πάγων as

thought, and all the moods that mould a state, hath he taught
himself; and how to flee the arrows of the frost, when 'tis hard
lodging under the clear sky, and the arrows of the rushing rain;
yea, he hath resource for all; without resource he meets nothing
that must come: only against Death shall he call for aid in vain;

on the first ι have been erased.—μόνωι L, with ον (not ου) over ωι from the first hand.
362 ἐπάξεται] Heindorf conject. ἐπεύξεται. Schneidewin, ἐπάσεται (so Semitelos,
placing a stop at ἔρχεται, and reading τὸ μέλλον "Αιδαν μόνον | θέλξειν οὐκ ἐπάσεται,
'only he will not find the spell which can charm Hades'). Rauchenstein, οὐκ ἐπαρκέσει. Pallis, ἐπίσταται. M. Schmidt, ἔπραξέ πα. Seyffert, διδάξεται. Wecklein,
πεπάσεται.

'inhospitable *hills*,' citing Moschion fr.
7. 5 (*Frag. Trag.* p. 633), who describes
primitive man as inhabiting ὀρειγενῆ
σπήλαια: but the context is against this.
As corrections of the MS. αἴθρια, there
is little to choose between ἐναίθρεια and
ὑπαίθρεια: Aesch. *Ag.* 335 has ὑπαιθρίων
πάγων: but after πάγων the loss of ἐν
would be easier than that of ὑπ. The
ι of αἰθρία could be long (as Solon 13.
22): but ῑ is not elsewhere found in the
derivatives; for in Cratinus Δηλιάδες fr. 5
we must read Ὑπερβορείους αἴθρια τιμῶντας
στέφῃ (not, as Blaydes gives it, Ὑπερ-
βορέους αἴθρῑα). The spelling ἐναίθρεια
is conjectural, but in *O. C.* 1088 L has
ἐπινικείῳ, as metre requires, for ἐπινικίῳ.
Below, v. 814, ἐπινύμφειος has been
conjectured: see n. there.— **βέλη**, the
'shafts' of piercing cold, or of lashing
rain. Cp. Plat. *Legg.* 873 E κεραυνός, ἤ
τι παρὰ θεοῦ τοιοῦτον βέλος ἰόν (some
such swift and sudden visitation): Aesch.
P. V. 371 βέλεσι πυρπνόου ζάλης (sent
forth from Aetna): *Il.* 1. 53 κῆλα θεοῖο
(of the pestilence).

360 παντοπόρος is at once a comment
on the achievements already enumerated
(cp. περιφραδής in 348), and a general
expression absolving the poet from further
detail: 'yes, there is nothing that he
cannot provide.' Isocr. may have had
this passage in mind in or. 3 § 6 (quoted
on 354), where an enumeration parallel
with that of Soph. is closed by a phrase
answering to παντοπόρος,—καὶ σχεδὸν
ἅπαντα τὰ δι' ἡμῶν μεμηχανημένα λόγος
ἡμῖν ἐστιν ὁ συγκατασκευάσας. We must
not point thus: βέλη· παντοπόρος, ἄπορος
κ.τ.λ., when the sense would be weakened,
and the construction perplexed ('all-pro-
viding, and in no case without resource,
he meets the future').

οὐδὲν ... τὸ **μέλλον** = οὐδὲν ὃ μέλλει

(ἔσεσθαι), nothing that is to be (cp. the
absolute τὸ μέλλον, τὰ μέλλοντα). So
Plat. *Lach.* 197 Α ἔγωγε ἀνδρεία καλῶ
οὔτε θηρία οὔτε ἄλλο οὐδὲν τὸ τὰ δεινὰ
ὑπὸ ἀγνοίας μὴ φοβούμενον=οὐδὲν ὃ μὴ
φοβεῖται. This negative form is as correct
as (though actually rarer than) the positive
πᾶν τὸ καλῶς ἔχον (Plat. *Rep.* 381 Α) for
πᾶν ὃ καλῶς ἔχει. Donaldson took τὸ
μέλλον adverbially: 'in regard to the
future, he comes to nothing without
resources.' Cp. 728, μηδὲν τὸ μὴ δίκαιον,
where μηδέν is subst., not adv.

361 f. **μόνον** and **μόνου** are alike
admissible; μόνον means, 'the only thing
that he will not achieve is to escape
death'; μόνου, 'the only thing that he
will not escape is death.' In this general
view of human achievement, μόνον seems
a little the better. **φεῦξιν—ἐπάξεται**,
procure means of escape from death.
ἐπάγεσθαι, prop. 'to bring into one's own
country'; usu. said of calling in allies to
help one; or of importing foreign pro-
ducts: Thuc. 4. 64 ξυμμάχους δὲ οὐδέποτε
...ἐπαξόμεθα: id. 1. 81 ἐκ θαλάσσης ὧν
δέονται ἐπάξονται. Then often fig., of
calling in anything to one's aid: Plat.
Legg. 823 Α τὸ δὲ δὴ παρὸν ἡμῖν τὰ νῦν
οἷον μάρτυρα ἐπαγόμεθα· δηλοῖ μὲν ἂν ὃ
βουλόμεθα: 'we call to our help, as a
witness, the example which is actually
present with us; it will show what we
mean.' *Gorg.* 492 Β αὐτοὶ ἑαυτοῖς δεσπό-
την ἐπαγάγοιντο τὸν τῶν πολλῶν ἀνθρώπων νόμον τε καὶ λόγον καὶ ψόγον ('*call in*
to rule them'). Menander Ὑδρία fr. 2
γέροντα δυστυχοῦντα, τῶν θ' αὑτοῦ κακῶν |
ἐπαγόμενον λήθην, ἀνέμνησας πάλιν
('seeking to procure forgetfulness of his
troubles'). The word is admirably suitable and vivid here: man looks to every
side for succour against the foe that is
ever in the land,—Death; but from no

6 νόσων δ' ἀμηχάνων φυγὰς ξυμπέφρασται.

ἀντ. β'. σοφόν τι τὸ μηχανόεν   365
2 τέχνας ὑπὲρ ἐλπίδ' ἔχων τοτὲ μὲν κακόν, ἄλλοτ'
  ἐπ' ἐσθλὸν ἔρπει·
3 νόμους *γεραίρων χθονὸς θεῶν τ' ἔνορκον δίκαν,
4 ὑψίπολις· ἄπολις, ὅτῳ τὸ μὴ καλὸν   370
5 ξύνεστι τόλμας χάριν. μήτ' ἐμοὶ παρέστιος
6 γένοιτο μήτ' ἴσον φρονῶν, ὃς τάδ' ἔρδει.   375

---

363 ἀμηχάνων L, with ουσ written over ων by a late hand. (Dübner says, ' ων ex
ουσ factum a m. rec.'; but ων is from the first hand, and has not been touched.)
365 σοφόν τι] Heimsoeth conject. δεινόν τι: Schmidt, τοῖόν τι: Gleditsch, τοσόνδε.
366 ὑπερ ἐλπίδ' L (not ὑπερελπίδ').—ἔχων] ἔχον r: cp. 344.   **367** τοτὲ L, ποτὲ r.
368 παρείρων MSS. (with glosses πληρῶν, τηρῶν, στέργων).—Reiske conject. γεραίρων.
Dindorf, παραιρῶν. Schaefer, γὰρ αἴρων. Schneidewin, τ' ἀείρων. Pallis, τε τηρῶν.

---

quarter can he find help. It is surprising
that so many recent critics should have
confidently condemned ἐπάξεται, and
sought to replace it by conjectures (see
cr. n.).

363 f. ἀμηχάνων, such as seem to
baffle all treatment: *El.* 140 ἀμήχανον |
ἄλγος: Simonides *ap.* Plat. *Prot.* 344 c
ἀμήχανος συμφορά.—**φυγάς**, like φεῦξιν:
Eur. *Helen.* 799 λέκτρων...φυγάς, means
of escape from the union; cp. Ar. *Eq.*
759 κἀκ τῶν ἀμηχάνων πόρους εὐμηχάνους
πορίζων.—**ξυμπέφρασται**, here midd., as
Aesch. *Suppl.* 438 καὶ δὴ πέφρασμαι: cp.
O. C. 1016 n.

365—375 The ode closes with a
more direct reference to the incident
which suggested its theme. The daring
ingenuity shown by the unknown breaker
of Creon's edict is an instance of the
subtlety which leads to ruin. The implied contrast with Creon—ὑψίπολις by
his care for the laws—is effective in view
of the destined περιπέτεια.

365 f. σοφόν τι...ἔχων: lit., possess-
ing, in his resourceful skill, a thing subtle
beyond belief: σοφόν τι is predicate, and
in apposition with τὸ μηχανόεν τέχνας.
Cp. Thuc. 2. 89 μέγα τι τῆς διανοίας τὸ
βέβαιον ἔχοντες ἀντιτολμῶσιν: 'they are
strong in the confidence of their spirit
when they confront the foe.' There is
no ground for altering σοφόν into δεινόν,
τοῖον, or the like.—**τὸ μηχανόεν τ.**, the
inventive quality in his skill: for τέχνας,
cp. *O. T.* 380 n.; for the absence of τᾶς,
cp. above, 10 (κακά). Cp. Thuc. 1. 90

τὸ...βουλόμενον καὶ ὕποπτον τῆς γνώμης:
2. 61 ἐν τῷ ὑμετέρῳ ἀσθενεῖ τῆς γνώμης.

367 τοτὲ μὲν...ἄλλοτ'. L has τοτὲ
here: cp. *El.* 739 τότ' (*i.e.* τοτὲ) ἄλλος,
ἄλλοθ' ἅτερος: Plat. *Phaedr.* 237 E τοτὲ
μὲν ἡ ἑτέρα, ἄλλοτε δὲ ἡ ἑτέρα κρατεῖ. Cp.
O. C. 1745 n. There is no reason, then,
for reading ποτὲ μέν here with inferior
MSS., though it is equally good (Plato has
ποτὲ μὲν answered by ποτὲ δέ, by ἐνίοτε
δέ, or by αὖθις δέ).—**ἐπ'** with κακόν as
well as ἐσθλόν: cp. 212 n. on κἀς.

368 γεραίρων, 'honouring,' is in my
belief a certain correction of the MS.
παρείρων. The latter = 'weaving in,' as
a thread into a texture, or a flower into a
wreath: for the genuine fig. use of it, see
Xen. *Symp.* 6. 2 μεταξὺ τοῦ ὑμᾶς λέγειν
οὐδ' ἂν τρίχα, μὴ ὅτι λόγον, ἄν τις παρεί-
ρειε: 'while you are speaking, one could
not put in a hair, much less a speech'
(so close and continuous is the texture
of your speaking). Here, παρείρων has
been explained as, 'weaving the laws
(etc.) into the texture of his life'; but,
even if we grant that so strange a phrase
would be possible with words added to
express 'the texture of his life,' it is certainly impossible without them. Dindorf
proposed παραιρῶν as = 'wresting,' 'vio-
lating' (a strange sense), and pointed at
δίκαν· 'he comes to evil (though at other
times to good) when he violates the
laws,' etc. ΓΕΡΑΙΡΩΝ could easily
generate ΠΑΡΕΙΡΩΝ. γεραίρειν, prop.
to distinguish by gifts of honour, is also a
general poet. synonym for τιμᾶν: cp. Her.

but from baffling maladies he hath devised escapes.

Cunning beyond fancy's dream is the fertile skill which _{2nd anti-} brings him, now to evil, now to good. When he honours ^{strophe.} the laws of the land, and that justice which he hath sworn by the gods to uphold, proudly stands his city: no city hath he who, for his rashness, dwells with sin. Never may he share my hearth, never think my thoughts, who doth these things!

Semitelos, παροίκων ('dwellers' in the land), with εὐορκῶν (='φυλάττων εὐσεβῶς') for ἔνορκον. **370** ὑψίπολις] ῥυσίπολις Iernstedt. **373** μή τέ μοι (not μήτε μοι) L: μήτ' ἐμοὶ r. **374** μήτ' ἴσον] In L more than one letter has been erased after τ' (Dübner suggests ισ, Campb. εγ). **375** ἔρδει L (not ἔρδοι: the ε is clear, and has not been touched).

---

5. 67 ἐτίμων τὸν Ἄδρηστον καὶ δὴ πρὸς τὰ πάθεα αὐτοῦ τραγικοῖσι χοροῖσι ἐγέραιρον. Ar. *Th.* 960 γένος Ὀλυμπίων θεῶν | μέλπε καὶ γέραιρε φωνῇ.

369 θεῶν τ' ἔνορκον δίκαν, Justice, which men swear to observe, taking oaths by the gods (ὅρκοι θεῶν: *O. T.* 647 n.): =ὅρκοις θεῶν κεκυρωμένην.

370 f. ὑψίπολις seems best taken as =ὑψηλὴν πόλιν ἔχων: cp. Pind. *P.* 8. 22 ἁ δικαιόπολις...νᾶσος (Aegina). In *O.* 2. 8 Theron, tyrant of Acragas, is called ὀρθόπολις in an active sense, as =ὀρθῶν τὴν πόλιν. In *O. T.* 510 ἀδύπολις=ἀνδάνων τῇ πόλει: but it is harder to suppose that ὑψίπολις could have been intended to mean, 'standing high in his city.' Nor would that be the fittest sense. The loyal citizen makes the prosperous city; and her prosperity is his. See on 189. In this clause the Chorus thinks especially of Creon (191 τοιοῖσδ' ἐγὼ νόμοισι τήνδ' αὔξω πόλιν).—**ἄπολις.** Where the typical citizen is a law-breaker, the city is ruined, and the evil-doer is left citiless. So Creon had described law-breaking as ἄτην...ἀστοῖς (185). The contrast with ὑψίπολις shows that the sense is not merely, 'when a man breaks the law he becomes an exile' (Lys. or. 21 § 35 ἀντὶ ...πολιτῶν ἀπόλιδας). The central thought is the power of human wit to make or mar the πόλις, according as the man is moral or immoral.—**τὸ μὴ καλόν**, the generic μή, such a mood as is not good.— **τόλμας χάριν**, by reason of ('thanks to') his audacity, with ξύνεστι, not with ἄπολίς (ἐστι). In *O. T.* 888 δυσπότμου χάριν χλιδᾶς is not precisely similar, since it goes with κακά νιν ἕλοιτο μοῖρα. Others

point at ξύνεστι, taking τόλμας χάριν with μήτ' ἐμοὶ κ.τ.λ.: but μήτ' should clearly be the first word in that sentence.

372 ff. παρέστιος. Cp. *O. T.* 249 n., where Oed. invokes a curse on himself, should the murderer become ξυνέστιος with him: also *ib.* 240 n. Hor. *Carm.* 3. 2. 26 *vetabo, qui Cereris sacrum Vulgarit arcanae, sub isdem Sit trabibus, fragilemve mecum Solvat phaselon.* Schneidewin cp. also Eur. fr. 848 (the dishonourer of parents) μή μοι γένοιτο μήτε συνθύτης ποτέ, κ.τ.λ., and Callim. *Hymn.* 6. 117 (to Demeter) μὴ τῆνος ἐμὶν φίλος, ὅς τοι ἀπεχθής, | εἴη, μήθ' ὁμότοιχος.—**ἴσον φρονῶν**, 'may he not become like-minded with me,' is another way of saying, 'may I never come to share his sentiments.' Cp. *Il.* 15. 50 ἴσον ἐμοὶ φρονέουσα, 'likeminded with me': Ar. *Av.* 634 ἐμοὶ φρονῶν ξυνῳδά. In a narrower sense (not intended here) τὰ αὐτὰ φρονεῖν was said of agreement in politics, *idem sentire de republica:* Her. 1. 60 τωὐτὸ φρονήσαντες, 'having made common cause' (the στασιῶται of Megacles and Lycurgus).

375 ἔρδει, L's reading, should be kept. The indic. is, of course, compatible with generality: for such an indic. after an optative, cp. Dem. or. 4. 51 νικῴη δ' ὅ τι πᾶσιν ὑμῖν μέλλει συνοίσειν. It is also rather in favour of the indic. that the speaker is here thinking of an actual case. The optat. **ἔρδοι** would be abstract, 'any one who should conceivably do these things,' and would be equally correct: cp. on 666.

376 The choral ode has closed with an allusion to the unknown *man* (ὅς: cp. 248 τίς ἀνδρῶν, 319 ὁ δρῶν). At this mo-

ἐς δαιμόνιον τέρας ἀμφινοῶ
τόδε· πῶς εἰδὼς ἀντιλογήσω
τήνδ' οὐκ εἶναι παῖδ' Ἀντιγόνην;
ὦ δύστηνος
καὶ δυστήνου πατρὸς Οἰδιπόδα,   380
τί ποτ'; οὐ δή που σέ γ' ἀπιστοῦσαν
τοῖς βασιλείοισιν ἄγουσι νόμοις
καὶ ἐν ἀφροσύνῃ καθελόντες;

ΦΥ. ἥδ' ἔστ' ἐκείνη τοὔργον ἡ 'ξειργασμένη·
     τήνδ' εἵλομεν θάπτουσαν. ἀλλὰ ποῦ Κρέων;   385
ΧΟ. ὅδ' ἐκ δόμων ἄψορρος ἐς δέον περᾷ.
ΚΡ. τί δ' ἔστι; ποίᾳ ξύμμετρος προὔβην τύχῃ;
ΦΥ. ἄναξ, βροτοῖσιν οὐδέν ἐστ' ἀπώμοτον·
     ψεύδει γὰρ ἡ 'πίνοια τὴν γνώμην· ἐπεὶ

---

376 ἐς] Reiske conject. εἰ [*i.e.* 'I marvel whether this portent is supernatural'], and presently πῶς δ'.—ἀμφινοοῶ L, the first o blotted.   **378** τήνδ' οὐκ εἶναι] Hermann conject. μὴ οὐ τήνδ' εἶναι.   **380** καὶ δυστήνου] Meineke conject. κἀκ (or παῖ) δ. **382** βασιλείοισ ἄγουσι L, βασιλείοισιν ἄγουσι Triclinius. So in 931 L has τοῖσ for τοῖσιν.

---

ment Antigone is led in by the Guard.—
ἀμφινοῶ: cp. *O. C.* 316 (where Antigone can scarcely believe her eyes, on seeing Ismene,) ἆρ' ἔστιν; ἆρ' οὐκ ἔστιν; ἡ γνώμη πλανᾷ; For ἐς, cp. φοβεῖσθαι εἴς τι, *O. T.* 980 n.—**δαιμόνιον τέρας**, a portent sent by gods,—so astounding as to require a supernatural cause. Xen. *Mem.* 1. 3. 5 εἰ μή τι δαιμόνιον εἴη.

377 f. πῶς εἰδὼς κ.τ.λ.: 'How, when I know (that she *is* Antigone, *sc.* ὅτι ἐστί), shall I maintain that she is *not?*' (οὐκ εἶναι=ὅτι οὐκ ἐστί). A simple verb of 'saying' regularly takes οὐ with inf. in oratio obliqua: λέγω οὐκ εἶναι=ὅτι οὐκ ἐστί. If this verb of saying is negatived, the negative with the inf. is still οὐ: πῶς λέξω οὐκ εἶναι; Here, ἀντιλογέω has the construction of a simple verb of saying: πῶς ἀντιλογήσω οὐκ εἶναι; Hermann conjectured μὴ οὐ τήνδ' εἶναι (which is palaeographically very improbable). μὴ οὐκ εἶναι would be the normal constr. after πῶς ἀντιλογήσω, if ἀντιλογέω were viewed in its special quality as a verb of 'denying.' ἀρνοῦμαι μὴ εἶναι: πῶς ἀρνήσομαι μὴ οὐκ (or simply μή, *O. T.* 1388 n.) εἶναι; Cp. below, 443 n. It may be noted that, when ἀντιλέγω means to 'deny,' it is more often followed by ὡς (or ὅτι) οὐ with the finite

verb; when followed by μή and inf., it more often means 'to protest against' a measure; Thuc. 3. 41 ἀντέλεγε...μὴ ἀποκτεῖναι Μυτιληναίους: Xen. *Cyr.* 2. 2. 20 αἰσχρὸν ὂν (=οὐ δεῖ) ἀντιλέγειν τὸ μὴ οὐχὶ τὸν πλεῖστα πονοῦντα...μεγίστων ἀξιοῦσθαι. —**ἀντιλογήσω** might be deliberative aor., but is rather fut. ind. (cp. *O. T.* 1419, *O. C.* 310).

379 f. ὦ δύστηνος: nom. for voc., *O. C.* 185 n.—**δ. πατρός**, gen. of origin: *O. C.* 214 n.—**Οἰδιπόδα** occurs as gen. in *O. T.* 495, but as voc. *ib.* 1194.

381 ff. τί ποτ'; Cp. *Ph.* 1210.—**οὐ δή που**: cp. *O. T.* 1472 οὐ δὴ κλύω που...;—**ἀπιστοῦσαν**=ἀπειθοῦσαν, cp. 219, 656.—**ἄγουσι.** It is more probable that the final ιν of βασιλείοισιν should have dropped out in L (see cr. n.) than that Soph. should have written ἀπάγουσι. At Athens ἀπάγω and ἀπαγωγή were technical terms for a process of summary arrest by which any citizen could bring before the magistrates a person taken in a criminal act (ἐπ' αὐτοφώρῳ). We have seen (on v. 158) that a word with a technical Attic sense was not necessarily excluded from Attic poetry. But ἀπάγω would surely jar here. Allowing for the difference between a technicality and a

Enter the Guard, on the spectators' left, leading in
ΑΝΤΙΓΟΝΕ.

What portent from the gods is this?—my soul is amazed. Anapaests.
I know her—how can I deny that yon maiden is Antigone?
O hapless, and child of hapless sire,—of Oedipus! What
means this? Thou brought a prisoner?—thou, disloyal to the
King's laws, and taken in folly?

GUARD.

Here she is, the doer of the deed:—we caught this girl
burying him:—but where is Creon?

CH. Lo, he comes forth again from the house, at our need.

CR. What is it? What hath chanced, that makes my
coming timely?

GU. O King, against nothing should men pledge their
word; for the after-thought belies the first intent. I could

—βασιλείοις ἀπάγουσι Boeckh (for which Wecklein suggests ἐσάγουσι or προσάγουσι).
384 In L the speaker is designated by αγ, before which S has written φύλαξ in the margin:
cp. 223.—ἐξειργασμένη L (without art.): ἡ 'ξειργασμένη r and Brunck. **386** ἄψορρος]
The ἄ made from ὔ in L.—εἰς δέον r (including A): εἰς μέσον L. Nauck writes εἰς
καιρὸν: Semitelos, αἰσίως. Wecklein conject. ἐς καλόν. **387** ξύμμετροσ ἐξέβην L,
with προύβην written above by S. ποία ξύμμετρος προύβη τύχη r.—Bergk conject.

---

colloquialism, it would be nearly as bad
as, 'Have they taken you up?'—καὶ
connects ἀπιστοῦσαν with καθελόντες
(not with ἐν ἀφροσύνῃ): cp. *O. C.* 737 n.

384—581 Second ἐπεισόδιον. Antigone, brought before Creon, avows and
justifies her deed. Creon declares that
she shall die. Ismene, when led in
(531), associates herself with the act,
but is not permitted by her sister to
claim any part in it. Creon orders that
both sisters shall be kept prisoners.

384 ἐκείνη, she whom we sought:
cp. *O. C.* 138 ὅδ' ἐκεῖνος ἐγώ, n.—τοὔργον
ἥ 'ξειργ.: for the order, cp. 324.

386 ἐς δέον: cp. *O. T.* 1416 ἐς δέον
πάρεσθ' ὅδε | Κρέων: so *ib.* 78 εἰς καλὸν·
Ai. 1168 ἐς αὐτὸν καιρόν. L has εἰς μέσον,
i.e. 'he comes forth in public' (so that
you, and all, can speak with him).
The phrase occurs elsewhere in Soph.,
but never with ref. to entrance on the
stage: *Ph.* 609 ἔδειξ' Ἀχαιοῖς ἐς μέσον·
(showed him publicly); *Ai.* 1285 τὸν
κλῆρον ἐς μέσον καθεὶς (*i.e.* among the
others): *Tr.* 514 ἴσαν ἐς μέσον (into the
arena). Here, ἐς δέον is not only far the
better phrase, but is confirmed by Creon's
question in the next v., ποίᾳ ξύμμετρος...

τύχῃ; A, and almost all the later MSS.,
have εἰς δέον, which may, doubtless, have
been a conjecture suggested by *O. T.* 1416,
—as is held by those who believe all our
MSS. to have come from L; but it looks
more like a true reading which L has
somehow missed. Cp. on 831.

387 ξύμμετρος, commensurate with,
i.e. here, opportune for. *O. T.* 84 ξύμμετρος γὰρ ὡς κλύειν: *ib.* 1113 ξυνᾴδει τῷδε
τἀνδρὶ σύμμετρος.

388 ἀπώμοτον, *abiurandum:* there
is nothing, the possibility of which men
ought to deny on oath: οὐκ ἔστιν ὅ τι
ἀπομνύναι χρὴ βροτοὺς μὴ οὐκ ἂν γενέσθαι.
Archilochus fr. 76 χρημάτων ἄελπτον οὐδέν
ἐστιν οὐδ' ἀπώμοτον | οὐδὲ θαυμάσιον. Eu-
polis Πόλεις fr. 25 τί δ' ἔστ' Ἀθηναίοισι
πρᾶγμ' ἀπώμοτον;

389 ψεύδει = falsifies (like ψευδοποιεῖν):
Thuc. 3. 66 τὴν...ψευσθεῖσαν ὑπόσχεσιν.—
ἡ 'πίνοια, here, the *after*-thought, αἱ
δεύτεραι φροντίδες. But usually the ἐπὶ
in ἐπινοέω, ἐπίνοια, denotes *advance*,—
'forming a design,' or 'inventing': Ar.
Eq. 90 οἶνον σὺ τολμᾷς εἰς ἐπίνοιαν λοιδο-
ρεῖν ; Cp. Lucian Προμηθεὺς εἶ ἐν λόγοις
7 τό γε μεταβουλεύεσθαι Ἐπιμηθέως ἔργον,
οὐ Προμηθέως ἐστίν.

σχολῇ ποθ᾽ ἥξειν δεῦρ᾽ ἂν ἐξηύχουν ἐγώ, 390
ταῖς σαῖς ἀπειλαῖς, αἷς ἐχειμάσθην τότε·
ἀλλ᾽ ἡ γὰρ ἐκτὸς καὶ παρ᾽ ἐλπίδας χαρὰ
ἔοικεν ἄλλῃ μῆκος οὐδὲν ἡδονῇ,
ἥκω, δι᾽ ὅρκων καίπερ ὢν ἀπώμοτος,
κόρην ἄγων τήνδ᾽, ἡ καθῃρέθη τάφον 395
κοσμοῦσα. κλῆρος ἐνθάδ᾽ οὐκ ἐπάλλετο,
ἀλλ᾽ ἔστ᾽ ἐμὸν θοὔρμαιον, οὐκ ἄλλου, τόδε.
καὶ νῦν, ἄναξ, τήνδ᾽ αὐτός, ὡς θέλεις, λαβὼν
καὶ κρῖνε κἀξέλεγχ᾽· ἐγὼ δ᾽ ἐλεύθερος
δίκαιός εἰμι τῶνδ᾽ ἀπηλλάχθαι κακῶν. 400

ΚΡ. ἄγεις δὲ τήνδε τῷ τρόπῳ πόθεν λαβών;
ΦΥ. αὕτη τὸν ἄνδρ᾽ ἔθαπτε· πάντ᾽ ἐπίστασαι.
ΚΡ. ἦ καὶ ξυνίης καὶ λέγεις ὀρθῶς ἃ φής;

ξύμμετρ᾽ ἐξέβην.   **390** σχολῇ ποθ᾽ ἥξειν (ἥιξειν L) δεῦρ᾽ ἂν ἐξηύχουν ἐγώ MSS.
Wecklein conject. δεῦρό μ᾽ for δεῦρ᾽ ἄν.   Meineke, ἥκειν for ἥξειν, or δεῦρό γ᾽ for δεῦρ᾽
ἄν.   Blaydes, ποτ᾽ ἐλθεῖν, or γ᾽ ἂν ἐλθεῖν, for ποθ᾽ ἥξειν.   F. W. Schmidt, δεῦρ᾽, ἄναξ,
ηὔχουν.   **392** ἐκτὸς] Seyffert conject. ἄτοπος: Gleditsch, ἄλογος: Pallis, εἰκὸς.—
ἐλπίδας] In L the first hand wrote ἐλπίδα, but σ has been added (by the first hand itself, I think) above the α.   Some think that the ρὰ of χαρὰ was added by S: this seems

---

390 ἐξηύχουν ἄν, I could have vowed,
σχολῇ ἥξειν ποτὲ δεῦρο, that it would be
long before I ever came hither.   Cp. Eur.
Helen. 1619 οὐκ ἄν ποτ᾽ ηὔχουν οὔτε σ᾽
οὔθ᾽ ἡμᾶς λαθεῖν | Μενέλαον, ὦναξ, ὡς
ἐλάνθανεν πάρων: 'I should never have
expected that he would escape us'; where
(as the order of words shows) ἄν goes
with ηὔχουν,—the suppressed protasis
being, as here, εἰ ἤρωτά τις, 'if any one
had asked me.'   So Lys. or. 12 § 22 ἐγὼ
δ᾽ ἐβουλόμην ἂν αὐτοὺς ἀληθῆ λέγειν, 'I
could wish' (the ref. there being to present time), *sc.* εἰ δυνατὸν ἦν.   Cp. *Ph.*
869 n.   The needless emendations of this
verse have aimed at disjoining ἄν from
ἐξηύχουν and attaching it to the infin.,
or else at removing it altogether.   But,
though the φύλαξ had actually said (in
the 'aside' at 329) that he did not mean
to come back, he was not therefore de-
barred from using this turn of phrase; 'I
could have vowed that I would not come
back.'—σχολῇ (cp. 231), here iron., 'not
in a hurry' (*O. T.* 434 n.); Shaksp. *Tit.
Andron.* 1. 2. 301 'I'll trust by leisure
him that mocks me once.'
    391 ταῖς σαῖς ἀπειλαῖς, 'by reason
of thy threats': cp. 335 (νότῳ) n., 588

(πνοαῖς), 956 (ὀργαῖς).   Here, the causal
dat. seems also to suggest occasion ('at
the time of your threats'): see on 691 λόγοις.—ἐχειμάσθην: *Ph.* 1460 χειμαζομένῳ
(ἐμοί), in my sore trouble.
    392 ἡ...ἐκτὸς (τῶν ἐλπίδων) καὶ παρὰ
ἐλπίδας.   I cannot parallel this zeugma
of preps. with a case suited only to the
second (in *Il.* 17. 760 περί τ᾽ ἀμφί τε
τάφρον both preps. take acc.): and yet
it seems to be genuine, the phrase being
so energetic and compact.   ἐκτός is certainly supported by 330, while ἄτοπος,
ἄλογος, and εἰκός are all very improbable substitutes.   Nor can I think, with
Schütz, that ἐκτός is here adverb: 'the
outside joy' (*i.e.* outside of one's calcu-
lations).
    393 f. οὐδὲν ἔοικε μῆκος, is not at all
(adv.) like in greatness, ἄλλῃ ἡδονῇ, to
any other pleasure; *i.e.* is vastly greater
than any other.   For the adv. οὐδέν, cp.
Plat. *Lys.* 220 c τὸ φίλον...οὐδὲν τούτοις
ἔοικε.   For μῆκος=*amplitudo*, Empedo-
cles 15 ἐξ οἵης τιμῆς τε καὶ ὅσσου μήκεος
ὄλβου: so Pindar speaks of μακρὸς ὄλβος
(*P.* 2. 26), μακροτέρα ἀρετά (*I.* 4. 21),
Aristotle of μακρὰ τιμήματα (*Pol.* 3. 5. 6,
opp. to βραχέα *ib.* 4. 4. 24), μακρὰ οὐσία

have vowed that I should not soon be here again,—scared by thy threats, with which I had just been lashed: but,—since the joy that surprises and transcends our hopes is like in fulness to no other pleasure,—I have come, though 'tis in breach of my sworn oath, bringing this maid; who was taken showing grace to the dead. This time there was no casting of lots; no, this luck hath fallen to me, and to none else. And now, Sire, take her thyself, question her, examine her, as thou wilt; but I have a right to free and final quittance of this trouble.

CR. And thy prisoner here—how and whence hast thou taken her?

GU. She was burying the man; thou knowest all.

CR. Dost thou mean what thou sayest? Dost thou speak aright?

very doubtful. The ρ is somewhat small and fine; but cp. the λ of ἐλπίδα, and the οσ of ἀπώμοτοσ in 394. **393 f.** Nauck condenses these two verses into one, which he places in the text: πέπεικεν, ἥκω καίπερ ὧν ἀπώμοτος. Mekler rejects vv. 392—394 as spurious.—ὄρκων] L has ου over ων from the first hand. **395** καθευρέθη L.— καθῃρέθη an anonymous critic in *Class. Journ.* xvii. 58: and so many recent edd. **402** ἔθαπτε] ἔθαπτεν L. **403** ξυνίῃς] ξυνίεισ L, as *O. T.* 628, *El.* 1347, and ἵεισ *El.* 596. Some hold, with Brunck, that the Attic 2nd sing. pres. was ἱεῖς, and of τίθημι, τιθεῖς. But see Porson, Eur. *Or.* 141, and Ellendt *s.v.* ἵημι.

(*ib.* 4. 4. 5), and Soph. himself of μακρὸς πλοῦτος (*Ai.* 130). For ἔοικε Wolff-Bellermann cp. Thuc. 7. 71 ὁ...φόβος ἦν... οὐδενὶ ἐοικώς ('great beyond example'), Xen. *De Vect.* 4. 31 οὐδενὶ τῶν παρεληλυθότων ἐοικός ('far greater than any of the past'); and for the sentiment, Eur. fr. 554 ἐκ τῶν ἀέλπτων ἡ χάρις μείζων βροτοῖς | φανεῖσα μᾶλλον ἢ τὸ προσδοκώμενον.— Nauck's treatment of this verse and the next has no justification: see cr. n.

394 δι' ὅρκων...ἀπώμοτος, though I had sworn with oaths (sworn solemnly) not to come. Cp. *Ai.* 1113 ὅρκων οἷσιν ἦν ἐνώμοτος: Ar. *Ran.* 150 ἐπίορκον ὅρκον ὤμοσεν.

395 f. καθῃρέθη (cp. 383 καθελόντες) is clearly better here than L's καθευρέθη: and the compound καθευρίσκω is nowhere found in classical Attic.—τάφον κοσμοῦσα, paying the due rites of burial (τάφον = ταφήν, cp. 490), by sprinkling the dust and pouring the libations on the corpse. κοσμέω was specially said of obsequies: cp. 901, *El.* 1139 λουτροῖς ἐκόσμησ'.—ἐπάλλετο, as when lots were shaken in a helmet (*Ai.* 1285; cp. *El.* 710). His ἕρμαιον is the luck of being the first to bring the glad tidings,—as his former mission was ironically called τοῦτο τἀγαθόν (275). In the

discovery and seizure of Antigone he had no greater share than his comrades (432).

399 f. κρῖνε=ἀνάκρινε, question: *Ai.* 586 μὴ κρῖνε, μὴ 'ξέταζε.—δίκαιός εἰμι: the only certain instance in Tragedy of the personal constr. (Thuc. 1. 40 δίκαιοί γ' ἐστε...ἰέναι); for in Eur. *Hipp.* 1080 πολλῷ γε μᾶλλον σαυτὸν ἤσκησας σέβειν | ἢ τοὺς τεκόντας ὅσια δρᾶν, δίκαιος ὤν, the latter words are more pointed if ironical ('just man though thou art'): and Aesch. *Eum.* 55 καὶ κόσμος οὔτε πρὸς θεῶν ἀγάλματα | φέρειν δίκαιος is different ('proper to bring'). But Ar. has this use, *Nub.* 1283 ἀπολαβεῖν...δίκαιος εἶ, and *ib.* 1434.— ἀπηλλάχθαι, perf., for good and all: *O. T.* 1050.

401 f. Observe the order of the words as marking his amazement. For the double interrog. cp. *Il.* 21. 150 τίς πόθεν εἶς ἀνδρῶν; *Ph.* 243 τίνι | στόλῳ προσέσχες τήνδε γῆν, πόθεν πλέων;—πάντ' ἐπίστασαι: one of the formulas which often close a messenger's speech, as *Tr.* 484 πάντ' ἐπίστασαι λόγον: *Ai.* 480 πάντ' ἀκήκοας λόγον: *ib.* 876 πάντ' ἀκήκοας: *Ph.* 241 οἶσθα δὴ τὸ πᾶν.

403 ἦ καί, *O. T.* 368 n. The first καί here is not 'both.'—ὀρθῶς, 'rightly': *i.e.* do your words express what you really

ΦΥ. ταύτην γ᾽ ἰδὼν θάπτουσαν ὃν σὺ τὸν νεκρὸν
ἀπεῖπας. ἆρ᾽ ἔνδηλα καὶ σαφῆ λέγω;   405
ΚΡ. καὶ πῶς ὁρᾶται κἀπίληπτος ᾑρέθη;
ΦΥ. τοιοῦτον ἦν τὸ πρᾶγμ᾽. ὅπως γὰρ ἥκομεν,
πρὸς σοῦ τὰ δείν᾽ ἐκεῖν᾽ ἐπηπειλημένοι,
πᾶσαν κόνιν σήραντες ἣ κατεῖχε τὸν
νέκυν, μυδῶν τε σῶμα γυμνώσαντες εὖ,   410
καθήμεθ᾽ ἄκρων ἐκ πάγων ὑπήνεμοι,
ὀσμὴν ἀπ᾽ αὐτοῦ μὴ βάλῃ πεφευγότες,
ἐγερτὶ κινῶν ἄνδρ᾽ ἀνὴρ ἐπιρρόθοις

---

404 ἰδὼν Brunck: ἴδον L : εἶδον r.   **406** κἀπίληπτος] κἀπίλημπτοσ L.—ᾑρέθη] εὑρέθη, with η over ευ from the first hand.   The correction meant was ᾑρέθη (not ηὑρέθη, for L regularly gives ευ in the aor., impf., and pf. of εὑρίσκω) which the schol., too, read: ποίῳ τρόπῳ αὐτὴν συνελάβεσθε καὶ κατειλήφατε;   **407** ἥκομεν] ἱκόμην Kvíčala.

---

mean to say? (Not, merely, 'truly,' *i.e.* in accordance with the fact: cp. 99 n.)

404 τὸν νεκρόν: antecedent with art. drawn into relative clause: *O. C.* 907 n. νῦν δ᾽ οὕσπερ αὐτὸς τοὺς νόμους εἰσῆλθ᾽ ἔχων, | τούτοισιν κ.τ.λ.

405 ἆρ᾽ ἔνδηλα: said triumphantly: Aesch. *Ag.* 268 ΧΟ. πῶς φής…; ΚΛ. Τροίαν Ἀχαιῶν οὖσαν· ἦ τορῶς λέγω; Cp. *Ai.* 1158 οὐδείς ποτ᾽ ἄλλος ἦ σύ. μῶν ᾐνιξάμην;

406 ὁρᾶται…ᾑρέθη: historic pres. combined with aor., as *Ai.* 31 φράζει τε κἀδήλωσεν: cp. 419, *Tr.* 359 ff., *O. T.* 118 f.—ἐπίληπτος, seized in the act = ἐπ᾽ αὐτοφώρῳ.   Her. 3. 69 ἐπίλαμπτος… ἀφάσσουσα (τὰ ὦτα) ἔσται, 'will be caught feeling the ears.' [Dem.] or. 25 § 80 τοὺς ἐπιλήπτους (the epileptic) φησὶν ἰᾶσθαι, αὐτὸς ὢν ἐπίληπτος πάσῃ πονηρίᾳ.

407 ἥκομεν. The occupation of the guards was temporarily gone when they perceived that the burial, which they had been set to prevent, had been effected (255). Creon, speaking to their deputy, sent them back to their post, with orders to discover the culprit (306). ἥκομεν (imperf.) simply refers to their taking up their station again near the body. It need not imply that they had escorted their comrade on his way to Creon. We could not take ἥκομεν…ἐπηπειλημένοι as merely plur. for sing., and then refer σήραντες, etc., to the guards collectively. Nor is the conject. ἱκόμην needed.

408 f. τὰ δείν᾽ ἐκεῖν᾽. Creon's threats

were addressed to all the guards: cp. 305 ff.—τὸν | νέκυν: so *O. C.* 351 τὰ τῆς | οἴκοι διαίτης: *Ph.* 263 ὃν οἱ | δισσοὶ στρατηγοί: *El.* 879 κἀπὶ τοῖς | σαυτῆς κακοῖσι. So Ar. *Eccl.* 452 οὐδὲ τὸν | δῆμον. Aesch. places the art. thus only when it is a *pronoun* (*Ag.* 7 τῶν: *Theb.* 385, *Eum.* 137 τῷ). In Eur. no instance seems to occur.

411 καθήμεθ᾽ is better taken as plpf. than pf., for, though ἥκομεν is ambiguous, we have a series of historical tenses in 415—421. Ar. sometimes uses and sometimes omits the augment, as *Ach.* 638 ἐκάθησθε, *Eccl.* 304 καθῆντο (both proved by metre); and if our MSS. can be trusted, classical prose, too, admitted both forms, as Aeschin. or. 2 § 89 ἐκαθήμην, Dem. or. 18 § 169 καθῆτο. In the five pluperfects furnished by Attic inscriptions of 428—325 B.C. the syllabic augment is always added, but there is no epigraphic evidence in the particular case of ἐκαθήμην (see Meisterhans, p. 77).—ἄκρων ἐκ πάγων, with καθήμεθα, 'on the hill-top.' The corpse lay on the highest part of the Theban plain (1110, 1197), with rising ground (πάγοι) behind or around it.   The guards posted themselves on this rising ground, facing the corpse, and with their backs to the wind. The use of ἐκ (or ἀπό), with a verb denoting *position*, occurs only in a few places of poetry; but it is certainly genuine, and deserves attention, for its true force has not (I think) been observed. (1) *Il.* 14. 153 Ἥρη δ᾽ εἰσεῖδε χρυσόθρονος ὀφθαλμοῖσιν | στᾶσ᾽

GU.   I saw her burying the corpse that thou hadst forbidden
to bury.   Is that plain and clear?

CR.   And how was she seen? how taken in the act?

GU.   It befell on this wise.   When we had come to the
place,—with those dread menaces of thine upon us,—we
swept away all the dust that covered the corpse, and bared
the dank body well; and then sat us down on the brow
of the hill, to windward, heedful that the smell from
him should not strike us; every man was wide awake,
and kept his neighbour alert with torrents of threats,

---

408 δεῖν'] δεῖν' L.   **410** εὖ] Reiske conject. αυ.   **411** ὑπήνεμοι] Keck and
Naber conject. ὑπήνεμον (to go with ὀσμήν): Tournier, ἀπήνεμοι: Semitelos, σκοπού-
μενοι.   **412** βάληι L: βάλοι H. Stephanus.   **413** κινῶν r: κεῖνον L.   Nauck and

---

ἐξ Οὐλύμποιο ἀπὸ ῥίου.   Here, ἀπὸ ῥίου
goes with εἰσεῖδε: but ἐξ Οὐλύμποιο, however much εἰσεῖδε may have influenced it,
at least cannot be disjoined from στᾶσ'.
(2) Eur. *Ph.* 1009 ἀλλ' εἶμι καὶ στὰς ἐξ
ἐπάλξεων ἄκρων | σφάξας ἐμαυτὸν σηκὸν
εἰς μελαμβαθῆ | δράκοντος, ἔνθ' ὁ μάντις
ἐξηγήσατο, | ἐλευθερώσω γαῖαν.   It is im-
possible to sever στάς from ἐξ ἐπ., even
if we partly explain ἐξ by σφάξας.   (3) *ib.*
1224 Ἐτεοκλέης δ' ὑπῆρξ' ἀπ' ὀρθίου
σταθεὶς | πύργου κελεύσας σῖγα κηρῦξαι
στρατῷ.   The position of σταθείς forbids
us to sever it from ἀπ' ὀρθ. π., even
though ὑπῆρξε or κελεύσας is used to explain ἀπό.   (4) Eur. *Tro.* 522 ἀνὰ δ'
ἐβόασεν λεὼς | Τρῳάδος ἀπὸ πέτρας
σταθείς.   A similar case.   In all these
passages, a picture is presented, and we
have to glance from a remoter to a nearer
object.   The mental eye is required to
measure the space between Hera on
the peak of Olympus, and Poseidon on
the plain of Troy; between Megareus
on the walls of Thebes, and the cavern
into which his corpse is to fall.   And, in
each case, ἐκ or ἀπό denotes the *quarter*
in which the remoter object is to be
looked for.   This, which might be called
the 'surveying' use, is distinct from that
in which the prep. has a pregnant force,
as being directly suggestive of motion (οἱ
ἐκ Σικελίας ἥξουσι); but it springs from
the same mental tendency,—viz., to take
a rapid glance over the dividing interval.
Cp. ἵστασθαι πρός τινος ('on his side').
So here: in the foreground of the picture
is the corpse, which they have just laid
bare.   Now look to the hillocks behind
it; in that quarter you will see the guards

at their post.—I have not cited *Od.* 21.
419 τόν ῥ' ἐπὶ πήχει ἑλὼν ἕλκεν νευρὴν
γλυφίδας τε | αὐτόθεν ἐκ δίφροιο καθήμε-
νος, because there ἐκ δίφροιο goes with
ἕλκεν, not with καθήμενος (he drew the
bow, just from the chair, where he sat).
—ὑπήνεμοι, under the wind, *i.e.*, so that
it blew from behind them, not in their
faces, as the next v. explains.   (At v. 421
the dust is blown in their faces, but that
is by the sudden, gusty σκηπτός.)   The
idea of 'sheltered,' which ὑπήνεμος usu.
implies, is less prominent here, yet quite
admissible, if we suppose them to sit just
below the summits of the πάγοι.   Cp. Xen.
Oec. 18. 6 ἐκ τοῦ προσηνέμου μέρους, on the
side *towards which* the wind blows, opp.
to ἐκ τοῦ ὑπηνέμου, to windward.   Theophr.
Causs. Plantt. 3. 6. 9 opposes πνευματώδης
καὶ προσήνεμος τόπος to τὰ ὑπήνεμα: and
Arist. *Hist. An.* 9. 15 ἐν προσηνέμῳ to ἐν
ἐπισκεπεῖ.

412 βάλη, the 'vivid' subjunct. (instead of βάλοι), after a secondary tense;
while in v. 414 we have the normal optat.
(ἀκηδήσοι).   For this combination cp.
Xen. *An.* 3. 5. 17 παρήγγειλαν, ἐπειδὴ
δειπνήσειαν,...ἀναπαύεσθαι, καὶ ἔπεσθαι
ἡνίκ' ἄν τις παραγγείλη.

413 ἐγρτί: see on ἀστακτί, *O. C.*
1251.   Each man was careful to keep
wide awake, and also to see that his
comrades did so.—κινῶν, urging to vigi-
lance.   Plat. *Rep.* 329 D βουλόμενος ἔτι
λέγειν αὐτὸν ἐκίνουν καὶ εἶπον, ὦ Κέφαλε,
κ.τ.λ.   The conject. νεικῶν is needless.
For the subg. instead of the plur. (κινοῦν-
τες) in partitive apposition, see on φύλαξ
ἐλέγχων φύλακα, 260.—ἐπιρρόθοις κακοῖσιν, lit., with obstreperous taunts,

---

κακοῖσιν, εἴ τις τοῦδ᾽ *ἀκηδήσοι πόνου.

χρόνον τάδ᾽ ἦν τοσοῦτον, ἔστ᾽ ἐν αἰθέρι   415
μέσῳ κατέστη λαμπρὸς ἡλίου κύκλος
καὶ καῦμ᾽ ἔθαλπε· καὶ τότ᾽ ἐξαίφνης χθονὸς
τυφὼς ἀείρας σκηπτόν, οὐράνιον ἄχος,
πίμπλησι πεδίον, πᾶσαν αἰκίζων φόβην
ὕλης πεδιάδος, ἐν δ᾽ ἐμεστώθη μέγας   420
αἰθήρ· μύσαντες δ᾽ εἴχομεν θείαν νόσον.
καὶ τοῦδ᾽ ἀπαλλαγέντος ἐν χρόνῳ μακρῷ,
ἡ παῖς ὁρᾶται, κἀνακωκύει πικρᾶς
ὄρνιθος ὀξὺν φθόγγον, ὡς ὅταν κενῆς
εὐνῆς νεοσσῶν ὀρφανὸν βλέψῃ λέχος·   425
οὕτω δὲ χαὔτη, ψιλὸν ὡς ὁρᾷ νέκυν,

Semitelos conject. νεικῶν: Hense, κεντῶν.   **414** ἀφειδήσοι MSS.: ἀκηδήσοι Bonitz.
Golisch proposed ἀφ᾽ εὑδήσοι (*Jahr. Phil.* p. 176, 1878), and so, by an independent

---

the adj. expressing the loud, continuous noise of tongues. The ἐπι- does not mean 'bandied to and fro': see *Tr.* 263 πολλὰ μὲν λόγοις | ἐπερρόθησε. In fr. 521 ἐπίρροθα δώματα='open to reproach.' Elsewhere (as with Aesch.) ἐπίρροθος= 'helper' (ἐπιρροθέω, to come with shouts to the rescue). Cp. ἐρρόθουν 259 n., 290.

414 ἀκηδήσοι: fut. opt. in orat. obliqua; the direct form of the threat would be (κλαύσει) εἰ ἀκηδήσεις (or ἐὰν ἀκηδήσῃς). Cp. *Ph.* 374 ἤρασσον κακοῖς | τοῖς πᾶσιν... | εἰ τἀμὰ κεῖνος ὅπλ᾽ ἀφαιρήσοιτό με: he said (ὄλοιο), εἰ ἀφαιρήσει. *Ai.* 312 δεῖν᾽ ἐπηπείλησ᾽ ἔπη, | εἰ μὴ φανοίην (he said, εἰ μὴ φανεῖς). ἀκηδέω had been used by Hom. *Il.* 14. 427, 23. 70, Aesch. *P. V.* 508, and recurs in later poetry. The MS. ἀφειδήσοι cannot be defended as='play the prodigal with,' *i.e.* 'be careless of.' ἀφειδεῖν πόνου could mean only to be unsparing of labour. In Thuc. 4. 26 ἀφειδὴς ὁ κατάπλους καθειστήκει is explained by the next words, ἐπώκελλον γὰρ τὰ πλοῖα τετιμημένα χρημάτων: they were 'unsparing' of their boats, since a value had been set on the latter. Bonitz, to whom ἀκηδῆσοι is due, refers to Apoll. Rhod. 2. 98 οὐδ᾽ ἄρα Βέβρυκες ἄνδρες ἀφείδησαν βασιλῆος, where Choeroboscus has preserved the true ἀκήδησαν. In the schol. on *Ai.* 204 φειδόμενοι occurs by error for κηδόμενοι.

415—421 The incident of the storm was a dramatic necessity, to account for Antigone reaching the corpse unobserved. A powerful picture is compressed into seven lines. (Cp. *O. C.* 1315 ff. for a like instance of self-restraint in description.)

416 f. κατέστη, prop., had taken its place. There is a Homeric echo here: *Il.* 8. 66 ὄφρα μὲν ἠὼς ἦν καὶ ἀέξετο ἱερὸν ἦμαρ, | τόφρα μάλ᾽ ἀμφοτέρων βέλε᾽ ἥπτετο, πῖπτε δὲ λαός· | ἦμος δ᾽ ἠέλιος μέσον οὐρανὸν ἀμφιβεβήκει, | καὶ τότε δὴ χρύσεια πατὴρ ἐτίταινε τάλαντα.—**χθονὸς** (*from* the ground) with ἀείρας: cp. *O. T.* 142 βάθρων | ἵστασθε, n.

418 τυφώς, the whirlwind: the σκηπτός is the storm of dust (κονιορτός) which it lifts from the ground. The word σκηπτός usu.='a thunderbolt,' and by its deriv. ought at least to mean a storm swooping on the earth from the sky; but the schol. attests its use in a larger sense; σκηπτὸς δὲ λέγεται πᾶν πνεῦμα θυελλῶδες, ὅταν συνερείδῃ τῇ γῇ, καὶ πάλιν ἄνω αἴρῃ· τὸ δὲ τοιοῦτο καὶ στρόβιλόν τινες καλοῦσι, παρὰ τὸ στροβεῖν.—**οὐράνιον ἄχος,** a trouble in the sky (cp. *O. C.* 1466 οὐρανία...ἀστραπή), since the cloud of dust darkened the sky: schol. τὸ λυποῦν τὸν αἰθέρα, καθὸ ταράσσει αὐτόν: only ἄχος is rather what annoys *us* than what annoys the (personified) οὐρανός. In these lines the poet describes the actual physical if any one should be careless of this task.

So went it, until the sun's bright orb stood in mid heaven, and the heat began to burn : and then suddenly a whirlwind lifted from the earth a storm of dust, a trouble in the sky, and filled the plain, marring all the leafage of its woods; and the wide air was choked therewith : we closed our eyes, and bore the plague from the gods.

And when, after a long while, this storm had passed, the maid was seen; and she cried aloud with the sharp cry of a bird in its bitterness,—even as when, within the empty nest, it sees the bed stripped of its nestlings. So she also, when she saw the corpse bare,

---

conjecture, Semitelos reads (1887). **420** ἐν δ' ι : ἔνθ' L. **423** πικρᾶς] πικρῶς Bothe. **424** In L two letters have been erased before κενῆσ, perh. ἐκ.

---

effects produced by the storm. He mentions the destruction of foliage ; and we need some reference also to the main point of all—the obscuring of the air. Therefore I should not take οὐράνιον ἄχος as = 'a *heaven-sent* plague' ; that is presently said by θείαν νόσον (421). A third version—'a trouble rising *high as* heaven' (like οὐράνιον πήδημα, etc.)—is also possible, but less suitable here than either of the others. In Aesch. *Suppl.* 809 ἴυξε δ' ὀμφὰν οὐρανίαν, the adj. clearly = οὐρανομήκη, and so perh. in *Pers.* 572 ἀμβόασον οὐράνι' ἄχη, though there (as in *Ai.* 196 ἄταν οὐρανίαν φλέγων) 'heaven-sent' is at least equally fitting.—For the tribrach in the 5th place, see *O. T.* 719 n.

419 f. πίμπλησι (histor. pres., between ἔθαλπε and ἐνεμεστώθη, cp. 406), viz., with dust and scattered leaves.—αἰκίζων, maltreating, λυμαινόμενος, by breaking the branches and tearing off the leaves.—ἐν δ' ἐμεστ., tmesis: cp. 1274, *El.* 713 ἐν δὲ πᾶς ἐμεστώθη δρόμος. Distinguish the adv. ἐν δέ (and withal), *O. T.* 27 n.

421 f. μύσαντες. μύω (from μῦ, a sound made with closed lips) = 'to be shut,' said of the eyes, the lips, or any opening (*Il.* 24. 637 οὐ γάρ πω μύσαν ὄσσε): but the aor. part. regularly meant, 'with eyes shut': Plat. *Gorg.* 480 c παρέχειν μύσαντα καὶ ἀνδρείως ὥσπερ τέμνειν καὶ κάειν ἰατρῷ. There was a proverb, μύσαντα φέρειν ('to grin and bear it'), Meineke *Com.* 3, p. 4.—νόσον, the scourge of the storm : cp. 1141.—ἐν χρ. μακρ. : for the prep. see *O. C.* 88 n.

423 πικρᾶς, in its bitterness. Else-

where πικρός, said of persons, means 'embittered,' and so 'hostile,' etc. (as *Ai.* 1359). But there is no reason why πικρός should not also mean 'embittered' in the sense, 'with a bitter feeling of anguish.' There is a pathos in this which is lost by reading πικρῶς, 'shrilly.' Nor could πικρᾶς mean merely 'piercing,' as if the epithet of the cry were given to the bird itself. In *O. C.* 1610 φθόγγος πικρός, and in *Ph.* 190 πικρὰ οἰμωγή, mean not merely a 'shrill,' but a 'bitter,' cry ; and so conversely here, the epithet πικρά, while primarily denoting anguish, also suggests the shrill sound.

425 εὐνῆς...λέχος would be a weak pleonasm for 'nest'; it is better to take εὐνῆς as the nest, and λέχος as the resting-place of the young birds within it. The phrases λέκτρων εὐναί, λέκτρων κοῖται, κοίτης λέκτρον, etc., said of the *marriage*-bed, are not properly similar, meaning rather, 'the bed on which they slept,' etc.: *i.e.* εὐναί or κοῖται refer to the act of sleeping. κενῆς is certainly pleonastic with νεοσσῶν ὀρφανόν (cp. *Ph.* 31 κενὴν οἴκησιν ἀνθρώπων δίχα, and *O. T.* 57 n.), yet hardly anticipates it; the bird, approaching its nest, feels that it is κενή, then peeps in, and, sure enough, the λέχος is ὀρφανόν.

426 οὕτω δέ, 'so, I say, she': for δέ introducing the apodosis in a simile cp. *El.* 25 ὥσπερ γὰρ ἵππος εὐγενής...θυμὸν οὐκ ἀπώλεσεν | ..., ὡσαύτως δὲ σὺ | ἡμᾶς τ' ὀτρύνεις κ.τ.λ.: so *Tr.* 112 ff., πολλὰ γὰρ ὥστ'...οὕτω δὲ τὸν Καδμογενῆ.—ψιλόν, *sc.* κόνιος, stripped of the dust which she had sprinkled on it (409). Cp. *O. C.* p. 279.

86 ΣΟΦΟΚΛΕΟΥΣ

γόοισιν ἐξώμωξεν, ἐκ δ' ἀρὰς κακὰς
ἠρᾶτο τοῖσι τοὔργον ἐξειργασμένοις.
καὶ χερσὶν εὐθὺς διψίαν φέρει κόνιν,
ἔκ τ' εὐκροτήτου χαλκέας ἄρδην πρόχου   430
χοαῖσι τρισπόνδοισι τὸν νέκυν στέφει.
χἠμεῖς ἰδόντες ἱέμεσθα, σὺν δέ νιν
θηρώμεθ' εὐθὺς οὐδὲν ἐκπεπληγμένην·
καὶ τάς τε πρόσθεν τάς τε νῦν ἠλέγχομεν
πράξεις· ἄπαρνος δ' οὐδενὸς καθίστατο,   435
*ἅμ' ἡδέως ἔμοιγε κἀλγεινῶς ἅμα.
τὸ μὲν γὰρ αὐτὸν ἐκ κακῶν πεφευγέναι
ἥδιστον· ἐς κακὸν δὲ τοὺς φίλους ἄγειν
ἀλγεινόν. ἀλλὰ πάντα ταῦθ' ἥσσω λαβεῖν
ἐμοὶ πέφυκε τῆς ἐμῆς σωτηρίας.   440
ΚΡ. σὲ δή, σὲ τὴν νεύουσαν ἐς πέδον κάρα,

429 εὐθύς] αὖθις Reiske. διψὰν ἐκφέρει κόνιν L. ι had been written over ν; a later hand erased it, and accented a. In the marg. S has written γρ. διψίαν φέρει, and so A reads, with other later MSS. Dindorf conject. διψάδ' ἐμφέρει. But ἐκφέρει was a mere

---

427 ff. γόοισιν ἐξώμωξεν: cp. O. T. 65 ὕπνῳ γ' εὕδοντα, n.—ἐκ δ'...ἠρᾶτο, tmesis: cp. n. on 106.—διψίαν: cp. 246.

429 φέρει κόνιν. A difficulty presents itself. The essence of the symbolical rite was the sprinkling of dust. She had done that (245). Was it not, then, done once for all? In Horace (C. 1. 28. 35) the passer-by is free when the dust has been thrown; he can go his way. I have never seen this question put or answered. The only answer which I can suggest is that, at her first visit, she had not brought the χοαί. (Cp. on 245 ff.) Perhaps the rite was considered complete only if the χοαί were poured while the dust still covered the corpse.

430 f. The πρόχους, or 'out-pourer,' was a jug, especially a water-jug, with a handle, and had, of course, various forms; some of the types given by Guhl and Koner (p. 147, fig. 198, 26—31) resemble modern water-jugs for washing.—εὐκρότητος, 'well-hammered,' and so 'well-wrought,' is the epith. of a knife (δωρίς, sc. κοπίς) in Eur. El. 819.—ἄρδην (for ἀέρδην, from αἴρω) is found with πηδᾶν (Ai. 1279) and φέρειν (Eur. Alc. 608), but is usu. fig., as with ἀπολλύναι. Here, ἄρδην

ἐκ πρόχου στέφει=ἄρασα τὸν πρόχουν στέφει.

431 χοαῖσι. In Od. 10. 519 the three χοαί to the dead are of (1) hydromel, (2) wine, (3) water: see O. C. 479 n.—τρισπόνδ., instead of the simple τρισίν: cp. on 346 σπ. δικτυοκλώστοις. χοαί were to the νέρτεροι, as σπονδαί to the ὕπατοι: λοιβαί could mean either (O. C. 477).—στέφει: El. 51 τύμβον... | λοιβαῖσι πρῶτον καὶ καρατόμοις χλιδαῖς | στέψαντες.

432 f. ἱέμεσθα, pres.: for the ῑ, cp. O. C. 1279 n.—σὺν δὲ...θηρώμεθ', tmesis, as El. 746 σὺν δ' ἑλίσσεται | τμητοῖς ἱμᾶσι. But σύν is adv. ib. 299 σὺν δ' ἐποτρύνει: cp. above, 85.

434 f. ἠλέγχομεν, proceeded to prove against her, i.e. taxed her with, her past and present deeds. We should not supply αὐτήν: the verb governs τὰς πράξεις only: cp. Plat. Theaet. 161 E ἐλέγχειν τὰς ἀλλήλων φαντασίας τε καὶ δόξας (examine into). It would be natural to say, ταῦτα ἐλέγχω αὐτήν, but hardly τὰς πράξεις ἐλέγχω αὐτήν.—ἄπαρνος... οὐδενός=οὐδὲν ἀπαρνουμένη, the gen. with the adj. corresponding to the acc. with the verb; cp. κωλυτικός, ποιητικός τινος etc.—καθίστατο, she did not take up the lifted up a voice of wailing, and called down curses on the doers of that deed. And straightway she brought thirsty dust in her hands; and from a shapely ewer of bronze, held high, with thrice-poured drink-offering she crowned the dead.

We rushed forward when we saw it, and at once closed upon our quarry, who was in no wise dismayed. Then we taxed her with her past and present doings; and she stood not on denial of aught,—at once to my joy and to my pain. To have escaped from ills one's self is a great joy; but 'tis painful to bring friends to ill. Howbeit, all such things are of less account to me than mine own safety.

CR. Thou—thou whose face is bent to earth—

---

blunder like ἐξέβην in 387. **434** πρόσθεν] πρόσθε L. (Cp. 402, 462.) **436** ἅμ' Dindorf: ἀλλ' MSS. **439** ταῦθ'] τἄλλ' Blaydes. **440** πέφυκεν L.

---

position of denying anything. Her *attitude* towards the charge was one of simple confession. καθίστασθαι with a predicative adj. expresses definite assumption of a character, or complete attainment of a state; Thuc. 3. 102 ξύμμαχον καθεστήξει (will have definitely allied itself): 6. 15 πολέμιοι καθέστασαν: 4. 78 τοῖς πᾶσι...ὕποπτον καθεστήκει: 2. 59 ἄποροι καθεστῶτες: 4. 26 ἀφειδὴς...καθεστήκει: 6. 59 χαλεπωτέρα...ἡ τυραννὶς κατέστη. So *Ai.* 306 ἔμφρων...καθίσταται: *O. T.* 703 φονέα...καθεστάναι.

436 ἅμ' for the MS. ἀλλ' (AM for ΑΛΛ) is certain; καθίστ. would be unmeaning with the adverbs, and we cannot supply a new verb. Cp. Thuc. 7. 77 § 6 σιτία ἅμα κομίζειν, where ἅμα (for the MS. ἄλλα) is due to Reiske. Besides ἅμα μὲν ...ἅμα δέ ('partly'...'partly'), we also find double ἅμα, (a) where the clauses are linked by καί, as here; Plat. *Gorg.* 496 B ὧν ἅμα τε ἀπαλλάττεται ἄνθρωπος καὶ ἅμα ἔχει (cp. *ib.* 497 A): (b) with partic. and finite verb: id. *Tim.* 38 B ἵνα ἅμα γεννηθέντες ἅμα καὶ λυθῶσιν. Verg. *G.* 3. 201 *simul arva fuga, simul aequora verrens.* Cp. Hor. *S.* 1. 7. 11 *Inter | Hectora Priamiden animosum atque inter Achillen.*

438 φίλους φησί, διὰ τὸ εἶναι τὴν Ἀντιγόνην τοῦ βασιλικοῦ γένους (schol.): he is a δοῦλος of the family. Cp. Eur. *Med.* 54 χρηστοῖσι δούλοις συμφορὰ τὰ δεσποτῶν | κακῶς πίτνοντα.

439 f. πάντα ταῦθ' refers to ἐς κακὸν δὲ...ἀλγεινόν: 'all these things'='all such objects as the safety of friends.'

λαβεῖν, 'to obtain,' epexeg. of ἥσσω: cp. 638: *Ph.* 81: *El.* 1015 προνοίας οὐδὲν ἀνθρώποις ἔφυ | κέρδος λαβεῖν ἄμεινον: where, as here, we have a gen. depending on the comparat., instead of ἤ with nom.—Semitelos takes λαβεῖν as=ὑπολαβεῖν: 'all these considerations are naturally lower in my estimate than my own safety.' Similarly Campbell; 'It is in my nature' (ἐμοὶ πέφυκε—a questionable sense) 'to take less account of all this than of my own safety.' But such a use of λαμβάνειν does not seem warranted by Thuc. 2. 42 τὴν τιμωρίαν...ποθεινοτέραν λαβόντες, or by such phrases as λαμβάνειν τι ἐν πόθῳ (*O. C.* 1679).—Blaydes's τἄλλ' for ταῦτ' is attractive, but unnecessary; and palaeographically it is not probable.

441 σὲ δή, κ.τ.λ. *sc.* καλῶ. Eur. *Helen.* 546 σὲ τὴν ὄρεγμα δεινὸν ἡμιλλωμένην | τύμβου 'πὶ κρηπῖδ' ἐμπύρους τ' ὀρθοστάτας, | μεῖνον. Ar. *Av.* 274 ΕΤ. οὗτος, ὦ σέ τοι. ΠΕ. τί βωστρεῖς; The abrupt acc. calls the person's attention in a rough and harsh way. A governing verb is sometimes added, as *El.* 1445 σέ τοι, σὲ κρίνω, ναὶ σέ, τὴν ἐν τῷ πάρος | χρόνῳ θρασεῖαν. *Ai.* 1226 σὲ δὴ τὰ δεινὰ ῥήματ' ἀγγέλλουσί μοι | τλῆναι... | σέ τοι, τὸν ἐκ τῆς αἰχμαλωτίδος λέγω. Eur. *Med.* 271 σὲ τὴν σκυθρωπὸν καὶ πόσει θυμουμένην, | Μήδειαν, εἶπον, etc. Antigone has her eyes bent on the ground: she is neither afraid nor sullen, but feels that Creon and she can never come to terms. There is nothing in common between their thoughts. Cp. 499.

φής, ἢ καταρνεῖ μὴ δεδρακέναι τάδε;
ΑΝ. καὶ φημὶ δρᾶσαι κοὐκ ἀπαρνοῦμαι τὸ μή.
ΚΡ. σὺ μὲν κομίζοις ἂν σεαυτὸν ᾗ θέλεις
    ἔξω βαρείας αἰτίας ἐλεύθερον·   445
    σὺ δ᾽ εἰπέ μοι μὴ μῆκος, ἀλλὰ συντόμως,
    *ᾔδησθα κηρυχθέντα μὴ πράσσειν τάδε;
ΑΝ. ᾔδη· τί δ᾽ οὐκ ἔμελλον; ἐμφανῆ γὰρ ἦν.
ΚΡ. καὶ δῆτ᾽ ἐτόλμας τούσδ᾽ ὑπερβαίνειν νόμους;
ΑΝ. οὐ γάρ τί μοι Ζεὺς ἦν ὁ κηρύξας τάδε,   450
    οὐδ᾽ ἡ ξύνοικος τῶν κάτω θεῶν Δίκη
    *τοιούσδ᾽ ἐν ἀνθρώποισιν ὥρισεν νόμους·
    οὐδὲ σθένειν τοσοῦτον ᾠόμην τὰ σὰ
    κηρύγμαθ᾽, ὥστ᾽ ἄγραπτα κἀσφαλῆ θεῶν

442 καταρνεῖ] καταρνῆι L.   443 τὸ μή] τὸ ἡ L, with μ written above by the first hand,
and a letter (σ?) erased before ἡ.—τὸ μὴ οὐ Hermann.   444 ᾗ L: οἶ r, and so Blaydes.
445 ἐλεύθερον] ἐλεύθερος Pallis.   446 συντόμως L. Some later MSS. have σύντομα
(as A, V), or σύντομον (V⁴).   447 ᾔδει στὰ L: ᾔδησθα Cobet.   448 ᾔδη] ᾔδειν

442 φὴς δεδρακέναι, ἢ καταρνεῖ μὴ
δεδρ., a zeugma. καταρνεῖ. In this compound (found only here) κατά gives the
notion of 'downright,' 'explicit': cp. κα-
ταφάναι (to affirm), κατάδηλος. μή regularly precedes the inf. when ἀρνεῖσθαι
means 'to deny,' but not when it means
'to refuse': Plat. Phaedr. 256 A ἀπαρνη-
θῆναι τὸ αὐτοῦ μέρος χαρίσασθαι.
443 καὶ......κοὐκ, corresponding with
the alternatives in Creon's question: for
the conjunctive form, cp. 1192: [Eur.]
Rhes. 164 ναί, καὶ δίκαια ταῦτα κοὐκ ἄλλως
λέγω.—τὸ μή: for the art., cp. 78.   τὸ
μὴ οὐκ is unnecessary, though it would
be normal: cp. O. T. 1387 οὐκ ἂν ἐσχό-
μην | τὸ μὴ 'ποκλῆσαι, n.
444 f. σὺ μέν. If she had denied
the charge, the φύλαξ must have been
detained; now, he can go. κομίζοις ἂν
σ. gives a contemptuous permission. So
in gentle command, Ph. 674 χωροῖς ἂν
εἴσω, Tr. 624 στείχοις ἂν ἤδη. Cp. Eur.
Ph. 1636 κόμιζε σαυτὴν...δόμων ἔσω.—ἔξω
with β. αἰτίας, after which ἐλεύθερον is
pleonastic: cp. Ai. 464 γυμνὸν φανέντα
τῶν ἀριστείων ἄτερ: and see n. on κενῆς
above, v. 424.
446 μῆκος, adv., 'at great length,'
like μακράν, τέλος, etc. If we read σύντομον or σύντομα, μῆκος might be obj.
acc. to εἰπέ, but συντόμως seems right.
Cp. Aesch. Pers. 698 μή τι μακιστῆρα

μῦθον ἀλλὰ σύντομον λέγων | εἰπὲ καὶ
πέραινε πάντα.
447 ᾔδησθα, not ᾔδης τὰ, is certainly
right. This 2nd pers. occurs in seven
places of drama, two of which require it
(Eur. El. 926, Cycl. 108), while the other
five admit it (this v., Tr. 988, Ar. Nub.
329, Th. 554, Eccl. 551). Similarly ᾖσθα
is either necessary or admissible whenever
it occurs in Attic drama.   Ar. Lys. 132
has ἔφησθα, and ἔφης nowhere: but the
case for ἔφησθα as the sole classical form
seems less strong than for ᾔδησθα and
ᾖσθα. ἔφησθα is required in four Homeric
passages (Il. 1. 397, 16. 830: Od. 3. 357,
23. 71), but ἔφης in one, Il. 22. 331 Ἕκ-
τορ, ἀτάρ που ἔφης Πατροκλῆ᾽ ἐξεναρίζων,
and in another it is traditional, 22. 280
ἤτοι ἔφης γε (where ἔφησθα is unlikely).
The ending is -σθα, not -θα, σ being an
integral part of it : Curtius compares Lat.
-sti (dedi-sti), and Gothic -st (saisô-st,
thou sowedst), Gk Verb pp. 34 ff. Besides οἶσθα, ᾔδησθα, ᾖσθα, and ἔφησθα,
the forms which take σθα are the Hom.
εἶσθα ('thou wilt go'); the presents indic.
διδοῖσθα (Il. 19. 270) and τίθησθα (Od. 9.
404, 24. 476) ; and a few subjunctives and
optatives (as βάλῃσθα, βάλοισθα).—κηρυχθέντα, the plur. partic. impersonal, as
570 ἡρμοσμένα, 576 δεδογμένα : a use more
freq. with adjectives, as ἀδύνατα, δίκαια
(cp. O. C. 485 n.), esp. verbals (below, 677).

dost thou avow, or disavow, this deed?

AN. I avow it; I make no denial.

CR. (*To Guard.*) Thou canst betake thee whither thou
wilt, free and clear of a grave charge. [*Exit Guard.*
(*To* ANTIGONE.) Now, tell me thou—not in many words,
but briefly—knewest thou that an edict had forbidden this?

AN. I knew it: could I help it? It was public.

CR. And thou didst indeed dare to transgress that law?

AN. Yes; for it was not Zeus that had published me that
edict; not such are the laws set among men by the Justice who
dwells with the gods below; nor deemed I that thy decrees
were of such force, that a mortal could override the unwritten

---

L.—ἐκφανῆ L, with μ above κ from the first hand. **451** ξύνοικος] ξύνεδρος Blaydes.
452 οἳ τούσδ᾽ . . ὥρισαν MSS. Semitelos, οἳ τούς γ᾽ : Wakefield, ἢ τούσδ᾽ . . ὥρισεν :
Valckenaer, τοιούσδ᾽ . . ὥρισεν. Wunder and others reject the verse.

---

448 ἤδη: on the form cp. *O. T.* 1525
n.—τί δ᾽ οὐκ ἔμελλον, sc. εἰδέναι; 'why
was I not likely to know it?' = 'of course
I knew it.' Plat. *Rep.* 605 c πάνδεινὸν
που (ἐστί). τί δ᾽ οὐ μέλλει (sc. εἶναι), εἴπερ
γε δρᾷ αὐτό; Xen. *H.* 4. 1. 6 τὸν δ᾽ υἱὸν...
ἑώρακας αὐτοῦ ὡς καλός ἐστι;—τί δ᾽ οὐ
μέλλω (sc. ἑωρακέναι);—ἐμφανῆ. I prefer this to L's ἐκφανῆ, not because Soph.
does not elsewhere use ἐκφανής, but because, in the two places where Aesch.
has used it, it has the sense of *emerging
into view* (*Pers.* 398, the Greeks going
into action at Salamis, or of *standing out*
among other objects which are less distinct (ἀνδρὸς ἐκφανὲς τέκμαρ, *Eum.* 244).
The sense required here is simply, 'public.'

449 καὶ δῆτ᾽, 'And you *indeed* dared
...?' Not, 'And *then*' (*i.e.* with that
knowledge), which would be κᾆτα.

450 Ζεύς is opposed to Creon's edicts,
not only as supreme god and therefore
guardian of all religious duty, but also in
each of his two special qualities,—as
χθόνιος (*O. C.* 1606 n.),—and as οὐράνιος,
since the denial of burial pollutes the
realm of οἱ ἄνω θεοί (1072).

451 f. τῶν κάτω θεῶν. For this
rare gen. (instead of the regular dat.)
with ξύνοικος, cp. Lycurgus *In Leocr.*
§ 145 οὗτος ἐν ταύτῃ τῇ χώρᾳ σύνοικος
ὑμῶν γενήσεται. So *O. C.* 1382 Δίκη
ξύνεδρος Ζηνός. 'The Justice that dwells
with the gods below' is their personified right to claim from the living
those religious observances which devote
the dead to them. A person who

omits such observances is defrauding
Hades of his own: see 1070. This Justice,
then, 'has not ordained such laws' as
Creon's; it has not *forbidden* kinsfolk to
bury their dead; on the contrary, it has
bound them to do so. **τοιούσδ᾽**...**ὥρισεν**
is a certainly true correction of the MS.
οἳ τούσδ᾽...**ὥρισαν**. With the latter, οἳ
are either Zeus and Δίκη,—which would
be the natural sense,—or οἱ κάτω θεοί:
and τούσδε νόμους are the laws of sepulture. But, after **τάδε** in 450, referring
to Creon's edicts, the demonstrative pronoun here also should refer to them.
Creon has just called his own laws
τούσδε νόμους (449). If Antigone, immediately afterwards, used τούσδε νόμους
to describe the divine laws, the stress
on τούσδε would be extremely awkward. Further, τοιούσδ᾽ ὥρισεν has a
pathetic force which renders it incom-
parably finer here than the somewhat
tame statement of fact, 'who have appointed the laws of burial among men.'

454 f. ἄγραπτα...νόμιμα. Arist.
Rhet. 1. 13 § 2 distinguishes (1) ἴδιος
νόμος, the particular law which each community defines for itself, which is partly
written, partly (so far as consisting in
custom) unwritten: (2) κοινὸς νόμος, the
universal, unwritten law of nature (ὁ κατὰ
φύσιν). ἔστι γάρ, ὃ μαντεύονταί τι πάντες,
φύσει κοινὸν δίκαιον καὶ ἄδικον, κἂν μηδεμία
κοινωνία πρὸς ἀλλήλους ᾖ μηδὲ συνθήκη,
οἷον καὶ ἡ Σοφοκλέους Ἀντιγόνη φαίνεται λέγουσα, ὅτι δίκαιον, ἀπειρημένον
(=in spite of the edict), θάψαι τὸν Πολυνείκην, ὡς φύσει ὂν τοῦτο δίκαιον. (Here he

νόμιμα δύνασθαι θνητὸν ὄνθ' ὑπερδραμεῖν·   455
οὐ γάρ τι νῦν γε κἀχθές, ἀλλ' ἀεί ποτε
ζῆ ταῦτα, κοὐδεὶς οἶδεν ἐξ ὅτου 'φάνη.
τούτων ἐγὼ οὐκ ἔμελλον, ἀνδρὸς οὐδενὸς
φρόνημα δείσασ', ἐν θεοῖσι τὴν δίκην
δώσειν. θανουμένη γὰρ ἐξῄδη, τί δ' οὔ;   460
κεἰ μὴ σὺ προὐκήρυξας· εἰ δὲ τοῦ χρόνου
πρόσθεν θανοῦμαι, κέρδος αὔτ' ἐγὼ λέγω.
ὅστις γὰρ ἐν πολλοῖσιν, ὡς ἐγώ, κακοῖς
ζῆ, πῶς ὅδ' οὐχὶ κατθανὼν κέρδος φέρει;
οὕτως ἔμοιγε τοῦδε τοῦ μόρου τυχεῖν   465
παρ' οὐδὲν ἄλγος· ἀλλ' ἄν, εἰ τὸν ἐξ ἐμῆς

---

455 θνητὸν ὄνθ'] θνητὰ φύνθ' Bothe.   **456** οὐ γάρ] οὐ μήν in Plutarch's quotation, *Mor.* 731 C, doubtless by a slip of memory.—νῦν γε κἀχθές] Arist. twice quotes this v.: (1) *Rhet.* 1. 13 § 2, where Q (= Marcianus 200) and Yᵇ (= Vat. 1340) have τε instead of γε, and Q has καὶ χθές. (2) *ib.* 1. 15 § 6 where all have γε κἀχθές.

---

quotes vv. 456 f.) Cp. *O. T.* 865 ff. νόμοι... | ὑψίποδες, οὐρανίαν | δι' αἰθέρα τεκνωθέντες, with notes there. Thuc. 2. 37 (νόμοι) ὅσοι ἄγραφοι ὄντες αἰσχύνην ὁμολογουμένην φέρουσι. When 'the unwritten laws' are thus called νόμοι, the latter word is used figuratively. νόμιμα, observances sanctioned by usage, is the more correct word: so Plat. *Legg.* 793 A observes that τὰ καλούμενα ὑπὸ τῶν πολλῶν ἄγραφα νόμιμα cannot properly be called νόμοι, but still must be taken into account: δεσμοὶ γὰρ οὗτοι πάσης εἰσὶ πολιτείας, μεταξὺ πάντων ὄντες τῶν ἐν γράμμασι τεθέντων τε καὶ κειμένων καὶ τῶν ἔτι τεθησομένων.—ἀσφαλῆ, they stand fast for ever, like the θεῶν ἔδος ἀσφαλὲς αἰεί (*Od.* 6. 42).—θνητὸν ὄντ', 'one who is a mortal,'—*i.e.* Creon; but it is needless to supply σέ from τὰ σά: the expression is the more forcible for being general. Cp. Eur. fr. 653 οὐ θαῦμ' ἔλεξας, θνητὸν ὄντα δυστυχεῖν: *Alc.* 799 ὄντας δὲ θνητοὺς θνητὰ καὶ φρονεῖν χρεών. Bothe's θνητὰ φύνθ', rashly adopted by Nauck, is a wanton change, which the ambiguity of the neut. pl. makes still worse.—ὑπερδραμεῖν, out-run, and so fig., prevail over: Eur. *Ph.* 578 ἦν δ' αὖ κρατηθῇς καὶ τὰ τοῦδ' ὑπερδράμῃ, and his cause prevail (Canter's certain corr. of ὑπεκδράμῃ): *Ion* 973 καὶ πῶς τὰ κρείσσω θνητὸς οὖσ' ὑπερδράμω; (prevail against Apollo). It has been proposed to refer θνητὸν ὄνθ' to

Antigone: but if she said, 'I did not think your edicts so strong that I, a mortal, could prevail over divine law,' δύνασθαι would rather imply that, if she had been able, she would have been willing to do so. Besides, ὑπερδραμεῖν is more naturally said of the law-giver who sets his law above the other law.

456 f. νῦν γε κἀχθές. Cp. Her. 2. 53 μέχρι οὗ πρώην τε καὶ χθές. Plat. *Legg.* 677 D ὡς ἔπος εἰπεῖν, χθὲς καὶ πρώην γεγονότα (where the phrase is presently strengthened into τὸν ἀτεχνῶς χθὲς γενόμενον). The usu. Attic form was χθὲς καὶ πρώην, though πρώην καὶ χθές also occurs. Cp. Catullus 61. 137 *hodie atque heri.* So *heri et nudius tertius.* Tryphon, an Alexandrian grammarian of the Augustan age, is quoted by Apollonius *De Adverb.* p. 556, 32 as saying, χθές ἀττικώτερον τοῦ ἐχθές: but the reverse seems to be the case. Attic Comedy supports ἐχθές against χθές in a majority of cases; though χθές may have been preferred, even in prose, after a vowel.—ζῆ: cp. *O. T.* 482 ζῶντα (of the oracles which are operative, effectual), and *ib.* 45 n.—'φάνη, with prodelision of the temporal augment in the 6th place, as ὡς ἐγὼ 'φάνην *O. C.* 974 n.

458 f. τούτων (sc. τῶν νομίμων)... τὴν δίκην, the penalty belonging to these laws: *i.e.* the penalty of breaking them. The emphasis on τούτων

and unfailing statutes of heaven.   For their life is not of to-day
or yesterday, but from all time, and no man knows when they
were first put forth.

Not through dread of any human pride could I answer to
the gods for breaking *these*.   Die I must,—I knew that well
(how should I not?)—even without thy edicts.   But if I am
to die before my time, I count that a gain: for when any one
lives, as I do, compassed about with evils, can such an one find
aught but gain in death?

So for me to meet this doom is trifling grief; but if I had

---

457 ταῦτα] τοῦτο Arist. *Rh.* I. 13 § 2.   Victorius supposed that Arist. thus
purposely altered ταῦτα, to suit his own words introducing the citation, ὡς φύσει ὂν
τοῦτο δίκαιον (see comment. on 454 f.).   Rather it was a mere slip: cp. comment.
on 223.—'φάνη] φάνη L.   **458** ἐγὼ οὐκ] ἐγ' οὐκ L.   **460** ἐξῄδη Brunck:
ἐξῄδειν L.   **462** πρόσθεν] πρόσθε L.—αὖτ' L, αὖτ' r.

---

shows that, like ταῦτα just before, it refers
to the νόμιμα: we cannot, therefore, render, 'the penalty of such an act' (*sc. τοῦ
ὑπεροδραμεῖν*).—**ἐν θεοῖσι**, the forensic ἐν,
denoting the tribunal: Plat. *Legg.* 916 B
διαδικαζέσθω δὲ ἐν τισι τῶν ἰατρῶν: *Gorg.*
464 D εἰ δέοι ἐν παισὶ διαγωνίζεσθαι: Lys.
or. 13 § 35 ὁ δὲ δῆμος ἐν τῷ δικαστηρίῳ ἐν
δισχιλίοις ἐψηφίσατο (*sc. ποιεῖν τὴν κρίσιν*).
Cp. *O. T.* 677 ἐν...τοῖσδ', n.

460 f. δώσειν. The fut. inf. and
the pres. inf. are equally common after
μέλλω in Soph. (*O. T.* 967 n.).—**θανουμένη γάρ** introduces the reason for her
conduct. 'It was not likely that I should
obey your edicts, and thereby incur
punishment after death, for the sake of
avoiding immediate death. *For*, as to
death, I knew already that I must die
some time or other; and if it is to be a
little sooner, so much the better.'—**τί δ'
οὖ**; *sc.* ἔμελλον ἐξειδέναι (448).

461 f. κεἰ μὴ σὺ προὐκήρυξας: Even
if thou hadst not proclaimed death as the
penalty of infringing the edict.   The apodosis might be either (*a*) ἐξῄδη ἄν, implied
in τί δ' οὔ; or (*b*) ἔδει ἄν με θανεῖν, implied
in θανουμένη.   But (*a*) is best: 'I should
have known it, even if you had not brought
it publicly to my knowledge.'   For καὶ εἰ
cp. *O. T.* 305 n.—**τοῦ χρόνου**, the natural
term of life (cp. *O. T.* 963): expressed
below by πρίν μοι μοῖραν ἐξήκειν βίου (896).
—**αὖτ'**, *i.e.* αὐτό.   Cp. *El.* 1267 εἰ σε θεὸς
ἐπόρισεν | ἀμέτερα πρὸς μέλαθρα, δαιμόνιον
| αὐτὸ τίθημ' ἐγώ: fr. 154 ἔχοιμ' ἂν αὐτὸ
μὴ κακῶς ἀπεικάσαι.   **αὖτε** (L) would mean,
'again,' 'on the other hand' (so far from

thinking it a loss).   The epic αὖτε is used
by Soph. in one lyric passage (*Tr.* 1010);
by Aesch. both in lyrics and in trimeters;
never by Eur.   The simpler αὐτό is more
probable here.

464 φέρει = φέρεται (*O. C.* 6 n.).—The
woman uses the masc. gender in putting
the general case.   Cp. Eur. *Med.* 1017
οὔτοι μόνη σὺ σῶν ἀπεζύγης τέκνων· | κού-
φως φέρειν χρὴ θνητὸν ὄντα συμφοράς.

465—468 Kvičala and Wecklein reject these four verses, despairing of the
difficulties found in vv. 466, 467, which
have been variously amended; see Appendix.   The alleged difficulties are, (1)
παρ' οὐδὲν ἄλγος: (2) the mention of the
mother only: (3) the position of θανόντ',
which might suggest the sense, 'slain by
my mother': (4) ᾐσχόμην (as L has it).
Before dealing with these points, I would
call attention to a trait which the im-
pugners of these verses have overlooked,
and which speaks strongly for the genuineness of the passage as a whole, corrupt
though it be in certain words.   That trait
is the clause **τοῖσδε δ' οὐκ ἀλγύνομαι** in
468, returning upon the thought παρ' οὐδὲν ἄλγος in 466.   This series of three
clauses, in which the second is opposed
to the first, and the third re-iterates the
sense of the first, is peculiarly Sophoclean:
cp. *Ai.* 1111 οὐ γάρ τι τῆς σῆς οὕνεκ' ἐ-
στρατεύσατο | γυναικός,... | ἀλλ' οὕνεχ' ὅρ-
κων οἷσιν ἦν ἐνώμοτος, | σοῦ δ' οὐδέν:
similar instances are *O. T.* 337 f., *Tr.*
431 ff.   This touch would hardly have
come from an interpolator.

466 ἄλγος, nom., *sc.* ἐστί: **παρ' οὐδέν,**

μητρὸς θανόντ᾽ ἄθαπτον ἠνσχόμην νέκυν,
κείνοις ἂν ἤλγουν· τοῖσδε δ᾽ οὐκ ἀλγύνομαι.
σοὶ δ᾽ εἰ δοκῶ νῦν μῶρα δρῶσα τυγχάνειν,
σχεδόν τι μώρῳ μωρίαν ὀφλισκάνω.　　　　470

ΧΟ. δηλοῖ τὸ γέννημ᾽ ὠμὸν ἐξ ὠμοῦ πατρὸς
τῆς παιδός· εἴκειν δ᾽ οὐκ ἐπίσταται κακοῖς.

ΚΡ. ἀλλ᾽ ἴσθι τοι τὰ σκλήρ᾽ ἄγαν φρονήματα
πίπτειν μάλιστα, καὶ τὸν ἐγκρατέστατον

---

467 ἠισχόμην νέκυν L: with marg. gloss by S, ἠνεσχόμην ὑπερεῖδον. The later MSS. have ἠίσχόμην (L²), ἠνσχόμην (A, V³), ἠσχόμην (Vat. b), ἰσχόμην (E, V⁴), ἠνεσχόμην (R, Vat.), or ἠνειχόμην (V). See comment.　　　**471 f.** δηλοῖ]

---

adv.: 'is a pain in no appreciable degree,' is a pain not worth a thought: as he might have said, οὐδαμοῦ ἄλγος ἐστί. The normal use of παρ᾽ οὐδέν, 'of no account,' is either (a) with the verb εἶναι, as *O. T.* 982 ταῦθ᾽ ὅτῳ | παρ᾽ οὐδέν ἐστι, or (b) with a verb meaning 'to esteem,' as above, v. 34, τὸ πρᾶγμ᾽ ἄγειν | οὐχ ὡς παρ᾽ οὐδέν. The only peculiarity here is that, instead of a word in the general sense, '*is esteemed*' (ἄγεται), we have a virtual equivalent, tinged with the special thought of the moment, viz., '*is a pain*.' Exactly so in *El.* 1327 we have πότερα παρ᾽ οὐδὲν τοῦ βίου κήδεσθ᾽ ἔτι, instead of πότερα παρ᾽ οὐδὲν τὸν βίον ἄγετε. Thus the suspicions as to the genuineness of παρ᾽ οὐδὲν ἄλγος are illusory.

ἀλλ᾽ ἄν. For the position of ἄν (to which objection has been taken) cp. *El.* 333 ἀλγῶ 'πὶ τοῖς παροῦσιν· ὥστ᾽ ἄν, εἰ σθένος | λάβοιμι, δηλώσαιμ᾽ ἂν οἷ᾽ αὐτοῖς φρονῶ: *ib.* 439 ἀρχὴν δ᾽ ἄν, εἰ μὴ τλημονεστάτη γυνὴ | πασῶν ἔβλαστε, τάσδε δυσμενεῖς χοὰς | οὐκ ἂν ποθ᾽, ὃν γ᾽ ἔκτεινε, τῷδ᾽ ἐπέστεφε.

467 ἄθαπτον ἠνσχόμην νέκυν, had allowed him to be an unburied corpse. For ἄθαπτον without ὄντα, cp. Arist. *Hist. An.* 8. 8 δύναται δ᾽ ἄποτος ἀνέχεσθαι (*sc.* ὤν): and *O. T.* 412 n. L has ἠίσχόμην, and ἠνσχόμην appears only as one of several readings in the later MSS.,—the other readings being manifestly impossible. The first question is, Could an Attic poet have used ἠνσχόμην for ἠνεσχόμην? We can only say that we find nothing really like it, and that no support for it can be drawn from the Homeric forms in which ἀνά suffers apocope, viz., ἄνσχεο = ἀνασχοῦ (*Il.* 23. 587

etc.), ἀνσχήσεσθαι (*Il.* 5. 104), ἄνσχετά (*Od.* 2. 63), ἀνσχεθέειν (*Od.* 5. 320). Still, there is force in Prof. Tyrrell's remark (*Classical Review*, vol. II. p. 140) that 'ἠνσχόμην is just the form in which an Attic poet would have applied apocope of ἀνά, inasmuch as he would have felt that he was only sacrificing the redundant augment.'

In my first edition I placed in the text the emendation of Semitelos (1887) ᾔσχυναν κύνες. Cp. *Il.* 22. 74 ἀλλ᾽ ὅτε δὴ πολιόν τε κάρη πολιόν τε γένειον | αἰδῶ τ᾽ αἰσχύνωσι κύνες κταμένοιο γέροντος. If the ες of κύνες had been obliterated, νέκυν would easily have arisen (esp. after ν); and a change of υ into ο would have taken ᾔσχυναν far towards ἠίσχόμην. But, while I still hold that this brilliant conjecture has no small degree of probability, I also recognise the justice of the criticism that the context here decidedly favours a verb in the first person.

Other emendations will be found in the Appendix. Most of them assume that we must have ἠνεσχόμην (or ἀνεσχόμην), and therefore alter the words θανόντ᾽ ἄθαπτον and νέκυν in various ways, —usu. omitting νέκυν. The verses produced by these processes are wretched, while, from a palaeographical point of view, they are pure conjectures, which do not attempt to account for the tradition in L.—Two points remain. (1) τὸν ἐξ ἐμῆς | μητρός. This is like saying, 'the son of the same womb.' Cp. Eur. *I. T.* 497 πότερον ἀδελφὼ μητρός ἐστον ἐκ μᾶς; Yet it has been seriously urged by many critics, as a ground for change, that a mention of the *father* was indispensable. ἐμῆς need not be altered to ὁμῆς (Seyffert) suffered my mother's son to lie in death an unburied corpse, that would have grieved me ; for this, I am not grieved. And if my present deeds are foolish in thy sight, it may be that a foolish judge arraigns my folly.

CH. The maid shows herself passionate child of passionate sire, and knows not how to bend before troubles.

CR. Yet I would have thee know that o'er-stubborn spirits are most often humbled ; 'tis the stiffest iron, baked to

---

δῆλον Nauck.—τὸ γέννημ'] M. Schmidt gives τι γέννημ' (with ἡ παῖς ὄν for τῆς παιδός): Semitelos, γονὴν λῆμ'. For τῆς παιδός Mekler conject. πεφυκός.—ἐπίσταται] L has the second τ in an erasure, perh. from σ. The final ι had been omitted, and has been added above α by the first hand. **474** πίπτει Boeckh.

---

or μιᾶς (Meineke). (2) τὸν ἐξ ἐμ. | μητρὸς θανόντ'. It is quite true that, when written, these words have an awkward ambiguity ; but they would have had none when spoken, since a slight pause after μητρός would have been required to bring out θανόντ'. This is the right test to apply in the case of a play written to be acted.

470 σχεδόν τι, 'almost,' iron., 'it might perhaps be said that...': so *El.* 608 (also at the close of a defiant speech), εἰ γὰρ πέφυκα τῶνδε τῶν ἔργων ἴδρις, | σχεδόν τι τὴν σὴν οὐ καταισχύνω φύσιν. Cp. *ib.* 550 εἰ δὲ σοὶ δοκῶ φρονεῖν κακῶς | γνώμην δικαίαν σχοῦσα, τοὺς πέλας ψέγε (end of a speech): also *Ai.* 1038, *O. C.* 1665.—μώρῳ μωρίαν: cp. 754. The παρήχησις gives bitterness, as (*O. T.* 371).—ὀφλισκάνω with dat., as Eur. *Bacch.* 854 γέλωτα Θηβαίοις ὀφλεῖν, etc. ; but in this use it can also take πρός τινα or παρά τινι (Plato). Cp. *O. T.* 511.

471 f. These two verses give a moment of stillness before the storm breaks forth. So at *O. T.* 404 four verses of the chorus divide the angry speech of Oedipus from the retort of Teiresias.—τὸ γέννημα τῆς παιδός (the offspring consisting in the maiden) the maiden his offspring, δηλοῖ (*sc.* ὄν) ὠμόν, shows herself fierce, ἐξ ὠμοῦ πατρός, from a fierce sire (*i.e.* by the disposition inherited from him). Cp. 20 δηλοῖς...καλχαίνουσα (n.) : the omission of ὄν is somewhat bold, but possible for poetry ; cp. 709 ὤφθησαν κενοί: Plat. *Legg.* 896 B δέδεικται ψυχὴ τῶν πάντων πρεσβυτάτη. γέννημα occurs below, 628, *O. T.* 1167, and *Tr.* 315, meaning always 'that which is begotten,' the offspring. So in Plato the word always means the thing produced ; for in *Sophist.* 266 D, τὸ δ᾽ ὁμοιωμάτων τινῶν

γέννημα, where Ast takes it as = 'confectio,' the sense is, 'the other a product (consisting in) certain images.' In Aesch. *P. V.* 850 ἐπώνυμον δὲ τῶν Διὸς γεννημάτων | τέξεις κελαινὸν Ἔπαφον, the word, if genuine, would certainly mean 'begetting'; but Wieseler's correction, γέννημ' ἀφῶν ('an offspring called after the touch of Zeus'), is highly probable. For τὸ γέννημα τῆς παιδός as = ἡ γεννηθεῖσα παῖς, cp. 1164 τέκνων σπορᾷ, *El.* 1233 γοναὶ σωμάτων ἐμοὶ φιλτάτων (her brother), Eur. *Med.* 1098 τέκνων...βλάστημα. Here, the thought would have been complete without τῆς παιδός ('the offspring shows the father's fierceness'), which is added, as if by an after-thought, for the further definition of τὸ γέννημα. I cannot believe that Soph. intended τὸ γέννημα τῆς παιδός to mean, 'the inborn disposition of the maiden,'—an unexampled sense for γέννημα. On the other hand, all the emendations are unsatisfactory and improbable. The language, though somewhat peculiar, appears to be sound.

472 εἴκειν...κακοῖς, not 'to succumb' to them, but to bend before them (as trees before a storm, 713), with a prudent view to self-preservation. Cp. Aesch. *P. V.* 320 σὺ δ᾽ οὐδέπω ταπεινός, οὐδ᾽ εἴκεις κακοῖς, | πρὸς τοῖς παροῦσι δ᾽ ἄλλα προσλαβεῖν θέλεις.

473 f. ἀλλ᾽ ἴσθι τοι: so oft. in threatenings: cp. 1064 : *Tr.* 1107 ἀλλ᾽ εὖ γέ τοι τόδ᾽ ἴστε: *El.* 298 ἀλλ᾽ ἴσθι τοι τίσουσά γ᾽ ἀξίαν δίκην.—πίπτειν, instead of the regular πίπτοντα : this inf. after οἶδα (as = 'I know that...', not, 'I know how to...') is not rare in poetry ; cp. *O. T.* 691, *Ph.* 1329, Aesch. *Pers.* 173, 431, 435 : so after ἐπίσταμαι above, 293, and 1092.

σίδηρον ὀπτὸν ἐκ πυρὸς περισκελῆ   475
θραυσθέντα καὶ ῥαγέντα πλεῖστ᾽ ἂν εἰσίδοις·
σμικρῷ χαλινῷ δ᾽ οἶδα τοὺς θυμουμένους
ἵππους καταρτυθέντας· οὐ γὰρ ἐκπέλει
φρονεῖν μέγ᾽ ὅστις δοῦλός ἐστι τῶν πέλας.
αὕτη δ᾽ ὑβρίζειν μὲν τότ᾽ ἐξηπίστατο,   480
νόμους ὑπερβαίνουσα τοὺς προκειμένους·
ὕβρις δ᾽, ἐπεὶ δέδρακεν, ἥδε δευτέρα,
τούτοις ἐπαυχεῖν καὶ δεδρακυῖαν γελᾶν.
ἦ νῦν ἐγὼ μὲν οὐκ ἀνήρ, αὕτη δ᾽ ἀνήρ,
εἰ ταῦτ᾽ ἀνατὶ τῇδε κείσεται κράτη.   485
ἀλλ᾽ εἴτ᾽ ἀδελφῆς εἴθ᾽ ὁμαιμονεστέρα

476 ἐσίδοισ L, with ει over ε from the first hand.   **482 f.** L inverts the order of these two vv., but S has corrected the error by writing β᾽ before 483 and α᾽ before 482 in the left-hand marg.   **484** νῦν] τἄρ᾽ Elmsley.   **485** ἀνα-τὶ L: ἀνατεὶ r.—κείσεται] πείσεται Semitelos (Blaydes had conjectured εἰ ταῦτά μου γυναικὶ πείσεται κράτη). Nauck proposes ἐάσεται.   **486** ὁμαιμονεστέραισ

---

475 ὀπτὸν... περισκελῆ, tempered to hardness: for the proleptic adj., cp. Thuc. 2. 75 ᾕρετο τὸ ὕψος...μέγα, Eur. *El.* 376 (πενία) διδάσκει δ᾽ ἄνδρα τῇ χρείᾳ κακὸν (to be bad).—περισκελής, dried or parched all round, from σκέλλω, *torrere*: cp. *Il.* 23. 190 μὴ πρὶν μένος ἠελίοιο | σκήλει᾽ ἀμφὶ περὶ χρόα ἴνεσιν: hence, fig., αἱ περισκελεῖς φρένες (*Ai.* 649): cp. *retorridus*. From the same rt come σκληρός, σκελετός (skeleton), and ἀσκελής (dried),—this last having a fig. sense in the Homeric ἀσκελὲς αἰεί ('stubbornly,' *Od.* 1. 68).—ἐκ πυρός, *by means of* fire; cp. 990 : *Ph.* 710 ἐξ ὠκυβόλων τόξων...αὐύσειε...φορβάν.

476 θραυσθέντα καὶ ῥαγέντα, 'broken and shivered.' ῥαγέντα is here the stronger word, in so far as it pictures the fragments of the ruptured iron flying asunder, while θραυσθέντα merely says that the iron is broken into pieces. As Heinrich Schmidt observes, the foremost idea in ῥηγνύναι is that of the separation of the parts,—the *rent* or *rift* being brought before us ; in θραύειν, that of a whole being broken into small pieces (*Synonymik der Gr. Sprache*, vol. III. pp. 304 ff.).

477 f. χαλινῷ δ᾽. Cp. *O. C.* 714 ἵπποισιν τὸν ἀκεστῆρα χαλινόν, n. For σμικρῷ cp. *Ai.* 1253 μέγας δὲ πλευρὰ βοῦς ὑπὸ σμικρᾶς ὅμως | μάστιγος ὀρθὸς εἰς ὁδὸν πορεύεται.—καταρτυθέντας, brought under discipline, made docile. καταρτύω =to equip, or prepare (*O. C.* 71): then,

like ἁρμόζω (*O. C.* 908), in a fig. sense, to bring into order, regulate, by a course of training: cp. Plat. *Legg.* 808 D (a child is the ὑβριστότατον θηρίων), ὅσῳ μάλιστα ἔχει πηγὴν τοῦ φρονεῖν μήπω κατηρτυμένην (not yet brought under discipline) : Plut. *Mor.* 38 C (the sensuous impulses, αἱ ἐφ᾽ ἡδονὴν ὁρμαί, are disastrous) ἂν ἐᾷ τις ἀφέτους, ᾗ πεφύκασι, χωρεῖν, καὶ μὴ...καταρτύῃ τὴν φύσιν (discipline the character). Plut. *Them.* 2 τοὺς τραχυτάτους πώλους ἀρίστους ἵππους γίνεσθαι φάσκων, ὅταν ἧς προσήκει τύχωσι παιδείας καὶ καταρτύσεως (education and discipline). In Aesch. *Eum.* 473 the act. perf. part. κατηρτυκὼς (ἱκέτης) is said to be a term applied to a horse whose mouth was 'fully furnished' with teeth (*i.e.* which had shed its foal's teeth), and hence, 'broken in,' 'tamed' : at any rate, it must be kept distinct from the passive καταρτυθείς as used here.

478 f. Suspicion has fallen on ἐκπέλει, which occurs only here : Hesych. explains it by ἔξεστι, and ἐξέπελεν by ἐξεγένετο. He would hardly have invented the imperf., if he had not met with it in literature : and the metrical convenience of such a synonym for ἔξεστι is a further reason for believing that it was current.—ὅστις : for the omission of the anteced. τούτῳ, see on 35 : for the gender, on 464.—τῶν πέλας : cp. fr. 83 ('tis better to conquer by any means) ἢ δοῦλον αὐτὸν ὄντα τῶν πέλας κλύειν.

hardness in the fire, that thou shalt oftenest see snapped and shivered; and I have known horses that show temper brought to order by a little curb; there is no room for pride, when thou art thy neighbour's slave.—This girl was already versed in insolence when she transgressed the laws that had been set forth; and, that done, lo, a second insult,—to vaunt of this, and exult in her deed.

Now verily I am no man, she is the man, if this victory shall rest with her, and bring no penalty. No! be she sister's child, or nearer to me in blood than

L first hand; but the letters ισ have been partially erased. ὁμαιμονεστέρας r (including A). The schol. in L read the gen.: εἴτε ἐξ ἀδελφῆς ἐμῆς εἴτε οἰκειοτέρας καὶ συγγενικωτέρας κ.τ.λ. The Roman ed., indeed, gives οἰκειοτέρα καὶ συγγενικωτέρα: but L's authority for the scholium is the better.

480 ff. αὕτη δ'. Creon began by addressing Antigone (473). He now denounces her to the Chorus. Cp. O. T. 1078 αὕτη δ' ἴσως, κ.τ.λ. (of Iocasta).— ὑβρίζειν μὲν...ὕβρις δ': epanaphora (O. T. 25 n.). The sense is, 'Her *disobedience* was an act of consummate insolence; and her *defiance* now makes it worse.' ἐξη-πίστατο, 'knew thoroughly,' with bitterness; cp. 686; Eur. fr. 796 ὅστις σωφρο-νεῖν ἐπίσταται. τότ' is explained by ὑπερβαίνουσα.—τοὺς προκ., which had been set forth: cp. O. T. 865, Eur. I. T. 1189 τὸν νόμον...τὸν προκείμενον.—τού-τοις, neut., these deeds: cp. 468 κείνοις ...τοῖσδε.—δεδρακυῖαν γελᾶν=to exult *in* having done it. For the partic., cp. Ar. Vesp. 1007 κοὐκ ἐγχανεῖταί σ' ἐξαπατῶν Ὑπέρβολος.

484 f. νῦν, 'now,' *i.e.* 'under these circumstances,' is better than νυν or τάρ' here.—εἰ ταῦτα...κράτη, if this victory shall remain on record for her, without bringing her any punishment. For κράτη, deeds of might, and so prevalence, victory, cp. *El.* 476 Δίκα, δίκαια φερομένα χεροῖν κράτη: *ib.* 689 οὐκ οἶδα τοιοῦθ' ἀν-δρὸς ἔργα καὶ κράτη. For κείσεται, cp. Pind. *I.* 4. 17 τὶν δ' ἐν Ἰσθμῷ διπλόα θάλλοισ' ἀρετά, | Φυλακίδα, κεῖται, 'for thee, Phylacidas, a double glory of valour is *laid up* at the Isthmus.' So, here, κείσεται means, 'placed to her credit,' 'permanently secured to her'; cp. the colloquialism, 'to *score* a success.' Other interpretations are:—(1) 'If this royal power of mine shall have been instituted without penalty for her.' For the word κράτη, this sense is tenable (cp. 60, 166, 173, O. T. 237): it is the whole phrase that appears strained. And ταῦτ'

(said with bitter emphasis) evidently refers to Antigone's acts; cp. 483 τού-τοις. Semitelos reads πείσεται: 'If this sovereignty of mine' (here Creon lifts his sceptre) 'shall yield to her without punishing her.' The verb would, however, be strange, and somewhat weak. (2) 'If these edicts shall have been set forth without penalty for her.' This last gives an impossible sense to κράτη. Ar. *Ran.* 1126 ff. illustrates the poetical ambiguity of κράτη, the debate there being whether, by πατρῴα κράτη, Aesch. meant, 'a victory over a father,' or 'power derived from a father.'—For the form of ἀνατί, cp. O. C. 1251 n.: for ταῦτα without τά, *ib.* 471.

486 f. ἀδελφῆς, (child of) a sister, ἀδελφιδῆ: for the gen., cp. 380, 825.—εἴθ' ὁμαιμονεστέρα, 'or nearer in blood to me than any member of my family.' The gen. ὁμαιμονεστέρας (see cr. n.) would mean, 'or (child of) one nearer in blood to me,' etc. She could be the child of no one nearer than a sister, unless it were of a mother or of a daughter; and it is far-fetched to suppose that Creon means, 'my niece,—aye, my sister, or my grand-daughter.' All that he means is, 'my niece,—aye, or the nearest relation possible.' This is more simply and clearly said by the nom. ὁμαιμονεστέρα. If the comparative were here restricted to the regular Sophoclean sense of the positive ὅμαιμος and ὁμαίμων, as meaning brother or sister (see on O. C. 330), then the gen. could be explained in another way, viz., as a rhetorical hyperbole: 'sister's child, or child of one who was thrice my sister,' —like Plato *Lysis* 210 ς ὁ πατὴρ καὶ ἡ μήτηρ καὶ εἴ τι τούτων οἰκειότερόν ἐστι.

τοῦ παντὸς ἡμῖν Ζηνὸς ἑρκείου κυρεῖ,
αὐτή τε χἠ ξύναιμος οὐκ ἀλύξετον
μόρου κακίστου· καὶ γὰρ οὖν κείνην ἴσον
ἐπαιτιῶμαι τοῦδε βουλεῦσαι τάφου.   490
καί νιν καλεῖτ'· ἔσω γὰρ εἶδον ἀρτίως
λυσσῶσαν αὐτὴν οὐδ' ἐπήβολον φρενῶν·
φιλεῖ δ' ὁ θυμὸς πρόσθεν ἡρῆσθαι κλοπεὺς
τῶν μηδὲν ὀρθῶς ἐν σκότῳ τεχνωμένων.
μισῶ γε μέντοι χὤταν ἐν κακοῖσί τις   495
ἁλοὺς ἔπειτα τοῦτο καλλύνειν θέλῃ.

487 ἑρκίου L: ἑρκείου r.   **490** βουλεῦσαι] Keck conject. φροντίσαι: Mekler, ἐπι-
ψαῦσαι: Semitelos, συλλαβεῖν: Metzger, τόνδε κηδεῦσαι τάφον.   **494** ὀρθῶς] ὀρθὸν

Hyperbole is congenial to Creon's excitement; cp. 1040. But the addition, τοῦ
παντὸς Ζ. ἑρκείου, ill suits this, while, on
the other hand, it agrees well with the
nom. ὁμαιμονεστέρα. On the whole, then,
I incline to prefer the nom.; but the
point is a nice one, and the gen. is quite
tenable.—κυρεῖ (οὖσα), = ἐστί: cp. O. T.
362 φονέα...κυρεῖν.

487 τοῦ παντὸς Ζηνὸς ἑρκείου = πάντων τῶν οἰκείων (schol.): so Eustath. 1930,
30 ἑρκεῖον Δία ἐκεῖνος (Sophocles) τοὺς ἐν
οἴκῳ πάντας δηλοῖ. The altar of Ζεὺς
ἑρκεῖος stood in the court-yard (αὐλή) in
front of the Greek house; ἕρκος denoting
the buildings which enclose the αὐλή, or,
sometimes, the space so enclosed, the αὐλή
itself. In Od. 22. 334 Phemius thinks of
passing from the μέγαρον into the αὐλή, Διὸς
μεγάλου ποτὶ βωμὸν | Ἑρκείου. (Cp. my
Introd. to Homer, p. 58.) This is the altar
at which Peleus was sacrificing, αὐλῆς ἐν
χόρτῳ (Il. 11. 774 : cp. Athen. 5, p. 189
F): as in Plat. Rep. 328 C there is sacrifice
in the αὐλή. So in Her. 6. 68 Demara-
tus supplicates his mother especially by
τοῦ Ἑρκείου Διὸς τοῦδε (whose altar or
image he is touching, καταπτόμενος).
Priam is slain πρὸς...κρηπίδων βάθροις...Ζη-
νὸς ἑρκείου (Eur. Tro. 16),—ἐπὶ τῇ ἐσχάρᾳ,
τοῦ Ἑρκείου (Paus. 4. 17. 4): cp. Ovid Ibis
286, Cui nihil Hercei profuit ara Iovis.
In Cratinus jun., Χείρων 1 ff. (c. 350 B.C.),
a returned exile says, ξυγγενεῖς | καὶ
φράτορας καὶ δημότας εὑρὼν μόλις | εἰς
τὸ κυλικεῖον ἐνεγράφην (put on the feast-
ing-list—παρὰ προσδοκίαν for εἰς τὸ γραμ-
ματεῖον)· Ζεὺς ἔστι μοι | ἑρκεῖος, ἔστι
φράτριος: where ἑρκεῖος corresponds
with ξυγγενεῖς. Dionysius 1. 67 expresses the attributes of the Roman Pe-

nates by the words πατρῷοι, γενέθλιοι,
κτήσιοι, μύχιοι, ἑρκεῖοι (for ἑρκίους in his
text should be ἑρκείους : so L has ἑρκίου
here).—In relation to the family, Ζεύς is
also γενέθλιος (Pind. O. 8. 16: cp. ξύναιμος, 659), ὁμόγνιος, and ἐφέστιος (as pre-
siding over household life : Ai. 492, Her.
1. 44).—For the god's name used to
denote that which he protects, cp. Eur.
Hec. 345 πέφευγας τὸν ἐμὸν ἱκέσιον Δία, =
my supplication, with its consequences.

488 ἀλύξετον. The pres. ind. ἀλύσκω
occurs in Apollon. Rhod., and the pres.
part. in Od.; otherwise we find only the
fut. (usu. ἀλύξω, but ἀλύξομαι, Hes. Op.
363) and aor. ἤλυξα (once midd., ἐξαλύ-
ξωμαι Ai. 656). The gen. μόρου follows
the analogy of ἀπολύεσθαι, ἀπαλλάττεσθαι,
etc. The regular constr. of the verb is
w.th the acc. (as in the Homeric κῆρας
ἀλύξας), and so Eur. always has an acc.
with ἐξήλυξα. In El. 627 θράσους | τοῦδ'
οὐκ ἀλύξεις, the gen. is not like this, but
causal ('for this boldness'). Oppian's
ἐξήλυξε μόροιο (Hal. 3. 104) was obviously
suggested by our verse. So in Ph. 1044.
Soph. has ventured on τῆς νόσου πεφευγέναι, thinking, doubtless, of the Homeric
πεφυγμένος ἦεν ἀέθλων.

489 f. καὶ γὰρ οὖν, for indeed: cp.
771 εὖ γὰρ οὖν, O. C. 980 οὐ γὰρ οὖν, ib.
985 ἀλλ' ἐν γὰρ οὖν.—ἐπαιτιῶμαι κείνην,
I accuse her, βουλεῦσαι ἴσον τοῦδε
τάφου, of having had an equal share in
plotting this burial. For the inf. after
ἐπαιτιᾶσθαι cp. El. 603 ὃν πολλὰ δή με σοὶ
τρέφειν μιάστορα | ἐπῃτιάσω. Ar. Vesp.
1446 Αἴσωπον οἱ Δελφοί ποτε ... φιάλην
ἐπῃτιῶντο κλέψαι. Plat. Critias 120 C
εἴ τίς τι παραβαίνειν αὐτῶν αἰτιῷτό τινα.
For the substantival ἴσον with gen., cp..

any that worships Zeus at the altar of our house,—she and her kinsfolk shall not avoid a doom most dire; for indeed I charge that other with a like share in the plotting of this burial.

And summon her—for I saw her e'en now within,—raving, and not mistress of her wits. So oft, before the deed, the mind stands self-convicted in its treason, when folks are plotting mischief in the dark. But verily this, too, is hateful,—when one who hath been caught in wickedness then seeks to make the crime a glory.

Nauck (ascribing it to Tournier, whose text, however, has ὀρθῶς). **496** θέλη L., with ει deleted between λ and η.

Eur. *Ion* 818 ὁμοῖος εἶναι τῆς τύχης τ' ἴσον φέρειν: id. *Ph.* 547 δωμάτων ἔχων ἴσον.—Another construction is possible: ἴσον ἐπαιτιῶμαι κείνην τοῦδε τοῦ τάφου, βουλεῦσαι: 'I charge her equally with this burial,—*i.e.* with plotting it.' The constr. with the gen. is frequent (Aesch. *P. V.* 974 ἦ κάμὲ γάρ τι ξυμφορᾶς ἐπαι-τιᾷ;): the objection here is that the epexegetic infin. βουλεῦσαι, requiring a case different from that governed by ἐπαιτιῶμαι, ought to come last: cp. Plat. *Crito* 52 B οὐδ' ἐπιθυμία σε ἄλλης πόλεως οὐδ' ἄλλων νόμων ἔλαβεν εἰδέναι: Eur. *Med.* 1399 χρῄζω στόματος | παίδων ὁ τάλας προσ-πτύξασθαι. In *O. T.* 644 εἰ σέ τι | δέ-δρακ', ὀλοίμην, ὧν ἐπαιτιᾷ με δρᾶν, ὧν might represent either (*a*) τούτων ὧν, δρᾶν being epexegetic, or (*b*) τούτων ἅ (acc. governed by δρᾶν); the latter is simplest. —βουλεῦσαι, of plotting mischief, as *Tr.* 807 τοιαῦτα...πατρὶ βουλεύσασ' ἐμῷ: *Ai.* 1055 στρατῷ...βουλεύσας φόνον.

491 καί νιν καλεῖτ', 'And now call her.' This is the καί so frequent in the orators, when the speaker turns to call for witnesses, documents, etc.: Lys. or. 16 § 13 καί μοι ἀνάβηθι, or. 13 § 35 καί μοι ἀνάγνωθι τὸ ψήφισμα.

492 λυσσῶσαν...οὐδ' ἐπ.: cp. *O. T.* 58 n.: Her. 9. 55 μαινόμενον καὶ οὐ φρε-νήρεα.—**ἐπήβολον**, 'in possession of' (*compos*), a word used by Aesch. (*P. V.* 444 φρενῶν, *Ag.* 542 νόσου), but not by Eur. It belonged to the diction of Ionian epos, appearing first in *Od.* 2. 319 (οὐ γὰρ νηὸς ἐπήβολος οὐδ' ἐρετάων), and is used by Herod.; Plato, too, admits it (as *Euthyd.* 289 B ἐπιστήμης ἐπηβόλους). Düntzer would derive it from ἐπί and ἄβολος ('meeting with'), assumed from the late verb ἀβολέω as=ἀντιβολέω (Ap. Rhod. 3. 1148); but it is more likely that it was simply an epic metrical license for

ἐπίβολος. The sense seems to come from ἐπιβάλλομαι as='to throw oneself on' a thing, and so take possession of it.

493 f. ὁ θυμὸς τῶν...τεχνωμένων, the mind of those who are planning nothing aright (planning utter mischief) in the dark, **φιλεῖ κλοπεὺς ᾑρῆσθαι**, is apt to stand convicted of its treason, **πρόσθεν**, before-hand,—*i.e.* before the treasonable deed has been done. For the order of words (ὁ θυμός being divided from the attributive gen. by the predicate), cp. Thuc. 2. 8 ἡ δὲ εὔνοια παρὰ πολὺ ἐποίει τῶν ἀν-θρώπων μᾶλλον ἐς τοὺς Λακεδαιμονίους. *Ismene* has not yet been caught in a disloyal act; but her guilty conscience has already shown itself. **κλοπεύς** here answers to κλέπτειν as='to do by stealth or fraud,' *Ai.* 1137 πόλλ' ἂν κακῶς λάθρᾳ σὺ κλέψειας κακά. It denotes the plotter's treachery towards the State, not the betrayal of the plotter by his own conscience (as some have taken it). **ᾑρῆσθαι** κλοπεύς (without ὤν), as *O. T.* 576 φονεὺς ἁλώσομαι: the perf. (expressing that the exposure is already decisive), like ᾑρῆσ-θαι *ib.* 1050.—**τεχνωμένων** midd., as usual; cp. *Ph.* 80 τεχνᾶσθαι κακά. This is better than to make it pass., as a gen. absol., ('when utter mischief is being contrived,') a constr. which seems to require the change of ὀρθῶς to ὀρθῶν, since τὰ μηδὲν ὀρθῶς could hardly mean, 'things which (are) in no wise well,' *sc.* ἔχοντα. οἱ μηδὲν ὀρθῶς τεχνώμενοι=those who plan nothing in such a way as to be right (the generic μή): cp. *Ph.* 407 παντὸς ἂν λόγου κακοῦ | γλώσσῃ θιγόντα καὶ παν-ουργίας, ἀφ' ἧς | μηδὲν δίκαιον ἐς τέλος μέλλοι ποιεῖν.

495 f. γε μέντοι: cp. *O. T.* 442 n. '(I hate such plotting in the dark :) however, I certainly hate this also,—when a de-tected traitor seeks to glorify the treason.'

ΑΝ. θέλεις τι μεῖζον ἢ κατακτεῖναί μ' ἑλών;

ΚΡ. ἐγὼ μὲν οὐδέν· τοῦτ' ἔχων ἅπαντ' ἔχω.

ΑΝ. τί δῆτα μέλλεις; ὡς ἐμοὶ τῶν σῶν λόγων
ἀρεστὸν οὐδέν, μηδ' ἀρεσθείη ποτέ·   500
οὕτω δὲ καὶ σοὶ τἄμ' ἀφανδάνοντ' ἔφυ.
καίτοι πόθεν κλέος γ' ἂν εὐκλεέστερον
κατέσχον ἢ τὸν αὐτάδελφον ἐν τάφῳ
τιθεῖσα; τούτοις τοῦτο πᾶσιν ἁνδάνειν
λέγοιτ' ἄν, εἰ μὴ γλῶσσαν ἐγκλήοι φόβος.   505
ἀλλ' ἡ τυραννὶς πολλά τ' ἄλλ' εὐδαιμονεῖ,
κἄξεστιν αὐτῇ δρᾶν λέγειν θ' ἃ βούλεται.

ΚΡ. σὺ τοῦτο μούνη τῶνδε Καδμείων ὁρᾷς.

497 L prefixes ΑΓ (by error for ΑΝ).—τι] τί L.   **500** ἀρεσθείη] ἀρέστ' εἴη Elmsley.
504 ἀνδάνει L, with most of the later mss., but A and V³ have ἀνδάνειν.   **505** ἐγ
κλείσοι L: ἐκκλείσοι or ἐγκλήσοι r: ἐγκλῆσαι Erfurdt: ἐγκλήοι Schaefer. Cp. cr. n.
on *O. T.* 1388.   **506 f.** These two vv. are rejected as spurious by A. Jacob, who

---

Ismene's guilty terror is contrasted with
Antigone's impudent hardihood,—as
Creon deems it. **μισῶ...ὅταν**, like μέμ
νησαι ὅτε...ἐποίησας (Xen. *Oec.* 2. 11),
οἶδ' ἡνίκ' Αἴας εἷλκε (Eur. *Tro.* 70) etc.—
ἔπειτα, like εἶτα, as *Ai.* 760 ὅστις ἀνθρώ
που φύσιν | βλαστὼν ἔπειτα μὴ κατ' ἄνθρω
πον φρονῇ.—**καλλύνειν**, to make καλός
(fr. 786 πρόσωπα καλλύνουσα, of the waxing moon), here, to make specious : so
Plat. *Legg.* 944 Β εὐδιάβολον κακὸν καλ
λύνων (a soldier excusing himself for
ὅπλων ἀποβολή).

497 f. **θέλεις τι μεῖζον**, *sc.* ποιεῖν,—
not that θέλω could not take a simple
acc., but a Greek would mentally supply
a general inf. to balance κατακτεῖναι: cp.
Thuc. 3. 85 ἀπόγνοια...τοῦ ἄλλο τι (*sc.*
ποιεῖν) ἢ κρατεῖν τῆς γῆς.—**ἑλών**: cp.
O. T. 641 κτεῖναι λαβών.—**ἐγὼ μὲν οὐδέν**.
He desires nothing more,—and will take
nothing less.—**ἅπαντ' ἔχω**: cp. Eur. *Or.*
749 τοῦτο πάντ' ἔχω μαθών ('tell me that,
and I am satisfied').

500 ἀρεστὸν οὐδέν, not ἀρεστὸς οὐδείς:
cp. *O. T.* 1195 βροτῶν | οὐδέν.—**μηδ'
ἀρεσθείη**. Cp. 686. If sound (as it seems
to be), this is a solitary example of the
aor. pass. ἠρέσθην as = 'became pleasing,'
and must be defended by the pass. (or
midd.) ἀρέσκομαι as used by Herod., 6.
128 ἠρέσκοντο, 'they were approved' (or,
'they pleased'): 9. 79 μήτε Αἰγινήτῃσι
ἅδοιμι μήτε τοῖσι ταῦτα ἀρέσκεται (those
who approve this course). Considering

the Ionic affinities of Attic Tragedy, this
use of ἀρέσκομαι in Ionic prose seems a
sufficient warrant for a corresponding use
of ἠρέσθην, whether we take it as properly
passive ('was approved'), or as a pass.
form used to supplement the middle
('pleased'). I do not add Eur. fr. 942
θεοῖς ἀρέσκον, because there I should read
θεοὺς ἀρέσκον, 'propitiate the gods,' the
Attic use of the midd.; cp. Xen. *Mem.* 4.
3. 16 νόμος δὲ δήπου πανταχοῦ ἐστι κατὰ
δύναμιν ἱεροῖς θεοὺς ἀρέσκεσθαι, 'to propitiate the gods with sacrifice. The Attic
passive meant 'I am pleased,' Thuc. 1.
129 τοῖς λόγοις τοῖς ἀπὸ σοῦ ἀρέσκομαι,
5. 37 οἱ βοιωτάρχαι ἠρέσκοντο, but occurs
only in pres. and impf.: ἠρέσθην, as the
corresponding aor., appears only in later
Greek, as Paus. 2. 13. 8 οὐκ ἀρεσθεὶς τῷ
δοθέντι πώματι. The traditional ἀρεσθείη,
then, is at least not less probable than
Hermann's **ἀρεσθείην**, when the whole
question is viewed in the light of attested
usage. As to Elmsley's neat **ἀρέστ' εἴη**,
a fatal objection to it is the change to
the impers. plur.; as if one said, 'not one
of your words pleases me; and never may
I feel pleasure:' (without, 'in them').

501 τἀμά, a general phrase, 'my
views.' Cp. *El.* 1050 οὔτε γὰρ σὺ τἄμ'
ἔπη | τολμᾷς ἐπαινεῖν οὔτ' ἐγὼ τοὺς σοὺς
τρόπους.—**ἔφυ** with partic. ('are naturally
...'), cp. *O. T.* 9 πρέπων ἔφυς.

502 καίτοι marks the transition to
another and higher point of view than

An. Wouldst thou do more than take and slay me?

Cr. No more, indeed; having that, I have all.

An. Why then dost thou delay? In thy discourse there is nought that pleases me,—never may there be!—and so my words must needs be unpleasing to thee. And yet, for glory— whence could I have won a nobler, than by giving burial to mine own brother? All here would own that they thought it well, were not their lips sealed by fear. But royalty, blest in so much besides, hath the power to do and say what it will.

Cr. Thou differest from all these Thebans in that view.

is followed by Dindorf, Meineke, Nauck, and M. Schmidt.—In L there has been an attempt to make πολλὰ τἄλλ' out of πολλά τ' ἀλλ'.—δρᾶν, omitted in the text of L, has been added above the line by an early corrector.

Creon's. '*Thou* wilt never approve my deed. *And yet* how could I have won a better claim to the approval of all who judge rightly?' In καίτοι πόθεν κλέος γ' the absence of caesura gives a slower movement, just as in v. 44: she communes with her own thought. κλέος... εὐκλεέστερον, like δύσπνοοι πνοαί (587), φρένες δύσφρονες (1261), πόνοι δύσπονοι (1277): *Ph.* 894 ξύνηθες...ἔθος. Distinguish the case of the adj. compounded with a noun merely cognate in sense to the subst.; above, v. 7 n.

503 ff. ἐν τάφῳ τιθεῖσα, *i.e.* symbolically, by sprinkling dust and pouring χοαί: cp. 80, 395, and *O. C.* 1410 n.—τούτοις πᾶσι λέγοιτο ἄν, by all these it would be said, τοῦτο ἀνδάνειν (αὐτοῖς), that this seems good to them: for dat. with pres. pass. (a constr. usually restricted to the pf. pass.) cp. Menander *Sentent.* 511 τἀληθὲς ἀνθρώποισιν οὐχ εὑρίσκεται. If the datives were taken with ἀνδάνειν, λέγοιτο ἄν would be too indefinite. At the same time the proximity of ἀνδάνειν has influenced the construction. ταὐτὸ has been suggested, but there is nothing suspicious in τούτοις τοῦτο, which Nauck groundlessly condemns.—The pres. ἐγκλήοι is required by the sense, since the act is a continuing one; ἐγκλῆσαι would refer to some given moment or particular occasion. The mss. favour the aor., but most of the recent edd. rightly give the pres.

506 f. ἀλλ' ἡ τυραννίς. '(If these men dared to say what they think, they would applaud me.) *But* royalty has the advantage of being able to do and say what it pleases, without being opposed in word or deed':—and so these men are

silent. These are two excellent and vigorous lines,—not only free from the slightest internal mark of spuriousness, but admirably suited to their place, both by thought and by expression. It was an extraordinary freak of arbitrary criticism to reject them. The reasons assigned for doing so deserve mention only for their curious weakness; as (*a*) ἀλλ' ἡ ought to be ἡ γάρ—Dindorf: (*b*) Antigone should not mention the *advantages* of the τυραννίς—A. Jacob: (*c*) Creon could not be reproached with δρᾶν λέγειν θ' ἃ βούλεται—Nauck: of which last objection Bellermann, in his simple and triumphant vindication of these verses, justly says that it is 'wholly unintelligible.' (*d*) Wecklein, too, has effectively defended them. We may add that Creon's reply in v. 508, which refers primarily to vv. 504 f., does not therefore ignore vv. 506 f., since these two vv. cohere closely with the former: vv. 504—507 express a single thought. For similar references in tragedy to the τυραννίς, as it was viewed by Greeks in the historical age, cp. Aesch. *P. V.* 224 f., Eur. *Ion* 621—632.

508 f. μούνη: τῶνδε refers to the Chorus: for the Ionic form, cp. 308, 705.—τοῦτο...ὁρᾷς, seest this,='takest this view'; viz., that thy deed is right, and that only my power prevents its being publicly approved. A very rare use of ὁρᾶν: indeed, I know no strictly similar instance, for we cannot compare *O. T.* 284, where see n.: still, it is natural enough. Cp. Plat. *Phaedr.* 276 A ἄλλον ὁρῶμεν λόγον. So we say, 'I do not see it,'='I cannot take that view.' μούνη τῶνδε: cp. 101 κάλλιστον...τῶν προτέρων, n.—ὑπίλλουσιν (for the spelling cp. n. in

ΑΝ. ὁρῶσι χοὖτοι· σοὶ δ᾽ ὑπίλλουσιν στόμα.

ΚΡ. σὺ δ᾽ οὐκ ἐπαιδεῖ, τῶνδε χωρὶς εἰ φρονεῖς;   510

ΑΝ. οὐδὲν γὰρ αἰσχρὸν τοὺς ὁμοσπλάγχνους σέβειν.

ΚΡ. οὔκουν ὅμαιμος χὠ καταντίον θανών;

ΑΝ. ὅμαιμος ἐκ μιᾶς τε καὶ ταὐτοῦ πατρός.

ΚΡ. πῶς δῆτ᾽ ἐκείνῳ δυσσεβῆ τιμᾷς χάριν;

ΑΝ. οὐ μαρτυρήσει ταῦθ᾽ ὁ κατθανὼν νέκυς.   515

ΚΡ. εἴ τοί σφε τιμᾷς ἐξ ἴσου τῷ δυσσεβεῖ.

ΑΝ. οὐ γάρ τι δοῦλος, ἀλλ᾽ ἀδελφὸς ὤλετο.

ΚΡ. πορθῶν δὲ τήνδε γῆν· ὁ δ᾽ ἀντιστὰς ὕπερ.

ΑΝ. ὅμως ὅ γ᾽ Ἅιδης τοὺς νόμους τούτους ποθεῖ.

ΚΡ. ἀλλ᾽ οὐχ ὁ χρηστὸς τῷ κακῷ λαχεῖν *ἴσους.   520

ΑΝ. τίς οἶδεν εἰ κάτωθεν εὐαγῆ τάδε;

---

509 ἱπίλλουσιν L: ὑπίλλουσι r (as A), or ὑπείλουσι (V⁴).   **513** μιᾶς τε MSS.: μιᾶς γε Hermann.—πατρός] Tournier conject. γεγώς.   **514** δυσσεβῶι L, with ηι over ὦι: δυσσεβεῖ or δυσσεβῇ r.—τιμᾶισ L, with gl. ἀντὶ τοῦ νέμεις.   **516** εἰ τοῖ σσφε L: εἴ τοί σφε r.   **518** ποοθῶν δε (without acc.) L. Most of the later

---

Appendix on 340), lit., 'turn' (or 'roll') 'under,' said of an animal putting its tail between its legs; cp. Eur. fr. 544 (from his Οἰδίπους,— referring to the Sphinx) οὐρὰν δ᾽ ὑπίλασ᾽ ὑπὸ λεοντόπουν βάσιν | καθέξετ᾽. Veig. Aen. 11. 812 (a terrified wolf) caudamque remulcens Subiecit pavitantem utero. Here, 'keep down' the utterance of their thoughts; 'make their lips subservient' to thee. Cp. σαίνειν, adulari.—Euphony commends, though metre does not require, the ν ἐφελκυστικόν, which L gives. Cp. 571.

510 f. σὺ δ᾽ οὐκ ἐπαιδεῖ; And art thou not ashamed of it (cp. ἐπαισχύνομαι), if thou thinkest otherwise than they do?—thinkest, namely, that thou art free to act on thy own views, regardless of thy king. For the sake of argument, he concedes their possible *sympathy* with her, but insists on their loyal *behaviour*. She answers, 'No, I am not ashamed, for I am doing nothing shameful.'

512 f. ὅμαιμος always of brother and sister in Soph.: O. C. 330 n.—**ἐκ μιᾶς τε**. The soundness of the text is thoroughly vindicated by Plat. *Legg*. 627 C (quoted by Schneidewin), πολλοὶ ἀδελφοί πού γένοιντ᾽ ἂν ἑνὸς ἀνδρός τε καὶ μιᾶς υἱεῖς, which also confirms the MS. τε against the conjecture γε.

514 f. πῶς δῆτ᾽: why, then, dost thou render (to Polyneices) a tribute impious in the sight of Eteocles?—*i.e.*, which

places the latter on the same level with the former.—ἐκείνῳ, ethic dat., 'in his judgment': cp. 904, O. C. 1446 ἀνάξιαι... πᾶσιν, and *ib*. 810 n., O. T. 40. We cannot well render, 'impious *towards* him,' which would be πρὸς or εἰς ἐκεῖνον: nor can the dat. be one of 'interest,' as though δυσσεβῇ were equivalent to βλαβεράν. The next verse agrees well with ἐκείνῳ being ethic dat.: 'he will not so testify,' ='he will not say that he thinks my act impious.'—χάριν is usu. explained as acc. of the inner object, like τιμᾷς τιμήν. But it would evidently be awkward to have an objective acc. added, as τιμῶ χάριν αὐτόν. Rather **τιμᾷς** is here slightly deflected from the sense, 'to honour by observance,' 'to observe duly,' as Eur. *Tro*. 1210 οὓς Φρύγες νόμους | τιμῶσιν, Ion 1045 τὴν εὐσέβειαν...τιμᾶν, and means, 'to render duly,' as religious observance requires. So I should take it also in the parallel phrase, Eur. *Or*. 828 πατρῷαν | τιμῶν χάριν, duly rendering grace to thy sire.—ὁ κατθανὼν νέκυς: cp. 26.

516 εἴ τοι, *siquidem*: O. T. 549.—σφε: cp. 44 n.—ἐξ ἴσου, *only* on a level with, as O. T. 1019. So ἴσον='equally *little*' (Her. 2. 3), or 'equally *vain*' (id. 8. 79): and id. 8. 109 τά τε ἱρὰ καὶ τὰ ἴδια ἐν ὁμοίῳ ἐποιέετο, *i.e.* made sacred things of (only) the same account as things profane. Cp. 393.

517 οὐ γάρ τι δοῦλος. No, Eteocles

AN. These also share it; but they curb their tongues for thee.

CR. And art thou not ashamed to act apart from them?

AN. No; there is nothing shameful in piety to a brother.

CR. Was it not a brother, too, that died in the opposite cause?

AN. Brother by the same mother and the same sire.

CR. Why, then, dost thou render a grace that is impious in his sight?

AN. The dead man will not say that he so deems it.

CR. Yea, if thou makest him but equal in honour with the wicked.

AN. It was his brother, not his slave, that perished.

CR. Wasting this land; while *he* fell as its champion.

AN. Nevertheless, Hades desires these rites.

CR. But the good desires not a like portion with the evil.

AN. Who knows but this seems blameless in the world below?

MSS. have δέ, but a few γε. The older edd. give γε: most of the recent, δέ. **519** ὁμῶς Mekler.—τουσ νόμουσ τούτουσ MSS.: schol. marg. of L, γρ. τοὺς νόμουσ ἰσουσ.—Semitelos writes ὁμοὺς (for ὅμως) ..τούτοις. **520** λαχεῖν L: λαβεῖν r.— ἴσος MSS. Bergk conject. ἴσα (which Nauck adopts), or ἴσον. Nauck also suggests ἴσους (if τούτους be kept in 519). **521** κάτω'στὶν MSS. In L, γρ. κάτωθεν is written

---

cannot complain, for Polyneices was not his slave—his natural inferior—but his brother, and had the same claim on me that he had. Creon insists on the difference between the loyal man and the disloyal. Antigone dwells on the fact that both men had the same claim on her natural piety, and (519) on her sense of religious duty.

518 πορθῶν δέ: for δέ introducing an objection, cp. *O. T.* 379: for the partic., *ib.* 1001, 1011.—ὁ δ᾽, but the other (perished) ἀντιστὰς ὑπὲρ τῆσδε γῆς, as this land's champion. ὕπερ is paroxytone as virtually following its case, since the gen. is supplied from τήνδε γῆν. Cp. *Ai.* 1231 τοῦ μηδὲν ἀντέστης ὕπερ.

519 τούτους, the reading of the MSS., has been rejected by nearly all modern editors in favour of ἴσους, which the Scholiast mentions as a variant. But the simple τούτους is perfectly suitable, —'these laws,' the laws of sepulture (τὸ θάπτειν, as a schol. paraphrases); and everything that ἴσους would convey is already expressed by ὅμως. 'One was the country's foe, the other its champion —granted. *Nevertheless* Hades desires these laws,'—*i.e.* even in the case of the foe. A corruption of ἴσους into τούτους

is very improbable. Rather ἴσους was merely one of those conjectures which so often appear in the margin of the MSS., having for their object the supposed improvement of a point. The MS. ἴσος in 520 does not strengthen the case for ἴσους here.

520 The MS. λαχεῖν ἴσος is usu. explained, 'equal in respect to obtaining (rites),' *i.e.* with an equal claim to rites. The phrase is not only without any parallel, but seems impossible. ἴσος λαχεῖν νόμιμα would be very strange; ἴσος λαχεῖν, absolutely, is stranger still. The train of thought strongly favours ἴσους, as Nauck suggests and Semitelos reads. 'Hades may desire these rites; but the good man does not (desire) to receive only the same rites as the wicked': *i.e.* Eteocles will not be satisfied with the equality merely because Polyneices was his brother (517): he will think of the contrast between that brother's merits and his own. The dead can be said λαγχάνειν νόμους (of burial), in the sense of obtaining that which the νόμοι give. Therefore we need not write ἴσον or ἴσα.

521 f. κάτωθεν, simply 'below': cp. 1070, Eur. *Alc.* 424 τῷ κάτωθεν ἀσπόνδῳ θεῷ: Dem. or. 23 § 28 ὁ κάτωθεν νόμος,

ΚΡ. οὔτοι ποθ᾽ οὑχθρός, οὐδ᾽ ὅταν θάνῃ, φίλος.
ΑΝ. οὔτοι συνέχθειν, ἀλλὰ συμφιλεῖν ἔφυν.
ΚΡ. κάτω νυν ἐλθοῦσ᾽, εἰ φιλητέον, φίλει
    κείνους· ἐμοῦ δὲ ζῶντος οὐκ ἄρξει γυνή.   525

ΧΟ. καὶ μὴν πρὸ πυλῶν ἥδ᾽ Ἰσμήνη,
    φιλάδελφα κάτω δάκρυ᾽ *εἰβομένη·
    νεφέλη δ᾽ ὀφρύων ὕπερ αἱματόεν
    ῥέθος αἰσχύνει,
    τέγγουσ᾽ εὐῶπα παρειάν.   530

ΚΡ. σὺ δ᾽, ἣ κατ᾽ οἴκους ὡς ἔχιδν᾽ ὑφειμένη

above. **523** οὔτοι συνέχθειν] In L the first hand seems to have written οὐ τοινυν εχειν, but added θ above χ, and S completed the correction. **524** νυν] νῦν L. **525** ἄρξει] L has ει in erasure, prob. from η. **527** δάκρυα λειβόμενα L, δάκρυα

the law below (=the continuation of a law already cited). We need not understand here, 'if these things are approved *from* below.' κάτω 'στὶν has the MS. authority: but it is most improbable that Soph. would have given such a needlessly unpleasing verse, and the change is sufficiently explained by a later belief that the sense required κάτω.—εὐαγῆ, right in respect to ἄγος, *i.e.* free from it, pure (*O. T.* 921). She means: 'who can tell if Eteocles, in the world below, will not think it consonant with piety that Polyneices should be honoured?' Perhaps earthly feuds are made up there. Creon answers, 'No,—foe once, foe always,—even in death: Eteocles *will* resent it.' Cp. *Od.* 11. 543 where the spirit of Ajax in Hades will not speak to Odysseus—κεχολωμένη εἵνεκα νίκης | τήν μιν ἐγὼ νίκησα.—There would be far less point in Creon's words if we took them to mean, '*my* dead foe is still my foe' (cp. *Ai.* 1348, 1372).

523 οὔτοι συνέχθειν. 'Even if my brothers hate each other still, my nature prompts me, not to join Eteocles in hating Polyneices, but to love each brother as he loves me': cp. 73 φίλη...φίλου μέτα. Cp. Polybius 1. 14 φιλόφιλον δεῖ εἶναι τὸν ἀγαθὸν ἄνδρα καὶ φιλόπατριν, καὶ συμμισεῖν τοῖς φίλοις τοὺς ἐχθροὺς καὶ συναγαπᾶν τοὺς φίλους. Eur. imitates our verse, *I. A.* 407 (Agam. to Menelaus) συσσωφρονεῖν γάρ, οὐχὶ συννοσεῖν ἔφυν, 'nay, my sympathies are with prudence, not with frenzy.'

524 f. νῦν, as *Ai.* 87, *Tr.* 92, *Ph.* 1196, but νῦν *O. T.* 658, and oft.—κείνους =τοὺς ἐκεῖ, the dead. Nauck proposes νεκρούς, which would be a deplorable change. For the pause after the emphatic word, cp. 46 n.

526 f. καὶ μήν introducing the new person: *O. C.* 549 n. At Creon's command (491), two πρόσπολοι had gone to bring Ismene. The door from which she now enters is that by which she had left the stage (99). It is supposed to lead to the γυναικωνῖτις (cp. 578).—εἰβομένη, the correction of Triclinius for the MS. λειβομένη, enables us to keep δάκρυα, instead of changing it to δάκρυ, when φιλάδελφα must be taken as adv. (cp. *O. T.* 883 n.). The Schol. so took it (he paraphrases by φιλαδέλφως), and it would seem, therefore, that he read δάκρυ λειβομένη. But, though this constr. is quite admissible, it would be far more natural that φιλάδελφα should agree with δάκρυα. In *O. C.* 1251 we have λείβων δάκρυον: neither λείβω nor εἴβω occurs elsewhere in Soph.; and the only other place in Tragedy where εἴβω has good support is Aesch. *P. V.* 400, where Hermann, by reading δακρυσίστακτον ἀπ᾽ ὄσσων ῥαδινῶν δ᾽ εἰβομένα ῥέος, for the MS. δακρυσίστακτον δ᾽...λειβομένα, restores the metre. But κατὰ δάκρυον εἴβειν and δάκρυα λείβειν were equally familiar as Homeric phrases; and if an Attic poet could use the latter, there was certainly no reason why he should not use the former. I may remark, too, that κάτω points to a reminiscence of the phrase

CR. A foe is never a friend—not even in death.

AN. 'Tis not my nature to join in hating, but in loving.

CR. Pass, then, to the world of the dead, and, if thou must needs love, love them.   While I live, no woman shall rule me.

Enter ISMENE *from the house, led in by two attendants.*

CH. Lo, yonder Ismene comes forth, shedding such tears as fond sisters weep; a cloud upon her brow casts its shadow over her darkly-flushing face, and breaks in rain on her fair cheek.

CR. And thou, who, lurking like a viper in my house,

λειβομένα or δάκρυα λειβομένη r. δάκρυ' ειβομένη Triclinius: δάκρυ λειβομένη Wex.
528 αἱματόεν] ἱμερόεν M. Schmidt, adding the words ἱσταμένη | τὸ πρὶν after ὕπερ.
531 ἥ] ἡ L.—ὑφειμένη] ὑφημένη Brunck. Cp. schol., ἡ γὰρ ἔχιδνα λάθρᾳ καθεζο-

---

with εἴβειν, for Homer never says κατὰ δάκρυα λείβειν. Nothing is more natural than that εἰβομένη should have become λειβομένη in the MSS., the latter word being much the commoner.—**κάτω**, adv., 'downwards': cp. 716, fr. 620 ὦτα κυλλαίνων κάτω. Nauck's objection, that κάτω εἰβομένη could not stand for κατειβομένη, would have force only if κάτω were necessarily a prep., substituted for κατά. He proposes καταὶ (cp. καταιβάτης).

528 f. νεφέλη δ' ὀφρύων ὕπερ, a cloud of grief (resting) on her brow,—as dark clouds rest on a mountain-summit: cp. Eur. *Hipp.* 173 στυγνὸν δ' ὀφρύων νέφος αὐξάνεται: Aesch. *Theb.* 228 τὰν ἀμήχανον | κἀκ χαλεπᾶς δύας ὑπερθ' ὀμμάτων | κρημναμέναν νεφέλαν: so συννεφὴς = συννοφρυωμένος. Cp. *Deme supercilio nubem* (Hor. *Ep.* 1. 18. 94). The cloud of sorrow is associated with the rain of tears: cp. Shaksp. *Ant.* 3. 2. 51 *Will Caesar weep?—He has a cloud in 's face.* —**αἱματόεν**, here, '*suffused with* blood,' darkly flushed. This application of αἱματόεις to the human face seems unparalleled, though in *Anthol. P.* 6. 154 Leonidas of Tarentum (*c.* 280 B.C.) has φύλλα τε πεπταμένων αἱματόεντα ῥόδων. Eur. *Phoen.* 1487 was less daring when he called a dark blush τὸν ὑπὸ βλεφάροις | φοίνικ' ('crimson'), ἐρύθημα προσώπου. It recalls the well-known fragment of Ion in Athen. 603 E, where the schoolmaster objects to Phrynichus's ἐπὶ πορφυρέαις παρῇσι, on the principle, οὐ κάρτα δεῖ τὸ καλὸν τῷ μὴ καλῷ φαινομένῳ εἰκάζειν,—and Sophocles makes a lively defence of it. Shaksp. uses 'bloody' for 'blood-red': *Hen. V.* 1. 2. 101 *unwind your bloody flag.*—**ῥέθος** = πρόσωπον, as Eur. *H. F.* 1203 πάρες ἀπ'

ὀμμάτων | πέπλον, ἀπόδικε, ῥέθος ἀελίῳ δεῖξον. Cp. Eustathius 1090, 27 ἰστέον ὅτι ῥέθεα οἱ μὲν ἄλλοι τὰ μέλη φασίν, Αἰολεῖς δὲ μόνοι, κατὰ τοὺς παλαιούς, τὸ πρόσωπον ῥέθος καλοῦσιν. This suggests that the Attic dramatists had lyric precedent for this use of ῥέθος: as Lycophron (173) may also have had for using it as = σῶμα. The Homeric use is confined to the phrase ἐκ ῥεθέων (thrice in *Il.*, never in *Od.*).—**αἰσχύνει**, *i.e.* overcasts its sunny beauty: cp. Thomson, *Spring* 21, *Winter ...bids his driving sleets* Deform the day delightless.

531 σὺ δ' with φέρ', εἰπέ (534).— ὑφειμένη, *submissa*, 'lurking,' as a viper lurks under stones: Arist. *H. A.* 8. 15 αἱ δ' ἔχιδναι ὑπὸ τὰς πέτρας ἀποκρύπτουσιν ἑαυτάς. Eur. *H. F.* 72 σῴζω νεοσσοὺς ὄρνις ὣς ὑφειμένη, like a cowering hen (ὑφειμένους Kirchhoff). The word may also suggest a contrast between Antigone's bolder nature and the submissive demeanour of Ismene (cp. *El.* 335 νῦν δ' ἐν κακοῖς μοι πλεῖν ὑφειμένη δοκεῖ, 'with shortened sail'). But we should not render it by 'submissive'; its primary reference is to the image of the ἔχιδνα. Others render, 'having crept in,' *clam immissa*. The act. can mean to 'send in secretly' (see on ὑφείς, *O. T.* 387), but the pass. ὑφίεσθαι does not seem to occur in a corresponding sense.—**ἔχιδνα**: cp. *Tr.* 770 (the poison works) φονίας | ἐχθρᾶς ἐχίδνης ἰὸς ὥς. So of Clytaemnestra (Aesch. *Cho.* 249): Eur. *Andr.* 271 ἐχίδνης καὶ πυρὸς περαιτέρω: cp. *Ion* 1262. This image for domestic treachery is quaintly illustrated by the popular notions mentioned in Arist. *Mirab.* 165 (p. 846 b 18 Berl. ed.) τοῦ περκνοῦ ἔχεως τῇ ἐχίδνῃ συγγινομένου,

λήθουσά μ' ἐξέπινες, οὐδ' ἐμάνθανον
τρέφων δύ' ἄτα κἀπαναστάσεις θρόνων,
φέρ', εἰπὲ δή μοι, καὶ σὺ τοῦδε τοῦ τάφου
φήσεις μετασχεῖν, ἢ 'ξομεῖ τὸ μὴ εἰδέναι;   535

ΙΣ. δέδρακα τοὖργον, εἴπερ ἥδ' ὁμορροθεῖ,
καὶ ξυμμετίσχω καὶ φέρω τῆς αἰτίας.

ΑΝ. ἀλλ' οὐκ ἐάσει τοῦτό γ' ἡ δίκη σ', ἐπεὶ
οὔτ' ἠθέλησας οὔτ' ἐγὼ 'κοινωσάμην.

ΙΣ. ἀλλ' ἐν κακοῖς τοῖς σοῖσιν οὐκ αἰσχύνομαι   540
ξύμπλουν ἐμαυτὴν τοῦ πάθους ποιουμένη.

ΑΝ. ὧν τοὖργον, Ἅιδης χοἰ κάτω ξυνίστορες·
λόγοις δ' ἐγὼ φιλοῦσαν οὐ στέργω φίλην.

ΙΣ. μήτοι, κασιγνήτη, μ' ἀτιμάσῃς τὸ μὴ οὐ
θανεῖν τε σὺν σοὶ τὸν θανόντα θ' ἁγνίσαι.   545

ΑΝ. μή μοι θάνῃς σὺ κοινά, μηδ' ἃ μὴ 'θιγες

μένη τῶν ἀνθρώπων ἐκπίνει τὸ αἷμα.—Semitelos conject. φοινία.   **533** ἄτα L, ἄτας r.
535 ἢ ἐξομῆι τό μ' εἰδέναι L. The acc. on τό has been altered from τὸ: the latter
points to the true reading. Cp. 544.   **536** εἰπερ ἥδ' ὁμορροθεῖ] εἴπερ ἥδ'· ὁμορροθῶ

ἡ ἔχιδνα ἐν τῇ συνουσίᾳ τὴν κεφαλὴν ἀπο-
κόπτει. διὰ τοῦτο καὶ τὰ τέκνα, ὥσπερ
τὸν θάνατον τοῦ πατρὸς μετερχόμενα, τὴν
γαστέρα τῆς μητρὸς διαρρήγνυσιν. (Cp.
Shaksp. *Per.* 1. 1. 64 *I am no viper, yet
I feed On mother's flesh*.)

532 λήθουσά μ' ἐξέπινες. It seems
unnecessary to suppose a confusion of
images. The venom from the echidna's
bite is here described as working insidi-
ously, and, at first, almost insensibly.
So Heracles says of the poison, which he
has already (*Tr.* 770) compared to the
echidna's, ἐκ δὲ χλωρὸν αἷμά μου | πέπω-
κεν ἤδη, *Tr.* 1055. Cp. *El.* 784 ἥδε γὰρ
μείζων βλάβη | ξύνοικος ἦν μοι, τοὐμὸν
ἐκπίνουσ' ἀεὶ | ψυχῆς ἄκρατον αἷμα.

533 ἄτα κἀπαναστάσεις. The dual is
commended, as against ἄτας, by a certain
scornful vigour; just as at 58 the dual has
an emphasis of its own. And the combination with a plural is no harsher than
(*e.g.*) Plat. *Laches* p. 187 A αὐτοὶ εὑρεταὶ
γεγονότε. Cp. *O. C.* 530 αὗται δὲ δύ' ἐξ
ἐμοῦ...παῖδε, δύο δ' ἄτα.—**ἐπαναστάσεις**,
abstract (like ἄτα) for concrete: so 646
πόνους (bad sons): κεῖνος ἡ πᾶσα βλάβη
(*Ph.* 622), ὄλεθρος, etc. **θρόνων**, object.
gen. (ἐπανίστασθαι θρόνοις). Creon suspects the sisters of being in league with

malcontent citizens (cp. 289), who wish
to overthrow his rule.
535 τὸ μή: cp. 443. [Dem.] or. 57
§ 59 οὐκ ἂν ἐξομόσαιτο μὴ οὐκ εἰδέναι. Plat.
Legg. 949 A ἐξαρνηθέντι καὶ ἐξομοσαμένῳ.
536 f. ὁμορροθεῖ, concurs, consents:
fr. 446 ὁμορροθῶ, συνθέλω, | συμπαραινέσας
ἔχω. Schol. *ad* Ar. *Av.* 851 ὁμορροθεῖν
δὲ κυρίως τὸ ἅμα καὶ συμφώνως ἐρέσσειν.
So *Orphic Argonaut.* 254 ὁμορροθέοντες,
'rowing all together' (cp. above on 259).
The image thus agrees with ξύμπλουν
in 541. Ismene remembers her sister's
words: 'even if you should change your
mind, I could never welcome you now as
my fellow-worker' (69). She says, then,
'I consider myself as having shared in
the deed—if my sister will allow me.'
Nauck sadly defaces the passage by his
rash change, εἴπερ ἥδ'· ὁμορροθῶ.
537 τῆς αἰτίας depends on both verbs.
ξυμμετίσχω having prepared the ear for
a partitive gen., no harshness is felt in
the reference of that gen. to φέρω also.
We cannot take the gen. with the first
verb only, and regard καὶ φέρω as parenthetic. Some real instances of such a
parenthetic construction are given in the
n. on 1279 f.; but the supposed examples
often break down on scrutiny. Thus in

wast secretly draining my life-blood, while I knew not that
I was nurturing two pests, to rise against my throne—come,
tell me now, wilt thou also confess thy part in this burial, or
wilt thou forswear all knowledge of it?

Is. I have done the deed,—if she allows my claim,—and
share the burden of the charge.

An. Nay, justice will not suffer thee to do that: thou didst
not consent to the deed, nor did I give thee part in it.

Is. But, now that ills beset thee, I am not ashamed to sail
the sea of trouble at thy side.

An. Whose was the deed, Hades and the dead are witnesses:
a friend in words is not the friend that I love.

Is. Nay, sister, reject me not, but let me die with thee, and
duly honour the dead.

An. Share not thou my death, nor claim deeds to which

Nauck. **538** σ' added in L by S. **539** 'κοινωσάμην] κοινωσάμην L.
Cp. 457, 546. **541** ποιουμένην L, but a line has been drawn across the final ν.
544 τὸ μ' οὐ L, with η above μ from the first hand. Cp. 535. **546** μηδ'] μὴ

Ai. 274, ἔληξε κἀνέπνευσε τῆς νόσου, the
gen. goes with both verbs (cp. on *O. C.*
1113): for *O. C.* 1330, see n. there: in
Aesch. *P. V.* 331 πάντων μετασχὼν καὶ
τετολμηκὼς ἐμοί, the pron. might be dat.
of interest with the second partic.; but
we ought perhaps to read συντετολμηκώς
τ' ἐμοί.

538 f. ἀλλ' οὐκ ἐάσει σ': cp. *O. C.* 407
ἀλλ' οὐκ ἐᾷ τοὐμφύλον αἷμά σ', ὦ πάτερ.—
'κοινωσάμην: prodelision of the augment,
as 457 (n.): cp. *O. C.* 1602 ταχεῖ 'πόρευ-
σαν σὺν χρόνῳ.

541 ξύμπλουν: cp. Eur. *H. F.* 1225
καὶ τῶν καλῶν μὲν ὅστις ἀπολαύειν θέλει, |
συμπλεῖν δὲ τοῖς φίλοισι δυστυχοῦσιν οὔ.
I. T. 599 ὁ ναυστολῶν γάρ εἰμ' ἐγὼ τὰς
συμφοράς, | οὗτος δὲ συμπλεῖ.

542 f. Cp. *Ph.* 1293 ὡς θεοὶ ξυνί-
στορες.—**λόγοις**, and not ἔργοις. Cp. *Ph.*
307 λόγοις | ἐλεοῦσ·, they show compassion
in word (only). Theognis 979 μή μοι
ἀνὴρ εἴη γλώσσῃ φίλος ἀλλὰ καὶ ἔργῳ.

542 f. μή μ' ἀτιμάσῃς, do not reject
me (the word used by the suppliant Oed.,
O. C. 49, 286), **τὸ μὴ οὐ** (cp. 443 n.), so as
to hinder me from dying with thee, and
paying due honour to the dead. **ἁγνίσαι
τὸν θ.** is to make him ἁγνός, *i.e.* to give
him the rites which religion requires; as,
conversely, a corpse which is ἄμοιρος and
ἀκτέριστος is also ἀνόσιος (1071). Eur.
Suppl. 1211 ὑφ' αὐτῶν σώμαθ' ἡγνίσθη πυρί,
where their corpses *received the rites* of

fire, *i.e.* were burned. Cp. 196 n. If
Ismene shares in the penalty of the deed,
she will share in the merit.

546 μή μοι, not μή 'μοι, since the main
emphasis is on the verbal notion ('*share*
not my death,' rather than, 'share not *my*
death'): cp. 83 n. The combination μή
μοι...σὺ has a scornful, repellent tone (cp.
O. C. 1441 n.). **κοινά**, adv.: cp. *Ai.* 577:
O. T. 883 ὑπέροπτα (n.).—**μηδ' ἃ μὴ
'θιγες**. If this were an instance of θιγγάνω with acc., it would be a solitary
instance in Soph., who has θιγγάνω with
genitive in nine passages; in *Ph.* 667
παρέσται ταῦτά σοι καὶ θιγγάνειν, ταῦτα is
nom. The acc. with θιγγάνω is very rare in
classical Greek; cp. Alcman, *fr.* 38 ἅ μή
μοι θίγης. In Eur. *H. F.* 963, πατὴρ δέ
νιν | θιγὼν κραταιᾶς χειρὸς ἐννέπει τάδε, νιν
depends on ἐννέπει: cp. *Ai.* 764 ὁ μὲν γὰρ
αὐτὸν ἐννέπει· τέκνον, etc. In Theocr. 1.
59 οὐδέ τί πα ποτὶ χείλος ἐμὸν θίγεν, the
gen. αὐτοῦ is understood with προσέθιγεν,
and τι is adv., 'at all.' Nor does ψαύω
govern an acc. below in 859, 961 (where
see notes). Krüger (11. § 47. 12. 2) treats
ἅ here as a sort of adverb (*ib.* 11. § 46. 6. 9),
i.e., *in a case where* you did not put your
hand (to the deed, *sc.* τοῦ ἔργου); but this
is very awkward. Rather, I think, there
is an unusual kind of attraction, due to
the special form of the sentence. We
could not say (*e.g.*) ἃ μὴ ἐρᾷ τις, οὐ θηρᾶται,
(ἅ for ταῦτα ὧν). But here μηδ' ὧν μὴ

ποιοῦ σεαυτῆς· ἀρκέσω θνήσκουσ' ἐγώ.

ΙΣ. καὶ τίς βίος μοι σοῦ λελειμμένη φίλος;

ΑΝ. Κρέοντ' ἐρώτα· τοῦδε γὰρ σὺ κηδεμών.

ΙΣ. τί ταῦτ' ἀνιᾷς μ', οὐδὲν ὠφελουμένη;   550

ΑΝ. ἀλγοῦσα μὲν δῆτ', εἰ *γελῶ γ', ἐν σοὶ γελῶ.

ΙΣ. τί δῆτ' ἂν ἀλλὰ νῦν σ' ἔτ' ὠφελοῖμ' ἐγώ;

ΑΝ. σῶσον σεαυτήν· οὐ φθονῶ σ' ὑπεκφυγεῖν.

ΙΣ. οἴμοι τάλαινα, κἀμπλάκω τοῦ σοῦ μόρου;

ΑΝ. σὺ μὲν γὰρ εἵλου ζῆν, ἐγὼ δὲ κατθανεῖν.   555

ΙΣ. ἀλλ' οὐκ ἐπ' ἀρρήτοις γε τοῖς ἐμοῖς λόγοις.

ΑΝ. καλῶς σὺ μὲν τοῖς, τοῖς δ' ἐγὼ 'δόκουν φρονεῖν.

ΙΣ. καὶ μὴν ἴση νῷν ἐστιν ἡ 'ξαμαρτία.

ΑΝ. θάρσει· σὺ μὲν ζῇς, ἡ δ' ἐμὴ ψυχὴ πάλαι
τέθνηκεν, ὥστε τοῖς θανοῦσιν ὠφελεῖν.   560

δ' L.—'θιγες] θίγεσ L. Cp. 457, 539.   **547** θνήσκουσ' L. For the ι subscript. see comment on *O. T.* 118.   **548** φίλος has been suspected. Wecklein conject. μόνη: Hense, μένει: M. Schmidt, δίχα: Nauck, σοῦ γ' ἄτερ λελειμμένη.   **551** δῆτ', εἰ MSS. Dindorf conject. δή, κεῖ: Wolff, δή, τὸν.—γελῶ γ'] γελῶτ' L. Heath conject. γελῶ γ'.   **552** σετ' L (without acc.): σ' ἔτ' ι (σ' ἐπ' E).   **557** καλῶς σὺ μὲν τοι...τοῖσδ' L. The τ of τοι is in an erasure, which appears to show that τοι has not been made from τοῖσ. Dübner thinks that the first hand wrote μὲν γ' οὐ:

<hr />

'θιγες ποιοῦ σεαυτῆς would have been intolerable, on account of the second gen. after ποιοῦ. For the sake of compactness, and of clearly marking the object to ποιοῦ, the poet has here allowed ἄ to stand for ταῦτα ὧν. I do not compare *O. C.* 1106, αἰτεῖς ἅ τεύξει, holding that ἄ there = ταῦτα ἅ (not ὧν): see n.

547 ποιοῦ σεαυτῆς, a somewhat rare phrase. Her. 1. 129 ἑωυτοῦ ποιέεται τὸ Κύρου ἔργον. [Plat.] *Hipp. min.* 372 C ἐμαυτοῦ ποιούμενος τὸ μάθημα εἶναι ὡς εὔρημα. Dem. or. 19 § 36 εἰς αὑτὸν ποιούμενος (taking on himself) τὰ τούτων ἁμαρτήματα. In Thuc. 8. 9 ἑαυτοῦ...τὸν στόλον ἴδιον ποιήσασθαι, the gen. goes with the adj.—ἀρκέσω in the pers. constr., cp. *Ai.* 76 ἔνδον ἀρκείτω μένων, and *O. T.* 1061 n.

548 σοῦ λελειμμένη, bereft of thee. λείπομαί τινος, to lag behind, then, fig., to be deprived of, as *El.* 474 γνώμας λειπομένα, Eur. *Alc.* 406 νέος ἐγώ, πάτερ, λείπομαι φίλας | ...ματρός.—φίλος has been groundlessly suspected, for no other reason, seemingly, than because it is masc.

549 κηδεμών, alluding esp. to v. 47.

Cp. Xen. *Anab.* 3. 1. 17 ἡμᾶς δέ, οἷς κηδεμών...οὐδεὶς πάρεστιν, who would have no one *to plead our cause* (no 'friend at court,' such as the younger Cyrus had in his mother Parysatis). In *Π.* 23. 163 κηδεμόνες are the chief mourners for the dead. In Attic, though sometimes poet. for κηδεστής, the word did not necessarily imply kinship.

551 ἀλγοῦσα μὲν δῆτ', yes, indeed, it is to my own pain that I mock *thee*,—if I do mock. δῆτα assents (*O. T.* 445 n.) to οὐδὲν ὠφελουμένη: there is, indeed, no ὄφελος in it, but only ἄλγος.—ἐν σοί: cp. *Ai.* 1092 ἐν θανοῦσιν ὑβριστής, ib. 1315 ἐν ἐμοὶ θρασύς.—Heath's εἰ γελῶ γ', for εἰ γέλωτ', is supported by the accent γελῶτ' in L, and seems right. It smooths the construction; and εἰ γελῶ γ' better expresses that the taunt sprang from anguish, not from a wish to pain. Then γέλωτα γελῶ, without an epithet for the subst., is unusual.—Cp. *Ai.* 79 οὔκουν γέλως ἥδιστος εἰς ἐχθροὺς γελᾶν;

552 ἀλλὰ νῦν, *now*, at least: *O. C.* 1276 ἀλλ' ὑμεῖς γε, n.

554 κἀμπλάκω, and am I to miss the

thou hast not put thy hand: my death will suffice.

IS. And what life is dear to me, bereft of thee?

AN. Ask Creon; all thy care is for him.

IS. Why vex me thus, when it avails thee nought?

AN. Indeed, if I mock, 'tis with pain that I mock thee.

IS. Tell me,—how can I serve thee, even now?

AN. Save thyself: I grudge not thy escape.

IS. Ah, woe is me! And shall I have no share in thy fate?

AN. Thy choice was to live; mine, to die.

IS. At least thy choice was not made without my protest.

AN. One world approved thy wisdom; another, mine.

IS. Howbeit, the offence is the same for both of us.

AN. Be of good cheer; thou livest; but my life hath long been given to death, that so I might serve the dead.

---

but it seems equally possible that it was μέν σοι. There is no trace of erasure at the two dots after τοι. Of the later MSS., A and V³ have μὲν τοῖσ: others, μὲν θοῦ, μέν θ᾽ οὗ, or μέν τ᾽ οἴου: but none (I believe) μέντοι or μὲν σοί. The schol. in L has μέντοι in the lemma, but explains, σεαυτῇ καλῶς ἐδόκεις φρονεῖν, μὴ συμπράτ-τουσά μοι· ἐγὼ δὲ τούτοις κ.τ.λ. Hence Martin, καλῶς σὺ μὲν σοί. **560 ὥστε]** Wieseler conject. ὥς σε: Dobree, with the same view, proposed ὠφελεῖς ('and so you are helping a sister who is already as the dead': cp. 552).

---

fate? i.e. to be dissociated from it: delib. aor. subj., which can be used, not only in asking what one is to do, but also in expressions of despair as to what one must suffer (Tr. 973 τί πάθω;). For ἀμπλακεῖν cp. 910, 1234.

555 εἵλου, alluding to v. 78 f.—ζῆν: for the emphatic pause, cp. Ph. 907 οὔκουν ἐν οἷς γε δρᾷς· ἐν οἷς δ᾽ αὐδᾷς, ὀκνῶ.

556 ἐπ᾽ ἀρρήτοις...τοῖς ἐμ. λ. (but you did not choose death) without my words (my arguments against that course) having been spoken,—referring to vv. 49—68. For ἐπί with the negative verbal (= πρὶν τοὺς ἐμοὺς λόγους ῥηθῆναι) cp. Eur. Ion 228 ἐπὶ δ᾽ ἀσφάκτοις | μήλοισι δόμων μὴ πάριτ᾽ ἐς μυχόν ('before sheep have been slain, pass not,' etc.).

557 σὺ μὲν τοῖς: 'you seemed wise to the one side (Creon); I, to the other' (to Hades and the dead). Nauck pronounces the text unsound, objecting to the use of τοῖς: but that it was good Attic is sufficiently shown by Plat. Legg. 701 E (cited by Wolff) οὐ συνήνεγκεν οὔτε τοῖς οὔτε τοῖς (it profited neither party). Cp. O. C. 742, n. on ἐκ δὲ τῶν.—σὺ μὲν σοί, the schol.'s reading, is very inferior.—For the rhetorical χιασμός cp. O. T. 538 n. (and ib. 320).

558 καὶ μήν, and yet,—though I did shrink from breaking Creon's law,—I am now, morally, as great an offender as you, since I sympathise with your act.

559 f. θάρσει is not said with bitterness (that could hardly be, after 551): rather it means, 'Take heart to live,' as Whitelaw renders it. These two verses quietly express her feeling that their lots are irrevocably sundered, and exhort Ismene to accept the severance.—ἡ ἐμὴ ψυχή, my life, a periphrasis for ἐγώ, like O. C. 998 τὴν πατρὸς | ψυχήν...ζῶσαν (n.). —πάλαι, i.e. ever since she resolved to break the edict. (Cp. O. T. 1161.)—ὥστε τοῖς θ. ὠφελεῖν, so as to (with a view to) serving the dead. The dat., as with ἐπαρ-κεῖν: Ph. 871 ξυνωφελοῦντά μοι: Aesch. Pers. 842 ὡς τοῖς θανοῦσι πλοῦτος οὐδὲν ὠφελεῖ: Eur. Or. 665 τοῖς φίλοισιν ὠφε-λεῖν: Ar. Av. 419 φίλοισιν ὠφελεῖν ἔχειν. So ἐπωφελεῖν O. C. 441.—Dobree proposed to understand σε as subj. to the inf., 'so that (you) are helping the dead,' —i.e., your offer of help (552) is made to one who is already as good as dead. But σέ could not be thus understood; and this sense (which it has been sought to obtain by emendations, see cr. n.) would be frigid.

ΚΡ. τὼ παῖδε φημὶ τώδε τὴν μὲν ἀρτίως
    ἄνουν πεφάνθαι, τὴν δ' ἀφ' οὗ τὰ πρῶτ' ἔφυ.

ΙΣ. οὐ γάρ ποτ', ὦναξ, οὐδ' ὃς ἂν βλάστῃ μένει
    νοῦς τοῖς κακῶς πράσσουσιν, ἀλλ' ἐξίσταται.

ΚΡ. σοὶ γοῦν, ὅθ' εἵλου σὺν κακοῖς πράσσειν κακά.   565

ΙΣ. τί γὰρ μόνῃ μοι τῆσδ' ἄτερ βιώσιμον;

ΚΡ. ἀλλ' ἥδε μέντοι μὴ λέγ'· οὐ γὰρ ἔστ' ἔτι.

ΙΣ. ἀλλὰ κτενεῖς νυμφεῖα τοῦ σαυτοῦ τέκνου;

ΚΡ. ἀρώσιμοι γὰρ χἀτέρων εἰσὶν γύαι.

ΙΣ. οὐχ ὥς γ' ἐκείνῳ τῇδέ τ' ἦν ἡρμοσμένα.   570

ΚΡ. κακὰς ἐγὼ γυναῖκας υἱέσι στυγῶ.

---

563 οὐ γάρ ποτ'] ἀλλ' οὐ γὰρ Plutarch *Phoc.* 1, and *Mor.* 460 E. The grammarian Gregorius Corinthius (*c.* 1150 A.D.) p. 417 has ἀλλὰ γάρ. **564** πράσσουσιν] πράξασιν Plut. *Mor.* 460 E. πράττουσιν Gregorius *l.c.* **565** σοὶ γοῦν] καὶ has been deleted before σοὶ in L.—κακοῖς] L has ·ῃ· written above by S. Some of the later MSS. have κακῇ or (as A) κακῷ. **567** μέν σοι L, and so nearly all the later MSS.;

---

561 L gives τὼ παῖδε φημὶ as in *O. C.* 317 καὶ φημὶ, and this may probably be taken as the traditional accentuation, though some modern edd. write τὼ παῖδέ φημι, καί φημι. The justification of the oxytone φημὶ is in the emphasis which falls on it. Similarly it has the accent when parenthetic, as Lucian *Deor. Conc.* 2 πολλοὶ γάρ, φημί, οὐκ ἀγαπῶντες κ.τ.λ. —τὼ παῖδε...τὴν μὲν...τὴν δέ, partitive apposition: see on 21.—ἀρτίως, because Creon had hitherto regarded Ismene as being of a docile and submissive nature: cp. on 531 ὑφειμένη.

563 f. The apology is for her sister as well as for herself: even such prudence (cp. 68 νοῦν) as may have been inborn forsakes the unfortunate under the stress of their misfortunes.—βλάστῃ: cp. *El.* 238 ἐν τίνι τοῦτ' ἔβλαστ' ἀνθρώπων; *O. C.* 804 φύσας...φρένας (n.).—τοῖς κ. πράσσουσιν, dat. of interest: *Tr.* 132 μένει γὰρ οὔτ' αἰόλα νὺξ | βροτοῖσιν.—ἐξίσταται, stands aside, gives place (*Ai.* 672); and so, leaves its proper place, becomes deranged: cp. Eur. *Bacch.* 928 ἀλλ' ἐξ ἕδρας σοι πλόκαμος ἐξέστηχ' ὅδε. The converse phrase is commoner, ἐξίσταμαι τῶν φρενῶν: cp. 1105.—Schneidewin cp. Eur. *Antigone* fr. 165 ἄκουσον· οὐ γὰρ οἱ κακῶς πεπραγότες | σὺν ταῖς τύχαισι τοὺς λόγους ἀπώλεσαν,—which plainly glances at our passage. For similar allusions cp. *O. C.* 1116 n.

565 σοὶ γοῦν (cp. 45 n.) *sc.* ἐξέστη.—κακοῖς, *i.e.* Antigone: for the plur., cp. 10.

566 τῆσδ' ἄτερ explains μόνῃ: cp. on 445.—βιώσιμον is Ionic and poet.; the Attic word was βιωτός. It is needless to change τί (subst.) into πῶς. The more usual phrase was, indeed, impers., as Her. 1. 45 οὐδέ οἱ εἴη βιώσιμον: Plat. *Crito* 47 D ἆρα βιωτὸν ἡμῖν ἐστί; But, just as we can have ὁ βίος οὐ βιωτός ἐστι (cp. *O. C.* 1691), so also οὐδὲν βιωτόν ἐστι, no form of life is tolerable. Cp. *O. T.* 1337 τί δῆτ' ἐμοὶ βλεπτόν, ἢ | στερκτόν, ἢ προσήγορον | ἔτ' ἔστ', etc., where the only difference is that the subst. τί corresponds to an object. accus., and not as here to a cognate (βίον βιῶναι).

567 ἀλλά...μέντοι, 'nay, but...': cp. *Ph.* 524 ἀλλ' αἰσχρὰ μέντοι σοῦ γέ μ' ἐνδεέστερον | ξένῳ φανῆναι.—ἥδε μὴ λέγε, say 'not 'ἥδε,' speak not of her as still with thee, for she is already numbered with the dead. οἵδε are οἱ ἐνθάδε, the living (75), as κεῖνοι (525) are οἱ ἐκεῖ, the dead (cp. 76). The peculiarity is that we should have expected either (*a*) τήνδε, acc. to λέγε, or (*b*) τῆσδε, as a direct quotation from the last verse: cp. Dem. or. 18 § 88 τίς ἦν...; ὑμεῖς, ὦ ἄνδρες Ἀθηναῖοι. τὸ δ' ὑμεῖς ὅταν λέγω, λέγω τὴν πόλιν. If (*e.g.*) ὑμῶν had preceded ω ἄνδρες, Dem. would doubtless have said τὸ δ' ὑμῶν, or else ὑμᾶς δ'. Here.

CR. Lo, one of these maidens hath newly shown herself foolish, as the other hath been since her life began.

IS. Yea, O King, such reason as nature may have given abides not with the unfortunate, but goes astray.

CR. Thine did, when thou chosest vile deeds with the vile.

IS. What life could I endure, without her presence?

CR. Nay, speak not of her 'presence'; she lives no more.

IS. But wilt thou slay the betrothed of thine own son?

CR. Nay, there are other fields for him to plough.

IS. But there can never be such love as bound him to her.

CR. I like not an evil wife for my son.

---

but E has μέν τοι σοί: Brunck replaced μέντοι.   **568** ἀλλὰ κτενεῖς MSS. Nauck writes οὐ μὴ κτενεῖς.—νυμφια (without acc.) L: νυμφεῖα r.   **569** ἀρώσιμοι] In L an early hand has written ο above ω.—χἀτέρων εἰσὶν MSS.: Dindorf, εἰσὶ χἀτέρων. Nauck arranges vv. 569—574 as follows, bracketing 570 and 573 as spurious:— 569, 572, 571, 574; giving 572 and 574 to Ismene (with L).   **571** υἱάσιν L:

---

however, no fair objection would remain if we had ἀλλὰ τὸ ἥδε μὴ λέγε, *i.e.* 'never use the word ἥδε about her,'—which makes the sense more general than if he said, ἀλλὰ τῆσδε μὴ λέγε, *i.e.* 'do not say (that you cannot live without) ἥδε.' The question, then, seems to resolve itself into this:—Wishing to give the more general sense just indicated, could the poet say ἥδε instead of τὸ ἥδε? To show that the art. was not always required in such quotation, it is enough to cite Ar. *Eq.* 21 λέγε δὴ μόλωμεν, by the side of τὸ μόλωμεν *ib.* 26. While, then, I cannot produce any exact parallel for this ἥδε, I think it reasonable to suppose that colloquial idiom would have allowed it. Those who deny this have two resources. (1) To point thus: ἀλλ' ἥδε μέντοι—μὴ λέγ'· *i.e.* instead of adding οὐκ ἔστιν ἔτι after μέντοι, he breaks off his sentence—'do not speak of her.' So Bellermann. (2) Semitelos reads ἀλλ' ἥδε μέν σοι μὴ λέγ' ὡς ἄρ' [for οὐ γὰρ] ἔστ' ἔτι, 'do not say that you have *her* any longer.' As to σοι, see cr. n. above. Neither of these readings gives such a forcible sense as the vulgate.

568 νυμφεῖα, *sc.* ἱερά, 'nuptials,' as *Tr.* 7 (but *ib.* 920 'bridal-chamber,' as in sing. below, 1205); here = νύμφην. Cp. Eur. *El.* 481 σὰ λέχεα, thy spouse: and so εὐνή, etc.—Having failed to win Creon's pity for herself, Ismene now appeals to his feeling for his son. Haemon's coming part in the play is thus prepared.

569 ἀρώσιμοι, a poet. form (only here), analogous to the epic forms of adjectives

in which a short vowel is lengthened for metre's sake (cp. on 492). Though the verb was ἀρόω, the adj. with the suffix σιμο would properly be formed from the subst. ἄροσις (cp. *O. C.* 27 n.). Suidas gives ἀρόσιμον κλίμα· τὸ ἀροτριούμενον. For the metaphor cp. *O. T.* 1256 μητρῴαν ...ἄρουραν, and *ib.* 1485, 1497: Lucr. 4. 1107.

570 οὐχ ὥς γ' ('Another marriage is possible for him'). 'No, not in the sense of the troth plighted between him and her,'—not such a union of hearts as had been prepared there. ἡρμοσμένα ἦν, impers., lit., 'as things had been adjusted'; cp. on 447: Her. 1. 112 ἡμῖν κακῶς βεβουλευμένα ἔσται: id. 6. 83 τέως μὲν δή σφι ἦν ἄρθμια ἐς ἀλλήλους. The choice of the word has been influenced by the Ionic and poet. use of ἁρμόζειν as = to betroth (ἐγγυᾶν): Her. 3. 137 ἅρμοσται (perf. pass. as midd.) τὴν Μίλωνος θυγατέρα...γυναῖκα, he has become engaged to her: Pind. *P.* 9. 127 ἁρμόζων κόρᾳ | νυμφίον ἄνδρα. Cp. 2 Epist. Cor. 11. 2 ἡρμοσάμην γὰρ ὑμᾶς ἑνὶ ἀνδρὶ παρθένον ἁγνήν.

571 υἱέσι, the regular Attic dat. plur. (as Plat. *Rep.* 362 E, Ar. *Nub.* 1001, etc.), from the stem υἱυ-, which furnished also the Attic nom. and gen. plur., υἱεῖς; and the dual υἱῆ (or rather υἱεῖ, Meisterhans p. 63), υἱέοιν. The Attic forms of the sing. and the acc. plur. were taken from υἱο-, except that υἱέος, υἱεῖ were alternative forms for the gen. and dat. sing. Here L has the epic υἱάσιν, from a third stem, υἱ-, whence the Homeric forms υἷος, υἷι,

*ΑΝ. ὦ φίλταθ᾽ Αἷμον, ὥς σ᾽ ἀτιμάζει πατήρ.
ΚΡ. ἄγαν γε λυπεῖς καὶ σὺ καὶ τὸ σὸν λέχος.
*ΧΟ. ἦ γὰρ στερήσεις τῆσδε τὸν σαυτοῦ γόνον;
ΚΡ. Ἅιδης ὁ παύσων τούσδε τοὺς γάμους ἐμοί.   575
ΧΟ. δεδογμέν᾽, ὡς ἔοικε, τήνδε κατθανεῖν.
ΚΡ. καὶ σοί γε κἀμοί. μὴ τριβὰς ἔτ᾽, ἀλλά νιν
    κομίζετ᾽ εἴσω, δμῶες· ἐκ δὲ τοῦδε χρὴ
    γυναῖκας εἶναι τάσδε μηδ᾽ ἀνειμένας.
    φεύγουσι γάρ τοι χοὶ θρασεῖς, ὅταν πέλας   580
    ἤδη τὸν Ἅιδην εἰσορῶσι τοῦ βίου.

υἷσι r.   **572** The MSS. give this v. to Ismene.   The Aldine ed. (1502) and
that of Turnebus (1553) first gave it to Antigone; and so Boeckh.—αἷμων L.
αἷμον r.   **574** The MSS. give this verse to Ismene; Boeckh, to the Chorus.
575 ἐμοί L: ἔφυ r (including A). κυρεῖ is Meineke's conject.; μόνος Nauck's, who
also changes παύσων to λύσων.   **576** L gives this verse to the Chorus (not to
Ismene, as has sometimes been stated).   The later MSS. are divided; most of them
give it to Ismene.—ἔοικε] ἔοικεν L. Cp. 402.   **577** καὶ σοί γε κἀμοί] F. Kern

---

υἷα, υἷε, υἷες, υἷας: cp. Monro *Hom. Gr.*
§ 107.—The dat. of interest goes with
κακὰς γυναῖκας, not with **στυγῶ**: cp. Ar.
Nub. 1161 πρόβολος ἐμός, σωτὴρ δόμοις,
ἐχθροῖς βλάβη.

572 It is not of much moment that L,
like the later MSS., gives this verse to Ismene. Errors as to the persons occur not
seldom in L (see, *e.g.*, cr. n. to *O. C.*
837, and cp. *ib.* 1737); and here a mistake would have been peculiarly easy, as
the dialogue from v. 561 onwards has
been between Creon and Ismene. To me
it seems certain that the verse is Antigone's, and that one of the finest touches in
the play is effaced by giving it to Ismene.
The taunt, κακὰς γυναῖκας υἷέσι, moves
Antigone to break the silence which she
has kept since v. 560: in all this scene she
has not spoken to Creon, nor does she
now address him: she is thinking of Haemon,—of the dishonour to *him* implied in
the charge of having made such a choice,
—ὡς αἰεὶ τὸν ὁμοῖον ἄγει θεὸς ὡς τὸν ὁμοῖον.
How little does his father know the heart
which was in sympathy with her own. This
solitary reference to her love heightens in
a wonderful degree our sense of her unself-
ish devotion to a sacred duty. If Ismene
speaks this verse, then τὸ σὸν λέχος in 573
must be, 'the marriage of which you talk'
(like *El.* 1110 οὐκ οἶδα τὴν σὴν κληδόν'),
which certainly is not its natural sense.—
Αἷμον. L has αἷμων. Soph. would have

written AIMON : hence the tradition is
subject to the same ambiguity as in
ΚΡΕΟΝ. The analogy of δαῖμον would
probably have recommended the form
in o.

573 ἄγαν γε λυπεῖς, 'Nay, thou art
too troublesome,'—the impatient phrase
of one who would silence another, as *Ai.*
589 (Ajax to Tecmessa) ἄγαν γε λυπεῖς· οὐ
κάτοισθ᾽, etc.: so *ib.* 592 πόλλ᾽ ἄγαν ἤδη
θροεῖς.

574 The MSS. give this verse to
Ismene; but Boeckh is clearly right in
giving it to the Chorus. Ismene asked
this question in 568, and Creon answered:
she rejoined to this answer (570), and
Creon replied still more bitterly. She
could not now ask her former question
over again. But there is no unfitness in
the question being repeated by a new
intercessor, since to ask it thus is a form
of mild remonstrance.

575 ἐμοί, L's reading, is right. Creon
has been asked,—'Can you indeed mean
to deprive your son of his bride?' He
grimly replies, 'I look to the Death-god
to break off this match.' The ἔφυ in the
later MSS. was obviously a mere conjecture,—and a weak one.

576 This verse clearly belongs to the
Chorus, to whom L assigns it. The first
words of the next verse show this. Hermann objected that in similar situations
the Chorus usually has two verses. It is

AN. Haemon, beloved! How thy father wrongs thee!
CR. Enough, enough of thee and of thy marriage!
CH. Wilt thou indeed rob thy son of this maiden?
CR. 'Tis Death that shall stay these bridals for me.
CH. 'Tis determined, it seems, that she shall die.
CR. Determined, yes, for thee and for me.—(*To the two Attendants.*) No more delay—servants, take them within! Henceforth they must be women, and not range at large; for verily even the bold seek to fly, when they see Death now closing on their life.

[*Exeunt Attendants, guarding* ANTIGONE *and* ISMENE.— CREON *remains.*

conject. καὶ σοί γε κοινῇ.   **578** ἐκ δὲ τοῦδε χρὴ L. The τοῦδε has been made from τασδε: whether the latter was originally τάσδε or τᾶσδε, or accentless, is doubtful, but the circumflex has been added by the corrector just over the o, perh. to avoid blotting in the erasure over υ. The correction 8 had been written above before the letters ασ were altered in the text. The lemma of the schol. has ἐκ δὲ τᾶσδε. The later MSS. have ἐκ δὲ τοῦδε.   **579** γυναῖκασ εἶναι τᾶσδε (sic) μηδ' ἀνειμένασ L. So the later MSS., but with τάσδε or τοῦδε (A): which latter shows the same tendency as L's

true that this is usually the case. But *O. T.* 1312 is enough to show that there was no rigid rule; why, indeed, should there be? And, here, surely, πλέον ἥμισυ παντός.—δεδογμένα (ἐστί),=δέδοκται: cp. on 570 ἡρμοσμένα, 447 κηρυχθέντα. Cp. Menander Ἀρρηφόρος 1. 3 δεδογμένον τὸ πρᾶγμ'· ἀνερρίφθω κύβος.

577 καὶ σοί γε κἀμοί, sc. δεδογμένα. It is settled, for both of us: *i.e.,* I shall not change my mind, and it is vain for thee to plead. The datives are ethic. We might also understand, 'settled *by* thee, as by me,'—alluding to the words of the Chorus in v. 211 and in v. 220. But I now feel, with Mr T. Page, that this would be somewhat forced.—We must not point thus: καὶ σοί γε. καί μοι μὴ τρίβας, etc. (so Semitelos). This would be more defensible if, in 576, σοί had stood with δεδογμένα: but, as it is, the vagueness of the latter confirms καὶ σοί γε κἀμοί. Bellermann, giving 576 to Ismene, adopts Kern's καὶ σοί γε κοινῇ ('yes, and she shall die with you').—μὴ τρίβας, sc. ποιεῖσθε: cp. Ar. *Ach.* 345 ἀλλὰ μή μοι πρόφασιν, ἀλλὰ κατάθου τὸ βέλος: *Vesp.* 1179 μή μοί γε μύθους.—νιν, plur., as *O. T.* 868 (masc.), *O. C.* 43 (fem.), *El.* 436 (neut.), etc.

578 f. ἐκ δὲ τοῦδε, κ.τ.λ. Compare 484 ἦ νῦν ἐγὼ μὲν οὐκ ἀνήρ, αὕτη δ' ἀνήρ: 525 ἐμοῦ δὲ ζῶντος οὐκ ἄρξει γυνή: also 678 ff.

This much-vexed passage is sound as it has come down to us. Creon means: 'henceforth they must be *women,* and must not roam unrestrained.' The fact that a woman has successfully defied him rankles in his mind. Hence the bitterness of γυναῖκας here. The Attic notions of feminine propriety forbade such freedom as ἀνειμένας denotes. Cp. *El.* 516 (Clytaemnestra finding Electra outside the house) ἀνειμένη μέν, ὡς ἔοικας, αὖ στρέφει: Electra should be restrained, μή τοι θυραίαν γ' οὖσαν αἰσχύνειν φίλους. So pseudo-Phocyl. 216 (keep a maiden in-doors), μηδέ μιν ἄχρι γάμων πρὸ δόμων ὀφθῆμεν ἐάσῃς. Ar. *Lys.* 16 χαλεπή τοι γυναικῶν ἔξοδος. The emphasis of γυναῖκας here is parallel with the frequent emphasis of ἀνήρ (as Eur. *El.* 693 ἄνδρα γίγνεσθαί σε χρή, a *man*). Cp. *O. C.* 1368 αἴδ' ἄνδρες, οὐ γυναῖκες, εἰς τὸ συμπονεῖν.—All the emendations are weak or improbable. See Appendix.

580 f. χοἱ θρασεῖς. Remark how well the use of the masc. here suits the taunt conveyed in the last verse. πέλας (ὄντα)... εἰσορῶσι: cp. *O. C.* 29 πέλας γὰρ ἄνδρα τόνδε νῷν ὁρῶ: and see *ib.* 586 n.

582—625 Second στάσιμον. 1st strophe, 582—592,=1st antistr., 593—603. 2nd strophe, 604—614,=2nd antistr., 615—625. See Metrical Analysis.

στρ. ά. ΧΟ. εὐδαίμονες οἷσι κακῶν ἄγευστος αἰών.

2 οἷς γὰρ ἂν σεισθῇ θεόθεν δόμος, ἄτας

3 οὐδὲν ἐλλείπει, γενεᾶς ἐπὶ πλῆθος ἕρπον·   585

4 ὅμοιον ὥστε ποντίαις οἶδμα δυσπνόοις ὅταν

5 Θρήσσαισιν ἔρεβος ὕφαλον ἐπιδράμῃ πνοαῖς,

6 κυλίνδει βυσσόθεν κελαινὰν θῖνα, καὶ   590

7 δυσάνεμοι στόνῳ βρέμουσιν ἀντιπλῆγες ἀκταί.

ἀντ. ά.   ἀρχαῖα τὰ Λαβδακιδᾶν οἴκων ὁρῶμαι   593

2 πήματα *φθιτῶν ἐπὶ πήμασι πίπτοντ',   595

τᾶσδε, viz. to make the word the same in both vv.   **585 f.** γενεᾶσ | ἐπι πλῆθοσ (not ἐπιπλῆθοσ) L..—ἕρπον] L has ·ω· written above ο.   **587** ποντίαις] ποντίαισ ἀλὸσ L, the second ι of ποντίαισ having been added by an early hand.   ποντίας ἀλὸς the other MSS. Elmsley deleted ἀλός.   For ποντίαις Schneidewin conject. πόντιον : Dindorf, ποντίαν (with θῖνα).   **589** Θρήσσαισιν] θρηίσσηισιν L (the first ι from a corrector).   Θρήκηθεν Semitelos.   **591 f.** θῖνα καὶ δυσάνεμον | στόνωι βρέμουσι

The sentence of death just passed on Antigone leads the Chorus to reflect on the destiny of her house, and on the power of fate generally.—When a divine curse has once fallen upon a family, thenceforth there is no release for it. Wave after wave of trouble vexes it. Generation after generation suffers. These sisters were the last hope of the race; and now an infatuated act has doomed them also. —What mortal can restrain the power of Zeus? Human self-will and ambition may seem to defy him, but he is drawing them on to their ruin.—Anapaests (626—630) then announce the approach of Haemon.

582 κακῶν ἄγευστος, act., cp. *O. T.* 969 ἀψαυστος ἔγχους n.   Eur. *Alc.* 1069 ὡς ἄρτι πένθους τοῦδε γεύομαι πικροῦ. Her. 7. 46 ὁ...θεὸς γλυκὺν γεύσας τὸν αἰῶνα (having allowed men to taste the sweetness of life).

583 ff. σεισθῇ θεόθεν, *i.e.* by an ἀρά (likened to a storm, or earthquake, that shakes a building): when a sin has once been committed, and the shock of divine punishment has once been felt. In the case of the Labdacidae the calamities were traced to the curse called down on Laïus by Pelops, when robbed by him of his son Chrysippus (*O. T.* p. xix.).—ἄτας οὐδὲν ἐλλείπει, (for these men, οἷς = τούτοις οἷς) no sort of calamity is wanting. Some join ἐλλείπει with ἕρπον, on the analogy of

παύεσθαι with part., 'never fails to go'; but this constr. is at least very rare. In a probably spurious ψήφισμα *ap.* Dem. or. 18 § 92 we have οὐκ ἐλλείψει εὐχαριστῶν : but Xen. *Mem.* 2. 6 § 5 (adduced by Wecklein) is not an example, for there μὴ ἐλλείπεσθαι εὖ ποιῶν = 'not to be outdone in generosity.' Then in Plat. *Phaedr.* 272 B ὅ τι ἂν αὐτῶν τις ἐλλείπῃ λέγων = simply 'omit *in* speaking.'—γενεᾶς ἐπὶ πλῆθος. The phrase is bold, and somewhat strange; but I do not think that it is corrupt.   γενεᾶς here is the whole race, not (as in 596) a generation of the race. The words mean literally, '*over a multitude of the race*'; *i.e.*, the ἄτη does not cease with the person who first brought it into the family, or with his generation, but continues to afflict succeeding generations. The collective noun γενεᾶς justifies the use of πλῆθος: as he might have said, ἀπογόνων πλῆθος.   It is needless, then, to write γενεᾶν. We cannot understand, 'to the fulness of the race,' *i.e.* till the race has been exhausted.

586 ff. ὅμοιον, adv.: Plat. *Legg.* 628 D ὅμοιον ὡς εἰ...ἡγοῖτό τις.—ποντίαις (see cr. n.) is far the most probable reading. The loss of the second ι, leaving ποντίας, wou!d easily have brought in ἀλός, which the metre shows to be superfluous. In Greek poetry there is no objection to the three epithets with πνοαῖς: the whole phrase would be felt as meaning, 'stormy sea-

CH. Blest are they whose days have not tasted of evil. 1st strophe. For when a house hath once been shaken from heaven, there the curse fails nevermore, passing from life to life of the race; even as, when the surge is driven over the darkness of the deep by the fierce breath of Thracian sea-winds, it rolls up the black sand from the depths, and there is a sullen roar from wind-vexed headlands that front the blows of the storm.

I see that from olden time the sorrows in the house of 1st anti-strophe. the Labdacidae are heaped upon the sorrows of the dead;

(the β from τ?) δ' ἀντιπλῆγεσ ἀκταί· L. So the later MSS. (βρέμουσιν for βρέμουσι δ' Vat.). Bergk conject. δυσάνεμοι· Jacobs, δυσανέμῳ. **593 f.** Λαβδακιδᾶν] μ deleted before β in L.—οἴκων] Seyffert conject. δόμων: Wecklein, κλύων or σκοπῶν. —πήματα φθιμένων MSS. For φθιμένων Dindorf conject. φθιτῶν, comparing Eur. Alc. 100, where φθιτῶν has become φθιμένων in some MSS. He also conjectured πῆμά τ' ἄλλ' ἄλλοις, which Wecklein receives. Seyffert, πῆματ' ἐκφύντων.

winds from Thrace.' Construe: ὅταν οἶδμα, when a surge, ποντίαις δυσπν. Θρ. πνοαῖς, driven by stormy sea-winds from Thrace (instr. dat., cp. on 335 νότῳ), ἐπιδράμῃ ἔρεβος ὕφαλον, rushes over the dark depths of the sea (lit., the darkness under the surface of the sea). For δυσπν. πνοαῖς, cp. 502 n.: for Θρήσσαισιν, Aesch. Ag. 192 πνοαὶ δ' ἀπὸ Στρυμόνος μολοῦσαι, ib. 654 Θρῆκιαι πνοαί (and 1418): Il. 9. 5 (where the tumult in the breasts of the Greeks is likened to a storm) Βορέης καὶ Ζέφυρος, τώ τε Θρήκηθεν ἄητον.

590 ff. κελαινὰν θῖνα, the dark-coloured mud or sand that the storm stirs up from the bottom of the sea. θίς is masc. in Homer, Ar., and Arist., and that was prob. its usual gender. Soph. has it fem. again in Ph. 1124, and so it is in later writers. In the Il. θίς is always the sea-shore; in Od. that is its regular sense, but once (12. 45) it means 'heap.' It is used as here by Ar. Vesp. 696 ὥς μου τὸν θῖνα ταράττεις (my very depths). Verg. G. 3. 240 at ima exaestuat unda Vorticibus, nigramque alte subiectat arenam.—δυσάνεμοι should be read. δυσάνεμον could not here be adv. with βρέμουσιν, and must therefore be epithet of θῖνα, when it could mean only τὴν ὑπὸ ἀνέμων ταραχθεῖσαν (schol.), i.e. 'stirred up by the storm,'—a strained sense for it. Cp. Apoll. Rhod. 1. 593 ἀκτήν τ' αἰγιαλόν τε δυσήνεμον.—στόνῳ βρ.: cp. 427.—ἀντιπλῆγες (only here) ἀκταί, headlands which are struck in front, struck full, by the waves; in contrast with παραπλῆγες, 'struck obliquely': see Od. 5. 417 (Odysseus seeking a place to land) ἦν

που ἐφεύρω | ἠϊονάς τε παραπλῆγας λιμένας τε θαλάσσης ('shores where the waves strike aslant'). Soph. was doubtless thinking of the Homeric phrase.—Not (1) 'beating back the waves,' ἀντίτυποι: nor (2) 'beaten again,'—i.e. by the ever-returning waves. This last is impossible. —Cp. O. C. 1240 where Oed. is likened to a βόρειος...ἀκτὰ κυματοπλήξ. Oppian Cyn. 2. 142 κρημνοῖσι καὶ ὑδατοπλήγεσιν ἄκραις.

593 f. ἀρχαῖα, predicate: I see that, from olden time, the house-troubles (οἴκων πήματα) of the (living) Labdacidae are heaped upon the troubles of the dead. The dead are now Laïus, Oedipus, and his two sons. ἀρχαῖα carries us back to the starting-point of the troubles, —the curse pronounced on Laïus by Pelops (cp. on 583).—ὁρῶμαι, midd., as in Homer and Attic Comedy, but not in Attic prose; which, however, used the midd. περιορᾶσθαι (Thuc. 6. 103) and προορᾶσθαι (Dem. or. 18 § 281, etc.). Soph. has ὁρωμένη, midd., Tr. 306 (dial.); and so, too, εἰδόμην Ph. 351 (dial.), etc. Though οἴκων answers metrically to the first two syllables of ἀγευστος in 582, it is not suspicious, because the second syllable of the trochee can be irrational (a long for a short): see Metr. Anal. Conversely, φθιτῶν is metrically admissible, though its first syllable answers to the first of σεισθῇ in 583. This correction of φθιμένων is strongly confirmed by the similar error of the MSS. in Eur. Alc. 100 (see cr. n.).

3 οὐδ' ἀπαλλάσσει γενεὰν γένος, ἀλλ' ἐρείπει
4 θεῶν τις, οὐδ' ἔχει λύσιν. νῦν γὰρ ἐσχάτας ὑπὲρ
5 ῥίζας <ὃ> τέτατο φάος ἐν Οἰδίπου δόμοις,   600
6 κατ' αὖ νιν φοινία θεῶν τῶν νερτέρων
7 ἁμᾷ κόνις, λόγου τ' ἄνοια καὶ φρενῶν ἐρινύς.
στρ. β'. τεάν, Ζεῦ, δύνασιν τίς ἀνδρῶν ὑπερβασία κατάσχοι; 605

597 ἐρείπει r, ἐρίπει L. Seyffert conject. ἐπείγει.   **599 f.** νῦν γὰρ ἐσχάτας
ὑπὲρ (ὕπερ L) | ῥίζας τέτατο φάος MSS.—Hermann proposed three different emen-
dations: (1) ὑπὲρ | ῥίζας δ τέτατο, to which the schol. points. (2) ὑπὲρ ῥίζας
ἐτέτατο, so that a new sentence begins with κατ' αὖ. (3) ὅπερ | ῥίζας ἐτέτατο.
This last he preferred.—Nauck would change ὑπέρ into θάλος (acc. governed by
κατακμᾷ). Keeping ὑπέρ, Theod. Kock and others would substitute θάλος for φάος.

---

596 f. ἀπαλλάσσει, releases (by ex-
hausting the malignity of the ἀρά): so oft.
ἀπαλλάσσω τινὰ κακῶν, φόβου, etc.—γενεὰν γένος: cp. 1067 νέκυν νεκρῶν: Ai.
475 παρ' ἦμαρ ἡμέρα.—The subject to ἔχει
(ἀλλ' ἐρείπει θεῶν τις being parenthetical)
is 'the Labdacid house,' i.e. γενεά in the
larger sense (585), supplied from γενεάν
just before. This is simpler than to supply
πήματα as subject.—λύσιν, deliverance
from trouble, as O. T. 921, Tr. 1171.

599 νῦν γὰρ ἐσχάτας κ.τ.λ. (1) The
first question is,—are we to read ὃ τέτατο
or ἐτέτατο? If ἐτέτατο, then the sentence
is complete at δόμοις. A new sentence
beginning with κατ' αὖ would be intolerably abrupt: yet neither κᾆτ' nor καὶ ταύταν
appears probable. This difficulty would
be avoided by changing ὑπέρ into ὅπερ: but
then ῥίζας φάος must mean, 'the comfort (or hope) afforded by the ῥίζα,'—a
strange phrase. And τέτατο confirms
ὑπέρ as well as φάος. I therefore prefer
ὃ τέτατο. (2) The next point concerns
νιν. Reading ὃ τέτατο, Wecklein still
refers νιν to ῥίζας, not to φάος, saying that
the constr. is as though ἃς ὑπὲρ ἐσχάτας
ῥίζας had preceded. This is a grammatical impossibility. With ὃ τέτατο, νιν can
refer only to φάος. Can this be justified?
Thus, I think. The ἐσχάτη ῥίζα of the
family is the last remaining means of pro-
pagating it. A light of hope (φάος) was
'spread above' this 'last root,'—as sunshine above a plant,—because it was
hoped that the sisters would continue the
race. The sisters themselves are, properly speaking, the ἐσχάτη ῥίζα. But as
the word ῥίζα can also have an abstract
sense, denoting the chance of propagation,
the sisters can here be identified with the
hope, or φάος, which shines above the ῥίζα.

In Greek this is the easier since φάος was
often said of persons, as Il. 18. 102 οὐδέ
τι Πατρόκλῳ γενόμην φάος, Eur. Hec. 841
ὦ δέσποτ', ὦ μέγιστον Ἕλλησιν φάος. To
say καταμᾶν φάος (δόμων) is like saying,
'to mow down the hope of the race,'—in
this case, the two young lives. A further
reason against referring νιν to ῥίζα is that
the verb should then be, not καταμᾷ, but
ἐξαμᾷ, as Ai. 1178 γένους ἅπαντος ῥίζαν
ἐξημημένος: a root is not 'mowed down,'
in such a case, but cut out of the ground.
The proposed change of φάος into θάλος,
though not difficult in a palaeographical
sense, is condemned by τέτατο, which
does not suit θάλος, but exactly suits φάος.
Cp. Ph. 831 τάνδ' αἴγλαν ἃ τέταται τανῦν.
Od. 11. 19 ἀλλ' ἐπὶ νὺξ ὀλοὴ τέταται δει-
λοῖσι βροτοῖσι: Hes. Op. 547 ἀὴρ πυροφό-
ρος τέταται μακάρων ἐπὶ ἔργοις (rich men's
fields): Theogn. 1077 ὀρφνη γὰρ τέταται.
Plat. Rep. 616 B διὰ παντὸς τοῦ οὐρανοῦ
καὶ γῆς τεταμένον φῶς. As to the proposed substitution of θάλος for ὑπέρ, (with
φάος retained,) it would be as violent as
needless.—For ῥίζας cp. Pind. O. 2. 46
ὅθεν σπέρματος ἔχοντα ῥίζαν: El. 765
πρόρριζον...ἔφθαρται γένος: Lucian Tyr.
13 πανωλεθρίᾳ παντὸς τοῦ γένους καὶ ῥιζό-
θεν τὸ δεινὸν ἅπαν ἐκκεκομμένον.

601 f. κατ' αὖ...ἁμᾷ, = καταμᾷ αὖ,
'mows down in its turn' (not, 'otherwise
than we hoped'). In my first edition I
adopted the conjecture κοπίς. Prof.
Tyrrell's able defence of the MS. κόνις
(Classical Review, vol. II. p. 139), though
it has not removed all my difficulties, has
led me to feel that more can be said for
that reading than I had recognised. I
now prefer, therefore, to leave κόνις in
the text, and to re-state here the arguments for and against it.

and generation is not freed by generation, but some god strikes them down, and the race hath no deliverance.

For now that hope of which the light had been spread above the last root of the house of Oedipus—that hope, in turn, is brought low—by the blood-stained dust due to the gods infernal, and by folly in speech, and frenzy at the heart.

Thy power, O Zeus, what human trespass can limit? 2nd strophe.

601 κατ'] κᾶτ' L, but a line has been drawn through the ^. The later MSS. have κᾶτ', κατ', κᾱτ' (V⁴), κᾱτ' (L²), or κατά νιν. Gaisford, writing κᾱτ' with Brunck and others, reads ὑπὲρ | ῥίζας ἐτέτατο (see last note).—καὶ ταύταν Semitelos.
602 ἀμᾷ L, ἀμᾷ r.—κόνις MSS. The conjecture κοπίς has been made by several scholars independently. Gaisford gives the priority, though doubtfully ('ni fallor'), to John Jortin (ob. 1770). Heath ascribes it to Askew. Reiske also suggested it.
604 τεάν] Triclinius conject. τὰν σάν: Wecklein, σὰν ἄν: Nauck, τίς σάν.—δύναμιν L, with ·σ· over μ from the first hand. **605** ὑπερβασίᾳ r. Meineke con-

---

(1) If κόνις be right, κόνις θεῶν τῶν νερτέρων is the dust, belonging (due) to the gods infernal, which Antigone strewed on her brother's corpse; it is φοινία, because the corpse was gory. The strongest point in favour of κόνις is that it is in harmony with the following words, λόγου τ' ἄνοια καὶ φρενῶν ἐρινύς. The whole sense then is: 'She, too—the last hope of the race—is now to die,—for a handful of blood-stained dust (i.e., for a slight, yet obligatory, act of piety towards her slain brother)—and for those rash words to Creon,—the expression of her frenzied resolve.' On the other hand, the objection to κόνις is the verb **καταμᾷ**, which implies the metaphor of reaping. (See Appendix.) The proposed version, 'covers,' is impossible, and, if possible, would be unsuitable. What we want is a verb meaning simply 'destroys,' or 'dooms to death.' Now it is true that Greek lyric poetry often tolerates some confusion of metaphor (see on v. 117, and cp. O. T. p. lviii): the question is whether this example of it be tolerable. Prof. Tyrrell holds that it is excused by the tumult of feeling in the mind of the Chorus. That is, the metaphor of a young life 'mowed down' is not completed by a mention of the agent, the Destroyer: it is swiftly succeeded in the speaker's thought by a dramatic image of the cause, Antigone sprinkling the dust, and defying Creon. This is conceivable; but it is at least extremely bold.

(2) If we read κοπίς, then καταμᾷ is appropriate, and φοινία also has a more evident fitness. The great objection is the want of unison with λόγου τ' ἄνοια καὶ φρενῶν ἐρινύς. If the τ' after λόγου means

'both,' the κοπὶς νερτέρων is the deadly agency as seen in the girl's rash speech and resolve: if the τ' means 'and,' it is an agency to which these things are superadded. On either view the language is awkward. This must be set against the gain in unity of metaphor.

It has further been urged against κοπίς that the word is too homely. This may be so; but we lack proof. κοπίς seems to have been a large curved knife, known to the Greeks chiefly as (a) a butcher's or cook's implement, (b) an oriental military weapon. It does not follow, however, that the effect here would be like that of 'chopper,' or of 'scimitar,' in English. The dignity of a word may be protected by its simplicity; and κοπίς is merely 'that which cuts.' Pindar was not afraid of homeliness when he described a chorus-master as a κρατήρ, or an inspiring thought as an ἀκόνα (cp. O. C. 1052 n.). Nicander could say, of the scorpion, τοίη οἱ κέντροιο κοπίς (Ther. 780). If κοπίς be right, the change to κόνις may have been caused, not by a misreading of letters, but by mere inadvertence,—the copyist having the word κόνις in his thoughts at the moment: it has already occurred frequently (247, 256, 409, 429).—See Appendix.

603 λόγου...ἄνοια, folly shown in speech (defining gen.),—Antigone's answer to Creon (450 ff.): cp. 562 (ἄνουν), 383 (ἀφροσύνη). φρενῶν ἐρινύς, an erinys of (or in) the mind: i.e. the infatuated impulse which urged Antigone to the deed is conceived as a Fury that drove her to her doom. Schol. ὅτι οἰστρηθεῖσα ὑπὸ τῶν ἐρινύων...τοῦτο τετόλμηκεν.

604 τεάν, epic and Ion. (Hom., Hes.,

8—2

2 τὰν οὔθ' ὕπνος αἱρεῖ ποθ' ὁ *πάντ' ἀγρεύων,
3 οὔτε θεῶν *ἄκματοι μῆνες, ἀγήρως δὲ χρόνῳ
4 δυνάστας κατέχεις Ὀλύμπου μαρμαρόεσσαν αἴγλαν. 610
5 τό τ' ἔπειτα καὶ τὸ μέλλον
6 καὶ τὸ πρὶν ἐπαρκέσει

ject. ὑπέρβασις (Pallis ὑπέρβιος) ἄν.   Nauck, ἂν παρβασία.—κατάσχοι L, and so almost
all the later MSS.: E seems to be alone in κατάσχῃ.   606 παντογήρωσ L, with gl.
αἰώνιος above by S.   The letters γηρ are underlined.   παντογήρως was also read by
the Scholiast.   πανταγήρως A.—Bamberger conject. παντοθήρας.   Schneidewin,

---

Her., Pind., etc.); admitted by Aesch.
and Eur. in lyrics.—δύνᾰσιν: cp. 951.
A poetical form used by Pind., Eur. (in
dial. as well as in lyr.), etc.—κατάσχοι.
Epic usage admits the optat. (without ἄν)
where an abstract possibility is to be
stated, as Il. 19. 321 οὐ μὲν γάρ τι
κακώτερον ἄλλο πάθοιμι, 'for I could
not (conceivably) suffer anything worse.'
The Homeric instances are chiefly in
negative sentences (Od. 3. 231 being a
rare exception, ῥεῖα θεός γ' ἐθέλων καὶ
τηλόθεν ἄνδρα σαώσαι). Attic verse affords
some certain examples,—all in negative
sentences, or in questions when (as here)
a negative answer is expected. So Aesch.
P. V. 291 οὐκ ἔστιν ὅτῳ | μείζονα μοῖραν
νείμαιμ' ἢ σοί. Other instances are Aesch.
Ch. 172, 595: Ag. 620: Eur. Alc. 52.
Our passage is undoubtedly another genuine instance, and the attempts to alter
it (see cr. n.) are mistaken. Attic prose,
on the other hand, supplies no trustworthy
example: in most of those which are alleged ἄν should be supplied. I have discussed this question in O. C., Appendix
on v. 170, p. 273.—Men may overstep
their due limits: but no such ὑπερβασία
can restrict the power of Zeus. He punishes the encroachment.

606 The MS. παντογήρως is unques-
tionably corrupt. Sleep, the renewer of
vigour, could not be described as 'bringing old age to all.' Nor can the epithet
be explained as 'enfeebling all,' in the
sense of 'subduing them'; nor, again, as
'attending on all, even to old age.' The
neighbourhood of ἀγήρως is not in favour
of παντογήρως, but against it; in the case
of παντοπόρος—ἄπορος (360), and of ὑψίπολις—ἄπολις (370), there is a direct contrast between the two words. Either
πάντ' ἀγρῶν or πανταγρεὺς (see cr. n.)
would be good, if οὔτ' could be taken
from the next verse, and added to this.

But οὔτ' clearly belongs, I think, to the
next verse,—as will be seen presently.
Bamberger proposed παντοθήρας, or παντόθηρος. The former would be a subst.
like ἰχθυοθήρας, 'fisherman,' ὀρνιθοθήρας,
'fowler': the latter (which I should prefer),
an adj. like πολύθηρος, 'catching much'
(Heliodorus 5. 18), εὔθηρος, 'having good
sport.' παντόθηρος would suit the sense
well. But its probability depends on the
way in which we conceive the corrupt
παντογήρως to have arisen. It is evident
that the genuine ἀγήρως in the next line
had something to do with it. It seems
most likely that the eye of the transcriber
who first wrote παντογήρως had wandered
to ἀγήρως, and that by a mere inadvertence
he gave a like ending to the earlier word.
Now this might most easily have hap-
pened if the sixth letter of the earlier
series had been Γ, but would obviously
have been less likely if that letter had
been Θ. I therefore think it more probable
that παντογήρως arose from πάντ' ἀγρεύων
than from παντόθηρος. It is immaterial
that the last four letters of the latter are
nearer to the MS., since, on the view just
stated, the transcriber's error arose from
the fact that the consecutive letters ἀγ
were common to ἀγρεύων and ἀγήρως, and
that, from these letters onwards, he accidentally copied ἀγήρως. It may be added
that such an error would have been easier
with a separate word like ἀγρεύων than
with the second part of a compound like
παντόθηρος.—The verb ἀγρεύω, 'to catch'
(common both in verse and in prose) is
used by Soph. in fr. 507.—Soph. was
thinking of Il. 14. 244 ff. (Ὕπνος speaking to Hera), ἄλλον μέν κεν ἔγωγε θεῶν
αἰειγενετάων | ῥεῖα κατευνήσαιμι... | Ζηνὸς
δ' οὐκ ἂν ἔγωγε Κρονίονος ἆσσον ἱκοίμην,
| οὐδὲ κατευνήσαιμ', ὅτε μὴ αὐτός γε κελεύοι.

607 The MS. οὔτ' ἀκάματοι θεῶν
should answer metrically to 618 εἰδότι δ'

That power which neither Sleep, the all-ensnaring, nor the
untiring months of the gods can master; but thou, a ruler
to whom time brings not old age, dwellest in the dazzling
splendour of Olympus.

And through the future, near and far, as through the past,

πάντ' ἀγρευτάς. Wolff, πανταγρεύς. Wecklein, πάντ' ἀγρῶν (and formerly πάντ'
ἀφαυρῶν). Semitelos, πάντ' ἀγρώσσων.   **607** οὔτ' ἀκάματοι θεῶν MSS. Hermann conject. οὔτε θεῶν ἄκμητοι. See Appendix.   **608** The first hand in L
wrote ἀγήρωι: an early corrector changed ι to σ. Most of the later MSS. have
ἀγήρως, but a few ἀγήρω.   **612** ἐπαρκέσει] ἐπικρατεῖ Koechly, which Nauck

---

οὐδὲν ἕρπει. Far the best emendation is
οὔτε θεῶν ἄκματοι (Hermann ἄκμητοι).
This supposes merely a transposition of
two words, of which L affords undoubted
instances (cp. on 107), and the very
natural development of ἀκάματοι out of
the rarer form ἄκματοι. For the latter
cp. *Hom. hymn. Apoll.* 520 ἀκμήτοις δὲ
λόφον προσέβαν ποσίν. The word **θεῶν**
seems to me clearly genuine. Many recent editors have condemned it, because
Zeus is the marshaller of the seasons (*Il.*
2. 134 Διὸς μεγάλου ἐνιαυτοί, *Od.* 24. 344
Διὸς ὧραι, Plat. *Prot.* 321 A τὰς ἐκ Διὸς
ὥρας). How, then, could the poet say
that *Zeus* is not subdued by 'the months
of the gods'? The simple answer is that
the term θεῶν is not opposed to Zeus,
but includes him. Though Zeus (the Sky
Father) was more especially the ταμίας
ὡρῶν, that function can also be ascribed
to the gods collectively: see *e.g.* Plat.
Legg. 886 A οὐκοῦν, ὧ ξένε, δοκεῖ ῥάδιον
εἶναι ἀληθεύοντας λέγειν ὡς εἰσὶ θεοί;—
πῶς;—πρῶτον μὲν γῆ καὶ ἥλιος ἄστρα τε
τὰ ξύμπαντα καὶ τὰ τῶν ὡρῶν διακε-
κοσμημένα καλῶς οὕτως, ἐνιαυτοῖς τε
καὶ μησὶ διειλημμένα. Cp. *ib.* 809 D,
as illustrating another reason which made
the phrase **θεῶν μῆνες** so natural—the
fact, namely, that the ἑορταί were the
land-marks of the Calendar: τίνων δὴ πέρι
λέγομεν; ἡμερῶν τάξεως εἰς μηνῶν περιό-
δους καὶ μηνῶν εἰς ἕκαστον τὸν ἐνιαυτόν,
ἵνα ὧραι καὶ θυσίαι καὶ ἑορταὶ τὰ προσήκοντα ἀπολαμβάνουσαι ἑαυταῖς ἕκαστα...
θεοῖς μὲν τὰς τιμὰς ἀποδιδῶσι κ.τ.λ. And,
if **θεῶν** be genuine, then **οὔτε** belongs to
this verse, and we gain a fresh argument
against those emendations which would
append οὔτ' to v. 606: for οὔτ' | ἀκάματοι
θεῶν <νιν> is certainly not probable.
See Appendix.—All the immortals have
a *life* which is not worn out by those

months which they themselves control.
The distinction of Zeus is that his *su-
premacy* over gods and men is unalterable.
—**ἄκματοι**, untiring in their course: cp.
Il. 18. 239 ἠέλιον δ' ἀκάμαντα: Eur. fr.
597 ἀκάμας τε χρόνος.

608 f. I doubt whether the dat.
χρόνῳ could be instrumental or causal
here ('not made old *by* time'). It rather
seems to be an adverbial dat. of circumstance, 'not growing old with time' (as
time goes on). χρόνῳ oft.='at length'
(*O. C.* 437).—**μαρμαρόεσσαν** (only here)
=μαρμαρέαν. μαρμαίρω and its cognate
adj. are applied to any *sparkling* or *flashing* light (as of sun or stars, bright eyes,
gleaming metal). Cp. *Il.* 1. 532 ἀπ'
αἰγλήεντος Ὀλύμπου. A. Blackwall compares the language of St Paul in 1 Tim.
6. 15 ὁ μακάριος καὶ μόνος δυνάστης...φῶς
οἰκῶν ἀπρόσιτον.

611 f. τό τ' ἔπειτα (acc. of duration) is
what will immediately follow the *present*
moment (cp. Plat. *Parm.* 152 C τοῦ τε νῦν
καὶ τοῦ ἔπειτα), and is here distinguished
from τὸ **μέλλον**, the *more distant* future;
Plaut. *Pers.* 778 (quoted by Schneid.)
qui sunt, quique erunt (τὸ ἔπειτα), *quique fuerunt, quique futuri sunt posthac*
(τὸ μέλλον). It is much as if we said,
'to-morrow, and for all time.' Many have
compared Eur. *I. T.* 1263 τά τε πρῶτα |
τά τ' ἔπειθ' ἅ τ' ἔμελλε τυχεῖν: but even
if Seidler's ἅ τ', rather than ὅσ', be there
the true correction of the MS. ὅσα τ', the
parallelism is not strict, since τὰ ἔπειτα
would then mean 'what followed τὰ
πρῶτα,' not, 'what is to follow τὰ νῦν.'
—**καὶ τὸ πρίν** is usu. explained as a
compressed form of ὥσπερ καὶ τὸ πρὶν
ἐπήρκεσε: but this is at least much bolder
than the examples which are brought to
support it, as Dem. or. 18 § 31 καὶ τότε
καὶ νῦν καὶ ἀεὶ ὁμολογῶ, which would be

7 νόμος ὅδ'· οὐδὲν ἕρπει
8 θνατῶν βιότῳ *πάμπολύ γ' ἐκτὸς ἄτας.

ἀντ. β'. ἁ γὰρ δὴ πολύπλαγκτος ἐλπὶς πολλοῖς μὲν ὄνασις
ἀνδρῶν,   616
2 πολλοῖς δ' ἀπάτα κουφονόων ἐρώτων·
3 εἰδότι δ' οὐδὲν ἕρπει, πρὶν πυρὶ θερμῷ πόδα τις
4 προσαύσῃ. σοφίᾳ γὰρ ἔκ του κλεινὸν ἔπος πέ-
φανται,   621
5 τὸ κακὸν δοκεῖν ποτ' ἐσθλὸν

adopts. **613** ἕρπει MSS.: ἕρπειν Heath: ἕρπων Boeckh.   **614** πάμ̄|πολισ L.
The later MSS., too, have πάμπολις, but Campb. cites πάμπολῠ͞ν as written by the
first hand in one of them (Vat.), and corrected to πάμπολιν. πάμπολύ γ' Heath.
See Appendix.   **616** ὄνησις L, the final σ made from ν by an early corrector.

---

parallel only if it were καὶ νῦν καὶ ἀεὶ καὶ
τότε ὁμολογῶ: and νῦν τε καὶ πάλαι δοκεῖ
(181) is irrelevant, since πάλαι can take
the pres. (279). Rather, perh., **ἐπαρκέσει**,
'will hold good,' means, 'will be found
true,'—both in the future, and if we scan
the past.—For τὸ before πρίν, cp. O. C.
180 ἔτῐ; προβίβαζε. **ἐπαρκέσει**, will hold
out, hold good,=διαρκέσει: so only here,
perhaps, for in Solon fr. 5. 1 δήμῳ μὲν
γὰρ ἔδωκα τόσον κράτος ὅσσον ἐπαρκεῖ, we
must surely read ἀπαρκεῖ, with Coraës.
613 f. πάμπολύ γ' (Heath), for πάμπολις, is not only the best emendation,
but (in my belief) a certain one. I do not
know whether it has been noticed that
πάμπολῠ͞ν in one of the late MSS. (see cr. n.),
—a mere blunder for πάμπολις,—forcibly
illustrates the ease with which the opposite
change of πάμπολύ γ' into πάμπολις could
have occurred. The νόμος, then, is :—
' Nothing vast comes to (enters into) the
life of mortals, ἐκτὸς ἄτας, free from a curse
(cp. ἔξω...αἰτίας, 445)'—without bringing
ἄτη. Cp. Plat. Rep. 531 D πάμπολυ
ἔργον, Legg. 823 Β πάμπολύ τι πρᾶγμα,
ib. 677 Ε γῆς δ' ἀφθόνου πλῆθος πάμπολυ.
Too much power, or wealth, or prosperity
—anything so great as to be μὴ κατ' ἄνθρωπον—excites the divine φθόνος: the
man shows ὕβρις, and this brings ἄτη.
Cp. Her. 7. 10 ὁρᾷς τὰ ὑπερέχοντα ζῷα
ὡς κεραυνοῖ ὁ θεὸς οὐδὲ ἐᾷ φαντάζεσθαι, τὰ
δὲ σμικρὰ οὐδέν μιν κνίζει; ὁρᾷς δὲ ὡς ἐς
οἰκήματα τὰ μέγιστα αἰεὶ καὶ δένδρεα τὰ
τοιαῦτα ἀποσκήπτει τὰ βέλεα; φιλέει γὰρ
ὁ θεὸς τὰ ὑπερέχοντα πάντα κολούειν.
Diog. L. 1. 3. 2 (Zeus) τὰ μὲν ὑψηλὰ

ταπεινῶν, τὰ δὲ ταπεινὰ ὑψῶν. Soph. fr.
320 καλὸν φρονεῖν τὸν θνητὸν ἀνθρώποις
ἴσα.—ἕρπει: cp. Ai. 1087 ἕρπει παραλλὰξ
ταῦτα (come to men): for the dat., cp.
above, 186. The inf. ἕρπειν would be
admissible after οὐδέν, since this is not a
precept (like μὴ πλουτεῖν ἀδίκως), but a
statement of fact. In 706 L has ἔχει by
mistake for ἔχειν, and such errors are
frequent. And δοκεῖν in 622 might seem
to recommend ἕρπειν here. Yet ἕρπει
seems right. For this is not what the
νόμος says,—as δοκεῖν in 622 depends on
ἔπος πέφανται, and δράσαντι παθεῖν in
Aesch. Cho. 313 on μῦθος...φωνεῖ. The
constant fact, οὐδὲν ἕρπει, ἰς the νόμος.
Cp. Ph. 435 λόγῳ δὲ σ' ἐν βραχεῖ | τοῦτ'
ἐκδιδάξω· πόλεμος οὐδέν' ἄνδρ' ἑκὼν | αἱρεῖ
πονηρόν.—πάμπολις is impossible. For
the attempts to explain it, and for other
conjectures, see Appendix.
615—625 ἁ γὰρ δή κ.τ.λ. The γὰρ
introduces an explanation of the law just
stated. 'No inordinate desire comes to
men without bringing ἄτη. For hope,
which can be a blessing, can also be a
curse, by luring a man to pursue forbidden
things; and then he sins blindly, till the
gods strike him. The gods cause him to
mistake evil for good; and his impunity
is of short duration.' Creon is destined
to exemplify this. **πολύπλαγκτος**, roam-
ing widely—as a mariner over unknown
seas—in dreams of the future. Soph.
was perh. thinking of Pind. O. 12. 6 αἱ
γε μὲν ἀνδρῶν | πόλλ' ἄνω, τὰ δ' αὖ κάτω
ψεύδη μεταμώνια τάμνοισαι κυλίνδοντ' ἐλ-
πίδες, 'at least, the hopes of men are

shall this law hold good: Nothing that is vast enters into the life of mortals without a curse.

For that hope whose wanderings are so wide is to many men a comfort, but to many a false lure of giddy desires; and the disappointment comes on one who knoweth nought till he burn his foot against the hot fire.

2nd anti-strophe.

For with wisdom hath some one given forth the famous saying, that evil seems good, soon or late,

---

ὄνασις Brunck. **619** προσαύσηι L, with •αἴρει• (*i.e.* προσαίρει) written above by an early hand. The later MSS. have προσαύσῃ, προσψαύσῃ, προσαίρῃ, and προσάρῃ. **620** σοφία L, with ι written over α by a late hand. σοφίας Γ. **621** πέφανται] In L the ν has been erased. **622** ποτ'] Wecklein

---

oft tossed up and down, ploughing a sea of vain deceits.'—πολύπλαγκτος might also be act., 'causing men to err greatly'; but this is less fitting here.

616 πολλοῖς μὲν ὄνασις, by cheering them, and inciting to worthy effort. This clause is inserted merely for the sake of contrast with the next. When Greek idiom thus co-ordinates two clauses, the clause which we should subordinate to the other is that which has μέν; as here, '*though* a blessing to many.' So *O. C.* 1536 (n.), εὖ μὲν ὀψέ δ', 'late, though surely.'

617 ἀπάτα...ἐρώτων. The gen. is best taken as subjective, a cheating (of men) by desires; *i.e.*, ἔρωτες ἀπατῶσι. The ἐλπίς *is* such an ἀπάτη, because it ends in that. If the gen. were objective, the sense would be ἐλπὶς ἀπατᾷ ἔρωτας. This is equally possible, but hardly so natural. In 630, ἀπάτας λεχέων, the gen. is neither of these, but one of relation (a deceiving of him about his marriage). Cp. Hes. *Op.* 460 νεωμένη οὔ σ' ἀπατήσει, when ploughed again, the soil will not disappoint thee.—κουφονόων: see on 342.

618 f. The ἀπάτη, or final frustration of his desires, ἔρπει, creeps on him, οὐδὲν εἰδότι, knowing nothing. Others construe, οὐδὲν ἔρπει εἰδότι, nothing comes to him aware of it; *i.e.* he understands the true meaning of nothing that happens to him. This is somewhat forced; and that οὐδέν is object to εἰδότι is confirmed by Antiphon or. 1 § 29 οἱ δ' ἐπιβουλευόμενοι οὐδὲν ἴσασι πρὶν ἐν αὐτῷ ὦσι τῷ κακῷ γ' ἤδη. Cp. *Ai.* 964 τἀγαθὸν χεροῖν | ἔχοντες οὐκ ἴσασι, πρίν τις ἐκβάλῃ.

619 πρὶν...προσαύσῃ. Attic, like epic, poetry can use simple πρίν, instead of

πρὶν ἄν (308), with subjunct.: so *Ai.* 965 (see last n.), *Ph.* 917, *Tr.* 608, 946, etc. —προσαύσῃ (only here), 'burn against.' The simple verb occurs *Od.* 5. 490 ἵνα μή ποθεν ἄλλοθεν αὖοι (*sc.* πῦρ), 'kindle.' Attic had ἐναύω, 'kindle,' and ἀφαύω, 'parch.' The image here seems to be that of a man who walks, in fancied security, over ashes under which fire still smoulders (cp. Lucr. 4. 927 *cinere ut multo latet obrutus ignis*, Hor. *c.* 2. 1. 7 *incedis per ignes Suppositos cineri doloso*). There was a prov., ἐν πυρὶ βέβηκας (Suidas, etc.). —πόδα: cp. Aesch. *Ch.* 697 ἔξω κομίζων ὀλεθρίου πηλοῦ πόδα: *P. V.* 263 πημάτων ἔξω πόδα | ἔχει (and so *Ph.* 1260 ἐκτὸς κλαυμάτων, Eur. *Her.* 109 ἔξω πραγμάτων).—Some render προσαύσῃ 'bring to,' assuming an αὔω equiv. in sense to αἴρω: but the evidence for this is doubtful: see Appendix.

620 f. σοφία, modal dat., =σοφῶς: cp. *El.* 233 εὐνοίᾳ γ' αὐδῶ: so ὀργῇ (*O. T.* 405), θυμῷ (*O. C.* 659), etc.—ἔκ του, *i.e.* by some wise man of olden time:—not like the οὐκ ἔφα τις in Aesch. *Ag.* 369 (alluding to Diagoras). Cp. frag. adesp. 383 (schol. on *Tr.* 296) καὶ τοῦτο τοὔπος ἐστὶν ἀνδρὸς ἔμφρονος, | ὅταν καλῶς πράσσῃ τις, ἐλπίζειν κακά. For similar γνῶμαι in tragic lyrics, cp. Aesch. *Ag.* 750, *Ch.* 313. —πέφανται: *Tr.* 1 λόγος μὲν ἔστ' ἀρχαῖος ἀνθρώπων φανείς: *O. T.* 525, 848.

622 ff. τὸ κακὸν δοκεῖν ποτ' κ.τ.λ. The sense of ποτέ here is not 'sometimes,' but 'at one time or another,' 'at length,' as *Ph.* 1041 ἀλλὰ τῷ χρόνῳ ποτέ. A moment arrives when he makes the fatal error. ἄτη (ἀάω), as the heaven-sent influence that leads men to sin, is properly 'hurt done to the mind.' Milton, *Samson*

120 ΣΟΦΟΚΛΕΟΥΣ

6 τῷδ' ἔμμεν ὅτῳ φρένας
7 θεὸς ἄγει πρὸς ἄταν·
8 πράσσει δ' ὀλίγιστον χρόνον ἐκτὸς ἄτας.　　625

ὅδε μὴν Αἵμων, παίδων τῶν σῶν
νέατον γέννημ'· ἆρ' ἀχνύμενος
τῆς μελλογάμου
τάλιδος ἥκει μόρον Ἀντιγόνης,
ἀπάτας λεχέων ὑπεραλγῶν;　　630

ΚΡ. τάχ' εἰσόμεσθα μάντεων ὑπέρτερον.
ὦ παῖ, τελείαν ψῆφον ἆρα μὴ κλύων
τῆς μελλονύμφου πατρὶ λυσσαίνων πάρει;

conject. τότ'.　　**623** ἔμμεν' L: ἔμμεν Brunck.　　**625** ὀλίγωστὸν (sic) L, ωσ having been made from οσ: the accent on ι is crossed out. ὀλιγοστὸν r. ὀλίγιστον Bergk.
628 f. ἆρ' (sic) ἀχνύμενοσ | τῆσ μελλογάμου νύμφησ | τάλιδοσ ἥκει μόρον Ἀντιγόνησ L:

1676 *Among them he a spirit of phrenzy sent, Who hurt their minds.* Cp. βλαψίφρων, φρενοβλαβής. *Il.* 19. 137 ἀλλ' ἐπεὶ ἀασάμην, καί μευ φρένας ἐξέλετο Ζεύς. Theognis 403 σπεύδει ἀνήρ, κέρδος διζήμενος, ὅν τινα δαίμων | πρόφρων εἰς μεγάλην ἀμπλακίην παράγει, | καί οἱ ἔθηκε δοκεῖν, ἃ μὲν ᾖ κακά, ταῦτ' ἀγάθ' εἶναι, | εὐμαρέως, ἃ δ' ἂν ᾖ χρήσιμα, ταῦτα κακά. Lycurgus *in Leocr.* § 92 οἱ γὰρ θεοὶ οὐδὲν πρότερον ποιοῦσιν ἢ τῶν πονηρῶν ἀνθρώπων τὴν διάνοιαν παράγουσι· καί μοι δοκοῦσι τῶν ἀρχαίων τινὲς ποιητῶν ὥσπερ χρησμοὺς γράψαντες τοῖς ἐπιγιγνομένοις ταῦτα τὰ ἰαμβεῖα καταλιπεῖν· ὅταν γὰρ ὀργὴ δαιμόνων βλάπτῃ τινά, | τοῦτ' αὐτὸ πρῶτον, ἐξαφαιρεῖται φρενῶν | τὸν νοῦν τὸν ἐσθλόν, εἰς δὲ τὴν χείρω τρέπει | γνώμην, ἵν' εἰδῇ μηδὲν ὧν ἁμαρτάνει. The schol. on our verse quotes an unknown poet's lines, ὅταν δ' ὁ δαίμων ἀνδρὶ πορσύνῃ κακά, | τὸν νοῦν ἔβλαψε πρῶτον, ᾧ βουλεύεται. ('Quem Iuppiter vult perdere, dementat prius.' See n. in Appendix.)—The epic **ἔμμεν** (used also by Pind. and Sappho) occurs nowhere else in tragedy.

625 ὀλίγιστον, a superl. used not only in epic poetry but also by Attic writers (as Ar. and Plat.), is right here. The MS. ὀλιγοστόν cannot be defended by Ar. *Pax* 559 πολλοστῷ χρόνῳ, which is merely another form of πολλοστῷ ἔτει (Cratinus jun. Χείρ. 1); *i.e.* πολλοστός has its proper sense, 'one of many' (*multesimus*), and the χρόνος, like the ἔτος, is conceived

as the last of a series. So ὀλιγοστὸς χρόνος would mean, not, 'a fraction of time,' but, 'one in a small number of χρόνοι' or periods. In Arist. *Metaph.* 9. 1. 14 most MSS., and the best, have ὀλίγιστον...χρόνον: while A^b (cod. Laur. 87. 12) is the only MS. cited in the Berlin ed. (p. 1053 a 9) for ὀλιγοστόν. And otherwise ὀλιγοστὸς occurs only in later Greek, as Plut. *Anton.* 51 καταβὰς ὀλιγοστός, 'having gone to the coast *with a small retinue*'; *Caes.* 49 ὀλιγοστῷ τοσαύτην ἀμυνομένῳ πόλιν 'fighting so great a State *with a small force.*'—**πράσσει...ἐκτὸς ἄτας**, like πράσσει καλῶς: so πράσσειν κατὰ νοῦν (Plat. *Rep.* 366 B, Ar. *Eq.* 549). **ἄτας** is here 'calamity' (as in 584, 614), while in the last verse ἄταν is rather 'infatuation.'—Donaldson changed ἄτας here to ἄλγους, because the strophe (614) also ends with ἐκτὸς ἄτας. On the other hand Dindorf ejects ἐκτὸς ἄτας from 614 (leaving a lacuna). But I believe ἐκτὸς ἄτας to be genuine in both places, as οὐδὲν ἔρπει also is both in 613 and in 618. We have to remember, first, that Soph. (like other ancient poets) easily tolerated repetition of words (see on *O. C.* 554); secondly, that tragic lyrics could admit refrains, and might, by a kindred instinct, permit such verbal echoes as these.

626 f. μήν instead of the usu. καὶ μήν (526).—**νέατον**, 'youngest and last,' Megareus being dead (1303): cp. 807 τὰν νεάταν ὁδόν; so 808, *Ai.* 1185. As applied to him whose mind the god draws to mischief; and but for the briefest space doth he fare free of woe.

But lo, Haemon, the last of thy sons;—comes he grieving for the doom of his promised bride, Antigone, and bitter for the baffled hope of his marriage?

Enter HAEMON.

CR. We shall know soon, better than seers could tell us.—My son, hearing the fixed doom of thy betrothed, art thou come in rage against thy father?

over τάλιδοσ S has written τῆς νύμφης. Triclinius omitted the words τῆς μελλογάμου νύμφης. Brunck was the first who saw that νύμφης only should be deleted. **630** λέχεων L. **633** λυσσαίνων] Schol. in L, γρ. θυμαίνων.—Meineke conject. δυσμενών: Semitelos, πατέρα δεννάσων.

to a person, νέατος could not be said of a sole survivor unless he was *also* the latest-born. **γέννημ'**: cp. 471 n.—**ἀχνύμενος** with **μόρον** as internal acc.: cp. *Il.* 5. 361 ἄχθομαι ἕλκος.

628 In the MS. reading (see cr. n.) νύμφης is a gloss on **τάλιδος**: but τῆς **μελλογάμου** should be retained. Except in the lexicons, τάλις occurs only here and in a verse of Callimachus, αὐτίκα τὴν τάλιν παιδὶ σὺν ἀμφιθαλεῖ, quoted by the Schol., who says, τάλις λέγεται παρ' Αἰολεῦσιν ἡ ὀνομασθείσά τινι νύμφη. Hesychius has, τάλις· ἡ μελλόγαμος παρθένος καὶ κατωνομασμένη τινί· οἱ δὲ γυναῖκα γαμετήν· οἱ δὲ νύμφην. This shows that τάλις could mean, not only an affianced bride, but also a bride after marriage: just as νύμφη can mean either. The epithet τῆς **μελλογάμου** is not, then, superfluous; and τῆς μελλονύμφου in 633 is no argument against it. On the other hand **τάλιδος**, without the epithet, would have a crude effect. A passage in Pollux (3. 45) has been taken to prove that he had τῆς μελλογάμου in his text. It does not prove this,—nor the reverse. τῆς μελλογάμου in Pollux should be (as Semitelos saw) τὴν μελλόγαμον, and we should refer his words solely to v. 633. His point is simply that ἡ μελλόνυμφος is more correct than ἡ μελλονύμφη.—Curtius connects τάλις with τέρ-ην, tender; θρόνα, flowers: Sanskrit tár-una-s, youthful, tender, tál-unī, girl, young woman. He supposes the first idea to be that of a plant sprouting or blossoming (cp. θάλος). This at least agrees well with what we know as to the usage of τάλις.

630 ἀπάτας (gen. sing.) λεχέων, a de-

ceit practised on him, a disappointment, in regard to his marriage. The gen. λεχέων is one of relation, helped, perhaps, by the idea of privation (as if ἀπάτη were ἀποστέρησις).

631—780 Third ἐπεισόδιον. Haemon vainly intercedes with his father. They quarrel, and the son abruptly leaves the scene (765). Creon then commands that Antigone shall at once be immured in a rocky vault.

631 μάντεων ὑπέρτερον = βέλτιον ἢ μάντεις ἴσασιν (and better, therefore, than they could tell us). Schol. ὁ λόγος παροιμιακῶς, ὁπότε μὴ στοχασμῷ χρώμεθα, ἀλλ' αὐτόπται τῶν πραγμάτων γινόμεθα. Eur. *H. F.* 911 ΑΓ. ἄλαστα τὰν δόμοισι.—ΧΟ. μάντιν οὐχ ἕτερον ἄξομαι, 'I will not bring a seer, other than myself' (cp. *O. T.* 6), *i.e.* 'I need no seer to tell me that':—imitated by the author of the *Rhesus* 949 σοφιστὴν δ' ἄλλον οὐκ ἐπάξομαι, who also has 952 ἤδη τάδ'· οὐδὲν μάντεως ἔδει φράσαι. Cp. *O. C.* 403.

632 f. τελείαν announces that he will not yield.—ψῆφον: cp. 60.—**ἆρα μή**, like μῶν, 'can it be that...?' *El.* 446.—τῆς **μελλονύμφου**: for the gen., cp. Thuc. 1. 140 τὸ Μεγαρέων ψήφισμα, and n. on 11. —λυσσαίνων, the reading of the MSS., is a word not extant elsewhere, but as correctly formed as ὀργαίνω, χαλεπαίνω, etc. At first sight it seems too strong: λύσσα is 'raving.' But a certain vehemence of language characterises Creon (cp. 280 ff.). Instead of saying merely, 'have you come here in displeasure?' he says, 'have you come here to storm at me?' As **σοὶ μέν** shows, there is a tacit contrast with the sisters: he had described Ismene as λυσ-ἢ σοὶ μὲν ἡμεῖς πανταχῆ δρῶντες φίλοι;

ΑΙΜΩΝ.

πάτερ, σός εἰμι· καὶ σύ μοι γνώμας ἔχων   635
χρηστὰς ἀπορθοῖς, αἷς ἔγωγ᾽ ἐφέψομαι.
ἐμοὶ γὰρ οὐδεὶς *ἀξιώσεται γάμος
μείζων φέρεσθαι σοῦ καλῶς ἡγουμένου.

ΚΡ. οὕτω γάρ, ὦ παῖ, χρὴ διὰ στέρνων ἔχειν,
γνώμης πατρῴας πάντ᾽ ὄπισθεν ἑστάναι.   640
τούτου γὰρ οὕνεκ᾽ ἄνδρες εὔχονται γονὰς
κατηκόους φύσαντες ἐν δόμοις ἔχειν,
ὡς καὶ τὸν ἐχθρὸν ἀνταμύνωνται κακοῖς,
καὶ τὸν φίλον τιμῶσιν ἐξ ἴσου πατρί.
ὅστις δ᾽ ἀνωφέλητα φιτύει τέκνα,   645
τί τόνδ᾽ ἂν εἴποις ἄλλο πλὴν αὑτῷ πόνους

---

635 μοι] L has μου, the ν being joined to the following γ, as ι would not have been. μοι Γ.   **637** ἀξιωσ εσται L. As the letters εσ are contracted into one character somewhat like ε, L's reading is even nearer than it looks in our type

---

σῶσαν (492). I therefore think λυσσαίνων genuine, and a finer reading than the variant noted in L, **θυμαίνων**. The latter word is used by Hesiod, and in Attic comedy. Some recent edd. place it in the text.

634 σοὶ μέν: cp. 498.—**πανταχῆ δρῶντες**, 'however I may act.' *Ai.* 1369 ὡς ἂν ποιήσῃς, πανταχῆ χρηστός γ᾽ ἔσει. Her. 9. 27 πάντῃ γὰρ τεταγμένοι (wherever we may be posted) πειρησόμεθα εἶναι χρηστοί: id. 8. 110 πάντως ἔτοιμοι ἦσαν λέγοντι πείθεσθαι ('ready in every case').

635 f. σός: cp. *O. C.* 1323.—**γνώμας ἔχων χρηστάς**, having good counsels, **ἀπορθοῖς** (αὐτάς) **μοι**, thou settest them before me as rules. ἀπορθόω (a rare word) means, like ἀπευθύνω, (1) 'to straighten out,' and then (2) 'to guide in a straight course.' Plat. *Legg.* 757 E (praying the gods) ἀπορθοῦν τὸν κλῆρον πρὸς τὸ δικαιότατον, 'to direct the lot (for magistracies) in the best interests of justice.' Here the γνῶμαι are the κανόνες, *regulae*, which are to guide the youth's course: cp. fr. 430 ὥστε τέκτονος | παρὰ στάθμην ἰόντος ὀρθοῦται κανών. Eur. *El.* 52 γνώμης πονηροῖς κανόσιν ἀναμετρούμενος | τὸ σῶφρον.—Others understand: (1) ἀπορθοῖς γνώμας μοι, thou guidest *my* views, χρηστὰς ἔχων, having good views (of thine

own). Or (2) 'Having good views, thou guidest me,' supplying με with ἀπορθοῖς (like *O. T.* 104 ἀπευθύνειν πόλιν). But μοι would then be awkward. Cp. Plaut. *Trin.* 304 (a son to his father) *sarta tecta tua praecepta usque habui mea modestia.*

637 f. ἀξιώσεται, pass. ; cp. 210, *O. C.* 581 δηλώσεται, *O. T.* 672 στυγήσεται (n.). ἀξ. **μείζων φέρεσθαι**, will be *esteemed* more important to win (cp. 439 ἥσσω λαβεῖν): so Plat. *Theaet.* 161 D ὥστε καὶ ἄλλων διδάσκαλος ἀξιοῦσθαι δικαίως, 'to be justly ranked as a teacher.' The same use is implied in *Legg.* 917 D ὁπόσης ἂν τιμῆς ἀξιώσῃ τὸ πωλούμενον (at whatever price he may value...).—L's reading, **ἀξίως ἔσται**, though tenable, seems slightly less probable, when we observe that this adv. is regularly used either (a) with gen., ἀξίως ἑαυτῶν, etc., or (b) absol., in such phrases as Thuc. 3. 40 κολάσατε...ἀξίως τούτους, 'according to their deserts.' (So *O. T.* 133 ἀξίως='as the case required.') Thus we could say, οὗτος ὁ γάμος ἀξίως ἔσται μείζων φ., 'will *deservedly* (=on its merits) be a greater prize.' But it is less natural to say, οὐδεὶς γάμος ἀξίως ἔσται μ. φ., 'no marriage will *rightly* be preferred,' etc., where ἀξίως becomes a mere equiv. for δικαίως or προσηκόντως. The change of ἀξιώσεται into ἀξίως ἔσται would

Or have I thy good will, act how I may?

HAE. Father, I am thine; and thou, in thy wisdom, tracest for me rules which I shall follow. No marriage shall be deemed by me a greater gain than thy good guidance.

CR. Yea, this, my son, should be thy heart's fixed law,—in all things to obey thy father's will. 'Tis for this that men pray to see dutiful children grow up around them in their homes,— that such may requite their father's foe with evil, and honour, as their father doth, his friend. But he who begets unprofitable children—what shall we say that he hath sown, but troubles for

to ἀξιώσεται, Musgrave's correction. late MS. (Dresden a, 14th cent.). grave and Schaefer conject. ἱστάναι. **645** φυτεύει MSS.: φιτύει Brunck.

638 μείζων] μεῖζον is quoted from one **640** ὅπισθεν] ὅπιθεν L.—ἑστάναι] Mus- **643** ἀνταμύνονται L: ἀνταμύνωνται r. **646** πόνους] L has a marg. gl. by S, γρ. πέδας· ἵν' ᾖ, ἐμπόδιον, δεσμούς, κώλυμα τοῦ πράττειν ἃ βούλεται.

---

have been the easier, since the ordinary fut. was ἀξιωθήσομαι.—σοῦ **καλῶς ἡγουμ.**, (with **μείζων**), than thy good guiding: cp. Her. 1. 34 μετὰ δὲ Σόλωνα οἰχόμενον. —It is a mistake (I think) to detect a mental reserve in the participle ('than thy guiding, *if*, or *when*, it is good'). Haemon knows that his one chance of saving Antigone is first to mollify his father, and then to urge the argument from public opinion (688 ff.). His deference is unqualified.

639 γάρ in assent (*O. T.* 1117).—**διὰ στέρνων ἔχειν**, lit., 'to be disposed in one's breast,' = φρονεῖν, or διακεῖσθαι. The phrase differs in two points from others which seem like it. (1) The gen. with **διά** in such phrases regularly denotes a state or act of the mind, whereas στέρνων represents the mind itself. (2) **ἔχειν** in such phrases is always trans., the intrans. verb being εἶναι. Thus ἔχω τινά (or τι) δι' αἰσχύνης, αἰτίας, ὀργῆς, φυλακῆς, etc. But εἰμὶ δι' ἡσυχίης (Her. 1. 206), διὰ φόβου (Thuc. 6. 59), δι' ὄχλου (Ar. *Eccl.* 888). Here **οὕτω**, going with **ἔχειν**, shows that the verb is intrans.,—not trans., with ταῦτα understood.

640 (One ought to think thus),—that is, **ὅπισθεν ἑστάναι πατρ. γνώμης**, one ought to place oneself under the guidance of a father's counsel, **πάντα**, in all things (adv. neut. pl., *O. T.* 1197 etc.). Thus ἑστάναι depends on χρή,—the indefinite subject of ἔχειν (τινά) being continued with it; and the whole clause explains οὕτω. The image from a soldier posted behind his leader suits the military

tone in which Creon presently enforces the value of discipline (670). Cp. Plat. *Rep.* 471 D εἴτε καὶ ἐν τῇ αὐτῇ τάξει εἴτε καὶ ὅπισθεν ἐπιτεταγμένον. The phrase ὄπισθεν ἑστάναι γνώμης is a poetical equiv. for ἀκολουθεῖν τῇ γνώμῃ (Thuc. 3. 38).—We could also render,—'that all things rank second to a father's will': when **ἑστάναι** would depend on διὰ στέρνων ἔχειν as = νομίζειν. But ἑστάναι applies to the τάξις of persons more naturally than to the estimation of things: cp. Her. 9. 27 ἵνα δοκέει ἐπιτηδεότατον ἡμέας εἶναι ἑστάναι (in battle): and the constr. is also less simple. ἱστάναι (which Musgrave proposed) would suit that view better.

643 f. ὡς without ἄν, as 760, *O. T.* 359, and oft.—**ἀνταμύνωνται**, a neutral word: thus Thuc. 2. 67 τοῖς αὐτοῖς ἀμύνεσθαι, to retaliate; but 1. 42 τοῖς ὁμοίοις ἡμᾶς ἀμύνεσθαι, to reward: here **κακοῖς** defines it.—ἐξ ἴσου **πατρί** = ὥσπερ ὁ πατήρ (cp. 516): *O. C.* 171 ἀστοῖς ἴσα χρὴ μελετᾶν.—The son's part is τοὺς αὐτοὺς ἐχθροὺς καὶ φίλους νομίζειν,—the definition of a ξυμμαχία as dist. from a merely defensive ἐπιμαχία, Thuc. 1. 44. Cp. 523 n.: Pind. *P.* 2. 83 φίλον εἴη φιλεῖν· | ποτὶ δ' ἐχθρὸν ἅτ' ἐχθρὸς ἐὼν λύκοιο δίκαν ὑποθεύσομαι.

646 f. ἄλλο is most simply taken as governed by φῦσαι, though, if we had ἤ instead of πλήν, Greek idiom would rather lead us to supply ποιῆσαι: see on 497, and cp. *Ai.* 125 οὐδὲν ὄντας ἄλλο πλὴν | εἴδωλ'. This is better than to make ἄλλο object to εἴποις ('what could one say of him,' etc.).—**πόνους**: cp. 533.—

φῦσαι, πολὺν δὲ τοῖσιν ἐχθροῖσιν γέλων·
μή νύν ποτ', ὦ παῖ, τὰς φρένας <γ'> ὑφ' ἡδονῆς
γυναικὸς οὕνεκ' ἐκβάλῃς, εἰδὼς ὅτι
ψυχρὸν παραγκάλισμα τοῦτο γίγνεται,   650
γυνὴ κακὴ ξύνευνος ἐν δόμοις. τί γὰρ
γένοιτ' ἂν ἕλκος μεῖζον ἢ φίλος κακός;
ἀλλὰ πτύσας ὡσεί τε δυσμενῆ μέθες
τὴν παῖδ' ἐν Ἅιδου τήνδε νυμφεύειν τινί.
ἐπεὶ γὰρ αὐτὴν εἷλον ἐμφανῶς ἐγὼ   655
πόλεως ἀπιστήσασαν ἐκ πάσης μόνην,
ψευδῆ γ' ἐμαυτὸν οὐ καταστήσω πόλει,
ἀλλὰ κτενῶ. πρὸς ταῦτ' ἐφυμνείτω Δία
ξύναιμον· εἰ γὰρ δὴ τά γ' ἐγγενῆ φύσει
ἄκοσμα θρέψω, κάρτα τοὺς ἔξω γένους.   660

648 μὴ νῦν L: μὴ νύν Aldus (μὴ τοί νυν A).—τὰσ φρένασ ὑφ' ἡδονῆσ L. The γ' inserted after φρένας in some later MSS. was a conjecture of Triclinius. See

γέλων: cp. El. 1153 γελῶσι δ' ἐχθροί: Ai. 79 οὔκουν γέλως ἥδιστος εἰς ἐχθροὺς γελᾶν; 961 οἱ δ' οὖν γελώντων κἀπιχαιρόντων κακοῖς. **648** τὰς φρένας γ'. Recent edd. have usually scorned the simple insertion of γε, by which Triclinius healed the metre. But it should be noticed that γε may emphasise τὰς φρένας ἐκβάλῃς, and not merely τὰς φρένας: cp. 747: O.C. 1278 τοῦ θεοῦ γε προστάτην, where γε emphasises the whole phrase, not merely the word θεοῦ. The deprecatory force of γε, as seen in μὴ σύ γε (O. C. 1441 n.), also recommends it, even when we have not σύ. Cp. Eur. Hipp. 503 καὶ μή γε πρὸς θεῶν, εὖ λέγεις γάρ, αἰσχρὰ δέ, | πέρα προβῇς τῶνδ'. Without, then, thinking **φρένας γ'** certain, I think it far more probable than the next best remedy, **φρένας σύ γ' ἡδονῆς**. As to a third conjecture, σύ γ' ἡδονῆς, the phrase οὕνεκα ἡδονῆς γυναικὸς (pleasure in her) would be very awkward. Some strange emendations have been proposed: see Appendix.—**φρένας...ἐκβάλῃς**, cast off the restraint of reason, as O. T. 611 φίλον... ἐσθλὸν ἐκβαλεῖν, O. C. 631 εὐμένειαν ἐκβάλοι (reject friendship). The first idea is that of *casting out* of house or land, banishing. Somewhat similar is Plat. *Crito* 46 B τοὺς δὲ λόγους, οὓς ἐν τῷ ἔμπροσθεν ἔλεγον, οὐ δύναμαι νῦν ἐκβαλεῖν (reject). Cp. 683.—**ὑφ' ἡδονῆς**: Ai. 382

ἦ που πολὺν γέλωθ' ὑφ' ἡδονῆς ἄγεις. Here the word denotes sensuous impulse: cp. Eur. Ph. 21 ἡδονῇ δούς: Thuc. 3. 38 ἀκοῆς ἡδονῇ ἡσσώμενοι. **650** ψυχρόν, frigid, joyless: Eur. Alc. 353 ψυχρὰν μέν, οἶμαι, τέρψιν.—**παραγκάλισμα**: so Tr. 540 ὑπαγκάλισμα (of a wife); and so ἀγκάλισμα, ἐναγκάλισμα. The neuter gives a contemptuous tone. Cp. 320 λάλημα, 756 δούλευμα. Eur. Or. 928 τἄνδον οἰκουρήματα (of women), Aesch. Ag. 1439 Χρυσηΐδων μείλιγμα (Agamemnon). **651 f. δόμοις.** For the full stop after the 5th foot cp. O. T. 800.—**ἕλκος**, esp. an ulcer; said in Il. 2. 723 of a serpent's venomous bite; hence fitting here in ref. to the false friend, the ἔχιδνα in the house (531). So civil strife (στάσις ἔμφυλος) is described by Solon as πάσῃ πόλει...ἕλκος ἄφυκτον (4. 17).—**φίλος** is any one near and dear to us; the masc. is used, though the reference is to a wife, because the thought of domestic treason is put in the most general way: so (though with ref. to a woman) 464 κατθανών, 496 ἁλούς. Cp. Eur. Alc. 355 ἡδὺ γὰρ φίλους | κἂν νυκτὶ λεύσσειν, ὅντιν' ἂν παρῇ χρόνον (Admetus speaking of his wife: we might read φίλος). **653** πτύσας, with loathing: Aesch. P. V. 1069 (speaking of treason) κοὐκ ἔστι νόσος | τῆσδ' ἥντιν' ἀπέπτυσα μᾶλλον.—**ὡσεί**

himself and much triumph for his foes? Then do not thou,
my son, at pleasure's beck, dethrone thy reason for a woman's
sake; knowing that this is a joy that soon grows cold in
clasping arms,—an evil woman to share thy bed and thy home.
For what wound could strike deeper than a false friend? Nay,
with loathing, and as if she were thine enemy, let this girl go
to find a husband in the house of Hades. For since I have
taken her, alone of all the city, in open disobedience, I will not
make myself a liar to my people—I will slay her.

So let her appeal as she will to the majesty of
kindred blood. If I am to nurture mine own kindred
in naughtiness, needs must I bear with it in aliens.

Appendix.   **656** πάσασ L, πάσης r.   **658** ταῦθ' L, with r written above by
an early hand.   **659** τάτ' ἐγγενῆ (from ἐνγενῆ) L, with συγγενῆ written above
by S. The later MSS. have τάτ' or (as A) τάδ' ἐγγενῆ.—Erfurdt restored τά γ'.

τε δυσμενῆ (οὖσαν), and as if she were a
foe. For πτύσας connected by τε with an
adj. in a different case, see n. on 381 σέ
γ' ἀπιστοῦσαν... ἀγουσι...καὶ...καθε-
λόντες. In El. 234 we have μάτηρ ὥσεί
τις πιστά: but nowhere in Attic poetry
do we find the epic and lyric use of ὡσεί τε
as merely=ὡσεί (Il. 2. 780, Pind. I. 44,
etc.). And, as we have seen, it is needless to assume it here. Yet supposed
difficulties about φίλος and ὡσεί τε have
led Nauck to propose that vv. 652—654
should be made into two, thus: γένοιτ'
ἂν ἕλκος μεῖζον; ἀλλ' ἀποπτύσας | τὴν παῖδ'
ἐν Ἅιδου τήνδε νυμφεύειν μέθες.

654 νυμφεύειν here=γαμεῖσθαι, nu-
bere, as 816. But it also=γαμεῖν, uxorem
ducere: Eur. I. A. 461 Ἅιδης νιν, ὡς ἔοικε,
νυμφεύσει τάχα.

656 f. ἀπιστήσασαν: cp. 219.—
ψευδῆ: referring to his solemn and public
declaration, 184—210.

658 κτενῶ. For the emphatic pause,
cp. 72 θάψω, and n. on 46.—πρὸς ταῦτ',
after an announcement of resolve, and
before a defiant imperative, as O. T. 426,
O. C. 455, El. 820, Aesch. P. V. 992,
Ar. Ach. 959 etc. Similarly πρὸς οὖν
τάδε, Ar. Nub. 1030.—ἐφυμνείτω, repeatedly invoke (a scornful word): cp. 1305,
O. T. 1275 n.—Δία ξύναιμον: see on 487.

659 f. τά γ' ἐγγ. φύσει, those who,
by birth, are relatives: for the place of
the adverbial φύσει, cp. El. 792 τοῦ θανόντος ἀρτίως, Aesch. P. V. 216 τῶν παρεστώ-
των τότε. For the neut., instead of τοὺς
ἐγγενεῖς, cp. Ph. 448 τὰ μὲν πανοῦργα καὶ
παλιντριβῆ...τὰ δὲ | δίκαια καὶ τὰ χρήστ'.

—ἄκοσμα, unruly: so of Thersites, Il. 2.
213 ὅς ῥ' ἔπεα φρεσὶν ᾗσιν ἄκοσμά τε
πολλά τε ᾔδη, | μάψ, ἀτὰρ οὐ κατὰ κόσμον,
ἐριζέμεναι βασιλεῦσιν. Cp. 730.—θρέψω
with predicative adj., as 1080, O. T.
98, etc.—κάρτα τοὺς ἔξω γ., sc. ἀκόσμους
θρέψω. It is needless to supply a more
general verb, like ποιήσω: the ruler's relation to his people justifies θρέψω: cp.
O. T. 1 ὦ τέκνα. 'If I allow my own
kindred to be unruly, I shall be obliged
to tolerate unruliness in the citizens at
large. For my authority as a ruler will
be gone.'

661—671. Seidler transposes vv.
663—667, placing them after 671. The
object is to bring vv. 668—671 into immediate connection with 662. In this
there is one slight grammatical gain;
since, as the vv. stand in the MSS., τοῦτον
...τὸν ἄνδρα (668) means, 'the man who
acts thus' (viz., as described in vv. 666 f.).
But the order given in the MSS. is right.
The transposition obliterates one of the
finest touches in the speech. Creon demands that the obedience of the citizens to
the ruler shall be absolute (666 f.). And
then he supplements this demand with a
remark on the dignity of such obedience.
The man who so obeys gives the best
proof that he could also rule (668 ff.).
Seidler destroys the point of vv. 668 ff.
by placing them after 662.

The connection of thought in the whole
passage—which is slightly obscured by
compression—may be most clearly shown
by taking the verses in small consecutive
groups. (1) 659 f. If I tolerate disloyalty

ἐν τοῖς γὰρ οἰκείοισιν ὅστις ἔστ' ἀνὴρ
χρηστός, φανεῖται κἂν πόλει δίκαιος ὤν·
ὅστις δ' ὑπερβὰς ἢ νόμους βιάζεται,
ἢ τοὐπιτάσσειν τοῖς κρατύνουσιν νοεῖ,
οὐκ ἔστ' ἐπαίνου τοῦτον ἐξ ἐμοῦ τυχεῖν.   665
ἀλλ' ὃν πόλις στήσειε, τοῦδε χρὴ κλύειν
καὶ σμικρὰ καὶ δίκαια καὶ τἀναντία·
καὶ τοῦτον ἂν τὸν ἄνδρα θαρσοίην ἐγὼ
καλῶς μὲν ἄρχειν, εὖ δ' ἂν ἄρχεσθαι θέλειν,
δορός τ' ἂν ἐν χειμῶνι προστεταγμένον   670
μένειν δίκαιον κἀγαθὸν παραστάτην.
ἀναρχίας δὲ μεῖζον οὐκ ἔστιν κακόν.
αὕτη πόλεις ὄλλυσιν, ἥδ' ἀναστάτους
οἴκους τίθησιν· ἥδε *συμμάχου δορὸς

663—667 Seidler, whom Nauck and others follow, places these five verses after 671. See comment. **664** Doederlein conject. ἤτοι 'πιτάσσειν.—The first hand in L wrote κρατύνουσιν νοεῖ. A later hand has made this into κρατοῦσιν ἐννοεῖ, the reading of some later MSS. (including A). **666** στήσειε. In L the final ε was added by S. **672** δὲ L, with ·γάρ· written above by S. Many of the later MSS. (including A) read γάρ. Stobaeus Flor. 43. 26 has δέ. **673** πόλισθ' L, with τ written above by S. The later MSS.

---

in my own relatives, I shall encourage it in other citizens. (2) 661 f. For (γάρ) only a man who is firm (χρηστός) where his own relatives are concerned will be found to uphold justice in the State (i.e. will have the authority necessary for doing so). (3) 663 f. Now, I recognise disloyalty in any one who breaks the law and defies the government, as Antigone has done. (4) 666 f. Instead of so doing, the citizen is bound to obey the government in everything. (5) 668—671. There is nothing slavish in that; on the contrary, it shows that the citizen is not only a good subject, but would, if required, be a good ruler;—as he would also be a good soldier.—Then comes the general censure on unruliness (672—676). And then the conclusion:—I must vindicate my authority, and punish Antigone (677 —680).

663 f. ὑπερβάς, absol., having transgressed: Il. 9. 501 ὅτε κέν τις ὑπερβήῃ καὶ ἁμάρτῃ: so Plat. Rep. 366 A ὑπερβαίνοντες καὶ ἁμαρτάνοντες.—τοὐπιτάσσειν, prop. said of a master giving orders to slaves (O. C. 839): so ἐπιτάγματα are a despot's commands (Arist. Pol. 4. 4. 28). For the

art., cp. 78.—νοεῖ, as 44.—Antigone 'did violence to the laws' by her deed: she seemed 'to dictate to her rulers' when she proclaimed a law superior to theirs (450 ff.). Cp. 482 ff.

666 f. στήσειε: the optat. (instead of ὃν ἂν στήσῃ) puts the case in the most general way: any one whom she might conceivably appoint. Hence this optat. suits γνώμαι: cp. 1032: Tr. 92 τὸ γ' εὖ | πράσσειν, ἐπεὶ πύθοιτο, κέρδος ἐμπολᾷ: O. T. 315 (n.), ib. 979.—καὶ τἀναντία, i.e. καὶ μεγάλα καὶ ἄδικα. So oft. in euphemisms, Thuc. 4. 62 ἀγαθὸν ἤ...τὰ ἐναντία: Plat. Rep. 472 C εὐδαιμονίας τε πέρι καὶ τοῦ ἐναντίου. Cp. Leutsch Paroem. App. 1. 100 κρεισσόνων γὰρ καὶ δίκαια κἄδικ' ἔστ' ἀκούειν: and the verse cited by schol. on Aesch. P. V. 75 δοῦλε, δεσποτῶν ἄκουε καὶ δίκαια κἄδικα.

668 f. τοῦτον...τὸν ἄνδρα refers to the indefinite subject of κλύειν in 666:—the man who thus obeys. The looseness of grammatical connection would hardly be felt when the sense was so clear. Cp. 1035 (τῶν δ'). So in O. C. 942 αὐτούς refers to τὴν πόλιν in 939.—καλῶς...εὖ: for the change of word in the epanaphora

He who does his duty in his own household will be found
righteous in the State also. But if any one transgresses, and
does violence to the laws, or thinks to dictate to his rulers, such
an one can win no praise from me. No, whomsoever the city
may appoint, that man must be obeyed, in little things and
great, in just things and unjust; and I should feel sure that
one who thus obeys would be a good ruler no less than a good
subject, and in the storm of spears would stand his ground
where he was set, loyal and dauntless at his comrade's side.

But disobedience is the worst of evils. This it is that ruins
cities; this makes homes desolate; by this, the ranks of allies

---

have πόλεις τ' (as A), πόλεις δ' (L²), or πόλεις (V⁴). The choice is between
πόλεις ὅλλυσιν, ἥδ' (Dindorf), and πόλεις τ' ὅλλυσιν ἥδ' (Nauck). L has ἥδ' here
and in 674. ἥδ' is found in some later MSS. (V, Liv. a). See comment.
674 συμμάχηι L: σὺν μάχῃ r. Reiske and Bothe conjectured συμμάχου,
which has been generally received. Held, κἀν μάχῃ. M. Schmidt, σὺν τροπῇ,

---

cp. *O. C.* 1501 σαφὴς μὲν ἀστῶν ἐμφανὴς
δὲ τοῦ ξένου (n.).—ἄν with ἄρχειν (=ὅτι
ἄρχοι ἄν) as well as θέλειν.
670 f. δορός...χειμῶνι. Eur. *Suppl.* 474
πολὺς κλύδων | ἡμῖν τε καὶ σοὶ ξυμμάχοις
τ' ἔσται δορός.—προστεταγμένον, the regular term for placing soldiers at their posts:
Thuc. 2. 87 ἔπεσθε, χώραν μὴ προλείποντες
ᾗ ἄν τις προσταχθῇ.—παραστάτην, one
who stands beside one in the ranks (as
προστάτης in front and ἐπιστάτης behind):
Xen. *Cyr.* 3. 3. 21 (the gods are invoked
as) παραστάτας ἀγαθοὺς καὶ συμμάχους.
The Attic ἔφηβος, on beginning, at
eighteen, his term of service as a περί-
πολος, took an oath, οὐ καταισχυνῶ ὅπλα
τὰ ἱερά [the arms given to him by the
State], οὐδ' ἐγκαταλείψω τὸν παραστάτην ὅτῳ ἄν στοιχήσω (by whose side
he should be placed): Stob. *Serm.* 43. 48.
Thus for an Athenian audience this verse
would be effective, and would seem peculiarly appropriate when addressed to
the youthful Haemon.
673 πόλεις ὅλλυσιν, ἥδ' is far better
and more spirited than πόλεις τ' ὅλλυσιν
ἥδ': it is also strongly confirmed by the
similar passage, 296 ff., where we have
τοῦτο—τόδ'—τόδ', just as here αὕτη...ἥδ'...
ἥδ'. When πόλεις had become, as in L,
πόλις,—a corruption found also in Aesch.
Pers. 489,—τ' may have been added for
metre's sake. To ἥδε itself there is no
objection: it was certainly used in iambics by Soph. (fr. 253, fr. 503), no less
than by Aesch. (*Cho.* 1025, *Eum.* 414),

and by Eur. (*Hec.* 323, *H. F.* 30).—
Campb. reads πόλεις τ'...ἥδ', and regards
the anacoluthon as making the lines 'more
expressive.'
674 ff. συμμάχου is a certain correction of L's συμμάχηι. The meaning is,
'Disobedience causes allied forces (σύμμαχον δόρυ) to break up in flight.' It
turns union into disunion,—the hope of
victory into defeat. With σὺν μάχῃ the
sense would be, 'Disobedience, aiding
the spear (of the foe), causes rout.' But
this would represent disobedience as
merely one cause of defeat,—an incident
that turns the scale. It is evidently more
forcible to represent it as breaking up an
army which might otherwise have stood
united and firm.—τροπὰς καταρρήγνυσι,
lit., *causes* rout *to break forth*, *i.e.* breaks
up the army in rout. Cp. Athen. 130 c
ὁ γελωτοποιὸς εἰσῆλθε...καὶ πολλοὺς κατέρ-
ρηξεν ἡμῶν γέλωτας, 'and *caused* shouts of
laughter *to break forth* among us': (not,
'wreaked many witticisms upon us,'—as
Casaubon took it.) The only peculiarity
in the use of the verb is that it is here
equiv. to ποιεῖ καταρρήγνυσθαι. We cannot compare Theocr. 22. 172 νεῖκος ἀναρ-
ρήξαντας, 'having broken *into* strife' (said
of the parties to it), which is merely like
ῥῆξαι φωνήν, etc.—τῶν δ' ὀρθουμένων
(masc.), of those who have a prosperous
course: Thuc. 2. 60 πόλιν...ὀρθουμένην,
opp. to σφαλλομένην: 8. 64 ξυνέβη...τὴν
πόλιν ἀκινδύνως ὀρθοῦσθαι. Cp. 163, 167.—
τὰ πολλὰ σώματα, 'the greater number

τροπὰς καταρρήγνυσι· τῶν δ' ὀρθουμένων 675
σῴζει τὰ πολλὰ σώμαθ' ἡ πειθαρχία.
οὕτως ἀμυντέ' ἐστὶ τοῖς κοσμουμένοις,
κοὔτοι γυναικὸς οὐδαμῶς ἡσσητέα.
κρεῖσσον γάρ, εἴπερ δεῖ, πρὸς ἀνδρὸς ἐκπεσεῖν,
κοὐκ ἂν γυναικῶν ἥσσονες καλοίμεθ' ἄν. 680

ΧΟ. ἡμῖν μέν, εἰ μὴ τῷ χρόνῳ κεκλέμμεθα,
λέγειν φρονούντως ὧν λέγεις δοκεῖς πέρι.

ΑΙ. πάτερ, θεοὶ φύουσιν ἀνθρώποις φρένας,
πάντων ὅσ' ἐστὶ κτημάτων ὑπέρτατον.
ἐγὼ δ' ὅπως σὺ μὴ λέγεις ὀρθῶς τάδε, 685
οὔτ' ἂν δυναίμην μήτ' ἐπισταίμην λέγειν·

with στίχας for τροπὰς in 675. **676** πειθαρχία] πιθαρχία L. **678** γυναικὸς]
'Lege γυναικῶν ex v. 680 et Eustathio p. 759, 39': Porson *Adv.* p. 172. But
Eustathius, *l.c.*, after quoting 677 correctly, proceeds, καὶ οὐ γυναικῶν ἡσσητέα·
ἀντὶ τοῦ ἀμυντέον καὶ ἡσσητέον. The point which interested him was merely the
use of the verbal adj. in the plur. We cannot assume that he had γυναικῶν in
his text; see n. in Appendix on 292. **679 f.** Heimreich suspects both
these two verses. Bergk and Meineke reject 680. As Wecklein says (*Ars Soph.*

---

of lives,' differing from τοὺς πολλούς only
by bringing out the notion of personal
safety more vividly. Cp. *Ai.* 758 where
the masc. follows τὰ...σώματα.—ἡ
πειθαρχία: called τῆς εὐπραξίας | μήτηρ
by Aesch. *Th.* 225. The schol. quotes
Il. 5. 531 αἰδομένων δ' ἀνδρῶν πλέονες σόοι
ἠὲ πέφανται.

677 ἀμυντέ', the impers. neut. plur.,
as Her. 9. 58 ἐκείνοισι ταῦτα ποιεῦσι οὐκ
ἐπιτρεπτέα ἐστί, ἀλλὰ διωκτέοι εἰσί: Thuc.
1. 86 τιμωρητέα, 88 πολεμητέα, 118 ἐπι-
χειρητέα, etc.: so *O. C.* 495 ὁδωτά. Cp.
447, 576. Eur. *Or.* 523 ἀμυνῶ δ', ὁσονπερ
δυνατός εἰμι, τῷ νόμῳ. Thuc. 1. 140 τοῖς
κοινῇ δόξασι βοηθεῖν.—**τοῖς κοσμουμένοις**
(neut.), the regulations made by οἱ κοσ-
μοῦντες, the rulers: meaning here, his
own edicts. For the act. κοσμεῖν, cp.
Her. 1. 59 (Peisistratus) ἔνεμε τὴν πόλιν
κοσμέων καλῶς τε καὶ εὖ. And for the
pass. thus used, *ib.* 100 ταῦτα μὲν κατὰ
τὰς δίκας ἐποίεε (Deïoces), τάδε δὲ ἄλλα
ἐκεκοσμέατό οἱ: 'and the following
regulations had also *been made* by him.'—
Another view (also noticed by the Schol.)
makes **τοῖς κ.** dat. of οἱ κοσμούμενοι, 'the
rulers.' But (*a*) the only place which
might seem to favour this use of the midd.
is Thuc. 8. 24 (the Chians, the more they
prospered) τόσῳ καὶ ἐκοσμοῦντο ἐχυρώ-

τερον: but there the verb may well be
pass., 'the more securely was their government organised.' (*b*) As Creon is himself
at once ὁ ἀμύνων and ὁ κοσμῶν, it is more
natural that he should speak of his own
edicts than of 'the rulers.'—κόσμος was
said of a constitution, esp. oligarchical
(Thuc. 4. 76 μεταστῆσαι τὸν κόσμον καὶ ἐς
δημοκρατίαν...τρέψαι: 8. 72 μένειν ἐν τῷ
ὀλιγαρχικῷ κόσμῳ). The Cretan κόσμοι
were oligarchical magistrates, with military as well as civil powers (Arist. *Pol.*
2. 10).

678 κοὔτοι...ἡσσητέα: Ar. *Lys.* 450
ἀτὰρ οὐ γυναικῶν οὐδέποτ' ἔσθ' ἡττητέα |
ἡμῖν. (Cp. Milton, *Samson* 562 'Effemi-
nately vanquished.') Since ἡσσᾶσθαι is
only pass., its verbal in τέος can be only
pass.: as ἁλωτέον could mean only, 'one
must be taken.' But even in other cases
the verbal in τέος sometimes answers to
the pass., not to the act., sense of the
verb: as Xen. *Oec.* 7 § 38 ὅταν ἐκείνη
(the queen-bee) ἐκλίπῃ, οὐδεμία οἴεται τῶν
μελιττῶν ἀπολειπτέον εἶναι, ἀλλ' ἕπονται
πᾶσαι: *i.e.* ὅτι δεῖ ἀπολείπεσθαι (pass.),
'to be left behind': (for the stationary
bees could not be said ἀπολείπειν the
emigrant.)

679 f. δεῖ: for the pause, cp. 555.—
ἐκπεσεῖν: here absol., *to be displaced*,

are broken into headless rout: but, of the lives whose course
is fair, the greater part owes safety to obedience. Therefore we
must support the cause of order, and in no wise suffer a woman
to worst us. Better to fall from power, if we must, by a man's
hand ; then we should not be called weaker than a woman.

CH. To us, unless our years have stolen our wit, thou
seemest to say wisely what thou sayest.

HAE. Father, the gods implant reason in men, the highest
of all things that we call our own. Not mine the skill—far from
me be the quest!—to say wherein thou speakest not aright ;

---

em. p. 147), if 680 were condemned, 679 must go too.   **681** κεκλήμεθα L,
but with gl. σεσυλήμεθα written above : κεκλέμμεθα r.—Hartung conject. τῶν
φρενῶν: Schaefer, βεβλάμμεθα: whence Nauck, εἴ τι μὴ φρενῶν βεβλάμμεθα.
684 ὅσσ' L : ὅς r.—χρημάτων MSS.: but L has κτ written above by the first hand.
—ὑπέρτατον L : ὑπέρτερον r.   **685** λέγηισ L : λέγεις r.—Heimreich would change

---

thrust out : oft. of dethronement (ἐκπ.
τυραννίδος, ἀρχῆς, κράτους, Aesch.), or of
exile (χθονός, *O. C.* 766).—**κοὐκ ἄν...κα-
λοίμεθ' ἄν**: the doubled ἄν, as oft. in emphatic or excited utterances (*O. T.* 339 n.).
—These two verses (like so many others)
have been suspected merely because they
are not indispensable. A defence is perhaps hardly needed. It is enough to
remark that Creon's irritation under a
woman's defiance (484, 525, 579) naturally prompts this further comment on
the word γυναικός in 678. And the
phrase γυναικῶν ἥσσονες (680) has a
peculiar force as spoken to Haemon,—
whom Creon afterwards taunts as γυναικὸς
ὕστερον (746).
681 μέν : 498, 634.—**τῷ χρόνῳ**, by
our age: cp. 729 τὸν χρόνον, 'my years':
O. T. 963.—**κεκλέμμεθα**, are deceived : so
1218: *Tr.* 243 εἰ μὴ ξυμφοραὶ κλέπτουσί
με.
682 δοκεῖς λέγειν φρονούντως περὶ (τούτων περὶ) ὧν λέγεις. At first sight it is
natural to wish, with Herm., for δοκεῖς...
ὧν λέγεις λέγειν πέρι. Cp. 1057 ἃν λέγῃς
λέγων. But here it is fitting that λέγειν
should have the prominence of the first
place. And the undoubted harshness of
the order may be partly excused by observing that ὧν λέγεις is practically equiv.
to τούτων.
683 ff. θεοί. Creon had urged that
filial piety demands the submission of
the son's judgment to the γνώμη πατρῴα
(640); and had warned Haemon against
disregarding the voice of reason (648).

Haemon replies: 'Reason is the gift of
the gods. I dare not suggest that your
reasonings are wrong ; but other men, too,
may sometimes reason soundly. Now, I
know what the Thebans are saying of
your action ; and, as a son devoted to
your welfare, I ought to tell you.'—The
tact and deference which mark this speech
place Creon's αὐθάδεια in a stronger light.
—**κτημάτων**: cp. *O. T.* 549: Her.
5. 24 κτημάτων πάντων ἐστὶ τιμιώτατον
ἀνὴρ φίλος ξυνετός τε καὶ εὔνοος.
685 f. ἐγὼ δ' ὅπως : lit., 'I should not
be able to say (and may I never be capable
of saying !) in what respect (ὅπως) thou
dost not say these things rightly.' He
could not, if he would—and would not, if
he could—impugn his father's reasonings.
He only suggests that the case may have
also another aspect, which Creon has not
considered.—**μὴ** after ὅπως is generic, as
after ὅς, ὅστις (691, 696): I could not say
what point in thy argument is *such as not*
to be true :—just as we could have, οὐκ
οἶδα ὅ (or ὅ τι) μὴ ἀληθεύεις. The μή
might be taken with **ὀρθῶς** ('how thou
sayest *otherwise than* rightly'), but the
order of words is against this. [It cannot
be explained as substituted for οὐ through
the influence of the optatives.]—**μήτ' ἐπισταίμην.** For this verb as = 'to be capable
of,' cp. 472, *Tr.* 543 ἐγὼ δὲ θυμοῦσθαι μὲν
οὐκ ἐπίσταμαι | νοσοῦντι κείνῳ. For the
wish co-ordinated with the statement of
fact, cp. 500: *Tr.* 582 κακὰς δὲ τόλμας
μήτ' ἐπισταίμην ἐγὼ | μήτ' ἐκμάθοιμι, τάς
τε τολμώσας στυγῶ : and *ib.* 143.

γένοιτο μέντἂν χἁτέρῳ καλῶς ἔχον.
σοῦ δ᾽ οὖν πέφυκα πάντα προσκοπεῖν ὅσα
λέγει τις ἢ πράσσει τις ἢ ψέγειν ἔχει.
τὸ γὰρ σὸν ὄμμα δεινὸν ἀνδρὶ δημότῃ   690
λόγοις τοιούτοις οἷς σὺ μὴ τέρψει κλύων·
ἐμοὶ δ᾽ ἀκούειν ἔσθ᾽ ὑπὸ σκότου τάδε,
τὴν παῖδα ταύτην οἷ᾽ ὀδύρεται πόλις,
πασῶν γυναικῶν ὡς ἀναξιωτάτη
κάκιστ᾽ ἀπ᾽ ἔργων εὐκλεεστάτων φθίνει·   695
ἥτις τὸν αὑτῆς αὐτάδελφον ἐν φοναῖς
πεπτῶτ᾽ ἄθαπτον μήθ᾽ ὑπ᾽ ὠμηστῶν κυνῶν
εἴασ᾽ ὀλέσθαι μήθ᾽ ὑπ᾽ οἰωνῶν τινός·
οὐχ ἥδε χρυσῆς ἀξία τιμῆς λαχεῖν;

μὴ to δή, and omit v. 687.   **687** χἁτέρῳ] Erfurdt conject. χἁτέρως or χἁτέρᾳ.   The
schol. in L has δυνατόν σε [not δυνατὸν δὲ, as it has been reported] καὶ ἑτέρως καλῶς
μεταβουλεύσασθαι.   **688** σοῦ L, with ι written above by the first hand, and
gl. in marg. by S, σὺ δ᾽ οὐ πέφυκας.   **690** τὸ γὰρ σὸν L: τὸ σὸν γὰρ r.
691 τέρψει] τέρψηι L.   Nauck suspects this verse.   Autenrieth would place it before

---

687 καλῶς ἔχον (sc. τι: cp. O. T. 517
εἰς βλάβην φέρον), something good, some
true thought, **γένοιτο ἂν καὶ ἑτέρῳ**, might
come to (accrue to) another also. For
γένοιτο cp. Plat. Symp. 211 D εἴ τῳ γένοιτο
αὐτὸ τὸ καλὸν ἰδεῖν.   (The phrase γένοιτο
μέντἂν occurs also Ai. 86.)—Not : ' Yet it
might be found well for another' (to say
that you were wrong). Haemon seeks
to propitiate his father ; but that purpose
would scarcely be served by such a speech
as this—'Being your son, I do not con-
tradict you myself, though I think that
other people might very reasonably do so.'
688 f. σοῦ δ᾽ οὖν: 'but in any case
(i.e., whatever may be the worth of opinions different from yours) it is my natural
part to watch on your behalf,' etc.   For
δ᾽ οὖν cp. 722, 769: O. C. 1205 ἔστω δ᾽
οὖν ὅπως ὑμῖν φίλον.—The gen. **σοῦ** is
supported by the use of the gen. with
προκήδομαι (741), προταρβῶ (83), προνοῶ,
etc., and expresses the idea, 'in thy defence,' better than σοί would do. Cp.
Eur. Med. 459 τὸ σὸν...προσκοπούμενος.—
Herm. adopted the v. l. of the schol. in
L, **σὺ δ᾽ οὐ πέφυκας**, which Ellendt approves : but (a) πέφυκας is then less fitting,
and (b) δ᾽ οὖν commends the vulgate as
genuine.—For the repeated τις, cp. Aesch.
Eum. 889 μῆνίν τιν᾽ ἢ κότον τιν᾽. Thuc.

4. 62 εἴ τῳ τι ἔστιν ἀγαθὸν ἢ εἴ τῳ τὰ
ἐναντία.   (Distinguish Eur. Or. 1218 ἥν
τις,... | ἢ σύμμαχός τις ἢ κασίγνητος,—
anyone,—be he ally or brother : and Andr.
733 ἔστι γάρ τις οὐ πρόσω | Σπάρτης πόλις
τις, which, if sound, is a mere pleonasm.)
690 τὸ γὰρ σόν, not τὸ σὸν γάρ : so
O. T. 671 τὸ γὰρ σόν, οὐ τὸ τοῦδ᾽: ib.
1024 ἡ γὰρ πρὶν...ἀπαιδία.   In the case
of σόν, at least, this order seems to
strengthen, rather than diminish, the
emphasis. **ὄμμα**: cp. O. T. 447 οὐ τὸ
σὸν | δείσας πρόσωπον. Jeremiah i. 8 'Be
not afraid of their faces.'—**δημότῃ**, the
ordinary Theban citizen: cp. O. C. 78 n.
691 λόγοις τοιούτοις, causal dat. :
thy face is terrible to the citizen on account
of such words as shall displease thee : i.e.
the citizen imagines the stern king's face
growing darker at the sound of frank
speech, and restrains his lips. (Cp. 509.)
Doubts as to the dat. λόγοις τ. led Dindorf
to suppose the loss of one verse (or more)
after 690. Herwerden has suggested
something like κοὐδεὶς ποτ᾽ ἀστῶν ἐμφανῶς
χρῆται, πάτερ, | λόγοις τοιούτοις κ.τ.λ.
Nauck thinks that either v. 691 is wholly
spurious, or that the words λόγοις τοιούτοις
are corrupt. But, while the dat. is certainly bold—esp. with ἀνδρὶ δ. preceding
it—it is (I think) quite within the possi-

and yet another man, too, might have some useful thought. At least, it is my natural office to watch, on thy behalf, all that men say, or do, or find to blame. For the dread of thy frown forbids the citizen to speak such words as would offend thine ear; but I can hear these murmurs in the dark, these moanings of the city for this maiden; 'no woman,' they say, 'ever merited her doom less,—none ever was to die so shamefully for deeds so glorious as hers; who, when her own brother had fallen in bloody strife, would not leave him unburied, to be devoured by carrion dogs, or by any bird:— deserves not *she* the meed of golden honour?'

690, deleting the stop after ἔχει in 689. **695** ἀπ' L: ἐπ' r. **696** αὐτῆς] αὐτῆσ L. **697 f.** μήθ'...μήδ' (*sic*) L: μήθ'...μήθ' r.—For ἄθαπτον μήθ', Schneidewin proposed ἔθαπτεν μηδ': and Blaydes reads ἔθαψε, μηδ' (with μηδ' in 698).—κυνῶν] In L a *v. l.* λύκων is noted by S. **699** τιμαῖσ L, with γρ.

bilities of classical idiom. We should remember that Athenians were accustomed to use a simple dat. (of 'time' or 'occasion') in speaking of festivals,—as τραγῳδοῖς καινοῖς: cp. (*e.g.*) Plat. *Symp.* 174 A χθὲς γὰρ αὐτὸν διέφυγον τοῖς ἐπινικίοις, 'I eluded him yesterday *when he was holding* his sacrifice for victory.' So, here, the dat. λόγοις τοιούτοις, though properly causal, might sound to a Greek ear like, '*at* such words,' *i.e.* 'when such words are spoken.' The causal dat. in 391, ταῖς σαῖς ἀπειλαῖς, is similar. Cp. also Thuc. I. 84 εὐπραγίαις...οὐκ ἐξυβρίζομεν, where the notion, 'by reason of successes,' is similarly blended with the notion, 'in seasons of success.'—οἷς with τέρψει (cp. *O. C.* 1140, *Ph.* 460), κλύων epexegetic. If, however, the order had been κλύων τέρψει, then οἷς might have been for οὕς, by attraction. The μή is generic ('such that not...'), cp. 696. For the fut. midd. τέρψομαι (with pass. sense) cp. fr. 612 ὅπου γε μὴ δίκαια τέρψεται, and [Eur.] *Rhes.* 194. For the fut. ind. after a relative with μή, cp. *O. T.* 1412 n. —Nauck reads τέρψῃ (aor. midd.). This rare aor. ἐτερψάμην is epic, as *Od.* 12. 188 τερψάμενος ('having had delight'). It is not Attic, the Attic aor. in that sense being ἐτέρφθην (*O. C.* 1140).

692 f. ὑπὸ σκότου goes with ἀκούειν more naturally than with ὀδύρεται, and the sense is the same: *i.e.*, he is in the σκότος where the things are said: for the gen., cp. 65 n., and *Tr.* 539 μίμνομεν μιᾶς ὑπὸ | χλαίνης, which shows that we need

not here conceive the sounds as 'coming from under' the darkness. Cp. Xen. *Cyr.* 4. 6. 4 κατέσχεν ὑπὸ σκότου τὸν φθόνον. Eur. *Or.* 1457 ὑπὸ σκότου | ξίφη σπάσαντες. But ὑπὸ σκότῳ also occurs (Aesch. *Ag.* 1030, Eur. *Ph.* 1214).

695 κάκιστ'... εὐκλεεστάτων: cp. *O. T.* 1433 ἄριστος ἐλθὼν πρὸς κάκιστον. Plat. *Apol.* 30 A τὰ πλείστου ἄξια περὶ ἐλαχίστου ποιεῖται.—ἀπ' ἔργων, as their result: *Ai.* 1078 πεσεῖν ἂν κἂν ἀπὸ σμικροῦ κακοῦ.

696 ff. ἥτις with causal force (*O. C.* 962); hence, too, the generic μήθ'...μήδ' which belong to εἴασε (understood with the second μήθ'), not to ὀλέσθαι: 'being one who did not allow' (*quae non permiserit*).—αὐτάδελφον: cp. 1.—ἐν φοναῖς: cp. 1314. The phrases ἐν φονῇσιν and ἀμφὶ φονῇσιν are Homeric, and Her. uses the former (with art., 9. 76 ἐν τῇσι φονῇσι ἐόντας). The phrase ἐν φοναῖς is used by Pindar, Aesch., Eur., and (in parody) by Ar. But v. 1003 of this play— the only play of Soph. which contains the word—seems a solitary Attic instance of φοναῖς without ἐν.

699 χρυσῆς, a general epithet for what is brilliant or precious: thus Pind. *P.* 3. 73 ὑγίειαν...χρυσέαν, and even (*O.* 10. 13) στεφάνῳ χρυσέας ἐλαίας (the wreath of natural olive), as Olympia is μάτηρ χρυσοστεφάνων ἀέθλων (*O.* 8. 1) in a like sense. Cp. *O. T.* 157 ('golden' hope), *O. C.* 1052 (the 'golden' bliss of initiation).—There is no allusion to a χρυσοῦς στέφανος.—λαχεῖν can take either

. τοιάδ' ἐρεμνὴ σῖγ' ἐπέρχεται φάτις.　　　　700
ἐμοὶ δὲ σοῦ πράσσοντος εὐτυχῶς, πάτερ,
οὐκ ἔστιν οὐδὲν κτῆμα τιμιώτερον.
τί γὰρ πατρὸς θάλλοντος εὐκλείας τέκνοις
ἄγαλμα μεῖζον, ἢ τί πρὸς παίδων πατρί;
μή νυν ἓν ἦθος μοῦνον ἐν σαυτῷ φόρει,　　　705
ὡς φὴς σύ, κοὐδὲν ἄλλο, τοῦτ' ὀρθῶς ἔχειν.
ὅστις γὰρ αὐτὸς ἢ φρονεῖν μόνος δοκεῖ,
ἢ γλῶσσαν, ἣν οὐκ ἄλλος, ἢ ψυχὴν ἔχειν,
οὗτοι διαπτυχθέντες ὤφθησαν κενοί.
ἀλλ' ἄνδρα, κεἴ τις ᾖ σοφός, τὸ μανθάνειν　　710
πόλλ' αἰσχρὸν οὐδὲν καὶ τὸ μὴ τείνειν ἄγαν.
ὁρᾷς παρὰ ῥείθροισι χειμάρροις ὅσα
δένδρων ὑπείκει, κλῶνας ὡς ἐκσῴζεται·
τὰ δ' ἀντιτείνοντ' αὐτόπρεμν' ἀπόλλυται.
αὔτως δὲ ναὸς ὅστις ἐγκρατῆ πόδα　　　　715

καὶ στήλης in marg. by S. τιμῆς r.　　**701** ἐμοὶ made from ἐμοῦ in L.　　**703** εὐκλείας MSS.: εὐκλείᾳ Johnson.　　**705** After this v., Wecklein suspects the loss
of a v. such as μηδ' ἀξίου τοὺς ἄλλοθεν λόγους παρείς.　　**706** ὥς] Blaydes conject.
δ or ἅ.—ἄλλ ο, from ἀλλ' δ, (not ἀλλ' δ,) L: o and ω had been written above, but have

---

gen. or acc., the latter being more freq.
(*O. C.* 450 n.). But here the inf. is
rather epexegetic (cp. 1098 λαβεῖν), the
gen. depending on ἀξία.

700 ἐπέρχεται, spreads *over* (the town).
Cp. *Od.* 1. 299 οἷον κλέος ἔλλαβε... | πάν-
τας ἐπ' ἀνθρώπους. Cp. ὑφέρπειν, of secret
rumour, *O. T.* 786 n.

703 f. θάλλοντος, prospering, as *Ph.*
419 μέγα | θάλλοντές εἰσι νῦν ἐν Ἀργείων
στρατῷ.—μεῖζον εὐκλείας=μεῖζον ἢ εὔ-
κλεια.—πρὸς παίδων, on their part, from
their side: cp. *Tr.* 738 τί δ' ἔστιν, ὦ παῖ,
πρός γ' ἐμοῦ στυγούμενον; We understand
μεῖζον ἄγαλμά ἐστι τῆς ἐκείνων εὐκλείας.
—The conjecture εὐκλείᾳ is attractive,
(*a*) because θάλλω so oft. takes a dat. of
respect, as Hes. *Op.* 234 (ἀγαθοῦσι), Pind.
O. 9. 16 (ἀρεταῖσιν), etc.: (*b*) because the
strong sigmatism of the verse is thus
modified. But the words πρὸς παίδων
confirm εὐκλείας, since with εὐκλείᾳ we
should have expected παίδων alone. It is
true that πατὴρ θάλλων εὐκλείᾳ could
mean 'a father's fame' (cp. 638); but
one could not have, πρὸς παίδων τί
μεῖζον ἄγαλμα παίδων εὐκλείᾳ θαλλόντων;—

Triclinius wrongly joined εὐκλείας ἄγαλμα,
thinking of εὐκλείας γέρας (*Ph.* 478) and
στέφανον εὐκλείας μέγαν (*Ai.* 465).

705 f. νυν: cp. 524.—φόρει: Ar. *Eq.*
757 λῆμα θούριον φορεῖν: Eur. *Hipp.* 118
σπλάγχνον ἔντονον φέρων. So Shaksp.
Cymb. 3. 4. 146 'if you could *wear* a
mind | Dark as your fortune is': *Caes.*
5. 1. 113 'He *bears* too great a mind.'—
ἦθος=a way of *thinking:* the inf. depends on it, as on 'do not *think.*' ὡς
φὴς σύ, your way of speaking,=ὃ σὺ φῄς:
cp. *O. C.* 1124 (n.) καί σοι θεοὶ πόροιεν ὡς
ἐγὼ θέλω.—κοὐδέν, not καὶ μηδέν: it is
merely oratio obliqua for ὅτι τοῦτο καὶ
οὐδὲν ἄλλο ὀρθῶς ἔχει. The imperative
μή...φόρει does not affect this: cp. *Ai.*
1085 καὶ μὴ δοκῶμεν δρῶντες ἂν ἡδώμεθα |
οὐκ ἀντιτίσειν αὖθις ἂν λυπώμεθα. But
καὶ μηδέν could also have stood here,
since v. 705 could be regarded as equiv.
to, 'do not feel confident that...': see n.
on *O. T.* 1455.—τοῦτο, antecedent to ὡς
φῄς, emphatically placed: cp. *O. T.* 385.

707 f. μόνος with φρονεῖν only.—
ψυχήν: cp. 176. Theognis 221 ὅστις
τοι δοκέει τὸν πλησίον ἴδμεναι οὐδέν, | ἀλλ'

Such is the darkling rumour that spreads in secret. For me, my father, no treasure is so precious as thy welfare. What, indeed, is a nobler ornament for children than a prospering sire's fair fame, or for sire than sons'? Wear not, then, one mood only in thyself; think not that thy word, and thine alone, must be right. For if any man thinks that he alone is wise,—that in speech, or in mind, he hath no peer,—such a soul, when laid open, is ever found empty.

No, though a man be wise, 'tis no shame for him to learn many things, and to bend in season. Seest thou, beside the wintry torrent's course, how the trees that yield to it save every twig, while the stiff-necked perish root and branch? And even thus he who keeps the sheet of his sail

---

been erased.—φῆς] φημὶ L.—ἔχει L: ἔχειν Γ.   **707** αὐτὸς ἦ] αἰτῶν εὖ Priscian 17. 157.   **710** κεῖ τισ εῖ L: κεῖ τις ῆ Γ (κὴν τις ῆ A).   **711** ἄγαν] L has γαν in an erasure: the scribe had written μανθάν.   **712** παραρρείθροισι L.   **713** ἐκσωίζεται L.   **715** αὕτως] οὕτωσ L, made from αὔτωσ.—ὅστις] εἴτισ L, with ὁσ written above

---

αὐτὸς μοῦνος ποικίλα δήνε' (devices) ἔχειν, | κεῖνός γ' ἄφρων ἐστί, νόου βεβλαμμένος ἐσθλοῦ, | ἴσως γὰρ πάντες ποικίλ' ἐπιστάμεθα. Isocr. or. 3 § 43 joins Theognis, Hesiod and Phocylides as ἀρίστους...συμβούλους τῷ βίῳ τῷ τῶν ἀνθρώπων. They were read in schools.

709 οὗτοι after the collective ὅστις: Xen. Oec. 7. 37 ὃς ἂν κάμνῃ τῶν οἰκετῶν, τούτων σοι ἐπιμελητέον πάντων.—διαπτυχθέντες, when laid open. Cp. Eur. Hipp. 984 τὸ μέντοι πρᾶγμ', ἔχον καλοὺς λόγους, | εἴ τις διαπτύξειεν, οὐ καλὸν τόδε.   Andr. 330 ἔξωθέν εἰσιν οἱ δοκοῦντες εὖ φρονεῖν | λαμπροί, τὰ δ' ἔνδον πᾶσιν ἀνθρώποις ἴσοι. Also σκόλιον no. 7 in Bergk Poet. Lyr. (from Athen. 694 C, etc.) εἴθ' ἐξῆν ὁποῖός τις ἦν ἕκαστος | τὸ στῆθος διελόντ', ἔπειτα τὸν νοῦν | ἐσιδόντα, κλήσαντα πάλιν, | ἄνδρα φίλον νομίζειν ἀδόλῳ φρενί. The image might be suggested by various objects,— a casket, tables, fruit, or the like.—Cp. Shaks. Rom. 3. 2. 83 (of Romeo) 'Was ever book containing such vile matter So fairly bound?'—**κενοί**, sc. ὄντες: cp. 471.

710 f. ἄνδρα, subject to μανθάνειν, as O. T. 314 ἄνδρα δ' ὠφελεῖν κ.τ.λ.: for the place of τό, cp. 723, Tr. 65 σὲ... | τὸ μὴ πυθέσθαι instead of τὸ σὲ μὴ πυθέσθαι.— **κεῖ...ῆ**: see O. T. 198 n.—**τείνειν**, absol., here, like τείνειν τόξον or τείνειν πόδα, 'to strain the cord too tight,'—to be overrigid in maintaining one's own views. This poet. use should be distinguished from the ordinary intrans. use of τείνω,

like tendere, 'to have a direction,' or 'take one's way' (Xen. An. 4. 3. 21 ἔτεινον ἄνω πρὸς τὸ ὄρος).

712 παρὰ ῥείθρ.: for ᾱ before initial ῥ, cp. O. T. 847 (ἐμὲ ῥέπον), O. C. 900 ἀπὸ ῥυτῆρος.—**χειμάρροις**, here a neut. adj., as Eur. Tro. 449 ὕδατι χειμάρρῳ: usu. ὁ χειμάρρους (sc. ποταμός). Tozer, Geo. Gr. p. 84: 'The numerous torrents (χειμάρροι) are the natural result of the configuration of the country, for the steep limestone mountains have but little of a spongy surface to act as a reservoir for the rain... It is especially at the time of the autumn rains that the greatest floods take place, and the sudden swelling and violent rush of the stream has furnished Homer with some of his finest similes.' (Il. 4. 452 ff., 16, 384 ff.: imitated by Verg. Aen. 2. 305 ff., 12. 523.)—Antiphanes (c. 380 B.C.) parodies these verses (fr. incert. 10: Athen. 22 F).

713 f. ὑπείκει. Cp. Babrius fab. 36: an oak, torn up by the roots, is being swept down by a boiling torrent, and asks the reeds how they have managed to escape; when a reed (κάλαμος) answers;—σὺ μὲν μαχομένη ταῖς πνοαῖς ἐνικήθης, | ἡμεῖς δὲ καμπτόμεσθα μαλθακῇ γνώμῃ, | κἂν βαιὸν ἡμῶν ἄνεμος ἄκρα κινήσῃ.—**αὐτόπρεμνα**=αὐτόρριζα, πρόρριζα; Il. 9. 541 χαμαὶ βάλε δένδρεα μακρὰ | αὐτῇσιν ῥίζῃσι.

715 αὕτως, adv. from αὐτός (with 'Aeolic' acc.); see on O. T. 931.—**ναός**,

τείνας ὑπείκει μηδέν, ὑπτίοις κάτω
στρέψας τὸ λοιπὸν σέλμασιν ναυτίλλεται.
ἀλλ' εἶκε θυμοῦ καὶ μετάστασιν δίδου.
γνώμη γὰρ εἴ τις κἀπ' ἐμοῦ νεωτέρου
πρόσεστι, φήμ' ἔγωγε πρεσβεύειν πολὺ   720
φῦναι τὸν ἄνδρα πάντ' ἐπιστήμης πλέων·
εἰ δ' οὖν, φιλεῖ γὰρ τοῦτο μὴ ταύτῃ ῥέπειν,
καὶ τῶν λεγόντων εὖ καλὸν τὸ μανθάνειν.

ΧΟ. ἄναξ, σέ τ' εἰκός, εἴ τι καίριον λέγει,
μαθεῖν, σέ τ' αὖ τοῦδ'· εὖ γὰρ εἴρηται διπλᾶ.   725

by first hand.—ἐγκρατῇ] ἐγκρατεῖ L., with η written above by first hand: ἐγκρα-τῆς r.   717 τὸ λοιπὸν MSS.: Hermann conject. τὸ πλοῖον.—σέλμασι L. 718 θυμῶι L. So Ald., following Par. A, as usual. But θυμοῦ is in many of the later MSS., including L², V, V³ (first hand), V⁴, Aug. b, Dresd. a. See comment.

Doric for νεώς, allowed by tragedy even in iambics, as *Ai.* 872, Aesch. *Th.* 62, Eur. *Med.* 523: though ναῆς (953) and ναῖ occur only in lyrics. So ναός, temple (286), Ἀθάνα, κυναγός, ὁδαγός, ποδαγός (1196): and even in Att. prose λοχαγός, οὐραγός, ξεναγός.—ἐγκρατῇ, proleptic: cp. 475 περισκελῆ.—πόδα, the sheet: the πόδες were ropes attached to the two lower corners of the sail, whence their name. Eur. *Or.* 706 καὶ ναῦς γάρ, ἐντάθεισα πρὸς βίαν ποδί, | ἔβαψεν, ἔστη δ' αὖθις, ἣν χαλᾷ πόδα: a ship dips when strained too hard by the sheet (*i.e.* when the sheet is hauled too taut), but rights again, if one slackens.

716 f. μηδέν, generic (such an one as does not...).—κάτω στρέψας, *sc.* ναῦν, easily supplied from ναός: for κάτω, cp. 527: for στρέφω=ἀναστρέφω, *O. C.* 1453. Hermann's τὸ πλοῖον for τὸ λοιπόν is not only needless, but spoils the force of the phrase: '*thenceforth* voyages,' is an ironi-cal way of saying that the voyage comes to an abrupt end: cp. 311.—σέλμασιν, the rowers' benches: thus ὑπτίοις vividly suggests the moment of capsizing.

718 εἶκε θυμοῦ, 'cease from wrath,' lit., recede from it. The θυμός is con-ceived as ground from which he retires; so θυμοῦ περᾶν='to *go far in* wrath,' and is contrasted with εἴκειν: *O. T.* 673 στυγνὸς μὲν εἴκων δῆλος εἶ, βαρὺς δ', ὅταν | θυμοῦ περᾶσῃς. For the gen., cp. *Il.* 4. 509 μηδ' εἴκετε χάρμης | Ἀργείοις: ib. 5. 348 εἶκε, Διὸς θύγατερ, πολέμου καὶ δηϊο-τῆτος: Her. 2. 80 εἴκουσι τῆς ὁδοῦ: id. 7. 160 ὑπείξομεν τοῦ ἀρχαίου λόγου: Ar. *Ran.*

790 ὑπεχώρησεν αὐτῷ τοῦ θρόνου. Eur. has a somewhat similar phrase, *Hipp.* 900 ὀργῆς δ' ἐξανεὶς κακῆς, ἄναξ | Θησεῦ, τὸ λῷστον σοῖσι βούλευσαι δόμοις, where the sense is, 'having remitted thy wrath,' ἐξανεὶς [σεαυτὸν] ὀργῆς.—καὶ μετάστασιν δίδου, 'and concede a change': allow our pleading to change your mood. A change in Creon's mood implies a change in the whole situation. For the notions thus blended in μετάστασιν here, cp. Alexis fr. incert. 46 τῶν μετρίων αἱ μείζονες | λῦπαι ποιοῦσι τῶν φρενῶν μετάστασιν: Andoc. or. 2 § 18 οἴσειν ἔμελλεν...τοῦ τότε παρόν-τος κακοῦ μετάστασιν.—δίδου: a verb oft. used of *concession* to the remonstrance of friends: *Ai.* 483 παῦσαί γε μέντοι καὶ δὸς ἀνδράσιν φίλοις | γνώμης κρατῆσαι: *Tr.* 1117 δός μοι σεαυτόν, μὴ τοσοῦτον ὡς δάκνει | θυμῷ δύσοργος.—Others place a comma or point at εἶκε, taking καί as= 'also'; 'yield, *also* permitting thy wrath to change' (with διδούς); or 'yield: also permit,' etc. (an asyndeton, with δίδου). On this view, either θυμῷ or θυμοῦ is pos-sible. But the fatal objection to it is the weakness of καί, whether the 'also' is explained (*a*) as by Campbell (with δίδου) —'if you are angry, be *also* placable'; or (*b*) as by Wecklein (with διδούς)—'it is possible not only to moderate one's pas-sion, but *also* to desist from it,' which implies that he might yield while still angry.—See Appendix.

719 f. εἴ τις γνώμη πρόσεστι καὶ ἀπ' ἐμοῦ ν. (ὄντος), *i.e.*, if I also, younger though I am, can contribute a sound

taut, and never slackens it, upsets his boat, and finishes his
voyage with keel uppermost.

Nay, forego thy wrath; permit thyself to change. For
if I, a younger man, may offer my thought, it were far best,
I ween, that men should be all-wise by nature; but, otherwise—
and oft the scale inclines not so—'tis good also to learn from
those who speak aright.

CH. Sire, 'tis meet that thou shouldest profit by his words,
if he speaks aught in season, and thou, Haemon, by thy father's;
for on both parts there hath been wise speech.

and Appendix. **720** φήμ' L (not φῆμ'). **721** πλέω L: πλέων r. **725** αὖ
τοῦδ'] αὑτοῦ δ' L.—διπλᾶι L. (The ι is certainly from the first hand.) διπλᾶ r.
διπλῇ Hermann.

---

opinion. Cp. *O. C.* 292 τἀνθυμήματα |
...τἀπὸ σοῦ, the thoughts urged on thy
part. *El.* 1464 τελεῖται τἀπ' ἐμοῦ. For
the modest καί, cp. *O. T.* 1100 εἰ χρή τι
κἀμὲ...σταθμᾶσθαι: *Ph.* 192 εἴπερ κἀγώ τι
φρονῶ.—If κἀπ' were taken as καὶ ἐπί, it
must mean, 'in my case also.' Plat. *Rep.*
475 A ἐπ' ἐμοῦ λέγειν (to take me as an
instance). In *El.* 1469 I formerly thus
took κἀπ' ἐμοῦ θρήνων τύχῃ, but now think
that there, too, it is καὶ ἀπό.—πρεσβεύειν
=πρεσβύτατον εἶναι, to be the *best* thing:
Eur. *Her.* 45 οἷσι πρεσβεύει γένος, whose
birth has precedence (=the eldest): cp.
O. T. 1365 (πρεσβύτερον) n.

721 φῦναι, should be by nature: Pind.
O. 9. 107 τὸ δὲ φυᾷ κράτιστον ἅπαν (opposed to διδακταὶ ἀρεταί).—πάντ', adv.:
Tr. 338 τούτων ἔχω γὰρ πάντ' ἐπιστήμην
ἐγώ: *O. T.* 475 n.—The merit of listening to good advice is often thus extolled:
Hes. *Op.* 291 οὗτος μὲν πανάριστος, ὃς αὐ-
τὸς πάντα νοήσῃ· | ἐσθλὸς δ' αὖ κἀκεῖνος,
ὃς εὖ εἰπόντι πίθηται. Her. 7. 16 ἴσον
ἐκεῖνο, ὦ βασιλεῦ, παρ' ἐμοὶ κέκριται, φρο-
νέειν τε εὖ καὶ τῷ λέγοντι χρηστὰ ἐθέλειν
πείθεσθαι. Cp. Cic. *pro Cluentio* 31:
Livy 22. 29.

722 εἰ δ' οὖν, sc. μὴ ἔφυ τοιοῦτος.
This is better than to suppose that φιλεῖ
γάρ has changed the form of the sentence
(εἰ δ' οὖν τοῦτο μὴ ταύτῃ ῥέπει), since this
elliptical εἰ δ' οὖν was a familiar Attic
idiom: see Plat. *Apol.* 34 D εἰ δή τις ὑμῶν
οὕτως ἔχει—οὐκ ἀξιῶ μὲν γὰρ ἔγωγε, εἰ δ'
οὖν [sc. οὕτως ἔχει]—ἐπιεικῆ ἄν μοι δοκῶ
πρὸς τοῦτον λέγειν: 'If any one of you is so
disposed—I do not think that he ought to
be so, but *suppose that he is*—I think that
I might fairly say to him,' etc. Eur. *Hipp.*
507 εἴ τοι δοκεῖ σοι, χρῆν μὲν οὔ σ' ἁμαρ-

τάνειν· | εἰ δ' οὖν [sc. ἥμαρτες], πιθοῦ μοι
('you ought not to have erred,—but if
you *have*'). So, without ellipse, Aesch.
Ag. 1042 εἰ δ' οὖν ἀνάγκη τῆσδ' ἐπιρρέποι
τύχης, 'but if one *should* be doomed to
slavery' (then worthy masters are best).
Eur. fr. 463 λύπη μὲν ἄτη περιπεσεῖν...|
εἰ δ' οὖν γένοιτο, κ.τ.λ. Cp. δ' οὖν in
688 (n.).—τοῦτο...ταύτῃ: cp. *Ai.* 950
τάδ' ἔστη τῇδε: Aesch. *P. V.* 511 οὐ ταῦτα
ταύτῃ. μή is generic, going with ταύτῃ:
in a way other than this.—ῥέπειν to incline (as the scale of a balance does): so
Plat. *Legg.* 862 D τῇδε ῥέπειν, *Tim.* 79 E
ἐκείνῃ ῥέπον (to incline, or tend, in that
direction).

723 καὶ τὸ τῶν εὖ λεγόντων μανθάνειν
καλόν (ἐστι): for the place of εὖ, cp. 659:
for that of τό, 710. The simple gen., as
O. T. 545, etc.

724 f. σέ τ' doubled: cp. 1340, *O. T.*
637.—L's διπλᾶι really favours διπλᾶ
rather than Hermann's διπλῇ: for ι subscript is oft. wrongly added or omitted
(cp. 726 cr. n.); whereas ῃι was not likely
to become ᾱι here. Either word is admissible; but I slightly prefer διπλᾶ, for this
reason. It is true that the plur. of διπλοῦς
in poetry usu.=simply 'two' (51, 1232,
1320, *O. T.* 20, 1135). But Soph. has
at least one instance of the distributive
sense ('two sets'), viz., *O. T.* 1249,
where διπλοῦς=a twofold brood, *i.e.*
Oed., and his children. (I do not add
O. T. 288 διπλοῦς | πομπούς, taking it to
mean merely 'two,' not 'two sets.') And
in Attic prose the distributive use is not
rare: thus in Plat. *Legg.* 722 E διπλοῖ...
νόμοι are not 'two laws,' but 'two sets of
laws.' We have, then, good warrant for
διπλᾶ here as='two sets of arguments.'

136 ΣΟΦΟΚΛΕΟΥΣ

ΚΡ. οἱ τηλικοίδε καὶ διδαξόμεσθα δὴ
    φρονεῖν ὑπ' ἀνδρὸς τηλικοῦδε τὴν φύσιν;
ΑΙ. μηδὲν τὸ μὴ δίκαιον· εἰ δ' ἐγὼ νέος,
    οὐ τὸν χρόνον χρὴ μᾶλλον ἢ τἄργα σκοπεῖν.
ΚΡ. ἔργον γάρ ἐστι τοὺς ἀκοσμοῦντας σέβειν;   730
ΑΙ. οὐδ' ἂν κελεύσαιμ' εὐσεβεῖν εἰς τοὺς κακούς.
ΚΡ. οὐχ ἥδε γὰρ τοιᾷδ' ἐπείληπται νόσῳ;
ΑΙ. οὔ φησι Θήβης τῆσδ' ὁμόπτολις λεώς.
ΚΡ. πόλις γὰρ ἡμῖν ἁμὲ χρὴ τάσσειν ἐρεῖ;
ΑΙ. ὁρᾷς τόδ' ὡς εἴρηκας ὡς ἄγαν νέος;   735
ΚΡ. ἄλλῳ γὰρ ἢ 'μοὶ χρή *με τῆσδ' ἄρχειν χθονός;
ΑΙ. πόλις γὰρ οὐκ ἔσθ' ἥτις ἀνδρός ἐσθ' ἑνός.

726 οἱ] In L, the first hand has written ἦι above οἱ. This was meant to indicate a variant ἦ,—the ι being added by an error of a frequent kind (cp. 755 ἦισθ'). Dindorf wrongly supposed that it was meant to indicate a correction of διπλᾶι in 725 into διπλῆι. In that case it would have been written over or near διπλᾶι, not at the beginning of v. 726.—διδαξόμεσθα δὴ] διδαξόμεσθ' ἃ δεῖ Semitelos. **728** μηδὲν τὸ μὴ] μηδέν γ' ὃ μὴ Tournier: μηδέν γε μὴ K. Walter. **729** τἄργα]

On the other hand, **διπλῆ** is strange (though possible) as = 'in two ways,' *i.e.* 'on both sides.' It usu. means, 'doubly' (Eur. *Ion* 760 κεἰ θανεῖν μέλλω διπλῇ); or 'twice as much' (Plat. *Rep.* 330 C διπλῆ ἢ οἱ ἄλλοι). So, here, it would more naturally mean, 'twice over.'

726 f. καὶ with **διδαξ.**, shall we *indeed* be taught: *El.* 385 ἦ ταῦτα δὴ με καὶ βεβούλευνται ποιεῖν; *O. T.* 772 n. For διδαξ. as pass., cp. 637.—**δή**, an indignant 'then': the word ends a verse also in 923, *Tr.* 460, *Ph.* 1065, Eur. *Suppl.* 521, *Hipp.* 1093.—**τὴν φύσιν**, birth, and so age; *O. C.* 1295 ὧν φύσει νεώτερος.

728 f. μηδέν, *sc.* διδάσκου: **τὸ μὴ δίκ.** = ὃ μὴ δίκαιόν ἐστι: see on 360 οὐδὲν...τὸ μέλλον.—**τὸν χρόνον**, my years: cp. 681.— The change of **τἄργα** into τοὔργον (adopted by Nauck) is no gain. The sing. is taken as 'the cause' (which he defends). But he means, 'you should consider, not my age, but my conduct,—my merits': and this is expressed by τἄργα, just as in *O. C.* 265 ὄνομα μόνον δείσαντες· οὐ γὰρ δὴ τό γε | σῶμ' οὐδὲ τἄργα τάμά. Cp. Menander fr. incert. 91 μὴ τοῦτο βλέψῃς, εἰ νεώτερος λέγω, | ἀλλ' εἰ φρονούντων τοὺς λόγους ἀνδρῶν λέγω (v. l. φρονοῦντος...ἀνδρός: Bentley, φέρω).

730 ἔργον. Haemon has asked that

his ἔργα may be considered. Creon asks scornfully, 'Do you consider it an ἔργον—something which you can urge in your favour—to be the champion of a rebel?' ἔργον would not have been thus used alone, but for the desire to give τἄργα a derisive echo. The Attic associations of the word help, however, to explain this use. Thus ἔργον meant (*a*) a thing *worth doing*, as Ar. *Lys.* 424 οὐδὲν ἔργον ἑστάναι, it is *no use*... (cp. *Ai.* 852); so οὐδὲν προὔργου ἐστί, *non operae pretium est:* or (*b*), one's allotted task, as Ar. *Av.* 862, ἱερεῦ, σὸν ἔργον, θῦε. So here, without meaning so much as 'achievement' (*El.* 689), it could mean, 'useful act,' 'worthy task.'—**τοὺς ἀκοσμοῦντας**: so *Ph.* 387: cp. above 660, 677.—**σέβειν**, as 511.

731 οὐδ', not even: *O. C.* 1429 (n.) οὐδ' ἀγγελοῦμεν φλαῦρα. So far am I from showing honour to evil-doers, that I would not even wish others to do so. Without directly denying that Antigone can be described as ἀκοσμοῦσα, he denies that she is κακή. This involves the whole question between the divine and the human law.

732 τοιᾷδε...νόσῳ, that of being κακή. Others understand, τῷ εἰς τοὺς κακοὺς εὐσεβεῖν. But the sense of the dialogue runs thus:—'C. Do you approve of honour-

CR. Men of my age—are we indeed to be schooled, then, by men of his?

HAE. In nothing that is not right; but if I am young, thou shouldest look to my merits, not to my years.

CR. Is it a merit to honour the unruly?

HAE. I could wish no one to show respect for evil-doers.

CR. Then is not she tainted with that malady?

HAE. Our Theban folk, with one voice, denies it.

CR. Shall Thebes prescribe to me how I must rule?

HAE. See, there thou hast spoken like a youth indeed.

CR. Am I to rule this land by other judgment than mine own?

HAE. That is no city, which belongs to one man.

τοὔργον Hilberg. **731** οὐδ' ἂν] οὔ τᾶν Schneidewin. **734** ἀμὲ] ἄμμε L. **735** τόδ'] In L an early hand has changed o to a. **736** ἄλλωι γὰρ ἢ (sic) μοι χρῆ γε L. So (with χρή) most of the later MSS. Dobree's conject., ἄλλῳ γὰρ ἢ 'μοὶ χρή με, has been generally received.—Campbh. cites ἄλλον γὰρ ἢ με from M⁴, = cod. C. 24 sup. in the Ambrosian Library at Milan, a 15th cent. MS. **737** ἀνδρός ἐσθ'] ἀνδρὸσ ἔσθ' L.

---

ing law-breakers?—*H*. I should not dream of honouring wrong-doers.—*C*. Is not she, then, a wrong-doer?' Doubtless, Creon could also say,—'Does not she, then, honour wrong-doers (Polyneices)?' Here, however, his point is that *she* is a rebel,—not, that her brother was a traitor.—For the fig. use of νόσος, cp. 1052, and n. on 653.—ἐπείληπται, attacked, as by a disease: so the act., Thuc. 2. 51 (ἡ νόσος) δὶς...τὸν αὐτὸν...οὐκ ἐπελάμβανε. (Distinguish the sense of ἐπίληπτος in 406.)

733 Θήβης, possessive gen., not gen. with ὁμόπτολις, which = 'of the same city': the sense is, 'the united folk of Thebes,' = the whole city, πάνδημος πόλις (7). Cp. 693. The epic πτόλις is used both in lyr. and in dial. by Aesch. and Eur., but in neither by Soph.

734 ἡμῖν, plur. (instead of ἐμοί), combined with the sing. ἐμέ: cp. 1194: *Ai.* 1400 εἰ δὲ μή 'στι σοὶ φίλον | πράσσειν τάδ' ἡμᾶς, εἶμ', ἐπαινέσας τὸ σόν: *Ph.* 1394 εἰ σέ γ' ἐν λόγοις | πείσειν δυνησόμεσθα μηδὲν ὧν λέγω (and *ib.* 1219 ff.): Eur. *H. F.* 858 ἥλιον μαρτυρόμεσθα δρῶσ' ἃ δρᾶν οὐ βούλομαι: *Ion* 391 κωλυόμεσθα μὴ μαθεῖν ἃ βούλομαι.

735 ὡς ἄγαν νέος—despite the difference between your age and mine (726).

736 Dobree's με for γε is clearly right; γε would throw a false emphasis on χρή ('Now, *ought* I to rule...?'): the sense requires the stress to fall on ἄλλῳ ἢ 'μοί.

This dat. 'of interest' does not mean, 'for my own advantage' (or gain), but, 'to my own satisfaction,' *i.e.* 'according to my own views.' Haemon has made light of Creon's protest against dictation from Thebes. Creon rejoins, 'What, am I to rule Thebes in dependence on any other judgment than my own?' In Eur. *Suppl.* 410 Creon's herald says, πόλις γὰρ ἧς ἐγὼ πάρειμ' ἄπο | ἑνὸς πρὸς ἀνδρός, οὐκ ὄχλῳ, κρατύνεται.—For ἐμοί instead of ἐμαυτῷ, cp. Plat. *Gorg.* 474 Β ἐγὼ γὰρ δὴ οἶμαι καὶ ἐμὲ καὶ σὲ..ἡγεῖσθαι.—Though **χρή γε** is untenable, the dat. is no argument against it: χρή could be absolute, the dat. being still a dat. of interest. There is no certain Attic instance of χρή with dat. In Eur. *Ion* 1317 τοῖσι δ' ἐνδίκοις | ἱερὰ καθίζειν, ὅστις ἠδίκειτ', ἐχρῆν, Dobree's τοὺς δέ γ' ἐνδίκους is needless: the sense is, 'in the interest of the just, it was right,' etc. In Lys. or. 28 § 10 τοῖς ἄρχουσι τοῖς ὑμετέροις ἐπιδείξετε πότερον χρὴ δικαίοις εἶναι, we should read δικαίους, and just afterwards ὑφελομένους. Xen. has δεῖ with dat. and infin., if the text is sound in *An.* 3. 4. 35.

737 πόλις γὰρ οὐκ ἐσθ'. Cp. Arist. *Pol.* 3. 16 περὶ δὲ τῆς παμβασιλείας καλουμένης,—αὕτη δ' ἐστὶ καθ' ἣν ἄρχει πάντων κατὰ τὴν ἑαυτοῦ βούλησιν ὁ βασιλεύς,—δοκεῖ δέ τισιν οὐδὲ κατὰ φύσιν εἶναι τὸ κύριον ἕνα πάντων εἶναι τῶν πολιτῶν, ὅπου συνέστηκεν ἐξ ὁμοίων ἡ πόλις. For Plato, the

138 ΣΟΦΟΚΛΕΟΥΣ

ΚΡ. οὐ τοῦ κρατοῦντος ἡ πόλις νομίζεται;
ΑΙ. καλῶς ἐρήμης γ' ἂν σὺ γῆς ἄρχοις μόνος.
ΚΡ. ὅδ', ὡς ἔοικε, τῇ γυναικὶ συμμαχεῖ.   740
ΑΙ. εἴπερ γυνὴ σύ· σοῦ γὰρ οὖν προκήδομαι.
ΚΡ. ὦ παγκάκιστε, διὰ δίκης ἰὼν πατρί.
ΑΙ. οὐ γὰρ δίκαιά σ' ἐξαμαρτάνονθ' ὁρῶ.
ΚΡ. ἁμαρτάνω γὰρ τὰς ἐμὰς ἀρχὰς σέβων;
ΑΙ. οὐ γὰρ σέβεις, τιμάς γε τὰς θεῶν πατῶν.   745
ΚΡ. ὦ μιαρὸν ἦθος καὶ γυναικὸς ὕστερον.
ΑΙ. οὔ τἂν ἕλοις ἥσσω γε τῶν αἰσχρῶν ἐμέ.
ΚΡ. ὁ γοῦν λόγος σοι πᾶς ὑπὲρ κείνης ὅδε.
ΑΙ. καὶ σοῦ γε κἀμοῦ, καὶ θεῶν τῶν νερτέρων.

739 καλῶς· ἐρήμησγ' L: καλῶς γ' ἐρήμης Blaydes.   740 τῇ γυναικί] ταῖς γυναιξὶ
Tournier.   742 ὦ παγκάκιστε] ὦ παῖ κάκιστε in Plutarch's quotation (Mor. 483 c),
and so Porson wished to read (Adv. 172, Eur. Or. 301).   743 ὁρῶ] ὁρῶι L.
745 οὐ] Musgrave conject. εὖ.   747 οὐ κἂν L (meaning, doubtless, οὐκ ἂν, for
the κ of οὐκ is oft. thus detached in L, and joined to the next word): οὔ τἂν

τυραννίς is ἔσχατον πόλεως νόσημα, Rep.
544 c. Cic. de Rep. 3. 31 ubi tyrannus
est, ibi...dicendum est nullam esse rem-
publicam.
738 νομίζεται with gen., as O. C. 38
(n.).—In a different sense (and rather with
an allusion to demagogues) it is said in
Ph. 386 πόλις γὰρ ἔστι πᾶσα τῶν ἡγου-
μένων (like ἔστι τοῦ λέγοντος, O. T. 917).
739 καλῶς ἐρήμης γ' (L) is much
better than καλῶς γ' ἐρήμης (Blaydes and
Nauck): Soph. often thus adds γε to the
emphatic adj., as El. 365 οὐδ' ἂν σύ, σώ-
φρων γ' οὖσα: ib. 518 θυραίαν γ' οὖσαν:
Ph. 811 οὐ μήν σ' ἐνορκόν γ' ἀξιῶ θέσθαι.
740 Though at least one late MS.
(Paris E) has συμμαχεῖν, it is needless to
assume here the same mixed constr. as
Tr. 1238 ἀνὴρ δ' ὅδ', ὡς ἔοικεν, οὐ νεμεῖν
ἐμοί | φθίνοντι μοῖραν.
741 οὖν, indeed, in fact: cp. 489.—
προκήδομαι: cp. on προσκοπεῖν, 688.
742 ὦ παγκάκιστε: so Heracles to
his son Hyllus, Tr. 1124. Cp. O. C. 743
πλεῖστον...κάκιστος.—διὰ δίκης ἰὼν πατρί,
engaging in controversy with him, bandy-
ing arguments with him. Thuc. 6. 60
ἀρηθέντι διὰ δίκης ἐλθεῖν, to deny the
charge, and stand a trial. Xen. An. 3.
2. 8 πάλιν αὐτοῖς διὰ φιλίας ἰέναι...διὰ
παντὸς πολέμου αὐτοῖς ἰέναι. So διὰ μάχης
(Her. 6. 9), δι' ἔχθρας (Eur. Ph. 479).—
Cp. Plut. Mor. 483 c (a brother, in a

brother's defence, ought to brave the displeasure of parents): αἱ δὲ ὑπὲρ ἀδελφοῦ
παρ' ἀξίαν κακῶς ἀκούοντος ἢ πάσχοντος
ἀντιδικίαι καὶ δικαιολογίαι πρὸς αὐτοὺς
(the parents) ἄμεμπτοι καὶ καλαί· καὶ οὐ
φοβητέον ἀκοῦσαι (to have said to one) τὸ
Σοφόκλειον· ὦ παῖ κάκιστε (quoting this
v.)...καὶ γὰρ αὐτοῖς ἡ τοιαύτη δίκη (controversy) τοῖς ἐλεγχομένοις ποιεῖ τὴν ἧτταν
ἡδίω τῆς νίκης.
744 ἀρχάς, the king's powers or prerogatives, like κράτη (60, 166, 173): cp.
177, 797. Cp. Aesch. Ch. 864 ἀρχάς τε
πολισσονόμους | πατέρων θ' ἕξει μέγαν ὄλ-
βον (Orestes). Eur. I. A. 343 ἐπεὶ κατέ-
σχες ἀρχάς (Agamemnon).
745 οὐ γὰρ σέβεις: '(that plea is void),
for,' etc.: i.e. 'nay, but thou dost not...'
Creon has asked, 'Do I wrong, when I
reverence my royal office?' Haemon
answers, 'Nay, there can be no such
reverence, when you dishonour the gods.'
A king rules by the divine grace. He
sins against his own office when he uses
his power to infringe the majesty of the
gods.—τιμάς, esp. sacrifices (as in this
case the offerings to the νέρτεροι): cp. O.
T. 909 n.
746 ὦ μιαρόν. In Haemon's last
words Creon hears an echo of Antigone's
doctrine—that the θεῶν νόμιμα rank above
the human king's edict (453). Hence
γυναικὸς ὕστερον, 'inferior to her.' rank-

CR.   Is not the city held to be the ruler's?

HAE.   Thou wouldst make a good monarch of a desert.

CR.   This boy, it seems, is the woman's champion.

HAE.   If thou art a woman ; indeed, my care is for thee.

CR.   Shameless, at open feud with thy father!

HAE.   Nay, I see thee offending against justice.

CR.   Do I offend, when I respect mine own prerogatives?

HAE.   Thou dost not respect them, when thou tramplest on the gods' honours.

CR.   O dastard nature, yielding place to a woman!

HAE.   Thou wilt never find me yield to baseness.

CR.   All thy words, at least, plead for that girl.

HAE.   And for thee, and for me, and for the gods below.

Elmsley. [Porson on Eur. *Med.* 863 first pointed to the misunderstood crasis of τοι and ἄν as a source of MS. error, giving several examples; Elmsley on *Med.* 836 f. first applied the remark to this verse.]—The Aldine, following A and some other MSS., has οὐκ ἄν γ', and Brunck wrote οὐκ ἄν γ' ἕλοις κρείσσω με (for γε) τῶν αἰσχρῶν ποτέ.—οὐκ ἄν λάβοις Nauck.   **748** ὁ γοῦν] ὅ γ' οὖν L.

---

ing after her ; so *Ai.* 1366, *Ph.* 181. Not, 'unable to resist her influence' (through love), as though it were γυναικὸς ἥσσον : a meaning which ὕστερος could not have. The general sense is, however, the same, —viz., that he ranks behind a woman, who leads him.

747 'I may be inferior to a woman, but at least you will never find me yielding to base temptations.' It would have been αἰσχρόν if he had allowed fear or self-interest to deter him from pleading this cause. (Cp. 509.) Cp. *Tr.* 489 ἔρωτος...ἥσσων: fr. 844 ἥσσων...ὀργῆς.— οὔ τἄν is a certain correction of οὐκ ἄν (cp. *O. T.* 1445, 1469: *O. C.* 1351: *Tr.* 279: *Ai.* 456, 534, etc.). Against the weak conjecture οὐκ ἄν γ' is the repetition of γε: cp. on *O. C.* 387. Where τἄν has been corrupted in our MSS., it has most often become τ' ἄν, sometimes γ' ἄν or δ' ἄν. But a change of οὔ τἄν into οὐκ ἄν would also be easy in writing where, as in that of L, the κ of οὐκ was often attached to the next word (see cr. n.).—γε emphasises the whole phrase, ἥσσω τῶν αἰσχρῶν, not ἥσσω alone: cp. 648 n.

748 γοῦν: cp. *O. C.* 24 n. To plead *her* cause *is* to be ἥσσων τῶν αἰσχρῶν.

749 καὶ σοῦ γε. Creon is concerned, not merely as a king whose city will be punished by the gods, but as a man who is to be saved from incurring guilt.

750—757 Objections have been made to the traditional order of these verses, chiefly in two respects. (1) 755 εἰ μὴ πατὴρ ἦσθ' is—it is argued—the strongest thing said by Haemon, and ought therefore to come immediately before Creon's final outburst, ἀληθες; (758). How could it be followed by merely so mild a phrase as μὴ κώτιλλέ με?—We may reply:— Haemon says that, *if* Creon were not his father, he *would have* thought him mad. It is to this that μὴ κώτιλλέ με refers, meaning, 'Do not seek to deceive me by an affectation of filial deference.' (2) 757 βούλει λέγειν τι is too mild a remark—it is said—to form the climax of provocation to Creon's anger.   We may reply:—It is in substance, if not in form, such a climax, —for a father who holds that *unquestioning* obedience (640) is a son's first duty. It asserts Haemon's right to maintain his own views against his father's,—διὰ δίκης ἰέναι, as Creon put it (742). The traditional order seems, therefore, to be right.

Three modes of transposition have been proposed. (1) Enger puts 756 and 757 after 749.   Then κώτιλλε (756) refers to Haemon's plea that he has his father's cause, and that of religion, at heart. We lose nothing by such a transposition ; but neither do we gain.

(2) Donner (in his transl., ed. 1863) simply transposed verses 755 and 757, leaving the rest as they stand.   For this

ΚΡ. ταύτην ποτ' οὐκ ἔσθ' ὡς ἔτι ζῶσαν γαμεῖς.   750
ΑΙ. ἥδ' οὖν θανεῖται καὶ θανοῦσ' ὀλεῖ τινά.
ΚΡ. ἦ κἀπαπειλῶν ὧδ' ἐπεξέρχει θρασύς;
ΑΙ. τίς δ' ἔστ' ἀπειλὴ πρὸς κενὰς γνώμας λέγειν;
ΚΡ. κλαίων φρενώσεις, ὧν φρενῶν αὐτὸς κενός.
ΑΙ. εἰ μὴ πατὴρ ἦσθ', εἶπον ἄν σ' οὐκ εὖ φρονεῖν.   755
ΚΡ. γυναικὸς ὢν δούλευμα, μὴ κώτιλλέ με.
ΑΙ. βούλει λέγειν τι καὶ λέγων μηδὲν κλύειν;
ΚΡ. ἄληθες; ἀλλ' οὐ, τόνδ' Ὄλυμπον, ἴσθ' ὅτι,
χαίρων ἐπὶ ψόγοισι δεννάσεις ἐμέ.

750 ποτ' . . γαμεῖς.] πότ' . . γαμεῖς; L.   **751** ἥδ' οὖν L, and lemma schol.:
ἥδ' οὖν vulg.: ἢ δ' οὖν Hartung. Nauck conject. εἰ δ' οὖν.   **752** ἢ κἀπαπειλῶν. In L there has been an erasure at the letters απα, which are, however, by an early hand (the first, or S). The first hand had (I think) written ἢ
καὶ ἀπειλῶν. For an analogous error cp. O. C. 172 cr. n.   **755** ἦσθ'] ἦισθ' L.
Cp. 726.   **757** κλύειν r, λέγειν L.—Wecklein conject. ψέγειν τι καὶ ψέγων μηδὲν

---

it may fairly be said that 757 comes very
fitly after 754. On the other hand it
s..ems to me that 756 does not aptly
follow 757.

(3) Pallis arranges thus:—749, 756,
755, 754, 757, 750—753. Thus κενὰς
γνώμας (753) becomes the last sting.—
The fact is that, in a stormy altercation,
we do not look for a closely logical texture
and a delicately graduated *crescendo*. The
MS. order is (to my mind) the best; but
other arrangements are possible, and
would be nearly as good.

750 Creon, instead of replying to v.
749, abruptly repeats his resolve. οὐκ
ἔστιν ὡς ταύτην ἔτι ζῶσαν γαμεῖς (fut.)
ποτέ, it cannot be that you shall ever wed
her while she yet lives; *i.e.* she is to die
at once, and can become your bride, if
ever, only ἐν Ἅιδου (654). Cp. 1240.—
ὡς for the more usual ὅπως: so *Ph.* 196
οὐκ ἔσθ' ὡς οὐ.—The strange place of
ποτέ is explained by the strong emphasis
on ταύτην ('*her*, at *any* time, it is impossible that thou shouldest wed'). Soph.
often admits bold arrangements of words
(cp. *O. T.* 1245, 1251: *O. C.* 1428).

751 ἥδ' referring to ταύτην (cp. 296 f.).
At first sight ἡ δ' is attractive; but that
phrase is properly used with the imperat.,
and has a defiant or scornful tone (*O. T.*
669 ὁ δ' οὖν ἴτω: *Ai.* 961 οἱ δ' οὖν γελών-
των: Ar. *Ach.* 186 οἱ δ' οὖν βοώντων).
The quiet ἥδ' is more impressive here.—
ὀλεῖ τινά, *i.e. ἐμέ*: Creon understands

him to mean *σέ*. As vv. 763 f. show,
Haemon is resolved not to survive Antigone. But he has no thought of threatening his father's life: his frantic action at
v. 1231 was a sudden impulse, instantly
followed by remorse (1245). For the
sinister τις, cp. *Ai.* 1138 τοῦτ' εἰς ἀνίαν
τοὔπος ἔρχεταί τινι. Ar. *Ran.* 552 ff. κακὸν ἥκει τινί...δώσει τις δίκην. Thuc. 4.
68 εἰ...μὴ πείσεταί τις, αὐτοῦ τὴν μάχην
ἔσεσθαι.

752 ἦ ἐπεξέρχει καὶ ἐπαπειλῶν ὧδε
θρασύς; Dost thou go the length of e'en
threatening so boldly? The participial
clause defines the manner of ἐπεξέρχει,
and so is practically equiv. to ὥστε καὶ
ἐπαπειλεῖν etc. The καὶ here belongs to
the partic. (distinguish the composite ἢ
καὶ in question, *O. T.* 368). Eur. *Bacch.*
1346 ἀλλ' ἐπεξέρχει λίαν, (we have erred,)
but thou *goest too far* (in vengeance). Cp.
O. C. 438 τὸν θυμὸν ἐκδραμόντα μοι |
μείζω κολαστήν.

754 κλαίων, as *O. T.* 401, 1152.—
φρενώσεις, a poet. word, used by Xen.
Mem. 4. 1. 5 τοὺς ἐπὶ πλούτῳ μέγα φρο-
νοῦντας...ἐφρένου λέγων.

755 οὐκ εὖ φρονεῖν, as angrily refusing
(754) to hear reason.

756 δούλευμα: cp. on 650.—μὴ κώτιλλέ με, 'do not seek to cajole me,'—
referring to εἰ μὴ πατὴρ ἦσθ', as expressive
of filial respect. Creon means, 'do not
pretend that you have any of the feelings
with which a son ought to regard a father.'

CR. Thou canst never marry her, on this side the grave.

HAE. Then she must die, and in death destroy another.

CR. How! doth thy boldness run to open threats?

HAE. What threat is it, to combat vain resolves?

CR. Thou shalt rue thy witless teaching of wisdom.

HAE. Wert thou not my father, I would have called thee unwise.

CR. Thou woman's slave, use not wheedling speech with me.

HAE. Thou wouldest speak, and then hear no reply?

CR. Sayest thou so? Now, by the heaven above us—be sure of it—thou shalt smart for taunting me in this opprobrious strain.

λέγειν. **758** ἄληθες;] ἀληθέσ; L. (The first hand wrote merely a comma: S added the dot above it.) But in *O. T.* 350 (the only other instance in Soph.) L has ἄληθεσ (though without the note of interrogation). **759** ἐπί] Dobree conject. ἔτι: Musgrave, ἐπιψόγοισι.—δεννάσεις] δ' ἐννάσεις L, the δ substituted by S for another letter (λ?). So in *Ai.* 243 L has δ' ἐννάζων: and in Theognis 1211 (Bergk) one MS. has δ' ἔνναζε.

Cp. Theognis 363 εὖ κώτιλλε τὸν ἐχθρόν (cajole)· ὅταν δ' ὑποχείριος ἔλθῃ, | τῖσαί νιν, πρόφασιν μηδεμίαν θέμενος: id. 851 Ζεὺς ἀνδρ' ἐξολέσειεν Ὀλύμπιος, ὃς τὸν ἑταῖρον | μαλθακὰ κωτίλλων ἐξαπατᾶν ἐθέλει.

757 λέγειν...κλύειν; do you wish to speak, and yet not to hear? λέγειν τι has a euphemistic tone ('to say something strong, or harsh'), like δρᾶν τι (*El.* 336), but the τι could hardly be represented in translation without exaggerating it. λέγειν καὶ ἀκούειν was a familiar phrase for fair discussion (Thuc. 4. 22 λέγοντες καὶ ἀκούοντες περὶ ἑκάστου ξυμβήσονται: cp. *O. C.* 189). *El.* 628 πρὸς ὀργὴν ἐκφέρει, μεθεῖσά μοι | λέγειν ἃ χρῄζοιμ', οὐδ' ἐπίστασαι κλύειν: ib. 990 ἢ προμηθία | καὶ τῷ λέγοντι καὶ κλύοντι σύμμαχος. The words imply a claim of equality, and are also full of scorn: hence Creon's outburst. —Not: 'do you wish to taunt and not to be taunted in return?'—as if κλύειν = 'to have things said to one' (*Ai.* 1322 κλύοντι φλαῦρα συμβαλεῖν ἔπη κακά: *El.* 523 κακῶς δέ σε | λέγω κακῶς κλύουσα πρὸς σέθεν θαμά).

758 ἄληθες; the word which marks that Teiresias can no longer restrain his wrath against Oedipus (*O. T.* 350).—οὐ τόνδ' "Ολ., without μά: *O. T.* 660, 1088. Cp. *Ai.* 1389 Ὀλύμπου τοῦδ' ὁ πρεσβεύων πατήρ: *O. C.* 1655.—ἴσθ' ὅτι, adverbial: cp. 276 n.

759 χαίρων, *impune*, as *O. T.* 363, *Ph.* 1299.—ἐπὶ ψόγοισι δεννάσεις, lit.,

revile me with (continual) *censures*: ψόγος is merely censure, fault-finding, not necessarily implying offensive speech (cp. 689). δεννάζω, to reproach or revile: *Ai.* 243 κακὰ δεννάζων ῥήμαθ': [Eur.] *Rhes.* 925 (the Muse speaking of Thamyris) ὃς ἡμῶν πόλλ' ἐδέννασεν τέχνην. So Theogn. 1211 (if the verse be his, and not Anacreon's) μή μ' ἀφελῶς [ἀφίλως?] παίζουσα φίλους δέννα ζε τοκῆας, alluding to her saying that they had been slaves. Her. 9. 107 παρὰ δὲ τοῖσι Πέρσῃσι γυναικὸς κακίω ἀκοῦσαι δέννος μέγιστός ἐστι.—ἐπί with dat. is not merely 'with,' but implies a *continuing strain* of utterance: *El.* 108 ἐπὶ κωκυτῷ τῶνδε πατρῴων | πρὸ θυρῶν ἠχὼ πᾶσι προφωνεῖν: Eur. *Tro.* 315 ἐπὶ δάκρυσι καὶ | γόοισι τὸν θανόντα πατέρα... καταστένουσ' ἔχεις (thou art *ever* lamenting).—Others explain ἐπί as (*a*) 'in addition to,' which implies too sharp a contrast with δεννάσεις, esp. without καί: (*b*) 'with a view to,' *i.e.* 'in order to blame me.' Cp. Eur. *Ph.* 1555 οὐκ ἐπ' ὀνείδεσιν οὐδ' ἐπὶ χάρμασιν | ἀλλ' ὀδύναισι λέγω ('not *for* insult or spiteful joy, but *in* pain'). Here, however, that sense would be weak. —For Dobree's ἔτι, cp. Ar. *Plut.* 64 οὔτοι μὰ τὴν Δήμητρα χαιρήσεις ἔτι. It is plausible, and may be right. But I prefer ἐπὶ ψόγοισι, because (in the sense explained above) it is so fitting when an impatient man breaks off a dialogue which has irritated him throughout.

ἄγετε τὸ μῖσος, ὡς κατ' ὄμματ' αὐτίκα   760
παρόντι θνήσκῃ πλησία τῷ νυμφίῳ.

ΑΙ. οὐ δῆτ' ἔμοιγε, τοῦτο μὴ δόξῃς ποτέ,
οὔθ' ἥδ' ὀλεῖται πλησία, σύ τ' οὐδαμὰ
τοὐμὸν προσόψει κρᾶτ' ἐν ὀφθαλμοῖς ὁρῶν,
ὡς τοῖς θέλουσι τῶν φίλων μαίνῃ ξυνών.   765

ΧΟ. ἀνήρ, ἄναξ, βέβηκεν ἐξ ὀργῆς ταχύς·
νοῦς δ' ἐστὶ τηλικοῦτος ἀλγήσας βαρύς.

ΚΡ. δράτω, φρονείτω μεῖζον ἢ κατ' ἄνδρ' ἰών·
τὼ δ' οὖν κόρα τώδ' οὐκ ἀπαλλάξει μόρου.

ΧΟ. ἄμφω γὰρ αὐτὼ καὶ κατακτεῖναι νοεῖς;   770

ΚΡ. οὐ τήν γε μὴ θιγοῦσαν· εὖ γὰρ οὖν λέγεις.

ΧΟ. μόρῳ δὲ ποίῳ καί σφε βουλεύει κτανεῖν;

ΚΡ. ἄγων ἔρημος ἔνθ' ἂν ᾖ βροτῶν στίβος
κρύψω πετρώδει ζῶσαν ἐν κατώρυχι,

---

760 ἄγαγε L, ἄγετε r: ἄγ', ἄγε Wecklein.   **761** θνήσκει L.   **763** οὐδαμὰ]
οὐδαμᾶι L. Most of the later MSS. have οὐδαμᾶ, but Dresden a οὐδαμὰ, and Vat.
οὐδαμοῦ.   **765** μαίνῃ] In L the first hand wrote μαίνησι: another early hand,
deleting σ, wrote ε over α and εισ over ηι, thus indicating μαίνηι and μένεις (or
μενεῖς) as alternative readings. The later MSS. have μαίνῃ, μένεις, μενεῖς, μένῃς, or
μένῃ. The Schol. knew both μένῃς (which he explains first) and μαίνῃ.—ξυνών.
L has σ above ξ from first hand.   **766** ἀνήρ L, ἀνὴρ r.   **767** βαρύς made

---

760 f. ἄγετε. The plur. is addressed
to the two πρόσπολοι who had ushered
the sisters into the house (578, κομίζετ'
εἴσω, δμῶες). So at 491 the plur. is used,
καλεῖτ'. And, in general, such orders
are usu. given in the plur., or by τις with
3rd pers. (as *O. T.* 1069). Cp. 931 τοῖσιν
ἄγουσιν. This is against Wecklein's ἄγ',
ἄγε. The objection to L's ἄγαγε is not
only the sing. number, but also the fact
that the 2nd aor. imperat. act. (and midd.)
of ἄγω does not seem to have been used
in Attic.—τὸ μῖσος: *Ph.* 991 ὦ μῖσος
(Odysseus): so μίσημα, στύγος, στύγνημα.
—κατ' ὄμματ': Xen. *Hier.* 1. 14 οὐδεὶς...
ἐθέλει τυράννου κατ' ὀφθαλμοὺς κατηγορεῖν
('to his face').—παρόντι...πλησία. The
accumulation of words for 'presence'
marks his vehement anger: cp. Haemon's
pleonasm in 764, and *O. T.* 430.

762 ff. ἔμοιγε is placed as if it were
to be common to both the clauses (οὔτε...
τε), but the constr. changes: cp. *El.* 913
ἀλλ' οὐδὲ μὲν δὴ μητρὸς οὔθ' ὁ νοῦς φιλεῖ |
τοιαῦτα πράσσειν οὔτε δρῶσ' ἐλάνθανεν.—
For οὔτε followed by τε cp. *O.C.* 1397 (n.).

—οὐδαμά, neut. plur. adv.: this form is
required by metre in 830, as οὐδαμᾷ (Doric)
in 874: L always gives οὐδαμᾶι: see on
O. C. 1104.—ἐν ὀφθαλμοῖς, with them
(the instrumental ἐν, 962, 1003, 1201):
an epic phrase, *Il.* 1. 587 ἐν ὀφθαλμοῖσιν
ἴδωμαι, etc.: so oft. ἐν ὄμμασιν (*Tr.* 241).

765 ὡς: cp. 643.—τοῖς θέλουσι, *i.e.*
any who can endure it. Cp. the words
of Teiresias, 1087.—Haemon now finally
quits the scene. The deuteragonist is
thus set free for the parts of the Ἄγγελος
and the Ἐξάγγελος.

766 f. ἐξ ὀργῆς ταχύς, in haste *caused
by* wrath: cp. *Il.* 7. 111 μηδ' ἔθελ' ἐξ ἔριδος
σεῦ ἀμείμονι φωτὶ μάχεσθαι, out of mere
rivalry.—βαρύς, resentful: cp. *O. T.* 673
βαρὺς δ', ὅταν | θυμοῦ περάσῃς; so as epith.
of μῆνις (*O. C.* 1328) and ὀργή (*Ph.* 368).
The sense of βαρύ in 1251 is different.

768 μεῖζον ἢ κατ' ἄνδρα is said in
answer to their hint of fear:—let his passion touch the human limit, aye, or over-
pass it. *O. C.* 598 τί γὰρ τὸ μεῖζον ἢ κατ'
ἄνθρωπον νοσεῖς; For ἀνήρ=ἄνθρωπος, *ib.*
567.—ἰών: *Ph.* 351 εἰ τἀπὶ Τροίᾳ πέργαμ'

Bring forth that hated thing, that she may die forthwith in his
presence—before his eyes—at her bridegroom's side !

HAE.   No, not at my side—never think it—shall she perish ;
nor shalt thou ever set eyes more upon my face :—rave, then,
with such friends as can endure thee.   [*Exit* HAEMON.

CH.   The man is gone, O King, in angry haste ; a youthful
mind, when stung, is fierce.

CR.   Let him do, or dream, more than man—good speed to
him !—But he shall not save these two girls from their doom.

CH.   Dost thou indeed purpose to slay both ?

CR.   Not her whose hands are pure : thou sayest well.

CH.   And by what doom mean'st thou to slay the other ?

CR.   I will take her where the path is loneliest,
and hide her, living, in a rocky vault,

---

from βραχύσ in L.   **769** τάδ' (*sic*) .. τάδ' L : τὼ δ' .. τώδ' Dindorf.—μόρου L :
μόρων Vat., V⁴.   **770** αὐτὰ L : αὐτὼ Dindorf.—κατακτανῆναι (not κατακτῆναι) L :
κατακτεῖναι r.   **771** τήνδε (from τῆνδε) L, with γ above δ either from the first
hand (so Duebner) or from an early corrector. The same hand has written οι above
λέγεισ. Perh. εὖ γὰρ ἂν λέγοις was a *v. l.*   **773** ἄγων .. στίβος] Semitelos conject.
ἀγκὼν .. στίβου.—ἔνθ' ἂν made from ἔνθα ἂν in L.   **774** πετρώδη L with ει above
η from the first hand.

αἱρήσοιμ' ἰών : *Ai.* 304 ὅσην κατ' αὐτῶν
ὕβριν ἐκτίσαιτ' ἰών. So here it scornfully
suggests some daring enterprise.

769 f. For δ' οὖν cp. 688, 722.—τὼ
...τώδε : cp. 561 (τώ), *O. T.* 1472 (τοῖν),
O. C. 1600 (τώ), *El.* 977 (τώδε τώ)—all
fem.—Attic inscriptions of *c.* 450—
320 B.C. present numerous instances of
fem. dual τώ, τοῖν, τούτοιν, οἷν, but no
instance of fem. dual τά, ταῖν, ταύταιν, or
αἷν. (Meisterhans p. 50.) Hitherto the
gen. and dat. ταῖν, ταῖνδε, ταύταιν have
been retained even by those edd. who give
τώ, τώδε, etc. (cp. *O.T.* 1462, 1504: *O.C.*
445, 859, 1149, 1290, etc.). But, so far as
epigraphic evidence goes, the distinction
is arbitrary.—καί with the whole phrase
κατακτ. νοεῖς rather than with κατακτ.
alone (for no minor penalty is in view) :
cp. 726.

771 θιγοῦσαν : cp. 546.—γὰρ οὖν : cp.
489, 741.

772 καί with βουλεύει ; (her doom
having been fixed,) by what fate *do* you
purpose to slay her? For καί thus following the interrog., cp. 1314. Aesch. *Ag.*
278 ποίου χρόνου δὲ καὶ πεπόρθηται πόλις ;
Eur. *Hec.* 515 πῶς καί νιν ἐξεπράξατ' ;—
σφε=αὐτήν, Antigone : cp. 44 n.

773 ἔνθα=ἐκεῖσε ἔνθα, as *O. T.* 796 :
so *O. C.* 188 ἄγε...με... | ἵν' ἂν etc. Cp.
Ph. 486 μή μ' ἀφῆς | ἔρημον οὕτω χωρὶς
ἀνθρώπων στίβου.

774 πετρώδει...ἐν κατώρυχι, 'in a
rocky cavern'; schol., ἐν ὑπογείῳ σπηλαίῳ.
Verse 773 shows that Creon is not yet
thinking of any particular spot. And
κατῶρυξ shows that he is not thinking of
some merely natural grotto or cavern.
This word, usu. an adj., here a subst.,
means a cavern, or chamber, excavated
by man's hand : cp. Eur. *Hec.* 1002 χρυσοῦ παλαιαὶ Πριαμιδῶν κατώρυχες. So
the place is described by κατασκαφῆς
(891). The κατῶρυξ actually used was
near the furthest and highest part of
the plain, where Polyneices lay (1197).
What, then, was the poet's conception ?
He seems to suppose the existence of
tombs artificially constructed in the rocky
πάγοι (411) which bordered on the
Theban plain. In one of these tombs—
chosen for the remoteness of its situation
(773)—Antigone is to be immured. The
general type of sepulchral chamber supposed here can be illustrated from actual
remains which have been discovered in
Greece : see below on vv. 1216 ff.

φορβῆς τοσοῦτον ὡς ἄγος μόνον προθείς,   775
ὅπως μίασμα πᾶσ᾽ ὑπεκφύγῃ πόλις.
κἀκεῖ τὸν Ἅιδην, ὃν μόνον σέβει θεῶν,
αἰτουμένη που τεύξεται τὸ μὴ θανεῖν,
ἢ γνώσεται γοῦν ἀλλὰ τηνικαῦθ᾽ ὅτι
πόνος περισσός ἐστι τὰν Ἅιδου σέβειν.   780

στρ. ΧΟ. Ἔρως ἀνίκατε μάχαν, Ἔρως, ὃς ἐν κτήμασι πίπτεις,
2 ὃς ἐν μαλακαῖς παρειαῖς νεάνιδος ἐννυχεύεις,

---

775 ὡς ἄγος μόνον] Blaydes conject. ὅσον ἄγος φεύγειν, and many edd. have adopted ὅσον, while retaining μόνον. (Hartung, ὡς ἄγος φεύγειν.) Dindorf proposed : (1) ἔθος for ἄγος : (2) ὡς ἄγος φεύγειν μόνον | προθείς, ὅπως μίασμ᾽ ὑπεκφύγῃ πόλις : (3) ὡς ἄγος φεύγειν προθείς, deleting v. 776. Wecklein (*Ars Soph. em.* p. 27) suggested τρέπειν for μόνον. **776** ὑπεκφυγηι L : ὑπεκφύγοι ר. **778** που] ποῦ L. **779** γοῦν] γ᾽ οὖν L.

---

775 ὡς ἄγος μόνον, *sc.* εἶναι, so much as to be barely an expiation; only just enough to avoid the μίασμα. The conjectural change of ὡς into ὅσον (adopted by several edd.) would be necessary if the indic. ἐστί had to be supplied, since we could not say τοσοῦτον ὡς (instead of ὅσον) ἄγος ἐστί. That change is unnecessary, because it is the inf. εἶναι that is understood. Cp. Xen. *An.* 7. 3 § 22 ὅσον μόνον γεύσασθαι, and see n. on *O. C.* 790 for other instances where the inf. is expressed. The inf. is understood, as here, in Xen. *An.* 7. 8 § 19 ἔχοντες πρόβατα ὅσον θύματα (*sc.* εἶναι): so *ib.* 7. 3 § 20 ἔχων...ὅσον ἐφόδιον.—**ἄγος** was used by Soph. in his lost *Phaedra* to denote ἅγνισμα θυσίας (Hesych. 1. 63), *i.e.* 'an expiatory sacrifice' (cp. Aesch. *Eum.* 325 ἅγνισμα φόνου). In Aesch. *Cho.* 154 also ἄγος has been taken as='expiation,' but there it seems rather to be 'pollution.' Cp. the schol. here : ἔθος παλαιόν, ὥστε τὸν βουλόμενον καθειργνύναι τινὰ ἀφοσιοῦσθαι βραχὺ τιθέντα τροφῆς, καὶ ὑπενθόουν κάθαρσιν τὸ τοιοῦτο, ἵνα μὴ δοκῶσι λιμῷ ἀναιρεῖν· τοῦτο γὰρ ἀσεβές.—Curtius, *Etym.* 5th ed., § 118, would write ἅγος here. He distinguishes two roots. (1) ἀγ-, ἄγος, 'guilt,' ἐναγής, 'accursed'; Sanskr. *âg-as*, 'vexation,' etc. (2) ἀγ-, ἅγος, 'consecration, sacrifice,' ἅγιος, etc. : Sanskr. *jaǵ.* On the other hand the analogy of *piaculum* suggests that ἄγος might combine the sense of 'expiation' with that of 'pollution.'

Creon's edict had announced that the transgressor would be publicly stoned to death (36). It is to this that the anxious question of the Chorus alludes (772). Creon had already said that Antigone's doom was to be κάκιστος (489). But now, at least, he feels that he cannot inflict such a death on the maiden, his kinswoman. She shall die, not by stoning, but by starvation. The choice is not prompted by cruelty, but simply by the desire to avoid physical violence.

The danger of a μίασμα—to be avoided by a dole of food—has no relation to the special circumstances,—Antigone's royal birth, and the nature of her offence. In the ancient belief, that danger existed whenever a person was put to death by starvation. Two notions were probably blended; (*a*) that, if a little food was given, the death was nature's work, not man's; (*b*) that the νέρτεροι claimed an indemnity for the usual ἐναγίσματα. So the Greeks put Philoctetes ashore on desolate Lemnos, —ῥάκη προθέντες βαιὰ καί τι καὶ βορᾶς | ἐπωφέλημα σμικρόν (*Ph.* 274). So, too, when a Vestal was to be buried alive, the small vault in the Campus Sceleratus was furnished with a couch, a burning lamp, and a small table, on which the dole was placed,—bread, olives, milk, and a jug of water (Plut. *Num.* 10).

776 πᾶσ᾽: cp. on 178. The sense is, 'in order that the whole city may not be defiled' (as it otherwise would be): μίασμ᾽ ὑπεκφύγῃ=μὴ μιανθῇ.

777 ὃν μόνον σέβει. Polyneices had come to destroy the shrines of the θεοὶ with so much food set forth as piety prescribes, that the city may avoid a public stain. And there, praying to Hades, the only god whom she worships, perchance she will obtain release from death; or else will learn, at last, though late, that it is lost labour to revere the dead. [*Exit* CREON.

CH. Love, unconquered in the fight, Love, who makest havoc Strophe. of wealth, who keepest thy vigil on the soft cheek of a maiden;

780 This v. was accidentally omitted from the text of L, and added in the margin by the first hand.　**782** ὅς ʳ, ὅστ᾽ L.—κτήμασι] For the conjectures, see Appendix.

ἐγγενεῖς (199). By honouring him, and Hades (519), she has dishonoured those other gods.

778 τὸ μὴ θανεῖν in acc. with τεύξεται: cp. Aesch. *Ch.* 711 τυγχάνειν τὰ πρόσφορα: *O. C.* 1106 (n.): fr. 824 καὶ τὰ καὶ τὰ τυγχάνων. This comparatively rare constr. has here been influenced by αἰτουμένη: though it is unnecessary to refer the acc. to the partic. only, or to understand, 'will successfully ask.' See, however, Her. 5. 23 τὴν παρὰ Δαρείου αἴτησας ἔτυχε...δωρεήν: 9. 109 πάντα γὰρ τεύξεσθαι αἰτήσασαν: where, in both instances, the acc. depends on the partic. only.—We could not well take τὸ μὴ θανεῖν here as = ὥστε μὴ θανεῖν (like κωλύω τὸ μὴ ποιεῖν τι).

779 f. ἀλλὰ τηνικαῦτα: cp. 552.—τᾶν, instead of τοὺς ἐν, Ἅιδου: 659.

781—800 Third stasimon. Strophe 781—790 = antistr. 791—800.

After Creon's and Haemon's speeches, the comment of the Chorus was in a neutral tone (724). When Haemon departed in anger, they spoke words implying that allowance must be made for the heat of youth (767). This beautiful ode is in a kindred strain. If Haemon has sinned against great θεσμοί—loyalty to country and to father—at least he is under the influence of a god whom none can withstand.

The pathos of the maiden's fate is heightened by this plea for her lover. When she is led in by the guards, on her way to death, the Chorus avow that pity works with them even as love with Haemon (801—805). A perfect preparation is thus made for the lyric dialogue between the Chorus and Antigone (806—882).

781 ἀνίκατε μάχαν: *Tr.* 441 Ἔρωτι μέν νυν ὅστις ἀντανίσταται, | πύκτης ὅπως ἐς χεῖρας, οὐ καλῶς φρονεῖ. Eur. fr. 433 Ἔρωτα, πάντων δυσμαχώτατον θεόν. Plat.

Symp. 196 D καὶ μὴν εἴς γε ἀνδρίαν Ἔρωτι οὐδὲ Ἄρης ἀνθίσταται· οὐ γὰρ ἔχει Ἔρωτα Ἄρης, ἀλλ᾽ Ἔρως Ἄρη.

782 ἐν κτήμασι πίπτεις, who *fallest upon* men's possessions; who makest havoc of their wealth and fortunes. Cp. *Od.* 24. 526 ἐν δ᾽ ἔπεσον προμάχοις, 'they fell on the fore-fighters': so ἐμπίπτειν is oft. said of the attacks of disease or passion. Love makes men reckless of possessions: it can bring ruin on great houses and proud cities. Sophocles himself has given us the best commentary: see *Tr.* 431, referring to the capture of Oechalia by Heracles, who loved Iolè, the daughter of its king, Eurytus: ὡς ταύτης πόθῳ | πόλις δαμείη πᾶσα, κοὐχ ἡ Λυδία | πέρσειεν αὐτήν, ἀλλ᾽ ὁ τῆσδ᾽ ἔρως φανείς. The same thought is finely expressed by Eur., in a choral ode to Ἔρως, which this passage has certainly helped to inspire (*Hipp.* 525 ff.): Ἔρωτα δέ, τὸν τύραννον ἀνδρῶν, | ...οὐ σεβίζομεν, | πέρθοντα καὶ διὰ πάσας | ἰόντα συμφορᾶς | θνατοῖς, ὅταν ἔλθῃ. Troy was sacked for the sake of Helen,—ἑλέναυς, ἕλανδρος, ἑλέπτολις. Medea betrayed her father's treasure to Jason (cp. Eur. *Med.* 480). The *resistless power* of Love is the central thought of this ode. All that men prize most becomes his prey.—See Appendix.

783 f. ἐν μαλακαῖς παρειαῖς. Ion of Chios (*ap.* Athen. 603 E) describes Soph. as saying, ὡς καλῶς Φρύνιχος (the tragic poet, *flor. c.* 490) ἐποίησεν εἴπας· λάμπει δ᾽ ἐπὶ πορφυρέαις παρῇσι φῶς ἔρωτος. Plut. *Mor.* 760 D σκόπει τοίνυν...τοῖς ἀρηΐοις ἔργοις ὅσον Ἔρως περίεστιν, οὐκ ἀργὸς ὤν, ὡς Εὐριπίδης ἔλεγεν, οὐδὲ ἀστράτευτος, οὐδ᾽ ἐν μαλακαῖσιν [ἐννυχεύ]ων παρειαῖς νεανίδων.—ἐννυχεύεις, keepest thy vigil: perh. here an image suggested by a soldier's night-watch (like Horace's *pulcris excubat in genis, sc.* Cupido, *C.*

3 φοιτᾷς δ' ὑπερπόντιος ἔν τ' ἀγρονόμοις αὐλαῖς· 785
4 καί σ' οὔτ' ἀθανάτων φύξιμος οὐδεὶς
5 οὔθ' ἀμερίων * σέ γ' ἀνθρώπων, ὁ δ' ἔχων μέμηνεν.   790

ἀντ.   σὺ καὶ δικαίων ἀδίκους φρένας παρασπᾷς ἐπὶ λώβᾳ·
2 σὺ καὶ τόδε νεῖκος ἀνδρῶν ξύναιμον ἔχεις ταράξας·
8 νικᾷ δ' ἐναργὴς βλεφάρων ἵμερος εὐλέκτρου   795
4 νύμφας, τῶν μεγάλων πάρεδρος ἐν ἀρχαῖς

785—790 L divides the vv. thus: φοιτᾷς δ— | τ' ἀγρονόμοις— | καί σ'...ἀν|θρώ-
πων...μέμηνεν.   786 τ' ἀγρονόμοις] The first hand in L seems to have written
πατρονόμοις.   789 ἐπ' ἀνθρώπων L.   So most of the later mss., but Campb. cites
ἀπ' from Vat. (14th cent.).   Nauck conject. σέ γ' ἀνθρώπων: so also Blaydes (ed.
1859).   790 ὁ δ'] ὅδ' L.   795 νικᾷ δ' .. εὐλέκτρου.   Two vv. in L, the second

---

4. 13. 8); cp. Xen. An. 6. 4. 27 ἐν δὲ τοῖς
ὅπλοις ἐνυκτέρευον, and so νυκτοφυλακεῖν.
Shaksp. Rom. 5. 3. 94 'beauty's ensign
yet Is crimson in thy lips and in thy
cheeks.' Gray, Progress of Poesy 1. 3. 16
'O'er her warm cheek and rising bosom
move The bloom of young desire and
purple light of love.'
  785 f. ὑπερπόντιος: cp. 1301 : so
ἐκτόπιος (O. T. 1340), θαλάσσιος (ib. 1411),
θυραῖος (El. 313), παράκτιος (Eur. I. T.
1424), etc.   So Eur. fr. 434 ("Ερως) κἀπὶ
πόντον ἔρχεται.   Plut. Mor. 760 D quotes
an unknown poet, on "Ερως:—πῦρ καὶ
θάλασσαν καὶ πνοὰς τὰς αἰθέρος | περᾶν
ἕτοιμος.   Lucr. 1. 18 (Venus moves) per
maria ac montes fluviosque rapaces Frondi-
ferasque domos avium camposque virentes.
—ἔν τ' ἀγρ. αὐλαῖς. ἀγρόνομοι αὐλαί
=dwellings in ἀγρός νεμόμενος, pastoral
wilds: cp. 349 ἀγραύλου: O. T. 1103
πλάκες ἀγρόνομοι, upland pastures.   El.
181 ἀκτὴ βούνομος, a shore on which oxen
are pastured (cp. O. T. 26).—Some take
the sense to be, 'Love conquers not man
only, but fishes and wild beasts'; cp. fr.
856. 9 (Κύπρις) εἰσέρχεται μὲν ἰχθύων πλω-
τῷ γένει, | ἔνεστι δ' ἐν χέρσου τετρασκελεῖ
γονῇ.   (How could ὑπερπόντιος imply a
visit to the fish?)   Others find a reference
to Paris carrying Helen over the Aegean,
Aphrodite visiting Anchises in the pastures of Ida, etc.   Rather the poet is
merely saying, quite generally, how
boundless is the range of Love.
  787 f. οὔτ' ἀθανάτων: Tr. 443 (of
Love) οὗτος γὰρ ἄρχει καὶ θεῶν ὅπως θέλει:
fr. 856. 13 (Κύπρις) τίν' οὐ παλαίουσ' ἐς τρὶς
ἐκβάλλει θεῶν; Eur. fr. 434 "Ερως γὰρ

ἄνδρας οὐ μόνους ἐπέρχεται, | οὐδ' αὖ γυ-
ναῖκας, ἀλλὰ καὶ θεῶν ἄνω | ψυχὰς χαράσ-
σει.—σὲ...φύξιμός ἐστι,=σὲ δύναται φεύγειν.   Cp. Aesch. P. V. 904 ὁ πόλεμος
ἄπορα πόριμος: Ag. 1090 (στέγην) πολλὰ
ξυνίστορα | ...κακά: Xen. Cyr. 3. 3. 9
ἐπιστήμονες δ' ἦσαν τὰ προσήκοντα: Isae.
or. 5 § 26 ἔξαρνοί εἰσι τὰ ὡμολογημένα:
[Plat.] Alcib. II. 141 D οἶμαι δέ σε οὐκ
ἀνήκοον εἶναι ἐνιά γε...γεγενημένα.   Similarly with a subst., Plat. Apol. 18 B τὰ
μετέωρα φροντιστής.
  789 f. σέ γ' : for γε with the repeated
σε, cp. O. T. 1101, Ph. 1116.—The ms.
ἐπ' could mean only, 'in the case of' (and
so, 'among'): a use which is not ade-
quately supported by Aristeid. Pan. 1. 96
μόνῃ τῇ πόλει ἐπὶ τῶν Ἑλληνικῶν, where
he means, 'in the case of' (i.e., 'so far as
they are concerned').   Nor could ἐπ' be
an adverb ('moreover,' O. T. 181), as
some take it.—ὁ δ' ἔχων : Plat. Phaedr.
239 C ἀνὴρ ἔχων ἔρωτα.
  791 f. ἀδίκους proleptic: cp. on 475:
Tr. 106 εὐνάζειν ἀδακρύτων βλεφάρων
πόθον (so that they shall not weep).—
παρασπᾷς (cp. 298), a metaphor from a
driver jerking his horses aside out of their
course: El. 732 (the charioteer) ἔξω πα-
ρασπᾷ (sc. τοὺς ἵππους), pulls them aside,
out of the crowd of chariots.   The word
is fig. again in O. C. 1185 οὐ γάρ σε...
παρασπάσει | γνώμης, pluck thee from
thy resolve.
  794 ξύναιμον, not ξυναίμων, since νεῖ-
κος-ἀνδρῶν forms one notion: cp. 862:
El. 1390 τοὐμὸν φρενῶν ὄνειρον : Ph. 952
σχῆμα πέτρας δίπυλον: Aesch. Eum. 325
ματρῷον ἄγνισμα...φόνου.—ἔχεις with aor.

thou roamest over the sea, and among the homes of dwellers
in the wilds; no immortal can escape thee, nor any among
men whose life is for a day; and he to whom thou hast come
is mad.

The just themselves have their minds warped by thee Anti-
to wrong, for their ruin: 'tis thou that hast stirred up strophe.
this present strife of kinsmen; victorious is the love-
kindling light from the eyes of the fair bride; it is
a power enthroned in sway beside the eternal

---

beginning with ἵμερος.   **796** εὐλέκτρου] In L a letter (perh. ι) has been erased
between ε and κ.   **797 f.** πάρεδρος ἐν ἀρχαῖς MSS. In L the letters δρ are in an
erasure, from ργ. The Schol. notes that some read πάρεδρος, as Doric for παρέδρους.
This indicates that he knew no other variant. See comment. and Appendix.

---

part.: cp. 22.—**ταράξας**, *excitasti*. Dem.
or. 18 § 153 ἵν' εἰδῆτε ἡλίκα πράγματα ἡ
μιαρὰ κεφαλὴ ταράξασα αὕτη δίκην οὐκ
ἔδωκεν. In this sense later prose has also
συνταράττω.

795 f. ἐναργής, 'clearly seen,' 'present
to the lover's sight,' marks the vivid appeal to the senses, in contrast with the in-
visible and spiritual majesty of the θεσμοί
which Love overrides. For ἐναργής as
='before our eyes,' 'in bodily presence,'
cp. *O. C.* 910; *Tr.* 11, 224.—**βλεφάρων-
ἵμερος**, love-influence from the eyes, **εὐλέκτρου νύμφας**, of the fair bride. Both
genitives are possessive, but βλεφάρων
goes more closely with ἵμερος, denoting
the latter's source. Cp. 929: *O. C.* 729
ὀμμάτων... | φόβον...τῆς ἐμῆς ἐπεισόδου,
fear, shown in your eyes (possess. gen.), of
my entrance (objective gen.). In *Phaedr.*
251 B Plato describes ἵμερος as the desire
infused into the soul by an emanation
of beauty (κάλλους ἀπορροή) proceeding
from the beloved, and received through
the eyes of the lover (διὰ τῶν ὀμμάτων).
So the soul is spoken of (*ib.* E) as ἐποχε-
τευσαμένη ἵμερον, 'having refreshed herself
with the love-shower' or 'effluence of
beauty.' And ἵμερος itself receives fan-
ciful derivations, as *ib.* 251 C, ἐκεῖθεν μέρη
ἐπιόντα καὶ ῥέοντα, ἃ δὴ διὰ ταῦτα ἵμερος
καλεῖται (*i.e.* from ἰέναι μέρη and ῥεῖν):
while in *Crat.* 419 E it is explained by
ἱέμενος ῥεῖ. The real origin of the word
is prob. from rt. ἱς, 'wish,' whence ἰότητι,
and Ἰσ-μήνη, *Desiderata.* Curt. § 617.
So Soph. fr. 161 ὀμμάτων ἄπο | λόγχας
ἵησιν: 733 ὀμμάτειος πόθος: 430 (Hippo-
dameia speaking of Pelops), τοιάνδ' ἐν
ὄψει λίγγα θηρατηρίαν | ἔρωτος, ἀστραπήν
τιν' ὀμμάτων, ἔχει ('such a subduing arrow
of love, a lightning from the eyes'):

Aesch. *Ag.* 742 μαλθακὸν ὀμμάτων βέλος, |
δηξίθυμον ἔρωτος ἄνθος: *Suppl.* 1004
ὄμματος θελκτήριον | τόξευμ' ἔπεμψεν, ἱμέ-
ρου νικώμενος: Eur. *Hipp.* 525 Ἔρως,
Ἔρως δ κατ' ὀμμάτων | στάζεις πόθον,
εἰσάγων γλυκεῖαν | ψυχαῖς χάριν οὓς ἐπι-
στρατεύσῃ [*i.e.* 'on the eyes' of mortals:
better ὁ...στάζων, or else δς ἀπ'—.]—
εὐλέκτρου, epithet of Κύπρις in *Tr.* 515.
Cp. *Anthol. P.* 7. 649 εὐλεγχέος θαλάμου
(happy nuptials).

797 f. πάρεδρος ἐν ἀρχαῖς. I leave
these words in the text, without marking
them as corrupt, because the case against
them is not decisive, while no emendation
is certain. But I strongly suspect them.
If sound, they mean that the love inspired
by the maiden's eyes is a power 'enthroned in sway by the side of the great
laws.' The great laws are those 'unwritten' moral laws which most men feel
and acknowledge (cp. on 454 f.); here,
especially, the law of loyalty to country,
the law of obedience to parents. In
Haemon's case, love has shown that it is
at least of equal force with these θεσμοί.
For **πάρεδρος**, cp. *O. C.* 1267 Ζηνὶ σύνθα-
κος θρόνων | Αἰδώς: *ib.* 1382 Δίκη ξύνεδρος
Ζηνὸς ἀρχαίοις νόμοις. Pind. *O.* 8. 21
Διὸς ξενίου πάρεδρος | ...Θέμις. For **ἐν
ἀρχαῖς**, Eur. *Andr.* 699 σεμνοὶ δ' ἐν
ἀρχαῖς ἥμενοι κατὰ πτόλιν: *Or.* 897 ὃς ἂν
δύνηται πόλεος ἔν τ' ἀρχαῖσιν ᾖ. Cp. also
on 744.

The words answer metrically to φύξιμος
οὐδείς (788). The first two syllables of
πάρεδρος therefore represent a resolved
long syllable. Pindar affords some instances of such resolution (see Appendix),
and there is a probable example below
(970 ἀγχίπολις Ἄρης, where see n.). But
it is rare, and certainly unpleasing. As

148 ΣΟΦΟΚΛΕΟΥΣ

5 θεσμῶν· ἄμαχος γὰρ ἐμπαίζει θεὸς Ἀφροδίτα. 799

νῦν δ᾽ ἤδη ᾽γὼ καὐτὸς θεσμῶν
ἔξω φέρομαι τάδ᾽ ὁρῶν, ἴσχειν δ᾽
οὐκέτι πηγὰς δύναμαι δακρύων,
τὸν παγκοίτην ὅθ᾽ ὁρῶ θάλαμον
τήνδ᾽ Ἀντιγόνην ἀνύτουσαν. 805

στρ. α'. ΑΝ. ὁρᾶτ᾽ ἔμ᾽, ὦ γᾶς πατρίας πολῖται, τὰν νεάταν ὁδὸν
2 στείχουσαν, νέατον δὲ φέγγος λεύσσουσαν ἀελίου,
3 κοὔποτ᾽ αὖθις· ἀλλά μ᾽ ὁ παγκοίτας Ἅιδας ζῶσαν ἄγει

799 L divides thus: θεσμῶν· ἄμαχος γὰρ ἐμ|παίζει θεὸς Ἀφροδίτα. **800** ἐμπαίζει] Blaydes conject. ἐμπαίει: Herwerden, ἐνστάζει. **804** παγκοίταν L:

---

a whole, too, the phrase πάρεδρος ἐν ἀρχαῖς is suspicious. A yet stronger objection is the strangeness of describing the power which is *in conflict with* the θεσμοί as their assessor, or peer, in sway; an expression which would seem appropriate only if that power was working in harmony with them; as when Eur. (*Med.* 843) speaks of σοφίᾳ παρέδρους...ἔρωτας, | παντοίας ἀρετᾶς ξυνεργούς,—'the loves that sit with wisdom, co-workers of all excellence,'—those aspirations of the soul which assist intellectual effort.

The best line of emendation yet suggested is that of Semitelos, who writes ὥστε πέρα δρᾶν. He supposes that πέρα δρᾶν became, first, πάρεδρον (ΠΕΡΑΔΡΑΝ—ΠΑΡΕΔΡΟΝ). Then, πάρεδρον θεσμῶν seeming obscure, a marginal gloss ἐν ἀρχαῖς was added. This gloss came into the text, dislodging ὥστε: and πάρεδρον became πάρεδρος, to agree with ἵμερος. The original sense, then, was: 'the ἵμερος prevails, so that one transgresses the great θεσμοί.' Cp. *El.* 1506 ὅστις πέρα πράσσειν γε τῶν νόμων θέλει. This suits, too, the following lines, where the Chorus says, καὐτὸς (*i.e.*, like Haemon) θεσμῶν | ἔξω φέρομαι.—See Appendix.

800 ἐμπαίζει, 'wreaks her will' *in* that contest which νικᾷ implies. We find ἐμπαίζω with a dat. (1) of the object, as Her. 4. 134 ἐμπαίζοντας ἡμῖν, 'mocking us': (2) of the sphere, as Ar. *Th.* 975 χοροῖσιν ἐμπαίζει, 'sports in dances.' The ἐν of ἐμπαίζει here might also be explained as (*a*) in the ἵμερος, or the βλέφαρα, *i.e.* by their agency: or (*b*) 'on her victim.' But the interpretation first given appears

simpler. (Cp. Vergil's absol. use of 'illudere,' *G.* 1. 181, *Tum variae illudant pestes.*)

801 f. καὐτὸς θεσμῶν ἔξω: *i.e.* like Haemon, I also am moved to rebel against Creon's sentence, and to take Antigone's part.—φέρομαι, a proverbial image from the race-course: Ar. *Ran.* 993 μόνον ὅπως | μή σ᾽ ὁ θυμὸς ἁρπάσας | ἐκτὸς οἴσει τῶν ἐλαῶν, because some olives marked the limits of the course at the end of the race-course (schol. *ad loc.*), where the chariots turned, and where the horses were most likely to swerve or bolt. Plat. *Crat.* 414 B οὐ γὰρ ἐπισκοπεῖς με ὥσπερ ἐκτὸς δρόμου φερόμενον, ἐπειδὰν λεῖον ἐπιλάβωμαι (when I get on smooth ground). Aesch. *P. V.* 883 ἔξω δὲ δρόμου φέρομαι λύσσης | πνεύματι μάργῳ. Eur. *Bacch.* 853 ἔξω δ᾽ ἐλαύνων τοῦ φρονεῖν.—ἴσχειν δ᾽: cp. 817 ἔχουσ᾽: 820 λαχοῦσ᾽, by the rule of continuity (συνάφεια) in anapaestic systems. In lyrics such elision is rarer (see on 350).

803 πηγάς, not, the sources or springs, but the streams, of tears: so *Tr.* 852 ἔρρωγεν παγὰ δακρύων, and oft.: cp. *O. C.* 479, where πηγάς = the water gushing from the bowl. On the other hand in fr. 658 νυκτός...πηγάς = 'the sources of night' (the west).

804 f. παγκοίτην. The question between Doric and Attic forms in tragic anapaests cannot be decided by a rigid rule. It depends on the presence or absence of a lyric character. Thus in 110 f. the Doricisms are justified by the purely lyric stamp of the anapaests. Here, Attic forms are preferable. The lyric strains laws; for there the goddess Aphrodite is working her un-conquerable will.

But now at this sight I also am carried beyond the bounds of loyalty, and can no more keep back the streaming tears, when I see Antigone thus passing to the bridal chamber where all are laid to rest.

Kommos
1st
strophe.

AN. See me, citizens of my fatherland, setting forth on my last way, looking my last on the sunlight that is for me no more; no, Hades who gives sleep to all leads me living

---

παγκοίτην Wolff.   **809** λεύσουσαν L.   **810—816** L divides the vv. thus: κοῦ-ποτ— | Ἅιδας— | τὰν— | ἔγκληρον— | πώ μέ— | ὕμνησεν . . νυμφεύσω.   **810** παγ-κοίτας] πάγκοινος Blaydes.   **811** Ἅιδας] ἀΐδασ L.

---

of Antigone are brought into finer relief by the different tone of the choral ana-paests. Cp. 822, and see Appendix on 110.—Cp. *O. T.* 1578 (Death) τὸν ἀιέ-νυπνον. The word **θάλαμον** here has ref. to its special sense, 'bridal-chamber': cp. 891 νυμφεῖον, 1207 παστάδα. So oft. in epitaphs on the unmarried; *Anthol. P.* 7. 489 (by Sappho) Τιμάδος ἅδε κόνις, τὰν δὴ πρὸ γάμοιο θανοῦσαν | δέξατο Περσεφόνας κυάνεος θάλαμος. Kaibel *Epigrammata* 241 (on two young brothers) οἱ δισσοὶ συνόμαιμοι, ἰὼ ξένε, τῷδ' ὑπὸ τύμβῳ | ἄψαυστοι τέκνων κείμεθα κου-ριδίων· | Ἰκέσιος κἀγὼ νεαρὰν πληρούμενος ἥβαν | Ἕρμιππος κρυερὸν τόνδ' ἔχομεν θάλαμον.—ἀνύτουσαν with acc. of place, as *Ai.* 607 (ἀνύσειν), *O. C.* 1562 (ἐξανύσαι): cp. 231.

806—943 Fourth ἐπεισόδιον. An-tigone has now been brought out of the house by two of Creon's servants (οἱ ἄγοντες, 931) who are about to conduct her to her doom. She speaks of her fate to the Chorus, and they seek to comfort her,—while they intimate that she alone is to blame (853, 875). Creon enters (883); and, in obedience to his peremp-tory command, Antigone is presently led forth to death (943).

The structure of the κομμός (806—882) is as follows. 1st strophe (806—816) = 1st ant. (823—833). A system of choral ana-paests (817—822) comes after the strophe, and a similar system (834—838) after the antistrophe.— 2nd strophe (839—852) = 2nd ant. (857—871).—3rd str. (853—856) = 3rd ant. (872—875).—An epode forms the close (876—882). See Metrical Analysis.

806 ff. νεάταν...νέατον δέ. In such an epanaphora μέν regularly precedes δέ (as *O. T.* 25, 259; *O. C.* 5, 610, etc.); but there are numerous exceptions in Soph., as *O. C.* 1342 στήσω σ' ἄγων, | στήσω δ' ἐμαυτόν: *Ph.* 633 πάντα λεκ-τά, πάντα δὲ | τολμητά: *Tr.* 517 τότ' ἦν χερός, ἦν δὲ τόξων πάταγος: *ib.* 1147 κάλει τὸ πᾶν μοι σπέρμα σῶν ὁμαιμόνων, | κάλει δὲ τὴν τάλαιναν Ἀλκμήνην.—**νέατον**, in contrast with αὖθις, is best taken as adv.: Eur. *Tro.* 201 νέατον τεκέων σώματα λεύσσω: cp. the adv. τελευταῖον (*O. T.* 1183), ἔσχατον (*O. C.* 1550), πανύστατον, etc.—**κοῦποτ' αὖθις**, *sc.* ὀψομένη: *Ai.* 857 Ἥλιον προσεννέπω | πανύστατον δὴ κοῦ-ποτ' αὖθις ὕστερον.—Cp. the passage in Swinburne's *Erechtheus* where the maiden Chthonia, being about to die, speaks with the Chorus of Athenian Elders:—'People, old men of my city, lordly wise and hoar of head, | I, a spouseless bride and crown-less, but with garlands of the dead, | From the fruitful light turn silent to my dark unchilded bed.'

810 παγκοίτας=ὁ πάντας κοιμίζων. *Ai.* 831 καλῶ θ' ἅμα | πομπαῖον Ἑρμῆν χθόνιον εὖ με κοιμίσαι. Blaydes conjec-tures **πάγκοινος**, very plausibly. Cp. *El.* 138 τόν γ' ἐξ Ἀΐδα | παγκοίνου λίμνας. But these points may be noted. (1) Though we have had παγκοίτην so lately as in v. 804, such a repetition is no safe argu-ment for spuriousness: see on 76. (2) The 2nd and 3rd syllables of παγκοίτας = καί νιν in 828, and πάγκοινος therefore gives a more exact correspondence; but this proves nothing, since a spondee and a trochee are equally admissible. (See Metr. Analysis.) (3) παγκοίτας is *here*

4 τὰν Ἀχέροντος   812

5 ἀκτάν, οὔθ' ὑμεναίων ἔγκληρον, οὔτ' *ἐπινύμφειός

6 πώ μέ τις ὕμνος ὕμνησεν, ἀλλ' Ἀχέροντι νυμφεύσω·

σύστ. α'. ΧΟ. οὐκοῦν κλεινὴ καὶ ἔπαινον ἔχουσ'   817

ἐς τόδ' ἀπέρχει κεῦθος νεκύων,

οὔτε φθινάσιν πληγεῖσα νόσοις

οὔτε ξιφέων ἐπίχειρα λαχοῦσ',   820

ἀλλ' αὐτόνομος, ζῶσα μόνη δὴ

θνητῶν Ἀΐδην καταβήσει.

ἀντ. α'. ΑΝ. ἤκουσα δὴ λυγροτάταν ὀλέσθαι τὰν Φρυγίαν ξέναν

2 Ταντάλου Σιπύλῳ πρὸς ἄκρῳ, τὰν κισσὸς ὡς ἀτενὴς 825

---

814 ἐπινυμφίδιος MSS. (ἐπινυμφίδος Vat.). Dindorf conject. ἐπινύμφειος: Bergk,

a more expressive epithet than πάγκοινος ('receiving all'): eyes still bright with life and youth are to suffer the ἀτέρμονα νήγρετον ὕπνον.

811 f. ἄγει...ἀκτάν, a rare poet. constr. with ἄγω, as Ph. 1175 Τρῳάδα γᾶν μ' ἤλπισας ἄξειν: Aesch. Pers. 861 νόστοι... | εὖ πράσσοντας ἄγον οἴκους (so Porson for ἐς οἴκους). Cp. O. T. 178 ἀκτὰν πρὸς ἑσπέρου θεοῦ.

813 ff. οὔθ' ὑμεναίων...οὔτ' ἐπινύμφειος...ὕμνος. The ὑμέναιος has not been sung by friends escorting bride and bridegroom to their home; nor has the ἐπιθαλάμιον been sung in the evening at the door of the bridal chamber. (1) For the procession-song, cp. Il. 18. 492 νύμφας δ' ἐκ θαλάμων, δαΐδων ὑπὸ λαμπομενάων, | ἡγίνεον ἀνὰ ἄστυ· πολὺς δ' ὑμέναιος ὀρώρει. Ar. Pax 1332 ff. gives a specimen, with the refrain 'Ὑμήν, Ὑμέναι' ὦ. Cp. also Av. 1736. This was specially called the ἁρμάτειον μέλος (from the carriage conveying the newly-married couple), Etym. M. p. 145. (2) As to the ἐπιθαλάμιος (ὕμνος), or ἐπιθαλάμιον (μέλος), sung in the evening, see Phot. Bibl. p. 321 καὶ τὰ ἐπιθαλάμια δὲ τοῖς ἄρτι θαλαμευομένοις ἅμα οἱ ἠΐθεοι καὶ αἱ παρθένοι ἐπὶ τῶν θαλάμων ᾖδον. Extant specimens are Theocritus Idyll. 18 (for Helen and Menelaus), Catullus Carm. 61 and 62: for a burlesque, see Lucian Symp. 41. The word ὑμέναιος, though more specially denoting the procession-song, was a general term for a γαμήλιον ᾆσμα, and could denote the ἐπιθαλάμιος, in which 'Ὑμὴν ὦ 'Ὑμέναιε

was the usual refrain (Theocr. 18. 58, Catull. 61. 4 etc.): so Pindar P. 3. 17 οὐδὲ παμφώνων ἰαχὰν ὑμεναίων, ἄλικες | οἷα παρθένοι φιλέοισιν ἑταῖραι | ἑσπερίαις ὑποκουρίζεσθ' ἀοιδαῖς: Apollon. Rhod. 4. 1160 νυμφιδίαις ὑμέναιον ἐπὶ προμολῇσιν (threshold) ἄειδον. — οὔτε...ἔγκληρον,... οὔτε...ὕμνησεν: we expected οὔτε ὑμνηθεῖσαν : a finite verb is substituted for the second participial clause : cp. 255 f.: O.C. 348 πολλὰ μὲν...ἀλωμένη, | πολλοῖσι δ' ἡγεῖται, with n. there on 351.

ἐπινύμφειος, Dindorf's correction of ἐπινυμφίδιος, is strongly supported by these facts. (1) In O. C. 1088 Soph. certainly used ἐπινικείῳ instead of the usual ἐπινικίῳ. Cp. above, 358, ἐναίθρεια. (2) In Aesch. Cho. 334 ἐπιτύμβιος (restored with certainty by Herm.) had been corrupted into ἐπιτυμβίδιος. Bergk's ἐπὶ νυμφείοις ('for crown of nuptials') is quite possible (cp. n. on 568); but an epithet for ὕμνος is decidedly preferable here. Bergk relies on the schol., λείπει θύραις ἢ κοίταις, which suggests that the Schol. read ἐπὶ νυμφιδίοις (or νυμφείοις); but, if this were so, the fact would have little weight. The corruption would have been easy.—Herm. Schütz defends ἐπινυμφίδιος as metrically possible. But, though it is possible that a logaoedic dactyl might replace a spondee here, the latter is at least better suited to the grave and mournful rhythm. The antistrophic verse (831) ends with παγκλαύτοις. So v. 816 ends with νυμφεύσω, and 833 with κατευνάξει.

816 Ἀχέροντι νυμφεύσω: cp. on 654.

to Acheron's shore ; who have had no portion in the chant that brings the bride, nor hath any song been mine for the crowning of bridals ; whom the lord of the Dark Lake shall wed.

CH.   Glorious, therefore, and with praise, thou departest to that deep place of the dead : wasting sickness hath not smitten thee ; thou hast not found the wages of the sword ; no, mistress of thine own fate, and still alive, thou shalt pass to Hades, as no other of mortal kind hath passed.

AN.   I have heard in other days how dread a doom befell 1st anti-our Phrygian guest, the daughter of Tantalus, on the Sipylian strophe. heights ; how, like clinging ivy,

---

ἐπὶ νυμφείοις: Semitelos, ἐπὶ νυμφείαις, with εὐναῖς for ὕμνος.   **819** φθινάσι L.
822 θνατῶν ἀΐδαν L.   Dindorf writes Ἀΐδην: others, Ἅιδην.

---

820 ξιφέων (possessive gen.) ἐπίχειρα, 'the wages of swords,' i.e. the reward of strife with the sword,—viz. a violent death. The gen. after ἐπίχειρα always denotes that for which the reward is given, as Aesch. P. V. 318 ὑψηγόρου | γλώσσης, Ar. Vesp. 581 ταύτης (sc. τῆς δίκης), Plat. Rep. 608 c ἀρετῆς, [Dem.] Epist. p. 1484. 4 τῶν ... πεπονημένων. Here, ξιφέων can hardly be a subjective gen., 'the reward which the sword gives'; though the meaning is the same. The ironical sense of ἐπίχειρα occurs in Attic prose as well as verse ; Antiphon or. 1 § 20 ἡ μὲν διακονήσασα (in the murder) ἔχει τὰ ἐπίχειρα ὧν ἄξια ἦν (torture and death). Cp. El. 1382 τἀπιτίμια | τῆς δυσσεβείας. ξιφέων might be poet. plur. for sing., as in Eur. Andr. 812 ἔκ τε δεξιᾶς | ξίφη καθαρπάξουσιν, and Or. 1398 (cp. σκῆπτρα, etc.) ; but it is rather an ordinary plural.

821 f. αὐτόνομος, i.e. of your own free will. No one constrained her to do the act for which she suffers. She knew that death would be the consequence, and she chose it. The word is fitting, since she has set her laws (the θεῶν νόμιμα) above Creon's. The implied contrast is with the helpless victims of disease or of war.—The word could not mean, ' by an ordinance peculiar to your case,' i.e. ' by the unique doom of a living death.' —δή strengthens μόνη, as Tr. 1063.— Ἀΐδην seems preferable to Ἅιδην in the paroemiac. Cp. on 804.—Acc. of motion, like δόμους στείχειν (O. C. 643).

823 ff. ἤκουσα δή. The Chorus has

said, ' No mortal's fate was ever like thine.' She continues : ' I have heard before now (δή) how Niobe perished,—by a doom like mine.' To which the Chorus reply that Niobe was not a mere mortal (834).—The Theban princess remembers the fate of the Theban queen. Niobe, daughter of Tantalus, married Amphion, king of Thebes. She vaunted that she had borne many children, while Leto had borne only two. Wherefore those two, Apollo and Artemis, slew all her sons and daughters,—at Thebes, as said the Theban story ; but Niobe returned to her old home at Mount Sipylus, and was there turned to stone. (Ovid, Met. 6. 310, represents her as carried to Sipylus after the change.) Νιόβη was the title of lost plays by Aesch. and Soph.—λυγροτάταν, adverbial : cp. 305 (ὅρκιος): Ai. 966 ἐμοὶ πικρὸς τέθνηκεν.—ξέναν, in relation to Thebes ; the foreign wife of the Theban king. Pindar wrote a παιάν on Niobe's marriage, and said that the Lydian ἁρμονία was first used at Thebes on that occasion. (Plut. de Mus. 15.)

825 Ταντάλου, gen. of parentage : cp. 486, Ai. 172 Διὸς Ἄρτεμις: 952 Ζηνὸς ἡ δεινὴ θεός. Tantalus, son of Zeus, had his royal seat on Mount Sipylus, which belonged to Phrygia in the older and larger sense of that term. In Aesch. Νιόβη (fr. 153) he describes his realm as extending ' twelve days journey ' from Sipylus westward to Ida.

Σιπύλῳ. Mount Sipylus is in the country once called Maeonia, and after-

3 πετραία βλάστα δάμασεν· καί νιν *ὄμβροι τακομέναν,
4 ὡς φάτις ἀνδρῶν,
5 χιών τ᾽ οὐδαμὰ λείπει, τέγγει δ᾽ ὑπ᾽ ὀφρύσι παγ-
    κλαύτοις   830
6 δειράδας· ᾇ με δαίμων ὁμοιοτάταν κατευνάζει.

827 ff. L divides the vv. thus: πετραία— | ὄμβρῳ— | ὡς φάτις— | τάκει (τέγγει)— |
δειράδας— | δαίμων .. κατευνάζει.   **828** ὄμβρῳ MSS. ὄμβροι Musgrave, which
most edd. have received. Nauck, keeping ὄμβρῳ, changes χιών τ᾽ in 830 to αἰὼν

---

wards Lydia. It is a branch of the
Tmolus range (N. of which stood Sardis), and extends in a N.W. direction to
the Hermus. Magnesia 'ad Sipylum'
was on that river's left bank. From a
remote age volcanic forces were active in
this region, known to the Greeks as the
κατακεκαυμένη. Cp. Arist. *Meteor.* 2. 8
γενομένου σεισμοῦ τὰ περὶ Σίπυλον ἀνετρά-
πη. A city called Tantalis, once situated
at Sipylus, was said to have perished by
an earthquake, which made a lake. Tantalus, like Niobe, is a type of prosperity
plunged by ὕβρις into misery. Here, as
in the case of Sodom and Gomorrah,
some physical catastrophe was at the root
of the tradition.—See on 831.

826 f. ἀτενής, prop. 'strained,' 'intent' (*e.g.* ἀτενὴς ὄψις), or 'intense' (as
ἀτενεῖς ὀργαί): here it denotes the close
embrace of the ivy. Cp. *hederae sequaces*
(Persius *prol.*).—πετραία βλάστα δάμα-
σεν, the 'growth of stone' (the process
of petrifaction) 'subdued her,' *i.e.* passed
gradually over her whole form: cp. Ovid,
Met. 6. 301: Orba resedit | Exanimes
inter natos, natasque, virumque, | Diri-
guitque malis. Nullos movet aura capil-
los. | In vultu color est sine sanguine:
lumina maestis | Stant immota genis:
nihil est in imagine vivi. | Ipsa quoque
interius cum duro lingua palato | Con-
gelat, et venae desistunt posse moveri. |
Nec flecti cervix, nec bracchia reddere
gestus, | Nec pes ire potest: intra quoque
viscera saxumst. For αἴ in πετραία, cp.
1310 n.

828 ff. καί νιν ὄμβροι, κ.τ.λ. The
poet is thinking of Niobe's petrified form
among the lonely mountain-crags (*Il.* 24.
614 νῦν δέ που ἐν πέτρῃσιν, ἐν οὔρεσιν οἰο-
πόλοισιν, | ἐν Σιπύλῳ). 'The rain and the
snow never leave her, as she pines with
grief': *i.e.* she is amid the storms that
visit snow-crowned Sipylus throughout the

year. By these words the poet wishes to
call up a general image of bleak and storm-
beaten solitude. Niobe's own weeping is
then described by τέγγει δ᾽, etc. Now, if
we kept the MS. ὄμβρῳ, that dat. would
go closely with τακομέναν: 'as she melts,
flows down, with rain' (or 'with water'),
'the snow never leaves her.' Thus τέγγει
...δειράδας would be anticipated, and in
a prosaic manner; viz., by words suggesting that the appearance of weeping
is due to water trickling down the rock.
This is the true reason for preferring
ὄμβροι to ὄμβρῳ.   It is no argument
against ὄμβρῳ that χιών τ᾽ would answer
to τέγγει θ᾽ (for τε irregularly placed, cp.
O. T. 258 n.). With ὄμβροι, θ᾽ could still
follow τέγγει, but δ᾽ is better.—For the
constr. ὄμβροι...χιών τ᾽ οὐ λείπει (verb
agreeing in number with nearest subject)
cp. 1132 f.: *O. C.* 7 στέργειν γὰρ αἱ πάθαι
με χὼ χρόνος ξυνὼν | μακρὸς διδάσκει (n.).
—χιών is taken by Wecklein as = 'snow-
water' (Eiswasser). The only passage
which seems to favour that sense is Eur.
Tro. 1066 Ἰδαῖα...νάπη | χιόνι κατάρυτα
ποταμίᾳ, but there the adj. makes the
difference: 'snow carried down streams'
can be only 'snow-water.' In *Andr.* 215
Θρῄκην χιόνι τὴν κατάρρυτον means merely, 'on which snow falls thickly.' Cp.
Quintus Smyrnaeus 1. 293 ὑπαὶ Σιπύλῳ
νιφόεντι: cp. 763.

831 τέγγει δ᾽ ὑπ᾽ ὀφρύσι...δειράδας.
Though ὀφρύς and δειράς could be said of
a mountain, Soph. is here thinking simply
of the human form. παγκλαύτους (L)
might be proleptic (cp. n. on ἀδίκους, 791),
but παγκλαύτοις is better, since ὀφρύσι
seems to need an epithet.

The Niobe of Sipylus has usually been
identified with a colossal rock-image on
the N. side of the range. It is rudely
carved in relief, within a rectangular niche
on the face of a limestone cliff, and re-

the growth of stone subdued her; and the rains fail not, as men tell, from her wasting form, nor fails the snow, while beneath her weeping lids the tears bedew her bosom; and most like to hers is the fate that brings me to my rest.

(without τ'). He would, however, prefer οἴκτῳ to ὄμβρῳ. **830** οὐδαμὰ] οὐδαμᾶι L. **831** τάκει θ' L: τέγγει θ' r. δ' for θ' Bothe.—παγκλαύτουσ L: παγκλαύτοις or παγκλαύστοις r.

---

presents a woman seated on a throne. (See Stark, *Niobe*, pl. 1, Leips. 1863: cp. Baumeister, *Denkm.* p. 1029). Prof. W. M. Ramsay, however, holds that this image is the 'very ancient' ἄγαλμα of Cybele mentioned by Paus. 3. 22. 4. In two respects it differs from the ancient accounts of the Niobe (quoted below): (a) it does not 'weep,'—for the rainwater drops from the front of the niche, clear of the figure; and (b) the likeness to a human form grows, instead of vanishing, as one approaches. (*Journ. Hellen. Studies* III. 61 ff., 1882.) This has been confirmed by another traveller, Herr Schweisthal (as reported in the *Berl. Phil. Wochenschr.*, May 28, 1887, p. 704). He finds the true Niobe at no great distance from the Cybele, but nearer Magnesia, and in the vicinity of a stream (the Jarikkaia) which Humann, in his 'Excursion into Sipylus' (1881), had already identified with the Achelous of *Il.* 24. 616. It is a natural phenomenon,—the semblance—as seen from a distance—of a draped woman, seated high on the rocks; she looks towards the right, and lifts her right arm, as if in lament.

The best ancient description is by a poet whose native place was in that neighbourhood,—Quintus Smyrnaeus (1. 293–306):—'Her streaming tears still fall from the heights of the rugged cliff; and in sympathy with her the sounding waters of the Hermus make lament, and the lofty peaks of Sipylus, over which the mist that shepherds dread floats evermore. A great marvel is she to passers by, because she is like a sorrowful woman, who mourns some cruel grief, and weeps without stint. Such verily seems the figure, when thou gazest at it from afar; but when thou drawest near, lo, 'tis but a sheer rock, a cliff of Sipylus' (φαίνεται αἰπήεσσα πέτρη, Σιπύλοιό τ' ἀπορρώξ).

Nonnus was thinking of the effect *from the road*, when he wrote (2. 160), ἔσσομαι ὡς Νιόβη καὶ ἐγὼ λίθος, ὄφρα καὶ αὐτὴν |

λαϊνέην στενάχουσαν ἐποικτείρωσιν ὁδῖται. Pausanias, too, says that, at a certain distance from the cliff, δεδακρυμένην δόξεις ὁρᾶν καὶ κατηφῆ γυναῖκα, but that the illusion vanishes on a nearer approach (1. 21 § 3).

833 ὁμοιοτάταν, because the stone into which Niobe was changed may be likened to Antigone's rocky tomb: cp. *El.* 150 ἰὼ παντλάμων Νιόβα, σὲ δ' ἔγωγε νέμω θεόν, | ἅτ' ἐν τάφῳ πετραίῳ | αἰαῖ δακρύεις.—The Niobe in the Uffizi Gallery at Florence will occur to many as offering an ideal type of majestic sorrow and beauty not unworthy to be associated with Antigone, and yet suggesting a contrast no less than a resemblance; the contrast between the desolate mother, and the maiden who is going to join those whom she loves (897); between pride steadfast under divine anger, and the piety that has dared to offend man.

834—838 ἀλλὰ ... θανοῦσαν. The Chorus desire to console Antigone. There is no element of reproof in their words here. She has likened herself to Niobe. 'And yet Niobe'—the Chorus say—'was a goddess, while thou art a mortal. But (καίτοι) it will be a great glory for thy memory that thy fate was as the fate of a goddess, in life and in death.' 'In life' (ζῶσαν), and not only in death (θανοῦσαν), because Niobe, like Antigone, was in the fulness of her vitality when she met her doom. The moments of life through which Antigone is now passing are like the moments through which Niobe passed as she felt the beginning of the change into stone.—Why does Antigone rejoin, οἴμοι γελῶμαι? Because her thought had been, 'my doom is terrible and miserable as Niobe's'; but the Chorus had answered, 'It is indeed glorious for thee to be as Niobe.' She had looked for present pity. They had comforted her with the hope of posthumous fame. —See Appendix.

σύστ. β΄. ΧΟ. ἀλλὰ θεός τοι καὶ θεογεννής,
              ἡμεῖς δὲ βροτοὶ καὶ θνητογενεῖς.   835
              καίτοι φθιμένῃ μέγα κἀκοῦσαι
              τοῖς ἰσοθέοις *σύγκληρα λαχεῖν
              ζῶσαν καὶ ἔπειτα θανοῦσαν.

στρ. β΄. ΑΝ. οἴμοι γελῶμαι. τί με, πρὸς θεῶν πατρῴων,
            2 οὐκ *οἰχομέναν ὑβρίζεις, ἀλλ᾽ ἐπίφαντον;   840
            3 ὦ πόλις, ὦ πόλεως πολυκτήμονες ἄνδρες·
            4 ἰὼ Διρκαῖαι κρῆναι
            5 Θήβας τ᾽ εὐαρμάτου ἄλσος, ἔμπας ξυμμάρτυρας ὑμμ᾽
              ἐπικτῶμαι,   845
            6 οἷα φίλων ἄκλαυτος, οἵοις νόμοις

---

834 θεογεννῆσ L (not θεογενής, as Campb. gives it): the latter MSS. vary between
θεογεννής and θεογενής. Wieseler conject. θειογενής: M. Schmidt, καὶ θεῶν γέννημ᾽:
Nauck, θείου τε γένους (and formerly καὶ θεοῦ γέννης). **835** θνητογεννεῖσ L.
836 φθιμένα L, with ω above a from the first hand. φθιμένᾳ or φθιμέναν r.—
μέγ᾽ ἀκοῦσαι L: μέγα κἀκοῦσαι Seyffert: μέγα τἀκοῦσαι Wecklein. **837** τοῖσ
ἰσοθέοισ ἔγκληρα λαχεῖν L.—τοῖσι θεοῖσι σύγκληρα λαχεῖν Nauck (σύγκληρα Schaefer).
838 ζῶσαν .. θανοῦσαν. L has this v., which is also in most of the later MSS.;
but it is omitted by A, and consequently by the Aldine. Dindorf and others

---

834 θεός, sc. ἐκείνη μέν ἐστι (cp. 948).
The absence of a pron., to balance ἡμεῖς,
is unusual, but it is easy to carry on the
subject of τέγγει in 831. Niobe is of divine race, since her father was the son of
Zeus, and her mother the Pleiad Taygetè
(or Dionè, one of the Hyades). So in
Aesch. Νιόβη (fr. 157) her family is described as οἱ θεῶν ἀγχίσποροι (near kin),
...κοὔπω νιν ἐξίτηλον αἷμα δαιμόνων.—**θεογεννής**, god-begotten. The peculiarity is
that the word is formed directly from
γέννα, and not from the stem of the pass.
aor. in use: i.e., we should expect θεο-
γένννητος. But Pindar could coin θεότι-
μος (I. 5. 13) as=θεοτίμητος. Why, then,
should not a poet coin θεογεννής as=θεο-
γέννητος? It is of little moment that the
extant classical literature happens to present no strictly parallel compound with
γέννα (πρωτογεννής and πρωτογεννής being late Byzantine). **θειογενής** occurs in
Orac. Sibyll. (5. 261), but is not classical.
The Schol.'s paraphrase, θειοτέρου γένους
τυγχάνουσα, is no token (as some fancy)
that he read a gen., such as θείου τε
γένους.
836 **καίτοι** has an illative force, introducing the next step in the reasoning:

cp. 949, O. T. 855.—L's φθιμένα should
prob. be **φθιμένῃ** (see on παγκοίτην 804).
The variant φθιμένῳ (noted in L) is
warrantable as the masc. of general
statement (cp. 463): but it would be
extremely harsh, when ζῶσαν...θανοῦσαν
refers to the same person.—**κἀκοῦσαι**,
'e'en to have it said of her' (καί meaning,
'even if there is no other comfort'). This
seems a little more expressive than τά-
κοῦσαι (Wecklein), and also slightly more
probable palaeographically (cp. O. C. 172
cr. n.). The MS. **μέγ᾽ ἀκοῦσαι** is certainly
wrong, since a paroemiac could not begin
a new sentence. For ἀκούω (=λέγομαι,
audio) with inf., cp. Her. 3. 131 Ἀργεῖοι
ἤκουον μουσικὴν εἶναι Ἑλλήνων πρῶτοι.
837 **τοῖς ἰσοθέοις σύγκληρα**, a lot
shared by demigods. Plut. Mor. 103 F χρὴ
γὰρ οὐ μόνον ἑαυτὸν εἰδέναι θνητὸν ὄντα τὴν
φύσιν, ἀλλὰ καὶ ὅτι θνητῷ σύγκληρός
ἐστι βίῳ καὶ πράγμασι ῥᾳδίως μεθιστα-
μένοις πρὸς τοὐναντίον: i.e. that one shares
the lot of humanity at large.—The decisive objection to the MS. reading **ἔγκληρα** is the sense of the adj.; for ἔγκλη-
ρος always means either (1) act., having
a share in, as Eur. I. T. 682 ἔγκληρον...
κασιγνήτην, 'heiress,'=ἐπίκληρον, and so

CH. Yet she was a goddess, thou knowest, and born of gods; we are mortals, and of mortal race. But 'tis great renown for a woman who hath perished that she should have shared the doom of the godlike, in her life, and afterward in death.

AN. Ah, I am mocked! In the name of our fathers' 2nd gods, can ye not wait till I am gone,—must ye taunt me strophe. to my face, O my city, and ye, her wealthy sons? Ah, fount of Dircè, and thou holy ground of Thebè whose chariots are many; ye, at least, will bear me witness, in what sort, unwept of friends, and by what laws

---

reject it. But M. Seyffert defends it, and among recent edd. who retain it are Bellermann, Nauck, Wecklein, Pallis, Semitelos. **840** ὀλομέναν L: ὀλλυμέναν r. οὐλομέναν Triclinius. οἰχομέναν J. F. Martin and Wunder. **843** πολυκτήμονος Nauck. **844 ff.** Διρκαῖαι κρῆναι] Διρκαῖαι καὶ κρῆναι L (by dittographia).—L divides the vv. thus: ἰώ— | Θήβαστ᾿ | ξυμμάρτυρας— | οἵα— | πρὸς ἔργμα—ἔρ|χομαι—ποταινίου. **846** ὑμμ᾿] ὕμμ᾿ L.—ἐπικτῶμαι] In the marg. of L, γρ. ἐπιβῶμαι (by S). Bergk reads ὑμμ᾿ ἐπιβῶμαι with δύσμορα for δυσμόρῳ in 865: Blaydes, ὑμᾶς ἐπιβῶμαι, with δυσδαίμονι ib.—Musgrave conject. ἔτι κτῶμαι.

Hipp. 1011: or (2) pass., included in one's κλῆρος, as *H. F.* 468 ἔγκληρα πεδία ...κεκτημένος ('by inheritance'). Here, ἔγκληρα was perh. partly due to a reminiscence of ἔγκληρον in 814.—The change of τοῖς ἰσοθέοις into τοῖσι θεοῖσιν, though easy, is needless. The epic ῑ of ἰσόθεος might well be allowed in tragic lyrics or anapaests, like the ᾱ of ἀθάνατος (cp. 339 n.): and Aesch. once uses it, *Pers.* 80 ἰσόθεος φώς. [But ἰσόθεος has ῐ in Eur. *Tro.* 1169, *I. A.* 626 (dial.), as ἰσόνειρον has in Aesch. *P. V.* 547.] Note that the MS. τοῖς ἰσοθέοις ἔγκληρα would have arisen more easily from ΤΟΙΣΙΣΟΘΕΟΙΣΣΥΓΚΛΗΡΑ than from ΤΟΙΣΙΘΕΟΙΣΙΝΣΥΓΚΛΗΡΑ.

838 ζῶσαν...θανοῦσαν. The constr., φθιμένῃ μέγα ἐστίν, ἀκοῦσαι ζῶσαν σύγκληρα λαχεῖν (instead of ζώσῃ), is not rare: cp. Xen. *An.* 1. 2 § 1 Ξενίᾳ τῷ Ἀρκάδι ἥκειν παραγγέλλει λαβόντα τοὺς ἄνδρας [though shortly before, παραγγέλλει τῷ Κλεάρχῳ λαβόντι ἥκειν]: *ib.* 3. 1. 5 συμβουλεύει τῷ Ξενοφῶντι ἐλθόντα εἰς Δελφοὺς ἀνακοινῶσαι: *ib.* 3. 2. 1 ἔδοξεν αὐτοῖς προφυλακὰς καταστήσαντας συγκαλεῖν τοὺς στρατιώτας. The dat. with the inf. is, in such cases, equally right, but the acc. sometimes excludes an ambiguity. (Cp. on *O. T.* 913.) *El.* 479 ὕπεστί μοι...κλύουσαν is not similar.—I can see no reason to suppose the loss of a verse. The fact that six anapaestic verses (817—822) follow the strophe proves

nothing. Cp. on 110 f., and Append. on 155 ff.

839 γελῶμαι: see on 834 ff. Cp. Job xvii. 2: 'Are there not mockers with me?'

843 πολυκτήμονες, an epith. which also implies εὐγενεῖς: cp. *O. T.* 1070 πλουσίῳ χαίρειν γένει. So these Theban elders are called κοιρανίδαι (940), and in *O. T.* 1223 ὦ γῆς μέγιστα τῆσδ᾿ ἀεὶ τιμώμενοι: as Thebes itself, ἀγλααὶ (*O. T.* 153) and μεγάλαι (*ib.* 1203).

844 f. κρῆναι: so Polyneices appeals to Oed., πρὸς νύν σε κρηνῶν καὶ θεῶν ὁμογνίων (*O. C.* 1333, where see n.): and the dying Ajax invokes the κρῆναι of Troy (*Ai.* 862).—εὐαρμάτου: see n. on 148 f.—ἄλσος: cp. *El.* 5 (Argos) τῆς οἰστροπλῆγος ἄλσος Ἰνάχου κόρης, as the scene of Io's visitation by Hera. So Thebes is the 'sacred precinct' of Dionysus (cp. 154, 1137) and the other θεοὶ ἐγχώριοι.—ἔμπας, even if human sympathy fails me. Soph. has ἔμπας (=ὅμως) also in *Ai.* 122, 1338, and ἔμπᾱ *ib.* 563 (dial.).

846 ὕμμ᾿ (Aeolic and epic), as Aesch. *Eum.* 620: so dat. ὕμμι *O. C.* 247 (n.).—ἐπικτῶμαι, acquire, win: Aesch. *Eum.* 671 (ὅπως) καὶ τόνδ᾿ ἐπικτήσαιο σύμμαχον, θεά. In this general sense ἐπί is not inconsistent with what ἔμπας implies, viz. that she fails to win human sympathy.

847 οἵα: cp. on 823 (λυγροτάταν).—

7 πρὸς ἔργμα τυμβόχωστον ἔρχομαι τάφου ποταινίου·
8 ἰὼ δύστανος, *βροτοῖς οὔτε νεκροῖς κυροῦσα 850
9 μέτοικος, οὐ ζῶσιν, οὐ θανοῦσιν.

στρ. γ'. ΧΟ. προβᾶσ' ἐπ' ἔσχατον θράσους
2 ὑψηλὸν ἐς Δίκας βάθρον
3 προσέπεσες, ὦ τέκνον, πολύ. 855
4 πατρῷον δ' ἐκτίνεις τιν' ἆθλον.

ἀντ. β'. ΑΝ. ἔψαυσας ἀλγεινοτάτας ἐμοὶ μερίμνας,
2 πατρὸς τριπόλιστον οἶκτον τοῦ τε πρόπαντος

---

848 ἔργμα L (with two dots over γ, indicating ἔρμα). ἔργμα was the general reading, though V has ἔργμα, and Par. H (a copy of L) ἔρυμα. Schol. in marg. of L, ἔρμα, περίφραγμα. Brunck gave ἔργμα: Hermann, ἔρμα. **849** ποταινίου] ποταινείου (from ποτ' αἰνείου?) L, with ι over ει from the first hand. **851** οὔτ' ἐν βροτοῖσιν οὔτ' ἐν νεκροῖσιν | L. Triclinius changed βροτοῖσιν to βροτοῖς.— The corresponding words in the antistr. (v. 870) are κασίγνητε γάμων κυρήσας. Boeckh conject. βροτοῖς οὔτ' ἐν νεκροῖς κυροῦσα (with κασίγνητος in 870): Seyffert, βροτοῖς οὔτε νεκροῖς κυροῦσα: and so Wecklein, but with λοῦσα. Emperius, οὔτ' ἐν τοῖσιν ἐτ' οὔτε τοῖσιν, which Heinrich Schmidt receives, adding γ' after δύστανος. Gleditsch, ἰὼ δύσποτμος | βροτῶν, οὐδὲ νεκρὸς νεκροῖσιν. Cp. on 869 f. **853** ἔσχατον] ἐσχάτου F. Kern, and so Bellermann. **855** πολύν L: πολύ r. Dindorf (who,

---

φίλων ἄκλαυτος: cp. 1034: *Ai.* 910 ἄφαρκτος φίλων, and *O. C.* 1722 n.

848 ἔργμα τυμβόχωστον, an enclosure (prison) with a sepulchral χῶμα. The ἔργμα is the chamber in the rock, πετρώδης κατῶρυξ (774), in which she is to be immured: the χῶμα consists of the stones heaped up at the entrance, so as to close it: cp. 1216 ἁρμὸν χώματος λιθοσπαδῆ. For ἔργμα (εἴργω, to shut in) cp. Arist. *Part. Anim.* 2. 15. 1, where it is said that the eyelashes (βλεφαρίδες) protect the eyes, οἷον τὰ χαρακώματα ποιοῦσί τινες πρὸ τῶν ἐργμάτων, like the palings sometimes placed in front of fences (or hedges). The Berlin ed. (p. 958 b 18) there gives ἐργμάτων from the MSS. just as here L has ἔργμα, and as, conversely, MSS. of Pindar (*I.* 1. 27 etc.) give ἔργμα for ἔργμα=ἔργον. The old edd. of Arist. give ἐρυμάτων.—The reading ἔρμα (from ἐρείδω)='mound': *C. I.* 4599 ἐρισθενὲς ἔρμα θανοῦσιν: Kaibel *Epigr.* 1063. 4 κάγήραον ἔρμα. But this seems less fitting here than the notion of 'prison': cp. 886 περιπτύξαντες, 892 ἀείφρουρος.

849 ποταινίου, usu., 'recent,' 'fresh': here, 'of a new kind': cp. fr. 154. 5 ἠδονὰς ποταινίους. A tomb destined for the dead is to receive the living (cp. 821).

851 Though every treatment of this verse must remain subject to doubt, far the most probable (to my mind) is Seyffert's modification of Boeckh's βροτοῖς οὔτ' ἐν νεκροῖς κυροῦσα. This gives an exact correspondence with 870, κασίγνητε γάμων κυρήσας, and there is every reason to think that 870 is sound. Further, the origin of L's reading is elucidated. The first οὔτε is omitted (Aesch. *Ag.* 532 Πάρις γὰρ οὔτε συντελὴς πόλις, cp. *O. T.* 239); and this poetical license might easily have led a corrector to suppose that the first οὔτε had been lost. Again, the loss of κυροῦσα would have been easy after νεκροῖς.

852 μέτοικος: cp. 868, 890: see on *O. C.* 934. It is her doom, ζῶσα τυμβεύειν (888). She is not a dweller with the living, because her abode is the grave; nor with the dead, because she lives.— The similar phrase—perhaps imitated from this—in Eur. *Suppl.* 968 f., οὔτ' ἐν τοῖς φθιμένοις | οὔτ' ἐν ζῶσιν ἀριθμουμένα (Musgrave κρινομένα) has no such special point: the Argive widows merely mean that their life is a living death.

I pass to the rock-closed prison of my strange tomb, ah me unhappy! who have no home on the earth or in the shades, no home with the living or with the dead.

CH. Thou hast rushed forward to the utmost verge of daring; and against that throne where Justice sits on high thou hast fallen, my daughter, with a grievous fall. But in this ordeal thou art paying, haply, for thy father's sin.

3rd strophe.

AN. Thou hast touched on my bitterest thought,—awaking the ever-new lament for my sire and for all the doom given to

2nd antistrophe.

however, suspects a lacuna) conject. πάλιν: Schneidewin, ποδοῖν: Wolff, πόλει: Todt, πάθει: Seyffert, πολύς (as fem.): Bonitz, μόρῳ: Hartung, τάφῳ: Blaydes, μέγα. Wieseler points at τέκνον, joining πολύν with ἆθλον. **856** πατρῷον .. τιν' ἆθλον] Blaydes conj. πατρῴαν .. τιν' ἄταν: Seyffert, πατρῷον .. γενέθλον. —ἐκτείνεισ L, ἐκτίνεις Υ. Donaldson conj. ἐκτελεῖς: Pallis, ἐκπονεῖς. **857** ἔψαυσας] Blaydes writes ἔμνασας. **858** τριπόλιστον] Blaydes gives τριπόλητον: Hermann, τριπλοῦστὸν ('triplicatum'): Reiske, τριπάλαιστον (with οἶτον): Bergk τρίπαλτον (with τε after πατρός).—οἶκτον L, and so the later MSS., though in L² (cod. Laur. 31. 10) the κ has been erased, and in V οἶτον is indicated as a variant. οἶκον in the lemma of L's schol. was doubtless a mere slip. Brunck gave

---

853 ff. προβᾶσ'...πολύ: having advanced to the furthest limit of rashness, thou hast struck heavily (πολύ) against the lofty pedestal of Justice. We are to imagine the daring offender as going forward to a boundary where Justice sits enthroned, forbidding all further advance. Instead of pausing there, the rebel still rushes on, to cross the boundary—and, in doing so, dashes herself against the throne of the goddess. For βάθρον cp. Her. I. 183 (a sitting statue of Zeus) καὶ τὸ βάθρον (pedestal) οἱ καὶ ὁ θρόνος χρύσεός ἐστι. For προσέπεσες, Polyb. I. 39 προσπεσόντες εἴς τινα βραχέα (having come upon some shallows—in sailing). Cp. Aesch. Theb. 409 μάλ' εὐγενῆ τε καὶ τὸν Αἰσχύνης θρόνον | τιμῶντα καὶ στυγοῦνθ' ὑπέρφρονας λόγους. Ag. 383 λακτίσαντι μέγαν Δίκας βωμόν. Eum. 539 βωμὸν αἴδεσαι Δίκας, | μηδέ νιν κέρδος ἰδὼν ἀθέῳ ποδὶ λὰξ ἀτίσῃς. Solon fr. 4. 14 οὐδὲ φυλάσσονται σεμνὰ θέμεθλα Δίκης.—πολύ (adv.) =σφόδρα, violently.—Bellermann, adopting Kvíčala's general view, and also Kern's ἐσχάτον, renders: 'having advanced, with extreme rashness (Dem. or. 18 § 17 οὔτε δικαίως οὔτ' ἐπ' ἀληθείας οὐδεμιᾶς εἰρημένα), to the lofty threshold (βάθρον) of Justice, thou hast fallen heavily *down*': i.e., 'while, with the utmost boldness, thou wast obeying the command of Justice, thou hast been

hurled to destruction.' But (1) προσέπεσες could not mean this: we must at least have κατέπεσες. (2) The Chorus feel pity, indeed, for Ant., and recognise the praise of piety, which she has won (817, 872). But they also regard her collision with the city's law as an act of frantic folly (λόγου τ' ἄνοια καὶ φρενῶν ἐρινύς, 603); and they presently tell her that she has left Creon no choice but to punish her (874). By Δίκη they understand the law of the State,—not those θεῶν νόμιμα which Ant. preferred to obey.

856 πατρῷόν τινα......ἆθλον, 'some ordeal inherited from thy sire' (v. 2); τινά softens a statement into a conjecture; it is perhaps the work of the fate which he bequeathed. This is better than to take τινά closely with πατρῷον as='of the paternal kind.'—ἐκτίνεις, art paying (to the fates which exact it), like ἐκτίνω δίκην, τίσιν, ἄποινα.

857 ff. μερίμνας, gen. sing.: οἶκτον, acc. depending on ἔψαυσας...μερίμνας as =ἐποίησάς με μεριμνᾶν: cp. El. 122 τίνα | τάκεις ὧδ' ἀκόρεστον οἰμωγὰν | τὸν πάλαι ἐκ δολερᾶς ἀθεώτατα | ματρὸς ἁλόντ' ἀπάταις Ἀγαμέμνονα, where τὸν...'Ἀγαμέμνονα is governed by τίνα τάκεις...οἰμωγάν as =τί οἰμώξεις; see other examples in n. on 211 f. πατρός and πότμου are objective genitives with οἶκτον.—The objection

3 ἀμετέρου πότμου κλεινοῖς Λαβδακίδαισιν.　　　861
4 ἰὼ ματρῷαι λέκτρων
5 ἆται κοιμήματά τ' αὐτογέννητ' ἐμῷ πατρὶ δυσμόρου
　　ματρός,　　　865
6 οἵων ἐγώ ποθ' ἁ ταλαίφρων ἔφυν·
7 πρὸς οὓς ἀραῖος, ἄγαμος, ἅδ' ἐγὼ μέτοικος ἔρχομαι.
8 ἰὼ δυσπότμων κασίγνητε γάμων κυρήσας,
9 θανὼν ἔτ' οὖσαν κατήναρές με.　　　871

ἀντ. γ'. ΧΟ. σέβειν μὲν εὐσέβειά τις,

οἶτον, which Dindorf and others adopt. **861** πότμου] δόμου Hartung and Blaydes. **863** ματρῷαι r: πατρῷαι L. Cp. 980. **864** ἆται] ἆται L.— κοιμήματ' αὐτογενῆ | τ' L: κοιμήματά τ' αὐτογέννητ' r. Turnebus restored αὐτο-γέννητ'. **865** ἐμῷ L: ἁμῷ Triclinius, which gives a long syllable to correspond with the first syllable of ξυμμάρτυρας (846), but is unnecessary, since that syllable may be either long or short (see Metr. Anal.).—δυσμόρωι L: δυσμόρου r and schol.

to taking οἶκτον as acc. in apposition with ἔψαυσας...μερίμνας is that this would imply τὸ (σε) ψαῦσαι ἀλγ. ἐμοὶ μερίμνης οἶκτός ἐστιν: as Eur. Or. 1105 Ἑλένην κτάνωμεν, Μενέλεῳ λύπην πικράν, implies, τὸ Ἑλένην κτανεῖν Μενέλεῳ λύπη πικρὰ ἔσται: Aesch. Ag. 224 ἔτλα δ' οὖν | θυτὴρ γενέσθαι θυγατρός, γυναικοποίνων πολέμων ἀρωγάν, implies, τὸ θυτῆρα γενέσθαι ἀρωγὴ ἦν. Now, if we had, for instance, ἀνε-μνήσθην μερίμνης, it is conceivable that οἶκτον, as acc. in appos., should mean οἶκτου ἀφορμήν or ἔγερσιν. But when, as here, the subject of ἔψαυσας is distinct from the person who makes the lament, it seems impossible that οἶκτον should have this pregnant sense.—ἀλγ. μερίμνας is certainly not acc. plur. See on 546 and 961. No Greek hearer of these lyrics could take μερίμνας for anything but the usual gen. after ψαύω. If Soph. had intended the acc., he would at least have written ἀλγεινοτάταν...μέριμναν.—The interpretation given above would admit the reading οἶτον, 'doom,' which has, however, less authority (cr. n.). El. 166 τὸν ἀνήνυτον | οἶτον ἔχουσα κακῶν. But, as οἶτον πότμου is an impossible pleonasm, it would then be necessary to take τοῦ τε ...πότμου as depending on ἔψαυσας: for τριπόλιστον οἶτον could not be a parenthetic acc. in apposition with ἔψαυσας... μερίμνας πατρός. This would be very awkward. Further, οἶκτον is clearly the right word to introduce the lament ἰώ, etc., which actually follows.—τριπόλισ-

τον (οἶκτον), a lament which has often been renewed; a thrice-told tale of sorrow. πολέω = to turn up the soil with the plough: ἀναπολέω, to plough anew: then fig., to 'go over the same ground' again. Pind. N. 7. 104 ταῦτά...τρὶς τετράκι τ' ἀμπολεῖν: Ph. 1238 δὶς ταῦτα βούλει καὶ τρὶς ἀναπολεῖν μ' ἔπη; No πολίζω as =πολέω occurs, but Pind. once has ἀνα-πολίζω as =ἀναπολέω (P. 6. 3). Similarly a poet might well use τριπόλιστος as if πολίζω existed. It is needless to write τριπόλητον. The epic adj. is τρίπολος.— κλεινοῖς Λαβδακίδαισιν, dat. of interest after πότμου, all the fate for (i.e. appointed for) us, the Labdacidae, instead of the possessive gen., κλεινῶν Λαβδακιδᾶν. Cp. Eur. Ph. 17 ὦ Θήβαισιν εὐίπποις ἄναξ. It is needless to explain the dat. by pressing the deriv. of πότμος from πίπτω ('what falls to one'). Cp. on 571, and on 865 (ἐμῷ πατρί).—ἀμετέρου (=ἡμῖν) is here joined with the dat. of interest, as the possessive pron. is oft. joined with the gen. of the pers. pron. (τάμὰ δυστήνου κακά, O. C. 344). **863** ματρῷαι λέκτρων ἆται =ματρῴων λ. ἆται (see n. on 793), calamities of the mother's bed, i.e. springing from marriage with a mother. (So O. C. 526 γάμων .. ἆτα.) For the plur. ἆται in this sense, cp. O. C. 1244, El. 215.—L's πατρῷαι ('calamities of my father's marriage') is possible, but less good, since (a) the epithet μητρῷα denotes the bed to which he came: cp. O. T. 976 καὶ πῶς τὸ μητρὸς

us, the famed house of Labdacus.   Alas for the horrors of the
mother's bed! alas for the wretched mother's slumber at the side
of her own son,—and my sire!   From what manner of parents
did I take my miserable being!   And to them I go thus, accursed, unwed, to share their home.   Alas, my brother, ill-starred
in thy marriage, in thy death thou hast undone my life!

CH.   Reverent action claims a certain praise for reverence; 3rd antistrophe.

867 πρὸς οὖς..ἔρχομαι] Two vv. in L, divided at ἄ|δ' ἐγώ.   **869 f.** ἰὼ] ἰὼ
ἰὼ L.—κασίγνητε γάμων κυρήσας] A separate v. in L.—Wolff read ἰὼ ἰὼ κάσις
δυσπότμων γάμων κυρήσας, and in 851 (where see n.) ἰὼ δύστανος, οὔτ' ἐν βροτοῖς οὔτ'
ἐν νεκροῖσιν.   Bellermann suggests ἰὼ δυσπότμων ἰὼ γάμων κασίγνητε κύρσας = 851 ἰὼ
δύστανός γ' οὔτ' ἐν βροτοῖσιν οὔτ' ἐν νεκροῖσι.—For γάμων Morstadt conject. τάφων.
872 f. σέβειν μὲν εὐσέβειά τις] Musgrave conject. μιν for μέν.   Nauck, σέβειν μὲν
εὐσεβὲς νεκρούς, or σέβειν μὲν εὐσεβεῖς θέμις.   M. Schmidt, σέβειν μὲν εὐσέβειά τις |
κρείσσους· κράτος δ' ὅτῳ μέλει etc.   Semitelos, σέβειν μὲν εὐσέβεια τοὺς | κάτω· κράτος
δ' ὅτῳ μέλει etc.

λέκτρον οὐκ ὀκνεῖν με δεῖ; and (b) with
πατρῴαι the explanation by ἐμῷ πατρί,
etc., would have been less needed.
  864 f. κοιμήματα . . αὐτογέννητα . .
ματρός, the mother's union with her
own offspring; the adj. = μετὰ τοῦ αὐτῆς
γεννήματος: cp. O. C. 1463 κτύπος . .
διόβολος (= κτύπος τοῦ ἐκ Διὸς βέλους):
Aesch. Eum. 212 ὅμαιμος (= συγγενοῦς)
αὐθέντης φόνος.—ἐμῷ πατρί, dat. of interest, 'for my sire' (i.e. to his misery);
the whole phrase being equiv. to, 'a mother's incestuous union with our father.'
The dat. goes with the whole preceding
phrase, not with αὐτογέννητα only ('incestuous in relation to him'), nor with
κοιμήματα only ('sleep with him').   The
latter, which Wecklein assumes, implies
κοιμᾶσθαί τινι as = συγκ. τινί, an unproved
constr.; for Hes. Th. 213 οὔτινι κοιμη-
θεῖσα θεὰ τέκε Νὺξ ἐρεβεννή is of doubtful
genuineness, and even there οὔτινι could
go with τέκε.—δυσμόρου is far better than
δυσμόρῳ: without it, the words could
imply that only the father's sin merited
pity.
  866 f. οἵων (masc.) ποτέ is exclamatory: 'from what manner of parents'
(for the gen., cp. 38).   The exclamatory
οἷος is freq. in Soph. (cp. 1228, Tr. 997,
etc.), and ποτέ strengthens it just as it
strengthens the interrogative τίς or ποῖος
(O. T. 754, Ph. 222, etc.).   So the exclamatory οἷος is strengthened by ἄρα (Ai.
367, 910).—Most commentators make
οἵων neut. relative to κοιμήματα: 'such

(wedlock) as that from which I sprang.'
But ποτέ is fatal to this; for (a) it cannot
here mean, 'in former days'; that would
be too weak: (b) nor can οἵων ποτέ mean,
'of whatever kind they may have been'—
like ὅστις ποτέ.   Besides, the masc. οὖς
most naturally refers to persons denoted
by οἵων.   I have therefore pointed at
ματρός.—ἀραῖος, fem.: elsewhere this
adj. is always of three terminations.   So
Attic tragedy uses κοινός, ποθεινός, πτωχός,
φανερός, etc., as fem.: see O. C. 751 n.—
μέτοικος: see on 852.
  870 κασίγνητε.   Polyneices.   His
marriage with Argeia, daughter of the
Argive king Adrastus, was the seal of the
armed alliance against Thebes, and thus
the prime cause of Antigone's death
(O. C. 378).—Not Oedipus.   Such an
allusion would be too repulsive here.
In O. C. 535 ἀδελφεαί marks the climax
of horror, and the word is wrung from
unwilling lips.   Further, as the doom of
the whole race is in question (859), the
brother is fitly mentioned.
  871 θανὼν ἔτ' οὖσαν: so Electra says
of her brother Orestes, ὥς μ' ἀπώλεσας
θανών.   Cp. on O. T. 1453.—κατήναρες.
This act. aor. occurs in later poetry.   The
epic form of the compound is κατεναίρο-
μαι, aor. κατενηράμην.   Eur. uses the epic
ἐναίρω, ἤναρον, but only in lyrics.   Soph.
has κατηναρισμένας (κατεναρίζω) in dial.,
Ai. 26.
  872 σέβειν.   'Reverent action' (meaning her loyalty to Polyneices) 'is, in a

2 κράτος δ᾽, ὅτῳ κράτος μέλει,
3 παραβατὸν οὐδαμᾷ πέλει·
4 σὲ δ᾽ αὐτόγνωτος ὤλεσ᾽ ὀργά.   875

ἐπ. ΑΝ. ἄκλαυτος, ἄφιλος, ἀνυμέναιος ταλαίφρων ἄγομαι
τάνδ᾽ ἑτοίμαν ὁδόν.
οὐκέτι μοι τόδε λαμπάδος ἱρὸν
ὄμμα θέμις ὁρᾶν ταλαίνᾳ·   880
τὸν δ᾽ ἐμὸν πότμον ἀδάκρυτον
οὐδεὶς φίλων στενάζει.

ΚΡ. ἆρ᾽ ἴστ᾽, ἀοιδὰς καὶ γόους πρὸ τοῦ θανεῖν
ὡς οὐδ᾽ ἂν εἷς παύσαιτ᾽ ἄν, εἰ χρείη λέγειν;
οὐκ ἄξεθ᾽ ὡς τάχιστα; καὶ κατηρεφεῖ   885
τύμβῳ περιπτύξαντες, ὡς εἴρηκ᾽ ἐγώ,
ἄφετε μόνην ἔρημον, εἴτε χρῇ θανεῖν

---

874 οὐδαμᾶι L. **876 ff.** L divides the vv. thus: ἄκλαυτος— | ταλαίφρων— | τάνδ᾽— | μοι—ὁμ|μα—ἐ|μὸν— | φίλων ... στενάζει. For ταλαίφρων ἄγομαι τάνδ᾽ ἑτοίμαν ὁδόν Dindorf writes ἔρχομαι τὰν πυμάταν ὁδόν. (Reiske had conjectured τάνδε πυμάταν ὁδόν.) Heinrich Schmidt places ταλαίφρων after ἄγομαι. **879** ἱρὸν Dind., etc.: ἱερὸν MSS. **880** ταλαίναι L (not ταλαίνα). The final ι is from the first hand; but the word was first accented τάλαιναι, and then ταλᾶιναι. **884** χρεῖ᾽ ηι L: χρείη

---

sense, εὐσέβεια᾽: i.e. though it is not complete εὐσέβεια—which the Chorus regard as including loyalty to the State's laws— yet, so far as it goes, it deserves praise of the same kind. Cp. 924 τὴν δυσσέβειαν εὐσεβοῦσ᾽ ἐκτησάμην: by practising εὐσέβεια towards the dead, she had come to be thought, on the whole, δυσσεβής—as a law-breaker. The Chorus is here the apologist of Creon, and this concession is meant to emphasise the next sentence. Hence the purposed vagueness of σέβειν. The speaker avoids a direct reference to the peculiarly sacred and tender duty which Ant. had fulfilled. The proposed emendations (see cr. n.) would obliterate this touch.

873 f. κράτος δὲ οὐδαμᾷ παραβατὸν πέλει (τούτῳ), ὅτῳ κράτος μέλει: but an offence against authority cannot be permitted by him who has authority in his keeping. The antecedent to ὅτῳ, viz. τούτῳ, is an ethic dat., 'in his sight'; he must not look on and see the law broken. For this dat., cp. 904.—οὐδαμᾷ (Dor.): cp. 763.—For μέλει cp. 1335: Il. 2. 25

ᾧ λαοί τ᾽ ἐπιτετράφαται καὶ τόσσα μέμηλεν. The Chorus echoes Creon's saying (677).

875 αὐτόγνωτος, act., deciding for oneself, αὐτὴ γιγνώσκουσα, like μεμπτός, 'blaming,' ὕποπτος, 'suspecting,' etc. (O. C. 1031 n.). Not pass., 'resolved upon' (i.e. here, 'adopted') 'by one's own choice,' as Ellendt takes it ('ultro susceptus '), and as the Schol. perh. did, who gives, αὐθαίρετος καὶ ἰδιογνώμων τρόπος. —ὀργά, disposition: see n. on 354 ff. (ὀργάς).

878 ἑτοίμαν, imminent, i.e. for which everything is prepared; Il. 18. 96 αὐτίκα γάρ τοι ἔπειτα μεθ᾽ Ἕκτορα πότμος ἑτοῖμος: Plut. Mor. 706 C ἕτοιμον τὸ διαφθαρῆναι τοῖς μὴ βοηθοῦντα...τὸν λογισμὸν ἔχουσι (corruption is imminent for those who have not reason to aid them). Cp. 936.

879 τόδε λ. ἱρὸν ὄμμα=τῆσδε ἱερᾶς λαμπάδος ὄμμα (793 n.). Cp. Eur. I. T. 194 ἀλλάξας... | ἱερὸν..ὄμμ᾽ αὐγᾶς | ἄλιος. Ion 1467 ἀελίου δ᾽ ἀναβλέπει λαμπάσιν.

881 ἀδάκρυτον, predicate, with proleptic force: no friend mourns my fate, but an offence against power cannot be brooked by him who hath power in his keeping. Thy self-willed temper hath wrought thy ruin.

AN.   Unwept, unfriended, without marriage-song, I am led Epode. forth in my sorrow on this journey that can be delayed no more. No longer, hapless one, may I behold yon day-star's sacred eye ; but for my fate no tear is shed, no friend makes moan.

CR.   Know ye not that songs and wailings before death would never cease, if it profited to utter them?   Away with her—away!   And when ye have enclosed her, according to my word, in her vaulted grave, leave her alone, forlorn— whether she wishes to die,

---

Dawes.—Blaydes conject. παύσειεν for παῦσαιτ' ἄν: but prints, by another conject., παύσαιτ' ἄν, εἰ 'ξείη, 'κχέων. Semitelos, προτοῦ λέγων | ὡς οὐδ' ἄν εἰς παύσαιτ' ἄν, εἰ χρείη θανεῖν.   **885** ἄξεσθ' L, ἄξετ' r.   **887** ἀφεῖτε μόνην L. Aldus (with A) has μόνην ἀφῆτ'. Most of the later MSS. have ἀφεῖτε, ἄφειτε, or ἀφῆτε: but for ἄφετε Vat. is cited. Blaydes, with Brunck, reads ἄπιτε μόνην, a v. l. noted in A.—χρὴ L: Dindorf conject. χρῇ: Hermann, εἰ χρῄζει: Nauck λῇ.

(and so it remains) unwept. Soph. has several instances of the predicative adj. thus added to a subst. which has the art. and possessive pron.; as *O. T.* 671 τὸ γάρ σόν, οὐ τὸ τοῦδ', ἐποικτίρω στόμα | ἐλεινόν (n.): *El.* 1143 τῆς ἐμῆς πάλαι τροφῆς | ἀνωφελήτου. Cp. 791.

883 f. ἆρ' ἴστε, ὡς, εἰ χρείη λέγειν ἀοιδὰς καὶ γόους πρὸ τοῦ θανεῖν, οὐδ' εἷς ἂν παύσαιτο (λέγων); The constr. would have been clearer with λέγων instead of λέγειν, but the latter has naturally been conformed to χρείη. The conject. παύσειεν is admissible (cp. *O. C.* 1751 παύετε θρῆνον, παῖδες), but unnecessary, and scarcely probable. Prof. Postgate's suggestion, that ἀοιδὰς καὶ γόους are objects to ἴστε, is tenable; but against it is the fact that in such cases the object of the principal verb is almost invariably the anticipated subject of the dependent clause (as *O. C.* 1197 γνώσει κακοῦ | θυμοῦ τελευτὴν ὡς κακὴ προσγίγνεται); as if here we had, ἆρ' ἴστ' ἀοιδὰς ὡς μακραί εἰσι; An object is very rarely so anticipated, as in Isae. or. 10 § 18, ἴσως οὖν ἄν τις...τὸν χρόνον ὑμῶν θαυμάσειε, πῶς ποτε πολὺν οὕτως ἐλάσαμεν.—οὐδ' ἄν εἷς, more emphatic than οὐδεὶς ἄν: *O. T.* 281 n.

885 οὐκ ἄξεθ'. When the first of two or more commands is given by οὐ with fut. indic., that constr. is usually continued,

either (*a*) with καί, as Eur. *Andr.* 1066 οὐχ ὅσον τάχος | χωρήσεται τις...καὶ... λέξει...; or (*b*) with repeated οὐ, as Ar. *Lys.* 459 οὐχ ἕλξετ', οὐ παιήσετ', οὐκ ἀράξετε; Here a direct imperat. follows (887), and a note of interrogation must therefore be placed after τάχιστα.—κατηρεφεῖ, prop. 'roofed over,' oft. an epithet of a natural cave (*Od.* 13. 349 σπέος, Soph. *Ph.* 272 ἐν κ. πέτρᾳ), and in *El.* 381 of a chamber (στέγη) like this κατῶρυξ. The fact that Nauck wishes to change it into κατώρυχι (or κατωρυχεῖ) is a strong instance of μεταβολὴ πάντων γλυκύ.

886 περιπτύξαντες: see on 848 (ἔργμα). Cp. Eur. *Ph.* 1357 τειχέων περιπτυχαί. Kaibel *Epigr.* 468 λαΐνεος στήλη με πέριξ ἔχει.

887 χρῇ, wishes: 3rd pers. pres. ind. of χράω, with contraction into ῇ instead of ᾷ, as in διψῆν, ζῆν, κνῆν, πεινῆν, σμῆν, χρῆν (to give an oracle), χρῆσθαι, ψῆν. Schol., εἰ χρῄζει καὶ θέλει. If the nom. ζῶσα is sound, as it seems to be, in the next v., then χρῇ is certain: for εἰ χρῄζει has no probability. Only one other passage, however, gives unambiguous support to the forms χρῆς, χρῇ,—viz. Ar. *Ach.* 778, (the Megarian) οὐ χρῆσθα; σιγῆς, ὦ κάκιστ' ἀπολουμένα; 'will you not make a sound?' (οὐ θέλεις, sc. φωνεῖν;). There, indeed, Blaydes writes οὐ χρῇ τυ

εἴτ' ἐν τοιαύτῃ ζῶσα τυμβεύειν στέγῃ·
ἡμεῖς γὰρ ἁγνοὶ τοὐπὶ τήνδε τὴν κόρην·
μετοικίας δ' οὖν τῆς ἄνω στερήσεται.　　　　　890

ΑΝ.　ὦ τύμβος, ὦ νυμφεῖον, ὦ κατασκαφὴς
οἴκησις ἀείφρουρος, οἷ πορεύομαι
πρὸς τοὺς ἐμαυτῆς, ὧν ἀριθμὸν ἐν νεκροῖς
πλεῖστον δέδεκται Φερσέφασσ' ὀλωλότων·
ὧν λοισθία 'γὼ καὶ κάκιστα δὴ μακρῷ　　　　895
κάτειμι, πρίν μοι μοῖραν ἐξήκειν βίου.
ἐλθοῦσα μέντοι κάρτ' ἐν ἐλπίσιν τρέφω
φίλη μὲν ἥξειν πατρί, προσφιλὴς δὲ σοί,
μῆτερ, φίλη δὲ σοί, κασίγνητον κάρα·

---

888 ζῶσα τυμβεύειν L. The difficulty felt as to χρή in 887 is shown by two types of reading which appear in later MSS., viz. (1) ζῶσα τυμβεύει in A, R, etc.: (2) ζῶσαν τυμβεύειν in Vat., Aug. b, and a few other 14th cent. MSS. Triclinius wrote ζῶσα τυμβεύσει. Reiske conject. ζῶσαν ὑμνήσειν: Semitelos, ζῶσαν ὑμνῳδεῖν.—For τυμβεύειν Morstadt conject. νυμφεύειν.　　　**891** In L the first hand

---

σιγῆν; but the MSS. are supported by the testimony of Suidas and Hesychius to χρῆς as = χρήζεις. In the other four places where these forms are usu. read, they are not indispensable, χρή being possible; but in two, at least, they are much better than χρή, viz. *El.* 606 κήρυσσέ μ' εἰς ἅπαντας, εἴτε χρῆς κακήν, | εἴτε στόμαργον, κ.τ.λ.: and *Ai.* 1373 σοὶ δὲ δρᾶν ἔξεσθ' ἃ χρῇς. In the other two, χρή might well stand: Eur. fr. 910 πρὸς ταῦθ' ὅ τι χρῇ καὶ παλαμάσθω | καὶ πᾶν ἐπ' ἐμοὶ τεκταινέσθω: Cratinus Νόμοι fr. 2 νῦν γὰρ δή σοι πάρα μὲν θεσμοὶ | τῶν ἡμετέρων, πάρα δ' ἀλλ' ὅ τι χρῇς. Except in *Ach.* 778, the MSS. everywhere give χρή: and the variants in the next v. (see cr. n.) show that χρῆ was strange to the copyists, though known to the Scholiast.

888 ζῶσα τυμβεύειν, to live entombed. Elsewhere τυμβεύω = to entomb (*Ai.* 1063 σῶμα τυμβεῦσαι τάφῳ); or to bring as a funeral offering, *El.* 406 πατρὶ τυμβεῦσαι χοάς. Here it is intrans., = ἐν τύμβῳ εἶναι. Cp. σαλεύω, which means either (1) to put others on a σάλος,—to toss them: or (2) intrans., to be on a σάλος. So the intrans. θαλασσεύω = to be on the sea. παρθενεύω, which is trans. in classical Gk. ('to bring up a maiden'), is intrans. in Heliod. 7. 8 τὸ...παρθενεῦον τοῦ ἄστεος. —The conject. νυμφεύειν is not right. That taunt would be quite out of place

here. Creon says simply, 'I immure her,—I do not kill her; she can either die, or live,—but in the tomb.'—στέγῃ, iron.: cp. *El.* 381 ζῶσα δ' ἐν κατηρεφεῖ | στέγῃ χθονὸς τῆσδ' ἐκτὸς ὑμνήσεις κακά, *i.e.* in a cave, or subterranean cell.

889 ἁγνοί: see on 775. His thought is: (1) she had warning: (2) no blood has been shed.—τοὐπὶ τήνδε, in what concerns her. In this phrase with the *acc.*, ἐπί more often means, 'so far as depends on one': Eur. *Hec.* 514 ἡμεῖς δ' ἄτεκνοι τοὐπὶ σ': *Or.* 1345 σώθηθ' ὅσον γε τοὐπ' ἔμ': Thuc. 4. 28 (he told Cleon to try) τὸ ἐπὶ σφᾶς εἶναι (so far as the generals were concerned): Xen. *Cyr.* 1. 4. 12 ἄλλου τινὸς τὸ ἐπὶ σὲ ἀνάγκη ἔσται δεῖσθαι ἡμᾶς. In all these places ἐπί with *dat.* would equally suit the sense; but not so in this verse. Cp. 1348 τά γ' εἰς θεούς.

890 μετοικίας, cp. 852.—δ' οὖν, 688. —στερήσεται, 637.

891 f. ὦ τύμβος, nom. for voc.: cp. 379.—νυμφεῖον: cp. 1205.—κατασκαφὴς: see on 774....ἀείφρουρος = ἣ ἀεὶ φρουρήσει με, not, ἣν ἐγὼ ἀεὶ φρουρήσω (like Aesch. *P. V.* 31 τήνδε φρουρήσεις πέτραν): cp. 886.

893 f. ἀριθμὸν...πλεῖστον: she thinks of Laïus, her father and mother, and her two brothers.—ἐν νεκροῖς with δέδεκται: the queen of the nether world has greeted them as they passed through the πολύξενοι or to live a buried life in such a home. Our hands are clean as touching this maiden. But this is certain—she shall be deprived of her sojourn in the light.

AN. Tomb, bridal-chamber, eternal prison in the caverned rock, whither I go to find mine own, those many who have perished, and whom Persephone hath received among the dead! Last of all shall I pass thither, and far most miserably of all, before the term of my life is spent. But I cherish good hope that my coming will be welcome to my father, and pleasant to thee, my mother, and welcome, brother, to thee;

---

accented ὤ—ὤ—ὤ. The first ὤ has been made ὦ. **892** ἀείφρουροσ L: ἀείφρουρος r. **894** φερσέφασσ᾽ L (the first σ from ρ): Περσέφασσ᾽ r. **895** λοισθί᾽ ἀγὼ L. (The accent on the first ι is faint.) The difference between the contracted αγ and εγ in L may be seen by comparing vv. 913, 916.

πύλαι to Hades (*O. C.* 1569 f.). So Oedipus is led by Ἑρμῆς ὁ πομπὸς ἥ τε νερτέρα θεός (*ib.* 1548). As ἡ ἀφανὴς θεός she is associated with Hades (*ib.* 1556).
Φερσέφασσα has L's support here. That form occurs also in Eur. *Helen.* 175, but Περσέφασσα in Aesch. *Cho.* 490. The *Il.* and *Od.* have only Περσεφόνεια. Φερσεφόνεια occurs in *Hom. hymn.* 13. 2. Pindar uses Φερσεφόνα. Plato attests that, in his day, the popular form was Φερρέφαττα, which he explains as the goddess of wisdom, who enables men φερομένων ἐφάπτεσθαι, to grasp changing phenomena. People were afraid to utter the name Φερσεφόνη (*Crat.* 404 C). Attic inscrr. of the 4th cent. B.C. give Περσεφόνη, Φερσεφόνη, Φερρέφαττα (Meisterhans pp. 36 ff.). MSS. have Φερσέφαττα (which should perh. be Φερρέφαττα) in Ar. *Ran.* 671, *Th.* 287. A vase ascribed to *c.* 435 B.C. gives ΠΕΡΣΩΦΑΤΑ (*sic*, Baumeister *Denkm.* p. 424). Welcker cites ΦΕΡΕΦΑΣΑ from an Agrigentine vase (*Götterl.* 1. 393). We may infer that Soph., *c.* 440 B.C., might have used either Περσέφασσα or Φερσέφασσα. The testimony of our oldest and best MS., L, may therefore be allowed to turn the scale.—In Περσεφόνη, the φον is certainly φαν, as in Ἀργειφόντης, and this comes out more clearly in Περσέφασσα: cp. Τηλεφᾶσσα =Τηλεφάεσσα, Apollod. 3. 1. 1. The first part of the word is prob. φερ, φέρω; and the name meant originally, 'she who brings (vegetation) to the light.' The initial Π would then have been due to the following φ (cp. πέ-φυκα for φέ-φυκα).

The replacement of the initial Φ may have been prompted by a wish to mitigate the δυσφημία of the name by avoiding an association with πέρθω.
895 f. κάκιστα, as a law-breaker (cp. 59): δή with superl., see 58 n.—**μοῖραν**... **βίου**: cp. 461. **ἐξήκειν** of time, as *Ph.* 199.
897 f. ἐν ἐλπίσιν τρέφω = ἐλπίζω. ἐν ἐλπίδι (or ἐλπίσιν) εἰμί was a common phrase. Cp. ἐν πόθῳ λαβεῖν τι (*O. C.* 1678).—**φίλη μὲν... προσφιλὴς δέ**: cp. 669 καλῶς μὲν...εὖ δέ, n.
899 κασίγνητον κάρα. Eteocles. Whatever view may be taken of vv. 904—920, few would question the genuineness of 900—903: and if the latter are genuine, νῦν δέ shows that Polyneices is not meant here. She speaks first of those kinsfolk to whom she had rendered pious offices in the usual manner. Then she comes to him who is uppermost in her thoughts,—the brother whose case was different from that of the others. In v. 23 she spoke of the rumour that Eteocles had been duly buried. But nothing here implies her presence at his ἐκφορά. ἔλουσα κἀκόσμησα were acts preparatory to the πρόθεσις. The χοαί could be rendered afterwards. She loved both brothers (cp. on 523). If father and mother were named here, without any mention of Eteocles, the omission would suggest that from *him* she could expect no welcome,—a contradiction of her real feeling (515). Further, the brevity of this reference to Eteocles heightens the effect of what follows.

ἐπεὶ θανόντας αὐτόχειρ ὑμᾶς ἐγὼ   900
ἔλουσα κἀκόσμησα κἀπιτυμβίους
χοὰς ἔδωκα· νῦν δέ, Πολύνεικες, τὸ σὸν
δέμας περιστέλλουσα τοιάδ' ἄρνυμαι.
[καίτοι σ' ἐγὼ 'τίμησα, τοῖς φρονοῦσιν, εὖ.
οὐ γάρ ποτ' οὔτ' ἂν εἰ τέκνων μήτηρ ἔφυν,   905
οὔτ' εἰ πόσις μοι κατθανὼν ἐτήκετο,
βίᾳ πολιτῶν τόνδ' ἂν ᾑρόμην πόνον.
τίνος νόμου δὴ ταῦτα πρὸς χάριν λέγω;
πόσις μὲν ἄν μοι κατθανόντος ἄλλος ἦν,
καὶ παῖς ἀπ' ἄλλου φωτός, εἰ τοῦδ' ἤμπλακον·   910
μητρὸς δ' ἐν Ἅιδου καὶ πατρὸς κεκευθότοιν
οὐκ ἔστ' ἀδελφὸς ὅστις ἂν βλάστοι ποτέ.
τοιῷδε μέντοι σ' ἐκπροτιμήσασ' ἐγὼ
νόμῳ, Κρέοντι ταῦτ' ἔδοξ' ἁμαρτάνειν
καὶ δεινὰ τολμᾶν, ὦ κασίγνητον κάρα.   915

900—928 Dindorf rejects the whole of these 29 verses. **904** 'τίμησα] τίμησα
L: cp. 457.—K. Lehrs rejects vv. 904—920. So Wecklein and Nauck. Nauck
formerly omitted from νῦν in 902 to Κρέοντι in 914 inclusive (so that v. 902 should
read, χοὰς ἔδωκα· ταῦτ' ἔδοξ' ἁμαρτάνειν); and in 916 changed διὰ χερῶν to δὴ
Κρέων. **905** A. Jacob (*Quaest. Sophocleae*, 1821, p. 363) first condemned

---

900 ff. ὑμᾶς. This play supposes
Oedipus to have died at Thebes: see on
50.—**ἔλουσα κἀκόσμησα:** see nn. on
O. C. 1602 f. λουτροῖς τέ νιν | ἐσθῆτί τ'
ἐξήσκησαν ᾗ νομίζεται. Cp. below, 1201.
—**χοάς:** cp. 431.—**περιστέλλουσα:** here,
of sprinkling the dust and pouring the
χοαί: cp. the general sense of the word
in *Ai.* 1170 τάφον περιστελοῦντε. More
oft. of laying out the dead (like κοσμεῖν
here, and συγκαθαρμόζειν in *Ai.* 922):
Od. 24. 292 οὐδέ ἑ μήτηρ | κλαῦσε περι-
στείλασα. Verg. *Aen.* 9. 485 canibus date
praeda Latinis | Alitibusque iaces : nec te
tua funera mater | Produxi, pressive ocu-
los, aut vulnera lavi, | Veste tegens.—
δέμας: 205.

904—920 Few problems of Greek
Tragedy have been more discussed than
the question whether these vv., or some
of them, are spurious. Arist. (*Rhet.* 3.
16 § 9) quotes vv. 911, 912, and certainly had the whole passage in his text
of Soph. The interpolation, then, if
such it be, must have been made soon
after the poet's death; and has been im-

puted to his son Iophon (ὁ ψυχρός), or
some other sorry poet; or to the actors.
I confess that, after long thought, I cannot bring myself to believe that Soph.
wrote 905—912: with which 904 and
913—920 are in organic unity, and must
now stand or fall. Some remarks will
be found in the Appendix.

The main points (to my mind) are
briefly these. (1) The general validity
of the divine law, as asserted in 450—
460, cannot be intelligibly reconciled with
the limitation in vv. 905—907. (2) A
still further limitation is involved in 911 f.
She has buried her brother, not simply as
such, but because, while he lived, he was
an irreplaceable relative. Could she have
hoped for the birth of another brother, she
would not, then, have felt the duty to be
so binding. (3) The composition of vv.
909—912 is unworthy of Sophocles.

904 'τίμησα (cp. 'φάνη, 457 n.), with
εὖ (last word of v., as *O. C.* 642), I
honoured thee rightly, **τοῖς φρονοῦσιν,** in
the judgment of the wise; ethic dat.
(25 n.): cp. 514.

for, when ye died, with mine own hands I washed and dressed you, and poured drink-offerings at your graves; and now, Polyneices, 'tis for tending thy corpse that I win such recompense as this.

[And yet I honoured thee, as the wise will deem, rightly. Never, had I been a mother of children, or if a husband had been mouldering in death, would I have taken this task upon me in the city's despite. What law, ye ask, is my warrant for that word? The husband lost, another might have been found, and child from another, to replace the first-born; but, father and mother hidden with Hades, no brother's life could ever bloom for me again. Such was the law whereby I held thee first in honour; but Creon deemed me guilty of error therein, and of outrage, ah brother mine!

---

vv. 905—913 inclusive: and so Schneidewin, conjecturing in 914 Κρέοντι μέντοι, or μόνῳ Κρέοντι. Kvičala condemns 905—912. **907** ἂν ἠρόμην r: ἀνηρόμην L. **911** κεκευθότοιν] βεβηκότων Arist. *Rh.* 3. 16 § 9. τετευχότων (τυγχάνω) Clemens Alex. *Strom.* 6, p. 747, 30.

---

906 ἐτήκετο, lay mouldering: Plat. *Tim.* 82 E ὅταν...τηκομένη σάρξ ἀνάπαλιν εἰς τὰς φλέβας τὴν τηκεδόνα ἐξίῃ. So *tabum* of corpses, Verg. *Aen.* 8. 487.

907 βίᾳ πολιτῶν. This was Ismene's phrase (79). Antigone had believed that the city was on her side (509). This has been noted as a mark of spuriousness in the verse. But it cannot (I think) be fairly claimed as such; for, since the Chorus had seemed to fail in sympathy (838), she had regarded herself as ἄφιλος (876) in Thebes.

908 πρὸς χάριν: see on 30.

909 ff. Cp. Her. 3. 119, which clearly supplied, not merely the thought, but the form, of these verses:—ἀνὴρ μέν μοι ἂν ἄλλος γένοιτο, εἰ δαίμων ἐθέλοι, καὶ τέκνα ἄλλα, εἰ ταῦτα ἀποβάλοιμι· πατρὸς δὲ καὶ μητρὸς οὐκέτι μοι ζωόντων, ἀδελφεὸς ἂν ἄλλος οὐδενὶ τρόπῳ γένοιτο. Arist. *Rhet.* 3. 16 § 9 (if you introduce a trait of character which will seem improbable, the reason of it should be added): ἂν δ' ἄπιστον ᾖ, τότε τὴν αἰτίαν ἐπιλέγειν, ὥσπερ Σοφοκλῆς ποιεῖ παράδειγμα τὸ ἐκ τῆς Ἀντιγόνης, ὅτι μᾶλλον τοῦ ἀδελφοῦ ἐκήδετο ἢ ἀνδρὸς ἢ τέκνων· τὰ μὲν γὰρ ἂν γενέσθαι ἀπολόμενα [this = vv. 909, 910]· μητρὸς δ' ἐν ᾅδου κ.τ.λ. (he then quotes 911 f., with βεβηκότων,—a mere slip of memory: see on 223).

Three points in these vv. are strange. (1) The gen. abs. **κατθανόντος**, for which a gen. has to be evolved from **πόσις**. The gen. of that word was not in Attic use ('mihi non succurrit exemplum ubi πόσεος aut πόσεως legatur,' Pors. *Med.* 906). Why was not ἀνδρός used? It looks as if the composer who made up these verses from Her. 3. 119 (see above) had sought to impart a touch of tragic dignity by substituting πόσις for the historian's word, ἀνήρ. The gen. κατθανόντος cannot be taken (as some wish) with ἄλλος, 'different from the dead' (!). (2) ἀπ' ἄλλου φωτός. Why is it assumed that the first husband died before, or with, his child? The two hypotheses of loss should have been kept separate. We wanted something like καὶ παῖς ἂν ἄλλος, παιδὸς ἐστερημένη. (3) **τοῦδ'** means the first husband's child, but is most awkward.—As to οὐκ ἔστ' ἀδελφός κ.τ.λ., it may be somewhat inelegant; but it is not (as some urge) incorrect, since οὐκ ἔστιν ὅστις = οὐδείς.

913 ἐκπροτιμήσασ', 'having singled thee out for honour,' with ref. to the supposed cases in which she would *not* have paid the burial rites. The double compound occurs only here,—as ἐξαφοράω only in *O. C.* 1648.

καὶ νῦν ἄγει με διὰ χερῶν οὕτω λαβὼν
ἄλεκτρον, ἀνυμέναιον, οὔτε του γάμου
μέρος λαχοῦσαν οὔτε παιδείου τροφῆς,
ἀλλ᾽ ὧδ᾽ ἔρημος πρὸς φίλων ἡ δύσμορος
ζῶσ᾽ εἰς θανόντων ἔρχομαι κατασκαφάς·]   920
ποίαν παρεξελθοῦσα δαιμόνων δίκην;
τί χρή με τὴν δύστηνον ἐς θεοὺς ἔτι
βλέπειν; τίν᾽ αὐδᾶν ξυμμάχων; ἐπεί γε δὴ
τὴν δυσσέβειαν εὐσεβοῦσ᾽ ἐκτησάμην.
ἀλλ᾽ εἰ μὲν οὖν τάδ᾽ ἐστὶν ἐν θεοῖς καλά,   925
παθόντες ἂν ξυγγνοῖμεν ἡμαρτηκότες·
εἰ δ᾽ οἵδ᾽ ἁμαρτάνουσι, μὴ πλείω κακὰ
πάθοιεν ἢ καὶ δρῶσιν ἐκδίκως ἐμέ.

ΧΟ. ἔτι τῶν αὐτῶν ἀνέμων αὐταὶ
      ψυχῆς ῥιπαὶ τήνδε γ᾽ ἔχουσιν.   930

ΚΡ. τοιγὰρ τούτων τοῖσιν ἄγουσιν
      κλαύμαθ᾽ ὑπάρξει βραδυτῆτος ὕπερ.

ΑΝ. οἴμοι, θανάτου τοῦτ᾽ ἐγγυτάτω
      τοὔπος ἀφῖκται.

ΚΡ. θαρσεῖν οὐδὲν παραμυθοῦμαι   935
      μὴ οὐ τάδε ταύτῃ κατακυροῦσθαι.

---

917 οὔτε τοῦ] οὔ τέ του L (του from τοῦ): Schneidewin conject. οὔτε πω.
920 θανάτων .. κατασφαγάσ᾽ L: θανόντων .. κατασκαφάς τ.   **922 f.** Nauck
rejects these two vv.   **927** πλείω] Vauvilliers conject. μείω.   **928** ἐνδίκωσ
L, with κ written above ν by S.   **929 f.** ἔτι τῶν αὐτῶν ἀνέμων αὐταί | ψυχῆσ
ῥιπαὶ τήνδε γ᾽ ἔχουσιν L. For αὐταί Erfurdt wrote αὖται. Dindorf, thinking that
ψυχῆς was a gloss on ἀνέμων, and that αὐταί was afterwards added for metre's

---

916 διὰ χερῶν...λαβών, *i.e.*, by forcible
arrest, as though I were a criminal. Cp.
O.C. 470 δι᾽ ὁσίων χειρῶν θιγών (= 'with'),
Aesch. *Suppl.* 193 (ἱκτηρίας) ἔχουσαι διὰ
χερῶν.

917 ἀνυμέναιον: see on 814.

919 ἀλλ᾽: cp. on 810.—πρὸς φίλων
with ἔρημος (not with ἔρχομαι), forsaken
on the part of my friends. The sense of
πρός in *Ph.* 1070 is similar, though there
it goes with the verb; ἢ καὶ πρὸς ὑμῶν
ὧδ᾽ ἔρημος, ὦ ξένοι, | λειφθήσομαι δή...;

921 δαιμόνων δίκην, that which the
gods recognise (451), as distinguished
from the human δίκη (854) which she has
offended.

922 ff. If the gods allow her to suffer

for obeying them, is it not vain for her to
invoke them?—βλέπειν εἴς τινα (for help),
as *Ai.* 398, 514, *El.* 959.—τίνα...ξυμ-
μάχων, what ally (of all conceivable allies)?
—ἐπεί γε δή: cp. *Tr.* 484 ἐπεί γε μὲν δή.
For the place of δή, cp. 726.—τὴν δυσσέβειαν, the repute of it; *El.* 968 εὐσέβειαν
ἐκ πατρὸς | θανόντος οἴσει: Eur. *I. T.* 676
καὶ δειλίαν γὰρ καὶ κάκην κεκτήσομαι:
Med. 218 δύσκλειαν ἐκτήσαντο καὶ ῥᾳθυ-
μίαν: *Ion* 600 γέλωτ᾽ ἐν αὐτοῖς μωρίαν τε
λήψομαι.

925 f. The gods are allowing her to
perish. But it does not follow that they
approve of her doom: for they are sometimes slow in punishing wrong (*O. C.*
1536). Hence the dilemma, introduced

And now he leads me thus, a captive in his hands; no bridal bed, no bridal song hath been mine, no joy of marriage, no portion in the nurture of children; but thus, forlorn of friends, unhappy one, I go living to the vaults of death.]

And what law of heaven have I transgressed? Why, hapless one, should I look to the gods any more—what ally should I invoke,—when by piety I have earned the name of impious? Nay, then, if these things are pleasing to the gods, when I have suffered my doom, I shall come to know my sin; but if the sin is with my judges, I could wish them no fuller measure of evil than they, on their part, mete wrongfully to me.

CH. Still the same tempest of the soul vexes this maiden with the same fierce gusts.

CR. Then for this shall her guards have cause to rue their slowness.

AN. Ah me! that word hath come very near to death.

CR. I can cheer thee with no hope that this doom is not thus to be fulfilled.

---

sake, gives ἔτι τῶν αὐτῶν ἀνέμων ῥιπαὶ | τήνδε γ᾽ ἔχουσιν. **931** τοι γάρ τοι τούτων L. Dindorf conject. τοιγάρτοι καὶ: Wecklein, τοιγάρτοι νιν: Bothe, τοιγὰρ ταύτην.—τοῖσιν Γ: τοῖσ L. **933 f.** ἐγγυτάτωι L.—Lehrs, with whom Nauck agrees, assigns these two vv. to the Chorus. **935 f.** L gives these two vv. to Creon: Boeckh, to the Chorus. The Scholiast recognises both views.

---

by ἀλλ᾽ οὖν ('well then'). (1) If the gods approve of my doom, then, after suffering it, I shall become conscious (in the other world) that I have sinned. (2) But if they disapprove of it, and regard Creon as the sinner, then they will punish him at last. And I could wish him no sorer doom than mine.—ἐν θεοῖς: cp. 459.—ξυγγνοῖμεν = συνειδείημεν. Lys. or. 9 § 11 συνέγνωσαν δὲ καὶ αὐτοὶ σφίσιν ὡς ἠδικηκότες, 'became conscious that they had done wrong.' The word could also mean, ὁμολογήσαιμεν, 'confess': but in that sense it regularly takes either an inf., as Her. 1. 91 συνέγνω ἑωυτοῦ εἶναι τὴν ἁμαρτάδα: or a dependent clause, as Plat. Legg. 717 D ξυγγιγνώσκοντα ὡς εἰκότως...θυμοῖτ᾽ ἄν.—ἡμαρτηκότες belongs more closely to the verb than does παθόντες: cp. Plat. Phaed. 70 A (ἡ ψυχὴ) διασκεδασθεῖσα οἴχηται διαπτομένη. For the tragic masc. plur., when a woman speaks of herself, cp. El. 399.

927 f. οἵδε, Creon: cp. 10.—μὴ πλείω, i.e. she will be content if they suffer ἴσα. She can imagine no worse fate. The tame conjecture μείω would not express

this bitter feeling.—καὶ δρῶσιν, do on their part: O. C. 53 n.

929 f. ἀνέμων-ῥιπαὶ ψυχῆς, stormgusts of the soul: both genitives are possessive: cp. 795 βλεφάρων-ἵμερος...νύμφας —Dindorf's expulsion of αὐταὶ | ψυχῆς (cr. n.) is unwarranted. ψυχῆς interprets the figurative sense; for αὐταὶ after τῶν αὐτῶν cp. n. on 155 ff. (νέοχμος νεαραῖσι).

931 f. τούτων, neut., causal gen. (O. T. 48). After τήνδε γ᾽, this is better than ταύτην would be: τοιγάρτοι (whether with καὶ or with νιν) would be unpleasing.—κλαύμαθ᾽: cp. 754: so Ph. 1260 ἐκτὸς κλαυμάτων.—ὕπερ = ἕνεκα (O. T. 165 n.). οἴμοι follows, but the change of person excuses the breach of synapheia: so O. C. 139 τὸ φατιζόμενον is followed by ἰώ, and ib. 143 πρέσβυς by οὐ.

933 f. This threat (to the guards) 'has come very near to death,' i.e., 'portends imminent death for me.' The phrase is not fig., 'is bitter as death to hear' (being a prelude to death).

935 f. Said by Creon, clearly—not by the Chorus. 'I can give thee no encouragement (οὐδέν adv.) to hope that

ΑΝ. ὦ γῆς Θήβης ἄστυ· πατρῷον
καὶ θεοὶ προγενεῖς,
ἄγομαι δὴ κοὐκέτι μέλλω.
λεύσσετε, Θήβης οἱ κοιρανίδαι,   940
τὴν *βασιλειδᾶν μούνην λοιπήν,
οἷα πρὸς οἵων ἀνδρῶν πάσχω,
τὴν εὐσεβίαν σεβίσασα.

στρ. α΄. ΧΟ. ἔτλα καὶ Δανάας οὐράνιον φῶς
2 ἀλλάξαι δέμας ἐν χαλκοδέτοις αὐλαῖς·   945

937 γῆσ made from γῆ in L.   **939** δὴ is the reading of A: δὴ 'γὼ of L.   The
latter arose from the wish to make the paroemiac into a dimeter.   **940** οἱ] ὦ Pallis.
941 τὴν βασιλίδα μούνην λοιπήν L.   The correction βασιλειδᾶν, which recent edd. have
generally received, was first proposed by K. Winckelmann (Salzwedler Programm,
p. 30, 1852); afterwards by M. Seyffert, in his ed. (1865).   Triclinius conjectured

---

the doom is not to be ratified on this
wise' (*i.e.*, by death).   **μὴ οὐ**, not *μή*, on
account of οὐδέν (443 n.).—**κατακυροῦσθαι**,
pres. denoting what is to be; *Ph.* 113
αἱρεῖ τὰ τόξα ταῦτα τὴν Τροίαν μόνα. Attic
prose used κυροῦν or ἐπικυροῦν (γνώμην,
νόμον, ψήφισμα, etc.).   Cp. Creon's pe-
remptory word τελείαν in 632.—**ταύτῃ**
(722) combined with **τάδε**: cp. 39.
   938 θεοὶ προγενεῖς, ancestral, not
merely as protectors of the race, but also
as progenitors.   She thinks esp. of Ares
and Aphrodite, the parents of Harmonia,
wife of Cadmus: Aesch. *Theb.* 135 σύ τ',
Ἄρης, πόλιν Κάδμου ἐπώνυμον | φύλαξαι
κήδεσαί τ' ἐναργῶς. | καὶ Κύπρις, ἅτ' εἶ
γένους προμάτωρ, | ἄλευσον. Dionysus,
the son of 'Cadmean' Semele (1115), is
another of the deities meant.   προγενής,
born before one, a poet. word, unfamiliar
to good Attic prose, but used by Aristotle
and later writers, usu. in comparat. (as
οἱ προγενέστεροι, 'those who have gone
before us'): so οἱ μεταγενέστεροι.
   939 δὴ = ἤδη (*O. T.* 968), as in καὶ
δή.—**κοὐκέτι μέλλω**, and am no longer
(merely) about to be led away: cp. *O. C.*
1074 ἔρδουσ' ἢ μέλλουσιν; *Ph.* 1255 κἀμέ
τοι | ταὐτὸν τόδ' ὄψει δρῶντα κοὐ μέλλοντ'
ἔτι. Meineke's conjecture μελλῶ (=μέλ-
λησις, Aesch. *Ag.* 1356) was needless.—
Seyffert understands, 'I make no more
delay,'—said firmly and proudly: she
scorns to bring punishment on her guards
by detaining them longer.   But this does
not suit ἄγομαι δή.

   940 οἱ κοιρανίδαι, the Theban εὐπα-
τρίδαι of the Chorus: see on 843.   The
nom. with art., instead of voc.,='ye who
are princes of Thebes,' and so brings out
the implied reproach to their apathy.
This constr. usu. has a somewhat pe-
remptory tone, as Plat. *Symp.* 218 B οἱ δὲ
οἰκέται...πύλας...τοῖς ὠσὶν ἐπίθεσθε. It is
different when a voc. precedes the art. and
partic., as Ar. *Av.* 30 ὦνδρες οἱ παρόντες
ἐν λόγῳ: cp. on 100 f.
   941 βασιλειδᾶν, *i.e.*, of the race of the
Labdacidae.   This correction of **βασιλίδα**
is certain.   In Plat. *Critias* 116 C, τὸ τῶν
δέκα βασιλειδῶν γένος, the same corruption, βασιλιδῶν, occurs in the MSS.
Suidas has βασιλείδης· ὁ τοῦ βασιλέως
(where Küster wrongly proposed ὁ τοῦ
Βασιλείου).   In adding the patronymic
suffix ιδα to a stem in εν (βασιλευ), the υ
is dropped, as in the gen. plur. (βασιλέ-ων):
hence βασιλε-ίδης, βασιλείδης: cp. Πηλεί-
δης.—**μούνην**, ignoring Ismene; not in
bitterness (cp. on 559), but because she
feels that, in spirit at least, she herself is
indeed the last of the race.   It is otherwise
when Oed. speaks of his daughters as his
only children (*O. C.* 895); and when Electra says that she is ἄνευ τοκέων (187),—
since Clytaemnestra is a μήτηρ ἀμήτωρ
(1154).
   943 εὐσεβίαν. Epic and lyric poetry
could substitute -ια for -εια in fem. nouns
from adjectives in -ης: so *O. C.* 1043
προμηθίας: Pind. *P.* 12.4 εὐμενίᾳ: Aesch.
Eum. 534 δυσσεβίας: Eur. *H. F.* 696

AN. O city of my fathers in the land of Thebè! O ye
gods, eldest of our race!—they lead me hence—now, now—they
tarry not! Behold me, princes of Thebes, the last daughter of
the house of your kings,—see what I suffer, and from whom,
because I feared to cast away the fear of heaven!

[ANTIGONE *is led away by the guards.*

CH. Even thus endured Danaë in her beauty to change 1st
the light of day for brass-bound walls; strophe.

βασίλειαν: Bergk, Λαβδακιδᾶν: Doederlein, Οἰδιπόδα: Seidler and others, βασι-
ληΐδα. Emperius proposed λεύσσετε Θήβης τὴν κοιρανιδᾶν | μούνην λοιπήν, regarding
τὴν βασιλίδα as a gloss.   **943** εὐσέβειαν MSS.: εὐσεβίαν Triclinius, saying,
οὕτω χρὴ γράφειν ἰωνικῶς .. ἀλλὰ καὶ τὸ σεβίσασα ἀπὸ τοῦ σεβίζω ὀφείλεις λέγειν,
which shows that his text had σεβήσασα.   **944—954** L divides the vv.
thus: ἔτλα— | ἀλλάξαι— | αὐλαῖσ— | τυμβήρει— | καίτοι— | καὶ Ζηνὸσ— | σκε γο-
νᾶσ— | ἀλλ' ἁ— | οὔτ' ἄν νιν— | οὐ πύργοσ— | κελαιναὶ .. ἐκφύγοιεν.

εὐγενίας. The motive was metrical convenience. Such forms are not Ionic, as
Triclinius called them (cr. n.): thus
Herod. used ἀληθείη, not ἀληθίη: though
there are other cases in which Ionic substitutes ε for ει (as βαθέα, ἐπιτήδεος, etc.).—
σεβίσασα, of respecting a law or custom:
so *O. C.* 636, *Ai.* 713 (θέσμια...σέβων).
944—987 Fourth stasimon. 1st
strophe 944—954 = 1st antistrophe 955—
965. 2nd str. 966—976 = 2nd antistr.
977—987. See Metrical Analysis.
    As Antigone spoke the verses ending
at 943, the guards were in the act of
leading her forth. The choral ode may
have begun before she had vanished; but
she is not to be conceived as still present
when she is apostrophised (949, 987).
    A princess is about to be immured in a
rocky cell. The Chorus remember three
other royal persons who have suffered a like
fate—Danaë, Lycurgus and Cleopatra.
The only points which these cases have
in common with Antigone's are the facts
of noble birth and cruel imprisonment.
    All four cases illustrate the same
general truth—no mortal can resist fate.
Danaë and Cleopatra were innocent;
Lycurgus was guilty. But the Chorus do
not mean to suggest Antigone's guilt or
innocence; still less, to foreshadow the
punishment of Creon. On this side, the
ode is neutral, purely a free lyric treatment of the examples. Such neutrality
suits the moment before the beginning of
the περιπέτεια. Teiresias is soon to come.
    944 f. Acrisius, the father of Danaë,
was king of Argos. The oracle at Delphi
told him that he was to be slain by his

daughter's son. He therefore immured
the maiden in a chamber built for that
purpose within the precincts of his house
at Argos. Here Zeus visited her in the
golden rain; she bore Perseus; and
Acrisius sent mother and child adrift on
the Aegean in a chest; but Zeus heard
her prayer, and brought them safely to
the island of Seriphus. Both Soph. and
Eur. wrote a Δανάη: Soph. wrote also an
Ἀκρίσιος.
    καὶ Δανάας δέμας ἔτλα ἀλλάξαι οὐ-
ράνιον φῶς: note the bold order of words,
and cp. *Ph.* 598 f. (τίνος...πράγματος).
ἔτλα καί is a Homeric echo, from *Il.* 5.
382 ff. Aphrodite has been wounded by
Diomede: her mother Dionè comforts
her by saying that Ares, Hera, and Hades
have also suffered wounds: τέτλαθι, τέκνον
ἐμόν... | τλῆ μὲν Ἄρης... | τλῆ δ' Ἥρη... |
τλῆ δ' Ἀΐδης. So here we have *three*
examples—Danaë, Lycurgus, Cleopatra.
—**δέμας** in periphrasis (*Tr.* 908) here
suggests her youthful beauty.—**ἀλλάξαι**
οὐρ. φῶς ἐν χαλκοδ. αὐλαῖς, 'to give up
light, (so as to be) in a prison,' *i.e.* to
exchange the light *for* the darkness of a
prison. ἀλλάσσω τί τινος can mean either
to give, or to take, one thing in exchange
for another. When ἀλλάσσω is used
absolutely, with ref. to place, it more
naturally means 'to go to' (Eur. *Hec.* 483
ἀλλάξασ' Ἅιδα θαλάμους), not, as here,
'to leave': but ἀμείβω is freq. in both
senses. Cp. *Ph.* 1262 ἀμείψας...στέγας
(having quitted them).
    χαλκοδέτοις αὐλαῖς, 'a brass-bound
dwelling': poet. pl. for sing., like δώματα,
etc.: cp. 785. Pherecydes (*ap.* schol.

3 κρυπτομένα δ' ἐν τυμβήρει θαλάμῳ κατεζεύχθη·

4 καίτοι <καὶ> γενεᾷ τίμιος, ὦ παῖ παῖ,

5 καὶ Ζηνὸς ταμιεύεσκε γονὰς χρυσορύτους.　　　　950

6 ἀλλ' ἁ μοιριδία τις δύνασις δεινά·

7 οὔτ' ἄν νιν *ὄλβος οὔτ' Ἄρης, οὐ πύργος, οὐχ ἁλί-
κτυποι

8 κελαιναὶ νᾶες ἐκφύγοιεν.

ἀντ. α'.　　ζεύχθη δ' *ὀξύχολος παῖς ὁ Δρύαντος,　　　　955

2 Ἠδωνῶν βασιλεύς, κερτομίοις ὀργαῖς,

3 ἐκ Διονύσου πετρώδει κατάφαρκτος ἐν δεσμῷ.

---

948 καὶ after καίτοι was added by Hermann. Wieseler conject. καίτοι γ' ἦν: as γεν follows, a scribe reading ΓΕΝΓΕΝ might easily omit γ' ἦν.—γενεᾶι L: γενεὰ in Dresd. a was prob. either a late conject., or a mere error. (γέννα Aug. b, V⁴.)— Hartung conject. ἦν, ὦ παῖ (instead of ὦ παῖ, παῖ): and so Blaydes.　　**950** χρυσορρύτουσ L: χρυσορύτους Triclinius.　　**952** ὄλβος Erfurdt: ὄμβρος MSS.

Apoll. Rhod. 4. 1091) describes it as 'a brazen chamber (θάλαμον...χαλκοῦν) made under ground, in the court-yard (αὐλή) of his house.' Paus. (2. 23. 7) says that he saw at Argos κατάγεων οἰκοδόμημα, ἐπ' αὐτῷ δὲ ἦν ὁ χαλκοῦς θάλαμος (made by Acrisius): *i.e.* the θάλαμος itself was above ground;—as Horace calls it *turris aenea* (*C.* 3. 16. 1). By the epithet χαλκοῦς the legend evidently meant to denote the strength and security of the prison,—as though the doors were of bronze. But it is very probable that this epithet originally came into the story through a reminiscence of a tomb (like the 'treasury of Atreus' at Mycenae), to the walls of which bronze plates had been nailed. (Cp. *Introd. to Homer*, ch. II. § 25.) In Simonides fr. 37. 7 χαλκεογόμφῳ is said of the chest in which Danaë was sent adrift,—not of the θάλαμος.

946 τυμβήρει: cp. on 255.—κατεζεύχθη: was brought under the yoke, *i.e.*, was strictly confined. Her. 8. 22 εἰ... ὑπ' ἀναγκαίης μέζονος κατέζευχθε ἢ ὥστε ἀπίστασθαι, if ye are in the bondage of a control too severe, etc. Cp. ζεύχθη, 955.

948 ff. τίμιος, *sc.* ἦν: cp. 834. Hermann's καίτοι καὶ is preferable to Wieseler's καίτοι γ' ἦν, because the doubled καὶ is forcible, while καὶ Ζηνός (without a previous καὶ) would be somewhat weak. —ταμιεύεσκε, as a precious charge. Cp. Aesch. *Eum.* 660 τίκτει δ' ὁ θρώσκων:

ἡ δ' (the mother) ἅπερ ξένῳ ξένη | ἔσωσεν ἔρνος. The iterative form occurs in only three other places of trag.: 963: Aesch. *Pers.* 656 ἔσκεν, Aesch. fr. 305 κλαίεσκον. —χρυσορύτους, for metre's sake, like *Ai.* 134 ἀμφιρύτου: ρρ regularly follows a simple vowel, but ρ a diphthong (*O. C.* 469).—A bowl (κρατήρ) from Caere, of the 5th cent. B.C., shows the golden rain descending on Danaë; she is sitting on the bed in her chamber, and preparing to retire to rest. A second scene, on the same bowl, represents the moment when she is about to be placed, where Simonides imagines her, λάρνακι ἐν δαιδαλέᾳ. Both paintings are reproduced by Baumeister (*Denkm.* p. 407).

951 ἁ μοιριδία τις κ.τ.λ. The peculiar place of τις makes it really equiv. to a parenthetic thought: 'the power of fate (whatever it may be) is a dread power.' So, while the general sense is what would be ordinarily given by ἁ μοιριδία δύνασις δεινά τις (δύνασίς) ἐστιν, the actual order of the words is more expressive. This is not merely an instance of τις preceding the adj. (as though τις δεινά stood for δεινά τις, cp. *Ph.* 519). Nor, again, is it strictly parallel with ὅταν δ' ὁ κύριος | παρῇ τις (*O.C.* 288), where art. and subst. precede; though it is similar.

952 f. οὔτ'...ὄλβος: wealth cannot buy off fate; arms cannot vanquish it; walls cannot keep it out; flight beyond sea cannot elude it.—Bacchylides fr. 36

and in that chamber, secret as the grave, she was held close prisoner; yet was she of a proud lineage, O my daughter, and charged with the keeping of the seed of Zeus, that fell in the golden rain.

But dreadful is the mysterious power of fate; there is no deliverance from it by wealth or by war, by fenced city, or dark, sea-beaten ships.

And bonds tamed the son of Dryas, swift to wrath, that 1st anti-king of the Edonians; so paid he for his frenzied taunts, strophe. when, by the will of Dionysus, he was pent in a rocky prison.

955—965 L divides thus: ζεύχθη— | Ἠδωνῶν— | ὀργαῖσ— | πετρώδει— | οὕτω— | ἀνθηρόν . . κεῖ|νοσ— | ψαύων— | παύεσκε— | γυναῖκασ— | φιλαύλουσ . . μούσασ.
955 ὀξυχόλως mss. (in L from ὀξυλόχως): ὀξύχολος Scaliger.   **958** πετρώδει] ει made from η in L.

θνατοῖσι δ᾽ οὐκ αὐθαίρετοι | οὔτ᾽ ὄλβος οὔτ᾽ ἄκαμπτος "Ἄρης οὔτε παμφθέρσης στάσις, | ἀλλ᾽ ἐπιχρίμπτει νέφος ἄλλοτ᾽ ἐπ᾽ ἄλλαν γαῖαν ἀ πάνδωρος αἶσα.—**πύργος**, city-walls, with their towers (*O. T.* 56).—**οὔτ᾽** ...οὔτ᾽, followed by οὐ...οὐχ: so even when only one οὔτε has been used, 249 n.

955 f. ζεύχθη, was brought under the yoke. As κατεζεύχθη in 946 better suited the sense, 'was strictly confined,' so here the simple ζεύχθη better suggests the idea, 'was tamed by imprisonment.'—**ὀξύχολος** κ.τ.λ. = ὁ Δρύαντος ὀξύχολος παῖς: the adj. is epithet, not predicate. Verg. *Aen.* 3. 13 Terra procul vastis colitur Mavortia campis, | Thraces arant, *acri* quondam regnata Lycurgo.

The Ἠδωνοί, or Ἠδῶνες (Thuc. 2. 99), occupied in historical times the part of Thrace E. of the Strymon and W. of the Nestus. In earlier times they had dwelt further west, but had been driven eastward by the Macedonian conquest of Mygdonia.

Dionysus, when he came from Asia with his new rites, was opposed by Lycurgus in Thrace, as by Pentheus at Thebes. The Λυκούργεια of Aeschylus is known from the schol. on Ar. *Th.* 135. This trilogy consisted of Ἠδωνοί, Βασσαρίδες, Νεανίσκοι, with Λυκοῦργος as satyric drama. In *Il.* 6. 130 ff. Dionysus, pursued by Lycurgus, dives beneath the sea; Thetis receives him; and Zeus blinds Lycurgus.

κερτομίοις ὀργαῖς, causal dat. with ζεύχθη: was subjugated by reason of the bursts of fury in which he reviled

Dionysus. For the dat., cp. 391, 691: *El.* 838 χρυσοδέτοις ἔρκεσι κρυφθέντα γυναικῶν, (Amphiaraus) buried alive, by reason of a woman's golden snares. **ὀργαῖς** might be general, 'moods' (355), but here has its special sense, though plur.: cp. Aesch. *Eum.* 848 ὀργὰς ξυνοίσω σοι. The dat. could be taken as a modal dat. with ὀξύχολος ('in,' or 'with,' his ὀργαί), but this is less good.—We could not take ζεύχθη...ὀργαῖς as = 'was enslaved to (his own) fierce moods.'—The recurrence of **κερτομίοις** in 961 is noteworthy, but not a ground for suspicion (76 n.): cp. 613 οὐδὲν ἕρπει with 618: and 614 ἐκτὸς ἄτας with 625. The idea of κερτόμιος is mockery, or bitter jest: cp. *Ph.* 1235 κερτομῶν λέγεις τάδε; with the answer, εἰ κερτόμησίς ἐστι τἀληθῆ λέγειν. The word is illustrated by the whole scene in which Pentheus mocks and taunts Dionysus (Eur. *Bacch.* 451—514). So Aesch. fr. 59 made Lycurgus ask, ποδαπὸς ὁ γύννις; ('whence comes this womanish youth?').

957 ἐκ Διονύσου, by his command (*O. C.* 67 n.). Lycurgus, having been driven mad by Dionysus, did many violent deeds, until at last the Edonians were commanded by an oracle to imprison him in a cave on Mount Pangaeus (Apollod. 3. 5. 1). He was afterwards torn asunder by wild horses (*ib.*), or devoured by panthers (Hyginus *Fab.* 132).—**πετρώδει...δεσμῷ**, the cave. Cp. Plat. *Legg.* 864 E ἐν δημοσίῳ δεσμῷ δεθείς.—**κατάφαρκτος**: for the spelling, cp. on 241.

4 οὕτω τᾶς μανίας δεινὸν ἀποστάζει
5 ἀνθηρόν τε μένος. κεῖνος ἐπέγνω μανίαις   960
6 ψαύων τὸν θεὸν ἐν κερτομίοις γλώσσαις.
7 παύεσκε μὲν γὰρ ἐνθέους γυναῖκας εὐιόν τε πῦρ,
8 φιλαύλους τ' ἠρέθιζε Μούσας.   965

στρ. β'.   παρὰ δὲ Κυανεᾶν *πελάγει διδύμας ἁλὸς

---

960 ἀνθηρόν] Nauck conject. ἀτηρόν: Pleitner and Wolff, ἔνθηρον.—Schneidewin wrote ἀνθηρὸν τὸ μένος.   **961** ψαύων] Herwerden conject. χραίνων: M. Schmidt, θήγων: Nauck (formerly), θραύων: Mekler, σεύων.   **965** φιλαύλουσ L: φιλαύλους τ' γ: φιλαύλους δ' Seyffert, and so most recent edd.   **966—976** L divides the vv.

---

959 f. οὕτω, *i.e.*, under the discipline of the rocky prison.—**ἀνθηρόν,** bursting into flower, hence, fig., exuberant, or at its height: cp. Plat. *Polit.* 310 D πέφυκεν ἀνδρία...κατὰ μὲν ἀρχὰς ἀκμάζειν ῥώμῃ, τελευτῶσα δὲ ἐξανθεῖν παντάπασι μανίαις: Aesch. *Pers.* 821 ὕβρις...ἐξανθοῦσ'. So oft. ἄνθος=ἀκμή, as *Tr.* 998 τόδ' ἀκήλητον | μανίας ἄνθος.—**ἀποστάζει** =ἀπορρεῖ, 'trickles away,' so 'gradually passes off.' The fig. use of ἀνθεῖν being so familiar, the change of metaphor in ἀποστάζει would hardly be felt. Wecklein, indeed, conceives that the poet is thinking of a tumour, which bursts when it has attained its full size. Unity of metaphor can be bought too dearly.—Others understand: 'so dread and exuberant is the rage that *flows from madness*': *i.e.*, 'so dreadful was the excess of impiety into which L. had been led by his madness.' But here we look rather for some direct comment on his punishment. His abasement (ζεύχθη) is the theme of these verses. The reference to his crime comes later (962).

960 ff. ἐπέγνω τὸν θεόν, μανίας ψαύων (αὐτοῦ) ἐν κ. γλώσσαις: he came to know the god, when in madness he assailed him with taunts. He had mistaken Dionysus for an effeminate mortal (see on 955 f.). Cp. *Od.* 24. 216 πατρὸς πειρήσομαι... | αἴ κέ μ' ἐπιγνώῃ (recognise). ψαύω nowhere else takes an acc. in class. Greek (see on 546, 859), and it is unnecessary to regard this passage as a solitary example. Poetry, esp. lyric, allowed occasional boldness, and even harshness, in the arrangement of words (cp. 944: *O. T.* 1251 n.: *O. C.* 1428). Even in prose we could have (*e.g.*) ἐνίκησαν ἄφνω ἐπιπε-

σόντες τοὺς πολεμίους, though the partic. could not govern an acc. Here the order is only so far bolder, that τὸν θεόν divides ψαύων from ἐν κ. γλώσσαις: as if, in our example, a second qualification of ἐπιπεσόντες (such as νύκτωρ) followed τοὺς πολεμίους. But, since the meaning of ψαύων is already indicated by μανίαις, we are not mentally straining forward for a clue to be given by ἐν κερτ. γλώσσαις. That is, we are not forced to bind the words, ψαύων τὸν θεόν, closely together in our thought, but can easily take the sentence as though it were pointed thus:— ἐπέγνω, μανίαις | ψαύων, τὸν θεόν, ἐν κερτ. γλώσσαις.—**μανίαις,** modal (rather than causal) dat.—**ψαύων** like καθαπτόμενος (ἀντιβίοις ἐπέεσσι, *Od.* 18. 415), but also suggesting profanation,—ἀθίκτου θιγγάνων.—**ἐν**= 'with' (764 n.).—**γλώσσαις,** a bold use of the plur., due to the fact that the sing., with an adj., could so easily be fig., *e.g.* κακὴ γλῶσσα='slander': so κερτόμιοι γλῶσσαι='taunts.'

963 f. παύεσκε: see on 950.—**ἐνθέους γυναῖκας:** the Maenads attendant on Dionysus, cp. 1128, 1150, *O. T.* 212, *O. C.* 680.—**εὔιον...πῦρ,** the torches which the Bacchanals swing while they raise the cry εὐοῖ. In *O.T.* 211 the god himself is εὔιος. Cp. Eur. *Bacch.* 307 (Dionysus by night on Parnassus) πηδῶντα σὺν πεύκαισι δικόρυφον πλάκα.

965 Μούσας. An interesting illustration is afforded by a sarcophagus in Baumeister's *Denkmaeler*, p. 837. In the centre of the group is the raging Lycurgus, with uplifted axe, about to slay the Dionysiac nymph Ambrosia, who cowers at his feet. A Fury is on each side of him, urging him on. To the right is Dionysus,—about to

There the fierce exuberance of his madness slowly passed away. That man learned to know the god, whom in his frenzy he had provoked with mockeries; for he had sought to quell the god-possessed women, and the Bacchanalian fire; and he angered the Muses that love the flute.

And by 'the waters of the Dark Rocks, the waters of the 2nd twofold sea, strophe.

thus: παρά— | διδύμασ— | ἀκταὶ— | ἠδ' ὁ θρηικῶν— | ἵν'— | δισσοῖσι— | εἶδεν— |
τυφλωθὲν— | ἀλαὸν— | ἀραχθὲν— | χείρεσσι .. ἀκμαῖσι.   966 f. παρα δε (sic)
κυανέων πελάγεων (note the accent) πετρῶν | διδύμασ ἁλοσ L. Brunck omitted
πετρῶν. Κυανεᾶν F. Wieseler. For πελάγεων I conjecture πελάγει. See comment.

---

save the nymph by changing her into a vine; and behind him stand his followers. At the extreme left are three Muses—Urania, with globe; Clio, with roll; Euterpè, prob. with flutes. (Zoega seems clearly right in thus explaining the three women: others have made them Moirae.)—The close relation of Dionysus with the Muses is marked by one of his Attic titles, Μελπόμενος (Paus. 1. 2. 5), as conversely Apollo had the title Διονυσόδοτος (id. 1. 31. 4). Muses were sometimes said to have nursed him. (Cp. Welcker, Götterl. 2. 611.)

The monuments relating to the myth of Lycurgus have been critically treated by Michaelis (Annal. Inst. 1872, pp. 248–270). The Italian vase-paintings follow a version different from that of Soph., viz. that the frenzy of Lycurgus was wreaked on his own son and wife. A large Neapolitan vase gives two pictures: in one, we see his murderous rage; in the other, Dionysus sits on his throne in calm majesty, stroking his panther.

966 Cleopatra is the third example. Her father was the wind-god, Boreas: her mother, the Athenian Oreithyia, whom he carried off to his wild home in Thrace. Cleopatra married Phineus, king of the Thracian Salmydessus, on the w. coast of the Euxine, not far from the entrance to the Bosporus. She bore him two sons. He afterwards put her away, and imprisoned her. Her imprisonment is not directly mentioned here: but cp. Diod. 4. 44, who says of Heracles, when serving with the Argonauts, τὴν Κλεοπάτραν ἐκ τῆς φυλακῆς προαγαγεῖν. Phineus then married Eidothea, sister of Cadmus. Eidothea put out the eyes of Cleopatra's two sons, and caused them also to be imprisoned.

It is the fate of Cleopatra herself which Soph. means to compare with Antigone's: this is plain from 986. The fate of the sons is made so prominent only because nothing else could give us so strong a sense of the savage hatred which pursued the mother.

Soph. supposes the outline of the story to be familiar. Cleopatra has already been divorced and imprisoned. The poet chooses the moment at which Cleopatra's sons are being blinded by Eidothea, with the sharp shuttle in her blood-stained hands. Ares, the god of cruel bloodshed, beholds with joy a deed so worthy of his Thracian realm.

The name of Cleopatra (like that of Capaneus, 133) is not mentioned. Two strophes are given to this theme, partly, perh., as having an Attic interest (982). Soph. wrote two plays called Φινεύς. We know only that Cleopatra's sons were there called Ὄαρθος (?Παρθένιος H. Weil) and Κράμβος: and that the subsequent blindness of Phineus was represented as a punishment of his cruelty (schol. Apoll. Rhod. 2. 178). Eidothea was mentioned by Soph. in his Τυμπανισταί (schol. on 980),—a play which perh. concerned the Dionysiac worship, since the τύμπανον (kettle-drum) was used in his ὄργια as well as in those of Cybelè. Another version called her Idaea, daughter of Dardanus.

παρὰ δὲ Κυανεᾶν πελάγει 8. ἁλός. For the double possessive gen., cp. 795, 929. πελάγει...ἁλός, as Eur. Tro. 88 πέλαγος Αἰγαίας ἁλός, the Homeric ἁλὸς ἐν πελάγεσσιν, etc. The rocky islets on the N. side of the entrance from the Euxine to the Bosporus were regularly called Κυάνεαι simply (without νῆσοι or πέτραι, Her. 4. 85). L's πετρῶν has long been recognised as a gloss. But Wieseler's change

2 ἀκταὶ Βοσπόριαι †ἠδ' ὁ Θρηκῶν – ⏑ –
3 Σαλμυδησσός, ἵν' ἀγχίπολις Ἄρης　　　　　　970
4 δισσοῖσι Φινείδαις
5 εἶδεν ἀρατὸν ἕλκος
6 τυφλωθὲν ἐξ ἀγρίας δάμαρτος,
7 ἀλαὸν ἀλαστόροισιν ὀμμάτων κύκλοις,
8 *ἀραχθέντων ὑφ' αἱματηραῖς　　　　　　975
9 χείρεσσι καὶ κερκίδων ἀκμαῖσιν.

968 ff. ἀκταὶ βοσπόριαι | ἠδ' ὁ θρηκῶν σαλμυδησσσβσ | L. For ἠδ' (ἠδ' r) Triclinius wrote ἰδ'. Blaydes suggests ἵν' or καί: Semitelos τ' ἰδ'. After Θρηκῶν, Boeckh supplies ἄξενος: Meineke, ἠϊών: H. Schütz, δύσχιμος.—ἵν' ἀγχίπολισ ἄρησ I., with ·ον· written over ἵν' by S. Of the later MSS., some (as A, V) have ἀγχίπολις, others (as L², Vat., Vat. b, Aug. b, Dresd. a) ἀγχίπτολις. Dindorf

of πελαγέων into σπιλάδων is also erroneous.

L's accent, πελάγεων, points to the truth,—as similar small hints in that MS. have been found to do elsewhere also (cp. *O. C.* 1113 n.). The correction, πελάγει, is so easy that it may well have occurred to others; but I have not met with it. It removes the difficulty (insuperable, to my mind) of παρά with the genitive here. Those who read κυανεᾶν σπιλάδων, or κυανέων πελαγέων, are forced to take παρά as = '*extending from* the dark rocks (etc.) are the coasts.' But such a use is wholly unparalleled. As to 1123, see n. there. In Pind. *P.* 1. 75 ἀρέομαι | πὰρ μὲν Σαλαμῖνος Ἀθαναίων χάριν = '*from* Salamis' (*i.e.*, by celebrating it). In Ar. *Ach.* 68 the Ravenna has ἐτρυχόμεσθα παρὰ Καΰστρίων | πεδίων ὁδοιπλανοῦντες, while other MSS. have διὰ (also with gen. plur.); but there παρὰ Καΰστριον | πεδίον (Dindorf) is certain. In Pind. *P.* 3. 60 γνόντα τὸ πὰρ ποδός, 'having learned one's nearest business' (cp. *P.* 10. 63), παρά has its normal sense, = 'that which begins *from* one's foot,' = which is directly before one in one's path. The corruption of πελάγει into πελαγέων naturally followed that of Κυανεᾶν into κυανέων.

967 f. ἀκταὶ Βοσπόριαι, *sc.* εἰσί (cp. 948 n.). The Κυάνεαι are at the point where the coast of the Bosporus joins the western coast of the Euxine. The city Salmydessus stood just S. of the promontory of Thynias, about 60 miles N.W. of the entrance of the Bosporus, near the modern Midjeh. The name Salmydessus was given also to the tract of coast

tending s. of the town.—After Θρηκῶν a cretic has been lost (= -τον γονάν in 980). Boeckh supplies it with ἄξενος, which is at least simple and fitting. Cp. Aesch. *P. V.* 726 τραχεῖα πόντου Σαλμυδησσία γνάθος | ἐχθρόξενος ναύταισι, μητρυιὰ νεῶν. Schütz, referring to the schol. on 969, πέλαγος δέ ἐστι δυσχείμερον περὶ Θράκην, proposes δύσχιμος ('dangerous'), a word used by Aesch. and Eur., though not by Soph. But the want of a verb is somewhat awkward. Can the missing word be κλῄζεται? (Cp. *O. T.* 1451 n.: and for the sing., below, 1133.) Ships often grounded on the shallows (τέναγος) which stretched from Salmydessus into the Euxine. The Thracians had set up slabs (στῆλαι), marking off the coast into allotments for wrecking purposes. Before this was done, there had been much bloodshed between rival wreckers (Xen. *An.* 7. 5. 13).—The MS. †ἠδ' cannot be right. A short syll. is required (= the last syll. of ἔχοντες in 980). In my first ed. I adopted ἰδ', the conjecture of Triclinius. Prof. Tyrrell remarks (*Class. Review* vol. II. p. 141) that ἰδέ is not elsewhere elided in classical poetry. As ἠδέ could be elided, that may be accidental. Still, it should be noted along with the other facts,—that ἰδέ occurs nowhere else in tragedy, and that the hiatus after Βοσπόριαι must be excused, as in epic verse, by the ictus before caesura (*Introd. to Homer* p. 194): cp. *Il.* 14. 175 ἀλειψαμένη, ἰδὲ χαίτας | πεξαμένη. On the whole, I now prefer to leave ἠδ', with an obelus. Either Βοσπόριαι καὶ ὁ or Βοσπόριαί θ' ὅ τε would be possible.

are the shores of Bosporus, and Thracian Salmydessus; where
Ares, neighbour to the city, saw the accurst, blinding wound
dealt to the two sons of Phineus by his fierce wife,—the
wound that brought darkness to those vengeance-craving orbs,
smitten with her bloody hands, smitten with her shuttle for
a dagger.

(formerly) conject. ἄγχουρος. Seyffert, ἀρχέπολις. **972** ἀρατὸν] Hermann
conject. ἀρακτὸν: Schneidewin, ἀραῖον. **973** τυφλωθὲν MSS.: ἀραχθὲν Wunder.
975 ἀραχθὲν ἐγχέων L: the later MSS. have either this or ἀραχθὲν ἀχέων. Seidler
and Lachmann restored ἀραχθέντων. Nauck would prefer τυφλωθέντων here, and
ἀραχθὲν in 973.

---

970 ἀγχίπολις "Αρης. This reading
(L's) agrees metrically with the antistrophe
(981 ἀρχαιογόνων), if we suppose the 2nd
and 3rd syllables of ἀγχίπολις to represent
a resolved long syllable. Such a resolution
is rare, but not unexampled: see on 798.
We could avoid it by reading, with Gleditsch, ἀκταὶ Βοσπόριαι, ἵν' ὁ Θρῃκῶν ἄξενος
| Σαλμυδησσὸς "Αρης τ' ἀγχίπολις. But (a)
this does not explain how ἠδ' came into the
MSS.: and (b) it is evidently better to say,
'where Ares saw,' than, 'where Salmydessus and Ares saw.' The reference to the
god's cruel joy would thus lose much of its
force. If, on the other hand, **ἀγχίπολις**
is read, then "Αρης has ă, and in 981 we
must suppose the loss of a syllable after
ἀρχαιογόνων. But such a loss is very
improbable: that verse appears sound.
Neither ἄγχουρος nor ἀρχέπολις has any
likelihood.—Ares is 'neighbour to the
city' of Salmydessus because his home is
in Thrace (*Il.* 13. 301, etc.). There may
also be a special reference to some local
shrine. 'He saw the wound dealt': *i.e.*,
it was a deed such as he loves to see.

971 ff. Φινείδαις, dat. of interest, with
τυφλωθέν.—**ἀρατόν,** accursed, bringing a
curse on the authors of the wound. In
his dramatic treatment of the story, Soph.
had connected this blinding of the sons
with the punishment of blindness which
the gods afterwards inflicted on Phineus
himself (schol. Apoll. Rhod. 2. 178).—
ἕλκος τυφλωθέν. τυφλοῦν ἕλκος = to *inflict*
a *blinding* wound. Cp. *Ai.* 55 ἔκειρε...
φόνον, he *dealt* death *by hewing down*.
Eur. *Suppl.* 1205 τρώσῃς φόνον, (wherever) thou *dealest* the *death*-wound. Verg.
Aen. 11. 82 caeso *sparsuros* sanguine
flammam (caedere sanguinem = to *shed*
blood *by cutting*). In such pregnant
idioms the special verb = a general verb
plus the partic. of the special verb used

instrumentally: *e.g.,* τυφλῶ ἕλκος = ποιῶ
ἕλκος τυφλῶν.—ἐξ here = ὑπό of the direct
agent: for, as κερκίδων indicates, she did
it with her own hand. Distinguish ἐκ
Διονύσου in 957 (by his order).

974 ἀλαὸν...κύκλοις, sightless *for* the
orbs, *i.e.*, making them sightless. Cp.
Pind. *O.* 1. 26 καθαροῦ λέβητος, the puri-
fying cauldron. — **ἀλαστόροισιν.** The
form ἀλάστορος was used by Aesch. as
= ἀλάστωρ (fr. 87 πρευμενῆς ἀ., fr. 286 μέγαν
ἀ.). The form may have been generally
current, since Pherecydes used Ζεὺς Ἀλά-
στοροs instead of Ζ. Ἀλάστωρ (Cramer
Anecd. 1. 62). The blind orbs are ἀλά-
στοροι, 'avenging spirits,' in the sense
that they mutely appeal to the gods for
vengeance.—For the παρήχησις (*O. T.*
371) Wolff cp. *Il.* 6. 201 κὰπ πεδίον τὸ
Ἀλήϊον οἶος ἀλᾶτο.

975 ἀραχθέντων. So ἀράσσω is used
of Oed. striking his eyes with the περόναι
(*O. T.* 1276).—ὑπό with dat. of the instrument, as in the epic ὑπὸ χερσὶ δαμῆναι,
O. T. 202 ὑπὸ σῷ φθίσον κεραυνῷ.

976 κερκίδων, poet. plur. for sing.,
like βωμοί, σκῆπτρα, etc.—The κερκίς
(κρέκω, to strike the web in weaving) was
'like a large netting needle' (Rich *s.v.*
radius), 'rather longer than the breadth
of the web.' It was used for two purposes. (1) As a rod with which to strike
the threads of the woof, in order to con-
dense them. The flat blade called σπάθη
was a later substitute. In the modern loom
this is done by the moveable bar called
the 'batten.' (2) As a shuttle, *i.e.*, an
instrument for shooting the threads of the
woof (κρόκη) from one side of the loom
to the other, between the threads of the
warp (στήμων). In the East weavers
sometimes use a long reed for both these
purposes. Eur. *Tro.* 198 οὐκ Ἰδαίοις ἱσ-
τοῖς κερκίδα | δινεύουσ' ἐξαλλάξω ('no more,

ἀντ. β.　　κατὰ δὲ τακόμενοι μέλεοι μελέαν πάθαν　　　977
　2 κλαῖον, ματρὸς ἔχοντες ἀνύμφευτον γονάν·　　980
　3 ἁ δὲ σπέρμα μὲν ἀρχαιογόνων
　4 ἄντασ᾽ Ἐρεχθειδᾶν,
　5 τηλεπόροις δ᾽ ἐν ἄντροις
　6 τράφη θυελλαισιν ἐν πατρῴαις
　7 Βορεὰς ἄμιππος ὀρθόποδος ὑπὲρ πάγου,　　985
　8 θεῶν παῖς· ἀλλὰ κἀπ᾽ ἐκείνα
　9 Μοῖραι μακραίωνες ἔσχον, ὦ παῖ.

ΤΕΙΡΕΣΙΑΣ.

Θήβης ἄνακτες, ἤκομεν κοινὴν ὁδὸν
δύ᾽ ἐξ ἑνὸς βλέποντε· τοῖς τυφλοῖσι γὰρ
αὕτη κέλευθος ἐκ προηγητοῦ πέλει.　　　　990
ΚΡ. τί δ᾽ ἔστιν, ὦ γεραιὲ Τειρεσία, νέον;
ΤΕ. ἐγὼ διδάξω, καὶ σὺ τῷ μάντει πιθοῦ.

977—987 L divides thus: κατὰ δὲ— | μελέαν— | κλαῖον— | ἔχον|τεσ— | δὲ σπέρμα — | ἄντασ— | τηλεπόροισ— | τράφη— | βορεὰσ— | θεῶν— | μοῖραι . . παῖ. **980** μα- τρὸς r, πατρὸσ L. Cp. 863. **981 f.** Dindorf conject. ἀρχαιογόνοιο | . .

---

at the loom, will I send the shuttle flying across the warp').—Cp. Eur. *Hec.* 1170, where the women blind Polymestor with their brooches (πόρπαι = περόναι); and *O. T.* 1269 n.

977 f. κατά in tmesis, as *O. T.* 1198, *O. C.* 1689, etc.—*κατατακόμενοι* alludes to their imprisonment; cp. schol. on 980 τυφλώσασα τοὺς Κλεοπάτρας παῖδας ἐν τάφῳ καθεῖρξεν.—**μέλεοι μελέαν**: cp. 156: *O. T.* 479.

980 ματρὸς ἔχοντες ἀν. γονάν, having their origin from an unhappily-married mother. The epithet is made to agree with **γονάν**, not with **ματρός**, as in 793, *νεῖκος-ἀνδρῶν ξύναιμον*: *i.e.*, μητρὸς-γονή, mother-source, forms one notion. For *γονὰς ἔχειν* cp. *O. C.* 972 ὃς οὔτε βλάστας πω γενεθλίους πατρός, | οὐ μητρὸς εἶχον. For ἀνύμφ., cp. Eur. *Tr.* 144 ἄλοχοι μέλεαι...καὶ δύσνυμφοι: *Hipp.* 757 κακονυμφοτάταν ὄνασιν ('to bless her with a marriage most unblest'). *O. T.* 1214 ἄγαμον γάμον.—The comma should not be placed after **ματρός**, which is inseparable from the following phrase. Without ματρός, the words ἔχοντες ἀνύμφευτον γονάν could still mean, 'born from one who was unhappily married,' but would be harsh and obscure. The word **πάθαν**

refers to their own fate. Then **ματρὸς**... **γονάν** supplements this by indicating that they mourn for their mother's fate also.

981 f. σπέρμα, acc. of respect; *Od.* 15. 267 ἐξ Ἰθάκης γένος εἰμί.—**ἀρχαιογ.**: *Ai.* 202 γενεᾶς χθονίων ἀπ᾽ Ἐρεχθειδῶν.— **ἄντασ᾽ Ἐρ.**, attained unto them, could trace her lineage to them,—her mother Oreithyia being the daughter of Erechtheus. Remark that the acc. σπέρμα mitigates the boldness of ἄντασε, and also suggests its primary meaning—viz., that the genealogy is carried back to a point at which it *meets* the Erechtheid line. Cp. Her. 2. 143 (Hecataeus) γενεηλογήσαντί τε ἑωυτὸν καὶ ἀναδήσαντι τὴν πατριὴν ἐς ἑκκαιδέκατον θεόν.

983 τηλεπόροις, merely poet. for 'distant'; lit., to which it is a far journey. Not (I think), 'spacious' (*i.e.* 'in which one can go far'): nor, 'extending far into the mountains.' So in *Ai.* 564, τηλωπὸς οἰχνεῖ, the adj. is merely 'distant'; it has not its full sense, 'seen afar.' Boreas carried Oreithyia to a region of Thrace which the poets called 'Sarpêdon' (we see the association with ἁρπάζω)—not, seemingly, the promontory called 'Sarpedonion,' on the s. coast, but in the wilds

Pining in their misery, they bewailed their cruel doom, 2nd anti-strophe.
those sons of a mother hapless in her marriage; but she traced
her descent from the ancient line of the Erechtheidae; and in
far-distant caves she was nursed amid her father's storms, that
child of Boreas, swift as a steed over the steep hills, a daughter
of gods; yet upon her also the grey Fates bore hard, my
daughter.

Enter TEIRESIAS, *led by a boy, on the spectators' right.*

TE.   Princes of Thebes, we have come with linked steps,
both served by the eyes of one; for thus, by a guide's help,
the blind must walk.

CR.   And what, aged Teiresias, are thy tidings?

TE.   I will tell thee; and do thou hearken to the seer.

Ἐρεχθεῖδα, reading ἀγχίπτολις in 970.
Meineke conject. ὦ Ζεῦ: Bergk, ὦπα.

984 θνέλλησιν MSS.   **987** ὦ παῖ]
990 ἐκ] Blaydes conject. ἦκ.

---

of Haemus. It is of this that Soph. is thinking here: cp. fr. 575 ἡμεῖς δ᾽ ἐν ἄντροις, ἔνθα Σαρπηδὼν πέτρα. That verse is from the Τυμπανισταί, in which the story of Cleopatra was noticed (cp. on 966); and she was probably the speaker. Oreithyia bore two sons to Boreas, Calais and Zetes; and, besides Cleopatra, another daughter, Chionè.

985 ἄμιππος, swift as horses. Cp. *O. T.* 466 ἀελλάδων | ἵππων, 'storm-swift steeds.' In prose ἄμιπποι = foot-soldiers who, in the Boeotian army, were sometimes told off to run alongside the cavalry (Thuc. 5. 57, Xen. *H.* 7. 5. 23). Cp. Theogn. 715 ὠκύτερος δ᾽ εἴησθα πόδας ταχέων Ἁρπυιῶν | καὶ παίδων Βορέω.—ὀρθόποδος, steep. ὀρθόπους, 'erect upon one's feet,' seems to be here merely a poet. equiv. (suggested by metrical convenience) for ὄρθιος. This was the more natural, since πούς, κνήμη, etc., were so oft. said of mountains. In *O. T.* 866 ὑψίποδες, said of the eternal νόμοι, differs from ὀρθόπους here by implying movement ('of sublime range'). We need not, then, explain ὀρθόπους as = ὄρθιος τοῖς τοῦ ἀναβαίνοντος ποσί.

986 f. κἀπ᾽ ἐκείνᾳ…ἔσχον = καὶ ἐκείνῃ ἐπέσχον, from the intrans. ἐπέχω as = 'to direct (one's course) against a person,' 'to attack him': cp. *Od.* 19. 71 τί μοι ὧδ᾽ ἐπέχεις κεκοτηότι θυμῷ; ('assail me'):

ib. 22. 75 ἐπ᾽ αὐτῷ πάντες ἔχωμεν ('let us all have at him').—Others understand, 'extended even to her,' 'reached her,' which mars the personification.—μακραίωνες: Aesch. *Eum.* 172 παλαιγενεῖς... Μοῖραs.

988—1114 Fifth ἐπεισόδιον. Teiresias denounces the divine wrath. Creon, terror-stricken, hastens to bury Polyneices and to release Antigone.

988 f. ἄνακτες: cp. 843, 940.—δυ᾽ ἐξ ἑνὸς βλ., two seeing by the agency of one (ἐκ as in 973): cp. *O. C.* 33 τῆς ὑπέρ τ᾽ ἐμοῦ | αὑτῆς θ᾽ ὁρώσης. The words would usu. mean, 'two seeing, where only one saw formerly.' Cp. *O. C.* 1764, where the regular sense of πράσσειν καλῶς, 'to fare well,' has not hindered the poet from using it as = 'to do rightly.'

990 αὕτη κ., the blind have this kind of walking appointed for them,— viz., walking with the help of a guide. αὕτη κ. = αὕτη ἡ κ. (*O. C.* 471): κέλευθος is not predicate (like παῦλαν in *O. C.* 88), as if the sense were, 'this (αὕτη for τοῦτο) is walking for the blind,—viz. to walk with a guide.' We do not need the art. ἡ with ἐκ, because πέλει = not simply 'is,' but, 'is possible.' Cp. *O. C.* 848 οὔκουν ποτ᾽ ἐκ (by means of) τούτοιν γε μὴ σκήπτροιν ἔτι | ὁδοιπορήσῃς (the blind Oed.'s daughters).

991 τί δ᾽ ἔστιν: cp. 20 n.

ΚΡ. οὔκουν πάρος γε σῆς ἀπεστάτουν φρενός.

ΤΕ. τοιγὰρ δι' ὀρθῆς τήνδ' *ἐναυκλήρεις πόλιν.

ΚΡ. ἔχω πεπονθὼς μαρτυρεῖν ὀνήσιμα.   995

ΤΕ. φρόνει βεβὼς αὖ νῦν ἐπὶ ξυροῦ τύχης.

ΚΡ. τί δ' ἔστιν; ὡς ἐγὼ τὸ σὸν φρίσσω στόμα.

ΤΕ. γνώσει, τέχνης σημεῖα τῆς ἐμῆς κλύων.

εἰς γὰρ παλαιὸν θᾶκον ὀρνιθοσκόπον

ἵζων, ἵν' ἦν μοι παντὸς οἰωνοῦ λιμήν,   1000

ἀγνῶτ' ἀκούω φθόγγον ὀρνίθων, κακῷ

κλάζοντας οἴστρῳ καὶ βεβαρβαρωμένῳ·

καὶ σπῶντας ἐν χηλαῖσιν ἀλλήλους φοναῖς

ἔγνων· πτερῶν γὰρ ῥοῖβδος οὐκ ἄσημος ἦν.

εὐθὺς δὲ δείσας ἐμπύρων ἐγευόμην   1005

βωμοῖσι παμφλέκτοισιν· ἐκ δὲ θυμάτων

Ἥφαιστος οὐκ ἔλαμπεν, ἀλλ' ἐπὶ σποδῷ

---

994 ναυκληρεῖσ L: ἐναυκλήρεις Valckenaer.   **996** τύχης] Semitelos conject. κυρεῖς. Blaydes, νῦν ἀκμῆς ἐπὶ ξυροῦ.   **998** σημεῖα τῆς ἐμῆς r: τῆσ ἐμῆσ σημεῖα L

---

993 f. οὔκουν...γε: cp. 321 n.—**δι' ὀρθῆς**, sc. ὁδοῦ. A rare instance of the fem. adj. in such a phrase with διά, which regularly takes a subst. (742 n.); but it follows the analogy of the freq. phrases with ἐκ, as ἐξ εὐθείας: Tr. 395 ἐκ ταχείας, 727 ἐξ ἑκουσίας: Thuc. 3. 92 ἐκ καινῆς: Her. 5. 116 ἐκ νέης, 6. 85 ἐξ ὑστέρης, 8. 6 ἐκ τῆς ἀντίης, etc.—**ἐναυκλήρεις** is right. The seer hopes, indeed, that the mischief can still be repaired (1025 ff.), but he thinks that Creon has made a disastrous mistake (1015). He could hardly say, then, δι' ὀρθῆς...**ναυκληρεῖς**. Creon has only just become king; but he had formerly been regent for some years (cp. O. T. 1418). Aesch. has the verb in this fig. sense (Th. 652). Cp. 167 ὤρθου: O. T. 104 ἀπευθύνειν: ib. 923 κυβερνήτην.

995 πεπονθὼς ὀνήσιμα, ἔχω μαρτυρεῖν (πεπονθέναι). We could say, μαρτυρῶ σοι εὐεργετήσαντι (like σύνοιδα): but less well, μαρτυρῶ εὖ πεπονθώς. Cp. O. C. 1128 εἰδὼς δ' ἀμύνω τοῖσδε τοῖς λόγοις τάδε, with like emphasis on the partic., 'I have felt these benefits which I thus requite.'

996 φρόνει βεβώς, bethink thee that thou art placed. O. C. 1358 ἐν πόνῳ | ... βεβηκώς, n. Il. 10. 173 νῦν γὰρ δὴ πάντεσσιν ἐπὶ ξυροῦ ἵσταται ἀκμῆς, | ἢ μάλα λυγρὸς ὄλεθρος Ἀχαιοῖς, ἠὲ βιῶναι. Eur.

H. F. 630 ὧδ' ἔβητ' ἐπὶ ξυροῦ; Helen. 897 ἐπ' ἀκμῆς εἰμὶ κατθανόντ' ἰδεῖν.—**τύχης**, interpreting ξυροῦ, adds dignity and solemnity to the phrase.

997 ὡς, exclamatory. El. 1112 τί δ' ἔστιν, ὦ ξέν'; ὡς μ' ὑπέρχεται φόβος.

999 f. θᾶκον. Paus. (9. 16. 1) saw at Thebes, near the temple of Zeus Ammon, οἰωνοσκοπεῖον...Τειρεσίου καλούμενον. Near it was a shrine of Τύχη.—**λιμήν**, a place to which the birds came: schol. ὅρμος καὶ ἕδρα, ὅπου πάντα τὰ ὄρνεα προσέρχονται. Cp. Eur. Or. 1077 καὶ δῶμα πατρὸς καὶ μέγας πλούτου λιμήν ('receptacle'): Aesch. applied the same phrase to Persia (Pers. 250). Omens were taken, not only from the flight of birds, but also from the positions in which they settled,—from their sounds, —and from their mode of feeding. The λιμήν means a place to which they were lured by food, so that their συνεδρίαι (Aesch. P. V. 492), and the other signs, could be noted. Cp. Arist. H. A. 9. 1 ὅθεν καὶ τὰς διεδρίας καὶ τὰς συνεδρίας οἱ μάντεις λαμβάνουσι, διέδρα μὲν τὰ πολέμια τιθέντες, σύνεδρα δὲ τὰ εἰρηνοῦντα πρὸς ἄλληλα.—Herwerden conjectures οὐρανοῦ λιμήν, understanding a space of sky chosen as a field of augural observation (templum).

1001 ff. κακῷ, ill-omened (O. C. 1433).

CR. Indeed, it has not been my wont to slight thy counsel.

TE. Therefore didst thou steer our city's course aright.

CR. I have felt, and can attest, thy benefits.

TE. Mark that now, once more, thou standest on fate's fine edge.

CR. What means this? How I shudder at thy message!

TE. Thou wilt learn, when thou hearest the warnings of mine art. As I took my place on mine old seat of augury, where all birds have been wont to gather within my ken, I heard a strange voice among them; they were screaming with dire, feverish rage, that drowned their language in a jargon; and I knew that they were rending each other with their talons, murderously; the whirr of wings told no doubtful tale.

Forthwith, in fear, I essayed burnt-sacrifice on a duly kindled altar: but from my offerings the Fire-god showed no flame;

(cp. comment. on 106).　　**999** ὀρνιθοσκόπον] Nauck conject. οἰωνοσκόπον.
1000 οἰωνοῦ] Herwerden conject. οὐρανοῦ.　　**1002** Wecklein conject.
βεβαρβαρωμένως: Usener, βεβαρβαρωμένα.

—οἴστρῳ, 'gad-fly,' then fig., 'rage,' a word which often suggests divine stimulation: as Heracles asks, ποῦ δ' οἶστρος ἡμᾶς ἔλαβε; (Eur. *H. F.* 1144).—κλάζοντας, since φθόγγον ὀρνίθων = ὄρνιθας φθεγγομένους: *Il.* 17. 755 τῶν δ' ὥστε ψαρῶν νέφος ἔρχεται ἠὲ κολοιῶν | οὖλον κεκλήγοντες: *Od.* 12. 181 ἀλλ' ὅτε τόσσον ἀπῆν (sc. ἡ νηῦς) ὅσσον τε γέγωνε βοήσας, | ῥίμφα διώκοντες.—βεβαρβαρωμένῳ. To the seer, the voices of birds were usually εὔσημοι (1021). Conversely the sound of a strange language is likened to the twittering of birds: Her. 2. 57 ἕως δὲ ἐβαρβάριζε (ἡ γυνή), ὄρνιθος τρόπον ἐδόκεέ σφι φθέγγεσθαι. Aesch. used χελιδονίζειν as = βαρβαρίζειν (fr. 440, cp. *Ag.* 1050).

1003 ἐν χηλαῖσιν, 'with' them: 764 n. —φοναῖς, an adverbial dat. of manner, 'murderously.' Cp. *O. C.* 1318 εὔχεται κατασκαφῇ | Καπανεὺς τὸ Θήβης ἄστυ δηώσειν πυρί, where the first dat. is one of manner, like φοναῖς here, and the second (instrumental) answers to ἐν χηλαῖσιν. Elsewhere the Attic use of the subst. is limited to the phrase ἐν φοναῖς (696 n.). The Schol. has φοναῖς· ταῖς αἱμακτικαῖς: as though it were from an adj. φονός. So some recent edd. take it. Such an adj. could have come from the rt. φεν, but there is no trace of it.

1005 The feuds and friendships of birds (ἔχθραι τε καὶ στέργηθρα Aesch. *P. V.* 492) were among the signs noted by augurs. In this case there was a vague

omen of bloodshed (φοναῖς), but no clear sign. The seer now sought further light by another mode of divination.—ἐμπύρων, sc. ἱερῶν, burnt-sacrifice; where the omen was given by the manner in which the fire dealt with the offering. Eur. *Suppl.* 155 μάντεις δ' ἐπῆλθες, ἐμπύρων τ' εἶδες φλόγα; *Phoen.* 954 ἐμπύρῳ χρῆται τέχνῃ. *I. T.* 16 εἰς ἔμπυρ' ἦλθε (had recourse to). This was ἡ δι' ἐμπύρων μαντεία, *ignispicium*, while ἱεροσκοπία = *haruspicina*, divination by inspecting entrails. In Aesch. *P. V.*, 488—499, vv. 488—492 concern ὀρνιθομαντεία: vv. 493—5, ἱεροσκοπία: and vv. 496—9, ἔμπυρα.—ἐγευόμην, proceeded to make trial of: *Tr.* 1101 μόχθων μυρίων ἐγευσάμην: Plat. *Rep.* 475 c παντὸς μαθήματος γεύεσθαι.

1006 παμφλέκτοισι, fully kindled. Fuel was placed around the offerings on the altar, and ignited at several points. The epithet marks that the failure of the rite was not due to any negligence.—θυμάτων. The offering consisted of thigh-bones cut from a sheep (or ox), with some of the flesh adhering to them, and wrapped round with a double covering of fat. On the top of these thigh-bones were laid parts of the victim's intestines (σπλάγχνα), including the gall-bladder (χολή).

1007 Ἥφαιστος = πῦρ (n. on 120 ff.). It was a good sign if the fire at once seized on the offering, and blazed up in clear flames (Apoll. Rhod. 1. 436 σέλας... | πάντοσε λαμπόμενον θυέων ἄπο). It was

μυδῶσα κηκὶς μηρίων ἐτήκετο
κἄτυφε κἀνέπτυε, καὶ μετάρσιοι
χολαὶ διεσπείροντο, καὶ καταρρυεῖς   1010
μηροὶ καλυπτῆς ἐξέκειντο πιμελῆς.
τοιαῦτα παιδὸς τοῦδ' ἐμάνθανον πάρα
φθίνοντ' ἀσήμων ὀργίων μαντεύματα·
ἐμοὶ γὰρ οὗτος ἡγεμών, ἄλλοις δ' ἐγώ.
καὶ ταῦτα τῆς σῆς ἐκ φρενὸς νοσεῖ πόλις.   1015

1013 φθίνοντ'] Wecklein conject. φανέντ': Semitelos φανθέντα, with Nauck's
σεμνῶν for ἀσήμων.—μαντεύματα] Nauck μαγεύματα: M. Schmidt λατρεύματα.

a bad sign, if the fire was smothered in smoke, or played feebly around the flesh without consuming it. See Eur. *Ph.* 1255 μάντεις δὲ μῆλ' ἔσφαζον, ἐμπύρους τ' ἀκμὰς | ῥήξεις τ' ἐνώμων, ὑγρότητ' ἐναντίαν, | ἄκραν τε λαμπάδ', ἣ δυοῖν ὅρους ἔχει, | νίκης τε σῆμα καὶ τὸ τῶν ἡσσωμένων: the seers 'were watching for *points* of flame, or for *breaks* in it,—such flickering as portends evil'; *i.e.*, they were watching to see whether it would blaze up or die down. The ἄκρα λαμπάς is prob. the highest point of the fire, which, if towards the right side, meant victory; if towards the left, defeat. So Statius, *Theb.* 10. 599, where Teiresias offers ἔμπυρα, and his daughter reports the signs to him (as the παῖς does here): *Sanguineos flammarum apices* (=ἐμπύρους ἀκμάς) *geminumque per aras* | *Ignem, et clara tamen mediae fastigia lucis* (=ἄκραν λαμπάδα) | *Orta docet*: *tunc in speciem serpentis inanem* | *Ancipiti gyro volvi* ('as if creeping on its way without an aim, the fire played timidly around the offering'). In Seneca *Oed.* 307 Teiresias asks, *Quid flamma? Larga iamne comprendit dapes?* | *Utrumne clarus ignis et nitidus stetit,* | *Rectusque purum verticem caelo tulit,* | *An latera circum serpit incertus viae,* | *Et fluctuante turbidus fumo labat?*

1008 f. The fat wrapped about the thigh-bones ought to have caught fire, when the flesh on the bones would have been burned, and the bones themselves calcined. But here there was no flame; the kindled fuel lay in smouldering embers (σποδός). The heat caused a fatty moisture to exude from the covering of the thigh-bones. Trickling forth on the embers, this moisture emitted smoke, and sputtered as it threw particles

of the fat upwards. The gall-bladder, too, which lay on the top of the thigh-bones, instead of catching fire, was gradually inflated by the heat, till it burst, scattering the gall into the air. And now the melting of the fat which covered the thigh-bones had gone so far that it was no longer a covering, but merely a liquid that was streaming off them, while they themselves were left naked and intact. So utterly had the gods refused the offering.

μυδῶσα: cp. 410: *O. T.* 1278 φόνου μυδώσας σταγόνας.—**κηκὶς μηρίων**, a moisture exuding from them. For μηρία see on 1011. Cp. Aesch. *Cho.* 268 ἐν κηκῖδι πισσήρει φλογός, pitchy ooze of flame, *i.e.*, the funeral-fire of pine-wood from which pitch oozes. We might perh. join μηρίων ἐτήκετο, 'was distilled from them': but the other constr. is simpler, and τήκεσθαί τινος is not found elsewhere.—**ἐτήκετο** here=exuded: it goes with ἐπὶ σποδῷ (the embers of the fuel placed around the offering).—**ἀνέπτυε**, as particles of the fat crackled and were tossed upward on contact with the smouldering fire.

1010 χολαί. Arist. always uses the sing. χολή for the gall-bladder. In Plat. *Tim.* 82 E χολάς= 'kinds of bile,' the χολῆς εἴδη of 83 C. Here there was a metrical motive (διεσπείροντο) for the plur., which denotes not merely the gall-bladder, but also the gall dispersed from it. The gall-bladder, and the lobe of the liver, afforded omens, by colour and form, in ἱεροσκοπία (1005 n.): Aesch. *P. V.* 495 χολῆς λοβοῦ τε ποικίλην εὐμορφίαν: cp. Eur. *El.* 827 ff. But here, in ἔμπυρα, the χολή was simply a part of the burnt-offering,—added to the μηρία, because otherwise associated with divinaa dank moisture, oozing from the thigh-flesh, trickled forth upon the embers, and smoked, and sputtered; the gall was scattered to the air; and the streaming thighs lay bared of the fat that had been wrapped round them.

Such was the failure of the rites by which I vainly asked a sign, as from this boy I learned; for he is my guide, as I am guide to others. And 'tis thy counsel that hath brought this sickness on our state.

1015 ταῦτα had been omitted in L, but the first hand has added it above the line.

---

tion. Cp. the unknown poet in Clemens Alex. *Strom.* p. 851 (it is vain to think that the gods rejoice) ὀστῶν ἀσάρκων καὶ χολῆς πυρουμένης. So, too, Menander *ap.* Athen. 146 E οἱ δὲ τὴν ὀσφὺν ἄκραν | καὶ τὴν χολὴν ὀστᾶ τ' ἄβρωτα τοῖς θεοῖς | ἐπιθέντες αὐτοὶ τἆλλα καταπίνουσ' ἀεί.

καταρρυεῖς, running down, dripping, with the fat which was melting off them: Schol. καταρρεόμενοι, καθυγραινόμενοι. This use of the adj. is parallel with a frequent use of the verb, as Eur. *Tro.* 15 θεῶν ἀνάκτορα | φόνῳ καταρρεῖ: *Il.* 8. 65 ῥέε δ' αἵματι γαῖα: Eur. *Bacch.* 142 ῥεῖ δὲ γάλακτι πέδον, etc.—καταρρυεῖς could also mean, 'slipping down'; but it does not appear that the μηροί were displaced; they were merely bared.

1011 μηροί = μηρίων in 1008,—thigh-bones, with some flesh on them. μηρός is the ordinary word for 'thigh.' μηρία was the sacrificial word, denoting thigh-bones, with so much flesh as the sacrificer chose to leave upon them. The tendency to give the gods more bone than meat is noticed by the poets quoted on v. 1010 (ὀστῶν ἀσάρκων—ὀστᾶ ἄβρωτα), and by Hes. *Th.* 556 (where men offer ὀστέα λευκά to the gods),—as it is implied in the story there told, of Prometheus giving the worst parts of the ox to Zeus, and keeping the best for men. Since the bone was an essential part of the offering, μηρία cannot be merely, 'slices cut from the thighs.' In the Homeric phrase, κατὰ πίονα μηρία καίειν, the word means, like μηροί here, thigh-bones wrapped in fat, the κνίσῃ... κῶλα συγκαλυπτά of Aesch. *P. V.* 496. In *Od.* 3. 456 ἐκ μηρία τάμνον | πάντα κατὰ μοῖραν, the phrase is equiv. to the μηροὺς ἐξέταμον of the *Il.* (1. 460 etc.); *i.e.*, μηρία includes the bones. Only one ox is there in question, but πάντα = 'completely.' The Hom. μῆρα = μηρία (*Il.*

1. 464).—**καλυπτῆς** = 'which had been wrapped round them'; cp. *Il.* 21. 321 τόσσην οἱ ἄσιν καθύπερθε καλύψω, 'so thick a covering of silt will I lay on him.' This is better than to make the adj. active, 'covering,' like μεμπτός, 'blaming' (*Tr.* 446: cp. *O. T.* 969 n.). —**πιμελῆς** (πίων), prop., soft fat (*adeps*), as dist. from στέαρ, stiff fat, tallow (*sebum*). The fat was laid in a double layer round the μηρία: *Il.* 1. 460 μηρούς τ' ἐξέταμον κατά τε κνίσῃ ἐκάλυψαν, | δίπτυχα ποιήσαντες. So human bones are wrapped δίπλακι δημῷ, *Il.* 23. 243.— **ἐξέκειντο**, lay outside of, *i.e.*, had been bared of, the fat.

1012 f. τοιαῦτα, adverbially with φθίνοντα: cp. 848 οἷα n.—**ὀργίων μαντεύματα**, 'oracles derived from rites,' —the predictions which he could have made if the rites had given him a sign. They gave none; and so his hopes of reading the future came to nought (**φθίνοντα**: cp. *O. T.* 906 φθίνοντα... | θέσφατα). Cp. *Tr.* 765 (where Heracles offers burnt sacrifice) ὅπως δὲ σεμνῶν ὀργίων ἐδαίετο | φλὸξ αἱματηρά.—**ἀσήμων**, not giving the φλογωπὰ σήματα (Aesch. *P. V.* 498) which burnt offerings can yield. Such signs might be good or evil, according to the aspects of the fire (cp. 1007 n.). But here the fire had refused to burn at all. Like the birds, these rites also had left him without any definite sign—though with a strengthened presentiment of evil.

1014 ἡγεμών. Cp. Statius *Theb.* 10. 603: the daughter of Teiresias describes the omens to him, *patriasque illuminat umbras.*

1015 ἐκ, of cause, as *O. C.* 620 ἐκ σμικροῦ λόγου. Cp. 957, 973.—**φρενός**, counsel, as 993.—**νοσεῖ**, *i.e.*, has incurred a μίασμα: cp. 1141.

βωμοὶ γὰρ ἡμῖν ἐσχάραι τε παντελεῖς
πλήρεις ὑπ᾽ οἰωνῶν τε καὶ κυνῶν βορᾶς
τοῦ δυσμόρου πεπτῶτος Οἰδίπου γόνου.
κᾆτ᾽ οὐ δέχονται θυστάδας λιτὰς ἔτι
θεοὶ παρ᾽ ἡμῶν οὐδὲ μηρίων φλόγα,   1020
οὐδ᾽ ὄρνις εὐσήμους ἀπορροιβδεῖ βοάς,
ἀνδροφθόρου βεβρῶτες αἵματος λίπος.
ταῦτ᾽ οὖν, τέκνον, φρόνησον. ἀνθρώποισι γὰρ
τοῖς πᾶσι κοινόν ἐστι τοὐξαμαρτάνειν·
ἐπεὶ δ᾽ ἁμάρτῃ, κεῖνος οὐκέτ᾽ ἔστ᾽ ἀνὴρ   1025
ἄβουλος οὐδ᾽ ἄνολβος, ὅστις ἐς κακὸν
πεσὼν ἀκεῖται μηδ᾽ ἀκίνητος πέλει.
αὐθαδία τοι σκαιότητ᾽ ὀφλισκάνει.
ἀλλ᾽ εἶκε τῷ θανόντι, μηδ᾽ ὀλωλότα

1016 f. παντελεῖς] In L εἰ has been made from η: over which ει had been written. So in 1017 πλήρεις from πλήρης. **1021** εὐσήμους] In L there has been an erasure of two (or three) letters after εὐ. Nauck conj. οὐδ᾽ αἰσίους ῥοιβδοῦσιν ὄρνιθες βοάς. **1022** λίπος] Blomfield conject. λίβος.—Blaydes proposes (inter alia) ἀνδρ. βεβρῶτα σώματος λίπος, with ὄρνε᾽ in 1021. **1025** ἁμάρτηι L:

1016 βωμοί, the public altars of the gods, usu. raised on a base (κρηπίς) with steps (cp. 854, *O. T.* 182).—ἐσχάραι, portable braziers, used in private houses either for sacrifice to household deities (esp. Ἑστία), or for purposes of cooking. Harpocration *s.v.* quotes Ammonius of Lamprae (an Attic writer of the 1st cent. A.D., who left a treatise Περὶ βωμῶν καὶ θυσιῶν):—ἐσχάραν φησὶ καλεῖσθαι τὴν μὴ ἔχουσαν ὕψος,...ἀλλ᾽ ἐπὶ γῆς ἱδρυμένην. It stood on four legs, instead of having a pedestal like the βωμός (Ross *Inscr.* 3. 52 ἐσχάραν τετράποδον). It was used in sacrifice to the ἥρωες, who, not being θεοί, had no claim to βωμοί: Pollux 1. 8 ἐσχάρα δ᾽ ἰδικῶς δοκεῖ ὠνομάσθαι, ἐφ᾽ ἧς τοῖς ἥρωσιν ἀποθύομεν.—παντελεῖς, in their full tale, 'one and all.' So ὁλόκληροι or ὁλοσχερεῖς could be used, where the notion was that of a total to which no unit was lacking.—Not, 'receiving ἱερὰ τέλεια'; nor, 'serving for all rites' (τέλη).

1017 f. πλήρεις (εἰσὶν) are defiled, ὑπ᾽ οἰων. κ. κυνῶν, by birds and dogs, βορᾶς τοῦ...Οἰδ. γόνου, with their food, (torn) from the son of Oed. This sense of πλήρης belongs also to πλέως and μεστός, but esp. to ἀνάπλεως, as to ἀναπίμπλημι. The fig. sense of πλήρεις might

here allow us to take ὑπό with βορᾶς, but it goes more naturally with the agents. For the gen. γόνου, describing the source or material of the βορά, cp. Aesch. *Ag.* 1220 κρεῶν...οἰκείας βορᾶς, food supplied by their own flesh (οἰκείας instead of οἰκείων: cp. above, 793). δυσμόρου, adverbially with πεπτῶτος, instead of δυσμόρως: cp. 823 λυγροτάταν ὀλέσθαι, n. —Two other constructions are possible. (1) τοῦ...γόνου in appos. with βορᾶς: 'their food,—viz., the son': cp. 1040 βορὰν | φέρειν νιν. But this seems forced, when the reference is to dispersed morsels of his flesh. (2) τοῦ...γόνου as gen. absol., 'as,' or 'since,' he has fallen. Such a gen. absol., however, ought here to express, not, 'as he has fallen,' but, 'as he has been left unburied.'

1019 κᾆτ᾽, 'and then,' here='and so.' It usually means, 'and after that,' *i.e.*, 'and nevertheless' (*O. C.* 418).—θυστάδας, accompanying sacrifice: Aesch. *Theb.* 269 Ἑλληνικὸν νόμισμα θυστάδος βοῆς. Cp. *Il.* 9. 499 καὶ μὲν τοὺς (the gods) θυέεσσι καὶ εὐχωλῇς ἀγανῇσιν | λοιβῇ τε κνίσῃ τε παρατρωπῶσ᾽ ἄνθρωποι | λισσόμενοι.

1021 f. ὄρνυς, as *Il.* 24. 219; *El.* 149; Eur. *H. F.* 72, fr. 637: Ar. *Av.*

For the altars of our city and of our hearths have been tainted, one and all, by birds and dogs, with carrion from the hapless corpse, the son of Oedipus: and therefore the gods no more accept prayer and sacrifice at our hands, or the flame of meat-offering; nor doth any bird give a clear sign by its shrill cry, for they have tasted the fatness of a slain man's blood.

Think, then, on these things, my son. All men are liable to err; but when an error hath been made, that man is no longer witless or unblest who heals the ill into which he hath fallen, and remains not stubborn. Self-will, we know, incurs the charge of folly. Nay, allow the claim of the dead; stab not the

---

ἁμάρτοι Γ.—οὐκ ἔστ' L: οὐκέτ' ἔστ' Γ.   **1027** ἀκεῖται MSS. ἀκῆται Wunder.—
ἀΐνητος L: ἀκίνητος Γ.   Blaydes conject.   ἀνίκητος or ἀνίατος: M. Schmidt, ἀνή-
κεστος.—πέλει L, with η written above by the first hand.   **1029** τῷ θανόντι]
Heimsoeth conject. τῷ δέοντι: Nauck, τῷ φρενοῦντι: Wecklein, νουθετοῦντι:

---

168 (v. l. τίς ὄρνις οὗτος, a quotation from tragedy: v. l. τίς οὗτος ὄρνις;). But ὄρνῖς (Eur. *Bacch.* 1364, Ar. *Av.* 833, etc.) is said to have been normal in Attic. —The ruggedness of the rhythm gives a certain impressive slowness, perhaps purposed. When an iambic verse has no caesura in the 3rd or in the 4th foot, it almost always has the 'quasi-caesura' (elision) after the 3rd foot (as if εὐσήμους were εὐφημοῦσ'). For other exceptions, cp. *Ai.* 1091 Μενέλαε, μὴ γνώμας ὑπο-στήσας σοφάς: *Ph.* 101, 1064, 1369: Aesch. *Pers.* 509 Θρῆκην περάσαντες μόγις πολλῷ πόνῳ.—**εὐσήμους:** cp. on 1002.—**βεβρῶτες,** as if πάντες ὄρνιθες σιγῶσι had preceded. Cp. Her. 1. 87 ὡς ὥρα πάντα μὲν ἄνδρα σβεννύντα τὸ πῦρ, δυναμένους δὲ οὐκέτι καταλαβεῖν.—**ἀνδροφθόρου.** ἀν-δρόφθορον αἷμα=ἀνδρὸς ἐφθαρμένου αἷμα: cp. *Ph.* 208 αὐδὰ τρυσάνωρ: *O.C.* 711, n. on αὔχημα εὔιππον.
1025 f. **ἐπεί,** instead of ἐπάν, with subjunct.: *O.C.* 1225. The subject to ἁμάρτῃ (ἀνήρ, or τις) is quickly supplied by the next clause.—**ἄνολβος,** of folly, as *Ai.* 1156: so δύσποτμος, *O.T.* 888.
1027 ἀκεῖται. *Il.* 13. 115 ἀλλ' ἀκεώ-μεθα θᾶσσον· ἀκεσταί τοι φρένες ἐσθλῶν.— **ἀκίνητος:** cp. *O.T.* 336 ἄτεγκτος. Plat. *Tim.* 51 E τὸ μὲν ἀεὶ μετὰ ἀληθοῦς λόγου, τὸ δὲ ἄλογον· καὶ τὸ μὲν ἀκίνητον πειθοῖ, τὸ δὲ μεταπειστόν. *Il.* 15. 203 ἦ τι μετα-στρέψεις; στρεπταὶ μέν τε φρένες ἐσθλῶν.
1028 **αὐθαδία** (poet. for αὐθάδεια), self-will, incurs the reproach of σκαιότης (for ὀφλισκάνει cp. 470). As δεξιός is a

quick-witted man, of flexible and receptive mind, so σκαιός is one whose mental clum-siness makes him unapt to learn. σκαιότης, 'ineptitude,' is often associated with igno-rance and with inaccessibility to new ideas. Cp. Plat. *Rep.* 411 E; one who omits to cultivate his mind acts βίᾳ...καὶ ἀγριότητι, ὥσπερ θηρίον..., καὶ ἐν ἀμαθίᾳ καὶ σκαιό-τητι μετὰ ἀρρυθμίας τε καὶ ἀχαριστίας ζῇ. Lys. or. 10 § 15 ἡγοῦμαι...τοῦτον...οὕτω σκαιὸν εἶναι ὥστε οὐ δύνασθαι μαθεῖν τὰ λεγόμενα. Ar. *Vesp.* 1183 ὦ σκαιὲ κά-παίδευτε. So here σκαιότης expresses a stupidity that is deaf to remonstrance.
1029 f. **εἶκε τῷ θανόντι,** 'make a concession to the dead,' i.e., give him the burial rites which are his due. It is not as if he were a living foe, and prowess (ἀλκή) could be shown by resisting his claim. The words τῷ θανόντι have been groundlessly suspected (see cr. n.).— **κέντει,** stab. Cp. the scene in the *Iliad* where the Greeks prick Hector's corpse with their swords: *Il.* 22. 371 οὐδ' ἄρα οἵ τις ἀνουτητί γε παρέστη: and ib. 24. 421. For κεντεῖν of cowardly or treacherous wounding, cp. *Ai.* 1244 ἡμᾶς ἢ κακοῖς βαλεῖτέ που | ἢ σὺν δόλῳ κεντήσεθ' οἱ λελειμμένοι.—**ἐπικτανεῖν,** 'slay anew.' In comp. with verbs of killing, ἐπί usu.= either 'in addition' (*O.C.* 1733 ἐπενά-ριξον, n.), or 'over' a grave, etc., as usu. ἐπισφάττειν: but cp. 1288: Diog. Laert. 2. 17 § 135 (Menedemus) Βίωνος...ἐπιμε-λῶς κατατρέχοντος τῶν μάντεων νεκροὺς αὐτὸς ἐπισφάττειν ἔλεγε. Cp. *Ph.* 946 ἐναίρων νεκρόν.

κέντει. τίς ἀλκὴ τὸν θανόντ' ἐπικτανεῖν;   1030
εὖ σοι φρονήσας εὖ λέγω· τὸ μανθάνειν δ'
ἥδιστον εὖ λέγοντος, εἰ κέρδος λέγοι.

ΚΡ. ὦ πρέσβυ, πάντες ὥστε τοξόται σκοποῦ
τοξεύετ' ἀνδρὸς τοῦδε, κοὐδὲ μαντικῆς
ἄπρακτος ὑμῖν εἰμι, τῶν δ' ὑπαὶ γένους   1035
ἐξημπόλημαι κἀμπεφόρτισμαι πάλαι.
κερδαίνετ', ἐμπολᾶτε τἀπὸ Σάρδεων
ἤλεκτρον, εἰ βούλεσθε, καὶ τὸν Ἰνδικὸν
χρυσόν· τάφῳ δ' ἐκεῖνον οὐχὶ κρύψετε,
οὐδ' εἰ θέλουσ' οἱ Ζηνὸς αἰετοὶ βορὰν   1040

Semitelos, θεσπίζοντι. **1030** ἐπικτανεῖν] The first hand in L had inadvertently
written some other and longer word beginning with ἐπι-. κτανεῖν is in an erasure,
which extends beyond it to the space of four or five letters. **1031 f.** μανθάνειν |
δ' ἥδιστον L. **1034 f.** κοὐδὲ μαντικῆς | ἄπρακτος ὑμῖν εἰμι τῶν δ' ὑπαὶ
γένους MSS. (ὕμιν L). See comment. **1036** κἀμπεφόρτισμαι L, with κ written
above μ by an early hand. The later MSS. are divided between κἀμ- and κἀκ-:
A has the latter. **1037** τὰ προ σάρδεων L, with ὸν above τὰ from the first

---

1031 f. εὖ φρονήσας, having conceived kindly thoughts; a very rare use
of the aor. part. in this sense, instead of
εὖ φρονῶν. The aor. part. of φρονέω usu.
means, (1) 'having come to a sound
mind,' *O. T.* 649, and so Isocr. or. 8.
§ 141, εὖ φρονήσαντας: (2) 'having formed
a project,' as Her. 7. 145: (3) in the
phrase τὠυτὸ (or τὰ αὐτὰ) φρονήσαντες,
'having come to an agreement,' Her. 1.
60, 5. 72.—μανθάνειν δ': for the elision
(ἐπισυναλοιφή) see *O. T.* 29 n.: and cp.
above, 350.—εἰ...λέγοι: for the optative
in the γνώμη, see 666 n. With ἥδιστον
we supply ἐστί, as in *O. T.* 315.
1033 ὥστε = ὡς: *O. C.* 343.—σκοποῦ,
sc. τοξεύουσι: the gen. as with στοχάζομαι:
so *Il.* 4. 100 ὀϊστεύσον Μενελάου: 14. 402
Αἴαντος δὲ πρῶτος ἀκόντισε. Cp. 241.
1034 f. κοὐδὲ μαντικῆς κ.τ.λ.: not
even by seer-craft do ye leave me unat-
tempted: in your plots against me ye
resort even to seer-craft. Two points in
this phrase are notable. (1) ἄπρακτος
= 'not worked,' in the sense of, 'not
plotted against.' πράσσειν oft. = 'to intrigue'; and 'to intrigue *against* one'
might be expressed by πράσσειν περί τινος,
or ἐπί τινι, though ἐπιβουλεύω τινί is the
usu. phrase. But, while ἐπιβουλεύομαι
had a personal pass. use ('to be plotted
against'), we could not say πράσσονται,

'they are the objects of an intrigue.'
ἄπρακτος is therefore bolder than its prose
equivalent, ἀνεπιβούλευτος. Still, for
poetry, it seems possible. (2) μαντικῆς.
Such a gen., joined to a verbal adj. with
α privative, more often denotes the agent,
answering to a gen. with ὑπό after a pass.
verb, or to the subject of an act. verb:
cp. 847: *Tr.* 685 ἀκτῖνος...ἄθικτον (untouched *by* the ray). Here, the instrument, μαντική, is, in fact, personified as
the agent: *i.e.*, μαντικῆς does not correspond to the instrum. dat. in καὶ μαντικῇ
πράσσετε περὶ ἐμοῦ, but to the nom. in
καὶ μαντικὴ πράσσει περὶ ἐμοῦ ὑμῖν (ye
have even seer-craft practising on me).
An easier reading would be μαντικῇ.
The instrumental dat. is often retained
with the negative verbal; as Plat. *Symp.*
219 E χρήμασι...μᾶλλον ἄτρωτος ἢ σιδήρῳ:
fr. com. anon. 52 ἀνεπιβουλεύτου φθόνῳ.
But poetical usage seems to warrant
μαντικῆς.—The conjecture ἄπρατος (see
Appendix) would forestall the taunt
which now forms the climax, ἐξημπόλημαι.

τῶν δ' ὑπαὶ γένους, 'by the tribe
of those men.'—the μάντεις implied in
μαντικῆς. Creon, though he addresses
Teiresias, is speaking as much to the
Chorus as to him. If we read τῶν (without δ'), as relative, it would naturally

fallen; what prowess is it to slay the slain anew? I have sought
thy good, and for thy good I speak: and never is it sweeter
to learn from a good counsellor than when he counsels for thine
own gain.

CR. Old man, ye all shoot your shafts at me, as archers at
the butts;—ye must needs practise on me with seer-craft also;—
aye, the seer-tribe hath long trafficked in me, and made me their
merchandise. Gain your gains, drive your trade, if ye list, in the
silver-gold of Sardis and the gold of India; but ye shall not hide
that man in the grave,—no, though the eagles of Zeus should

hand. Notwithstanding the space after προ, the scribe may have meant προ-
σάρδεων to be one word, as it is in the lemma of the schol. But it is also possible
that he merely forgot to accent πρό. Some of the later MSS. have τὸν πρὸ σάρδεων
(as Vat.), others τὸν πρὸς σάρδεων (as A). Eustathius (p. 368. 30, 1483. 27) reads
τὸν πρὸς Σάρδεων, which Brunck gave. Musgrave defended τὸν πρὸ Σάρδεων.
Blaydes and Nauck restored τἀπὸ Σάρδεων.   **1038** βούλεσθε made from βού-
λεσθαι L.   **1040** οὐδ' εἰ] οὐ δὴ L.

---

refer to ὑμῖν: it could hardly refer to
μαντικῆς. The conjecture of Semitelos,
μαντικοῖς, would then be attractive. But
such a substitute for μάντεσι would be very
strange. And, if we keep L's τῶν δ', the
scornful demonstrative sufficiently interprets the reference to μάντεις.—ὑπαί in trimeters, as El. 711: Aesch. Ag. 892, 944,
Eum. 417.—γένους: cp. 1055.—For
other views of the passage, see Appendix.

1036 ἐξημπόλημαι. Creon means:
'The Thebans have bribed Teiresias to
frighten me. He has taken their money.
In return, he is to deliver me into their
hands. I am like a piece of merchandise
which has been sold for export, and put
on board the buyer's ship.' Cp. 1063.
Her. 1. 1 ἐξεμπολημένων (Ion.) σφι σχεδὸν
πάντων, when they had sold off almost
everything.—Neither ἐμφορτίζομαι nor ἐκ-
φορτίζομαι occurs elsewhere, except that
an old glossary (cited by Dind.) gives
ἐξεφορτίσατο, exoneravit ('unladed'). In
later Greek we find ἐμφοροῦσθαι ναῦν, ἔμ-
φορτος, and ἐκφορτοῦν (both act. and midd.).
Here, ἐμπεφόρτισμαι, the reading of the
first hand in L, marks the completion of
the sale by the delivery of the goods.
The Schol. quotes Callimachus (fr. 529),
ἐποιήσαντό με φόρτον.—The correction in
L, ἐκπεφόρτισμαι, is far inferior. It
would mean, 'unladed (as a cargo) from
a ship': not, 'made into a cargo,' nor,
'exported as a cargo.'—In Tr. 537 there
is a like association of ἐμπόλημα and
φόρτος (though the passage is not other-

wise similar). Cp. Shaks. Com. Err. 3.
1. 72 'It would make a man mad as a
buck, to be so bought and sold.'

1037 f. τἀπὸ Σάρδεων ἤλεκτρον:
electron, or silver-gold, from the gold-
mines of Tmolus in Lydia, the range s.
of Sardis. Croesus dedicated at Delphi
a lion of refined gold (χρυσὸς ἄπεφθος),
standing on a pedestal formed by 117
half-plinths, or ingots, of gold,—four
being of refined gold, and the rest of this
electron, or 'white gold' (λευκὸς χρυσός);
Her. 1. 50. The celebrity of this ἀνάθημα in Greece helps to explain the poet's
phrase. Stein on Her. l. c. shows that
the ratio of silver to gold in electron was
about 3 to 7. Pliny, who makes the
ratio only 1 to 4, describes electron both
as a natural blend of metals, and as an
artificial product (fit et cura,...addito ar-
gento, 33. 80).—Paus. 5. 12 § 7 distinguishes
the two senses of ἤλεκτρον, (1) silver-gold,
(2) amber. The latter is the ἤλεκτρον of
Herodotus (3. 115), and of Od. 15. 460,
where a Phoenician brings a golden ὅρμος,
—μετὰ δ' ἠλέκτροισιν ἔερτο ('strung with
amber beads').—τἀπὸ is a certain correction of L's τὰ προ (cr. n.): in class.
Greek ἤλεκτρον is always neut., as it is in
Paus. also.—'Ινδικὸν χρυσόν: Her. 3.
94 speaks of the 'Ινδοί as sending Dareius
an annual tribute of 360 talents in gold
dust (ψῆγμα).

1040 οἱ Ζηνὸς αἰετοί: Il. 24. 310 ὅς
τε σοὶ αὐτῷ | φίλτατος οἰωνῶν, καὶ εὐ
κράτος ἐστὶ μέγιστον. Pind. P. 4. 4 (the

φέρειν νιν ἁρπάζοντες ἐς Διὸς θρόνους,
οὐδ᾽ ὡς μίασμα τοῦτο μὴ τρέσας ἐγὼ
θάπτειν παρήσω κεῖνον· εὖ γὰρ οἶδ᾽ ὅτι
θεοὺς μιαίνειν οὔτις ἀνθρώπων σθένει.
πίπτουσι δ᾽, ὦ γεραιὲ Τειρεσία, βροτῶν   1045
χοἰ πολλὰ δεινοὶ πτώματ᾽ αἴσχρ᾽, ὅταν λόγους
αἰσχροὺς καλῶς λέγωσι τοῦ κέρδους χάριν.

ΤΕ. φεῦ·
      ἆρ᾽ οἶδεν ἀνθρώπων τις, ἆρα φράζεται

ΚΡ. τί χρῆμα; ποῖον τοῦτο πάγκοινον λέγεις;

ΤΕ. ὅσῳ κράτιστον κτημάτων εὐβουλία;   1050

ΚΡ. ὅσῳπερ, οἶμαι, μὴ φρονεῖν πλείστη βλάβη.

ΤΕ. ταύτης σὺ μέντοι τῆς νόσου πλήρης ἔφυς.

ΚΡ. οὐ βούλομαι τὸν μάντιν ἀντειπεῖν κακῶς.

ΤΕ. καὶ μὴν λέγεις, ψευδῆ με θεσπίζειν λέγων.

ΚΡ. τὸ μαντικὸν γὰρ πᾶν φιλάργυρον γένος.   1055

ΤΕ. τὸ δ᾽ ἐκ τυράννων αἰσχροκέρδειαν φιλεῖ.

1042 f. ὡς] ὡσ L.—τοῦτο μὴ τρέσας] Nauck conject. τοῦτο ταρβήσας. Blaydes, τοῦτο δὴ τρέσας, if παρήσω be kept: but he gives τοῦτο μὴ τρέσας .. παρῶ τῳ (his own conject.). **1046** After αἴσχρ᾽ two letters have been erased in L: the first

---

Delphian priestess) χρυσέων Διὸς αἰητῶν πάρεδρος (the golden eagles on the ὀμφαλός). Hor. *Carm.* 4. 4. 1 *ministrum fulminis alitem.*

1042 f. οὐδ᾽ ὥς, not even (I say) in that case,—repeating the supposition, ‹ὐδ᾽ εἰ θέλουσ᾽. Cp. *Il.* 9. 379 ff. οὐδ᾽ εἴ μοι δεκάκις τε καὶ εἰκοσάκις τόσα δοίη, | ... οὐδέ κεν ὡς ἔτι θυμὸν ἐμὸν πείσει᾽ Ἀγαμέμνων. *Od.* 22. 61 ff. οὐδ᾽ εἴ μοι πατρῷα πάντ᾽ ἀποδοῖτε | ...οὐδέ κεν ὡς ἔτι χεῖρας ἐμὰς λήξαιμι φόνοιο.—Attic prose, too, used καὶ ὥς, 'even in that case' (Thuc. 1. 44), οὐδ᾽ ὥς (id. 1. 132), etc.—**παρήσω.** οὐ μή, with the 2nd pers. fut. ind., prohibits; but with the 1st or 3rd pers. it can be used in emphatic denial, though the aor. subjunct. is more usual: *El.* 1052 οὔ σοι μὴ μεθέψομαί ποτε: see n. on *O. C.* 177. There is no reason, then, for suspecting the text (see cr. n.).

1044 θεοὺς μιαίνειν. Teiresias had said that the altars were defiled (1016). Creon replies that he will not yield, even if birds fly with the carrion up to the very throne of Zeus;—'*for no mortal can pollute the gods.*' Campbell takes this to be an utterance of scepticism,

like οὐκ ἔφα τις | θεοὺς βροτῶν ἀξιοῦσθαι μέλειν (Aesch. *Ag.* 369),—anticipating the Epicurean conception of gods who are neither pleased nor angered by men.

This view seems to do some injustice to the poet's dramatic psychology. I read the words quite differently. The most orthodox Greek piety held that 'no mortal could pollute the gods.' See, for example, Eur. *H. F.* 1232. Heracles, having recovered sanity after slaying his children, has covered his face, to hide it from the holy light of the sun. Theseus —who is a type of normal εὐσέβεια— makes him uncover, saying,—τί δ᾽; οὐ μιαίνεις θνητὸς ὢν τὰ τῶν θεῶν. The sun-god cannot be polluted by a mortal. The idea of religious μίασμα was that a mortal had contracted some impurity which disqualified him for communion with the gods. The tainting of an altar cut off such communion by bringing uncleanness to the very place where men sought to be cleansed. Creon excitedly imagines a seemingly worse profanation, and then excuses his apparent impiety by a general maxim which all would admit:—'no man can pollute the gods.'

bear the carrion morsels to their Master's throne—no, not for
dread of that defilement will I suffer his burial:—for well
I know that no mortal can defile the gods.—But, aged Teiresias,
the wisest fall with a shameful fall, when they clothe shameful
thoughts in fair words, for lucre's sake.

TE. Alas! doth any man know, doth any consider...
CR. Whereof? What general truth dost thou announce?
TE. How precious, above all wealth, is good counsel?
CR. As folly, I think, is the worst mischief.
TE. Yet thou art tainted with that distemper.
CR. I would not answer the seer with a taunt.
TE. But thou dost, in saying that I prophesy falsely.
CR. Well, the prophet-tribe was ever fond of money.
TE. And the race bred of tyrants loves base gain.

---

hand had written αἰσχράν.   **1049** χρῆμα] Nauck conject. γνῶμα or ῥῆμα.
1051 πλείστη] πλείστηι L, made from πλήστηι.   **1053** ἀντ' εἰπεῖν L.
1054 λέγων] λέγειν L, with ω written above by the first hand. Cp. *O. T.* 360.
1056 τὸ δ' ἐκ] Hartung conject. τὸ δ' αὖ: Bischopp and Seyffert, τὸ δέ γε.

'The sky-throne of Zeus is still more
sacred than his altar on earth: if defilement cannot reach him there, much less
here.' The sophism is of the kind with
which an honest but stubborn and wrong-
headed man might seek to quiet his
conscience. Creon reveres Zeus (304):
he feels for the majesty of the gods, and
refuses to believe that they can honour
the wicked (284 ff.). But his religious
sense is temporarily confused by his anger.
1046 πολλά, adv., = 'very,' with adj.:
O. C. 1514 n.
1047 καλῶς, = εὐπρεπῶς, in a bad
sense: Eur. *Hipp.* 505 τᾷσχρὰ δ' ἦν
λέγῃς καλῶς: Thuc. 5. 89 μετ' ὀνομάτων
καλῶν. So Eur. *Hec.* 1191 τἆδικ' εὖ
λέγειν: cp. *O. C.* 807.
1048 ἆρ' οἶδεν κ.τ.λ. Instead of
being angered by Creon's bitter words,
Teiresias is communing with the mournful
thought which they suggest—the thought
of human folly. His sorrowful exclamation here is like his πάντες γὰρ οὐ φρονεῖτ'
in the scene with Oedipus (*O. T.* 328).
1049 τί χρῆμα; Cp. Eur. *Hec.* 754
(Hecuba having said, ἱκετεύω,) ΑΓ. τί
χρῆμα μαστεύουσα; So oft. in questions,
as *Ai.* 228, *Ph.* 1231.—πάγκοινον, a
sneer at the generality of the seer's
exordium. What aphorism is this to be?
But the seer's thought has a terribly
definite point, as Creon is soon to feel
(1066).

1050 f. κτημάτων: cp. 684.—ὅσῳπερ
with superl., as *O. C.* 743 n. By μὴ
φρονεῖν Creon hints that the seer's clever-
ness has outrun his prudence (1046).
1052 νόσου: cp. 732: πλήρης, 1017.
1053 In ἀντειπεῖν κακῶς, ἀντί qualifies the whole phrase: *i.e.*, it means, 'to
revile in return,' ἀντιλοιδορεῖν, as ἀντι-
δρᾶν κακῶς (*O. C.* 1191) = ἀνταδικεῖν.
1054 καὶ μήν, 'and verily,' meaning
here, 'and *yet*,'—the adversative force
arising from the contrast between Creon's
profession and his practice. Cp. 221.—
λέγεις, *sc.* κακῶς τὸν μάντιν.—For the
metre, cp. 44, 502.
1055 γένος: 1035. Cp. Eur. *I. A.*
520 τὸ μαντικὸν πᾶν σπέρμα φιλότιμον
κακόν. *Helen.* 755 (of μαντική), βίου γὰρ
ἄλλως δέλεαρ ηὑρέθη τόδε, | κοὐδεὶς ἐπλού-
τησ' ἐμπύροισιν ἀργὸς ὤν,—*i.e.*, the seer's
client is never enriched (though the seer
himself is).
1056 τὸ δ' ἐκ τυράννων. The text is
sound. Instead of saying, 'the race of
tyrants' (*i.e.*, all the tyrants who exist),
he says, with more rhetorical force, 'the
race *bred* of tyrants,' *i.e.*, the tyrants
whose progenitors have also been tyrants.
Thus ἐκ expresses that the love of 'base
gain' is hereditary. For τύραννος in the
bad sense, see *O. T.* 873 n.—αἰσχροκέρδειαν: not in the literal sense in which
Creon imputed it to his servants (313),
but in this, that Creon secures an **un-**

ΚΡ. ἆρ' οἶσθα ταγοὺς ὄντας ἂν λέγῃς λέγων;
ΤΕ. οἶδ'· ἐξ ἐμοῦ γὰρ τήνδ' ἔχεις σώσας πόλιν.
ΚΡ. σοφὸς σὺ μάντις, ἀλλὰ τἀδικεῖν φιλῶν.
ΤΕ. ὄρσεις με τἀκίνητα διὰ φρενῶν φράσαι.   1060
ΚΡ. κίνει, μόνον δὲ μὴ 'πὶ κέρδεσιν λέγων.
ΤΕ. οὕτω γὰρ ἤδη καὶ δοκῶ τὸ σὸν μέρος.
ΚΡ. ὡς μὴ 'μπολήσων ἴσθι τὴν ἐμὴν φρένα.
ΤΕ. ἀλλ' εὖ γέ τοι κάτισθι μὴ πολλοὺς ἔτι
τρόχους ἁμιλλητῆρας ἡλίου τελῶν,   1065
ἐν οἷσι τῶν σῶν αὐτὸς ἐκ σπλάγχνων ἕνα

1057 λέγησ L, from λέγεισ. (The first hand has merely added strokes, denoting η, to the contracted character for ει, instead of altering the latter.)—λέγων] Keck conject. ψέγων.   **1061** μόνον δὲ μὴ 'πὶ] μόνον δ' ἐπὶ L, with μὴ written above ἐπὶ by first hand.   **1062** The first hand in L had placed a full stop at μέρος.   The first

---

worthy personal triumph by trampling on religion and silencing just remonstrance (505 ff.). Cp. *Ai.* 1349 μὴ χαῖρ', 'Ατρείδη, κέρδεσιν τοῖς μὴ καλοῖς.

1057 f. ἆρ' οἶσθα λέγων ταγοὺς ὄντας ἃ ἂν λέγῃς; knowest thou that whatever it pleases thee to say is said of men who are rulers? λέγω τινά τι=to say something *of* him. ἃ ἂν λέγῃς is a scornful euphemism, implying that he indulges in random abuse. ταγούς: only here in Soph.: oft. in Aesch. (in *P. V.* 96 Zeus is ὁ νέος ταγὸς μακάρων); once in Eur., *I. A.* 269 (Adrastus). Here the word is not specially =στρατηγός (8), but simply =βασιλεύς.

1058 ἐξ ἐμοῦ: cp. *O. T.* 1221 ἀνέπνευσα ...ἐκ σέθεν.—ἔχεις σώσας, merely =σέσωκας (cp. 22). The rare position of ἔχεις might suggest the prose sense ('thou hast saved, and keepest'); but that position occurs where ἔχω is merely the auxiliary (794; *Ai.* 22 ἔχει περάνας).

1060 τἀκίνητα διὰ φρενῶν, =τὰ διὰ φρενῶν ἀκίνητα, those secrets in my soul which ought to be let alone. Cp. *O. C.* 1526 ἃ δ' ἐξάγιστα μηδὲ κινεῖται λόγῳ, n. For the place of the adv. διὰ φρενῶν, cp. 659 n.: for διά, 639 n.: Aesch. *Th.* 593 βαθεῖαν ἄλοκα διὰ φρενὸς καρπούμενος.

1061 κίνει: a word used esp. of sacrilege: Her. 6. 134 κινήσοντά τι τῶν ἀκινήτων (in a temple): Thuc. 4. 98 ὕδωρ...κινῆσαι (to profane, by secular use, water reserved for sacrifices).—μόνον δέ, sc. κίνει.—ἐπὶ κέρδεσιν, *i.e.*, with a view to

receiving money from the Thebans for persuading me to bury Polyneices. So Oed. (*O. T.* 388) calls the seer, δόλιον ἀγύρτην, ὅστις ἐν τοῖς κέρδεσιν | μόνον δέδορκε.

1062 οὕτω γὰρ ἤδη: 'indeed, as matters stand (ἤδη), καὶ δοκῶ (λέξειν), I think that I *shall* speak thus—*i.e.*, not for gain—so far as thou art concerned.' The seer, with grave irony, gives a new turn to Creon's phrase, μὴ ἐπὶ κέρδεσιν, and says that the admonition is superfluous. The message which he has to utter is fraught with no κέρδη—for Creon. For the plur. κέρδη in this general sense, cp. 1326. τὸ σὸν μέρος here=*quantum ad te attinet*: a sense quite as correct for it as the more usual *quantum in te est* (*O. T.* 1509, *O. C.* 1366, *Tr.* 1215). For καί emphasising δοκῶ (λέξειν), cp. 726. Creon's reply (1063) refers to the covert threat: 'say what thou wilt, thou shalt not shake my purpose.'—The choice lies between this view and that of the Scholiast, who makes the verse interrogative:—οὕτω νομίζεις, ὅτι ἐπὶ κέρδεσι λέγω; *i.e.*, 'what, do I seem *now*—on thy part—to be speaking for money?' The points in favour of the Scholiast's interpretation are:—(*a*) The combination γάρ...καί (before the verb) suits an indignant question: cp. 770, *Tr.* 1124. (*b*) The tone of rising anger—which began at 1060—fitly preludes the outburst at 1064: cp. *O. T.* 343—350. But on the other hand:—(*a*) The indignation comes late, seeing that Creon has already used the same taunt four times (1036, 1047,

CR.   Knowest thou that thy speech is spoken of thy King?

TE.   I know it; for through me thou hast saved Thebes.

CR.   Thou art a wise seer; but thou lovest evil deeds.

TE.   Thou wilt rouse me to utter the dread secret in my soul.

CR.   Out with it!—Only speak it not for gain.

TE.   Indeed, methinks, I shall not,—as touching thee.

CR.   Know that thou shalt not trade on my resolve.

TE.   Then know thou—aye, know it well—that thou shalt not live through many more courses of the sun's swift chariot, ere one begotten of thine own loins

---

corrector (S) changed this into a mark of interrogation. **1064** πολλὰσ L, with ·οὐ· above ὰ from first hand. **1065** τροχοὺς mss.: τρόχους Erfurdt.—ἀμιλλητῆρας] Musgrave conject. ἀμιλλητῆρος.—ἠλίου τελῶν] Winckelmann conject. ἥλιον τελεῖν.

1055, 1059); not, indeed, in so directly personal a form, yet still openly enough. (b) Though the seer is angered (1085), it is dramatically better to conceive him as speaking here with a stern calmness. (c) It would be correct to say (e.g.) πέφασμαι λέγων, τὸ σὸν μέρος ('I have been represented as speaking..., so far as you could create such a belief'): but hardly, δοκῶ τὸ σὸν μέρος, as merely = δοκῶ σοι.— On the whole, then, the first view is best. —Others, which may be rejected, are:— (1) 'I think that I *shall* speak for your good.' But, if we are thus to supply ἐπὶ κέρδεσιν, and not οὐκ ἐπὶ κέρδεσιν, the verse must be interrogative. (2) 'So far as you are concerned, I do not expect to speak for my own profit'; i.e., I shall receive no thanks from you. (3) 'Do you really think that I shall find any satisfaction in speaking?'—i.e., it will be only pain for you, without advantage for me.

1063 ἴσθι ὡς μὴ ἐμπ., rest assured that thou art not to trade (1037) on my resolve; i.e., to make profit out of it (from the Thebans) by persuading me to surrender it. ὡς (which might have been absent) adds emphasis by marking the point of view at which he is to place himself. In such phrases it is more often added to a partic. in the accus., the object of the imperat. verb: Ph. 253 ὡς μηδὲν εἰδότ' ἴσθι μ' ὧν ἀνιστορεῖς: O. T. 848 n. But cp. Her. 1. 91 ἐπιστάσθω Κροῖσος ὡς ὕστερον...ἁλοὺς τῆς πεπρωμένης.—**φρένα**: cp. 993.

1064 f. ἀλλ' εὖ γέ τοι: 473 n.—μὴ ...τελῶν, that thou art not to accom-

plish, i.e., live through: μή is due to the imperat. κάτισθι (O. C. 78 n.). The easy correction, ἥλιον τελεῖν, has been received by some recent edd. (κάτισθι then has the constr. with inf., as 473 ἴσθι ...πίπτειν). It may be right. But τελῶν, if not a usual phrase, is a natural one; and it is more impressive here to say, '*thou shalt not live through* many days,' than, 'the sun shall not fulfil many days.' —τρόχους = δρόμους, 'courses.' The MS. τροχοὺς = 'runners,' i.e., κύκλους, wheels. The authority for this Attic distinction goes back at least to the Augustan age: see Chandler § 332 n. 1 (2nd ed.), who cites Ammonius p. 137 τροχοὶ ὀξυτόνως καὶ τρόχοι βαρυτόνως διαφέρουσι παρὰ τοῖς Ἀττικοῖς. φησὶ Τρύφων (in the Augustan age) ἐν δευτέρᾳ περὶ Ἀττικῆς προσῳδίας. τοὺς μὲν γὰρ περιφερεῖς τροχοὺς ὁμοίως ἡμῖν προφέρονται ὀξυτονοῦντες· τρόχους δὲ βαρυτόνως λέγουσι τοὺς δρόμους. This passage helps to explain why our MSS. all give τροχοὺς here. When Ammonius wrote (towards the end of the 4th cent. A.D.) τρόχος, 'course,' was known only as an Atticism, while τροχός, 'wheel,' was a common word.—ἀμιλλητῆρας, racing, rapid: Eur. Or. 456 γέροντι δεῦρ' ἁμιλλᾶται ποδί. Xen. An. 3. 4. 44 ὥρμησαν ἁμιλλᾶσθαι ἐπὶ τὸ ἄκρον.—The Schol. explains, τοὺς ἀλλήλους διαδεχομένους, 'successive'; perh. taking the word to mean, 'competitors,' i.e., 'vying in swiftness.' But that does not warrant his version.

1066 ἐν οἷσι = ἐντὸς ὧν, i.e., before they have elapsed: cp. O. C. 619 n.— τῶν σῶν...ἐκ σπλάγχνων ἕνα, a strong

νέκυν νεκρῶν ἀμοιβὸν ἀντιδοὺς ἔσει,
ἀνθ' ὧν ἔχεις μὲν τῶν ἄνω βαλὼν κάτω,
ψυχήν τ' ἀτίμως ἐν τάφῳ κατῴκισας,
ἔχεις δὲ τῶν κάτωθεν ἐνθάδ' αὖ θεῶν   1070
ἄμοιρον, ἀκτέριστον, ἀνόσιον νέκυν.
ὧν οὔτε σοὶ μέτεστιν οὔτε τοῖς ἄνω
θεοῖσιν, ἀλλ' ἐκ σοῦ βιάζονται τάδε.
τούτων σε λωβητῆρες ὑστεροφθόροι
λοχῶσιν Ἅιδου καὶ θεῶν Ἐρινύες,   1075
ἐν τοῖσιν αὐτοῖς τοῖσδε ληφθῆναι κακοῖς.
καὶ ταῦτ' ἄθρησον εἰ κατηργυρωμένος
λέγω· φανεῖ γὰρ οὐ μακροῦ χρόνου τριβὴ
ἀνδρῶν γυναικῶν σοῖς δόμοις κωκύματα.
ἐχθραὶ δὲ πᾶσαι συνταράσσονται πόλεις,   1080

1068 βαλὼν r: βάλλειν L, with ω above ει from first hand.   **1069** κατῴκισας L. κατοικίσας, the reading of some later MSS. (as E, L²), is adopted by Bothe, who omits τ' after ψυχήν, and by Bergk, who places τ' after ἀτίμως.   **1070** θεῶν] Semitelos conject. γόων, to go with ἄμοιρον.   **1078** τριβὴ L. The only trace of

---

fig. phrase, one whose life is nourished by thine own heart's blood,—the son begotten of thee. If the ref. were to the mother, σπλάγχνα could mean 'womb': cp. Kaibel *Epigr.* 691 ζωὴ δὲ πλείων μητρὸς ἐν σπλάγχνοις ἐμή (of a babe who died just after birth). So brothers and sisters are ὁμόσπλαγχνοι (511).

1067 νέκυν νεκρῶν: 596 n. The νεκροί are Polyneices and Antigone.—ἀντιδοὺς ἔσει, fut. perf.: cp. *O. C.* 816 n.

1068 ἀνθ' ὧν here = ἀντὶ τούτων ὅτι, 'because': so Ar. *Plut.* 434. The phrase more often means 'wherefore' (*O. C.* 1295): cp. *O. T.* 264 n.—ἔχεις βαλὼν κάτω τῶν ἄνω (τινά), thou hast thrust to the grave (one) of the living. For the omission of τις after the partitive gen., cp. *El.* 1322 κλύω | τῶν ἔνδοθεν χωροῦντος.

1069 Bothe, omitting τε after ψυχήν, takes the latter with τῶν ἄνω, 'a life belonging to the upper world.' We could then read either (a) ἀτίμως...κατοικίσας, or (b) with Bergk, ἀτίμως τ'...κατοικίσας or κατῴκισας. But I prefer the MS. reading, because (a) τῶν ἄνω as = τῶν ἄνω τινά has a certain tone of solemnity and mystery which befits the utterance: (b) τῶν ἄνω... ψυχήν is somewhat weak: (c) the words ψυχήν τ'...κατῴκισας, both by rhythm and by diction, naturally form one clause,

—paraphrasing and interpreting the darker utterance in v. 1068.—Schütz takes ἀνθ' ὧν as = ἀντὶ τούτων οὕς, and τῶν ἄνω as by attraction for τοὺς ἄνω: *i.e.*, 'on account of those persons whom, being alive, thou hast entombed.' Kern, too, so takes ἀνθ' ὧν, but makes τῶν ἄνω partitive ('on account of those among the living whom'); and so, I think, it must be on any view. But the parallelism of ἔχεις μέν...ἔχεις δέ plainly requires that ἀνθ' ὧν should apply in the same sense to both clauses. Schütz, however, has to supply it with ἔχεις δέ in the changed sense of ἀντὶ τούτων (neut.) ὅτι.—For οἱ ἄνω = οἱ ἐν φάει, cp. 890: *Ph.* 1348 ὦ στυγνὸς αἰών, τί μ' ἔτι δῆτ' ἔχεις ἄνω | βλέποντα, κοὐκ ἀφῆκας εἰς Ἅιδου μολεῖν;—Some take τῶν ἄνω as = τῶν ἄνω θεῶν: 'one belonging to the gods above.' This is too forced. —ἀτίμως, ruthlessly: cp. *O. C.* 428, *El.* 1181.

1070 f. ἔχεις δέ = κατέχεις δέ. Since in ἔχεις μέν...ἔχεις δέ the rhetorical effect depends simply on the repetition (ἐπαναφορά), the change of sense is immaterial. —τῶν κάτωθεν θεῶν, possess. gen. with νέκυν, a corpse belonging to them. For κάτωθεν = κάτω, 521 n.—ἄμοιρον, without its due μοῖρα of burial rites: *Ai.* 1327 νεκρὸν ταφῆς | ἄμοιρον. Others take τῶν shall have been given by thee, a corpse for corpses; because thou hast thrust children of the sunlight to the shades, and ruthlessly lodged a living soul in the grave; but keepest in this world one who belongs to the gods infernal, a corpse unburied, unhonoured, all unhallowed. In such thou hast no part, nor have the gods above, but this is a violence done to them by thee. Therefore the avenging destroyers lie in wait for thee, the Furies of Hades and of the gods, that thou mayest be taken in these same ills.

And mark well if I speak these things as a hireling. A time not long to be delayed shall awaken the wailing of men and of women in thy house.   And a tumult of hatred against thee stirs all the cities

---

a reading τριβῇ seems to be in A (τριβῆ). λόγου for χρόνου in E was probably a mere oversight.   **1080—1083** Wunder and Dindorf reject these four verses. **1080** ἐχθραί] Reiske conject. ἔχθρᾳ: Musgrave, ἔχθραις: Semitelos ἔχθραι .. συνταράσσουσιν.—συνταρασσόνται] Bergk conject. συνταράξονται.

κ. θεῶν with ἄμοιρον: 'without a portion in the gods below,' *i.e.*, not admitted to communion with them. But the phrase is a strange one; and the leading thought here is that the νέρτεροι are robbed of one who belongs to them.—**ἀκτέριστον** (1207), without offerings at the grave, κτερίσματα (*O. C.* 1410): cp. 204.—**ἀνόσιον**, 'unhallowed,' sums up the state of the dead who has received no rites: cp. 545 n. Cp. Shaksp. *Haml.* 1. 5. 77 'Unhousel'd, disappointed, unanel'd' [without sacrament—unprepared for death—without extreme unction].

1072 f. ὤν, *sc.* τῶν νεκρῶν, suggested by νέκυν. Others make it neut., 'such acts as these.' It cannot refer to οἱ κάτωθεν θεοί.—**βιάζονται**, *sc.* οἱ ἄνω θεοί: because it was an offence against the pure οὐράνιοι θεοί to keep a μίασμα in their presence. Cp. *O. T.* 1425 τὴν γοῦν πάντα βόσκουσαν φλόγα | αἰδεῖσθ' ἄνακτος Ἡλίου, and see n. there on 1427. The subject to βιάζονται might, indeed, be οἱ κάτωθεν θεοί, for Greek idiom is often bold in such transitions: but the verb suits a positive better than a negative wrong.

1074 τούτων, neut., causal gen.: cp. 931 n.—**λωβητῆρες**, though the subject is fem.: so *El.* 850 ἴστωρ: Aesch. *Ag.* 111 χερὶ πράκτορι: *ib.* 664 τύχη...σωτήρ: *Suppl.* 1040 θέλκτορι Πειθοῖ.—**ὑστεροφθό-ροι**, destroying after (though not, here, *long* after) the crime. Aesch. *Ag.* 58 (Zeus) ὑστερόποινον | πέμπει παραβᾶσιν

Ἐρινύν.   *Anthol.* 12. 229 ὑστερόπουν ἀξό-μενοι Νέμεσιν.

1075 f. λοχῶσιν: *El.* 490 ἁ δεινοῖς κρυπτομένα λόχοις χαλκόπους Ἐρινύς.—Ἄιδου καὶ θεῶν, possess. gen.; the Eri-nyes are their ministers, avenging their wrongs: so oft. πατρός, μητρός, Ἐρινύες. In *El.* 112 the Erinyes are σεμναί...θεῶν παῖδες.—**ληφθῆναι**, inf. of result: cp. 64 ἀκούειν. The omission of ὥστε is some-what bold, since the subject of the inf. is not that of λοχῶσιν. Cp. *O. C.* 385 ἐμοῦ θεοὺς | ὥραν τιν' ἕξειν ὥστε σωθῆναί ποτε.

1077 ff. κατηργ., prop., overlaid with silver (Her. 1. 98); hence, fig., bribed. Cp. Pind. *P.* 11. 41 μισθοῖο συνέθεν παρέ-χειν | φωνὰν ὑπάργυρον (a word prop. said of a gilded surface, with silver below). —οὐ μακρ. χρόν. τριβή=a time for which thou wilt not have long to wait. Some, less naturally, make these words a parenthesis with ἔσται understood, and supply ταῦτα as subject to φανεῖ. Cp. Ar. *Ran.* 156 θιάσους εὐδαίμονας | ἀνδρῶν γυναικῶν.

1080—1083 The πόλεις are the cities which had furnished contingents to the Argive expedition against Thebes. These cities are stirred with passionate hatred against Creon by the tidings that burial has been refused to their fallen warriors. There is no *direct* allusion to the war of the Epigoni,—the expedition which the sons of the fallen chiefs led against Thebes, and in which they de-stroyed it. Bergk's συνταράξονται might

ὅσων σπαράγματ᾽ ἢ κύνες καθήγνισαν
ἢ θῆρες, ἤ τις πτηνὸς οἰωνός, φέρων
ἀνόσιον ὀσμὴν ἑστιοῦχον ἐς πόλιν.
τοιαῦτά σου, λυπεῖς γάρ, ὥστε τοξότης
ἀφῆκα θυμῷ καρδίας τοξεύματα   1085
βέβαια, τῶν σὺ θάλπος οὐχ ὑπεκδραμεῖ.
ὦ παῖ, σὺ δ᾽ ἡμᾶς ἄπαγε πρὸς δόμους, ἵνα
τὸν θυμὸν οὗτος ἐς νεωτέρους ἀφῇ,
καὶ γνῷ τρέφειν τὴν γλῶσσαν ἡσυχωτέραν
τὸν νοῦν τ᾽ ἀμείνω τῶν φρενῶν ἢ νῦν φέρει.   1090

1081 σπαράγματ᾽] Seyffert conject. τὰ πράγματ᾽. Tournier, ἀπάργματ᾽.. καθύ-
βρισαν.—καθήγνισαν MSS. Burton gave καθήγισαν (from which καθήγνισαν has been
made in V); and so most of the recent editors. Bellermann keeps καθήγνισαν.
1083 πόλιν] Nauck and Seyffert write πόλον (but in different senses): for other

---

suggest such an allusion; but the pres.
συνταράσσονται is right. The reference
is to the feelings which *now* agitate the
cities. Those feelings are one day to produce the new war. Here the prophet notes
them only as signs of a still distant storm.
Having foretold a domestic sorrow for
the father, he now foreshadows a public
danger for the king.

It has been objected that the play
contains no hint of burial having been
denied to any one except Polyneices.
This is not exactly the case: the phrase
τῶν ἐχθρῶν κακά in v. 10 is such a hint.
But it was unnecessary for the poet to
state a fact which all his hearers would
assume. Every one knew how Creon
had refused burial to the Argives, and
how Theseus had recovered their corpses
by force of arms. In the *Supplices* of
Eur. the Chorus consists of widows and
mothers of the unburied warriors. No
Athenian exploit was more famous (Her.
9. 27; Isocr. *Paneg.* § 52, *Encom. Helen.*
§ 31, *Panath.* § 168; Plat. *Menex.* 244;
[Lys.] or. 2 §§ 4 ff.: [Dem.] or. 60 §§ 7 ff.).
The war of the Epigoni, which was included in the epic *Thebais* (Paus. 9. 9 § 5),
was dramatised both by Aesch. and by
Soph. ('Επίγονοι).

Just as, in the *O. C.* (1410 n.), Soph.
glances at the theme of his *Antigone*,
so here he might naturally glance—however indirectly—at a later chapter of
the Theban story,—whether his *Epigoni*
already existed, or was still in the future.
Dramatically, the reference is the more

fitting, since the legend represented
Teiresias as still living, and still zealous
for Theban welfare, when the Epigoni
came.—For other views of the passage,
see Appendix.

1081 ὅσων (fem.) σπαράγματα, mangled bodies *belonging* to them, as being
the corpses of their citizens. The possessive gen. in this sense is quite justifiable,
since σπαράγματα=σώματα ἐσπαραγμένα,
just as πτώματα=σώματα πεπτωκότα. (It
would be possible, but harsh, to make
ὅσων masc., as=ἐπεὶ τοσούτων: cp. *O. C.*
263 n.)

L's **καθήγνισαν**='hallowed' them, in
the sense of, ' gave burial rites to them ':
cp. Eur. *Or.* 40 μήτηρ πυρὶ καθήγνισται
δέμας (has had the funeral rite of fire):
Suppl. 1211 ἵν᾽ αὐτῶν σώμαθ᾽ ἡγνίσθη
πυρί. The *v. l.* **καθήγισαν** reaches the
same meaning (' buried') by a different
channel. καθαγίζω was properly ' to devote' or 'dedicate': Her. 1. 86 ἀκροθίνια
...καταγιεῖν θεῶν ὅτεῳ δή. Then, fig., to
devote to the gods below by the funeral
fire; Plut. *Anton.* 14 τὸ...σῶμα τοῦ Καίσα-
ρος ἐν ἀγορᾷ καθαγίσαι (' solemnly burn ').
Either **καθήγνισαν** or **καθήγισαν**, then,
is admissible. But (apart from L's support) καθήγνισαν seems preferable on two
grounds: (a) its primary sense lends force
to the grim irony: (b) the funereal sense
of καθαγίζω has only post-classical evidence.—Hesychius (καθαγίσω) says that
Soph. used καθαγίζω, not in the sense of
καθιερόω, but in that of μιαίνω:—a statement perh. founded on a misunderstanding

whose mangled sons had the burial-rite from dogs, or from wild beasts, or from some winged bird that bore a polluting breath to each city that contains the hearths of the dead.

Such arrows for thy heart—since thou provokest me—have I launched at thee, archer-like, in my anger,—sure arrows, of which thou shalt not escape the smart.—Boy, lead me home, that he may spend his rage on younger men, and learn to keep a tongue more temperate, and to bear within his breast a better mind than now he bears. [*Exit* TEIRESIAS.

---

emendations see Appendix. **1089** L has τρέφειν, not στρέφειν.—ἡσυχωτέραν
MSS.: ἡσυχαιτέραν Schaefer. **1090** ἢ] ὧν Brunck.—Schneidewin, ἢ νῦν φέρειν:
Herwerden, ἢ νῦν τρέφει: F. W. Schmidt, τῶν γε νῦν φέρειν φρενῶν.

---

of καθήγισαν here. The Schol. read the latter (μετὰ ἄγους ἐκόμισαν). But the fact that L has καθήγνισαν must be set against these doubtful testimonies.—For the irony, cp. *El.* 1487 πρόθες | ταφεῦσιν, ὧν τόνδ' εἰκός ἐστι τυγχάνειν (as Gorgias called vultures ἔμψυχοι τάφοι, Longin. π. ὕψους 3 § 2): Aesch. *Th.* 1020 ὑπ' οἰωνῶν ... | ταφέντ' ἀτίμως: Ennius *Ann.* 142 *volturu' crudeli condebat membra sepulcro:* Lucr. 5. 993 *viva videns vivo sepeliri viscera busto.*

1083 ἑστιοῦχον...πόλιν, the city containing the ἑστίαι of those on whose flesh the bird has fed. The sing. is used, although several πόλεις are concerned, since the case of one city is the case of all. For the adj., cp. Aesch. *Pers.* 510 ἥκουσιν ἐκφυγόντες, οὐ πολλοί τινες, | ἐφ' ἑστιοῦχον γαῖαν, 'the land of their homes.' Eur. *Andr.* 283 ἑστιοῦχον αὐλάν, the abode that contains his hearth. Here, the word serves to suggest a pollution of hearth and altar (1016). Pollution, in a ceremonial sense, could be brought by the ὀσμή, even without an actual transport of carrion. And it is only the birds that are said to carry the taint.—See Appendix on 1080 ff.

1084 ff. σου, 'at thee,' with ἀφῆκα: 1033 n.—θυμῷ, modal dat.: 620 n.— καρδίας τοξεύματα, heart-arrows, *i.e.,* arrows for thy heart. Cp. Eur. *Hec.* 235 καρδίας δηκτήρια: *Med.* 1360 τῆς σῆς γάρ, ὡς χρῆν, καρδίας ἀνθηψάμην.—Not, arrows *from* my (angry) heart, like ὄμματος... τόξευμα (Aesch. *Suppl.* 1004).—τῶν = ὧν: cp. *O. C.* 747 n.

1087 ὦ παῖ. Cp. *O. T.* 444 ἄπειμι τοίνυν· καὶ σύ, παῖ, κόμιζέ με.

1089 τρέφειν: cp. 660 n.—ἡσυχωτέραν, the MS. reading, has been prudently

retained by most of the recent edd. In Plat. *Charm.* 160 A the MSS. give ὁ ἡσυχώτατος, though two lines before they give ὡς ἡσυχαίτατα. A grammarian in Bekker *Anecd.* 98. 19 quotes ἡσυχώτερον. In Aesch. *Eum.* 223 the MSS. give ἡσυχαιτέραν, and in Plat. *Phileb.* 24 C ἡσυχαιτέρου. It is true that our MSS. have no great weight on such a point, and that, if the ω form had been the current one in later Greek, it would have been likely to oust an older form in αι. But we see that sometimes, at least, the MSS. could preserve the αι and the ω forms side by side. It seems safer, then, to suppose that the normal ω form and the irregular αι form were both in Attic use, than to assume that the αι form alone was tolerated. The dictum of Thomas Magister, (quoted by Dindorf,) p. 426 ἡσυχαίτερον· οὐχ ἡσυχώτερον, is indecisive without more evidence than we possess.

1090 τὸν νοῦν...τῶν φρενῶν ἀμείνω (τρέφειν) ἢ νῦν φέρει (αὐτόν). Cp. *Il.* 18. 419 τῆς ἐν μὲν νόος ἐστὶ μετὰ φρεσίν, there is understanding in their breasts: 22. 475 ἐς φρένα θυμὸς ἀγέρθη, the soul returned to her breast. The word φρήν being thus associated with the physical seat of thought and feeling, ὁ νοῦς τῶν φρενῶν was a possible phrase. So trag. adesp. fr. 240 (when divine anger visits a man) ἐξαφαιρεῖται φρενῶν | τὸν νοῦν τὸν ἐσθλόν. (Cp. 176 n. ad fin.)—φέρει: 705 n.—If we took τῶν φρενῶν with ἀμείνω, then ἢ must be changed to ὧν, with Brunck. In so compact a clause, ἢ could not be an irregular substitute for ὧν. Nor could ἢ νῦν φέρει be an epexegesis: 'better than his (present) mind,—(that is, better) than he now bears it.'

ΧΟ. ἀνήρ, ἄναξ, βέβηκε δεινὰ θεσπίσας·
ἐπιστάμεσθα δ᾿, ἐξ ὅτου λευκὴν ἐγὼ
τήνδ᾿ ἐκ μελαίνης ἀμφιβάλλομαι τρίχα,
μή πώ ποτ᾿ αὐτὸν ψεῦδος ἐς πόλιν λακεῖν.

ΚΡ. ἔγνωκα καὐτὸς καὶ ταράσσομαι φρένας·   1095
τό τ᾿ εἰκαθεῖν γὰρ δεινόν, ἀντιστάντα δὲ
ἄτῃ πατάξαι θυμὸν ἐν δεινῷ πάρα.

ΧΟ. εὐβουλίας δεῖ, παῖ Μενοικέως, λαβεῖν.

ΚΡ. τί δῆτα χρὴ δρᾶν; φράζε· πείσομαι δ᾿ ἐγώ.

ΧΟ. ἐλθὼν κόρην μὲν ἐκ κατώρυχος στέγης   1100
ἄνες, κτίσον δὲ τῷ προκειμένῳ τάφον.

ΚΡ. καὶ ταῦτ᾿ ἐπαινεῖς, καὶ *δοκεῖ παρεικαθεῖν;

1091 ἀνήρ] ἀνὴρ L.—After βέβηκε, ν has been erased in L.   **1092** ἐπιστάμεσθα г : ἐπιστάμεθα L.   **1094** λακεῖν from λαβεῖν L.   **1096** τό τ᾿ εἰκάθειν ..
ἀντιστάντα δε (without accent) L: the first hand has written τ above δε.—εἰκαθεῖν
Elmsley.   **1097** ἄτῃ πατάξαι θυμὸν ἐν δεινῷ πάρα MSS.—Seyffert conject. ἐν
δεινοῦ πέρα (Musgrave had already proposed πέρα, and Martin δεινῶν or δεινοῦ
πέρα).—Wecklein, ἐπὶ δεινῷ πάρα.—Nauck, ἄτῃ παλᾶσαι δεινὰ καὶ δεινῶν πέρα.—
M. Schmidt, ἀντιστάντι δὲ | ἄτῃ, μαλάξαι θυμὸν ἐν δεινοῖς, πάρα.—Semitelos, ἄτῃ

1092 f. ἐξ ὅτου: cp. 12 n.—**λευκὴν...
ἐκ μελαίνης**. The words could mean
either: (1) 'since this hair which clothes
my head, once dark, has been white': or
(2) 'since this hair,—once dark, now
white,—has clothed my head,' i.e., from
infancy. The first is the sense intended
here. There is a certain looseness of
expression, since the thought is, 'though
I am old, I can recall no such case';
whereas the period actually described
might be a comparatively short one. So
we can say, 'he has grown grey in the
service of his country,' meaning, 'he has
served it all his life.'—**ἀμφιβάλλομαι**: cp.
Rhianus (the elegiac poet of Crete,
c. 225 B.C.) Anthol. P. 12. 93 χαίρετε,
καλοὶ παῖδες, ἐς ἀκμαίην δὲ μόλοιτε | ἥβην,
καὶ λευκὴν ἀμφιέσαισθε κόμην. For the
1st pers. sing. following ἐπιστάμεσθα, see
734 n.
1094 μή. We might have had the οὐ
of oratio obliqua with λακεῖν, =ὅτι οὐκ
ἔλακε. But here we have μή, as after
πιστεύω and like verbs. So O. T. 1455
οἶδα, μήτε μ᾿ ἂν νόσον | μήτ᾿ ἄλλο πέρσαι
μηδέν (n.). Cp. O. C. 656 n., 797 n.
In such cases μή seems to add a certain
emphasis to the statement of fact (like
saying, 'I protest that I know no instance').—**λακεῖν**, infin. (instead of the

more usual partic.) after ἐπιστάμεσθα:
293 n. This verb is esp. used of prophecy: cp. Tr. 822 (where τοὔπος τὸ
θεοπρόπον is subject to ἔλακεν): Aesch.
Ag. 1426 (of Clytaemnestra) περίφρονα δ᾿
ἔλακες. The ref. is esp. to the seer's
denunciation of Oedipus, and his command regarding Megareus (1303 n.).
1095 ἔγνωκα, I have noted it = I know
it well; more emphatic than οἶδα: cp.
O. C. 553 n.
1096 For τε...δέ, instead of τε...τε,
cp. Tr. 285 ταῦτα γὰρ πόσις τε σὸς |
ἐφεῖτ᾿, ἐγὼ δὲ πιστὸς ὢν κείνῳ τελῶ: ib.
333 ὡς σύ θ᾿ οἳ θέλεις | σπεύδῃς, ἐγὼ δὲ
τἄνδον ἐξαρκῇ τιθῶ. See also O. C.
367 n., 442 n.: Ph. 1312 f. Here, δέ is
accentless in L, and the first hand has
written τ above; but, if the genuine reading had been τε...τε, the change to τε...δέ
was not likely to occur; and the antithesis
makes δέ very natural. Cp. Aesch. Ag.
206 βαρεῖα μὲν κὴρ τὸ μὴ πιθέσθαι, | βαρεῖα
δ᾿, εἰ τέκνον δαΐξω.
1097 f. ἄτῃ πατάξαι (170 n.) **θυμὸν**,
to smite my proud spirit with a curse.
ἀντιστάντα implies that he is stationary:
the image is not, then, like that in 854
(ἐς Δίκας βάθρον | προσέπεσες). Rather the
ἄτη is to be conceived as sweeping down
on him, like the torrent which destroys

CH. The man hath gone, O King, with dread prophecies. And, since the hair on this head, once dark, hath been white, I know that he hath never been a false prophet to our city.

CR. I, too, know it well, and am troubled in soul. 'Tis dire to yield; but, by resistance, to smite my pride with ruin— this, too, is a dire choice.

CH. Son of Menoeceus, it behoves thee to take wise counsel.

CR. What should I do, then? Speak, and I will obey.

CH. Go thou, and free the maiden from her rocky chamber, and make a tomb for the unburied dead.

CR. And this is thy counsel? Thou wouldst have me yield?

πατάξαι πημονὴν ('to punish an outrage by injury') δεινοῦ πέρα. **1098** L has λαβεῖν, as Cobet and Campbell report; not λακεῖν, as Elmsley and Dübner. β and κ are somewhat alike in L, but β resembles our *u*, while the left-hand stroke of κ is always higher than the right-hand stroke. See 1094, where λακεῖν has been made from λαβεῖν. The difference is usually plain; nor is there any doubt here. L² agrees with L, but has λαχεῖν κρέον in marg.: E has λαχεῖν. A, with the other MSS., has κρέον. **1102** δοκεῖς MSS.: I conjecture δοκεῖ. Nauck, λέγεις, or με λῇς.—παρεικάθειν MSS.: παρεικαθεῖν Elmsley.

---

trees that resist it (712).—ἐν δεινῷ πάρα (=πάρεστιν), it is open to me, as the dreadful alternative; lit., as a thing in the region of τὸ δεινόν. For ἐν δεινῷ cp. *El.* 384 νῦν γὰρ ἐν καλῷ φρονεῖν ('tis opportune). Eur. *Her.* 971 οὐκοῦν ἔτ' ἐστὶν ἐν καλῷ δοῦναι δίκην: *I. A.* 969 ἐν εὐμαρεῖ τε (sc. ἐστί) δρᾶν: *Helen.* 1277 ἐν εὐσεβεῖ γοῦν νόμιμα μὴ κλέπτειν νεκρῶν ('tis a matter of piety). Here, the only peculiarity arises from the fusion of two propositions, viz. (1) πάρεστιν, and (2) ἐν δεινῷ ἐστιν. The phrase would have been clearer if ὅν had been added to ἐν δεινῷ: cp. 471 n. It may be noticed that elsewhere also Soph. uses πάρεστι and παρ.ν of an *evil* lot: *Ai.* 432 νῦν γὰρ πάρεστι καὶ δὶς αἰάζειν ἐμοί: *El.* 959 ᾗ πάρεστι μὲν στένειν... | πάρεστι δ' ἀλγεῖν: *Ph.* 283 ηὕρισκον οὐδὲν πλὴν ἀνιᾶσθαι παρόν. This is a point in favour of the traditional πάρα.—Seyffert's ἐν δεινοῦ πέρα would be excellent, were it not for ἐν, which cannot be justified by the use of εἷς with superlatives (*O. C.* 563 n.). Cp. [Dem.] or. 45 § 73 δεινόν, ὦ γῆ καὶ θεοί, καὶ πέρα δεινοῦ. Wecklein conjectures ἐπὶ (for ἐν) δεινῷ: 'by resisting, it is possible that, *in addition to* the difficulty (of resistance), I may incur calamity.' But, apart from the risk of calamity, there was nothing in resistance that he could call δεινόν. There is no likelihood in conjectures which displace θυμόν, such as Nauck's (see cr. n.).

1098 The question between L's λαβεῖν, and the Κρέον of later MSS., is not an easy one to decide. If λαβεῖν is an error, then it must be explained by the scribe's eye having wandered to v. 1094. But it has not been noticed (I think) that the argument from v. 1094 is two-edged. There, the scribe of L wrote λαβεῖν, which was afterwards corrected to λακεῖν, either by his own hand or by another. It might be held, then, that he wrote λαβεῖν, by an error of the eye, in 1094, because his archetype had λαβεῖν in 1098. The epexegetic construction of the inf. (=ὥστε λαβεῖν αὐτήν, see examples on 489 f.) may have been a stumblingblock, leading transcribers to think it a redundant gloss; when Κρέον would have been the obvious resource. Everything considered, I prefer to retain λαβεῖν.

1100 f. κατώρυχος: 774 n.—κτίσον is here more than ποίησον, as it implies observance of solemn rites: cp. 1201 ff.: Aesch. *Cho.* 483 οὕτω γὰρ ἄν σοι δαῖτες ἔννομοι βροτῶν | κτιζοίατ'.

1102 I read the impers. δοκεῖ: 'and does it seem good (to you) that I should yield?' The dat. can be understood, as

ΧΟ. ὅσον γ᾽, ἄναξ, τάχιστα· συντέμνουσι γὰρ
　　θεῶν ποδώκεις τοὺς κακόφρονας βλάβαι.
ΚΡ. οἴμοι· μόλις μέν, καρδίας δ᾽ ἐξίσταμαι　　　　　1105
　　τὸ δρᾶν· ἀνάγκῃ δ᾽ οὐχὶ δυσμαχητέον.
ΧΟ. δρᾶ νυν τάδ᾽ ἐλθὼν μηδ᾽ ἐπ᾽ ἄλλοισιν τρέπε.
ΚΡ. ὧδ᾽ ὡς ἔχω στείχοιμ᾽ ἄν· ἴτ᾽ ἴτ᾽ ὀπάονες,
　　οἵ τ᾽ ὄντες οἵ τ᾽ ἀπόντες, ἀξίνας χεροῖν
　　ὁρμᾶσθ᾽ ἑλόντες εἰς ἐπόψιον τόπον.　　　　　　1110
　　ἐγὼ δ᾽, ἐπειδὴ δόξα τῇδ᾽ ἐπεστράφη,
　　αὐτός τ᾽ ἔδησα καὶ παρὼν ἐκλύσομαι.

1105 καρδίαι L. Most of the later mss. have καρδίας: but some καρδία (as A, L²), καρδίαν, or καρδία. In L there is an erasure before ἐξίσταμαι, the first hand having first written ἐξεπίσταμαι. Semitelos writes καὶ βίᾳ ᾿ξεπίσταμαι (=‘have been taught’ how to act). **1107** νῦν L. **1108** ἴτ᾽ ἴτ᾽] Triclinius conjecturally added the second ἴτ᾽. L has ἴτ᾽, as Elmsley read it: the rough breathing has been

in *Ph.* 526 ἀλλ᾽, εἰ δοκεῖ, πλέωμεν, and *ib.* 645. This correction is confirmed by Aesch. *Th.* 650 σὺ δ᾽ αὐτὸς ἤδη γνῶθι, τίνα πέμπειν δοκεῖ, where L has δοκεῖ with an accent erased over the ο,—showing that the use of the impers. verb without a dat., seeming strange, had suggested δόκει (imperat.). There, some of the later mss. have δοκεῖς. Here, L shares the error of the rest, and has **δοκεῖς**—generated, doubtless, from δοκεῖ by the same misapprehension as in Aesch. *l. c.* The decisive objection to **δοκεῖς** here is that it could mean only, ‘art thou minded to yield?’ (Aesch. *Ag.* 16 ὅταν δ᾽ ἀείδειν ἢ μινύρεσθαι δοκῶ); not, ‘dost thou think it right that I should yield?’—**παρεικαθεῖν**: for the form, see on *O. T.* 651.

1103 f. συντέμνουσι...τοὺς κ., cut them (*i.e.*, their careers) short, ‘cut them off.’ The compressed phrase, though not strictly correct, is natural.—**ποδώκεις**: cp. *Il.* 9. 505 ἡ δ᾽ Ἄτη σθεναρή τε καὶ ἀρτίπος: *Ai.* 837 Ἐρινῦς τανύποδας (who are ταχεῖαι, *ib.* 843): *O. T.* 418 δεινόπους ἀρά.—**βλάβαι**, ‘harms,’ ‘mischiefs,’ with ref. to the primary sense of βλάπτω, to disable, or stop: *Il.* 6. 39 (horses) ὄζῳ ἐνὶ βλαφθέντε μυρικίνῳ, ‘caught in’ a tamarisk branch: Aesch. *Ag.* 120 (a hare) βλαβέντα λοισθίων δρόμων, ‘stopped’ from running further. The βλάβαι θεῶν cannot, however, be properly regarded as personified beings; and therefore we should not write Βλάβαι. In Aesch. *Eum.* 491 εἰ κρατήσει δίκα τε καὶ βλάβα |

τοῦδε μητροκτόνου, where some write Δίκα—Βλάβα, the sense is, ‘if the cause and the wrong (=the wrongful cause) of Orestes shall prevail.’—**κακόφρονας**: for the ō before φρ, cp. 336 n.

1105 f. **μόλις μέν** (ἐξίστ.), ἐξίστ. δέ: cp. Eur. *Ph.* 1421 μόλις μέν, ἐξέτεινε δ᾽ εἰς ἧπαρ ξίφος: Ar. *Nub.* 1363 κἀγὼ μόλις μέν, ἀλλ᾽ ὅμως ἠνεσχόμην.—**ἐξίσταμαι καρδίας**, resign my cherished resolve: Plat. *Phaedr.* 249 D ἐξιστάμενος...τῶν ἀνθρωπίνων σπουδασμάτων, καὶ πρὸς τῷ θείῳ γιγνόμενος. This use of καρδία was suggested by the similar use of θυμός, with which Homer associates it as the seat of desire or passion (*Il.* 13. 784 νῦν δ᾽ ἀρχ᾽, ὅππῃ σε κραδίη θυμός τε κελεύει): thus πληροῦσα θυμόν (Eur. *Hipp.* 1328) = πληροῦσα ἐπιθυμίαν.—**τὸ δρᾶν**, acc. of inner object, defining the concession: *Ph.* 1252 ἀλλ᾽ οὐδέ τοι σῇ χειρὶ πείθομαι τὸ δρᾶν.—**δυσμαχητέον**: *Tr.* 492 θεοῖσι δυσμαχοῦντες.

1107 ἐπ᾽ ἄλλ᾽. τρέπε = ἄλλοις ἐπίτρεπε: Aesch. *Eum.* 434 ἢ κἀπ᾽ ἐμοὶ τρέποιτ᾽ ἂν αἰτίας τέλος; (‘would ye commit the decision of the charge to me’?) This is ‘tmesis’ in the proper sense,—where the prep. determines the special sense of the verb: cp. *Il.* 8. 108 οὓς ποτ᾽ ἀπ᾽ Αἰνείαν ἐλόμην = ἀφειλόμην.

1108 ὡς ἔχω, *i.e.*, forthwith: 1235: *Ph.* 819 δέξαι θανάσιμόν μ᾽ ὅπως ἔχω.—**στείχοιμ᾽** ἄν, optat. with ἄν expressing a fixed resolve: *O. T.* 343 οὐκ ἂν πέρα φράσαιμι: *O. C.* 45 οὐχ...ἂν ἐξέλθοιμ᾽ ἔτι.—ἴτ᾽ ἴτ᾽. The rhythm given by the tri-

CH. Yea, King, and with all speed; for swift harms from the gods cut short the folly of men.

CR. Ah me, 'tis hard, but I resign my cherished resolve, —I obey. We must not wage a vain war with destiny.

CH. Go, thou, and do these things; leave them not to others.

CR. Even as I am I'll go :—on, on, my servants, each and all of you,—take axes in your hands, and hasten to the ground that ye see yonder! Since our judgment hath taken this turn, I will be present to unloose her, as I myself bound her.

---

questioned, but is certain. The later MSS. have *ἴτ*, or (as A) *οἴτ'*. Nauck conject. *εἴτ'* or *ἀλλ'*: Mekler, *ἄνιτ'*.   **1111** δόξαι τῆδ' (*sic*) ἐπεστράφην L: δόξα τῆδ' ἐπεστράφη r.   The corruption in L (shared by L² and V⁴) evidently arose from failure to perceive that *τῆδ'* was an adverb.   **1112** αὐτός τ' ἔδησα] Semitelos conject. αὐτὸς πεδήσας.

---

brach suits this agitated utterance. **εἴ** would be no improvement (see cr. n.).

1109 οἵ τ' ὄντες οἵ τ' ἀπόντες, one and all. This was doubtless a familiar phrase: cp. 40 n. *El.* 305 τὰς οὔσας τέ μοι | καὶ τὰς ἀπούσας ἐλπίδας διέφθορεν. Plaut. *Trin.* 360 *comedit quod fuit quod non fuit.*—ἀξίνας. In Xen. *An.* 1. 5. 12 the ἀξίνη is used by one who is ξύλα σχίζων. Here it has usually been supposed that the ἀξῖναι were to cut wood for the burning of the corpse. But no regular πυρά was made; the remains of the corpse were burned with νεοσπάδες θαλλοί, branches freshly *plucked* from the trees in the plain (1201). On the other hand, some implement was needed to raise the τύμβος ὀρθόκρανος of earth (1203). It seems, then, as if Soph. referred to some kind of axe which could serve like the γενῆς of v. 249 (n.). No tool was used to break open Antigone's tomb; the stones were dragged away (1216).

1110 ἐπόψιον, pass., looked-upon, beheld, from here : hence=φανερόν (schol.), 'in view.' Cp. *O. C.* 1600 εἰς προσόψιον | πάγον, the hill which was in view. —As Creon speaks, he points with his hand in a direction to the left of the spectators. The region meant is the furthest and highest part of the Theban plain (1197), where the body of Polyneices still lay. In the πάγοι adjacent to it was the rocky tomb of Antigone (774 n.).—Hermann assumed the loss of some vv. after 1110, in which Creon described the ἐπόψιος τόπος,—explaining that he would first bury Polyneices, and then free Antigone. But what need

was there for this, when he was himself to accompany his servants? Besides, his men, like all the other Thebans, might be supposed to know the place meant; and the Chorus had already said what was to be done there. Equally baseless is Bergk's theory that vv. 1111 —1114 are an interpolation, designed to fill a gap in the original text. See the notes on them. Dindorf agrees with Bergk only so far as to suspect vv. 1111, 1112.

1111 ἐγὼ δ'. The sense is not: 'do *you* go and bury Polyneices, while *I* release Antigone.' Creon takes part in both acts (1196 ff.). But at this moment his foremost thought is of saving Antigone. If she dies, his son must die (1066). Therefore, while he glances at the burial-rites by telling his men to bring axes, he describes his own part by his *most urgent* task,—the release.— ἐπιστράφη, prop., 'turned round'; as a person faces about, Eur. *Alc.* 187 καὶ πολλὰ θάλαμον ἐξιοῦσ' ἐπεστράφη. τῇδ', this way, in this direction (*O. C.* 1547).

1112 αὐτός τ' ἔδησα κ.τ.λ. =ὥσπερ αὐτὸς ἔδησα, οὕτω καὶ αὐτὸς παρὼν ἐκλύσομαι. The co-ordination (parataxis) of clauses by τε...καί, as elsewhere by μέν... δέ, is peculiarly Greek. Cp. *O. T.* 419 βλέποντα νῦν μὲν ὄρθ', ἔπειτα δὲ σκότον (= dark then, *though* now thou hast sight): *O. C.* 853 οὔτε νῦν καλὰ | δρᾷς, οὔτε πρόσθεν εἰργάσω (=thou art not doing well now, *as* neither didst thou formerly): *ib.* 1202 (οὐ καλὸν) αὐτὸν μὲν εὖ | πάσχειν, παθόντα δ' οὐκ ἐπίστασθαι τίνειν (*while* receiving benefits, to be incapable of re-

δέδοικα γὰρ μὴ τοὺς καθεστῶτας νόμους
ἄριστον ἦ σῴζοντα τὸν βίον τελεῖν.

στρ. ά. ΧΟ. πολυώνυμε, Καδμείας νύμφας ἄγαλμα   1115
2 καὶ Διὸς βαρυβρεμέτα
3 γένος, κλυτὰν ὃς ἀμφέπεις
4 Ἰταλίαν, μέδεις δὲ
5 παγκοίνοις Ἐλευσινίας   1120

1114 σῴζοντα τὸν βίον] τὸν βίον σωίζοντα L.   **1115—1125** L divides thus : πολυώνυμε— | νύμφασ— | βαρυβρεμέτα— | κλυτὰν— | ἰτάλειαν . . παγ|κοίνουσ— | δηιοῦσ— | ὦ βακχεῦ— | ναίων— | ῥέεθρον— | τ' ἐπὶ . . δράκοντοσ | .   **1115** Καδμείας] Dindorf writes Καδμεῖας, and in 1126 διλόφοιο for διλόφου.—νύμφας ἄγαλμα

---

quiting them). Here, the rhetorical effect of the idiom is to place the two acts in bolder contrast. The middle ἐκλύομαι and the active ἐκλύω (Aesch. *P. V.* 326) are equivalent in poetry. They do not differ as λύω (said of the captor) from λύομαι (of the ransomer).—Nauck and others take the words figuratively ; 'As I have made the tangle, I will unravel it' (cp. 40 n.). This is surely wrong. See on v. 1111.

1113 f. δέδοικα μὴ...ἦ: cp. *O. T.* 747 δεινῶς ἀθυμῶ μὴ βλέπων ὁ μάντις ἦ. In both these places, 'I fear lest...' means 'I shrewdly suspect that...,' and δέδοικα μὴ might therefore have been followed by pres. indic., which expresses a fear that something is now going on (cp. 278 n. Ar. *Nub.* 493 δέδοικα...μὴ πληγῶν δέει).—**τοὺς καθεστ. νόμους**, the laws established by the gods,—the θεῶν νόμιμα of 454 f.—**σῴζοντα...τὸν βίον τελεῖν**=σῴζειν ἕως ἂν τελευτήσῃς : but the turn of phrase chosen unconsciously foreshadows Antigone's fate.

1115—1154 This ὑπόρχημα, or 'dance-song,' takes the place of a fifth stasimon. The Chorus hopes that Creon may be in time to save Antigone, and that his sin against the dead may be expiated without disaster. Hence this strain, full of gladness, invoking the healing presence (1144) of the bright and joyous god who protects Thebes. The substitution of a ὑπόρχημα for a stasimon is used with a like dramatic purpose in other plays. (1) *O. T.* 1086—1109: the Chorus hopes that Oedipus may prove to be of Theban birth. (2) *Ai.* 693—717, a joyous invocation of Pan, the Chorus believing that Ajax has indeed repented. (3) *Tr.* 633—662: the Chorus joyously anticipates the return of Heracles. In

each of these cases the beginning of the end is near.

1st strophe 1115—1125=1st antistr. 1126—1136: 2nd str. 1137—1145=2nd antistr. 1146—1154. See Metrical Analysis.

1115 f. πολυώνυμε, *i.e.*, worshipped by various special titles in different places. The reference of the epithet to local rituals is well brought out by Theocr. 15. 109 (Aphrodite) πολυώνυμε καὶ πολύναε. Most of the greater deities are called πολυώνυμοι by the poets ; but the word is peculiarly suitable to Dionysus, owing to the manner in which his cult was interwoven with other cults ; thus in relation to Demeter he was Ἴακχος ; to the Muses, Μελπόμενος ; to Hades, Ζαγρεύς. Dionysus was distinctively πολυειδὴς καὶ πολύμορφος (Plut. *Mor.* 389 c). Upwards of sixty titles given to him can be enumerated (see Preller, *Griech. Mythol.*).—**Καδμείας.** We should not write Καδμεῖας, and διλόφοιο in 1126, with Dindorf. Nor is it necessary to place νύμφας after ἄγαλμα, with Nauck. See Metrical Analysis.—**ἄγαλμα**, glory: Aesch. *Ag.* 207 τέκνον...δόμων ἄγαλμα.—**νύμφας**, bride, young wife. Semele, daughter of Cadmus and Harmonia, was beloved by Zeus, and was ensnared by Hera into praying him that he would come to her in the same guise as to Hera. He came to her, therefore, armed with his thunderbolts, and amid lightning, which destroyed her. She was great with child, and Zeus saved her son, Dionysus. **βαρυβρεμέτα** (for the ῠ, cp. 336 n.) alludes to this story. Ov. *Met.* 3. 298 (Jupiter, bound by his own oath, grants Semele's prayer) : *ergo maestissimus altum | Aethera conscendit, nutuque sequentia traxit | Nubila ; quis nimbos*

My heart misgives me, 'tis best to keep the established laws, even to life's end.

CH. O thou of many names, glory of the Cadmeian bride, 1st offspring of loud-thundering Zeus! thou who watchest over strophe. famed Italia, and reignest, where all guests are welcomed, in the sheltered plain of Eleusinian

MSS.: ἄγαλμα νύμφας Nauck.   **1119** ἰτάλειαν L: ᾿Ιταλίαν r.—R. Unger conject. ᾿Ικαρίαν (also suggested by Erfurdt): Bergk, Κιδαλίαν: M. Schmidt, Φιγαλίαν: Seyffert, φυταλίαν.—μέδεισ from μηδεῖσ L.   **1120** παγκοίνουσ L. The first hand sometimes writes υσ very like ισ: but normally it makes this distinction, that υ is joined to the σ, while ι is not; so in κόλποισ, 1121.

---

immixtaque fulgura ventis | *Addidit, et tonitrus, et inevitabile fulmen.*
1119 The traditional reading, ᾿Ιταλίαν, may be supported by these considerations. (1) Southern Italy, the seat of so many Greek colonies, was preeminently associated with the cultivation of the vine; and Sophocles has himself used the name which expresses that fact: *Triptolemus* fr. 538 Οἰνωτρία τε πᾶσα καὶ Τυρσηνικὸς | κόλπος Λιγυστική τε γῆ σε δέξεται. (2) The opening words of the ode, Καδμείας νύμφας ἄγαλμα, claim Thebes as the birth-place of Dionysus. Though Italy, then, is mentioned before Eleusis, Parnassus and Euboea, that precedence has not the effect of representing Italy as the head-quarters of the Dionysiac worship. Rather the mention of Italy just after Thebes serves to exalt the Theban god by marking the wide range of his power. And this reference to a distant country well suits the immediately following παγκοίνοις, expressing that Eleusis receives votaries from every part of the Greek world. (3) Athenian colonists founded Thurii, on the site of Sybaris, in 444—3 B.C.,—only two or three years before the probable date of this play. Thus, just at this time, the Athenian mind had been turned towards Southern Italy, and the allusion would strike a chord of sympathy in the audience. It may be worth remembering that the poet himself would naturally have felt a more than common interest in the new home of his friend Herodotus.

The only worthy rival of ᾿Ιταλίαν is the conjecture ᾿Ικαρίαν. This was the name of a deme in the N. E. of Attica, picturesquely situated in an upland valley bounded on the N. by the mountain-chain ('Aphorismo') which shuts in the plain of Marathon, and on the S. by Pentelicus. The site—at a place called 'Dionyso'—is proved by local inscriptions, found by members of the American School in 1888. The story was that, when Dionysus first entered Attica, he was received at Icaria by Icarius, whom he taught to make wine. Icaria was associated with the earliest celebrations of the rural Dionysia (thus the ἀσκωλιασμός, or dancing on greased wine-skins, was said to have been introduced by Icarius himself), and with the infancy of Attic drama in both kinds,—as it was also the birth-place of Thespis, and, at a later time, of the comic poet Magnes. Inscriptions and other remains show that, in the 5th century B.C., it was the seat of an active Dionysiac worship, with dramatic performances. These discoveries remind us that Sophocles might well have called Icaria κλυτάν. Prof. A. C. Merriam further points out that, in literature, the legend of Icaria is often associated with that of Eleusis (*American School at Athens: Seventh Annual Report,* 1887—88, p. 96). To Statius, *Theb.* 12. 619 (*Icarii Celeique domus*), may be added Apollod. 3. 14. 7, Lucian *De Salt.* 39 f., Nonnus 27. 283 ff., etc. But these facts remain: (1) ᾿Ιταλίαν is also suitable, and is in all the MSS.: (2) it widens the range ascribed to the god's power: (3) a corruption of ᾿Ικαρίαν into ᾿Ιταλίαν is not one to which the letters would readily lend themselves, and would have been the less likely to occur because Icaria was familiarly associated with Dionysus.

1120 f. παγκοίνοις, welcoming guests from every quarter to the Eleusinian Mysteries: schol. ἐν οἷς πάντες συνάγονται διὰ τὰς πανηγύρεις. Cp. *El.* 138 ἐξ ᾿Αΐδα παγκοίνου λίμνας. Pind. *O.* 6. 63

6 Δηοῦς ἐν κόλποις, Βακχεῦ, Βακχᾶν

7 ὁ ματρόπολιν Θήβαν

8 *ναιετῶν παρ' ὑγρὸν

9 Ἰσμηνοῦ ῥεῖθρόν <τ'> ἀγρίου τ' ἐπὶ σπορᾷ δρά-
　κοντος·　　　　　　　　　　　　　　　　　　1124

ἀντ. α'.　σὲ δ' ὑπὲρ διλόφου πέτρας στέροψ ὄπωπε

2 λιγνύς, ἔνθα Κωρύκιαι

3 στείχουσι Νύμφαι Βακχίδες,

1121 Δηοῦς] δηιοῦσ L.　　**1122** ὦ βακχεῦ· βακχᾶν μητρόπολιν L. Herm. deleted ὦ: Musgrave added ὁ before μητρόπολιν.—ματρόπολιν Dindorf.　　**1123 f.** ναίων παρ' ὑγρὸν ισμηνοῦ | ῥέεθρον L (the second ρ of ῥέεθρον from ν). Dindorf restored ναιετῶν. Triclinius gave ὑγρῶν . . ῥεέθρων (Hermann ῥείθρων). I conjecture ὑγρὸν . . ῥεῖθρόν τ'.　　**1126—1135** L divides thus: σὲ δ'— | στέροψ...ἐν|θα— | στείχουσι— | κασταλείασ τε— | σε νυσαίων— | κισσήρεισ— | πολυστάφυλοσ— | ἀμβρότων— | θηβαίασ ...ἀγυιάσ. |　　**1126** διλόφου MSS.: διλόφοιο Dindorf (cp. on. 1115).　　**1127 f.** ἔν|θα

πάγκοινον ἐς χώραν (Olympia).—**κόλποις**, recesses, *i.e.*, the sheltered Thriasian plain, enclosed by hills,—Aegaleos on the E., Cithaeron on the N., and the Kerāta range on N. w. and w. Cp. Ar. *Ran.* 373 ἐς τοὺς εὐανθεῖς κόλπους λειμώνων (where, though the scene is in Hades, the allusion is to the Initiated visiting Eleusis). So Pind *O.* 9. 87 Νεμέας... κατὰ κόλπον: *ib.* 14. 23 κόλποις παρ' εὐδόξου Πίσας. This is better than to refer κόλποις to the Bay of Eleusis, whose shores are the λαμπάδεσ ἀκταί of *O. C.* 1049 (where see nn.).—'Ελευσῑνίας: on the ῑ, see n. on this v. in Metr. Analysis. **Δηοῦς**=Δήμητρος: *Hom. h. Dem.* 47 πότνια Δηώ. In this connection the proper name of the god was Ἴακχος (1152), a young deity who was represented as the son of Cora (or of Demeter); cp. *O. C.* 682 n. Indeed, Arrian expressly distinguishes the Eleusinian Iacchus from the Theban Dionysus, *An.* 2. 16 § 3: Ἀθηναῖοι Διόνυσον τὸν Διὸς καὶ Κόρης σέβουσιν...καὶ ὁ Ἴακχος ὁ μυστικός (the chant of the initiated) τούτῳ τῷ Διονύσῳ, οὐχὶ τῷ Θηβαίῳ, ἐπᾴδεται. But, as Welcker remarks (*Götterl.* 2, p. 543), Dionysus was the general name, often substituted for the special title.

1122 Βακχεῦ. The omission of ὦ before this word, and the addition of ὁ before **ματρόπολιν**, are conjectural (cr. n.). But they are certainly right; for the antistrophic words (1133) answering to Βακχεῦ—Θήβαν, are χλωρά τ' ἀκτὰ | πολυστάφυλος πέμπει, which are unques-

tionably sound.—**ματρόπολιν**: cp. *O. C.* 707 n. Thebes is the 'mother-city' of the Bacchants, as being the city of Semele and the native place of Dionysus. It was the place at which the Dionysiac cult, coming from Asia Minor by way of Thrace, first established itself in Greece Proper. From Thebes the cult was propagated to Delphi, and associated with the worship of Apollo. See Eur. *Bacch.* 306. Cp. *O. T.* 210 n., *Tr.* 510.

1123 f. L has ὑγρὸν...ῥέεθρον, not ὑγρῶν...ῥεέθρων, which was merely a conjecture of Triclinius. And the use of παρά with the genit. is not only unexampled (see n. on 966), but here, at least, wholly unintelligible. Metre requires, however, that a long syllable (answering to the first syll. of Θηβαίας in 1135) should precede ἀγρίου. I obtain this by adding τ' after ῥεῖθρον. The second syll. of **ὑγρόν**, as the last of a verse, is common. **παρά** with acc. is correct in ref. to a river, the notion being that his abode extends along its banks: cp. *El.* 184 ὁ παρὰ τὸν Ἀχέροντα θεὸς ἀνάσσων: Xen. *An.* 4. 3 § 1 τοῦ πεδίου τοῦ παρὰ τὸν Κεντρίτην ποταμόν: *ib.* § 6 ἐστρατοπεδεύσαντο παρὰ τὸν ποταμόν. For the position of τ', cp. *O. T.* 258 n., *O. C.* 33 n. The sing. ῥεῖθρον is not less suitable than the plur.: cp. Aesch. *Pers.* 497, *P. V.* 790. For the epithet **ὑγρόν**, cp. *Od.* 4. 458 (Proteus) γίγνετο δ' ὑγρὸν ὕδωρ, 'running water.'—'Ισμηνοῦ: see n. on 103 f.

1125 ἐπὶ σπορᾷ δρ., 'over the seed

Δεὸ! O Bacchus, dweller in Thebè, mother-city of Bacchants, by the softly-gliding stream of Ismenus, on the soil where the fierce dragon's teeth were sown!

Thou hast been seen where torch-flames glare through smoke, above the crests of the twin peaks, where move the Corycian nymphs, thy votaries, ^{1st anti-strophe.}

κωρύκιαι νύμφαι | στείχουσι βακχίδεσ L. Blaydes places νύμφαι after στείχουσι. Dindorf gives νύμφαι στίχουσι (Hesych. στίχουσι· βαδίζουσι, πορεύονται. στίχωμεν· πορευθῶμεν, βαδίσωμεν). Pallis, στείβουσι νύμφαι. Rauchenstein, Κωρύκιον | νύμφαι νέμουσι. M. Schmidt, Κωρύκιαι | γνυφαί ('glens') τ' ἔχουσι Βακχίδες. (Hesych. explains γνυφή by νάπη.) Seyffert, ἔνθα Κωρυκίας | γνυφάς τ' ἔχουσι Βακχίδες. So Keck, but with νάπας τ' for γνυφάς τ', and Semitelos with εὐνάς τ'.

of the dragon,' *i.e.*, on the ground where Cadmus sowed the dragon's teeth, from which the ancestors of the Cadmeans sprang. Hence the Thebans are called σπαρτοὶ ἄνδρες (*O. C.* 1534 n.). The place where Cadmus sowed the teeth was shown on the s. side of Thebes, near the Ἠλέκτραι πύλαι (Paus. 9. 10. 1).—Not, '(ruling) over the dragon's seed,' as if σπορᾷ meant the Thebans.

1126 ff. The general sense is: 'and on the heights of Parnassus thou holdest thy revels by night amid the Corycian Nymphs, who brandish torches.'—**διλόφου πέτρας**: *i.e.*, two πέτραι, each with a λόφος (cp. 146 δικρατεῖς λόγχας, n.): two peaks, one of which stands on each side of a great recess in the steep cliffs above Delphi,—the cliffs called Φαιδριάδες, 'gleaming,' from their splendour in the morning sunshine (cp. Eur. *Ion* 86 ff.). These cliffs are about 2000 ft. above sea-level. The easternmost of the two peaks was called Ὑάμπεια: the westernmost, perh. Ναυπλία, but this is doubtful. Neither of them is the summit of Parnassus. That summit, called Λυκώρεια, rises high above them (about 8000 ft. above the sea). Misunderstanding δικόρυφος, the Roman poets gave a wrong impression by their 'biceps Parnassus,' which Lucan brings out when he says (5. 72) 'Parnassus gemino petit aethera colle.'

By **ὑπὲρ διλόφου πέτρας** Soph. means the high ground above these two lower peaks, but below the summit of Parnassus. This high ground is what Eur. calls the δικόρυφος πλάξ (Eur. *Bacch.* 307). It consists of uplands stretching about 16 miles westward from the summit,

and affording pasturage, interspersed with firs, and with pieces of arable land: wheat, oats, and barley are now grown there. These uplands were the scene of a Dionysiac τριετηρίς, a torch-festival, held every second year, at the end of winter, by women from the surrounding districts; even Attic women went to it (Paus. 10. 4. 3). Cp. Lucan 5. 73 *Mons Phoebo Bromioque sacer, cui numine misto | Delphica Thebanae referunt trieteria Bacchae:* and Macrobius *Sat.* 1. 18. 3. Here, however, the poet alludes, not to the human festival, but to supernatural revels.

λιγνύς is a smoky flame, such as a resinous pine-torch gives; **στέροψ** finely expresses the lurid and fitful glare flashing through the smoke.—**ὄπωπε**, gnomic perf., 'hath (oft) seen thee': *i.e.*, when the Nymphs brandish their torches, Dionysus is in the midst of them. It was the popular belief that dancing fires could be seen by night on Parnassus, when the god was holding his revels. Eur. *Ion* 716 (Parnassus) ἵνα Βάκχιος ἀμφιπύρους ἀνέχων πεύκας | λαιψηρὰ πηδᾷ νυκτιπόλοις ἅμα σὺν Βάκχαις: cp. *ib.* 1125: *Bacch.* 306: *Phoen.* 226: *I. T.* 1243.

Κωρύκιαι......Νύμφαι: Nymphs who haunt the Κωρύκιον ἄντρον and its neighbourhood. The name is from κώρυκος, 'a wallet' (and so, a hollow thing), and was given also to a cave on the Cilician coast. The Parnassian cave is near the top of a hill on the high table-land which lies at the base of the central cone,—about 7 miles N.E. of Delphi, and as many N.W. of Aráchova. It is a large stalactite cavern, consisting of an outer chamber of some 200 ft. in length, and an inner one

4 Κασταλίας τε νᾶμα.   1130
5 καί σε Νυσαίων ὀρέων
6 κισσήρεις ὄχθαι χλωρά τ' ἀκτὰ
7 πολυστάφυλος πέμπει,
8 ἀμβρότων ἐπέων
9 εὐαζόντων, Θηβαίας ἐπισκοποῦντ' ἀγυιάς·   1135

στρ. β'.   τὰν ἐκ πασᾶν τιμᾶς ὑπερτάταν πόλεων
2 ματρὶ σὺν κεραυνίᾳ·
3 καὶ νῦν, ὡς βιαίας ἔχεται   1140
4 πάνδαμος πόλις ἐπὶ νόσου,
5 μολεῖν καθαρσίῳ ποδὶ Παρνασίαν ὑπὲρ κλιτὺν
6 ἢ στονόεντα πορθμόν.   1145

1130 κασταλείασ L, with ι above ει from the first hand.   1134 ἀμβρότων L:
ἀβρότων Turnebus.—ἐπέων] Hartung conj. ἐπετῶν (Pallis, ἐπετᾶν).   1135 θηβαίασ
L. Θηβαίας Hermann (=1124 ὧν ἀγρίου τ').   1137—1145 L divides thus:
τὰν—| ὑπερτάταν· | ματρὶ—| καὶ νῦν—| ἔχεται—| ἐπὶ—| καθαρσίῳ—| ὑπὲρ...πορθ-
μόν. | 1137 f. τὰν ἐκ πασᾶν τιμᾶσ | ὑπερτάταν πόλεων L. The second α of
ὑπερτάταν seems to have been ω: and some letters have been erased above the line.
Dindorf conject. τὰν ἔκπαγλα τιμᾶς | ὑπὲρ πασᾶν πόλεων. Blaydes τὰν ἐξ ἀπασᾶν |

---

of about 100 ft.; the greatest breadth is
about 200 ft., and the greatest height, 40.
In 480 B.C., when the Persians were
coming, many of the Delphians took
refuge in it (Her. 8. 36). An old place
of sacrifice can still be seen in it; and an
inscription found there shows that it was
sacred Πανὶ καὶ νύμφαις (C. I. G. 1728).
Aesch. Eum. 22 σέβω δὲ νύμφας, ἔνθα
Κωρυκὶς πέτρα | κοίλη, φίλορνις, δαιμόνων
ἀναστροφή.

The simple transposition, στείχουσι
νύμφαι for νύμφαι στείχουσι, satisfies the
metre, and is far more probable than the
change of στείχουσι into στίχουσι,—a form
which, though noticed by Hesychius, is
not known to have been used by any Attic
writer of the classical age.

1130 Κασταλίας τε νᾶμα, sc. ὅπωπέ
σε. The Κασταλία is a stream which
flows from a fissure in the high cliffs
above Delphi. It issues near the easternmost of the two peaks (1126 ff., n.),—that
which was called Τάμπεια: and bounds
in cataracts, down a precipitous channel,
to Delphi, where its water was used for
all sacred purposes. Below Delphi it
joins the Pleistus (Aesch. Eum. 27). It
is now called Ἅγιος Ἰωάννης. It is fitly
mentioned here, since it rises on the edge

of the highlands which form the scene of
the revels.

1131 καί σε Νυσαίων. And from
Nysa in Euboea thou comest to visit
Thebes, with thy followers who cry εὐοῖ.
The Euboean Nysa was imagined near
Aegae (famous for its temple of Poseidon),
on the w. coast of the island, opposite
Anthedon. Cp. Stephanus Byz. and
Hesych. s.v. Νῦσα. That word prob. de-
noted a moist and fertile place: Welcker
would refer it to a lost νύω from rt. νυ
(νέω): Götterl. 1. 439. 'Dionysos' was
'the Zeus of Nysa' (Preller Myth. 1·
549). Legend placed a Nysa in Thrace
(Il. 6. 133), Macedonia, Thessaly, Boeotia,
Naxos, Caria, Lydia, Cilicia, Arabia,
Aethiopia, Libya, India, and even at
Parnassus. In a fragment of the Thyestes
Sophocles beautifully describes a wondrous
vine of Euboea, which puts forth leaves
and bears fruit in the same day: fr. 235
ἔστι γάρ τις ἐναλία | Εὔβοὶς αἶα· τῇδε
βάκχειος βότρυς | ἐπ' ἦμαρ ἔρπει, κ.τ.λ.

1132 κισσήρεις ὄχθαι, ivy-clad hills.
Usually ὄχθη = a river-bank, ὄχθος = a
hill: so Ph. 726 Σπερχειοῦ...παρ' ὄχθας,
and just afterwards (729) Οἴτας ὑπὲρ
ὄχθων. But the distinction is not always
observed; nor need we suspect our MSS.,

hard by Castalia's stream.

Thou comest from the ivy-mantled slopes of Nysa's hills, and from the shore green with many-clustered vines, while thy name is lifted up on strains of more than mortal power, as thou visitest the ways of Thebè:

Thebè, of all cities, thou holdest first in honour, thou, and thy mother whom the lightning smote; and now, when all our people is captive to a violent plague, come thou with healing feet over the Parnassian height, or over the moaning strait!

2nd strophe.

ὑπερτιμᾷς πόλεων. Wecklein proposed (*Ars Soph. em.* p. 76) τὰν ἔκπαγλα τιμᾷς | ὑπερτιμᾷς πόλεων, but in his ed. (1874) has πασᾶν instead of τιμᾷς.   **1140** καὶ νῦν L. Tournier conject. καιρός.   **1141** πάνδημοσ L: πάνδαμος Dindorf.—Boeckh added ἀμὰ before πόλις, in order to obtain a metrical correspondence with the MS. text of the antistrophic verse, 1150: but see n. there.—ἐπὶ] Musgrave conject. ὑπό.
1144 παρνησίαν L: Παρνασίαν r.

---

for the fact was noticed in antiquity (schol. on Aratus *Phaenom.* 33). Thus Pind. *P.* 1. 64 ὄχθαις ὕπο Ταϋγέτου: Eur. *Suppl.* 655 Ἰσμήνιον πρὸς ὄχθον.—The κισσός was to Dionysus what the δάφνη was to Apollo. The crowning with ivy (κίσσωσις) was a regular incident of his festivals: he was called κισσεύς, κισσοκόμης, κισσοχαίτης. Cp. Alciphron *Epist.* 2. 3 § 10 μὰ τὸν Διόνυσον καὶ τοὺς Βακχικοὺς αὐτοῦ κισσούς. Ov. *F.* 3. 767 *hedera est gratissima Baccho.*

1133 πολυστάφυλος: cp. *Il.* 2. 537 Χαλκίδα τ᾽ Εἰρέτριάν τε πολυστάφυλόν θ᾽ Ἱστίαιαν. As Histiaea, afterwards Oreus, was on the N. coast, we may suppose that the Homeric epithet—here borrowed by Soph.—would have been at least equally applicable to other parts of the island.—πέμπει, agreeing with nearest subject: 830 n.

1134 f. The words ἀμβρότων ἐπέων answer metrically to ναιετῶν παρ᾽ ὑγρόν (1123). There is no metrical reason, then, for altering the MS. ἀμβρότων, with Turnebus, to ἀβρότων. Cp. *O. T.* 158 ἄμβροτε Φάμα. There is no certain instance of ἄβροτος in Tragedy. Cp. Pind. *P.* 4. 299 ἀμβροσίων ἐπέων, 'divine strains.' Here the epithet suggests the mystic power of the invocation.—εὐαζόντων: see on εὔιον, 964: 'while divine chants resound with the cry *evoe*'; *i.e.*, while the bacchants escort thee on thy way to Thebes with chants of praise. The conjecture ἐπεταῶν is neat, but needless.

1137 f. τὰν ἐκ πασᾶν. There is no reason, metrical or other, for suspecting

the MS. reading here. See on 1146. τάν, Θήβαν, implied in Θηβαίας: cp. 668, 1072.—For ἐκ ('chosen out of') cp. 164: ὑπερτάταν, proleptic; cp. Eur. *I. A.* 573 μείζω πόλιν αὔξει: Plat. *Rep.* 565 C τοῦτον τρέφειν τε καὶ αὔξειν μέγαν.

1139 κεραυνίᾳ, destroyed by the lightning of Zeus: see on 1115 f. Works of art frequently associate Dionysus with his mother. Thus a fragmentary vase-painting shows him introducing her to Olympus (Welcker, *Alte Denkm.* III. pl. 13). On coins she is sometimes enthroned beside him. See Baumeister, *Denkm.* p. 443.

1140 f. ἔχεται ἐπὶ βιαίας νόσου, is captive to a violent (=a most grievous) plague. The νόσος is the divine anger which Thebes has incurred (1015). ἐπὶ νόσου seems to be like ἐπ᾽ εἰρήνης ('in time of peace' *Il.* 2. 797), ἐπὶ σχολῆς (Aeschin. or. 3 § 191): *i.e.*, the prep. expresses the continuing presence of the νόσος, and the whole phrase strictly means, 'the city is in distress, under the prevalence of a malady.' (We could scarcely compare ἐπὶ ξύλου, and suppose a metaphor from a rack or cross; cp. n. on 308 f.) Musgrave's ὑπό (for ἐπί) is tame. For ἔχεται cp. Plat. *Legg.* 780 B ὑπὸ πολλῆς ἀπορίας ἐχομένους. There is only a verbal likeness to Her. 6. 11 ἐπὶ ξυροῦ γὰρ ἀκμῆς ἔχεται (are poised) ἡμῖν τὰ πρήγματα.—For βιαίας cp. n. on 1310 δείλαιος. The text is sound, without Boeckh's conjectural insertion of ἀμὰ before πόλις: see on 1150.—πάνδαμος: cp. on 7.

1143 ff. μολεῖν: infin. for imperat.: cp. n. on 150 ff.—καθαρσίῳ: Dionysus ἀντ. β. ἰὼ πῦρ *πνειόντων χοράγ' ἄστρων, νυχίων

2 φθεγμάτων ἐπίσκοπε,

3 παῖ Διὸς γένεθλον, προφάνηθ',

4 *ὦναξ, σαῖς ἅμα περιπόλοις   1150

5 Θυίαισιν, αἵ σε μαινόμεναι πάννυχοι χορεύουσι

6 τὸν ταμίαν Ἴακχον.

1146—1154 L divides thus: ἰὼ— | χοραγὲ— | φθεγμάτων— | παῖ-- | προφά-
νηθι— | σαῖσ— | θυίασιν— | πάννυχοι— | χορεύουσι . . Ἴακχον. | **1146 f.** ἰὼ πῦρ
πνειόντων | χοραγὲ ἄστρων· καὶ νυχίων | L. (So the later MSS., some with χοράγ'.)
For πνειόντων, Brunck gave πνειόντων. Hermann, inserting τῶν before πῦρ, made
πνεόντων a spondee. He also deleted καὶ before νυχίων.—Wolff: ἰὼ πύρπνων
ἄστρων χοραγὲ καὶ νυχίων. (So Campbell, but with ὦ πῦρ πνεόντων.)—Semitelos: ἰὼ

---

was often invested with the attributes of
the Purifier and Healer, as καθάρσιος,
ἀλεξίκακος, ἀκέσιος, etc. Cp. Athen. 22 E,
and 36—37. This was one aspect of
the Delphian cult which associated him
with Apollo.—κλιτύν ⏑—, as *Tr.* 271:
but ——, *Od.* 5. 470 ἐς κλιτὺν ἀναβάς.
Here, the last syll. of the verse being
common, ὔν stands for ῦν.—πορθμόν, the
Euripus, between Euboea and Boeotia.
At Chalcis (Egripo) it is only 40 yards
across.—στονόεντα refers to the noise of
wind and water in the strait, with its
constantly changing currents. Strabo 9.
403 περὶ δὲ τῆς παλιρροίας τοῦ Εὐρίπου
τοσοῦτον μόνον εἰπεῖν ἱκανόν, ὅτι ἑπτάκις
μεταβάλλειν φασὶ καθ' ἡμέραν ἑκάστην καὶ
νύκτα. Livy (28. 6) explains this by the
squalls from the hills. Cp. Lucan's description of the Euripus, 5. 234, *Arctatus
rapido fervet qua gurgite pontus.*
1146 f. πνειόντων, Brunck's simple
correction of πνεόντων, heals the metre.
The MS. reading in 1137 f. is above all
reasonable suspicion; and these verses
now all agree with them. It is a sin against
all critical method to make violent
changes in 1137 f.—as Dindorf (followed
by Wecklein) does—in order to keep the
short syllable of πνεόντων here. Hermann's argument against πνειόντων,
which has deterred editors from admitting
it, was strangely weak. He said that
the first syllable of the epic πνείω never
occurs with ictus (*i.e.*, in arsis); and that,
if the tragic poets had used that form,
they would at least not have put an ictus
on the πνει. But Homer repeatedly has
πνοιῇ with ictus on the 1st syll. (as first

word of the verse): and as πνοιή to πνοή,
so is πνείω to πνέω. It is plain, therefore, that the Homeric absence of ictus
from the πνει of πνείω was purely an
accident of convenience in composition,
—the phrases being μένεα πνείοντες, ζε-
φυρίη πνείουσα, ἡδὺ μάλα πνείουσαν, πνείει
τε καὶ ἕρπει, etc. We need not dwell,
then, on the fact which makes a second
fallacy in the argument,—viz. that the
ictus on πνει here is only equal to that
which falls on οντ (see Metr. Anal.).
Tragic lyrics teem with epic forms and
phrases. ζάω was at least as familiar a
word as πνέω. Yet twice in lyrics Soph.
has ventured to use the epic ζώω: *El.*
157 οἷα Χρυσόθεμις ζώει: *O.C.* 1213 ζώειν.
Is it, then, reasonable to suppose that
the poet, requiring ——— instead of ⏑——,
would have hesitated to use the familiar
epic form πνειόντων? Nor is this all.
In Aesch. *Cho.* 621 the MSS. give πνέονθ'
ἁ κυνόφρων ὕπνῳ: where πνέονθ' ἁ=σύμ-
μετρον in the strophe (610), and the 1st
syllable is (pace Hermanni) necessarily
long, being that of a spondee (or trochee):
Heath's correction, πνείονθ', is therefore
certain.
Other conjectures are: (1) ἰὼ πύρπνων
ἄστρων χοραγὲ καὶ νυχών (G. Wolff).
The objection is that the contracted πύρ-
πνους and πύρπνουν do not justify πύρπνων
for πυρπνόων: cp. Eur. *Med.* 478 ταύρων
πυρπνόων ἐπιστάτην. (2) ὦ (for ἰὼ) πῦ
πνεόντων χοραγὲ καὶ νυχίων (Campbell).
Here πνεόντων is a spondee. But such
a synizesis seems very improbable. Remark, too, that L's χοραγὲ ἄστρων does
not warrant us in supposing that ἄστρων

O thou with whom the stars rejoice as they move, the stars
whose breath is fire; O master of the voices of the night;
son begotten of Zeus; appear, O king, with thine attendant
Thyiads, who in night-long frenzy dance before thee, the giver
of good gifts, Iacchus!

2nd anti-
strophe.

πῦρ παλλόντων χοράγ', ἄστρον νυχίων | φθεγμάτων. Cp. on 1149.   **1148** φθεγ-
μάτων] φεγγάτων Gleditsch, on a former conject. of Nauck's.   **1149** παῖ
διὸs L. In order to obtain a long syll. (=νῦν 1140), Pallis proposes Διὸs παῖ:
Seyffert, παῖ Δίον: Bothe, παῖ Ζηνόs.—Semitelos writes, ἐπισκόπει | γᾶν, Δηοῦs
γένεθλον.   **1150** προφάνηθι ναξίαισ L. Bergk restored προφάνηθ', ὦναξ.—
Musgrave had given προφάνηθ', ὦ Ναξίαις. See on 1141.   **1152** θυϊάσιν L:
Θυίαισιν Boeckh.

---

originally preceded χοραγέ. Neglect of
elision is frequent in L: thus, to take
one play only, the *O. C.* supplies these
examples: 266 τἀμά· ἐπεὶ: 694 ἔστιν δὲ
οἷον: 883 τάδε. ὕβρις: 915 κύρια ὧδε:
1026 θηρῶντα ἡ τύχη: 1210 ἴσθι, ἐάνπερ.
The deletion of καί before νυχίων is also
warranted by instances in which καί has
been thrust into L. Here, the καί would
decidedly enfeeble the passage.

χοράγ' ἄστρων. The sympathetic joy
of the elemental powers—stars, moon, and
sea—was especially associated with those
night-festivals in which Dionysus bore
his mystic character, as the young Ἴακχος
of the Eleusinian ritual, the companion
of Demeter and Cora (n. on *O. C.* 682 ff.).
See Eur. *Ion* 1078 ff., where the reference is to the Dionysus of the Great Mysteries at Eleusis: ὅτε καὶ Διὸς ἀστερωπὸς
| ἀνεχόρευσεν αἰθήρ, | χορεύει δὲ Σελάνα |
καὶ πεντήκοντα κόραι | Νηρέος. Hence
this crowning strain, which begins by
greeting him as χοραγὸς ἄστρων, fitly closes
with his Eleusinian name.—**νυχίων φθεγμάτων**, the songs, or wild cries, of his
worshippers. Eur. *Bacch.* 485 (Pentheus)
τὰ δ' ἱερὰ νύκτωρ ἢ μεθ' ἡμέραν τελεῖς;—
ΔΙ. νύκτωρ τὰ πολλά· σεμνότητ' ἔχει σκό-
τος. Plut. *Mor.* 291 A mentions, as
Boeotian festivals of Dionysus, the Ἀγρι-
ώνια and Νυκτέλια,—ὧν τὰ πολλὰ διὰ
σκότους δρᾶται. Ar. *Ran.* 340 (the Chorus
of the Initiated) ἔγειρε φλογέας λαμπάδας
ἐν χερσὶ τινάσσων, | Ἴακχ', ὦ Ἴακχε, | νυκ-
τέρου τελετῆς φωσφόρος ἀστήρ.

1149 παῖ Διὸs=καὶ νῦν ὡς (1140),
but is sound, since the second syllable
may be either long or short (see Metr.
Anal.).

1150 ὦναξ is a certain correction of

L's ναξίαισ. The latter, *i.e.* Ναξίαις,
may be rejected for two reasons. (1) vv.
1140 f. (καὶ νῦν—ἐπὶ νόσου) are clearly
sound, and the weak addition of ἀμά before πόλις is a pure guess, based on the
supposed genuineness of Ναξίαις here.
(2) Naxos was, indeed, peculiarly associated with Dionysus, through Ariadne's
story, and in other ways (Diod. 5. 50 ff.,
Plin. *N. H.* 4. 12. 22): but, here, Ναξίαις,
as the epithet of his followers, would be
inappropriate, since he is to visit Thebes
either from Parnassus or from Euboea
(1143 f.).

1152 f. Θυίαισιν (θύω, to sacrifice),
female votaries of Dionysus,—here, his
attendant Nymphs (*O. C.* 679 n.),—not
human worshippers. The pediment of
the temple at Delphi represented Dionysus with the Thyiads, and a setting sun
(Stephani, *Compt. rend.*, 1860, vol. 3 pp.
77 ff.). Similar names were Βάκχαι,
Λῆναι, Μαινάδες (this properly a general
epithet); and, in Macedonia, Κλώδωνες,
Μιμαλλόνες (Plut. *Alex.* 2). Plut. *Mor.*
389 C quotes some words of a thyiad
song, εὔιον ὀρσιγύναικα μαινομέναις Διόνυσον ἀνθέοντα τιμαῖς. In Elis a Dionysiac
festival was called τὰ Θυῖα (Paus. 6. 26.
1). Cp. Catull. 64. 255 ff.: Verg. *Aen.* 4.
301 ff.—**χορεύουσι** with acc. of the god,
as Pind. *I.* 1. 7 Φοῖβον χορεύων. Cp.
κόπτομαι, τίλλομαι, τύπτομαι with acc. of
person mourned.

1154 ταμίαν, dispenser (of their fortunes): cp. Plat. *Rep.* 379 E ὡς 'ταμίας'
ἡμῖν Ζεὺς 'ἀγαθῶν τε κακῶν τε τέτυκ-
ται.' Cp. **Ἴακχον**: see on χοράγ' ἄστρων
(1146).

1155—1352 Exodos. The threefold
catastrophe. Creon's remorse.

ΑΓΓΕΛΟΣ.

Κάδμου πάροικοι καὶ δόμων Ἀμφίονος,   1155
οὐκ ἔσθ' ὁποῖον στάντ' ἂν ἀνθρώπου βίον
οὔτ' αἰνέσαιμ' ἂν οὔτε μεμψαίμην ποτέ.
τύχη γὰρ ὀρθοῖ καὶ τύχη καταρρέπει
τὸν εὐτυχοῦντα τόν τε δυστυχοῦντ' ἀεί·
καὶ μάντις οὐδεὶς τῶν καθεστώτων βροτοῖς.   1160
Κρέων γὰρ ἦν ζηλωτός, ὡς ἐμοί, ποτέ,
σώσας μὲν ἐχθρῶν τήνδε Καδμείαν χθόνα,
λαβών τε χώρας παντελῆ μοναρχίαν
ηὔθυνε, θάλλων εὐγενεῖ τέκνων σπορᾷ·
καὶ νῦν ἀφεῖται πάντα. τὰς γὰρ ἡδονὰς   1165
ὅταν προδῶσιν ἄνδρες, οὐ τίθημ' ἐγὼ

1156 στάντ' ἄν] Nauck conject. πάντ' ἄν: Meineke, ἄν τιν': Semitelos, ὅτῳ συνόντ'
ἄν.   1157 ἂν from ἄμ, with an erasure after it, L.   1160 καθεστώτων]
Blaydes conject. ἐφεστώτων.   1161 ὡς ἐμοί, ποτέ] ὡς ἐμοί ποτε L.   1162 μὲν]
Hartung conject. γὰρ.   1163 λαβών τε] λαβόντε L.   1164 After θάλλων,
τε has been erased in L.   1165 ff. τὰς γὰρ ἡδονὰσ | ὅταν προδῶσιν· ἀνδρὸσ οὐ
τίθημ' ἐγώ· L. Then follows v. 1168 πλούτει τε. So too the later MSS. Athenaeus
7. 280 C supplies verse 1167, quoting 1165—1171 thus: τὰς γὰρ ἡδονὰς | ὅταν
προδῶσιν ἄνδρες, οὐ τίθημ' ἐγὼ | ζῆν τοῦτον, ἀλλ' ἐμψυχον ἡγοῦμαι νεκρόν. | πλούτει
τε ... πρὸς τὴν ἡδονήν. In 12. p. 547 C he quotes the same verses in the same

---

1155 δόμων goes with Κάδμου also:
cp. O. T. 417 μητρός τε καὶ τοῦ σοῦ πατρός: O. C. 1399 κελεύθου τῆς τ' ἐμῆς
δυσπραξίας. Cadmus founded Thebes; at
a later time, Amphion (Niobe's husband)
and his brother Zethus built a wall round
it (Apoll. Rhod. I. 740 ff.). The Thebans are πάροικοι (neighbours) δόμων,
as dwelling around the Καδμεία, the
Theban acropolis which was the seat of
Cadmus (cp. O. T. 20 n.).

1156 f. οὐκ ἔστι (τοιοῦτος ἀνθρώπου
βίος), ὁποῖον οὔτ' αἰνέσαιμι ἂν ποτε οὔτε
μεμψαίμην στάντα: there is no kind of
human life that I would ever praise, or
complain of, as fixed. The partic.
στάντα has a causal force, giving the
ground for the praise or blame. Prosperity may seem secure, or misery irre-
mediable; but no condition can be regarded as really stable (στάσιμον). Soph.
has given us a perfect comment on
στάντα (which Nauck calls 'undoubtedly'
corrupt) in fr. 786, and it is strange that
it should have escaped notice:—ἀλλ'
οὑμὸς ἀεὶ πότμος ἐν πυκνῷ θεοῦ | τρόχῳ
κυκλεῖται, καὶ μεταλλάσσει φύσιν· | ὥσπερ

σελήνης δ' ὄψις εὐφρόνας δύο | στῆναι δύ-
ναιτ' ἂν οὔποτ' ἐν μορφῇ μιᾷ,—cannot
remain fixed in one phase.—βίον is the
antecedent drawn into the clause and
case of the relative: O. C. 56 ὃν δ' ἐπι-
στείβεις τόπον | ...καλεῖται etc.: ib. 907
νῦν δ' οὕσπερ αὐτὸς τοὺς νόμους εἰσῆλθ'
ἔχων.—The only other tenable view would
be: οὐκ ἔστι (βίος τοιοῦτος στὰς) ὁποῖον
αἰνέσαιμι ἄν: there is no life so situated
that I could praise it. On this view,
στάντα would cohere closely with ὁποῖον,
having been attracted into the acc. like
βίον itself. This is not impossible; but,
if this were the construction, I should
wish to read ὁποίᾳ: cp. Ai. 950 οὐκ ἂν
τάδ' ἔστη τῇδε μὴ θεῶν μέτα.

1160 μάντις...τῶν καθεστώτων, a
prophet about them,—i.e. one who can
say how long they will last. The conjecture ἐφεστώτων ('imminent'), which
Nauck receives, is decidedly wrong for
two reasons. (1) Though we find Κῆρες
ἐφεστᾶσιν, etc., the perf. part. was regularly used as it is in Ai. 1072 τῶν ἐφεστώτων (masc.) κλύειν 'to obey the rulers';
and here a Greek would rather have sup-

Enter MESSENGER, *on the spectators' left hand.*

ME. Dwellers by the house of Cadmus and of Amphion, there is no estate of mortal life that I would ever praise or blame as settled. Fortune raises and Fortune humbles the lucky or unlucky from day to day, and no one can prophesy to men concerning those things which are established. For Creon was blest once, as I count bliss; he had saved this land of Cadmus from its foes; he was clothed with sole dominion in the land; he reigned, the glorious sire of princely children. And now all hath been lost. For when a man hath forfeited his pleasures, I count him not

---

words. Eustathius p. 957. 17 quotes τὰς γὰρ ἡδονὰς | ὅταν προδῶσιν ἄνδρα (*sic*), οὐ τίθημ' ἐγώ, and remarks that, after these words, τὰ ἀκριβῆ ἀντίγραφα have the verse, ζῆν τοῦτον, ἀλλ' ἔμψυχον ἡγοῦμαι νεκρόν. If his statement did not rest merely on Athenaeus, then, in the 12th cent., a century after L was written, there were MSS. extant which could have corrected it here; yet all our MSS. share its defect. This point should be noticed as favouring the view that all our MSS. come from L. The edition of Turnebus (Paris, 1553) was the first which incorporated v. 1167.—See Appendix.

---

posed the sense to be, 'no one in authority is a prophet.' (2) The point is that things may seem established, and yet be unstable.

1161 ὡς ἐμοί: Ai. 396 ἔρεβος ὦ φαεννότατον ὡς ἐμοί: cp. O. C. 20 n.

1162 ff. σώσας...ἐχθρῶν: the gen. as after λύω, ἐλευθερῶ: Ph. 919 σῶσαι κακοῦ: Eur. Or. 779 σωθῆναι κακῶν.—The regular constr. would have been ἦν ζηλωτός, σώσας μὲν χθόνα, λαβὼν δὲ μοναρχίαν. For δέ, τε has been substituted, as in Tr. 1012 πολλὰ μὲν ἐν πόντῳ κατά τε ὄρια πάντα καθαίρων: Ph. 1056 πάρεστι μὲν | Τεῦκρος,... | ἐγὼ θ': ib. 1136 ὁρῶν μὲν αἰσχρὰς ἀπάτας, | στυγνόν τε φῶτ'. Then in the second clause, λαβών τε, a new finite verb, ηὔθυνε, has been inserted, with the result that λαβών now begins a new sentence. Cp. 815 ὕμνησεν, n.—παντελῆ, complete; Plat. Legg. 698 Α ἡ παντελής...ἐλευθερία: cp. 737 n.—ηὔθυνε: cp. 178: O. T. 104 ἀπευθύνειν πόλιν. The temporal augment for verbs beginning with ευ is attested by Attic inscrr. of c. 403—321 B.C. (Meisterhans, p. 78).—εὐγενεῖ, not εὐγενῶν: 793 n.

1165 ἀφεῖται πάντα, all has been given up,—has slipped from his grasp, and been lost. Cp. Her. 8. 49 ἡ γὰρ Ἀττικὴ ἀπεῖτο ἤδη (to the Persians). The perf. pass. of ἀφίημι is always pass. in sense, usu. meaning either 'set free'

(as Isocr. or. 17 § 11), or, 'left free' (Plat. Critias 117 C, of open ground), or 'permitted' (Thuc. 5. 91). The only apparent instance of ἀφεῖμαι as a perf. midd. is Dem. or. 23 § 157 τοῦ μὲν τιμωρεῖσθαι τὸν Χαρίδημον ἀφεῖσθαι, ἀποστεῖλαι δ' ὑπόσπονδον. But there, as ἀποστεῖλαι suggests, we must surely read the 2nd aor. midd. ἀφέσθαι, which was frequent in this sense (Plat. Gorg. 458 C, etc.). If ἀφεῖται were midd. here, we should require πάντων: cp. Thuc. 2. 60 τοῦ κοινοῦ τῆς σωτηρίας ἀφίεσθε.

1166 προδῶσιν. προδιδόναι ἡδονάς could not mean merely, 'to resign' one's joys. It necessarily implies a fault on the loser's part; and it is precisely because Creon had committed such a fault that I believe προδῶσιν to be sound. The man accused of taking a bribe to break the law was described at 322 as ἐπ' ἀργύρῳ... τὴν ψυχὴν προδούς. Our word, 'to forfeit,' i.e. 'to lose by one's own fault,' seems fairly to represent the shade of meaning which distinguishes προδιδόναι ἡδονάς from ἀπολλύναι ἡδονάς. Creon's joys—the life of his son, and the good opinion of his subjects—have been sacrificed by him to the indulgence of stubborn self-will. Athenaeus, who twice quotes this passage (cr. n.), shows that c. 200 A.D. it was read as above: he is our oldest and best source for it. L's ἀνδρὸς must be con-

ζῆν τοῦτον, ἀλλ' ἔμψυχον ἡγοῦμαι νεκρόν.
πλούτει τε γὰρ κατ' οἶκον, εἰ βούλει, μέγα,
καὶ ζῆ τύραννον σχῆμ' ἔχων· ἐὰν δ' ἀπῇ
τούτων τὸ χαίρειν, τἄλλ' ἐγὼ καπνοῦ σκιᾶς   1170
οὐκ ἂν πριαίμην ἀνδρὶ πρὸς τὴν ἡδονήν.
ΧΟ. τί δ' αὖ τόδ' ἄχθος βασιλέων ἥκεις φέρων;
ΑΓ. τεθνᾶσιν· οἱ δὲ ζῶντες αἴτιοι θανεῖν.
ΧΟ. καὶ τίς φονεύει; τίς δ' ὁ κείμενος; λέγε.
ΑΓ. Αἵμων ὄλωλεν· αὐτόχειρ δ' αἱμάσσεται.   1175
ΧΟ. πότερα πατρῴας ἢ πρὸς οἰκείας χερός;
ΑΓ. αὐτὸς πρὸς αὐτοῦ, πατρὶ μηνίσας φόνου.
ΧΟ. ὦ μάντι, τοὔπος ὡς ἄρ' ὀρθὸν ἤνυσας.

1168 πλούτει from πλουτεῖ L.   βούλει is accentless in L, with an erasure above it.
1169 ζῆ] ζῆι L: ζῆ r (with gl. ζῆθι in V).   **1170 f.** ἐγὼ] Tournier proposes
to write ἄγω, and to delete v. 1171.—πριαίμην ἀνδρὶ] Gleditsch conject. ποιοίμην πάντα.

---

sidered in connection with the fact that L (like our other MSS.) omits v. 1167. L has a point at **προδῶσιν**, and its reading was (I suspect) understood thus: 'when (men) forfeit their pleasures, I do not count that the part of a man' (*i.e.* of one who can be really said to live). Hence I do not think that L's **ἀνδρὸς** really confirms Seyffert's conjecture, **καὶ γὰρ ἡδοναὶ** | ὅταν προδῶσιν ἀνδρός, 'when a man's pleasures *fail.*' For this use of προδιδόναι, cp. Her. 7. 187 οὐδέν μοι θωῦμα παρίσταται προδοῦναι τὰ ῥέεθρα τῶν ποταμῶν (that they failed = ἐπιλιπεῖν): id. 8. 52 τοῦ φράγματος προδεδωκότος, the barricade having failed (them). Xenophanes fr. 1. 5 **ἄλλος** δ' οἶνος ἑτοῖμος, ὃς οὔποτέ φησι προδώσειν. So with acc., [Dem.] or. 52 § 13 τὸν ὀφθαλμὸν αὐτὸν προδιδόντα (his eye-sight failing him). Yet here the phrase would seem a strange one. And if **ἄνδρες** was older than **ἀνδρός**, as we have reason to believe that it was, that fact would confirm the genuineness of **τὰς γὰρ ἡδονάς.**—See Appendix.

οὐ τίθημι with inf., as oft. with the midd. τίθεμαι; Plat. *Phaed.* 93 C τῶν οὖν τιθεμένων ψυχὴν ἁρμονίαν εἶναι. Cp. *El.* 1270 δαιμόνιον αὐτὸ τίθημ' ἐγώ.

1167 For ζῆν, ζῶν has been proposed: but the Epic and Ionic ζώς does not occur in Attic.—**τοῦτον** after the plur. as, conversely, ὅστις is followed by οὗτοι (709 n.), and νέκυν by ὧν (1072).—**ἔμψ. νεκρόν:** cp.

Ph. 1018 ἄφιλον, ἔρημον, ἄπολιν, ἐν ζῶσιν νεκρόν.

1168 f. πλούτει...ζῆ, the hypothetical imperat.: Antiphon fr. 130 (*ap.* Stob. *Flor.* 68. 37) φέρε δὴ καὶ παῖδες γενέσθωσαν· φροντίδων ἤδη πάντα πλέα. Dem. or. 20 § 14 οὐδὲ γὰρ εἰ πάνυ χρηστός ἐσθ', ὡς ἐμοῦ γ' ἕνεκα ἔστω, βελτίων ἐστὶ τῆς πόλεως τὸ ἦθος.—**εἰ βούλει:** Plat. *Rep.* 432 A τοὺς ἰσχυροτάτους καὶ τοὺς μέσους, εἰ μὲν βούλει, φρονήσει, εἰ δὲ βούλει, ἰσχύι. For the form ζῆ, cp. Eur. *I. T.* 699 ἀλλ' ἕρπε καὶ ζῆ καὶ δόμους οἴκει πατρός. But *Anthol. P.* 11. 57 πῖνε, γέρον, καὶ ζῆθι (by Agathias, *c.* 550 A.D.): and so *ib.* 10. 143 (author uncertain). **σχῆμα,** outward show, dignity, pomp: Plat. *Legg.* 685 C τὸ τῆς ἀρχῆς σχῆμα...οὐ σμικρόν.

1170 τὸ **χαίρειν:** *Ai.* 555 ἕως τὸ χαίρειν καὶ τὸ λυπεῖσθαι μάθῃς. Aesch. *Eum.* 301 ἔρρειν, τὸ χαίρειν μὴ μαθόνθ' ὅπου φρενῶν: *ib.* 423 ὅπου τὸ χαίρειν μηδαμοῦ νομίζεται. For the thought, cp. Simonides fr. 71 τίς γὰρ ἀδονᾶς ἄτερ θνατῶν βίος ποθεινὸς ἢ ποία τυραννίς; | τᾶς δ' ἄτερ οὐδὲ θεῶν ζαλωτὸς αἰών: where ἡδονή is as general as τὸ χαίρειν here. More often, however, the sentiment refers to sensuous ἡδοναί: cp. Mimnermus fr. 1 τεθναίην ὅτε μοι μηκέτι ταῦτα μέλοι: Antiphanes fr. incert. 51 (it is foolish to disparage ἔρως), εἰ γὰρ ἀφέλοι τις τοῦ βίου τὰς ἡδονάς, | καταλείπετ' οὐδὲν ἕτερον ἢ τεθνηκέναι.—**καπνοῦ σκιᾶς:** gen. of price

as living,—I hold him but a breathing corpse. Heap up riches
in thy house, if thou wilt; live in kingly state; yet, if there be
no gladness therewith, I would not give the shadow of a vapour
for all the rest, compared with joy.

CH. And what is this new grief that thou hast to tell for
our princes?

ME. Death; and the living are guilty for the dead.

CH. And who is the slayer? Who the stricken? Speak.

ME. Haemon hath perished; his blood hath been shed by
no stranger.

CH. By his father's hand, or by his own?

ME. By his own, in wrath with his sire for the murder.

CH. O prophet, how true, then, hast thou proved thy
word!

1175 αὐτόχειρ] Meineke conject. ἀρτίχειρ.
from first hand.—Herwerden conject. γόνος: Keck, κόρης.   **1177** φόνου] φόνωι L, with ου above

---

(nom., καπνοῦ σκιά). *Ph.* 946 οὐδ' οἶδ'
ἐναίρων νεκρὸν ἢ καπνοῦ σκιάν, | εἴδωλον
ἄλλως. Aesch. fr. 390 τὸ γὰρ βρότειον
σπέρμ' ἐφ' ἡμέραν φρονεῖ, | καὶ πιστὸν οὐδὲν
μᾶλλον ἢ καπνοῦ σκιά. So Soph. fr. 12
ἄνθρωπός ἐστι πνεῦμα καὶ σκιὰ μόνον. Cp.
Pind. *P.* 8. 95 σκιᾶς ὄναρ | ἄνθρωπος.
Aesch. *Ag.* 839 εἴδωλον σκιᾶς.
   1171 πριαίμην ἀνδρί. After a verb
of buying or receiving, the dat. of interest
denotes the person who has the thing
taken off his hands: Ar. *Ach.* 812 πόσου
πρίωμαί σοι τὰ χοιρίδια; *Il.* 15. 87 Θέμιστι
δὲ καλλιπάρῳ | δέκτο δέπας.—πρὸς τὴν
ἡδ., *compared with* it: fr. 327. 4 κᾆοτι
πρὸς τὰ χρήματα | θνητοῖσι τἆλλα δεύτερ':
Eur. fr. 96 ἀλλ' οὐδὲν ηὐγένεια πρὸς τὰ
χρήματα. Suppose that one could buy
either (1) wealth and power without joy,
or (2) joy without wealth and power; in
comparison with (2), (1) would be worth
nothing.—Not, '*in exchange for* pleasure,'
like Plat. *Phaed.* 69 A ἡδονὰς πρὸς ἡδονάς...
καταλλάττεσθαι: for the price is expressed
by καπνοῦ σκιᾶς.
   1172 f. βασιλέων = τυράννων, the royal
house. *Tr.* 316 μὴ τῶν τυράννων; is she
of the royal stock?—αἴτιοι θανεῖν, instead
of τοῦ θανεῖν: Antiphon or. 5 § 23 ἐγὼ
αἴτιος ἦν πεμφθῆναι ἄγγελον.—As vv.
1186 ff. show, Eurydicè is supposed to
be in the act of opening the palace-door,
to come out, when she overhears evil
tidings. If she is supposed to have
fainted (1188) immediately on hearing
the general announcement in v. 1173,

J. S. III.³

then her request in v. 1190 is the more
natural. Possibly the spectators were
allowed to catch a glimpse of her through
the partly opened doors; though the
Chorus announce her only at 1180.
   1174 φονεύει = ὁ φονεύς ἐστιν: cp.
O. T. 437 τίς δέ μ' ἐκφύει βροτῶν (is my
sire), where see n.—ὁ κείμενος: cp. Aesch.
Eum. 590 οὐ κειμένῳ πω τόνδε κομπάζεις
λόγον.
   1175 αὐτόχειρ could mean either 'by
a kinsman's hand,' or 'by his own hand.'
See n. on 56 αὐτοκτονοῦντε. Hence such
compounds sometimes receive a further
definition, as *Ai.* 841 αὐτοσφαγεῖς | πρὸς
τῶν φιλίστων ἐκγόνων. But in Aesch.
Eum. 336 αὐτουργίαι, without any such
addition, = 'murders of kinsfolk.' G. Wolff
ought not, however, to have compared
Xen. *H.* 6. 4. 35, ἀποθνῄσκει αὐτοχειρίᾳ
μὲν ὑπὸ τῶν τῆς γυναικὸς ἀδελφῶν, βουλῇ
δὲ ὑπ' αὐτῆς ἐκείνης, *i.e.*, 'by the deed of
their hands' (cp. above, v. 306), 'though
at her instigation.' Attic prose does not
use αὐτόχειρ or αὐτοχειρία in the pregnant
poetical sense (a slayer, or a slaying, of
kinsfolk), but merely in the general sense,
'doing with one's own hands,' etc. See
Plat. *Legg.* 872 B: *ib.* 865 B, etc.
   1177 f. φόνου, causal gen.: 931 (τούτων)
n.—ὀρθὸν ἤνυσας, hast fulfilled it, so that
it comes right (cp. 1136, n. on ὑπερτάταν):
O. T. 506 πρὶν ἴδοιμ' ὀρθὸν ἔπος: cp. *ib.*
853. *O. C.* 454 (μαντεῖα) ἁμοὶ Φοῖβος ἤνυ-
σέν ποτε.

14

ΑΓ. ὡς ὧδ' ἐχόντων τἆλλα βουλεύειν πάρα.

ΧΟ. καὶ μὴν ὁρῶ τάλαιναν Εὐρυδίκην ὁμοῦ   1180
δάμαρτα τὴν Κρέοντος· ἐκ δὲ δωμάτων
ἤτοι κλύουσα παιδὸς ἢ τύχῃ πάρα.

ΕΥΡΥΔΙΚΗ.

ὦ πάντες ἀστοί, τῶν λόγων ἐπῃσθόμην
πρὸς ἔξοδον στείχουσα, Παλλάδος θεᾶς
ὅπως ἱκοίμην εὐγμάτων προσήγορος.   1185
καὶ τυγχάνω τε κλῇθρ' ἀνασπαστοῦ πύλης
χαλῶσα, καί με φθόγγος οἰκείου κακοῦ
βάλλει δι' ὤτων· ὑπτία δὲ κλίνομαι
δείσασα πρὸς δμωαῖσι κἀποπλήσσομαι.

1179 τἆλλα βουλεύειν] Blaydes conject. τῶνδε βουλεύειν: Martin, τἆλλα μου κλύειν: Wecklein, τἆλλα συμβάλλειν. **1182** πάρα] Brunck conject. περᾷ. **1183** ὦ πάντες] Blaydes conject. ὦνακτες: Heimsoeth, ἄπωθεν (with ῥημάτων for τῶν λόγων): Hense, γέροντες.—τῶν λόγων L: τοῦ λόγου γ' A. **1184** θεᾶς] Nauck conject. βρέτας: Dorschel (ap. Wolff) σέβας. Semitelos, Παλλάδ' ὡς θεάν.

1179 ὡς with the gen. absol. (cp. 1063 n.) marks the point of view which is to be taken: 'in the certainty that matters stand thus.' **πάρεστι βουλ. τὰ ἄλλα**, 'ye may consider of the rest': *i.e.*, such are the facts; it only remains to deal with them as may seem best. **βουλεύειν**, to form plans, decide on a course of action, *O. T.* 619: **τὰ ἄλλα**, adverbial acc. of respect, 'as to what remains,' instead of περὶ τῶν ἄλλων (*Ai.* 551 τὰ δ' ἄλλ' ὅμοιος). —**ὧδ' ἐχόντων**, neut. gen. abs., without a subject: *Ai.* 981 ὡς ὧδ' ἐχόντων... | πάρα στενάζειν: *El.* 1344 τελουμένων εἴποιμ' ἄν: Aesch. *Pers.* 170 πρὸς τάδ', ὡς οὕτως ἐχόντων τῶνδε, σύμβουλοι λόγου | τοῦδέ μοι γένεσθε, Πέρσαι. Thuc. 1. 116 ἐσαγγελθέντων ὅτι...νῆες...πλέουσιν.

1180 καὶ μήν: 526 n.—**Εὐρυδίκην**: anapaest in 5th place: cp. 11 n. Schol.: Ἡσίοδος Ἡνιόχην αὐτὴν καλεῖ· ἵκετο δ' εἰς Κρείοντα καὶ Ἡνιόχην [τανύπεπλον, *sc.* Heracles: *Scut.* 83].—**ὁμοῦ** = ἐγγύς: Ar. *Pax* 513 καὶ μὴν ὁμοῦ 'στιν ἤδη. Soph. has it also as a prep.: *Ai.* 767 θεοῖς...ὁμοῦ = σὺν θ.: in *Ph.* 1218 νεὼς ὁμοῦ = πέλας νεώς.

1182 κλύουσα παιδός: gen. of connection, 'about' him: *O. C.* 307 κλύων σοῦ (n.), hearing of thee.

1183 ὦ πάντες ἀστοί, said to the

Chorus and the Messenger, as representing the Thebans generally. In Eur. *I. T.* 1422 Thoas says ὦ πάντες ἀστοί, not to the Chorus (of Greek women), but to the Tauri as represented by his attendants. So, too, in Ar. *Eccl.* 834 ὦ πάντες ἀστοί is said to an imaginary body of Athenian citizens, represented by two men on the stage. In *Lys.* 638 the Chorus say ὦ πάντες ἀστοί to the audience.

1184 f. Παλλάδος προσήγορος εὐγμάτων answers to Παλλάδα προσαγορεύω εὔγματα: *i.e.*, the first gen. is objective, while the second represents an 'inner' accus. A combination of genitives was easily tolerated by Greek idiom: cp. 795 βλεφάρων ἵμερος...νύμφας (n.): Xen. *Cyr.* 8. 3. 19 δεδμενοι Κύρου ἄλλος ἄλλης πράξεως. **προσήγορος**, active, as *O. T.* 1338: it is passive *ib.* 1437, *Ph.* 1353.—The shrine to which Eurydicè was going may be imagined as one of the two Παλλάδος ναοί at Thebes mentioned in *O. T.* 20 (n.). She was anxious to do her part in seeking to propitiate the angry gods (1019).—So Iocasta comes forth from the house to offer prayers at the altar of Apollo Λύκειος (*O. T.* 919), and Clytaemnestra at that of Apollo προστατήριος (*El.* 637).

1186 f. τυγχάνω τε...καὶ...βάλλει: just as she was loosing the bolt, she heard

ΜΕ. These things stand thus: ye must consider of the rest.

ΧΗ. Lo, I see the hapless Eurydicè, Creon's wife, approaching; she comes from the house by chance, haply,—or because she knows the tidings of her son.

Enter EURYDICÈ.

ΕΥ. People of Thebes, I heard your words as I was going forth, to salute the goddess Pallas with my prayers. Even as I was loosing the fastenings of the gate, to open it, the message of a household woe smote on mine ear: I sank back, terror-stricken, into the arms of my handmaids, and my senses fled.

1185 ὅπως] Wolff conject. ὅμμ' ὡς.   **1186** τε L, with γ written above τ by the first corrector S, (not, I think, by the first hand:) some of the later MSS. have γε: L² has δέ.   **1189** δμωαῖσι] In L, S has written ·es· over αῖ (*i.e.*, δμώεσσι).

---

the sound (cp. 1172 f. n.). For the temporal parataxis with τε...καί, cp. Xen. *An.* 1. 8 § 1 ἤδη τε ἦν ἀμφὶ ἀγορὰν πλήθουσαν καὶ πλησίον ἦν ὁ σταθμός: so *ib.* 4. 2. 12, 4. 6. 2, *Cyr.* 1. 4. 28. So with καί alone, *O. T.* 718 n.

κλῆθρα χαλῶσα πύλης ἀνασπαστοῦ, loosing the bolts of the door, so that it should be opened (proleptic, cp. 475, 881). For the fem. of the verbal in -τός, see *O. T.* 384 n.—κλῆθρα, 'bolts,' are bars of wood drawn across the doors inside, and held by staples or sockets (πυθμένες *O. T.* 1261) in the door-posts (σταθμοί). Such bars were usu. called μοχλοί, but even in prose we find the more general word κλῆθρα: Xen. *An.* 7. 1. 17 διακόπτοντες ταῖς ἀξίναις τὰ κλεῖθρα ἀναπεταννύουσι τὰς πύλας. There, as here, the plur. κλῆθρα, referring to only one gate, indicates that more than one bolt was used; so, too, Ar. *Lys.* 310 κἂν μὴ καλούντων τοὺς μοχλοὺς χαλῶσιν αἱ γυναῖκες, | ἐμπιμπράναι χρὴ τὰς θύρας. Cp. Aesch. *Cho.* 878 πύλας | μοχλοῖς χαλᾶτε, open the door by (withdrawing) the bars. Eur. *Med.* 1314 χαλᾶτε κλῆδας. Plut. *Pelop.* 11 ἐνδοῦναι καὶ χαλάσαι τὰς θύρας.

ἀνασπαστοῦ. These doors opened inwards. ἐπισπᾶν θύραν meant to shut the door after one, in going out. Cp. Xen. *H.* 6. 4. 36 ὡς δ' εἰσῆλθον, ἐπισπάσασα τὴν θύραν εἶχετο τοῦ ῥόπτρου (Thebè's object was to shut her brothers into the room, till they had killed Alexander of Pherae): 'when they had entered, she, [having gone out and] shut

the door, held the knocker,'—the ῥόπτρον being a metal ring on the outside of the door, which also served as ἐπισπαστήρ or handle (cp. Her. 6. 91). Plut. *Dion* 57 οἱ μὲν ἔξω τὰς θύρας ἐπισπασάμενοι κατεῖχον. (In *O. T.* 1244 πύλας...ἐπιρράξασα is said of Iocasta, within the room, shutting the doors; but they, too, opened inwards, see *ib.* 1261 ff.) Hence ἀνασπᾶν θύραν, 'to draw it back,' is the opposite of ἐπισπᾶν, and means 'to open it' (from within). That phrase was not actually current, ἀνοιγνύναι being the common word; but the poetical ἀνασπαστός here implies it. Polyb. 5. 39. 4 is not rightly compared: there, ὡς ἀνασπάσοντες...τὰς πυλίδας='intending to wrench the gates open,' from outside: cp. id. 2. 5. 5 τῆς ...γεφύρας ἀνασπάσαντες τὰς σανίδας, 'having torn up the floor of the bridge.'

φθόγγος, the Messenger's words. She had fainted before hearing more, perhaps, than vv. 1172 f., where see n.—οἰκεῖον, domestic (affecting her family): cp. 1249. —Distinguish οἰκ. πάθη (*Ai.* 260), οἰκ. ἄτας (*El.* 215) as='caused by oneself.'

1188 f. δι' ὤτων: *El.* 737 ὀξὺν δι' ὤτων κέλαδον ἐνσείσας θοαῖς | πώλοις: cp. *O. T.* 1386 f.—πρὸς δμωαῖσι, with κλίνομαι: a use of the dat. with πρός which has epic precedent, as *Il.* 20. 420 λιαζόμενον προτὶ γαίῃ, sinking to earth: *ib.* 21. 507 τὴν δὲ προτὶ οἷ | εἷλε πατὴρ Κρονίδης, took her to his arms: cp. *O. T.* 1302 n.—ἀποπλήσσομαι, as=λιποψυχῶ, only here: Hippocr. uses it of apoplexy.

14—2

ἀλλ' ὅστις ἦν ὁ μῦθος αὖθις εἴπατε·　　　1190
κακῶν γὰρ οὐκ ἄπειρος οὖσ' ἀκούσομαι.
ΑΓ. ἐγώ, φίλη δέσποινα, καὶ παρὼν ἐρῶ,
κοὐδὲν παρήσω τῆς ἀληθείας ἔπος.
τί γάρ σε μαλθάσσοιμ' ἂν ὧν ἐς ὕστερον
ψεῦσται φανούμεθ'; ὀρθὸν ἀλήθει' ἀεί.　　　1195
ἐγὼ δὲ σῷ ποδαγὸς ἐσπόμην πόσει
πεδίον ἐπ' ἄκρον, ἔνθ' ἔκειτο νηλεὲς
κυνοσπάρακτον σῶμα Πολυνείκους ἔτι·
καὶ τὸν μέν, αἰτήσαντες ἐνοδίαν θεὸν
Πλούτωνά τ' ὀργὰς εὐμενεῖς κατασχεθεῖν,　　　1200
λούσαντες ἁγνὸν λουτρόν, ἐν νεοσπάσιν
θαλλοῖς ὃ δὴ 'λέλειπτο συγκατήθομεν,
καὶ τύμβον ὀρθόκρανον οἰκείας χθονὸς
χώσαντες, αὖθις πρὸς λιθόστρωτον κόρης

1193 παρείσω L, with η above ει from S.　　　**1194** ἐς ὕστερον] ἐσύστερον L.
1195 ἡ ἀλήθει' L: ἀλήθει' Hermann.　　　**1197** πεδίον ἐπ' ἄκρων (sic) L. The
later mss. have either πεδίων ἐπ' ἄκρων (as V), or πεδίον ἐπ' ἄκρον (as A).　　　Pallis,

---

**1192 f. καὶ παρὼν ἐρῶ, κοὐδὲν
παρήσω**: I *both* will speak as one who
was present, *and* will omit nothing : *i.e.*,
as my knowledge is full, *so* shall the story
be told without reserve. For the parataxis, cp. 1112: *El.* 680 κἀπεμπόμην
πρὸς ταῦτα καὶ τὸ πᾶν φράσω: *Tr.* 626
ἐπίσταμαί τε καὶ φράσω σεσωσμένα. For
παρών as partic. of the imperfect, cp.
166 σέβοντας (n.). Verses 1192—1195
form the dramatic apology for a trait
which is manifestly open to criticism,—
viz., the fulness of harrowing details
communicated by the Messenger to this
unhappy mother, who has only just recovered from a swoon. (See esp. 1231
—1239.)
　　1194 f. ὧν = τούτοις ὧν: Xen. *Mem.*
I. 2. 6 διαλέγεσθαι παρ' ὧν λάβοιεν τὸν
μισθόν, to converse with any who might
pay them. Cp. 35 n.—**ὧν** with **ψεῦσται**
(=fabricators), as one could say, ταῦτα
ἐψεύσαντο. For **φανούμεθ'** after the sing.
verb, cp. 734 n.—**ὀρθόν**, not ὀρθή: *O. T.*
542 n.: *O. C.* 592.
　　1196 ποδαγός, Doric (cp. 715 ναός, n.),
'guide,' as Eur. *Ph.* 1715 σύ μοι ποδαγὸς
ἀθλία γενοῦ (Oed. to Antigone). Plat.
Legg. 899 A has ποδηγεῖν as='to guide.'
—The word is usu. taken here as merely

pedissequus, 'attendant.' But the sense
of 'guiding' is essential to it. Creon had
indicated the region (1110), but he need
not be supposed to know the spot where
the body lay, or even the exact situation
of Antigone's tomb. **ἐσπόμην**, 'attended,'
is compatible with guiding.
　　1197 πεδίον...ἄκρον=the furthest part
of the plain. Near this part were the
πάγοι on which the watchers sat (411),
and Antigone's tomb was in one of those
πάγοι (774 n.). Thebes had hills to the
N. of it, and stood on a low spur which
they throw out southward (117 ff., n.).
The ἄκρον πεδίον, then, is the plain's
northern edge, where it touches the lower
slopes of the hills. The 'furthest' was
thus also the highest part.—**νηλεές**, passive: *O. T.* 180.
　　1198 κυνοσπάρακτον: cp. 206, 1017.
Antigone had paid the rites while the
corpse was still intact (257), and in this
sense is said to have saved it from birds
and dogs (697: cp. 467).
　　1199 f. τὸν μέν, as opposed to Antigone:
but instead of τῆς δὲ νυμφεῖον, etc., we
have a change of construction (1204 αὖθις
κ.τ.λ.).—**ἐνοδίαν θεόν**, Hecatè, who was
conceived as a wandering goddess, haunt-
ing the places where roads met, and where

But say again what the tidings were; I shall hear them as
one who is no stranger to sorrow.

ME. Dear lady, I will witness of what I saw, and will leave
no word of the truth untold. Why, indeed, should I soothe
thee with words in which I must presently be found false?
Truth is ever best.—I attended thy lord as his guide to the
furthest part of the plain, where the body of Polyneices,
torn by dogs, still lay unpitied. We prayed the goddess of
the roads, and Pluto, in mercy to restrain their wrath; we
washed the dead with holy washing; and with freshly-plucked
boughs we solemnly burned such relics as there were. We
raised a high mound of his native earth; and then we turned
away to enter the maiden's nuptial chamber with rocky couch,

πάγων ἐπ' ἄκρων.   **1200** πλούτωνά τ' ὀργᾶσ from πλοῦτονά τ' ὀργᾶσ L.—κατα-
σχέθειν L: κατασχεθεῖν Elmsley.   **1202** δὴ λέλειπτο L: cp. on 539.

---

offerings were left for her. (Τριοδῖτις, *Tri-
via*: Theocr. 2. 36 ἃ θεὸς ἐν τριόδοισι.)
Sophocles in his Ῥιζοτόμοι gave an incan-
tation by Medea, invoking Helios and
Hecatè (fr. 490, schol. Apoll. Rhod. 3.
1214): Ἥλιε δέσποτα καὶ πῦρ ἱερόν, | τῆς
εἰνοδίας Ἑκάτης ἔγχος, | τὸ δι' Οὐλύμπου
πωλοῦσα φέρει (which she bears when she
moves through the sky, as Selenè), | καὶ
γῆς ναίουσ' ἱερὰς τριόδους, | στεφανωσα-
μένη δρυῒ καὶ πλεκταῖς | ὠμῶν σπείραισι
δρακόντων. The last two lines refer to a
custom of representing her as crowned
with serpents, and with chaplets of oak-
leaves. Creon invokes her along with
Pluto (Hades, *O. T.* 30 n.), because on
earth she represented the χθόνιοι. As
ἐνοδία, she was more especially associated
with Hermes ἐνόδιος and ψυχοπομπός:
hence she was sometimes called ἄγγελος.
—θεόν, fem., as 834: *O. C.* 1548 ἡ...
νερτέρα θεός, *ib.* 1556 τὰν ἀφανῆ θεόν
(Persephone). Cp. *ib.* 683 n.—εὐμενεῖς,
proleptic: 881 n.—κατασχεθεῖν: cp. on
1102.
    1201 f. λούσαντες ἁγν. λουτρόν (cog-
nate acc.): cp. on 901.—ἐν, 'with,' of
the instrument: 764 (n.), 962, 1003.—
θαλλοῖς, from the ὕλη πεδιάς close by
(420).—Boeckh thought that *olive*-boughs
were meant, citing a νόμος *ap.* [Dem.] or.
43 § 71 ἐὰν μὴ (ἐλαίᾳ)...ἐπὶ ἀποθανόντα δέῃ
χρήσασθαι. But that, surely, does not refer
to a πυρά. The olive, like the laurel, was
used for other purposes connected with
the dead,—viz., in crowning the corpse

for the πρόθεσις (cp. schol. Eur. *Ph.* 1626),
and in decking the κλίνη on which the
corpse was laid (Ar. *Eccl.* 1030).—ὅ δὴ
=ὅ τι δήποτε, implying that much of the
body had been destroyed. Cp. Her. 1.
160 ἐπὶ μισθῷ ὅσῳ δή· οὐ γὰρ ἔχω τοῦτό
γε εἰπεῖν ἀτρεκέως.—λέλειπτο: cp. 457
'φάνη n.—συγκατήθομεν. The σύν here
is perh. not merely 'completely,' but
implies the collecting of dismembered
pieces: as συγκατακαίω regularly=to burn
something 'along with' something else
(Xen. *An.* 3. 2. 27). Like εἰσεβαίνομεν
(1205), this is the imperf. of consecutive
action ('proceeded to burn,' = 'next
burned').
    1203 τύμβον. If the Homeric usage
was followed, when the flesh had been
burned the bones would be washed with
wine or oil, wrapped in fat, and placed
in an urn (λάρναξ). The urn having been
deposited in a grave (κάπετος), the τύμβος
(or σῆμα) would be raised over it. Cp.
Introd. to Homer, ch. II. § 33.—ὀρθόκρανον, lit., with head erect, so='high': cp.
ὑψικάρηνος, ὑψίλοφος (of hills). From
κρᾶν (κρανίον) we have also βούκρανος,
ταυρόκρανος.—οἰκείας, 'native,'—a thing
pleasing to the dead: so in *O. C.* 406
Oed. asks, ἦ καὶ κατασκιῶσι Θηβαίᾳ κόνει;
The father's prophecy for his sons was
fulfilled: of their father-land they obtained ὁπόσαν καὶ φθιμένοισιν κατέχειν
(Aesch. *Th.* 731: cp. *O. C.* 789).
    1204 f. αὖθις answers to τὸν μέν
(1199), as in 167 τοῦτ' αὖθις to τοῦτο μέν.

νυμφεῖον Ἅιδου κοῖλον εἰσεβαίνομεν.　　　　　1205
φωνῆς δ' ἄπωθεν ὀρθίων κωκυμάτων
κλύει τις ἀκτέριστον ἀμφὶ παστάδα,
καὶ δεσπότῃ Κρέοντι σημαίνει μολών·
τῷ δ' ἀθλίας ἄσημα περιβαίνει βοῆς
ἕρποντι μᾶλλον ἆσσον, οἰμώξας δ' ἔπος　　　　1210
ἵησι δυσθρήνητον· ὦ τάλας ἐγώ,
ἆρ' εἰμὶ μάντις; ἆρα δυστυχεστάτην
κέλευθον ἕρπω τῶν παρελθουσῶν ὁδῶν;
παιδός με σαίνει φθόγγος. ἀλλά, πρόσπολοι,
ἴτ' ἆσσον ὠκεῖς, καὶ παραστάντες τάφῳ　　　　1215
ἀθρήσαθ', ἁρμὸν χώματος λιθοσπαδῆ
δύντες πρὸς αὐτὸ στόμιον, εἰ τὸν Αἵμονος

1208 μολών] L has αθ written above ολ by S: this variant μαθών is in the text of some later MSS. (as V).　　**1209** ἄσημα] Nauck conject. ἄχημα.—περιβαίνει] Schaefer conject. περισαίνει: Wunder, περιπολεῖ.　　**1212** ἄρ' L.—εἰμὶ] L has the second ι in an erasure: εἰ μὴ had been written.　　**1215** παραστάντεσ .φ. τάφωι L.

For αὖθις as = 'afterwards,' cp. *Ai.* 1283, *Tr.* 270.—λιθόστρωτον, 'with floor of stone,' here suggests, 'affording no couch but one of stone,' in contrast with a real νυμφεῖον, which contains a λέχος εὔστρωτον... | χλαίνῃσιν μαλακῇς ἐστρωμένον (*Hom. hymn. Ven.* 157 f.).—κόρης νυμφεῖον· Ἅιδου, the maiden's death-bower: cp. 795 n., 929.

1206 κωκυμάτων, the word used by Teiresias (1079): here, as usu., for the dead: cp. 28, 204, 1302: so κωκυντός, *Ai.* 851 etc.—Cp. *El.* 683 ὀρθίων κηρυγμάτων.

1207 ἀκτέριστον ἀμφὶ παστάδα, near (*i.e.* from the quarter of) the bridal-chamber where no funeral-rites had been paid; *i.e.*, where Antigone had been made the bride of Death, without even such honours as befitted such nuptials. For ἀκτέριστος cp. 1071 n. The word παστάς seems to be here used simply as a poetical equivalent for θάλαμος. There is probably no reference to pillars of rock (natural or artificial) in the τάφος. On the uses of παστάς, see Appendix.

1209 ἀθλίας...ἄσημα βοῆς, indistinct sounds, consisting in an ἀθλία βοή: *i.e.*, as he drew nearer, the sounds resolved themselves into the mournful cry of a human voice. The genit. is thus a 'defining' one. Cp. *O. C.* 923 n. φωτῶν

ἀθλίων ἰκτήρια (suppliant objects consisting in unhappy persons). Below, in 1265, the form of ὤμοι ἐμῶν ἄνολβα βουλευμάτων is analogous, but the gen. is there partitive (see n.). Here, βοῆς could, indeed, be possessive ('sounds belonging to, *i.e.*, forming part of, a cry'). But the perspective of the description is better kept by the other view of the genitive, which supposes that a sound, ambiguous at a distance, defines itself as we approach.—περιβαίνει, with dat. instead of the normal acc.; this dat. denotes the person interested, *i.e.*, here affected through the senses: *O. C.* 372 εἰσῆλθε τοῖν τρὶς ἀθλίοιν ἔρις (n.): *Tr.* 298 ἐμοὶ γὰρ οἶκτος... εἰσέβη. For the image, cp. *O. C.* 1477 ἀμφίσταται | διαπρύσιος ὄτοβος: *Od.* 6. 122 ὥς τέ με κουράων ἀμφήλυθε θῆλυς ἀϋτή.

1210 f. μᾶλλον ἆσσον: cp. Aesch. *Th.* 673 μᾶλλον ἐνδικώτερος: Eur. *El.* 222 μᾶλλον ἐχθίους: Plat. *Legg.* 781 A λαθραιότερον μᾶλλον καὶ ἐπικλοπώτερον.—ἔπος (= θρῆνον) δυσθρήνητον: see n. on 7.—ὦ τάλας: cp. *O. T.* 744 n.

1213 f. τῶν παρελθουσῶν: cp. 100 f. κάλλιστον...τῶν προτέρων, n.—σαίνει, 'greets my ear.' As σαίνω was properly said of a dog wagging its tail or fawning so it could be said of a sight or a sound the caverned mansion of the bride of Death. And, from afar off, one of us heard a voice of loud wailing at that bride's un-hallowed bower ; and came to tell our master Creon.

And as the King drew nearer, doubtful sounds of a bitter cry floated around him ; he groaned, and said in accents of anguish, 'Wretched that I am, can my foreboding be true ? Am I going on the wofullest way that ever I went ? My son's voice greets me. — Go, my servants, — haste ye nearer, and when ye have reached the tomb, pass through the gap, where the stones have been wrenched away, to the cell's very mouth, — and look, and see if 'tis Haemon's

---

The meaning of this φ is simply (I think) that the scribe's eye had caught the word φθοράν in 1224. Having written φ, he judged it simpler to leave it (with dots) than to change it by erasure into τ. **1216** ἀθρήσαθ᾽, ἀρμὸν] Semitelos conject. ἀθρεῖτε, θαλάμων.—χώματος] Seyffert conject. χάσματος: Tournier, δώματος.—λιθοσπαδῇ. In L, ι has been erased after ῆ. Cp. on 726.

---

which *appeals for recognition* by vividly striking our senses. Like *arridere*, the word usually implied a sensation of pleasure (*O. C.* 319 n.). But it could also denote, as here, a recognition attend-ed by pain. So in Eur. *Hippol.* 862 f., where Theseus recognises the seal on the tablets left by his dead wife, he says τύποι...προσσαίνουσί με.

1215 ὠκεῖς, adverbial: cp. 823, 847 : *Tr.* 927 δρομαία βᾶσ᾽.

1216 ἀρμὸν χώματος λιθοσπ., an opening in the stones heaped up at the entrance, made by dragging some of them away. Cp. 848 ἔργμα τυμβόχωστον. Haemon, in his frenzy of despair, had broken into the tomb by wrenching away part of this rude wall-work. The gap remained as he had made it. He had reached the spot only a short time before Creon (cp. on 1223).

ἀρμόν. The word ἀρμός means, (1) a fastening : Eur. *Med.* 1315 ἐκλύεθ᾽ ἁρμούς, undo the fastenings of the doors : (2) the chink between two things which are joint-ed together: so in Plut. *Alex.* 3 a furtive listener is described as τῷ τῆς θύρας ἁρμῷ προσβαλὼν (τὴν ὄψιν), 'having put his eye to the chink in the door.' So here ἁρμός is an aperture, just wide enough to admit of a man going through (cp. **δύντες**).— ἁρμός (with its derivatives ἁρμοῖ, ἁρμόζω, ἁρμονία), and ἀρπεδόνη (or ἀρπεδών), 'rope,' are connected with the causative form of the root *ar*, *ar-pajā-mi*, 'to fasten': see Curt. *Etym.* § 488.

1217 στόμιον. Having passed through the gap, they will find themselves in a narrow passage. They are to·go along this passage to the very mouth (στόμιον) of the sepulchral chamber into which it opens.

The kind of tomb which the poet here imagines is perhaps best represented, in Greece, by the rock-tombs of Nauplia, and of Spata in Attica. These consist of chambers worked horizontally into the rock, and approached by a passage or δρόμος, answering to that which Creon's men have to traverse before they reach the στόμιον of the tomb. The general type seems to have been determined by that of the more elaborate domed tombs, such as the so-called 'Treasury of Atreus' at Mycenae, which, like these ruder copies, were entered by a δρόμος. Indeed, the Nauplia tombs indicate a rough at-tempt to reproduce the dome (θόλος). [See Helbig, *Das Homer. Epos aus den Denkm. erläutert*, p. 53, with the sources quoted there in nn. 5, 6.]

The phrase λοίσθιον τύμβευμα (1220) might suggest a recess *within* the prin-cipal chamber, like that in the 'Treasury of Atreus'; but it is simpler to take it as merely 'the furthest part of the tomb.' We may observe that the words κατῶρυξ (774) and κατασκαφής (891) are suf-ficiently explained if we suppose that the δρόμος leading to the chamber sloped downwards from the entrance.

φθόγγον συνίημ', ἢ θεοῖσι κλέπτομαι.
τάδ' ἐξ ἀθύμου δεσπότου *κελευσμάτων
ἠθροῦμεν· ἐν δὲ λοισθίῳ τυμβεύματι   1220
τὴν μὲν κρεμαστὴν αὐχένος κατείδομεν,
βρόχῳ μιτώδει σινδόνος καθημμένην,
τὸν δ' ἀμφὶ μέσσῃ περιπετῆ προσκείμενον,
εὐνῆς ἀποιμώζοντα τῆς κάτω φθορὰν
καὶ πατρὸς ἔργα καὶ τὸ δύστηνον λέχος.   1225
ὁ δ' ὡς ὁρᾷ σφε, στυγνὸν οἰμώξας ἔσω
χωρεῖ πρὸς αὐτὸν κἀνακωκύσας καλεῖ·
ὦ τλῆμον, οἷον ἔργον εἴργασαι· τίνα
νοῦν ἔσχες; ἐν τῷ συμφορᾶς διεφθάρης;

1218 Reiske conject. φόβοισι κλέπτομαι: Tournier, θεοῖσι βλάπτομαι. **1219** τάδ' ἐξ ἀθύμου] Nauck reads ὀξυθύμου, ascribing that conject. to J. P. Pompe van Meerdervoort, and referring to Naber *Mnem. nov.* 9. 219 f.—Heath conject. τάδ' οὖν ἀθύμου: Pallis, τάδ' οὐκ ἄθυμοι: Seyffert, τάδ' ἐξ ἑτοίμου: Semitelos, τάδ' εἰκάθοντες.—κελεύσμασιν MSS. Dindorf writes κελεύμασιν, the form given by L in Aesch. *Pers.* 397, *Ch.* 751. Burton conject. κελευσμάτων. **1222** μιτώδει] The first

---

1218 θεοῖσι: dat. of agent with *pres. pass.*: see n. on 503 ff.—κλέπτομαι, am deluded: 681 n.—Cp. *O. C.* 316 ἦ γνώμη πλανᾷ;

1219 The simple correction, κελευσμάτων for κελεύσμασιν, is (I think) certainly right. Cp. Aesch. *Pers.* 397 ἔπαισαν ἅλμην βρύχιον ἐκ κελεύσματος (and similarly Eur. *I. T.* 1405): Her. 6. 50 ἔλεγε δὲ ταῦτα ἐξ ἐπιστολῆς τῆς Δημαρήτου. With κελεύσμασιν, we have only two tolerable resources. (1) To join κελεύσμασιν ἐξ ἀθύμου δεσπότου, 'orders given by him.' But, though τοῖς ἐξ ἀθ. δεσπ. κελεύσμασιν could be defended by τὴν ἐξ ἐμοῦ δυσβουλίαν (95), the phrase without the article is very strange. In phrases which might appear similar, it will be found that a verb has influenced the use of ἐκ with gen.: thus *Ai.* 137 σὲ δ' ὅταν... | λόγος ἐκ Δαναῶν κακόθρους ἐπιβῇ: Aesch. *Ag.* 1366 ἦ γὰρ τεκμηρίοισιν ἐξ οἰμωγμάτων | μαντευσόμεσθα τἀνδρὸς ὡς ὀλωλότος; here, however, it is impossible to take ἐξ ἀθύμου δεσπότου with ἠθροῦμεν, and to make κελεύσμασιν a mere epexegesis ('looked, at our master's instigation, *i.e.*, by his command').

(2) The alternative is to amend ἐξ ἀθύμου. Only one correction is probable, viz. ὀξυθύμου. The decisive objection to this is the sense. It could mean only,

'swift to wrath,' like ὀξύχολος (955). It could not mean merely, 'agitated' (by alarm). But Creon is no longer proud or fierce; he has been humbled: his late words (1211 ff.) expressed only grief and fear.

Dindorf writes κελεύμασιν, holding this to be the older Attic form (cr. n.). The fact appears to be that both κέλευμα and κέλευσμα are well attested in our MSS. of some authors: and there is no evidence from inscriptions. As regards the verb, Lobeck (on *Ai.* 704) remarks that, while ἐκελεύσθην is far commoner than ἐκελεύθην, κεκέλευμαι and κεκέλευσμαι are both well attested for the best age. But Veitch's statement on this point is more accurate. While ἐκελεύθην is extremely rare in classical Greek, κεκέλευμαι is nearly (if not quite) unknown to it. It would be very rash, then, to affirm that Soph. must have used the non-sigmatic form of the noun.

1221 αὐχένος: the gen. of the part, as with verbs of seizing, etc.: Arist. *H.A.* 9. 50. 7 ὅταν κρεμάσωσι (τὰς ὗς) τῶν ὀπισθίων ποδῶν: so κρεμῶμεν with gen., Ar. *Plut.* 312: *Il.* 17. 289 (τὸν) ποδὸς ἔλκε: *Od.* 3. 439 βοῦν δ' ἀγέτην κεράων.

1222 μιτώδει, thread-like, *i.e.*, formed by a thread-wrought fabric (the σινδών), and not, as usual, by a cord. μίτρος (ὁ), voice that I know, or if mine ear is cheated by the gods.'

This search, at our despairing master's word, we went to make; and in the furthest part of the tomb we descried *her* hanging by the neck, slung by a thread-wrought halter of fine linen; while *he* was embracing her with arms thrown around her waist,—bewailing the loss of his bride who is with the dead, and his father's deeds, and his own ill-starred love.

But his father, when he saw him, cried aloud with a dread cry, and went in, and called to him with a voice of wailing:—'Unhappy, what a deed hast thou done! What thought hath come to thee? What manner of mischance hath marred thy reason?

---

hand in L wrote μιτωίδη, adding ει above the η. S inserted ρ between τ and ω, and accented ω, but without deleting the accent on ι. A few of the later MSS. have μιτρώδει, either in the text (as V⁴), or as a correction (V¹, V³): it is also the Aldine reading. **1226** στυγὸν L, with ν above γ from an early hand. **1228** οἷον] ποῖον L. **1229** συμφοράσ (not ξ-) L.

---

the thread of the warp: Eur. *I. T.* 817 ὕφηνα καὶ τόδ' εἶδος εὐμίτοις πλοκαῖς (I wrought this scene, too, with threads deftly woven).—**σινδόνος.** σινδών (prob. from Ἰνδ-, *Sind*) was a general term for a smooth, fine texture, as βύσσος was the specific word for a kind of fine linen: Her. 2. 86 describes mummies as swathed σινδόνος βυσσίνης τελαμῶσι (where see Stein). Thuc. 2. 49. 4 τῶν πάνυ λεπτῶν ἱματίων καὶ σινδόνων. Diog. Laert. 6. 90 tells of an Athenian (*c.* 300 B.C.) being reprimanded by the ἀστυνόμοι for luxuriousness, ὅτι σινδόνα ἠμφίεστο.—Antigone used her veil (κάλυμμα: cp. Ar. *Lys.* 532).

1223 Haemon has thrown his arms around her waist (ἀμφὶ μέσσῃ περιπετῆ), embracing her (προσκείμενον), where she hangs lifeless. But verses 1236–1240 require us to suppose that Antigone's body is then stretched on the ground. We are left to understand that Haemon, while uttering his lament (1224 f.), has lifted the corpse, so as to extricate it from the noose, and has laid it down. Cp. *O. T.* 1266 (where Oed. finds Iocasta hanging), χαλᾷ κρεμαστὴν ἀρτάνην.—μέσσῃ: cp. 1236: fr. 235. 5 (iambics). Eur. has this form only in lyr.; Aesch. nowhere.—περιπετῆ, act.; but pass. in *Ai.* 907 ἔγχος περιπετές ('on which he fell'), unless I am right in suspecting that there we should read, τόδ' ἔγχος περιπετοῦς κατηγορεῖ, 'shows that he

fell upon it.' Cp. *O. C.* 1620 ἐπ' ἀλλήλοισιν ἀμφικείμενοι, n.

1224 f. εὐνῆς...τῆς κάτω, his bride who is dead. Cp. Eur. *Tro.* 831 αἱ μὲν εὐνάς (husbands), αἱ δὲ παῖδας, | αἱ δὲ ματέρας γεραιάς. It would be awkward to understand, 'the ruin of his marriage, (which is to be only) in the world below.' —πατρὸς ἔργα: he does not know that Creon is listening.—λέχος, marriage, as in 573. This word, too, could mean 'bride' (*Ai.* 211): it is v. 1224 that decides our version.

1226 σφε, Haemon: 44 n.—στυγνόν, bitter,—the notion of 'sad,' 'gloomy,' coming from that of 'hateful': cp. Moschus 3. 68 καὶ στυγνοὶ (*tristes*) περὶ σῶμα τεὸν κλαίουσιν Ἔρωτες.

1228 f. οἷον ἔργον: *i.e.*, Haemon's forcible entrance into Antigone's tomb.—τίνα νοῦν ἔσχες; lit., 'what thoughts hast thou conceived?'—the aor. meaning, as usu., not 'had,' but 'came to have.' So *El.* 1013 f. νοῦν σχὲς...εἰκαθεῖν, 'form the purpose to yield': *ib.* 1465 νοῦν ἔσχον, ὥστε συμφέρειν τοῖς κρείσσοσιν.—ἐν τῷ συμφορᾶς, by what manner of calamity: *i.e.*, 'what cruel god hath deprived thee of thy reason?' *Ai.* 314 κἀνήρετ' ἐν τῷ πράγματος κυροῖ ποτε: *Ph.* 174 ἐπὶ παντὶ τῷ χρείας: Eur. *Helen.* 1195 ἐν τῷ δὲ κεῖσαι συμφορᾶς;—διεφθάρης, mentally: *Il.* 15. 128 μαινόμενε, φρένας ἠλέ, διέφθορας: Eur. *Helen.* 1192 διέφθαρσαι φρένας;

ἔξελθε, τέκνον, ἱκέσιός σε λίσσομαι.   1230
τὸν δ' ἀγρίοις ὄσσοισι παπτήνας ὁ παῖς,
πτύσας προσώπῳ κοὐδὲν ἀντειπών, ξίφους
ἕλκει διπλοῦς κνώδοντας· ἐκ δ' ὁρμωμένου
πατρὸς φυγαῖσιν ἤμπλακ'· εἶθ' ὁ δύσμορος
αὑτῷ χολωθείς, ὥσπερ εἶχ', ἐπενταθεὶς   1235
ἤρεισε πλευραῖς μέσσον ἔγχος· ἐς δ' ὑγρὸν
ἀγκῶν' ἔτ' ἔμφρων παρθένῳ προσπτύσσεται·
καὶ φυσιῶν ὀξεῖαν ἐκβάλλει ῥοὴν
λευκῇ παρειᾷ φοινίου σταλάγματος.
κεῖται δὲ νεκρὸς περὶ νεκρῷ, τὰ νυμφικὰ   1240

1232 ἀντειπών ὄλωσ L, with ξίφουσ written above ὄλωσ by the first hand.
The final ν of ἀντειπών has been made from ο, and ὄ has been written above
the line, by the first hand.—Wecklein thinks that ὄλωσ came from κολεῶν [rather
κολεοῦ] written over ξίφους: but ἕλκει did not require such explanation.—
Seyffert conject. βέλους: Dindorf, ἔπος.—Nauck thinks the whole verse spurious.
1234 εἶθ' ὁ] In L the first hand wrote εἰ δύσμορος: S made εἰ into εἶθ' ὁ.
1235 αὑτῷ] αὑτῶι L.   **1236** μέσσον] Nauck conject. πηκτόν: Pallis, δισσόν.

1230 f. ἱκέσιος, adverbial: cp. 1215
ὡκεῖς, n. He extends his right hand in
supplication.—ὄσσοισι: Aesch. admits
ὄσσοις, and Eur. both ὄσσοις and ὄσσων,
in iambics no less than in lyrics.—παπτήνας: with an acc. this verb usu. = 'to
look around for,' as Il. 4. 200.
   1232 πτύσας προσώπῳ. Haemon
is momentarily insane with despair and
rage: the very words αὑτῷ χολωθείς,
1235, indicate the transport of frenzy
which these verses were meant to depict.
Nothing could do more violence to the
language, or more injury to the dramatic
effect, than the Scholiast's theory that
πτύσας προσώπῳ has a merely figurative
sense, 'with an expression of loathing on
his face.' When the figurative sense of a
word (like πτύσας) is to be marked by a
qualifying addition (like προσώπῳ), that
addition must not be such as equally to
suggest the literal sense. Thus a social-
ist riot might be called 'a fire not of
Hephaestus' (Eur. Or. 621); but it would
not be equally happy to describe it as
'a fire kindled by the tables of the rich.'
πτύσας προσώπῳ, instead of ἐπιπτύσας
προσώπῳ (πατρός), is merely an instance
of the boldness with which poetry could
use a simple dative to express the object
to (or against) which an action is directed.
Such a dat. is often equivalent to (a) ἐπί
with dat., (b) ἐπί, πρός, or εἰς, with acc.,

—in various relations, and with various
shades of meaning. Thus we have such
phrases as κακοῖς γελῶν (Ai. 1042) = κακοῖς ἐπεγγελῶν: Ph. 67 λύπην...'Αργείοις
βαλεῖς = ἐμβαλεῖς: Eur. Suppl. 322 τοῖς
κερτομοῦσι γοργὸν ὡς ἀναβλέπει, how she
looks up sternly at her revilers: Il. 7. 101
τῷδε δ' ἐγὼν αὐτὸς θωρήξομαι, against him:
ib. 23. 635 ὅς μοι ἀνέστη, against me: and
below 1236 ἤρεισε πλευραῖς = ἐπήρεισε.
Prose would have πτύσας εἰς (or ἐπί)
πρόσωπον.
   1233 f. διπλοῦς κνώδοντας ξίφους, his
cross-hilted sword. κνώδοντες are the two
projecting cross-pieces at the point where
the hilt joins the blade. The hilt (κώπη)
of the Greek sword had no guard, nor
had it always the cross-pieces; but these,
when used, served partly to protect the
hand. The κνώδοντες, or cross-hilt, can
be seen on some of the swords given by
Guhl and Koner, p. 244, fig. 277 (a, d).
The cross-hilt was sometimes simply a
straight cross-bar; sometimes the side
next the hand was rounded. Cp. Silius
Italicus Pun. 1. 515 pressumque ira simul
exigit ensem, | Qua capuli statuere morae.
—κνώδων (κνάω, ὀδούς) meant properly
any tooth-like prong or spike: see Xen.
Cyneg. 10. 3, where boar-spears (προβόλια)
have κνώδοντας ἀποκεχαλκευμένους στι-
φρούς, stout teeth forged of bronze, projecting from the shaft a little below the

Come forth, my child! I pray thee—I implore!' But the boy glared at him with fierce eyes, spat in his face, and, without a word of answer, drew his cross-hilted sword :—as his father rushed forth in flight, he missed his aim ;—then, hapless one, wroth with himself, he straightway leaned with all his weight against his sword, and drove it, half its length, into his side ; and, while sense lingered, he clasped the maiden to his faint embrace, and, as he gasped, sent forth on her pale cheek the swift stream of the oozing blood.

Corpse enfolding corpse he lies; he hath won his nuptial

1238 ῥοὴν L. The schol. in L has: τὴν πνοὴν τοῦ φοινίου σταλάγματος ἐκβάλλει τῇ λευκῇ αὐτῆς παρειᾷ, ὅ ἐστιν, αἷμα ἐξέπνευσεν. The last words show that πνοὴν was not a slip for ῥοήν, but was in the Scholiast's text. Most of the later MSS. (including A) have πνοὴν: but a few have ῥοὴν (as L², V, V⁴, Aug. b).— Blaydes conject. σφαγὴν, and ἐμβάλλει for ἐκβάλλει. **1240** περι νεκρῶι L: but it does not follow that the scribe meant the two words to form one.

---

head (λόγχη). In *Ai.* 1025, τοῦδ' αἰόλου κνώδοντος, 'this gleaming spike,' is the end of the sword-blade projecting through the body of Ajax. So in Kaibel *Epigr.* 549. 11 (an epitaph of the 1st cent. A.D.) φασγάνου κνώδοντι=' with the point (not, ' edge ') of the sword': the ref. is to thrusting, not cutting.—The Scholiast wrongly explains **διπλοῦς κνώδοντας** by διπλᾶς ἀκμάς, 'double edge.' This interpretation was obviously suggested by διπλοῦς (since a sword is often called δίστομον or ἀμφήκες), while the true sense of κνώδων was not accurately remembered: thus the Schol. vaguely calls it τὸ ὀξὺ τοῦ ξίφους.

ἐκ δ' ὅρμ., tmesis: cp. 427.—φυγαῖσιν, dat. of manner (620 n.). The poet. plur. of φυγή, when it does not mean 'remedies' (364), usu. means 'exile' (Eur. *El.* 233). The gen. might be absol., but is more simply taken with ἤμπλακ'.

Haemon, in his madness, meant to kill his father. He had harboured no such purpose before (see on 753); and his frantic impulse is instantly followed by violent remorse. Arist. (*Poet.* 14) observes that it is not conducive to a properly tragic effect (οὐ τραγικόν, ἀπαθές) if a person contemplates a dreadful act, and then desists from it, in the light of sober thought or fuller knowledge : διόπερ οὐδεὶς ποιεῖ ὁμοίως εἰ μὴ ὀλιγάκις (such incidents in Tragedy are rare), οἷον ἐν Ἀντιγόνῃ Κρέοντα ὁ Αἵμων. It need not be assumed that Arist. meant to censure Sophocles; it is more natural to suppose

that he cited the exception as one justified by the circumstances. But it should further be noticed that Aristotle was not accurate in taking this incident as the exception which illustrated his rule. For Haemon did not abandon his dreadful purpose; he was simply foiled by his father's flight. And then, in swift remorse, he actually did τῶν ἀνηκέστων τι.

1235 ff. ὥσπερ εἶχ': cp. 1108.— ἐπεντάθεις, lit., 'stretched,' or 'strained,' against the sword : *i.e.*, pressing his right side against the point of the sword, which at the same time he drove home with his right hand.—πλευραῖς, used as though ἤρεισε were ἐπήρεισε: cp. Pind. *P.* 10. 51 ἄγκυραν ἔρεισον χθονί. For the verb cp. Eur. *Andr.* 844 (ξίφος) ἀπόδος,...ἵν' ἀνταίαν | ἐρείσω πλαγάν.—μέσσον, predicative, denoting the point up to which he drove it in : *Ai.* 899 κεῖται κρυφαίῳ φασγάνῳ περιπτυχής.—ἔγχος = ξίφος: *Ai.* 95, 658, etc.—ἐς δ' ὑγρὸν ἀγκῶν', since π. προσπτύσσεται = παρθένον λαμβάνει : cp. the beautiful lines in Eur. *Ph.* 1439 (the dying Eteocles): ἤκουσε μητρός, κἀπιθεὶς ὑγρὰν χέρα | φωνὴν μὲν οὐκ ἀφῆκεν, ὀμμάτων δ' ἄπο | προσεῖπε δακρύοις.

1238 φυσῶν, breathing hard : ῥοὴν is governed by ἐκβάλλει only. But in Aesch. *Ag.* 1389 the compound governs the acc.: κἀκφυσιῶν ὀξεῖαν αἵματος σφαγὴν | βάλλει μ' ἐρεμνῇ ψακάδι φοινίας δρόσου.—ῥοὴν is plainly right: the bad variant, πνοήν, was perh. suggested by φυσῶν.

τέλη λαχὼν δείλαιος ἕν <γ᾽> Ἅιδου δόμοις,
δείξας ἐν ἀνθρώποισι τὴν ἀβουλίαν
ὅσῳ μέγιστον ἀνδρὶ πρόσκειται κακόν.

ΧΟ. τί τοῦτ᾽ ἂν εἰκάσειας; ἢ γυνὴ πάλιν
φρούδη, πρὶν εἰπεῖν ἐσθλὸν ἢ κακὸν λόγον.   1245

ΑΓ. καὐτὸς τεθάμβηκ᾽· ἐλπίσιν δὲ βόσκομαι
ἄχη τέκνου κλύουσαν ἐς πόλιν γόους
οὐκ ἀξιώσειν, ἀλλ᾽ ὑπὸ στέγης ἔσω
δμωαῖς προθήσειν πένθος οἰκεῖον στένειν.
γνώμης γὰρ οὐκ ἄπειρος, ὥσθ᾽ ἁμαρτάνειν.   1250

ΧΟ. οὐκ οἶδ᾽· ἐμοὶ δ᾽ οὖν ἥ τ᾽ ἄγαν σιγὴ βαρὺ
δοκεῖ προσεῖναι χἠ μάτην πολλὴ βοή.

ΑΓ. ἀλλ᾽ εἰσόμεσθα, μή τι καὶ κατάσχετον
κρυφῇ καλύπτει καρδίᾳ θυμουμένῃ,
δόμους παραστείχοντες· εὖ γὰρ οὖν λέγεις·   1255
καὶ τῆς ἄγαν γάρ ἐστί που σιγῆς βάρος.

1241 ἕν γ᾽ Ἅιδου] ἐν αἴδου L, with most of the later MSS.: but L², with a few others, has εἰν. Brunck wrote ἐν Ἀΐδου. Heath conject. ἕν γ᾽: Vauvilliers, εἰς Ἅιδου δόμους: Semitelos, Ἐνοδίας δόμοις: Mekler, ἐν σκότου δόμοις: Nauck, ἐν γαίας μυχοῖς. **1245** ἢ was omitted by the first hand in L, and added by S. **1248** ἀξιώσειν] Pallis conject. ἀξιοῦν χεῖν: Burges, ὀξὺν ἥσειν: Blaydes, ἐξανήσειν:

1241 τέλη, rites : *O. C.* 1050 n.—**ἕν γ᾽ Ἅιδου**. Though εἰν occurs nowhere else in tragic iambics, it might fairly be defended, in a ῥῆσις of epic colour, as a reminiscence of the Homeric εἰν Ἀΐδαο. But I decidedly prefer Heath's **ἕν γ᾽** ('in that world, though not in this'), because it adds point and pathos to what would otherwise be a somewhat tame statement of fact. Cp. 750. For another (probable) loss of **γε** in this play, cp. 648. For **ἕν γε**, cp. *O. T.* 1380 ἕν γε ταῖς Θήβαις : *O. C.* 153 ἕν γ᾽ ἐμοί : *Ph.* 685 ἴσος ἕν γ᾽ ἴσοις : Eur. fr. 349 ὡς ἕν γ᾽ ἐμοὶ κρίνοιτ᾽ ἂν οὐ καλῶς φρονεῖν.

1242 δείξας...τὴν ἀβουλίαν: for the constr., cp. n. on 883 f. For δεικνύναι said of a warning example, see *El.* 1382 καὶ δεῖξον ἀνθρώποισι τἀπιτίμια | τῆς δυσσεβείας οἷα δωροῦνται θεοί : cp. *O. T.* append. on 622 ff.

1243 πρόσκειται: cp. 94 n.

1244 f. τί τοῦτ᾽ ἂν εἰκάσ., *sc.* εἶναι: what wouldst thou conjecture this to be (or, to mean)? The optat. ending used here was the usual one in Attic : cp. *O.T.*

843 n.—**ἐσθλὸν ἢ κακόν**: cp. on 40.— A silent exit is similarly a prelude to disaster in the case of Deianeira (*Tr.* 813). Iocasta, too, quits the scene, not, indeed, without a word, yet with a reticence which is called σιωπή (*O. T.* 1075).

1246 τεθάμβηκ᾽: cp. *O. C.* 1140 θαυμάσας ἔχω (n.): and so oft. τεθαύμακα. —**βόσκομαι**: cp. fr. 863 ἐλπὶς γὰρ ἡ βόσκουσα τοὺς πολλοὺς βροτῶν.

1247 f. γόους...ἀξιώσειν = to think them ἄξιοι, *i.e.*, meet. This use of ἀξιόω is freq. in regard to persons, as *Ai.* 1114 οὐ γὰρ ἠξίου τοὺς μηδένας (esteem them). On the other hand, ἄξιος, as applied to actions, oft. = 'proper,' 'becoming': as Ar. *Eq.* 616 νῦν ἄρ᾽ ἄξιόν γε πᾶσίν ἐστιν ἐπολολύξαι. But, if ἀξιοῖ τινα could mean, 'he thinks a person estimable,' poetry, at least, could surely say, ἀξιοῖ τι, 'he thinks a thing proper.' The text, then, seems sound.—**ὑπὸ στέγης**: for the gen., cp. 692 n.

1249 προθήσειν governs πένθος : στένειν is epexeg. (for them to mourn): cp. 216 n. She will 'set the grief before

rites, poor youth, not here, yet in the halls of Death; and he
hath witnessed to mankind that, of all curses which cleave to
man, ill counsel is the sovereign curse.

[EURYDICÈ *retires into the house.*

CH.   What wouldst thou augur from this? The lady hath
turned back, and is gone, without a word, good or evil.

ME.   I, too, am startled; yet I nourish the hope that, at
these sore tidings of her son, she cannot deign to give her
sorrow public vent, but in the privacy of the house will set
her handmaids to mourn the household grief. For she is not
untaught of discretion, that she should err.

CH.   I know not; but to me, at least, a strained silence seems
to portend peril, no less than vain abundance of lament.

ME.   Well, I will enter the house, and learn whether indeed she is not hiding some repressed purpose in the depths of
a passionate heart. Yea, thou sayest well: excess of silence,
too, may have a perilous meaning.   [*Exit* MESSENGER.

Semitelos, ἐξαύσειν.   **1250** Blaydes conject. ἄμοιρος for ἄπειρος : Semitelos, δεινῶν
for γνώμης.   Meineke, Dindorf and Nauck reject the verse.   **1251** ἐμοὶ δ'] ἐμοι
δ' L: ἔμοιγ' Brunck.—σιγὴ from σιγῇ L.   **1253** ἀλλ'] Pallis conject. τάχ'.—
κατάσχετον] Musgrave conject. κατὰ σκότον.   **1254** θυμουμένηι L: a line has been
drawn through the ι.   Some of the later MSS. have θυμουμένη.   **1256** ἐστί που]
Bergk conject. ἔσθ' ὅπου.   Nauck suspects the verse (*Jahr. f. Philol.*, 65. 250).

---

them' by making a lament, after which
her handmaids, sitting around her, will
wail in chorus. *Il.* 24. 746 (Andromache
has bewailed Hector,) ὡς ἔφατο κλαίουσ'·
ἐπὶ δὲ στενάχοντο γυναῖκες. | τῇσιν δ' αὖθ'
Ἑκάβη ἀδινοῦ ἐξῆρχε γόοιο.
1250 γνώμης...οὐκ ἄπειρος.   The
reading has been unjustly suspected.
γνώμη, 'judgment,' or 'discretion,' is
here regarded as an influence moulding
the character from without.   The phrase
means, then, 'not uninformed by discretion,'—not unversed in its teachings.
Cp. Plat. *Rep.* 519 B τοὺς ἀπαιδεύτους καὶ
ἀληθείας ἀπείρους, 'uninformed by truth.'
1251 f. δ' οὖν: 688 n. προσεῖναι:
so oft. of attendant circumstances (or of
characteristic attributes):   *Tr.* 250 τοῦ
λόγου δ' οὐ χρὴ φθόνον, | γύναι, προσεῖναι.
—Cp. 720.
1253 f. εἰσόμεσθα, μή τι...καλύπτει,
'we shall know (about our fear) lest (μή)
she is concealing,' *i.e.*, whether we are
right in fearing that she conceals something. As Goodwin says (*Moods and
Tenses*, § 46, N. 5 *a*), this passage is one

of the most favourable to the view that
μή has an *interrogative* force, and yet here
also μὴ καλύπτει plainly expresses a fear.
The pres. *indic.* is used, because the fear
is strictly present; there is no thought that
the thing feared can possibly be pre-
vented. Before assuming that μή could
have the force of εἰ οὐ ('whether not'),
we should require an example in which
the clause with μή, after a verb like οἶδα,
expressed something which is not *feared*
(but hoped; or else regarded with neither
fear nor hope). As if here we had, εἰσόμεσθα μὴ ζήσειν ἔτι μέλλει. Cp. 278 n.
The use of μή in *direct* question (*O. C.*
1502) is, of course, elliptical: *e.g.*, μὴ
οὕτως ἔχει; comes from (δέδοικα) μὴ οὕτως
ἔχει.—καὶ ('indeed') goes with the whole
phrase κατάσχετον...καλύπτει: cp. 770n.
—κατάσχετον, a poet. word, here = 'repressed' (cp. *El.* 1011 κατάσχες ὀργήν):
usu., 'possessed' (by a god, or by passion), like κάτοχος.
1255 δόμους παραστείχοντες, advancing into the house: Eur. *Med.* 1137
παρῆλθε νυμφικοὺς δόμους.

222   ΣΟΦΟΚΛΕΟΥΣ

ΧΟ. καὶ μὴν ὅδ' ἄναξ αὐτὸς ἐφήκει
    μνῆμ' ἐπίσημον διὰ χειρὸς ἔχων,
    εἰ θέμις εἰπεῖν, οὐκ ἀλλοτρίαν
    ἄτην, ἀλλ' αὐτὸς ἁμαρτών.   1260

στρ. α΄. ΚΡ. ἰὼ
    2 φρενῶν δυσφρόνων ἁμαρτήματα
    3 στερεὰ θανατόεντ'·
    4 ὦ κτανόντας τε καὶ
    5 θανόντας βλέποντες ἐμφυλίους·
    6 *ὤμοι ἐμῶν ἄνολβα βουλευμάτων.   1265
    7 ἰὼ παῖ, νέος νέῳ ξὺν μόρῳ,
    8 αἰαῖ αἰαῖ,
    9 ἔθανες, ἀπελύθης,
    10 ἐμαῖς οὐδὲ σαῖσι δυσβουλίαις.

στρ. β΄. ΧΟ. οἴμ' ὡς ἔοικας ὀψὲ τὴν δίκην ἰδεῖν.   1270

    ΚΡ. οἴμοι,
    2 ἔχω μαθὼν δείλαιος· ἐν δ' ἐμῷ κάρᾳ

1259 f. ἀλλοτρίαν | ἄτην] Musgrave conject. ἀλλοτρίας | ἄτης.   **1261—1269** L divides thus: ἰὼ — | ἁμαρτήματα — | θανατόεντ' — | θανόντασ — | ἐμφυλίουσ — | ἰώ μοι — | βουλευμάτων — | ἰὼ παῖ — | αἰ αἰ — | ἔθανεσ — | ἐμαῖσ ... δυσβουλίαισ.   **1263** κτανόντας τε καὶ are written as a single word in L, καί being denoted by a contraction.   **1265** ἰώ (not ἰὼ) μοι L, with the other MSS.: ὤμοι

1257 καὶ μήν: 526.—**ἐφήκει**: *Ai.* 34 καιρὸν δ' ἐφήκεις.—The Messenger now goes into the palace. The same actor returns at 1277 as ἐξάγγελος.

1258 μνῆμ', as the epithet **ἐπίσημον** shows, means that the son's corpse is a memorial of the father's unwisdom.—**διὰ χειρός**: cp. 916.

1259 f. εἰ θέμις εἰπεῖν (cp. *O. C.* 1556), because it is a heavy charge against the King, that he has caused his son's death.—**ἄτην**, in apposition with μνῆμα: the corpse is an ἄτη, because the death was caused by Creon's infatuation. **ἀλλοτρίαν** here answers to οἰκεῖος as = 'caused by one-self' (cp. on 1187).—**ἁμαρτών** is causal: he is bringing a corpse, not through the fault of others, but *because* he himself has erred. For the partic. in the nom., opposed to a clause of different form, cp. Dem. or. 23 § 156 εἶδεν, εἴτε δή τινος εἰπόντος εἴτ' αὐτὸς συνείς. See also 381 f.

1261—1347 This κομμός is composed of four strophes and four anti-

strophes, which correspond as follows. (1) 1st strophe 1261—1269 = 1st antistr. 1284—1292. (2) 2nd str. 1271—1277 = 2nd ant. 1294—1300. (3) 3rd str. 1306—1311 = 3rd ant. 1328—1333. (4) 4th str. 1317—1325 = 4th ant. 1339—1347.

The lyric strophes and antistrophes are divided from each other by iambic trimeters, spoken by the Chorus or by the Messenger.—See Metrical Analysis.

1261 f. φρενῶν δυσφρόνων: 502 n. Cp. Aesch. *Th.* 874 ἰὼ ἰὼ δύσφρονες, 'misguided ones.' More often, δύσφρων = 'gloomy,' or 'malignant.'—**στερεά**, with ref. to his own αὐθάδεια, cp. 1028. So Plat. *Polit.* 309 B τὸ στερεὸν ἦθος. Cp. *Ai.* 925 ἔμελλες χρόνῳ | στερεόφρων ἄρ' ὧδ' ἐξανύσειν κακὰν | μοῖραν.

1263 f. ὦ...βλέποντες. Like Antigone (937), Creon now calls the Theban Elders to witness. Cp. n. on 162—210. —**κτανόντας** refers to Creon himself (for the plur., cp. 10), as **θανόντας** to

Enter CREON, *on the spectators' left, with attendants, carrying the shrouded body of* HAEMON *on a bier.*

CH. Lo, yonder the King himself draws near, bearing that which tells too clear a tale,—the work of no stranger's madness,—if we may say it,—but of his own misdeeds.

CR. Woe for the sins of a darkened soul, stubborn sins, fraught with death! Ah, ye behold us, the sire who hath slain the son who hath perished! Woe is me, for the wretched blindness of my counsels! Alas, my son, thou hast died in thy youth, by a timeless doom, woe is me!—thy spirit hath fled,—not by thy folly, but by mine own!

Kommos.
1st strophe.

CH. Ah me, how all too late thou seemest to see the right!

CR. Ah me, I have learned the bitter lesson! But then,

2nd strophe.

Turnebus.   **1266** ξὺν μόρῳ] ξυμμόρωι L.   **1267** αἶ αἶ αἶ L: αἰαῖ αἰαῖ
Dindorf.   **1268** ἀπελύθης] Keck conject. ἀπεσύθης.   **1270** ἰδεῖν] L has γρ.
ἔχειν in marg. from S.—Pallis conject. μαθεῖν.   **1271—1277** L divides thus:
.οἴμοι | ἔχω— | θεὸσ— | ἔπαισεν— | οἴμοι, λακπάτητον— | φεῦ φεῦ | ἰὼ πόνοι .. δύσπονοι.

Haemon: for the παρήχησις, cp. *Ph.* 336 ὁ κτανών τε χὠ θανών.—ἐμφυλίους = συγγενεῖς: cp. *O. T.* 1406 αἷμ' ἐμφύλιον (n.): *O. C.* 1385 γῆς ἐμφυλίου, 'the land of thy race.'

1265 ἐμῶν ἄνολβα βουλευμάτων, the unhappy (counsels) among my counsels (partitive gen.); *i.e.*, the unhappiness involved in my counsels. See on 1209. This poetical periphrasis has the effect of making the idea expressed by ἄνολβα stand out with a quasi-substantival force, and so is slightly stronger than ὦμοι ἐμὰ ἄνολβα βουλεύματα. It would be possible, but it is neither requisite nor fitting, to supply ἁμαρτήματα (1261) with ἄνολβα, placing only a comma at ἐμφυλίους.—For ἄνολβος, of folly, cp. 1026.

1266 νέος νέῳ ξὺν μόρῳ, 'young, and by an untimely death,' is a pleonasm, but a natural one. The Schol. explains νέῳ by καινοπρεπεῖ ('a death of a strange kind'). This sense is possible (cp. Aesch. *Suppl.* 712 ἀπροσδοκήτους τούσδε καὶ νέους λόγους), but is far less fitting here. νέῳ ξὺν μόρῳ, suggesting the thought that his years had been few, recalls Andromache's lament,—ἆνερ, ἀπ' αἰῶνος νέος ὤλεο (*Il.* 24. 725).

1268 ἀπελύθης: cp. 1314, where the midd. aor. has the same sense. In later Greek ἀπολύεσθαι and ἀπόλυσις came to be used of any 'departure': thus in Polyb. 3. 69 τὴν ἀποχώρησιν...ἐποιοῦντο is presently varied to ἐποιοῦντο τὴν ἀπόλυσιν. Here, however, the word has a distinctly poetical colour, and suggests the release of ψυχή from σῶμα,—though without the feeling expressed by the words, ἀπολύεις τὸν δοῦλόν σου...ἐν εἰρήνῃ (St Luke ii. 29). A fragment of Plutarch (Wyttenbach, p. 135) attests a familiar use of ἀπολύεσθαι and ἀπόλυσις with reference to death. Eustathius quotes this v., and v. 1314, in support of a like statement (p. 548, 52).

1269 ἐμαῖς οὐδὲ σαῖσι. οὐδέ here = καὶ οὐ: cp. 492. The negative form would be οὐκ ἐμαῖς ἀλλὰ σαῖς (*El.* 1470).

1272 ff. ἔχω μαθὼν = μεμάθηκα (21 n.), though here with a slightly stronger emphasis than that of an ordinary perf.: 'I have fully learned.'—No change is required in 1273. The soundness of the metre is confirmed by the antistrophic verse (1296), which is free from suspicion. Construe: ὁ δὲ θεὸς ἐν τῷ ἐμῷ κάρᾳ ἔπαισέ με, μέγα βάρος ἔχων. Three points claim

3 θεὸς τότ᾽ ἄρα τότε μέγα βάρος μ᾽ ἔχων
4 ἔπαισεν, ἐν δ᾽ ἔσεισεν ἀγρίαις ὁδοῖς,
5 οἴμοι, λακπάτητον ἀντρέπων χαράν.   1275
6 φεῦ φεῦ, ὦ πόνοι βροτῶν δύσπονοι.

ΕΞΑΓΓΕΛΟΣ.

ὦ δέσποθ᾽, ὡς ἔχων τε καὶ κεκτημένος,   1278
τὰ μὲν πρὸ χειρῶν τάδε φέρων, τὰ δ᾽ ἐν δόμοις
ἔοικας ἥκειν καὶ τάχ᾽ ὄψεσθαι κακά.   1280

1273 θεὸς τότ᾽ ἄρα τότε μέγα βάρος μ᾽ ἔχων MSS.—Erfurdt places θεὸς after τότ᾽ ἄρα. Meineke would write με μέγα βάρος for μέγα βάρος μ᾽. Enger (followed by Nauck) gives τότε θεὸς τότ᾽ ἄρα μέγα βάρος ἔχων. **1275** λακπάτητον] In L the first hand omitted the last three letters; S has added them above the line.—A has the *v. l.* λεωπάτητον (with γρ. λαοπάτητον), prompted by the wish to make an iambic senarius. Another *v. l.* was λαξπάτητον, or λὰξ πατητὸν (λαξ πατητὸν E).   **1276** ὦ πόνοι]

---

notice. (1) The place of με. This was possible, because μέγα βάρος, without ἔχων, could have stood as an adverbial cognate acc.: hence ἔχων is rather a superfluity than a word for which the ear was waiting. Greek poetry (esp. lyric) often has bold arrangements of words: cp. 944, 960 (n.). (2) **μέγα βάρος ἔχων** = σφόδρα βαρὺς ὤν. Cp. 300: *Od.* 24. 249 γῆρας | λυγρὸν ἔχεις: *ib.* 1. 368 ὕβριν ἔχοντες. (3) **ἐν δ᾽ ἐμῷ κάρᾳ** might have been followed by ἐνήλατο, or the like; but, ἔπαισε being used, the enclitic με was required to make it clear. The charge of redundancy would be just only if ἐμῷ were followed by ἐμέ.—For the image, cp. 1345: Aesch. *Ag.* 1175 δαίμων ὑπερβαρὴς ἐμπίτνων: and see *O. T.* 263 n. Triclinius understood the blow on the head to mean a disordering of the intellect (ἀντὶ τοῦ, ἐξέστησε τὰς ἐμὰς φρένας). But it is simply a poetical picture of the fell swoop with which the god descended on his victim,—taking possession of him, and driving him astray. Perhaps ἐμβρόντητος helped to suggest the other view. For the form of the dat. **κάρᾳ**, cp. *O. C.* 564 n.—**ἐν δ᾽ ἔσεισεν**, tmesis (420).—**ἀγρίαις ὁδοῖς**: cp. Pind. *P.* 2. 85 ἀλλ᾽ ἄλλοτε πατέων ὁδοῖς σκολιαῖς, in paths of guile.

1275 λακπάτητον, proleptic (475). The form λαξπάτητον, which Eustathius treats as the normal one (adding, ὅ τινες .. διὰ τοῦ κ γράφουσιν), is defended by Ellendt. He thinks that the κ form came

from correctors who supposed that ξπ was an impossible combination for Attic Greek. We find, indeed, ἐξπηχυστί Soph. fr. 938, and the 'Attic' forms ἔξπουν, ἔξκλινον, ἐξμέδμινον (*O. T.* 1137 n.). But, though λαξπάτητον may well have been admissible, it is evident that the κ form would be recommended by ease of pronunciation. The compound occurs only here.—**ἀντρέπων**, as though it were an altar, a statue, or a fair building. Cp. Aesch. *Ag.* 383, *Eum.* 539 (quoted on 853 ff.).—For the apocope of ἀνά in comp., cp. *O. C.* 1070 ἄμβασις, *Tr.* 528 ἀμμένει, *ib.* 839 ἄμμιγα, *Ai.* 416 ἀμπνοάς (all lyr.). In *Tr.* 396 (dial.) Herm. conjectured κἀννεώσασθαι for καὶ νεώσασθαι. It is unknown whether ἄγχαξε (fr. 883) occurred in lyr. or in dial. Cp. *Introd. to Homer,* Appendix, p. 197.

1276 φεῦ φεῦ, ὦ. The hiatus is excused by the pause.—πόνοι .. δύσπονοι: cp. 502 n.

1278 ὡς ἔχων τε καὶ κεκτημένος. Creon is actually touching (or helping to support) his son's corpse (1258 διὰ χειρὸς ἔχων, 1297 ἔχω μὲν ἐν χείρεσσιν). And meanwhile his wife lies dead within the house. The Messenger therefore says that Creon has come as one who both *has in hand* (ἔχων), and *has in store* (κεκτημένος). ἔχων is explained by τὰ μὲν πρὸ χειρῶν .. φέρων, and κεκτημένος by τὰ δ᾽ ἐν δόμοις. Cp. Plat. *Theaet.* 197 B οὐ τοίνυν μοι ταὐτὸν φαίνεται τῷ κεκτῆσθαι τὸ ἔχειν. οἶον εἰ ἱμάτιον πριάμεmethinks, oh then, some god smote me from above with crushing weight, and hurled me into ways of cruelty, woe is me,—overthrowing and trampling on my joy! Woe, woe, for the troublous toils of men!

Enter MESSENGER *from the house.*

ME. Sire, thou hast come, methinks, as one whose hands are not empty, but who hath store laid up besides; thou bearest yonder burden with thee; and thou art soon to look upon the woes within thy house.

ἰὼ πόνοι L.   **1278** ΕΞΑΓΓΕΛΟΣ] The designation in L is οἰκέτης here, and at v. 1282: ἄγγελος at vv. 1293, 1301, 1312, 1315.   **1279** πρὸ χειρῶν] προχειρῶν L.— τάδε] ταδε (not τὰ δὲ) from ταδε, L.—τὰ δ' ἐν δόμοισ L first hand. A corrector has made τὰ δ' into τάδ'.   **1280** τάχ' L. Some of the later MSS. have τά γ' (as A), others τάδ' (as V⁴).—ὄψεσθαι] ὄψεσθε L. Dindorf states (after Dübner) that the final ε has been made by a late hand into αι: but (as can be seen in the autotype facsimile, p. 63 B) there has been no such attempt at correction.—See comment.

νός τις καὶ ἐγκρατὴς ὢν μὴ φοροῖ, ἔχειν μὲν οὐκ ἂν αὐτὸν αὐτό, κεκτῆσθαι δέ γε φαῖμεν. So *ib.* 198 D; the chase after knowledge has a view either to (*a*) τὸ κεκτῆσθαι, possession, or (*b*) τὸ ἔχειν, holding, ready for use, that which is already possessed,—ἣν ἐκέκτητο μὲν πάλαι, πρόχειρον δ' οὐκ εἶχε τῇ διανοίᾳ. Cp. *Rep.* 382 B (men do not like) τῷ ψυχῇ περὶ τὰ ὄντα ψεύδεσθαί τε καὶ ἐψεῦσθαι καὶ ἀμαθῆ εἶναι καὶ ἐνταῦθα ἔχειν τε καὶ κεκτῆσθαι τὸ ψεῦδος: where ψεύδεσθαι answers to ἔχειν τὸ ψεῦδος,—to be deceived at a given time on a given matter; and ἐψεῦσθαι to κεκτῆσθαι τὸ ψεῦδος, —the settled incapacity for apprehending realities. In *Crat.* 393 A he says that ἄναξ and ἕκτωρ mean the same thing; οὐ γὰρ ἄν τις ἄναξ ᾖ, .. δῆλον .. ὅτι κρατεῖ τε αὐτοῦ καὶ κέκτηται καὶ ἔχει αὐτό (where ἕκτωρ has suggested both verbs).— The point of the phrase here is missed when it is taken as merely, 'possessing sorrows in the fullest sense of possession.' **1279 f.** πρὸ χειρῶν: cp. Eur. *Tro.* 1207 καὶ μὴν πρὸ χειρῶν αἵδε σοι σκυλευμάτων | Φρυγίων φέρουσι κόσμον (they are carrying robes, *ib.* 1220). *I. A.* 36 δέλτον τε γράφεις | τήνδ' ἣν πρὸ χερῶν ἔτι βαστάζεις. Thus the phrase means merely, 'visible in the hands,' without implying that the hands are outstretched. —**τάδε**, with adverbial force, 'yonder': so 155, 386, 526, 626, 805, 868, 1257. **τὰ δ' ἐν δόμοις** κ.τ.λ. The regular constr. would have been, ἔοικας ἥκειν ὡς ἔχων τε καὶ κεκτημένος,—τὰ μὲν πρὸ χειρῶν

τάδε φέρων, τὰ δ' ἐν δόμοις τάχ' ὀψόμενος. The present form has arisen thus. (1) Since **τὰ μὲν .. φέρων** interprets ἔχων, the poet wished it to come immediately after ἔχων τε καὶ κεκτημένος. (2) **ἔοικας ἥκειν**, although thus postponed, ought still to have been followed by τάχ' ὀψόμενος. But the place of ἔοικας in the long sentence now prompted the change of τάχ' ὀψόμενος into **καὶ τάχ' ὄψεσθαι.** The sentence, as it stands, would have seemed less boldly irregular to the Greek ear than it does to us, because Greek idiom so readily permitted the change of a second participial clause into a clause with a finite verb. (Cp. 256 ἐπῆν: 816 ὑμνήσεν.) Thus there would be nothing unusual in the following :—ἥκεις, τὰ μὲν φέρων, τὰ δὲ ἔοικας τάχα ὄψεσθαι. Here, instead of ἥκεις, we have ἔοικας ἥκειν, and the place of ἔοικας has led to ἥκειν and ὄψεσθαι being linked by καί.

Since **τὰ δ' ἐν δόμοις** is governed by ὄψεσθαι only, the words **ἥκειν καὶ** form a parenthesis, being equivalent to ἥκων. This is a rare constr., and alleged examples should be scrutinised before acceptance (cp. 537 n.); but there are some undoubted instances. Cp. Xen. *H.* 7. 3. 7 ὑμεῖς τοὺς περὶ Ἀρχίαν . . . (οὐ ψῆφον ἀνεμείνατε, ἀλλὰ) ὁπότε πρῶτον ἐδυνάσθητε ἐτιμωρήσασθε. Thuc. 6. 68 § 3 ἐξ ἧς (κρατεῖν δεῖ ἢ) μὴ ῥᾳδίως ἀποχωρεῖν. Plat. *Legg.* 934 E διδασκέτω (καὶ μανθανέτω) τὸν .. ἀμφισβητοῦντα. [Lys.] *In Andoc.* § 33 ἐπιτιμᾷ (καὶ ἀποδοκιμάζει) τῶν ἀρχόντων τισί. *Anthol. P.* 7. 664 Ἀρχίλοχον

ΚΡ. τί δ' ἐστιν αὖ κάκιον *ἐκ κακῶν ἔτι;
ΕΞ. γυνὴ τέθνηκε, τοῦδε παμμήτωρ νεκροῦ,
δύστηνος, ἄρτι νεοτόμοισι πλήγμασιν.

ἀντ. α΄. ΚΡ. ἰώ,

2 ἰὼ δυσκάθαρτος Ἅιδου λιμήν,   1284
3 τί μ' ἄρα τί μ' ὀλέκεις;   1285
4 ὦ κακάγγελτά μοι
5 προπέμψας ἄχη, τίνα θροεῖς λόγον;
6 αἰαῖ, ὀλωλότ' ἄνδρ' ἐπεξειργάσω.
7 τί φής, ὦ παῖ, τίνα λέγεις μοι νέον,

1281 τί δ' εστιν (sic) αὖ κάκιον ἢ κακῶν ἔτι; L.—J. Pflugk (whom Schneidewin follows) conject., τί δ' ἔστιν; ἢ κάκιον αὖ κακῶν ἔτι; So Emperius, but with ἤ.— Reiske, τί δ' ἐστιν αὖ; κάκιον ἢ κακῶν ἔτι; So Wecklein and Bellermann.— Canter, τί δ' ἔστιν αὖ κάκιον ἐκ κακῶν ἔτι; So Brunck and Hermann.—Herm. also proposed, κάκιον ὂν κακῶν ἔτι; which Schütz prefers.—G. H. Müller, τί δ' ἔστι δὴ κάκιον αὖ κακῶν ἔτι;—Blaydes, τί δ' ἐστιν αὖ κάκιον ἢ τὰ νῦν ἔτι;— Heiland (Progr. Stendal. 1851) would delete the verse, so that the five vv. (1278—80, 1282 f.) might answer to 1301—1305. Mekler agrees with him.   **1282** τέθ-νηκεν L.—Nauck conject. τέθνηχ', ἢ τοῦδε γεννήτωρ νεκροῦ: Semitelos, τέθνηκ' ἐκ τοῦδε πημάτων νεκροῦ: Pallis, μήτηρ τέθνηκεν τοῦδε παμμόρου νεκροῦ.

(καὶ στᾶθι καὶ) εἴσιδε. Others, indeed, take καὶ τάχα as = 'full soon,' and ὄψεσθαι as depending on ἥκειν: 'thou seemest to have come in order to see full soon,' etc. This final inf. is tenable (O. T. 198 n.). But I know no example of καὶ τάχα as = 'full soon,' like καὶ μάλα, καὶ λίαν, etc. And, even if it were possible, it would here be weak.—See Appendix.

1281 τί δ' ἔστιν. In order to form a judgment on this difficult verse, a careful scrutiny of Sophoclean usage is required. (1) The reading closest to the MSS. would be, τί δ' ἔστιν αὖ; κάκιον ἢ κακῶν ἔτι; This involves merely a change of punctuation, and of accent (ἢ for ἤ). But it suggests these difficulties. (a) The interrogative ἤ occurs about 50 times in Soph.: and in every instance it is the first word of the interrogative clause. Only a vocative sometimes precedes it, as O. C. 1102 ὦ τέκνον, ἢ πάρεστον; so ib. 863, Ph. 369. Eur., indeed, does not always observe this rule: El. 967 τί δῆτα δρῶμεν; μητέρ' ἢ φονεύσομεν; In Eur. Hec. 1013 I should point thus, ποῦ δῆτα; πέπλων ἐντὸς ἢ κρύψασ' ἔχεις; (ἢ Valckenaer for ἤ). But, if we read κάκιον ἢ κακῶν ἔτι here, it would be a solitary departure from the practice of Soph., as seen in fifty other

examples. (b) The formula τί δ' ἔστι (cp. on v. 20) occurs 21 times in Soph. (including Ph. 733, where the MSS. give τί ἔστι without δ') as a question complete in itself. But there is not one instance of τί δ' ἔστιν αὖ; which is, indeed, ill-suited to the rhythm of the tragic senarius.

(2) Transposing αὖ and ἤ, we could read, τί δ' ἔστιν; ἢ [or better, ἤ] κάκιον αὖ κακῶν ἔτι; But: (a) if this had been the original order, it is most improbable that ἤ and αὖ would have changed places. The sense would have been perfectly clear, whereas with αὖ...ἤ (the order in the MSS.) it is obscure. (b) The prominent place of αὖ in the MSS. is confirmed by many like instances: e.g. 1172: O. C. 1500 τίς αὖ παρ' ὑμῶν κοινὸς ἠχεῖται κτύπος; Ph. 1089 τίπτ' αὖ μοι τὸ κατ' ἆμαρ | ἔσται; ib. 1263 τίς αὖ παρ' ἄντροις θόρυβος ἵσταται βοῆς;

(3) Canter gave, τί δ' ἔστιν αὖ κάκιον ἐκ κακῶν ἔτι; The change of ἐκ to ἢ would have been peculiarly easy before initial κ (ΚΑΚΙΟΝΕΚΑΚΟΝ for ΚΑΚΙΟΝΕΚΚΑΚΟΝ). For ἐκ, cp. Tr. 28 ἀεί τιν' ἐκ φόβου φόβον τρέφω. Il. 19. 290 ὥς μοι δέχεται κακὸν ἐκ κακοῦ αἰεί. Eur. Ph. 371 ἀλλ' ἐκ γὰρ ἄλγους ἄλγος αὖ σέ δέρκομαι | ...ἔχουσαν. On the grounds stated above, I prefer this

CR. And what worse ill is yet to follow upon ills?

ME. Thy queen hath died, true mother of yon corpse—ah, hapless lady!—by blows newly dealt.

CR. Oh Hades, all receiving, whom no sacrifice can appease! 1st anti-
Hast thou, then, no mercy for me? O thou herald of evil, strophe.
bitter tidings, what word dost thou utter? Alas, I was already
as dead, and thou hast smitten me anew! What sayest thou,
my son? What is this new message that thou bringest—

1284—1292 L divides thus: ἰὼ ἰὼ—δυσκάθαρ|τοσ—ὀλέκεισ· | ἰὼ— | προπέμ-ψασ— | αἰαῖ— | τί φηῖσ— | σφάγιον— | γυναικεῖον...μόρον. | **1284** In L the first hand wrote χο before these vv.; a later hand changed it to κρε. **1286** ἰὼ L: ὦ r. **1287** λόγον] In L the first hand wrote λόγωι, and then changed it to λόγων: a later hand has made λόγον. **1288** αἰαῖ] αἶ αἶ L.—ἄνδρ'] ἄνδρα L. Cp. on 1147. **1289** τί φηῖσ ὦ παῖ· τίνα λέγεισ μοι νέον λόγον L.—R. Enger, omitting λόγον with Seidler, reads ὦ τίν' αὖ for ὦ παῖ τίνα, which Wecklein receives. Nauck prefers παῖ; τίν' αὖ.—Donaldson, τί φῆς; τίνα λέγεις νέον μοι νέῳ, which Dindorf adopts. And so Schütz would read, only with the MS. λόγον (followed by a note of interrogation) instead of νέῳ.

reading. The comparat. **κάκιον** means merely that the sum of his misery will be greater: not that he can conceive a calamity sorer than his son's death. Cp. *O. T.* 1364 f. εἰ δέ τι πρεσβύτερον ἔτι κακοῦ κακόν, | τοῦτ' ἔλαχ' Οἰδίπους.

1282 f. παμμήτωρ: schol. ἡ κατὰ πάντα μήτηρ: true mother; whose grief for her son would not suffer her to survive him; and whose act shows the same passionate temperament as his. Contrast μήτηρ ἀμήτωρ (*El.* 1154). παμμήτωρ usu. =ἡ πάντων μήτηρ (n. on 338). Cp. παμβασιλεία as = 'monarchy in the fullest sense' (n. on 737).—**νεοτόμ.**: adj. compounded with a word cognate in sense to the subst.: cp. 7 n. **ἄρτι** ('a moment ago') gives precision to the less definite νεοτόμοισι: *Tr.* 1130 τέθνηκεν ἀρτίως νεοσφαγής (cp. *Ai.* 898): Plat. *Legg.* 792 E τὸν ἀρτίως νεογενῆ.

1284 δυσκάθαρτος Ἅιδου λιμήν (nom. for voc., 1211). The 'haven' or 'receptacle' of Hades,—that nether world in which he receives the dead (810, 893)—is 'hard to be appeased,' in the sense that Hades is ever demanding fresh victims. The life of Haemon has already been exacted by Hades as a penalty for the offence of Creon against the νέρτεροι. But even this atonement (καθαρμός) has not proved enough. δυσκάθαρτος is used here as if one could say καθαίρω (for ἰλάσκομαι) θεόν: but that constr. does not occur. Cp. *O. C.* 466 καθαρμὸν...δαιμόνων (n.), such an atone-

ment as belongs (is due) to them. Plat. *Rep.* 364 E λύσεις τε καὶ καθαρμοὶ ἀδικημάτων.—For λιμήν cp. 1000: *Anth. P.* 7. 452 μνήμονες Εὐβούλοιο σαόφρονος, ὦ παριόντες, | πίνωμεν· κοινὸς πᾶσι λιμὴν Ἀΐδης.

1286 f. κακάγγελτα is equiv. to two distinct epithets, κακά and ἀγγελλόμενα, so that the whole phrase = 'tidings of dire woes.' Cp. 146 δικρατεῖς λόγχας (n.).—**προπέμψας**, said to the ἐξάγγελος, as the *herald* of the tidings. This use of προπέμπω comes from its sense of 'escorting' (*O. C.* 1667): we should not compare *El.* 1155 φήμας λάθρᾳ προὔπεμπες ὡς φανούμενος | τιμωρὸς αὐτός ('didst send forth,' from thy secret place of exile); nor, again, *Ph.* 1205 βελέων τι προπέμψατε ('produce,' 'furnish'): but rather *Ph.* 1265 μῶν τί μοι νέα | πάρεστε πρὸς κακοῖσι πέμποντες κακά;

1288 ἐπεξειργάσω: see on 1030.

1289 ff. ὦ παῖ, said to the Messenger. It has been objected that, at such a time, Creon could not use those words except with reference to Haemon (as in 1266, 1340). From a modern literary point of view, the objection is just. But we should remember how very familiar ὦ παῖ actually was as a mode of address, whether by elders to juniors, or by masters to slaves. Here it is used, not as to a slave, but merely as to a younger man; there is in it a certain pathetic appeal for sympathy. (Cp. ὦ παῖ, ὦ τέκνον, as said by the Messenger to Oed. in *O. T.* 1008, 1030.) Enger's conjecture, ὦ τίν'

8 αἰαῖ αἰαῖ,   1290
9 σφάγιον ἐπ' ὀλέθρῳ
10 γυναικεῖον ἀμφικεῖσθαι μόρον;

ΧΟ. ὁρᾶν πάρεστιν· οὐ γὰρ ἐν μυχοῖς ἔτι.

ἀντ. β'. ΚΡ. οἴμοι,
2 κακὸν τόδ' ἄλλο δεύτερον βλέπω τάλας.   1295
3 τίς ἄρα, τίς με πότμος ἔτι περιμένει;
4 ἔχω μὲν ἐν χείρεσσιν ἀρτίως τέκνον,
5 τάλας, τὸν δ' ἔναντα προσβλέπω νεκρόν.
6 φεῦ φεῦ μᾶτερ ἀθλία, φεῦ τέκνον.   1300

ΕΞ. ἥδ' *ὀξυθήκτῳ βωμία περὶ *ξίφει

1290 αἶ αἶ αἶ L: αἰαῖ αἰαῖ Dindorf.   **1291** ἐπ' ὀλέθρῳ] ἐπολέθρωι
L.   **1293** L gives this v. to the ἄγγελος.   Erfurdt first assigned it to the
Chorus.   **1294—1300** L divides thus: οἴμοι | κακὸν— | τίσ ἄρα— | ἔχω— |
τάλασ— | προσβλέπω— | φεῦ φεῦ . . τέκνον. | **1297** τέκνον] Wecklein writes
νεκρόν.   **1298** τὸν δ' ἔναντα] L has τάδ' ἐναντία· | προσβλέπω νεκρόν: but in the

---

αὖ (instead of ὦ παῖ τίνα), has not much
palaeographical probability. It gives,
indeed, a closer correspondence with
1266. But the form of dochmiac which
the ms. reading gives here is equally
correct. (See Met. Analysis.) Seidler
was certainly right in omitting λόγον (see
cr. n.): and that remedy suffices.
  Construe: τίνα νέον σφάγιον γυναικεῖον
μόρον λέγεις ἀμφικεῖσθαί μοι ἐπ' ὀλέθρῳ,
'what new death,'—the bloody death of a
woman,—dost thou describe as heaped
on destruction (i.e., superadded to Haemon's death), for my sorrow (μοι)?' (Cp.
595 πήματα φθιτῶν ἐπὶ πήμασι πίπτοντ'.)
γυναικεῖον=γυναικός: cp. Aesch. Pers.
8 νόστῳ τῷ βασιλείῳ.—The notion expressed by ἀμφικεῖσθαι ἐπ' ὀλέθρῳ seems
to be, strictly, that of death entwined
with death, like corpse embracing corpse
(1240). The verb ἀμφικεῖσθαι prop. = 'to
be set around' (as a wall round a city).
Perhaps the bold phrase here was partly
prompted by the fact that persons embracing each other could be described
(O. C. 1620 n.) as ἐπ' ἀλλήλοισιν ἀμφικείμενοι. I prefer this view.
  But another version is possible, if μοι
is taken with ἀμφικεῖσθαι : 'besetting
me,' ἐπ' ὀλέθρῳ, for (my) ruin. Cp. 1285

τί μ' ὀλέκεις; For ἐπί, cp. Thuc. 4. 86 οὐκ
ἐπὶ κακῷ, ἐπ' ἐλευθερώσει δέ. The difficulty is that ἀμφικεῖσθαι cannot well be
said of one sorrow (Eurydicè's death),
and that, therefore, we have to evolve
from the epithet νέον the notion of a
circle of woes of which this μόρος is one.
Thus the image would be much more
obscurely expressed than that in Ai. 351,
ἴδεσθέ μ' οἷον ἄρτι κῦμα φοινίας ὑπὸ ζάλης |
ἀμφίδρομον κυκλεῖται, ('behold what a
surge hath but now burst around me and
hemmed me in, under stress of a deadly
storm,') where Ajax is sitting in the
midst of the carnage which he has
wrought. It is altogether improbable
that ἀμφικεῖσθαι alludes to Eurydicè's
corpse having been brought (by the ἐκκύκλημα) into such a position that Creon
stood between it and Haemon's. See
1298, where Creon speaks of her as being
ἔναντα.
  1294 ὁρᾶν πάρεστιν. The corpse
of Eurydicè, and probably also the altar
at which she fell (1301), are now shown
to the spectators by means of the ἐκκύκλημα. The precise mechanism of this
contrivance is unknown; but the texts
leave no doubt as to its general nature. It
was a small stage, with space enough for

woe, woe is me!—of a wife's doom,—of slaughter heaped on slaughter?

CH. Thou canst behold: 'tis no longer hidden within.

[The doors of the palace are opened, and the corpse of EURYDICÈ *is disclosed.*

CR. Ah me,—yonder I behold a new, a second woe! What 2nd anti destiny, ah what, can yet await me? I have but now raised strophe. my son in my arms,—and there, again, I see a corpse before me! Alas, alas, unhappy mother! Alas, my child!

ME. There, at the altar, self-stabbed with a keen knife,

marg. S has written, γρ. τόνδ' (*sic*, not τὸν δ') ἔναντα.   **1301** ἥδ' (*sic*) ὀξύθηκτοσ· ἡ δὲ βωμία πέριξ L. Arndt conject. ἥδ' ὀξυθήκτῳ βωμία περὶ ξίφει. For βωμία, he afterwards proposed πτώσιμος. See Appendix.

---

three or four persons; and was low enough to admit of an actor stepping off it with ease. It was pushed on through the central stage entrance, and was usually brought sufficiently far forward to allow of actors entering or making their exit behind it. Here, the corpse of Eurydicè is evidently in full view of the house (cp. 1299). Soph. has used the ἐκκύκλημα in two other plays: *El.* 1458 (the corpse of Clytaemnestra, with Orestes and Pylades beside it); and in *Ai.* 344 (Ajax in his tent among his victims). See Albert Müller, *Gr. Bühnenalterthümer*, pp. 142 ff. (1886).

Recent explorations in the Dionysiac theatre at Athens have given rise to a theory that there was no permanent raised stage or proscenium before the Roman age. Even if this could be proved, it would still, however, remain certain that some such expedient as the ἐκκύκλημα was used in the fifth century. This is proved by the texts of Aesch., Soph., and Eur., as well as by the two scenes of Ar. where the tragic ἐκκύκλημα is parodied (*Ach.* 408—479; *Thesm.* 95—238). Ar. has the words ἐκκυκλεῖν and ἐσκυκλεῖν. Wecklein thinks that the ἐκκύκλημα was employed when a part of the interior of the house was to be disclosed, but the ἐξώστρα when merely a single object was to be shown; and that the ἐξώστρα was used here (*N. Jahrb.* 1870, vol. 101, p. 572: *Philol.* 31. 451). The meaning of ἐξώστρα is, however, doubtful.

1297 χείρεσσιν (976), though in an iambic verse, is excused by the lyric character of the whole κομμός. Eur. once admits it in dial., *Alc.* 756 ποτῆρα δ' ἐν χείρεσσι κίσσινον λαβών, where Monk needlessly proposed ποτήριον δ' ἐν χερσί.

1298 ἔναντα: an epic form, sometimes admitted in Attic poetry. Eur. *Or.* 1478 (lyr.) ἔναντα δ' ἦλθεν | Πυλάδης. Ar. *Eq.* 342 τῷ καὶ πεποιθὼς ἀξιοῖς ἐμοῦ λέγειν ἔναντα; Triclinius gave here the Hellenistic form ἔναντι (St Luke i. 8), which seems to be confined to the LXX., Apocrypha, and N.T.; see n. by Moulton in his ed. of Winer's Grammar, p. 591 (8th Engl. ed.).

1301 ἥδ': he indicates the dead body of Eurydicè, now made visible by the ἐκκύκλημα.—Arndt's first emendation is given in the text. His later substitution of πτώσιμος for βωμία was not an instance of second thoughts being wiser. The altar meant is that of Ζεὺς Ἑρκεῖος in the αὐλή of the house (487). The objection made to βωμία here is to the effect that one could say βώμιος ἐφέζεται or ἵσταται, but not βώμιος ποιεῖ τι: *i.e.* that the verb must refer directly to the assuming of the position denoted by βώμιος. It is quite true that this is usually the case; Eur. *Suppl.* 93 βωμίαν ἐφημένην: *O. T.* 32 ἑζόμεσθ' ἐφέστιοι: and cp. above, 785 f. But here βωμία is not merely an adverbial word, to be taken closely with λύει. It is rather an instance of an adj. used with the force of a participle, and virtually

λύει κελαινὰ βλέφαρα, κωκύσασα μὲν
τοῦ πρὶν θανόντος Μεγαρέως κλεινὸν *λάχος,
αὖθις δὲ τοῦδε, λοίσθιον δὲ σοὶ κακὰς
πράξεις ἐφυμνήσασα τῷ παιδοκτόνῳ.   1305

στρ. γ΄. ΚΡ. αἰαῖ αἰαῖ,
2   ἀνέπταν φόβῳ. τί μ᾽ οὐκ ἀνταίαν
3   ἔπαισέν τις ἀμφιθήκτῳ ξίφει;
4   δείλαιος ἐγώ, *αἰαῖ,   1310
5   δειλαίᾳ δὲ συγκέκραμαι δύᾳ.

1302 λύει] Bergk conject. μύει: Wieseler, κλήει.—κελαινὰ] λ from ν in L.   **1303** κλέι-
νὸν λέχος MSS.   Seyffert conject. κενὸν λέχος.   Bothe, κλεινὸν λάχος (Blaydes, αἰνὸν
λάχος; Semitelos, καινὸν λάχος).   Pallis, κλεινὸν δέμας.   Gleditsch, κλεινὸν σθένος.
Meineke, κλεινὸν τέλος.   **1304** δὲ σοὶ] δέ σοι L.—For σοὶ Pallis writes σὰς.
1305 πράξεις] Nauck conject. ἀρὰς: Heimsoeth, βάξεις.   **1306** αἰαῖ αἰαῖ] αἲ αἲ αἲ αἲ
(from αἲ) L.   **1307—1311** L divides thus: ἀνέπταν— | τί μ᾽ οὐκ— | ἔπαισεν— |

---

equivalent to βωμία στᾶσα: *i.e.* it means,
'having taken her place at the altar,' she
slew herself. Cp. *O. C.* 83 ὡς ἐμοῦ μόνης
πέλας (*sc.* οὔσης): and see above on 471.
Further: even if it were necessary to bind
βωμία closely with λύει, it would be bold
to say that poetry could not permit this
slight modification in the ordinary use of
the word, when we remember how free
was the adverbial use of adjectives in
poetry (*e.g.*, *Ai.* 217 νύκτερος Αἴας ἀπελω-
βήθη).

ξίφει. A sacrificial knife, which lay
on the altar. Cp. Eur. *Alc.* 74 (Death
speaks) στείχω δ᾽ ἐπ᾽ αὐτήν, ὡς κατάρξωμαι
ξίφει. For the prep. cp. *Ai.* 828 πεπτῶτα
τῷδε περὶ νεορράντῳ ξίφει.

Next to Arndt's, the best conjecture
seems that of Blaydes, ἥδ᾽ ὀξυθήκτῳ
σφαγίδι βωμίᾳ πέρι. In favour of Arndt's
we may observe:—(*a*) the MS. πέριξ (a
word not used by Soph., and nowhere
common) was not likely to have originated
from πέρι alone: whereas it could easily
arise from περὶ ξίφει, if ἰφει had been
blotted or lost. (*b*) The MS. ἤδε (or ἡ
δὲ) is just the kind of feeble make-shift
which is sometimes found in the MSS.,
where a verse had come down in a
mutilated state: see, *e.g.*, on *O. T.* 943 f.,
1264 f.—For other conjectures, see Appendix.

1302 λύει κελαινὰ βλέφαρα, allows
her eyes to close in darkness. λύει = re-

laxes: the eyelids are deprived of power
to remain open. The phrase has been
suggested by the epic λῦσε δὲ γυῖα, λέλυντο
δὲ γυῖα, etc., and seems quite intelligible;
though, doubtless, it would have been
more natural to say κλήει, as Soph. has
done in fr. 640, βλέφαρα κέκληται. In
[Eur.] *Rhes.* 8 we have λῦσον βλεφάρων
γοργωπὸν ἕδραν, of *opening* the eyes; but
that has no bearing on the different use
here. Wolff brings what at first sight
is a perfect parallel: *Anthol. P.* 3. 11
ἄνθ᾽ ὧν ὄμματ᾽ ἔλυσε τὰ Γοργόνος ἐνθάδε
Περσεύς. But unfortunately neither he
nor Bellermann has observed the meaning. It is not, '*caused* the Gorgon's eyes
to close,' but '*uncovered* the Gorgon's
head.' The epigram refers to Perseus
bringing Medusa's head to Seriphos, and
therewith petrifying Polydectes, who had
married Danaë, and sent her son on his
perilous mission.—The objection to μύει
is that elsewhere the verb has these
usages:—(1) intrans.,—ὄμματα μύει, the
eyes close, or μύομεν, we shut our eyes.
(2) trans., as *Anth. P.* 9. 558 ὕπνος ἔμυσε
κόρας (with the post-classical ῠ), 'caused
to close.' That is, there is no classical
example of such a phrase as μύει ὀφθαλ-
μούς, she shuts her eyes.

1303 Μεγαρέως. Cp. Aesch. *Theb.*
474 Μεγαρεύς, Κρέοντος σπέρμα, τοῦ σπαρ-
τῶν γένους, where he is one of the Theban
warriors who guard the gates: his patriotic

she suffered her darkening eyes to close, when she had wailed
for the noble fate of Megareus who died before, and then for
his fate who lies there,—and when, with her last breath, she
had invoked evil fortunes upon thee, the slayer of thy sons.

CR. Woe, woe! I thrill with dread. Is there none to 3rd
strike me to the heart with two-edged sword?—O miserable strophe.
that I am, and steeped in miserable anguish!

δείλαιοσ— | δειλαίᾳ ... δύᾳ. | **1307** ἀνταίαν] L has γρ. καιρίαν in the margin,
from S.   **1310** δείλαιος ἐγώ· φεῦ φεῦ MSS. In L the first hand had written
συγκέκραμαι δύαι (from the next v.) immediately after ἐγώ. Those words have been
erased, and φεῦ φεῦ written in their place; not (I think) by a later hand, but
by the first scribe himself. The error was, indeed, one which could not escape
him.—For φεῦ φεῦ, Erfurdt conject. αἰαῖ (=the second ἴτω in 1332): Gleditsch
repeats ἐγώ.   **1311** In L δείλαιαι has been made from δειλαία.

---

death is foreshadowed *ib.* 477 θανὼν
τροφεῖα πληρώσει χθονί. The story is
thus told by Eur. (*Phoen.* 930—1018),
who calls him Menoeceus. While the
Argives are pressing Thebes, Creon and
Eteocles send for Teiresias. The seer
says that Ares is wroth, because Cadmus
of old slew the god's offspring, a dragon
(or serpent?) which had its lair outside
the walls. One of the Cadmean race,
sprung from the dragon's teeth, must die
to appease him. Now, Creon and his
two sons are the only pure-bred σπαρτοί
left. And Haemon is married. The
seer therefore suggests that Menoeceus
should die. Menoeceus pretends that he
means to fly to Delphi. Creon leaves
the scene, in order to provide him with
money for the journey. Menoeceus then
rushes to the top of a tower on the walls,
where he cuts his throat, and falls into
the dragon's former den (σηκὸν ἐς μελαμ-
βαθῆ | δράκοντος, *Ph.* 1010, see n. above
on 411). Statius, who also calls him
Menoeceus, tells the story in *Theb.* 10.
589—782, and, like Eur., makes the son
practise a pious fraud in order to hinder
his father from preventing the sacrifice.—κλεινὸν λάχος: cp. Eur. *Ph.* 1013,
where he says, στείχω δὲ θανάτου δῶρον
οὐκ αἰσχρὸν πόλει | δώσων, νόσου δὲ τήνδ'
ἀπαλλάξω χθόνα. Statius *Th.* 10. 670
where Virtus says to Menoeceus, *rape
nobile fatum.* λάχος is freq. in poetry,
and is used by Xen. The MS. λέχος
would be forced as an allusion to the
dragon's den (θαλάμαι, Eur. *Ph.* 931, or
σηκός, *ib.* 1010) into which the corpse fell.

And it could not here be a general word
for 'grave.'
    1304 f. κακὰς πράξεις=δυσπραξίας.
A solitary instance of the plur. in this
sense; as, conversely, *Tr.* 879 is the only
instance of the sing. πρᾶξις as='mode of
doing,' instead of 'fortune' (*O. C.* 560 n.).
In Eur. *El.* 1305 κοιναὶ πράξεις, κοινοὶ δὲ
πότμοι, the sense is, 'actions.' But the
peculiarity here does not warrant a suspicion (see cr. n.). It is equally exceptional, the other way, when πράσσειν καλῶς
means 'to act well' (*O. C.* 1764 n.).—
ἐφυμνήσ.=ἐπαρασαμένη: cp. 658 n.
    1307 f. ἀνέπταν, aor. referring to a
moment just past; we should use the
pres.: cp. *O. C.* 1466 ἔπτηξα θυμόν: *Ai.*
693 ἔφριξ' ἔρωτι περιχαρὴς δ' ἀνεπτάμην:
cp. *O. T.* 337 n. The act. aor. ἔπτην is
once used in lyrics by Aesch. (*P. V.* 555
προσέπτα), and once by Eur. (*Med.* 440,
ἀνέπτα). It is a poetical form, but occurs
in late prose (Arrian, Lucian, etc.).—
φόβῳ, with fear of the curses invoked by
Eurydicè.—**ἀνταίαν**, sc. πληγήν (*O. C.*
544 n.), a blow which strikes one full on
the breast: *El.* 195 παγχάλκων ἀνταία |
γενύων ὡρμάθη πλαγά: Eur. *Andr.* 844
ἵν' ἀνταίαν | ἐρείσω πλαγάν. But διανταία
=a thrust which passes through the body:
Aesch. *Cho.* 639 ξίφος | διανταίαν ὀξυπευ-
κὲς ὠντᾷ.
    1310 f. δείλαιος, but in 1311 δειλαίᾳ
with αῖ: cp. *O. C.* 442 οἱ τοῦ πατρὸς τῷ
πατρί: *ib.* 883 ἆρ' οὐχ ὕβρις τάδ'; ὕβρις:
Ph. 296 ἀλλ' ἐν πέτροισι πέτρον: *ib.* 827
ὕπν'...ὕπνε (with ῡ in the first place, but
ῠ in the second): *El.* 148 ἆ Ἴτυν, αἰὲν

ΕΞ. ὡς αἰτίαν γε τῶνδε κἀκείνων ἔχων
    πρὸς τῆς θανούσης τῆσδ᾽ ἐπεσκήπτου μόρων.
ΚΡ. ποίῳ δὲ κἀπελύσατ᾽ ἐν φοναῖς τρόπῳ;
ΕΞ. παίσασ᾽ ὑφ᾽ ἧπαρ αὐτόχειρ αὐτήν, ὅπως   1315
    παιδὸς τόδ᾽ ᾔσθετ᾽ ὀξυκώκυτον πάθος.

στρ. δ'. ΚΡ. ὤμοι μοι, τάδ᾽ οὐκ ἐπ᾽ ἄλλον βροτῶν
    2 ἐμᾶς ἁρμόσει ποτ᾽ ἐξ αἰτίας.
    3 ἐγὼ γάρ σ᾽ ἐγὼ ἔκανον, ὦ μέλεος,
    4 ἐγώ, φάμ᾽ ἔτυμον. ἰὼ πρόσπολοι,   1320
    5 ἄγετέ μ᾽ ὅ τι *τάχιστ᾽, ἄγετέ μ᾽ ἐκποδών,
    6 τὸν οὐκ ὄντα μᾶλλον ἢ μηδένα.

ΧΟ. κέρδη παραινεῖς, εἴ τι κέρδος ἐν κακοῖς·
    βράχιστα γὰρ κράτιστα τὰν ποσὶν κακά.

1313 μόρων] μόρωι L.   The later MSS. have μόρων, μόρω (as A), or μόρων (as Aug. b and
T).   1314 ἐν φοναῖς] L has εισ φονάσ written by S above ἐν φοναῖσ.   1317 ὤμοι
MSS. (ὦι μοι μοι L).   Erfurdt gave ἰώ μοι for the sake of closer metrical agreement with 1339, ἄγοιτ᾽ ἄν.—ἐπ᾽ ἄλλον] Pallis conject. ἐπ᾽ ἄλλῳ.   1319 ἐγὼ γάρ
σ᾽ ἐγὼ ἔκανον ὦ μέλεοσ L, with most of the later MSS.: but Aug. b has ἔκτανον,
and so the Aldine.   Hermann inserted a second σ᾽ after ἐγώ.   Nauck proposes
ἐγὼ γάρ σ᾽ ἔκτανον, ὦ μέλεος, and in 1341 σέ τ᾽ αὖ τάνδ᾽· οὐδ᾽ ἔχω, ὦ μέλεος.

Ἴτυν ὀλοφύρεται.—The following are a
few among many instances of αἰ before ο:
827 πετραία: 1131 Νυσαίων: 1140 βιαίας:
Od. 20. 379 ἔμπαιον: Tyrt. 10. 20 γε-
ραιούς: Aesch. Suppl. 385 (lyr.) ἱκταίου
(Dind. ἱκτίου): Eur. El. 497 (dial.)
παλαιόν. For the repetition cp. 379,
977.—συγκέκραμαι, 'blended with' anguish, i.e. steeped in it: (Whitelaw:
'Fulfilled with sorrow, and made one
with grief.') Cp. Ai. 895 οἴκτῳ τῷδε
συγκεκραμένην, 'her soul is steeped in the
anguish of that wail': Ar. Plut. 853
οὕτω πολυφόρῳ συγκέκραμαι δαίμονι, where
the words just before, ὡς ἀπόλωλα δεί-
λαῖος (850), might suggest that the
parody glanced at our passage.
    1312 f. ὡς αἰτίαν...ἔχων, as being
responsible for, = ὡς αἴτιος ὤν.   So Aesch.
Eum. 579 Apollo, defending the accused
Orestes, says, αἰτίαν δ᾽ ἔχω | τῆς τοῦδε
μητρὸς τοῦ φόνου, I am responsible for
(not, 'am accused of') the deed.   In this
sense of the phrase, ἔχω = παρέχω: cp.
Thuc. 2. 41 ἀγανάκτησιν ἔχει, gives cause
of resentment; id. 2. 61 ἔχει αἴσθησιν,
makes itself felt.   But in prose αἰτίαν ἔχω

usu. = 'to bear the blame' for a thing,
i.e. to be held responsible for it: Her. 5.
70 εἶχον αἰτίην τοῦ φόνου τούτου: Plat.
Apol. 38 C ὄνομα ἕξετε καὶ αἰτίαν...ὡς
Σωκράτη ἀπεκτόνατε.—τῶνδε...μόρων, that
of Haemon: κἀκείνων, that of Megareus
(1303 f.).   For the plur., cp. El. 205
τοὺς ἐμὸς ἴδε πατὴρ | θανάτους αἰκεῖς.—
ἐπεσκήπτου, wast denounced.   In Attic
law ἐπισκήπτομαί τινι (midd.) meant, to
take proceedings against a witness for
perjury (ψευδομαρτυριῶν): Isae. or. 5 § 9
πρὶν ἐπεξελθεῖν οἷς ἐπεσκήψατο τῶν μαρ-
τύρων.   The rare pass. occuis in Plat.
Legg. 937 B ἐὰν δούλη ἐπισκηφθῇ τὰ ψευδῆ
μαρτυρῆσαι.
    1314 κἀπελύσατ᾽, quitted life: see
on 1268 ἀπελύθης.   For καί, cp. 772 n.—
ἐν φοναῖς: 696 n.
    1315 f. ὑφ᾽ ἧπαρ, expressing move-
ment, 'home to' it: cp. Tr. 930 ὁρῶμεν
αὐτὴν ἀμφιπλῆγι φασγάνῳ | πλευρὰν ὑφ᾽
ἧπαρ καὶ φρένας πεπληγμένην.   Eur. Or.
1063 παίσας πρὸς ἧπαρ φασγάνῳ.—ὀξυκώ-
κυτον, by the household (cp. 1079): she
herself heard the news in silence (1256).
    1317 f. τάδ᾽ οὐκ ἐπ᾽ ἄλλον βροτῶν

ΜΕ. Yea, both this son's doom, and that other's, were laid to thy charge by her whose corpse thou seest.

ΚΡ. And what was the manner of the violent deed by which she passed away?

ΜΕ. Her own hand struck her to the heart, when she had learned her son's sorely lamented fate.

ΚΡ. Ah me, this guilt can never be fixed on any other 4th strophe. of mortal kind, for my acquittal! I, even I, was thy slayer, wretched that I am—I own the truth. Lead me away, O my servants, lead me hence with all speed, whose life is but as death!

ΧΗ. Thy counsels are good, if there can be good with ills; briefest is best, when trouble is in our path.

1320 ἐγὼ φᾶμ' ἔτυμον L. Semitelos conject. ἐγώ, φαμί, σύννομ'. **1322 f.** ἄγετέ μ' ὅτι τάχοσ, ἄγετέ μ' ἐκ ποδῶν (sic, not ἐκποδῶν) L. Unless the os of τάχος is lengthened before the pause, the dochmiac requires either (a) a long syllable there, or (b) the addition of one short. Hence (a) Erfurdt proposed τάχιστ' instead of τάχος. Many edd. receive this. Enger, ἄγ' ἄγεθ' ὅτι τάχος μ', ἀπάγετ' ἐκποδών. Meineke, ἄγετέ μ', ὅτι τάχος μ' ἀπάγετ' ἐκποδών. Pallis, ἄγετέ μ' ὅτι τάχος, τίθεσθέ μ' ἐκποδών. (b) Schöne, ἀπάγετέ μ' ὅτι τάχος, ἄγετέ μ' ἐκποδών. **1327** βράχιστα γὰρ κράτιστα] In L, S notes a v. l., κράτιστα γὰρ τάχιστα.

ἁρμόσει ποτέ, the guilt can never fit (= be fixed upon) another man, ἐξ ἐμᾶς αἰτίας, (being transferred) from my responsibility, —i.e., so as to leave me blameless. For the intrans. ἁρμόσει, cp. O. T. 902 (n.), El. 1293. ἐκ here is not for ἀπό, but is used as if we had, οὔποτε ἐξ ὑπαιτίου ἀναίτιος φανοῦμαι (cp. Tr. 284 ἐξ ὀλβίων ἄζηλον εὑροῦσαι βίον). Thus ἐξ ἐμᾶς αἰτίας is really a compressed way of saying, 'by change from a state of things in which the αἰτία (blame) was mine.'
1319 f. μέλεος: for the nom., cp. 1211.—φᾶμ' ἔτυμον, i.e., this is the simple truth: I was virtually, though not actually, his slayer.
1322 ὅ τι τάχιστ'. This (Erfurdt's) emendation seems the simplest and best cure for the metre (see cr. n.). It is worth noticing that Soph. has this phrase in a closely similar passage, O. T. 1340 ἀπάγετ' ἐκτόπιον ὅ τι τάχιστά με. He has ὅσον τάχος thrice, and ὡς τάχος eight times, but ὅ τι τάχος nowhere else.
1325 τὸν οὐκ ὄντα μᾶλλον ἢ μηδένα, one who exists no more than a nonentity. In μηδένα, μή has its generic force: one who is such as to be a mere cipher. Cp.

Ai. 1114 οὐ γὰρ ἠξίου τοὺς μηδένας. O. T. 1019 καὶ πῶς ὁ φύσας ἐξ ἴσου τῷ μηδενί; (dat. of ὁ μηδείς,—he who is μηδείς in respect to consanguinity). Here τὸν μηδέν would have been equally fitting: cp. Ai. 1231 ὅτ' οὐδὲν ὢν τοῦ μηδὲν (the dead) ἀντέστης ὕπερ.—Postgate suggests (Trans. Cambridge Phil. Soc., 1886, p. 58) that this use of the oblique cases of μηδείς in sing., and of οὐδείς and μηδείς in plur., may have come from an attraction of the neuter by the masc. article: e.g., τοὺς μηδένας from τοὺς μηδέν. We do not find ὁ μηδείς. When it became declinable, the phrase could dispense with the article; e.g., τὸν μηδέν could be simply μηδένα.
1326 f. κέρδη: the plur. more often refers to money (1061); but cp. El. 767 ἢ δεινὰ μέν, κέρδη δέ.—τὰ γὰρ ἐν ποσὶ κακὰ κράτιστά (ἐστι) βράχιστα (ὄντα): instead of, κράτιστόν ἐστι τὰ...κακὰ βράχιστα εἶναι. For the personal constr., cp. O. T. 1368 κρείσσων γὰρ ἦσθα μηκέτ' ὢν ἢ ζῶν τυφλός, and n. ib. 1061. For the omission of ὄντα, cp. the oracle μὴ κίνει Καμάριναν· ἀκίνητος γὰρ ἀμείνων (sc. οὖσα), ap. Stephanus Byz. s. v. Καμάρινα.—**τὰν**

ἀντ. γ'. ΚΡ. ἴτω ἴτω,

  2 φανήτω μόρων ὁ κάλλιστ' *ἔχων   1329

  3 ἐμοί, τερμίαν ἄγων ἀμέραν,

  4 ὕπατος· ἴτω ἴτω,

  5 ὅπως μηκέτ' ἆμαρ ἄλλ' εἰσίδω.   1333

ΧΟ. μέλλοντα ταῦτα· τῶν προκειμένων τι χρὴ

    πράσσειν· μέλει γὰρ τῶνδ' ὅτοισι χρὴ μέλειν. 1335

ΚΡ. ἀλλ' ὧν ἐρῶ μέν, ταῦτα συγκατηυξάμην.

ΧΟ. μή νυν προσεύχου μηδέν· ὡς πεπρωμένης

    οὐκ ἔστι θνητοῖς συμφορᾶς ἀπαλλαγή.

1330 ἔχων Pallis: ἐμῶν MSS.   **1333** ἆμαρ ἀλλ' L.   **1336** ἐρῶ L. The later MSS. have ἐρῶ μὲν (V ἐρῶμεν). Bothe writes ἐρῶμεν. Schneidewin, ἐρῶμαι. F. W. Schmidt, ἐρῶ 'γώ. Dindorf, ἐρῶ, τοιαῦτα. Seyffert, ἐρῶ γ', ἅπαντα. Blaydes, ἐρῶ γε τυγχάνειν κατηυξάμην.—Nauck thinks that ἐρῶ ταῦτα is right, and that in 1314 we should perh. read κάλύετ' for κἀπελύσατ', the schol. there having τίνι τρόπῳ, φησίν,

---

ποσίν, before our feet, claiming immediate attention. Cp. Eur. *Alc.* 739 ἡμεῖς δέ, τοὐν ποσὶν γὰρ οἰστέον κακόν, | στείχωμεν, ὡς ἂν ἐν πυρᾷ θῶμεν νεκρόν. So Pind. *P.* 8. 32 τὸ δ' ἐν ποσί μοι τράχον, my present theme.

1329 ff. μόρων ὁ κάλλιστ' ἔχων. I have adopted ἔχων, a conjecture of Pallis for ἐμῶν, on the following grounds. (1) The phrase μόρων ἐμῶν could mean nothing but, 'of all fates possible for me.' This, however, is most strange. In 1313 μόρων meant 'violent deaths': so Aesch. *Th.* 420 αἱματη|φόρους μόρους. Hence it has been proposed to render μόρων ἐμῶν here, (a) 'the deaths caused by me': as Hermann, 'veniat caedium per me factarum suprema, exoptatissime mihi ultimum diem adducens.' (b) Figuratively, 'the many deaths that I have died'; cp. 1288 ὀλωλότ' ἄνδρ' ἐπεξειργάσω. But neither version is tolerable. (2) Triclinius proposed to make ἐμῶν fem., and to take it with τερμίαν: when it would at least be necessary to write ἐμᾶν (sc. ἀμερᾶν). But, either with ἐμῶν or with ἐμᾶν, the relation of ὁ κάλλιστ' ...ἄγων or ὁ κάλλιστ' ...ἄγων to the gen. μόρων is exceedingly awkward. 'That one among fates which *best* brings my last day,' cannot be explained as an equivalent for, 'that best of fates which brings it'; *i.e.*, for μόρων ὁ κάλλιστος, ὁ...ἄγων.

Both these difficulties (which to me

seem insuperable) are removed by reading μόρων ὁ κάλλιστ' ἔχων, the best of fates. That ἔχων could have been changed to ἐμῶν, either by conjecture or by accident, is shown by v. 575, where at the end of the verse L has the probably true ἐμοί, while other MSS. have ἔφυ. (If κύνες is right in 467, and ξίφει in 1301, these, too, are instances of final words corrupted.) A question of punctuation remains. The comma might follow either ἔχων or ἐμοί. I prefer the latter. Cp. *Ai.* 394 ἰὼ σκότος, ἐμὸν φάος, | ἔρεβος ὦ φαεννότατον, ὡς ἐμοί.

1332 ὕπατος, an emphatic repetition of ὁ κάλλιστ' ἔχων,—'supreme of fates,'—far best. It has been usual to take ὕπατος here as 'last.' But neither ὕπατος nor ὑπέρτατος ever bears that sense in classical Greek. Pindar often uses ὕπατος as 'best,' but never as 'last': *O.* 1. 100, *P.* 6. 42 and 10. 9, *N.* 10. 32. In post-classical poetry ὕπατος sometimes means 'last,' but that use was imitated from the Lat. *supremus* and *summus.* Thus in an epitaph on an Italian, a certain Aelius, Apollonides writes (*Anthol. P.* 7. 233), νοῦσον ὅτ' εἰς ὑπάτην ὤλισθανε, τέρμα τ' ἄφυκτον | εἶδεν. Whether the Apollonides of the Anthology was or was not he of Nicaea, who dedicated to Tiberius a commentary on Timon's Σιλλοί (Diog. Laert. 9. 109), at least he belonged to that age. This is proved by

CR. Oh, let it come, let it appear, that fairest of fates for me, that brings my last day,—aye, best fate of all! Oh, let it come, that I may never look upon to-morrow's light!

CH. These things are in the future; present tasks claim our care: the ordering of the future rests where it should rest.

CR. All my desires, at least, were summed in that prayer.

CH. Pray thou no more; for mortals have no escape from destined woe.

ἐλύετο..;).—L here gives the temporal augment in συγκατηυξάμην. So *Ph.* 1019 L has ηὔξάμην: *Tr.* 610 ηὔγμην: *ib.* 764 κατηύχετο. An Attic inscr. of 362 B.C. gives ηὖχθαι (Meisterhans, p. 78). **1337** προσεύχου] One MS. of the 14th cent. (Aug. b) has κατεύχου, which Benedict had conjectured.

---

his words in *Anthol. P.* 9. 287, Ἡελίου νῆσον ὅτ' εἶχε Νέρων, alluding to the residence of Tiberius at Rhodes (*c.* 6 B.C.— 2 A.D.). The epigram was written after Tiberius had been adopted by Augustus in 4 A.D., as he is called Ζῆνα τὸν ἐσσόμενον, and perhaps after he had come to the throne (14 A.D.). It would be interesting to know whether ὕπατος as ='last' can be carried back beyond the Roman, or later Alexandrian, age; I can find no trace of it.

1334 f. μέλλοντα, belonging to the future. To Creon's wish for death the Chorus replies, in effect, 'Sufficient unto the day is the evil thereof.'—τῶν προκειμένων: the duties which lie immediately before us; meaning here especially the obsequies of the dead.—For τι cp. *O. C.* 500 ἀλλ' ἐν τάχει τι πράσσετον.—τῶνδ' =τῶν μελλόντων.—ὅτοισι χρὴ μέλειν, *i.e.*, τοῖς θεοῖς. Cp. *Ph.* 1036 θεοῖσιν εἰ δίκης μέλει, | ἔξοιδα δ' ὡς μέλει γε.

1336 ἐρῶ μέν: for μέν cp. n. on 11. It merely gives a slight emphasis to ἐρῶ. —συγκατηυξάμην: κατά expresses that the prayer is solemn; σύν, that it sums up his desires. (For this force of σύν cp. 1202.) Cp. *O. C.* 585 ἐνταῦθα γάρ μοι κεῖνα συγκομίζεται ('by that boon I reap all the rest').—Nauck thinks that L's reading, ἀλλ' ὧν ἐρῶ, ταῦτα συγκατηυξάμην, is sound, and that in the corresponding verse, 1314, we should perh. read, ποίῳ δὲ **καλύετ'** (for κἀπελύσατ') ἐν φοναῖς τρόπῳ; He refers to the scholium on 1314: τίνι τρόπῳ, φησίν, ἐλύετο, καὶ ἐφέρετο εἰς φονάς; ἀντὶ τοῦ, ποίῳ τρόπῳ εἰς φόνον ἔπεσεν; Now, this does not point, I think, to the Scholiast's having ἐλύετο in his text, though it suggests that he had εἰς φονάς. He used the simple

verb in his paraphrase in order to bring out the literal sense (as he took it) of ἀπελύσατο. This is shown by ἐφέρετο and ἔπεσεν: he understood, 'she was set free (as a runner in a race is dismissed from the starting-post), and rushed (ἐφέρετο) to bloodshed.'—Further, the origin of L's reading is manifest. ἐρῶ μέν had become ἐρῶμεν (as it actually is in at least one later MS.). Then the plur. ἐρῶμεν seemed too harsh with the sing. συγκατηυξάμην immediately following (though, in fact, it would have been quite defensible, cp. 734 n.), and was changed to ἐρῶ (μεν disappearing). Semitelos would read with L here, and yet leave 1314 unaltered. He refers to *Ai.* 905 where L has τίνος ποτ' ἄρ' ἔπραξε χειρὶ δύσμορος corresponding with 951 ἄγαν ὑπερβριθὲς ἄχθος ἤνυσαν. But there ἔπραξε is surely corrupt: Hermann gives ἔρξε, and Wecklein ἔπαθε.

1337 προσεύχου, without θεοῖς or θεούς. Cp. Her. 1. 48 ὡς τὸ ἐκ Δελφῶν ἤκουσε, αὐτίκα προσεύχετό τε καὶ προσεδέξατο.—Campbell thinks that 'the rationalism of the day appears in this advice of the Chorus.' But such an interpretation ill accords with the tone of the Chorus, which presently insists on the duty of piety towards the gods (1348). Nor does it seem in harmony with the pervading spirit of the poet's work. Rather Creon is exhorted to recognise, with pious resignation, the fixity of the divine decrees. Cp. the closing words of the *Oed. Col.*, ἀλλ' ἀποπαύετε μηδ' ἐπὶ πλείω | θρῆνον ἐγείρετε· | πάντως γὰρ ἔχει τάδε κῦρος. Brunck compared *Aen.* 6. 376 (Aeneas to Palinurus in the shades) *Desine fata deum flecti sperare precando.*

ἀντ. δ. ΚΡ. ἄγοιτ' ἂν μάταιον ἄνδρ' ἐκποδών,
  2 ὅς, ὦ παῖ, σέ τ' οὐχ ἑκὼν *κατέκανον   1340
  3 σέ τ' *αὖ τάνδ', ὤμοι μέλεος· οὐδ' ἔχω
  4 πρὸς πότερον ἴδω, πᾷ *κλιθῶ· πάντα γὰρ
  5 λέχρια τὰν χεροῖν, τὰ δ' ἐπὶ κρατί μοι   1345
  6 πότμος δυσκόμιστος εἰσήλατο.

ΧΟ. πολλῷ τὸ φρονεῖν εὐδαιμονίας
    πρῶτον ὑπάρχει· χρὴ δὲ τά γ' εἰς θεοὺς
    μηδὲν ἀσεπτεῖν· μεγάλοι δὲ λόγοι   1350

1339—1346 L divides thus: ἄγοιτ'— | δσ, ὦ παῖ— | δσ, σέ τ'— | ὄπᾱ— | πάντα— | λέχρια— | πότμος...εἰσήλατο. | **1339** ἐκποδών] ἐκ ποδῶν L, with μ above κ from first hand. **1340** σέ τ' ι: σέ γ' L.—κατέκανον MSS.: κατέκανον Wilhelm Schneider: κάκτανον Hermann: ἔκτανον Musgrave. **1341** σέ τ' αὐτὰν L: σέ τ' αὖ τάνδ' Seidler. L has δσ before σέ τ', doubtless by inadvertent repetition from 1340: Hermann deleted it. **1342 f.** ὄπᾱ πρὸσ πρότερον ἴδω· πᾶ καὶ θῶ· | L. For πρότερον, some of the later MSS. (including A) have πότερον. For καὶ θῶ, Musgrave conjectured

---

1339 ἄγοιτ' ἄν, an entreaty: cp. *O.C.* 725. The opt. with ἄν had a different tone in 444.—μάταιον here expresses rash folly: cp. *O. T.* 891 ματάζων: *Tr.* 565 ματαίαις χερσί.

1340 f. κατέκανον is the best, as it is the simplest, emendation of κατέκτανον (see cr. n.). Though the pres. κατακαίνω is not classical, the aor. is frequent: Xen. uses it (*An.* 3. 1. 2, etc.).—σέ τ' αὖ τάνδ' is a certain correction of σέ τ' αὐτάν. Here the latter would be like saying, 'and actually *thee*,'—as if the slaying of Haemon had been comparatively venial. It cannot be naturally explained as meaning, 'the mother with the son.'

1342 f. πρὸς πότερον...πάντα γάρ. The reading of this verse cannot be certainly determined. The traditional text (see cr. n.) exceeds the metre. My own view is as follows:

(1) The MS. ὄπᾳ should be struck out. It evidently came in from the margin, having been a gloss on πᾷ, meant to show that πᾷ κλιθῶ is not a direct question, but depends on οὐδ' ἔχω. Retaining ὄπᾳ, we should have to suppose a double question: 'nor do I know in what direction, (or) to which thing, I am to look.' This is not only very awkward, but very weak. The hiatus after ἔχω, though not unexampled, is at least another point against ὄπᾳ.

(2) L has πάντα γάρ in a line by itself: but, considering the caprices of lyric division in that MS. (as in the rest), we cannot urge that fact as a hint of interpolation. If ὄπᾳ was a spurious addition to 1342, then πάντα γάρ might easily have been carried over. Again, the words πάντα γάρ are not indispensable; yet the effect of λέχρια τὰν χεροῖν, without them, would be rather oddly abrupt. Therefore we are by no means warranted (I think) in ejecting πάντα γάρ.

(3) κλιθῶ, for καὶ θῶ, is certain. On this last point there is now a general agreement.—The resulting dochmiac differs from that in 1320 only by the 'irrational' long (the ω of ἴδω) for short (the first of ἔτυμον): and this is admissible. See Metrical Analysis.—Other views are noticed in the Appendix.

πρὸς πότερον, i.e., to the corpse of Haemon at his side, or to that of Eurydicè in front of him (1297 ff.).—ἴδω, deliberative subjunct. in the indirect question, depending on οὐκ ἔχω: cp. n. on *O. T.* 72.—πᾷ κλιθῶ, in what direction I am to lean, i.e., where I am to find any support: my son and my wife have fallen: all my fortunes lie in ruin. πᾷ here answers to the dat. after κλίνομαι when it means 'to lean against' a thing, as *Od.* 6. 307 (she sits) κίονι κεκλιμένη.—Not merely,

CR.   Lead me away, I pray you; a rash, foolish man; who ^{4th anti-} have slain thee, ah my son, unwittingly, and thee, too, my wife— strophe. unhappy that I am!   I know not which way I should bend my gaze, or where I should seek support; for all is amiss with that which is in my hands,—and yonder, again, a crushing fate hath leapt upon my head.

[As CREON *is being conducted into the house, the Coryphaeus speaks the closing verses.*

CH.   Wisdom is the supreme part of happiness; and reverence towards the gods must be inviolate.   Great words

κλιθῶ. ὅπᾳ was first omitted by Seidler.   See Appendix.   **1344 f.** λέχρια τάδ᾽ ἐν χεροῖν L, and so most of the later MSS.: for τάδ᾽, Aug. b and Dresd. a give τά τ᾽. Brunck gave λέχρια τὰν χεροῖν: Kayser, λέχρια τὰ πρὸ χεροῖν.   **1347—1353** These six verses are rejected by Fr. Ritter.   **1349** τά τ᾽ εἰσ θεοὺσ L.   For τά τ᾽ Triclinius gave τά γ᾽.—Dindorf writes χρὴ δ᾽ ἐς τὰ θεῶν: Blaydes, χρὴ δ᾽ ἐς τοὺς θεούς: also conjecturing (as Wecklein does, *Ars Soph. em.* p. 167) χρὴ δὲ τὰ πρὸς θεούς.

'whither I am to betake myself,' ποῖ τράπωμαι; This is shown by λέχρια.

1344 f. λέχρια τὰν χεροῖν. τὰν seems right (see cr. n.): the MS. τάδ᾽ ἐν would come from ΤΑΕΝ. Creon is still touching the corpse of Haemon. The phrase τὰ ἐν χεροῖν would mean, figuratively, 'the matters with which I am engaged' (so ἔχειν τι ἐν χερσί, Her. 1. 35). Here, the words take a dramatic force from their literal sense. 'All is amiss with that which I handle.' Creon has, indeed, mismanaged the work which his hands found to do; and the proof of it is the corpse which he is touching. λέχριος = 'slanting,' 'oblique.' As ὀρθός means either 'straight' or 'upright,' so λέχριος can mean either 'moving sideways' (*O.C.* 195), or, 'not upright,' 'slanting.' Cp. πλάγιος, the ordinary prose equiv. of λέχριος, which has the second sense in Philemon Ἀγύρτης 5 σχήματα | πλάγι᾽ ἐστὶ τἄλλα, τοῦτο δ᾽ ὀρθὸν θηρίον, man alone is *erect*, while other creatures (*i.e.* quadrupeds) are bent earthward (cp. Sallust, *Cat.* 1 pecora quae natura *prona...* finxit). So, here, λέχρια means primarily 'awry':—τὰ πράγματα οὐκ ὀρθῶς ἔχει. Cp. Shaksp. *Rich. II.* 2. 4. 24 *And crossly to thy good all fortune goes.* But it is further tinged with the sense of 'prone,' applicable to the corpse. The Scholiast

here has usu. been understood as explaining λέχρια by πλάγια καὶ πεπτωκότα. But he meant only πλάγια to explain λέχρια, while πεπτωκότα referred to πότμος... εἰσήλατο: this is clear (I think) from his whole phrase, πλάγια καὶ πεπτωκότα, τὰ μὲν ἐν χερσί, τὰ δὲ ἐπὶ τῇ κεφαλῇ.

τὰ δ᾽ ἐπὶ κρατί μοι κ.τ.λ., while on the other hand: for the adverbial τὰ δ᾽, see *O. T.* 666 n. These words refer to the deaths of Eurydicè and Antigone, as τὰ ἐν χεροῖν referred to the death of Haemon. It is quite possible to read **τάδ᾽**, as = 'thus'; but then **τὰ ἐν χεροῖν** would denote *all* his woes, and so we should lose the dramatic blending of a literal with a figurative sense.—**εἰσήλατο:** cp. on 1271 f.

1347 f. εὐδαιμονίας πρῶτον, the most important element in it. Cp. Plat. *Rep.* 389 D σωφροσύνης δέ, ὡς πλήθει, οὐ τὰ τοιάδε μέγιστα, ἀρχόντων μὲν ὑπηκόους εἶναι, κ.τ.λ.—**τά γ᾽ εἰς θεούς:** cp. 889 n.: *O. T.* 706 (n.) τό γ᾽ εἰς ἑαυτόν. *Ph.* 1441 εὐσεβεῖν τὰ πρὸς θεούς.—For the sentiment, cp. 1050 f.

1349 ff. μεγάλοι...λόγοι: cp. 127 n. —For the position of τῶν ὑπεραύχων, cp. 944 f. Δανάας...δέμας.—**πληγὰς...ἀποτείσαντες,** as the price: cp. Her. 2. 65 ἀποτίνει ζημίην (a fine). So *ib.* 5. 56 οὐδεὶς ἀνθρώπων ἀδικῶν τίσιν οὐκ ἀποτείσει.

μεγάλας πληγὰς τῶν ὑπεραύχων
ἀποτείσαντες
γήρᾳ τὸ φρονεῖν ἐδίδαξαν.

1351 Nauck would place μεγάλας πληγὰς after τῶν ὑπεραύχων.   Semitelos thinks

---

1352 γήρᾳ, without a prep.: so Eur. *Hec.* 203, etc.: but this is poetical, prose

of prideful men are ever punished with great blows, and, in
old age, teach the chastened to be wise.

that the two latter words may have crept in from a gloss, 'ἀντὶ τῶν ὑπεραύχων,' on
μεγάλοι λόγοι.

---

preferring ἐν γήρᾳ, ἐν τῷ γήρᾳ, or ἐπὶ
γήρως.—τὸ φρονεῖν, so soon after 1347:

cp. on 76, 625 (ἐκτὸς ἄτας), 956 (κερτομίοις).
—ἐδίδαξαν, gnomic aor. (709).

APPENDIX.

Verses 2 f.   ἆρ' οἶσθ' ὅ τι Ζεὺς τῶν ἀπ' Οἰδίπου κακῶν
     ὁποῖον οὐχὶ νῷν ἔτι ζώσαιν τελεῖ;

The view taken in the commentary—that ὅ τι is subject to ἐστί understood—seems to have been first proposed by W. Schneider, then by Neue; it was advocated by Bonitz (*Beiträge* II. 17); and it is now received by Bellermann. What is new in my note, so far as I know, is the attempt to show how associations of colloquial idiom may have helped to soften the apparent harshness, and, more especially, to excuse the hyperbaton of Ζεύς. Here, at any rate, we approach the root of the difficulty which these verses present. The ultimate question is,—how much irregularity would the spoken language of the day have tolerated in such a sentence? We do not know: we can but study the evidence of contemporary analogies.

At one time I inclined to the only theory which dispenses with the assumption of irregularity. This consists in taking τελεῖ with both clauses: ἆρ' οἶσθ' ὅ τι Ζεὺς τῶν...κακῶν (τελεῖ), ὁποῖον οὐχὶ νῷν ἔτι ζώσαιν τελεῖ; Then,—τελεῖ being, in this case, better regarded as *fut.*,—the sense would be, 'what will Zeus fulfil, which he will not fulfil *while we live?*'—that condition being emphasised by the form of the sentence. Grammatically, this is blameless. Cp. Plat. *Legg.* p. 710 D πάντα σχε-δὸν ἀπείργασται τῷ θεῷ, ἅπερ (*sc.* ἀπεργάζεται) ὅταν βουληθῇ διαφερόντως εὖ πρᾶξαί τινα πόλιν: where the relative clause, expressing the condi-tion, ὅταν βουληθῇ...πόλιν, is parallel with our gen. absol., νῷν ἔτι ζώσαιν. If the τελεῖ after ζώσαιν stood after κακῶν, the parallelism of form would be complete: except, indeed, that the Platonic sentence is a little bolder, since it is natural to supply ἀπεργάζεται (or ἀπειργάσατο) rather than ἀπείργασται. Yet, admissible as this construction is, it is undoubtedly harsh. And that harshness—especially at the outset of the play—is a strong argument against it.

Two other interpretations have been suggested by those who take ὅ τι as a pronoun. (*a*) ὁποῖον is resumptive of ὅ τι. 'Knowest thou *what* evil,—*what sort of* evil,—he does not fulfil?'—an emphatic pleonasm. The Scholiast seems to have acquiesced in this:—εἶπεν δὲ διττῶς· πρῶτον μὲν ὅ τι, ἔπειτα δὲ ὁποῖον, ἀρκοῦντος θατέρου. But this seems weak; and it is certainly jerky. Others modify this view by taking οὐχί with ὁποῖον *only:* 'Knowest thou what of the ills—nay, what *not*—is being fulfilled by Zeus,' etc. But, 'knowest thou *what* of the ills...' (ὅ τι *without* οὐχί) would have implied, not *less* than her meaning, but the *reverse* of it. (*b*) Two questions are combined in ὅ τι ὁποῖον (as in τίς πόθεν εἶ;)—'what, (*and*) of what kind?' This view, proposed by Zehlicke (Greifsw. 1826), has been rightly rejected by A. Boeckh (*Ueber die Ant.* p. 175).—Wecklein's comment is, 'ὅ τι ὁποῖον, *quid quale,* welches Leid, wie es immer heissen mag': *i.e.,* 'what woe,—of whatever sort it may be.' I do not see how the words could yield this sense.

If we read ὅτι, the conjunction, then ὁποῖον is substituted for the direct ποῖον. 'Knowest thou that Zeus fulfils—what not?' In favour of this, we might, perhaps, suggest two points. (1) The double question, being somewhat awkward, may have made it easier to slide into the irregular relative construction with ὁποῖον. (2) The familiarity of the combination οἶδ' ὅτι—strongly illustrated by its use as an adverbial parenthesis (275 n.)—may have made it easier to treat οἶσθ' ὅτι, after some intervening words, as if ὅτι did not exist. On the other hand, the harshness of the construction is aggravated by the shortness of the sentence. We cannot compare *O. T.* 1401, where the MSS. give ἆρά μου μέμνησθ' ὅτι | οἷ' ἔργα δράσας ὑμὶν εἶτα δεῦρ' ἰὼν | ὁποῖ' ἔπρασσον αὖθις; For there —even if ὅτι is kept—it is obviously impossible that μέμνησθ' ὅτι οἷα δράσας, etc., should be a fusion of μέμνησθ' ὅτι τοιαῦτα δράσας with μέμνησθ' οἷα δράσας: the alternative—to treat οἷα and ὁποῖα as exclamatory— though not (to my mind) tolerable, would be a less evil: but clearly ὅτι should there be τι. It has been suggested, indeed, that ὁποῖον is not substituted for ποῖον, but is itself a direct interrogative. This has been supported by the analogy of ὁπότερος in direct question. Plat. *Lysis* 212 C ναί· ὁπότερος οὖν αὐτῶν ποτέρου φίλος ἐστίν; Heindorf there cites *Euthyd.* 271 A ὁπότερον καὶ ἐρωτᾷς, ὦ Κρίτων; *Rep.* 348 B ὁποτέρως οὖν σοι...ἀρέσκει; Let it be assumed that the readings are sound in those places. Still, there is at least no similar instance of ὁποῖος: nor is ὁποῖον here the *first word* of a direct question.

The proposed emendations are all unsatisfactory. They are of three classes.

(1) Those which alter v. 2, leaving v. 3 untouched.—Bothe: ἆρ' οἶσθά τι Ζεύς.—Meineke: ἆρ' οἶσθα δὴ Ζεύς.

(2) Those which alter v. 3, leaving v. 2 untouched.—Dindorf: ἐλλεῖπον for ὁποῖον.—Paley: οὐκ ἔσθ' ὁποῖον οὐχὶ νῷν ζώσαιν τελεῖ (*Journ. Phil.* x. p. 16). He thinks that ἔτι was a gloss (due to the frequency of its combination elsewhere with ζῆν), and that, when ἔτι had crept into the text, οὐκ ἔσθ' was erroneously omitted.—Blaydes: ἢ ποῖον, or τὸ λοιπόν, for ὁποῖον.

(3) Those which change, or transpose, words in both verses.— Heimsoeth (*Krit. Stud.* I. 211): ἆρ' οἶσθά πού τι τῶν ἀπ' Οἰδίπου κακῶν | ὁποῖον οὐ Ζεὺς νῷν ἔτι ζώσαιν τελεῖ;—Nauck: ἆρ' οἶσθ' ὅ τι Ζεὺς

νῶν ἔτι ζώσαιν τελεῖ | ὁποῖον οὐχὶ τῶν ἀπ' Οἰδίπου κακῶν; As Moriz
Schmidt says, this would naturally mean, 'Knowest thou what Zeus
fulfils for us, which does not belong to the woes from Oedipus?'—
Moriz Schmidt (1880): ἆρ' ἔσθ' ὅ τι Ζεὺς τῶν ἀπ' Οἰδίπου κακῶν—ἔοικεν
οὐχὶ νῶν ἔτι ζώσαιν τελεῖν; He prefers ἔσθ' to οἶσθ' on the ground that,
after the latter, ὅτι would naturally be taken as the conjunction. (But
cp. Plat. *Theaet.* 197 D κατασκευάζομεν οὐκ οἶδ' ὅ τι πλάσμα.) The
origin of ὁποῖον was, he supposes, a marginal gloss ὁποιονδήποτε, referring to κακῶν.—Semitelos compresses the two vv. into one: ἆρ' οἶσθ'
ὅ τι Ζεὺς οὐχὶ νῶν ζώσαιν τελεῖ;

4 οὔτ' ἄτης ἄτερ. It is difficult to avoid the conclusion that we have
to choose between two views. One is that the words ἄτης ἄτερ are
sound, but that there has been some confusion of negatives. I shall
return presently to this theory, which has lately been gaining ground in
Germany. The other view is that the words ἄτης ἄτερ conceal a corruption, but that the process which led to it can no longer be traced.

It must never be forgotten—it is indeed the capital condition of
sound criticism here—that οὔτ' ἄτης ἄτερ was already the traditional
reading in the time of Didymus, *c.* 30 B.C.[1] The practice of writing
explanations, 'glosses,' in the margin of MSS. was common in the later
age to which our MSS. belong; but we are not entitled to suppose that
it existed in the earlier Alexandrian age, from which the MSS. of 30 B.C.
had come down. Therefore we cannot assume, as Porson did, that ἄτερ
arose from a marginal gloss ἀτηρ`, *i.e.* ἀτηρόν, representing the *sense* of
some other word or phrase which originally stood in the text. Again:
it is possible that ἄτης ἄτερ arose from a dittographia, ἄτης ἄτης, and
that the word which originally followed ἄτης bore no likeness to ἄτερ.
But this also would be a bold assumption. And, apart from such
hypotheses, we can only be guided by the letters of οὔτ' ἄτης ἄτερ. No
reading can claim to be more than a guess, unless it is such that a mis-
writing of it might have generated those words.

This distinction between the clue of sense and the clue of writing
at once sets aside a large number of conjectures. Among the rest,
which suits the letters, not one, I think, suits the context. If, then,
the words οὐκ ἄτης ἄτερ are corrupt, they probably arose by some accident, or series of accidents, of another kind than mere mis-writing. And
if this is so, we may chance, indeed, to hit the truth by a conjecture;
but we can no longer prove it.

The attempts to explain οὔτ' ἄτης ἄτερ *without* supposing a confusion
of negatives have only a historical interest, and can be briefly dismissed.
(1) Triclinius suggested two versions, both of which make ἄτερ an
adverb, = χωρίς. (*a*) 'There is nothing painful, there is no excepted
form of ἄτη (lit., nothing of ἄτη, apart),...that I have not seen'; *i.e.*, ἄτερ
= ἄτερ ὄν. (*b*) 'Nothing painful, no sort of ἄτη, ἄτερ (ἐστί), *is apart*,' *i.e.*

[1] Schol. in L: Δίδυμος φησὶν ὅτι ἐν τούτοις τὸ ἄτης ἄτερ ἐναντίως συντέτακται τοῖς
συμφραζομένοις· λέγει γὰρ οὕτως· οὐδὲν γάρ ἐστιν οὔτε ἀλγεινόν, οὔτε ἀτηρόν, οὔτε
αἰσχρὸν ὃ οὐκ ἔχομεν ἡμεῖς. ἄτης ἄτερ δέ ἐστι τὸ ἀγαθόν.

'is absent.'—(2) Seidler: 'There is nothing painful, there is no shame or dishonour (such as can come) *without guilt*' (ἄτης ἄτερ), *i.e.*, 'no un-merited shame or dishonour.'—(3) Boeckh : 'There is nothing painful, nor—*leaving aside the curse upon our race* (ἄτης ἄτερ)—is there any shame or dishonour that I have not seen.' Thus the parenthesis, ἄτης ἄτερ, refers to the fatal deeds and woes of the Labdacidae, while αἰσχρόν and ἄτιμον refer to the dishonouring of Polyneices by Creon.—(4) A modification of the last view would give the parenthesis a more general sense; 'nor—*leaving aside the ruin of our fortunes*—is there any disgrace or dishonour.'

The theory that the poet himself was betrayed into an error by the accumulation of negatives deserves to be very carefully weighed. As a general rule, mistakes of the kind which people easily make in hurried or involved speaking have a somewhat larger scope in the ancient classical texts than in days when a writer's proof-sheets are revised for press,—with close criticism in prospect. Yet modern literature is by no means free from them ; and, in particular, the multiplication of negatives has always been apt to cause irregularities,—even in short sentences. Abbott (*Shaksp. Grammar* § 405) quotes Ascham's *Schole-master*, 37, 'No sonne, were he never so olde of yeares, might not marry': Shaks. *C. of E.* 4. 2. 7, 'First he denied you had in him no right'; etc. Bellermann brings two German instances (both from good writers, and in short sentences): Lessing's *Emilia Galotti* 11. 6 : 'Wie wild er schon war, als er nur hörte, dass der Prinz dich *nicht ohne Missfallen* gesehen!' And in a letter from Schiller to Goethe (Nov. 23, 1795): 'Da man sich *nie bedacht* hat, die Meinung über meine Fehler zu *unterdrücken.*' It is true that, in these examples, the irregularity consists in having a negative too much, while in Sophocles we should have to suppose a negative too little. Still, since two negatives precede the first οὔτ', the origin of the error would be similar[1].

The simplest form of the confusion-theory is to suppose that Sophocles wrote οὐδὲν γὰρ οὔτ' ἀλγεινὸν οὔτ' ἄτης ἄτερ | οὔτ' αἰσχρὸν οὔτ' ἄτιμόν ἐσθ', κ.τ.λ., meaning, 'there is nothing either painful or *not* without ἄτη,—instead of οὔτ' οὐκ ἄτης ἄτερ. Another form of it is that advocated by Hermann Schütz (*Sophokleische Studien*, 1886), pp. 6 ff., who would point thus: οὐδὲν γὰρ οὔτ' ἀλγεινὸν οὔτ' ἄτης ἄτερ· | οὔτ' αἰσχρὸν οὔτ' ἄτιμόν ἐσθ', etc. He understands : 'Nothing is not-painful or free from ἄτη.' Setting out, like Hermann, from the fact that οὐδὲν οὐκ ἀλγεινόν ἐστι means πάντα ἀλγεινά ἐστι, he supposes that the poet meant to say, οὐδὲν γὰρ οὐκ ἀλγεινὸν οὐδ' ἄτης ἄτερ ἐστί, but, wishing to co-ordinate the clauses, slid into the incorrect οὔτ' ...οὔτ'. That is, we have to suppose that οὔτ' ἀλγεινόν = οὔτ' οὐκ ἀλγεινόν. But I much prefer the simpler view first stated, for these reasons. (*a*) It is much easier to suppose that the influence of a *preceding* οὔτε should

---

[1] In Thuc. 7. 75 § 4 οὐκ ἄνευ ὀλίγων (ἐπιθειασμῶν) used to be explained as a like error, for οὐκ ἄνευ οὐκ ὀλίγων. But this seems impossible. Nor can ὀλίγων be explained (with Classen) as ='in a faint voice.' Either ἄνευ or ὀλίγων (probably the latter) is corrupt.

have caused a *second* οὔτε to be used instead of οὔτ᾽ οὐκ, than it is to suppose that the first οὔτε should have been so used. (*b*) It seems clear that the words from οὐδὲν to ἄτιμόν ἐσθ᾽ formed a single sentence. The sense is greatly weakened by having a point after ἄτερ. (*c*) In v. 5 we should then require οὐδ᾽...οὐδ᾽, unless we assumed a further inaccuracy in the use of οὔτ᾽...οὔτ᾽.

The negatives will supply a solution of a different kind if, instead of supposing they were originally confused, we suppose that the *second* οὔτε has been corrupted, from οὐκ or from οὐδ᾽. With οὐκ ἄτης ἄτερ the sense would be, 'Nothing either painful—not without ἄτη—or shameful,' etc. The ἄλγος, or mental anguish, was not unattended by ἄτη, external calamity. With οὐδ᾽ ἄτης, the only difference would be that the clause would then be linked to ἀλγεινόν : 'Nothing either painful (and not harmless), or shameful,' etc. Cp. *O. T.* 1282 στεναγμός, ἄτη, θάνατος, αἰσχύνη, κακῶν | ὅσ᾽ ἐστὶ πάντων ὀνόματ᾽, οὐδέν ἐστ᾽ ἀπόν. The great attraction of this remedy is that it changes only one letter ; the drawback is the somewhat forced sense.

We may now consider the conjectural emendations of ἄτης ἄτερ. Apart from the hypothesis of a marginal gloss or of a dittographia, the letters of ἄτης ἄτερ are our only safe guides. Mr E. Maunde Thompson has kindly given me the aid of his palaeographical learning and skill in an attempt to find some approximate limits for the corruption. We have to start from the fact that no variant seems to have been known in 30 B.C. About 230 B.C. Ptolemy Euergetes had acquired for Alexandria a standard text of the dramatists which had been written at Athens about 330 B.C.[1] If the words οὐκ ἄτης ἄτερ stood in the text of 330 B.C., inscriptions supply the only form of writing by which the possibilities of change can certainly be measured. But it is otherwise if the text of 330 B.C. had a different reading, and if οὐκ ἄτης ἄτερ arose after that text had been brought to Alexandria. The papyri of the Ptolemaic age give Greek writing of the 2nd century B.C. It is a beautiful linked handwriting, firm and yet easy,—quite unlike the formally carved letters on contemporary stone. Such a handwriting presupposes at least a century of development. We may therefore believe that the forms of letters in the papyri of 250 B.C. were essentially the same as in those of 150 B.C. Now, one trait of the Ptolemaic writing is the well-marked distinction between letters which rest on the line, and letters which go below it. Thus the tails of φ and ρ are long, so that there was small chance of any confusion between such letters and, for instance, θ and ο. Hence, if we suppose ἄτης ἄτερ to have been a Ptolemaic corruption from a Ptolemaic archetype, we must, at any rate, be reluctant to part with ρ : while, on the other, we must hesitate to introduce φ. The letter τ could have come from λ (written somewhat awry), or, more easily, from γ, or π. The form of the Ptolemaic ς was such that, if ἄτη had been written with a mere linking-stroke (–) after it, a careless scribe might have evolved ἄτης.

---

[1] See the Introduction to the Laurentian MS. of Sophocles, part II., pp. 13 f., where I have collected and examined the authorities.

A final -ον might have been represented by a contraction, or else lost by accident. Hence Ptolemaic writing would explain how ἄτης ἄτερ might have arisen (*e.g.*) from ἄτης πέρ(α), or ἄτην περῶν, or ἀλάστορον: but not from ἄτην φέρον, or ἄτην ἄγον, or ἀτηφόρον. It may be added that ε was usually large in proportion to ο, and that a confusion between them, though quite possible, is so far less probable. The subjoined transcript (made by Mr Thompson) shows how οὔτ᾽ ἄτης ἄτερ would have appeared in a Ptolemaic MS. of *c.* 250 B.C.:

It must always be remembered that these data are relevant only if we suppose the corruption to have taken place at Alexandria later than about 250 B.C. They cannot be safely used if the Ptolemaic copies were merely repeating an older Attic blunder; for we do not know how far the Attic handwriting of the 4th cent. B.C. resembled the Ptolemaic.

I subjoin a classified list of the conjectures known to me.

1. Conjectures which retain οὔτ᾽ ἄτης, but change ἄτερ.—Robinson Ellis (*Journ. Philol.* vol. XXI. p. 37): ἀτάρ, = *sed vero*, 'nay,' with cumulative force.—Wecklein (*Ars Soph. em.* p. 70): πέρα.—London ed. of 1722: μέτα.—Porson: ἔχον.—Hermann: γέμον.—Sallier and Bothe: ἄπερ.—Bergk: ὅπερ (omitting verse 5).—In the *Journal of Education* (May 1, 1888) Prof. L. Campbell remarked that I have made 'no reference to one [view], which, but for the abrupt transitions which it involves, would be at least plausible,—supposing vv. 4—6 to be an apostrophe to the shade of Œdipus, and reading οὔτ᾽ ἄτης, πάτερ.' It had escaped the memory of my friendly critic that it was I myself who suggested this emendation, in a letter written to him in the spring (I think) of 1886. I mentioned it also to Mr E. M. Thompson; but I did not care to print it in my first edition: and I record it now, only to show that it was not overlooked.—The conjecture of Buchholz, given below (under '5.'), was not then known to me.

2. Conjectures which keep ἄτερ, but change ἄτης.—Koraes: ἄγης [what is ἄγης ἄτερ is ἄζηλον].—Ast: ἄκους.

3. Changes of ἄτης ἄτερ into two other words.—Brunck: ἄτην φέρον or ἀτηρὸν αὖ.—Donaldson: ἄτην ἄγον.—Musgrave: ἄτῃ σαγέν ('loaded with calamity').—Semitelos: ἀτήρ᾽ ἄπερ.—Blaydes: ἀτηρὸν οὔτ᾽.—Pallis: ἄγαν βαρύ.—Hartung: ἀτηρὸν ὧδ᾽.

4. Changes of ἄτης ἄτερ into one word.—Johnson: ἀάατον ('noxium'). —Brunck: ἀτήριον [implying ἀτήρ, from ἄω, contracted for ἀάω, as λυτήριος implies λυτήρ].—Dindorf: ἀτήσιμος [as if formed, through ἄτησις, from ἀτάομαι].—Pallis: ὑπερβαρές.—Blaydes:—ἀτηφόρον, ὀλέθριον, or δύσφορον, or δυσχερές.—ἀλάστορον had occurred to me, but it seems impossible that it should have been used as = ἄλαστον. Cp. on. v. 974.

5. Conjectures which change both οὔτ᾽ and ἄτης ἄτερ.—Buchholz: οἷδ᾽ ἄτλης, πάτερ.—Moriz Schmidt: ἔσθ᾽ ὁποιονοῦν.

23 ff. 23 Ἐτεοκλέα μέν, ὡς λέγουσι, σὺν δίκῃ
24 χρησθεὶς δικαίᾳ καὶ νόμῳ κατὰ χθονὸς
25 ἔκρυψε τοῖς ἔνερθεν ἔντιμον νεκροῖς.

The attempts to correct this passage have been of two classes: I. those which disturb the present number of verses: II. those which are confined to verbal emendation.

I. 1. Wunder, whom several editors have followed, rejected verse 24. Such a theory fails to explain the origin of that verse. And the result is intrinsically bad. The honours paid to Eteocles are then dismissed too curtly. It is indispensable to the coming contrast that they should be described with some emphasis.

2. The latter objection applies equally to compressions of vv. 23, 24 into a single verse. This verse has been variously shaped. A. Jacob proposed Ἐτεοκλέα μὲν σὺν δίκῃ κατὰ χθονός. Instead of σὺν δίκῃ, Kayser suggests ὡς νόμος, Dindorf ὡς λόγος, Schneidewin ᾗ (or ἢ) δίκῃ, and Kolster (*Philol.* v. 223) ὡς νόμῳ. Pallis gives Ἐτεοκλέα μὲν σὺν δίκῃ τε καὶ νόμῳ.

3. F. Kern supposes the loss of one or more verses after v. 23. This, of course, opens indefinite possibilities as to the origin of χρησθεὶς δικαίᾳ in 24.

II. 1. Among the merely verbal emendations, the simplest are those which change only χρησθείς.—For this word, Moriz Seyffert proposed χρηστός.—F. W. Schmidt, χρηστοῖς [adopted by Bellermann, as meaning, 'just, *in the sight of the good*'; and by Wecklein, as 'meet *for patriots*'].—Nauck, κρίσει.

2. Changes of χρησθεὶς δικαίᾳ.—Wiesler proposed χρηστὸς δίκαια, with a comma after δίκῃ, so that δίκαια should be in appos. with the sentence.—Hermann Schütz (*Jahr. f. kl. Philol.*, 1876, p. 176) proposed χρῆσθαι δικαιῶν. In the note on 23 f. I suggest that this emendation would be improved by the further change of καὶ νόμῳ into τῷ νόμῳ. In his *Sophokleische Studien* (Gotha, 1886), p. 11, I find that Schütz himself now proposes this improvement. [Engelmann would read νῦν (for σὺν) δίκῃ | χρῆσθαι δικαιῶν καὶ νόμῳ.]—John W. Donaldson, in his ed. (1848), first conjectured προσθεὶς δίκαια, which he placed in the text. The same emendation was afterwards made by Jul. Held (*Observv.* p. 3, Schweidnitz, 1854).—Wecklein (*Ars Soph. em.* p. 107) proposes μνησθεὶς δίκης δὴ (or δικαίων).

3. A few emendations are of larger scope.—Moriz Schmidt:—Ἐτεοκλέα μέν,—πιστός, ὡς λέγει, δίκης | κρίσει δικαίᾳ κἀννόμῳ,—κατὰ χθονὸς | ἔκρυψε etc.—Semitelos: Ἐτεοκλέα μέν, ὡς λέγουσιν, ἔνδικον | κρίνας, δικαίῳ καὶ νόμῳ κατὰ χθονὸς | ἔκρυψε.

After my commentary on vv. 23 f. had been printed, I discovered that the conjecture σὺν δίκης | χρήσει had been made before,—viz., by Gerh. Heinrich Müller, in his *Emendationes et interpretationes Sophocleae* (Berlin, 1878), p. 51; and that Madvig had thought of σὺν τύχης (for δίκης) χρήσει. In one respect, however, I have not been anticipated,—viz., in the statement of the considerations by which the emendation was suggested to me, and by which it may be defended. Even if it should find little acceptance, still many students will probably feel that this is a case where we have to choose between gentle remedies,—among which σὺν δίκης χρήσει may ask a hearing,—and violent remedies which part company with the tradition. It may well be, of course, that the fault really lies deeper—and beyond discovery now.

110 ff. Some edd. change γᾷ (110), γᾶν, ὑπερέπτα (113) to the forms in η, because no other Doric forms occur in these anapaests. Anapaests held an intermediate place between dialogue and lyrics proper. According to the context in which they occur, they are sometimes more nearly akin to the former, and sometimes to the latter. Now, in the lyrics of Attic Tragedy the Doric α was a conventional mark of lyric style. The question of retaining it in any given set of anapaests must therefore be governed by the consideration just stated, and cannot be settled by an inflexible rule. In this passage the anapaests are essentially part of the choral song; and the Doric forms γᾷ, γᾶν, ὑπερέπτα, are therefore appropriate. They serve to maintain the continuity of lyric character. It is otherwise with the anapaests spoken by the Chorus just after the third stasimon (801—805), and in the following kommos (815—822). There, it is evident that the anapaests have the tone of dialogue rather than of lyrics; they are intended to afford a relief, or a contrast, to the lyrics before and after them. (Cp. n. on 804 f.) In them, accordingly, it seems clearly best to write παγκοίτην (804), and θνητῶν ᾿Αΐδην (822). Some cases occur elsewhere which are on the border-line; but, as a general rule, it is not difficult to decide. The MSS. almost invariably give the Doric forms in anapaests, which the transcribers regarded as following ordinary lyric usage.

138 ff.   εἶχε δ᾿ ἄλλᾳ τὰ μέν, |
                  ἄλλα δ᾿ ἐπ᾿ ἄλλοις, κ.τ.λ.

This, Erfurdt's reading, is a very gentle correction of L's εἶχε δ᾿ ἄλλᾳ τὰ μὲν ἄλλα τὰ δ᾿ ἐπ᾿ ἄλλοις, and has the peculiar merit of suggesting how the vulgate arose,—viz., by a confusion between ἄλλᾳ, ἄλλα on the one hand, and between τὰ μέν, τὰ δέ on the other. Dindorf's objection to the short μέν at the end of the verse is obviated by the pause (cp. on 1276). And, since the immediately preceding words, βακχεύων κ.τ.λ., have indicated the threats of Capaneus, the reference in τὰ μέν is perfectly clear. The irony of εἶχε δ᾿ ἄλλᾳ is also tragic. It is surprising, then, that Erfurdt's correction has not found more general acceptance.

The other emendations fall under three heads. (1) Those which keep at least one ἄλλᾳ.—Hermann: εἶχε δ᾿ ἄλλᾳ μὲν ἄλλᾳ· τὰ δ᾿ ἐπ᾿ ἄλλοις.—Emperius: εἶχε δ᾿ ἄλλᾳ μὲν ἄλλ᾿, | ἄλλα δ᾿ ἐπ᾿ ἄλλοις.—

Wecklein : εἶχε δ' ἄλλᾳ τὰ τοῦδ', | ἄλλα δ' ἐκ' ἄλλοις. [So in ed. 1874 : formerly εἶχε δ' ἄλλᾳ τάδ' ἄρ', *Ars Soph. em.* p. 12.]—Hense : εἶχε δ' ἄλλᾳ τάλαντ'· | ἄλλα δ' ἐπ' ἄλλοις.—Musgrave : εἶχε δ' ἄλλᾳ τὰ δεῖν'· | ἆθλα δ' ἐπ' ἄθλοις.—G. Wolff : εἶχε δ' ἄλλα τὰ Διός· | ἄλλα δ' ἐπ' ἄλλοις. (2) Those which change ἄλλᾳ into another part of ἄλλος.— Seyffert : εἶχε δ' ἄλλος τὰ μέν· | ἄλλα δ' etc.—Semitelos : εἶχε δ' ἄλλους δέος· | ἄλλα δ' ἐπ' ἄλλοις. (3) Those which change ἄλλᾳ into some other word or words.—Blaydes : εἶχε ταύτᾳ τὰ μέν, | ἄλλα δ' ἐπ' ἄλλοις.— Gleditsch : εἶλε τόνδ' ἄδε μοῖρ'· | ἄλλα δ' etc.—Kayser : ἔσχε δ' Ἄιδα λαχάν· | ἄλλα δ' etc. [Nearer to the letters than either of these would be εἶχε δ' ἄδ' αἶσά νιν,—the pause excusing the short νιν, as it excuses μέν.]

155 ff. The traditional text has :

155 ἀλλ' ὅδε γὰρ δὴ βασιλεὺς χώρας
156 Κρέων ὁ Μενοικέως νεοχμὸς
157 νεαραῖσι θεῶν ἐπὶ συντυχίαις
158 χωρεῖ· τίνα δὴ μῆτιν ἐρέσσων
159 ὅτι σύγκλητον τήνδε γερόντων
160 προὔθετο λέσχην
161 κοινῷ κηρύγματι πέμψας;

Verse 156, now a tripody, must be either shortened to a monometer, or lengthened to a dimeter. Taking the first alternative, Dindorf omits νεοχμός, while Hartung omits Μενοικέως, reading Κρέων ὁ νεοχμὸς νεαραῖσι θεῶν|. Bergk would omit Κρέων ὁ Μενοικέως and also θεῶν, reading (with νεοχμοῖς for νεαραῖσι) νεοχμὸς νεοχμοῖς ἐπὶ συντυχίαις. But it seems far more probable that the verse should be lengthened to a dimeter, by supplying one anapaest or its equivalent (see comment. on 155 ff.).

When this has been done, one difference still remains between this system of anapaests and that in vv. 141—147 ; viz., that the monometer, v. 160, answers to a dimeter, v. 146. Such a discrepancy seems to have been permissible. There is no ground for thinking that the correspondence between anapaestic systems was necessarily of the same precision as that between lyric strophes, while there is some evidence the other way. Thus the anapaestic system in 110—116 is, according to the most probable text, shorter by a monometer than that in 127— 133. This small difference of detail was quite compatible with a general regularity of effect in such systems (cp. note on vv. 100—161, p. 27).

Many critics, however, have required a rigidly complete correspondence with 141—147. They have therefore supplied the metrical equivalent of three anapaests. The supplements are shown by brackets. (1) Erfurdt : [τῆσδ' ἄρτι] Κρέων ὁ Μενοικέως [παῖς | φανθεὶς] νεοχμὸς νεαραῖσι θεῶν.—(2) Hermann : [ὃς τῆσδε] Κρέων [παῖς] ὁ Μενοικέως| [νεοχμῶς] νεοχμὸς νεαραῖσι θεῶν.—(3) Boeckh : Κρέων ὁ Μενοικέως, [νέον εἰληχὼς | ἀρχήν,] νεοχμὸς νεαραῖσι θεῶν.—(4) Wolff : Κρέων ὁ Μενοικέως, νεοχμὸς [νεοχμοῖς | ταγὸς ταχθείς,] νεαραῖσι θεῶν.—(5) Wecklein : Κρέων ὁ Μενοικέως [οἴκων ἔξω | ταγὸς] νεοχμὸς νεαραῖσι θεῶν.—Moriz Schmidt and Herm. Schütz take a like view, but leave a lacuna.

292 λόφον δικαίως εἶχον, ὡς στέργειν ἐμέ. The following are the passages in which Eustathius refers to this verse. On *Il.* 10. 573: παρὰ Σοφοκλεῖ τὸ ὑπὸ ζυγῷ νῶτον εὐλόφως φέρειν. On *Od.* 5. 285: τῷ Σοφοκλεῖ ἐν τῷ κάρα σείοντες οὐδ᾽ ὑπὸ ζυγῷ νῶτον εὐλόφως εἶχον. Cp. also on *Od.* 10. 169 ὁ τραγικὸς Οἰδίπους (an oversight for Κρέων) φησὶ τῶν τινας πολιτῶν μὴ ἐθέλειν ὑπὸ ζυγῷ νῶτον εὐλόφως φέρειν. On *Il.* 23. 508 νῶτος εὔλοφος παρὰ Σοφοκλεῖ. The very way in which these references are made suffices to show how preposterous it is to re-write the verse in accordance with them. G. Wolff has brought together a number of instances in which Eustathius has made similar slips. For example:—(1) *El.* 66 δεδορκότ᾽ ἐχθροῖς ἄστρον ὡς λάμψειν ἔτι, cited on *Il.* 2. 135 δεδορκὼς ἄστρον ὡς λάμψειν: (2) *O. T.* 161 κυκλόεντ᾽ ἀγορᾶς θρόνον εὐκλέα, cited on *Il.* 24. 1 Σοφοκλῆς που κυκλόεντα θῶκον ἀγορᾶς εὐκλεῆ: (3) *ib.* 1035 δεινόν γ᾽ ὄνειδος, cited on *Il.* 17. 105 καλόν γ᾽ ὄνειδος: (4) *Ai.* 445 φωτί, cited on *Il.* 6. 367 ἀνδρί: (5) *ib.* 1219 ἄκραν, cited on *Il.* 6. 397 ἱερήν. Such instances, which could easily be multiplied, detract nothing from the merit of Eustathius in his proper field; they merely show that his incidental literary references were usually made from memory, and that his memory was not infallible. We cannot treat his quotations as if they possessed a critical value for the texts of authors to whom he casually alludes. So much is equally true of Aristotle.

318 L here has τί δαὶ ῥυθμίζεις. δαί, a colloquial form of δή, is not read in any other passage of Soph., but is supported by L in Aesch. *P. V.* 933 (where τί δ᾽ ἄν should be read), and *Cho.* 900 (where Porson rightly gave ποῦ δή). As Ar. and Plato show, δαί was commonly used in short phrases expressing surprise, like τί δαί; πῶς δαί; τί δαὶ λέγεις; etc. In this verse δαί is clearly unsuitable, while on the other hand δέ constantly follows τί in such questions. The Triclinian gloss, διὰ τὸ μέτρον, suggests that δέ was changed to δαί by a corrector who did not know that δέ could be long before ῥ. In Plat. *Gorg.* 474 c where τί δὲ δὴ αἴσχιον is right, some MSS. have τί δαὶ δή: and in many other places δαί seems to have supplanted δέ or δή. (In Ar. *Ach.* 912, however, the metre permits δαί, which some edd. have changed to δέ.) Porson on Eur. *Med.* 1008 says, 'assentior Brunckio δαί e tragicis eximenti'; but the case of Eur. is different from that of Aesch. or of Soph. Thus in *Ion* 275 (τί δαὶ τόδ᾽;) it is quite possible that the colloquial style of the passage should have led Euripides to prefer δαί. Each passage in which the MSS. ascribe δαί to him should be tested by our sense of the degree in which, there, he meant to reproduce the language of every-day life.

340 Here, as in 509, I have preferred the spelling ἴλλω to εἴλλω, though without regarding it as certain. Cobet (*Var. Lect.* 361) pronounces confidently for ἴλλω, though without convincing reasons. The fact is that the MS. evidence is small in amount and doubtful in quality; and there is no epigraphic evidence. In Eur. fr. 544, οὐρὰν δ᾽ ὑπίλασ᾽, the MSS. of Athen. 701 B give ὑπήλασ᾽ or ὑπήκας: those of Aelian *De Nat. An.* 12. 7 give ὑπήλλασ᾽ or ὑπίλλασ᾽. Erotianus (gloss. Hippocr.

001

p. 378) gives ὑπείλλει. See Nauck, *Fragm. Trag.* p. 420; and cp.
Schweighäuser on Athen. *l. c.* (vol. 8, p. 366). In Plat. *Tim.* 40 B
εἰλλομένην and ἰλλομένην are among the various readings of the MSS.
(others being these same forms aspirated, and εἱλομένην, εἱλουμένην,
εἱλουμένην): so, again, *ib.* 76 B, 86 E. In Arist. *De Cael.* 2. 13 the
Berlin editors (p. 293 *b* 31) give ἴλλεσθαι, as also *ib.* 14 (p. 296 *b* 26),
noting εἰλεῖσθαι as a *v. l.* in the first passage, and εἰλεῖσθαι in the
second. Here, the corruption in L, ἀποτρύετ᾽ ἀπλομένων, arose from
ΑΠΟΤΡΥΕΤΑΙΙΛΟΜΕΝΟΝ (ἀποτρύεται ἰλομένων), ΙΙ having been substituted for the doubled iota, ΙΙ. This passage, then, must be added
to the testimony for ἴλλω *versus* εἴλλω. So, too, must ἰπίλλουσιν
(L) and ὑπίλλουσι (A, with other MSS.), in 509. In Ar. *Nub.* 762,
where most MSS. have εἴλλε, the Ravenna has ἴλλε. This last seems
the most significant of all the facts which can be gathered from
the MSS. That is, there is no testimony for εἴλλε which can fairly
be set against this. There is no instance in which εἴλλε is supported by a manuscript excelling the other MSS. of the same author as
much as the Ravenna excels the other MSS. of Aristophanes. I cannot,
therefore, concur with Dr Rutherford (who does not notice *Ant.* 340
and 509, or Arist. *De Caelo* 2. 13) in thinking that 'the evidence for the
spelling εἴλλω is...much greater than that for ἴλλω' (*New Phryn.*, p. 90).
I should rather have thought that the MS. evidence, so far as it goes, is
slightly in favour of ἴλλω. It is true that our MSS. sometimes wrongly
changed ει to ι, as in ἔτισα for ἔτεισα: but, in regard to ἴλλω, we have
to consider whether the doubling of λ might not have induced a
weakening of the initial diphthong into ι.

350 f. λασιαύχενά θ᾽ ἵππον ἔξεται ἀμ|φίλοφον ζυγόν L.—The emen-
dations may be divided into two classes.

I. The following retain ἀμφίλοφον ζυγόν, either as acc. or nom.

(i) Brunck: ὑπάξεται for ἔξεται. This would be the simplest
remedy. But the future tense is impossible. In this context, nothing
but a present tense would be endurable. The gnomic aor. ὑπήγαγεν
(Blaydes) must also, therefore, be rejected. It is, indeed, too far from
the letters to be probable. (ii) Gustav Jacob: ὁπλίζεται ('Man fits the
horse with a yoke'). This is now received by Bellermann, who formerly
proposed ἐθίζεται (also with double acc.). He compares ἀμφιέννυμί
τινά τι, etc. (iii) Dindorf: ἀέξεται, 'ut iugum equos ἀέξεσθαι dicatur,
qui iugo adhibito dociliores et sollertiores redduntur' (*i.e.*, the yoke
'improves' the horse!)—(iv) G. Wolff: ἔσας ἄγει ('having put the yoke
on the horse, he leads him').—(v) Campbell: ὑφέλκεται.—(vi) Blaydes,
in his text, ὀχμάζει ὑπ᾽.

II. In the following, ἀμφίλοφον ζυγόν is modified.—(i) Schöne and
Franz, ὀχμάζεται ἀμφὶ λόφον ζυγῷ (so Wecklein), or ζυγῶν (so Donald-
son). Receiving ὀχμάζεται, (ii) Schneidewin, ἀμφιλοφῶν ζυγόν, (iii)
Kayser, ἀμφιλόφῳ ζυγῷ, (iv) Blaydes, *inter alia*, ἀμφιβαλών ζυγόν.—(v)
Schütz, ἐφέξεται ἀμφὶ λόφον ζυγῶν.—(vi) Seyffert, ἀνάσσεται ἀμφιλόφῳ

ζυγῷ.—(vii) Semitelos, κρατεῖ δὲ μηχαναῖς ἀγραύλους | θῆρας ὀρεσσιβάτας, λασιαύχενά θ᾽ | ἵππον, ὃν ἐξετέ᾽ ἀμφὶ λόφον ζυγοῖ.—(viii) Pallis, λασιαύχενόν θ᾽ | ἵππον ζεύξατ᾽ ἐν ἀμφιλόφῳ ζυγῷ.

466 f. L gives εἰ τὸν ἐξ ἐμῆς | μητρὸς θανόντ᾽ ἄθαπτον ἠισχόμην νέκυν. The later MSS. have ἠισχόμην (ἠσχόμην), ἠνσχόμην, ἠσχόμην, ἰσχόμην, ἠνεσχόμην, or ἠνειχόμην. Leaving aside the mere corruptions, ἠισχόμην and ἠσχόμην, we see that the other MS. readings represent two different kinds of endeavour to amend the passage. One was ἰσχόμην: along with which we might have expected to find ἐσχόμην: and, in fact, ἐσχόμην and ἠσχόμην were the readings known to Eustathius (p. 529. 20, on *Il.* 5. 120). The other assumed the aor. or imperf., of ἀνέχομαι, contracted or uncontracted.

Hermann, who thought ἰσχόμην defensible ('non spernendum'), adopted ἐσχόμην. He took it, seemingly, in the sense of ἠνεσχόμην. This, as all would now admit, is impossible. Brunck adopted the portentous ἠνεχόμην from Pierson. Dindorf defends ἠνσχόμην as = ἠνεσχόμην: but see comment. Most of the other emendations assume either (1) ἠνεσχόμην, or (2) ἀνεσχόμην.

(1) Blaydes: μητρὸς θανόντ᾽ ἄθαπτον ὄντ᾽ ἠνεσχόμην.—Nauck: παρ᾽ οὐδέν᾽ ἀλλ᾽ ἄθαπτον εἰ τὸν ἐξ ἐμῆς | μητρὸς πατρός τε τὸν θανόντ᾽ ἠνεσχόμην.—Tournier: παρ᾽ οὐδέν᾽ ἄλγος δ᾽ ἦν ἄν, εἰ τὸν ἐξ ἐμῆς | μητρὸς πατρός τε μὴ ταφέντ᾽ ἠνεσχόμην.—Pallis, more boldly still, assumes the double compound: εἰ τὸν ἐξ ἐμῆς | μητρὸς φανέντ᾽ (or τραφέντ᾽) ἄθαπτον ἐξηνεσχόμην.

(2) G. Wolff: εἰ τὸν ἐξ ἐμῆς | μητρός θ᾽ ἑνός τ᾽ ἄταφον ἀνεσχόμην νέκυν.—Seyffert: εἰ τὸν ἐξ ὁμῆς | μητρὸς θανόντ᾽ ἄταφον ἀνεσχόμην νέκυν. —Moriz Schmidt: παρ᾽ οὐδέν᾽ ἀλλ᾽ ἄλγιστ᾽ ἄν, εἰ τὸν ἐξ ἐμῆς | ταφέντ᾽ ἄθαπτον ὧδ᾽ ἀνεσχόμην νέκυν (understanding χειρός with ἐμῆς).

Any reader who will consider these conjectures will find, I think, that they justify the remarks made in my note on this passage.

578 f. ἐκ δὲ τοῦδε χρὴ | γυναῖκας εἶναι τάσδε.—The following emendations have been proposed. (1) Dindorf: εὖ δὲ τάσδε χρὴ | γυναῖκας ἵλαι μηδ᾽ ἀνειμένας ἐᾶν. So Meineke, but with εἴρξαι instead of ἵλαι. Herwerden (*Obs. cr. in fragm. Com.* p. 134) improves this to εἴρξαι. And Nauck accordingly gives εὖ δὲ τάσδε χρὴ | γυναῖκας εἴρξαι μηδ᾽ ἀνειμένας ἐᾶν. He would prefer, however, to place ἐᾶν *before* ἀνειμ., with Madvig (*Adv.* 1. 216). (2) Bergk adopts the insertion of ἐᾶν and the omission of τάσδε in 579, but would refrain from further change: ἐκ δὲ τοῦδε χρὴ | γυναῖκας εἶναι μηδ᾽ ἐᾶν ἀνειμένας. The change of subject for the infinitives would, however, be very harsh. (3) Seyffert: εὖ δετὰς δὲ χρὴ | γυναῖκας εἶναι τάσδε μηδ᾽ ἀνειμένας. Engelmann substituted ἐκδετὰς for εὖ δετάς. This is one of those conjectures which are taking at first sight, but which reflection condemns. δετός occurs only in the subst. δετή, a faggot. Nor were the royal maidens to be put in bonds; they were merely to be detained in the house.

601 f. κατ' αὖ νιν...ἀμᾷ κόνις. The primary sense of ἀμᾶν was probably 'gather': the special sense 'cut,' 'mow,' was derived from the gathering of crops. The passages in which the verb occurs are of three classes. (1) Those which refer to reaping or mowing, and which therefore throw no light on the question whether 'gather' or 'cut' was the original notion. (2) Those which require the sense 'gather': as *Il.* 24. 165 (κόπρον) καταμήσατο χερσὶν ἑῆσιν, 'heaped it up' on himself: imitated by Josephus, *Bell. Iud.* 2. 21. 3 καταμώμενοι τῆς κεφαλῆς κόνιν. *Od.* 5. 482 εὐνὴν ἐπαμήσατο, 'heaped up a couch': *ib.* 9. 247 (γάλα) ἐν ταλάροι-σιν ἀμησάμενος, 'having collected.' (3) Those which require the sense, 'cut': as *Il.* 3. 359 (and 7. 253) διάμησε χιτῶνα. *Od.* 21. 300 ἀπ' οὔατα... | ῥῖνάς τ' ἀμήσαντες.

If, however, the MS. κόνις is retained in v. 602, the fact that καταμᾷ originally meant 'gathers in,' and only secondarily 'cuts down,' will not help to obviate the confusion of metaphor; for the metaphor is still borrowed from the gathering of the harvest.

Some critics have proposed to translate καταμᾷ 'covers.' Now, the version 'covers' would be suitable only if the φοινία θεῶν τῶν νερτέρων κόνις were the dust of the grave which is to hide Antigone: whereas it surely means the dust, due to the νέρτεροι, which she sprinkled on her brother's gory corpse. But how could καταμᾷ mean 'covers'? Prof. Lewis Campbell says:—'As καταμᾶσθαι κόνιν is 'To cover oneself with dust,' so, by a poetical inversion, the dust may be said καταμᾶν, 'To cover,' or 'Sweep out of sight.'' But καταμᾶσθαι κόνιν derives the sense, 'to cover oneself with dust,' only through its literal sense of 'heaping up dust for (or on) oneself.' Does, then, 'poetical inversion' allow us to say, κόνις καταμᾷ με, when we mean, καταμῶμαι κόνιν? On this point I can only repeat what I said in my first edition (commentary on vv. 601 f.);—''Poetical inversion' has its limits. 'He pulls down a pail of water upon himself.' This operation would not be correctly described by saying, 'the pail of water pulls him down.''

In the *Journal of Education* (May 1, 1888) Prof. Campbell suggests, however, another explanation, different from the 'poetical inversion'; viz., that ἀμάω may be 'a homonym with more than one meaning.' That is, besides the rt. ἀμα, 'gather,' there may have been another ἀμα, meaning 'cover.' To this we can only reply that the sense 'gather' (with its derivative 'cut,' 'mow') suffices everywhere else, and that this one passage seems inadequate ground for assuming another root with a different sense. As to the Homeric ᾱ in the act. ἀμάω, Dr Leaf (on *Il.* 18. 34) has pointed out that it occurs only under ictus, and therefore lends no support to the hypothesis of two distinct verbs.

With regard to the usage of the word κοπίς, a few words may be added in supplement to the commentary. (1) Ar. fr. 184, κοπίδι τῶν μαγειρικῶν, is enough to indicate that, if the kitchen use of the implement was the most familiar to Athenians, other kinds of κοπίς were also known to them. (2) The military κοπίς, as used by some orientals, occurs in Xen. *Cyr.* 2. 1. 9, where Cyrus describes the ordinary equipment of the Persian nobles called ὁμότιμοι as θώραξ,...γέρρον...

κοπὶς δὲ ἢ σάγαρις εἰς τὴν δεξιάν. Again, in *Cyr.* 6. 2. 10, the Asiatic troops of Cyrus are armed with ἀσπίς, δόρυ, and κοπίς. That the blade of the κοπίς was of a curved form is shown by its being distinguished from the Dorian σφαγίς, of which the blade was straight : cp. Eur. *El.* 811, 837. It is unknown whether the military κοπίς was a small curved sword, like a scimitar, or a curved blade on a long handle, like a 'bill.' At any rate the fact that it was current in Attic prose as the name of a warlike weapon tends to show that, for Attic ears, it cannot have been a word of such homely sound as 'chopper'; and Euripides, at least, did not think it out of keeping with the tone of a tragic ῥῆσις. (3) The image of Death thus armed might be illustrated by Eur. *Or.* 1398 ὅταν αἷμα χυθῇ κατὰ γᾶν ξίφεσιν | σιδαρέοισιν Ἅιδα. Eur. fr. 757 βίον θερίζειν ὥστε κάρπιμον στάχυν. Apoll. Rh. 3. 1186 Ἄρεος ἀμώοντος. Hor. *Ep.* 2. 2. 178 *metit Orcus | grandia cum parvis.*

606 f. L has ὁ παντογήρως | οὔτ' ἀκάματοι θεῶν. These words answer metrically to 617 f. -νόων ἐρώτων | εἰδότι δ' οὐδὲν ἔρπει. The conjectures have followed one of two courses, according as παντογήρως is (1) retained, or replaced by a metrical equivalent : (2) replaced by – ◡ –, while οὔτ' is brought back from v. 607.

(1) Hermann : ὁ παντογήρως | οὔτε θεῶν ἄκμητοι. [He afterwards preferred, ἀκάματοι θεῶν οὐ.] The Doric ἄκματοι should, however, be written. Schneidewin conjectured οὔτ' ἐτέων ἄκματοι.—Heath and Brunck had proposed a simple transposition (with οὐδέ), οὐδὲ θεῶν ἀκάματοι. But ἄκματοι is metrically better, and would most easily have arisen from ἀκάματοι. For the form, cp. *Hom. hymn. Ap.* 520, ἄκμητοι δὲ λόφον προσέβαν ποσίν. It is unnecessary, then, to write οὔτε θεῶν ἀκμῆτες, with Blaydes.—Dindorf : ὁ παντογήρως | οὔτ' ἄκοποι θεῶν νιν.— Neue, whom Hartung follows : ὁ παντογήρως | ἀκάματοί τε θεῶν οὐ.— Nauck (omitting θεῶν) : ὁ παντογήρως | οὔτ' ἀκάμαντες.

(2) Donaldson : ὁ παγκρατὴς οὔτ' | ἀκάματοι θέοντες. So Wolff, but with ὁ πανταγρεύς.—Wecklein desires a verb in the place of θεῶν : as ὁ πάντ' ἀγρῶν, οὔτ' | ἀκάματοι φθίνουσιν. He also thought of φθεροῦσιν. Mekler prefers σκεδῶσιν.

613 f. The mss. give οὐδὲν ἔρπει | θνατῶν βιότῳ πάμπολις ἐκτὸς ἄτας. On πάμπολις the Schol. has, ὁ κατὰ πᾶσαν πόλιν ἔρπων νόμος, ὅ ἐστι, πάντες ἄνθρωποι. Triclinius took the sense to be : 'the law never (οὐδέν as adv.) comes (= is never applicable to) the life of men, in any of their cities, without ἄτη' : *i.e.*, when any mortal thinks to rival the sovereignty of Zeus, he incurs ἄτη. This interpretation, which tortures the language without fitting the context, requires no refutation. Boeckh reads ἔρπων. Receiving this, Prof. Campbell explains :—' This principle (the sovereignty of Zeus) will last the coming time, and the time to come, as well as the time past, never swerving, as it moves onward, from calamity to the life of mortals in all their cities.' Are we, then, to understand that the attitude of mortals towards the sovereignty of Zeus has been, and

will be, *everywhere and always,* such as to bring down divine wrath? There are other difficulties; but this suffices.

Wecklein, adopting Heath's πάμπολύ γ' in his text, conjectures πλημμελές (*Ars Soph. em.* p. 47), which D'Ooge receives. It means 'nothing wrong,' *i.e.,* nothing out of harmony with the sovereignty of Zeus. But πάμπολύ γ' is far better in this general maxim, and is also far nearer to the letters.—Hartung, admitting Lange's παντελές, reads οὐδέν' ἕρπειν | θνατῶν βίοτον παντελὲς ἐκτὸς ἄτας, 'that no mortal life performs its course to the end (παντελὲς adv.) without ἄτη.'—Schneidewin sought a similar sense by reading οὐδὲν ἕρπει | θνατῶν βίοτον τὸν πολὺν ἐκτὸς ἄτας, *i.e.,* 'no mortal (οὐδὲν = οὐδείς) goes through the greater part of life without ἄτη.' Pallis: οὐδέν' ἕρπειν | θνατῶν βίοτου πρὸς τέλος ἐκτὸς ἄτας.—Bergk invented a form παμπᾶδίς as = παμπήδην ('altogether').

619 προσαύσῃ. The following are the principal pieces of evidence for an αὔω = αἴρω. (1) Alcman fr. 94 τὰν Μῶσαν καταύσεις. Eustathius explains this by ἀφανίσεις: cp. Ar. *Nub.* 972 τὰς Μούσας ἀφανίζων. (2) Hesychius: καταυσαι· καταυλῆσαι [καταντλῆσαι Lobeck], καταδῦσαι. (3) Pollux 6. 88 ἐξαῦσαι τὸ ἐξελεῖν. (4) *Etym. M.* p. 346. 58 gives ἐξαυστήρ as 'a flesh-hook,' for taking meat out of the pot (= κρέαγρα). Lobeck (on *Ai.* 805, p. 296 f., 3rd ed.) would add the *v. l.* προσάρῃ [and προσαίρῃ] here, regarding them as glosses on the true sense of προσαύσῃ. But it is surely far more probable that προσάρῃ and προσαίρῃ were merely conjectures, (generated, probably, by a corruption,) which sought to give a clear and simple word, suited to the context. And, on the other hand, two things are certain,—viz., that προσαύω could mean to 'burn against,' and that such a sense is specially fitting here. It may be granted that there was an αὔω = αἴρω, but there is no proof that an Attic writer would have used αὔω, or any compound of it, in that sense. And there is one piece of evidence the other way. Pollux (see above) quotes ἐξαῦσαι as = 'to take out,' from αὔω = αἴρω: yet it is known that an Attic writer used ἐξαῦσαι as = 'to roast,' from αὔω 'to kindle': Plat. com. Ἑορταί fr. 9 τὸ δὲ ὀπτῆσαι ἐξαῦσαι (*ap.* Eustath. p. 1547. 48, on *Od.* 5. 490, αὔοι).

622 The Greek verses given in the note, ὅταν δ' ὁ δαίμων, κ.τ.λ., were probably the original of 'Quem Iuppiter vult perdere, dementat prius.' They are cited, with this Latin verse added in brackets, by James Duport (Regius Professor of Greek at Cambridge, 1639—1654) in his *Gnomologia Homerica* (Cambridge, 1660), p. 282. He is illustrating *Od.* 23. 11, μάργην σε θεοὶ θέσαν. Joshua Barnes, in the 'Index prior' to his Euripides (Camb., 1694), has, 'Deus quos vult perdere, dementat prius, incerta v. 436.' On that verse itself, p. 515, another version is given, viz., 'At quando numen miserias paret viro, Mens laesa primum.' And in the margin he cites 'Franciados nostrae' v. 3, 'certe ille deorum | Arbiter ultricem cum vult extendere dextram | Dementat prius.' It was suggested to me that the line 'Quem Iuppiter' etc. had first appeared in Canter's Euripides. I have looked through both the editions, but without finding it. His duodecimo ed. (Antwerp, 1571) has an appendix of 16 pages, 'Euripidis sententiae aliquot insigniores breviter collectae et Latinis versibus redditae': but 'Quem Iuppiter' is not among them. His folio ed. (of 1614) does not seem to contain it either. Publilius Syrus 610 has 'stultum facit fortuna quem volt perdere.' This shows that part of the line, at least, was familiar *circ.* 50 B.C. The use of *dementat* as = *dementem facit* proves, of course, a post-classical origin.

648   The older MSS. have τὰς φρένας ὑφ' ἡδονῆς. Triclinius wrote φρένας γ'—rightly, I think (see comment.). Critics have proposed various other remedies, which may be classified thus. (1) Changes confined to ὑφ'. Hermann, πρὸς ἡδονῆς: Blaydes, δι' ἡδονήν: Hertel, σύ γ' ἡδονῆς (Meineke, σύ γ' ἡδονῇ): Seyffert, χύθ' ἡδονῆς (*i.e.* χυτά, adv., as = 'at random,' *temere*). (2) Larger changes.—Kayser, φιληδίᾳ for ὑφ' ἡδονῆς.—Stürenburg, κακόφρονος (do.).—Wecklein, τῶν φρενῶν ὑφ' ἡδονῆς | ...ἐκπέσῃς.—Semitelos, μή νυν ποτῷ [ποτάομαι—'be fluttered'], παῖ, τὰς φρένας, μήθ' [*imo* μηδ'] ἡδονάς, | κ.τ.λ.—Papageorgius, removing the note of interrogation after γέλων in 647, writes γέλων | ὑφ' ἡδονῆς· μή νύν ποτ', ὦ παῖ, τὰς φρένας, against metre.

718   L gives ἀλλ' εἶκε θυμῷι καὶ μετάστασιν δίδου. For θυμῷ, several of the later MSS. have θυμοῦ. Porson was content to propose ἀλλ' εἶκε θυμόν, comparing *O. C.* 1178 τάδ' εἰκαθεῖν, etc. Hermann conjectured, ἀλλ' εἶκε, θυμῷ καὶ μετάστασιν διδούς, 'sed cede, irae etiam intermissionem faciens.' (He does not say how he understood καί, which he renders by the equally ambiguous *etiam*.) Afterwards, while adhering to this text and punctuation, he preferred to retain δίδου with Gaisford; 'quae est per asyndeton instantius precantis oratio.'—Dindorf: ἀλλ' εἶκε, καὶ θυμῷ μετάστασιν δίδου. (So Pallis, but with θυμοῦ.)

The bolder treatments of the verse have usually been directed against θυμῷ or θυμοῦ. Schneidewin: ἀλλ' εἶκε δή μοι, or ἀλλ' εἶκέ θ' ἡμῖν. —Martin: ἀλλ' εἶκε μύθῳ. (So Nauck.)—Meineke: ἀλλ' εἶκε δήμῳ. (He afterwards acquiesced in εἶκε θυμῷ as = 'yield in thy mind,' but then desired καὶ ματάστασιν τίθου as = μετάστηθι.)—Mekler: ἀλλ' εἶκε καὶ σύ. —Mr J. G. Smith suggests, ἀλλ' εἴ γε θυμοῖ: this is ingenious, but the γε is unsuitable.

782   ἐν κτήμασι πίπτεις. These words have provoked a curious variety of interpretation and of conjecture. Besides the version defended in my note, the following have been proposed. (1) 'Love attacks rich men.' (Hermann: 'Non videtur mihi dubitari posse quin κτήματα pro opulentis ac potentibus dixerit.') (2) 'Love attacks cattle': κτήμασι = κτήνεσι (Brunck). (3) 'Love falls on his slaves,' *i.e.* falls on men, so as to enslave them,—κτήμασι being proleptic. This was Schneidewin's view, who compared Lucian *Dial. Deor.* 6. 3 where Hera describes Zeus as ὅλως κτῆμα καὶ παιδιὰ τοῦ Ἔρωτος. But surely it is one thing for Hera to say that Zeus is 'the very chattel and plaything of Love,' and quite another thing to suppose that Sophocles

here meant to say, ' Love falls upon his chattels.' κτῆμα, in this sense, suits humorous prose, but not elevated poetry.

The conjectures have been numerous. (1) Keeping the rest, instead of κτήμασι Dindorf proposes λήμασι (1860 Oxon. 3rd ed.), or ἐν τ' ἀνδράσι (1863 Leipsic 4th ed.) : Blaydes, σώμασι (or νεάνισι as a trisyll.) : Hartung, στήθεσι: Meineke, δώμασι: Musgrave, σχήμασι (*titulos dignitatesque invadis*). Seyffert, βλέμμασι. (2) Some would change the verb, with or without changing κτήμασι. Blaydes: εἰν ὄμμασι παίζεις (or -ν ἴζεις). He also mentions an old conject., εἰν ὄμμασιν ἵπτῃ ('*harmest through the eyes*'?).—Pallis: ἐν δέργμασιν ἵζεις.—Semitelos: ἐν κτήμασι τίκτει ('art born amid wealth').

797 f. τῶν μεγάλων **πάρεδρος ἐν ἀρχαῖς** | θεσμῶν. If πάρεδρος is sound here, the first two syllables are equivalent to the first long syllable of a dactyl. The following examples are furnished by Pindar. In each case I give the antistrophic verse along with the verse in which the example occurs. The example itself is printed in thicker type.

(1) *Ol.* 10 (11).

1st epode v. 17
καὶ χάλκ|εος Ἄρ|ης| τράπε δὲ | Κύκν|εια μάχ|α καὶ ὑ|πέρβι|ον Λ ||
2nd ep. v. 40
οὐ πολλ|ὸν ἴδε | πατρ|ίδα πολ|·ὺ | **κτέανον ὑπ|ὸ** στερε|ῷ πυρ|ὶ Λ ||

(2) *Pyth.* 11.

1st strophe v. 4 ματρὶ | πὰρ Μελί|αν χρυσ|έων | ἐς ἄδυτ|ον τριπόδ|ων Λ ||
1st antistr. v. 9 ὄφρα | Θέμιν ἱερ|ὰν Πυθ|ῶν|ά τε καὶ | ὀρθοδίκ|αν

(3) *Nem.* 7.

4th str., v. 70   Εὐ|ξενίδα πάτρ|αθε | Σώ|γενες ἀπ|ομνύω Λ ||
4th antistr., v. 78 κολλ|ᾷ χρυσὸν | ἔν τε | λευκ|ὸν ἐλέφ|ανθ' ἁμᾷ Λ ||

[Here, ξενῖδᾰ πάτρ=ᾳ χρῦσὸν. This is a very rare instance of ῠ in the subst., though χρῡσεος is frequent.]

(4) *Isthm.* 3.

4th str., v. 57 θεσπεσί|ων ἐπέ|ων λοιπ|οῖς ἀθ|ύρειν ||
4th ant., v. 63 ἔρνεἳ | Τελεσιάδ|α. τόλμ|ᾳ γὰρ | εἰκὼς ||

In the third and fourth of these examples, it will be observed that the resolution of the long syllable into ◡ ◡ has the special excuse of a proper name.

836—838 L gives the verses thus :

836 καίτοι φθιμένα [with ω over a] μέγ' ἀκοῦσαι
837 τοῖς ἰσοθέοις ἔγκληρα λαχεῖν
838 ζῶσαν καὶ ἔπειτα θανοῦσαν.

The following opinions on this passage claim notice. (1) Hermann, omitting v. 838, transposed the two other verses thus :—

$$\kappa\alpha\acute{\iota}\tau o\iota\ \phi\theta\iota\mu\acute{\epsilon}\nu\omega\ \tau o\hat{\iota}s\ \acute{\iota}\sigma o\theta\acute{\epsilon}o\iota s$$
$$\acute{\epsilon}\gamma\kappa\lambda\eta\rho\alpha\ \lambda\alpha\chi\epsilon\hat{\iota}\nu\ \mu\acute{\epsilon}\gamma'\ \acute{\alpha}\kappa o\hat{\upsilon}\sigma\alpha\iota.$$

Thus the pivot of his criticism was the belief that $\mu\acute{\epsilon}\gamma'$ $\acute{\alpha}\kappa o\hat{\upsilon}\sigma\alpha\iota$, being sound, should close a paroemiac. So Dindorf, too, formerly gave the passage (3rd ed. Oxon., 1860). [In his 6th Leipsic ed. (cur. Mekler, 1885) it is, $\kappa\alpha\acute{\iota}\tau o\iota\ \phi\theta\iota\mu\acute{\epsilon}\nu\omega\ \tau o\hat{\iota}\sigma\iota\ \theta\epsilon o\hat{\iota}\sigma\iota\nu\ |\ \sigma\acute{\upsilon}\gamma\kappa\lambda\eta\rho\alpha\ \lambda\alpha\chi\epsilon\hat{\iota}\nu\ \mu\acute{\epsilon}\gamma'\ \acute{\alpha}\kappa o\hat{\upsilon}\sigma\alpha\iota.$] Bergk also rejects 838. (2) G. Wolff refers to the schol. on 834 : $\kappa\alpha\rho\tau\epsilon\rho\epsilon\hat{\iota}\nu\ \sigma\epsilon\ \chi\rho\acute{\eta},\ \acute{\omega}s\ \kappa\alpha\grave{\iota}\ \acute{\eta}\ N\iota\acute{o}\beta\eta\ \acute{\epsilon}\kappa\alpha\rho\tau\acute{\epsilon}\rho\eta\sigma\epsilon\nu,\ \kappa\alpha\acute{\iota}\tau o\iota\ \theta\epsilon\iota o\tau\acute{\epsilon}\rho o\upsilon\ \gamma\acute{\epsilon}\nu o\upsilon s$ $\tau\upsilon\gamma\chi\acute{\alpha}\nu o\upsilon\sigma\alpha.\ T\alpha\nu\tau\acute{\alpha}\lambda o\upsilon\ \gamma\grave{\alpha}\rho\ \mathring{\eta}\nu\ \tauο\hat{\upsilon}\ \Delta\iota\acute{o}s.$—$\Pi\alpha\rho\alpha\mu\upsilon\theta o\acute{\upsilon}\mu\epsilon\nu os\ \alpha\mathring{\upsilon}\tau\acute{\eta}\nu,\ \theta\epsilon\grave{o}\nu$ $\phi\eta\sigma\grave{\iota}\ \tau\grave{\eta}\nu\ N\iota\acute{o}\beta\eta\nu.$ Hence Wolff inferred that the Schol. read a verse, now lost, in which Antigone was exhorted to be patient ($\kappa\alpha\rho\tau\epsilon\rho\epsilon\hat{\iota}\nu$). He suggested $\sigma\grave{\epsilon}\ \delta\grave{\epsilon}\ \kappa\alpha\grave{\iota}\ \tau\lambda\hat{\eta}\nu\alpha\iota\ \pi\rho\acute{\epsilon}\pi o\nu\ \acute{\omega}s\ \kappa\epsilon\acute{\iota}\nu\eta\nu$, to come immediately before $\zeta\hat{\omega}\sigma\alpha\nu\ \kappa\alpha\grave{\iota}\ \acute{\epsilon}\pi\epsilon\iota\tau\alpha\ \theta\alpha\nu o\hat{\upsilon}\sigma\alpha\nu$. He also changed the full stop after $\theta\nu\eta\tau o\gamma\epsilon\nu\epsilon\hat{\iota}s$ to a comma, and $\kappa\alpha\acute{\iota}\tau o\iota$ to $\kappa\alpha\grave{\iota}\ \tau\hat{\omega}$. The obvious reply to Wolff's theory is that the Schol.'s paraphrase, $\kappa\alpha\rho\tau\epsilon\rho\epsilon\hat{\iota}\nu\ \sigma\epsilon\ \chi\rho\acute{\eta}$, etc., refers to what the Chorus *suggests*,—not, necessarily, to what it *says*,— 'Niobe was a goddess, and you are a mortal' (and mortals expect suffering: therefore, if she was patient, you well may be so).

(3) Wecklein, too, assumes the loss of a verse. In 836 f. he reads

$$\kappa\alpha\acute{\iota}\tau o\iota\ \phi\theta\iota\mu\acute{\epsilon}\nu\omega\ \mu\acute{\epsilon}\gamma\alpha\ \tau\acute{\alpha}\kappa o\hat{\upsilon}\sigma\alpha\iota$$
$$\tau o\hat{\iota}\sigma\iota\ \theta\epsilon o\hat{\iota}\sigma\iota\nu\ \sigma\acute{\upsilon}\gamma\kappa\lambda\eta\mu\alpha\ \lambda\alpha\chi\epsilon\hat{\iota}\nu,$$

and indicates a lacuna between these verses and $\zeta\hat{\omega}\sigma\alpha\nu\ \kappa\alpha\grave{\iota}\ \acute{\epsilon}\pi\epsilon\iota\tau\alpha$ $\theta\alpha\nu o\hat{\upsilon}\sigma\alpha\nu$. His grounds are not G. Wolff's, but merely (*a*) the unsatisfactory sense, (*b*) the fact that at vv. 817 ff. we have six, and not five anapaests. [On this point, see Appendix on 155 ff.] Nauck's view is similar.

(4) Bellermann is disposed to agree with those who, like Hermann, Dindorf, and Bergk, reject 838. He remarks : 'Besonders auffallend ist $\zeta\hat{\omega}\sigma\alpha\nu$, da im *Leben* Antigones und Niobes keinerlei Ähnlichkeit gefunden werden kann.' This objection I venture to think that I have answered ; see n. on 834—838, p. 153.

(5) Semitelos gives :—

$$\kappa\alpha\acute{\iota}\ \tau\omega\ \phi\theta\iota\mu\acute{\epsilon}\nu\omega\nu\ \theta\alpha\hat{\upsilon}\mu\acute{\alpha}\ \gamma'\ \acute{\alpha}\kappa o\hat{\upsilon}\sigma\alpha\iota$$
$$\tau o\hat{\iota}\sigma\iota\ \theta\epsilon o\hat{\iota}\sigma\acute{\iota}\nu\ \sigma'\ \acute{\epsilon}\gamma\kappa\lambda\eta\rho\alpha\ \lambda\alpha\chi\epsilon\hat{\iota}\nu$$
$$\zeta\hat{\omega}\sigma\alpha\nu\ \kappa\alpha\grave{\iota}\ \acute{\epsilon}\pi\epsilon\iota\tau\alpha\ \theta\alpha\nu o\hat{\upsilon}\sigma\iota\nu,$$

i.e., 'Many among the dead will marvel to hear that in *life* thou didst win the same lot as a goddess (Niobe), and afterwards (after thy death) the same lot as the dead.' Are the dead to marvel, then, at the appearance among them of one who had seemed to be lifted out of the ranks of ordinary mortals?

904—920 This famous passage affords one of the most interesting exercises for criticism which can be found in ancient literature. Is it indeed the work of Sophocles? Or was it interpolated, after his death, by his son Iophon? The anonymous Life of Sophocles records a statement by the biographer Satyrus[1] (*c.* 200 B.C.) that the poet died in the act of reading the *Antigone* aloud. It has been suggested that he may then have been employed in revising the play, with a view to reproducing it; and that Iophon, in completing the task, may have brought in these verses. Another possibility is that they were due to the actors, whose innovations Lycurgus sought to check as early as *c.* 330 B.C. At any rate these verses were recognised in the text of Sophocles at the time when Aristotle composed his *Rhetoric*,—*i.e.*, not later than *c.* 338 B.C.

The first impression which the passage tends to produce is well described in the simple and direct words of Goethe, as reported by Eckermann. 'In the course of the piece, the heroine has given the most admirable reasons for her conduct, and has shown the noble courage of a stainless soul; but now, at the end, she puts forward a motive which is quite unworthy of her, ('ganz schlecht,') and which almost borders on the comic.' And then Goethe expresses the hope that scholars will prove the passage to be spurious.

Among those who think it genuine, few, perhaps, would say that it is good. A large majority would allow that, at the best, it requires some apology. The question comes to this:—Can the faults of the passage, as they appear to a modern taste, be excused by a peculiarity in ancient modes of thought? Or are they such as to make it inconceivable that any great poet, ancient or modern, should have embodied the passage in a work of art?

At v. 458 Antigone said that she had buried her brother, in defiance of Creon's edict, because she deemed that no mortal 'could override the unwritten and unfailing statutes of heaven.' 'Not through dread of any human pride could I answer to the gods for breaking these.' 'The justice that dwells with the gods below' (451) requires that rites should be paid to the dead by the living; and, among the living, that duty falls first upon the kinsfolk. This is a perfectly intelligible principle; and everything else that Antigone says or does is in harmony with it. But here she startles us by saying that she would *not* have braved Creon, and obeyed the gods, if it had been merely a husband or a child that had been lying unburied. Yet her religious duty would have been as clear—on her own principle—in those cases as in this. Would she have been prepared, then, to suffer that punishment beyond the grave which she formerly professed to fear (459)? Or does she now suppose that the gods would pardon a breach of the religious duty in any case except that of a brother? Whichever she means, her feet slip from the rock on which they were set; she suddenly gives up that which, throughout the drama, has been the immovable basis of her action,—the universal and unqualified validity of the divine law.

---

[1] See *O. C.* p. xli.

But this is not all. After saying that she would not have thus buried husband or child, she adds this explanation. 'The husband lost, another might have been found, and child from another, to replace the first-born; but, father and mother hidden with Hades, no brother's life could ever bloom for me again.' She has not buried even her brother, then, simply because he was her brother; but because he was her last brother, and there could not now be any more. The inference is that, if Polyneices had not been a relative unique in his own kind, she might have thought twice. This astonishing view is at once explained by the origin of the verses which contain it (909—912). They are a tolerably close metrical version—and a very poor one, too—of the reason given by the wife of Intaphernes for saving her brother rather than her husband or one of her children. (Her. 3. 119: see comment. on 909 ff.)

Now, the 'primitive sophism' employed by the wife of Intaphernes, and the tendency to exalt the fraternal tie, are things which we may certainly recognise as characteristic of that age. And it is true that Aeschylus has some quaint subtleties of a similar kind: as when Apollo defends Orestes on the ground that a man's mother is not, properly speaking, his parent (*Eum.* 658); and when Athena votes for Orestes because she herself had had no mother at all (736).

But all that is beside the question here. We have to ask ourselves:— In adopting the argument used by the wife of Intaphernes, could a great poet have overlooked the absurdities involved in transferring it from the living to the dead? Moriz Seyffert suggests an excuse, to this effect:— 'She means that, if she had not buried him, she would not have had his love when (in the course of nature) she joined him in the world below.' But such a motive would have been independent of the fact that no other brother could be born to her. And another brother—also dear to her—was already in the world of the dead (cp. 899 n.). The plain fact is that the composer who adapted the words from Herodotus was thinking only of the rhetorical opportunity, and was heedless of everything else. Remark particularly verse 908, which prefaces the four verses paraphrased from the historian:—τίνος νόμου δὴ ταῦτα πρὸς χάριν λέγω; There is a certain tone of clumsy triumph in that, strongly suggestive of the interpolator who bespeaks attention for his coming point. The singularities of diction in vv. 909—912 have been noticed in the commentary.

The considerations which have been stated above render it incredible to me that Sophocles should have composed vv. 905—912: with which v. 913 on the one side, and v. 904 on the other, closely cohere. A. Jacob,—who, in 1821, first brought arguments against the genuineness of the passage, —was content to reject vv. 905—912. And Schneidewin, sharing his view, proposed μέντοι (or μόνῳ, to precede Κρέοντι) for νόμῳ in v. 914. The sequence would then be,

904 καίτοι σ᾽ ἐγὼ ᾽τίμησα τοῖς φρονοῦσιν εὖ.
914 Κρέοντι μέντοι ταῦτ᾽ ἔδοξ᾽ ἁμαρτάνειν, κ.τ.λ.

But v. 904 has thoroughly the air of a preface to a specific self-justification. If it was followed merely by the statement, 'Yet Creon thought me wrong,' both v. 904 and v. 914 would be very weak. Again, it is evident that v. 913 could not directly follow v. 903, since the νόμος mentioned in 914 would not then have been stated. Now observe, on the other hand, how fitly v. 921 would follow 903 :—

τὸ σὸν
903 δέμας περιστέλλουσα τοιάδ᾽ ἄρνυμαι.
921 ποίαν παρεξελθοῦσα δαιμόνων δίκην;

Verse 921 is in every way worthy of Sophocles; nor does any just suspicion rest on 922—928. I agree, then, with those who define the interpolation as consisting of vv. 904—920.

H. Macnaghten (*Journ. Philol.* XXIV. 171—177, 1896) thinks that τοιάδ᾽ ἄρνυμαι in 903 means, 'I win a like recompense,'—viz., *love*, such as she had already merited from her parents, and from Eteocles. Verses 904—912 were interpolated by some one who took τοιάδ᾽ ἄρνυμαι (as it has usually been taken) to mean 'the recompense of a cruel death.' In 913 f. (the verses which originally came next after 903) τοιῷδε... νόμῳ means 'the law which bids honour the dead.' But surely the words τοιάδ᾽ ἄρνυμαι must be read in the light of 891—896 : they can only refer to her *doom*. Thus indeed, as the able critic says, they have been universally understood 'for more than 2000 years.'

In conclusion, it will be proper to state the principal arguments (not already noticed) which have been used to defend the authenticity of the passage.

(1) Bellermann's defence (in the Wolff-Bellerm. ed., pp. 83 f.) is, perhaps, the most ingenious. He argues, in effect :—She does not give up her original motive,—the religious duty. But she feels that this duty has degrees, answering to degrees of relationship. No one could be held bound to *give his life* in order to bury a stranger ; and so, from the zero point, the scale of obligation rises, till it becomes strongest in the case of a brother. Here, then, as everywhere, her sole motive is the divine command. She merely says :—'I can imagine breaking that command in any case—yes, in a husband's or in a child's —*sooner than* in the case of this brother.' This is psychologically natural. The duty which occupies us at a given moment is apt to seem the most imperative ; and the mind seizes on every thought that can enforce it. It does not follow that, if the supposed cases had been real, Antigone would then have acted as she now imagines. She knew the feelings of a sister ; she had never known those of wife or mother.

To this I should reply :—The sliding-scale theory of the religious duty here involves a fallacy, from the Greek point of view. Greeks distinguished between the obligation in respect to θυραῖοι and in respect to οἰκεῖοι. A husband and child are on the same side of that line as a brother. [In Her. 3. 119 οἰκήιοι is the term which comprehends all three relationships.] It is true that, if the dead had been a mere stranger, she could not have been deemed ἐναγής (cp. 255 f. n.) for declining to bury him at the cost of her own life. But her duty towards husband or child would have been the same in kind as her duty towards her brother. Besides, Bellermann's subtlety invests the crude and blunt sophistry of the text with an imaginative charm which is not its own. If the psychological phase which he supposes in the heroine had been expressed by the poet, such an expression must have preserved the essential harmony between her recent and her present attitude of mind.

Thudichum[1] also holds that Antigone is still loyal to her former principle. But now—so near to death, and condemned by all—she wishes to declare, in the most impressive manner, how overmastering was the sense of religious duty which he obeyed. It was not through insolence that she defied the State. She would have deferred to it in almost any imaginable case—but here she could not.—This is in general accord with Bellermann's view, but differs from it in giving the passage a more external character;—one of self-defence rather than of self-communing; and that is no gain, either in dignity or in pathos.

(2) Boeckh and Seyffert, in their editions of the play, take a bolder line. They agree in thinking that Antigone has abandoned the lofty ground on which she had formerly justified her action.

Boeckh concedes that this passage 'destroys the grandeur of her conduct.' She has now attained to a perception that she did wrong in breaking Creon's law. And, at the moment when that noble illusion fails her, 'the poet permits her to catch at such support as sophistry can lend to despair.'

Seyffert's conception is more refined; it is, in fact, related to Boeckh's much as the harmonising theory of Bellermann is related to that of Thudichum. She had acted, says Seyffert, from an elevated sense of religious duty. She finds herself condemned by all. The enthusiasm of her religious faith has been chilled; she is helpless and hopeless; her troubled thoughts fall back on the one thing of which she still feels sure,—the deep human affection which bound her to her brother.

Now, of Seyffert's view we may say, first, what has been said of Bellermann's,—that it is an idealising paraphrase of a crude text. But there is a further and yet graver objection,—one which applies alike to Seyffert and to Boeckh. After this disputed passage, and at the very moment when she is being led away to death, she says:— 'If these things are pleasing to the gods, when I have suffered my doom, I shall come to know my sin; but if the sin is with my judges, I could wish them no fuller measure of evil than they, on their part, mete wrongfully to me.' (925 ff.) Here the poet identifies his heroine, in one of her latest utterances, with the principle on which the catastrophe turns. Creon *is* punished by the gods; and his punishment is the token that they approve of Antigone's conduct. In the very last words which

---

[1] *Jahresbericht d. Gymn. z. Büdingen.* Schulj. 1857—8, pp. 33 ff., quoted by Semitelos, p. 600.

she speaks she describes herself as τὴν εὐσεβίαν σεβίσασα. (943.)
Thus, in two different places—both of them subsequent to the suspected passage—she stands forth distinctly as the representative of
the great law which had inspired her act. Is it probable—would it be
endurable—that at a slightly earlier moment,—in vv. 905—912,—she
should speak in the tone of one to whom that divine law had proved
a mockery and a delusion,—who had come to feel that thence, at least,
no adequate vindication of her conduct could be derived,—and who was
now looking around her for such excuse, or such solace, as could be
found on a lower range of thought and feeling?

No ; if this passage is to be defended at all, it must be defended from
such a point of view as that taken by Bellermann, not from that of
Seyffert or of Boeckh. Goethe's wish can never be fulfilled. No one
will ever convince every one that this passage is spurious. But every
student of the *Antigone* is bound to reflect earnestly on this vital
problem of the text,—the answer to which must so profoundly affect our
conception of the great drama as a whole.

966 f. Wieseler's conjecture, παρὰ δὲ κυανεᾶν σπιλάδων (for πελαγέων)
διδύμας ἁλός, published in 1857 (*Ind. Lect. Götting.* p. 10), has been
received by some editors. Bergk proposed Κυανεᾶν σπιλάδας, to avoid
παρά with the genitive, which is, indeed, an insuperable objection to
σπιλάδων : but then, with the change of case, the probability of the
emendation is still further diminished.

Other readings are :—Wecklein, παρὰ δὲ κυανέων (*sic*) σπιλάδων διδύμας
πέτρας (for ἁλός). | Meineke, παρὰ δὲ κυανέων τεναγέων διδύμας ἁλός, com-
paring Scymnus Perieget. 724 εἶτ' αἰγιαλός τις Σαλμυδησσὸς λεγόμενος |
ἐφ' ἑπτακόσια στάδια τεναγώδης ἄγαν.—Hartung alters more boldly :—
παρὰ δὲ Κυανέων (*sic*) διδύμαις ἁλὸς | ἀκταῖς Βοσπορίαις Θρῃκῶν Ἄρης |
Σαλμυδήσιος ἀγχιπτόλεμος.

1034 f. The MSS. give κοὐδὲ μαντικῆς | ἄπρακτος ὑμῖν εἰμι τῶν δ' ὑπαὶ
γένους.

(1) For ἄπρακτος, H. Stephanus conjectures ἄπρατος : Nauck, ἄγευστος : Pallis, ἄτρωτος or ἄπληκτος.

(2) The words τῶν δ' ὑπαὶ γένους have given rise to many conjectures, which, as I cannot but think, are unnecessary. Brunck is content
with τῶν for τῶνδ', and Blaydes with τῶν γένους ὕπο. But others have
sought to obtain the sense, 'and by my kinsmen': thus Hermann, τῶν
δ' ὑπ' ἐγγενῶν· Dindorf (omitting εἰμί) τῶν δὲ συγγενῶν ὕπο : Schneidewin,
τῶν δ' ὑπ' ἐν γένει : Nauck, τοῖσι δ' ἐν γένει. Donaldson, again, proposes
τῶν ὑπ' ἀργύρου. Seyffert, γόνους (for γένους), to be taken with ἐξημπόλημαι: *i.e.*, 'by whom I have long since been relieved of my son' ('who
have long since alienated my son's loyalty from me'!).—Wolff strangely
proposed μῶν for τῶν δ'.—Moriz Schmidt supposes that either two or
four verses for the Chorus have been lost after 1032. Then πρέσβυ in
1033 would be said by Creon to the Chorus, not to Teiresias. He also
thinks that one verse of Creon's has dropped out after 1034.

1080—1083 Boeckh denies that there is any reference, direct or indirect, to the war of the Epigoni. He takes the verses as merely stating a general axiom: 'All cities, becoming hateful [ἐχθραί, to the gods], are convulsed by calamity,'—when dogs, etc., defile their altars with carrion. This, surely, robs the seer's words of all force and point. Schneidewin, agreeing with Boeckh, takes ἐχθραί as 'hateful to the Erinyes' (1075). Semitelos, favouring the same view, amends thus: ἔχθραι [the subst., for ἐχθραί, adj.] δὲ πᾶσαι συνταράσσουσιν πόλεις, i.e., 'intestine factions.'— Kvičala would place verses 1080—1083 immediately after v. 1022, when ἐχθραί, as 'hateful *to the gods*,' would be interpreted by the neighbouring θεοί in 1020.

Erfurdt, with whom Hermann agrees, supposes a reference to the war of the Epigoni. My commentary has shown how far, and in what sense, I think that view correct. Wex finds an allusion to the war made by Athens on Thebes, in order to enforce burial of the Argives. But then, as Herm. says, Athens must have been specially indicated.

In 1081 Seyffert writes τὰ πράγματ' for σπαράγματ', with καθήγισαν, understanding, 'Hostile to thee, all the cities will be [Bergk's συνταρά- ξονται] in tumult, whose *affairs* have been polluted by birds,' etc., that carry pollution ἐστιοῦχον ἐς πόλον (for πόλιν), 'to the region near the altars.' His idea was that the affairs of the cities would be impeded by unfavourable auspices.—Nauck also conjectures ἐστιοῦχον ἐς πόλον, but refers it to the birds :—'the sky that contains their homes,'—the πόλος that is their πόλις (Ar. *Av.* 179).—Other emendations of πόλιν are the following. Dobree (*Adv.* 2. 31), σποδόν : Blaydes, δόμον, πέδον, πυράν, or φλόγα : Wieseler, πάλην as = τέφραν, σποδόν.—Schneidewin would write ἐς φλογοῦχον ἑστίαν (or ὀμφαλόν) : Semitelos, ἄστεως ἐς ὀμφαλόν, comparing Pind. fr. 45. 3.

1165 f. τὰς γὰρ ἡδονὰς | ὅταν προδῶσιν ἄνδρες.—The conjectures are of two classes, according as they retain τὰς γὰρ ἡδονάς, or require καὶ γὰρ ἡδοναί. (1) Blaydes proposes τὰς γὰρ ἡδονὰς | ὅταν προδῷ τις, ἄνδρ' ἔτ'. Mekler, τὰς γὰρ ἡδονὰς | ὅταν προδῷ σῶμ' ἀνδρός. Both these use the verb in the same sense as if we retained προδῶσιν ἄνδρες. The only object, then, is to avoid the plur. ἄνδρες before τοῦτον : but the plur. is quite admissible.—Herm. Schütz suggests τὰς γὰρ ἡδονὰς | ὅταν προῶσιν ἄνδρες. The act., though much rarer in this sense than the midd., is defensible : cp. Thuc. 8. 32 τὰς ναῦς...προήσειν. But the open οω is unexampled in tragic dialogue, though we find open οε (as in αὐτοέντης, προείπας). I had thought of παρῶσιν ('remit,' then, 'give up,' *O. C.* 1229 n.), but now believe προδῶσιν to be sound.—(2) Wecklein ὅταν γὰρ ἡδοναὶ | βίον προδῶσιν ἀνδρός.—Semitelos : καὶ γὰρ ἡδοναὶ | ὅτου 'ποδρῶσιν ἀνδρός ('when a man's pleasures take flight').—Hartung (omitting 1167) : καὶ γὰρ ἡδοναὶ | οὓς ἂν προδῶσιν, ἄνδρας οὐ τίθημ' ἐγώ.—Seyffert's reading has been noticed in the commentary.

1207 In the history of the word παστάς two points, at least, are clear. (1) Writers of the 5th and 4th centuries B.C. used the word to denote a portico, or a corridor, supported by pillars. In Her. 2. 148 παστάδες are pillared corridors dividing, and connecting, the groups of chambers in the Labyrinth near Lake Moeris. In Her. 2. 169 παστάς is a structure like a gallery, or cloister, built on to one side of an open court (αὐλή) in a temple. Doors opened from the παστάς into a sepulchral chamber. In Xen. *Mem.* 3. 8. 9 παστάδες are the open porticoes, or verandahs, of dwelling-houses, which receive the winter sunshine. (2) The word παστάς was especially associated with the θάλαμος or bedroom of a married couple. In Eur. *Or.* 1371 a Phrygian slave escapes from Helen's apartments in the house of Menelaus by climbing παστάδων ὑπὲρ τέρεμνα, *i.e.* over the roof-beams above the colonnade or peristyle (παστάδες) of the women's court. Theocritus (24. 46) uses παστάς as = θάλαμος,—the bed-room of Amphitryon and Alcmenè: ἀμφιλαφὴς δ' ἄρα παστὰς (the wide chamber) ἐνεπλήσθη πάλιν ὄρφνης. So παστός in Lucian *Dial. Mort.* 23. 3: νεανίαν, οἷος ἦν ἐκ τοῦ παστοῦ (as he came forth from the bridal chamber).

Then the word is often *joined with* θάλαμος in epitaphs on young brides or maidens: *Anthol. P.* append. 248 οὔπω νυμφείου θαλάμου καὶ παστάδος ὥρης | γευσαμένην: *ib.* 9. 245 δυσμοίρων θαλάμων ἐπὶ παστάσιν οὐχ Ὑμέναιος | ἀλλ᾽ Ἅιδης ἔστη πικρογάμου Πετάλης (by Antiphanes, 1st cent. B.C.). So παστός, Kaibel *Epigr.* 468 ἐκ δέ με παστῶν νύμφην κἀιχ (*sic*) θαλάμων ἥρπασ᾽ ἄφνως Ἀΐδας.

The three last passages suggest that παστάς was *a part* of the θάλαμος, which could stand poetically for the whole. But what part? We might suppose, an external portico. Against this, however, is the fact that the παστός is once, at least, placed definitely *within* the θάλαμος, as though it were a synonym for the marriage-bed: *Anthol. P.* 7. 711 χρύσεων παστὸς ἔσω θαλάμων. Possibly it was some arrangement of pillars specially associated with the interior of the θάλαμος,—whether in a recess containing the bed, or otherwise.

Here, I believe that the poet used παστάς simply for θάλαμος, without reference to any columnar character of the rocky tomb.—The word is probably compressed from παραστάς (pilaster, *anta*): thus παραστάδες can mean, 'a vestibule' (Eur. *Ph.* 415), as παστάς also can (*Anth.* 6. 172).

1279 f. τὰ μὲν πρὸ χειρῶν τάδε φέρων, τὰ δ᾽ ἐν δόμοις
ἔοικας ἥκειν καὶ τάχ᾽ ὄψεσθαι κακά.

The following conjectures illustrate the difficulties which some critics have felt here. (1) Musgrave proposed, τὰ μὲν πρὸ χειρῶν, τὰ δ᾽ ἐφορῶν, τά γ᾽ ἐν δόμοις | ἔοικας ἥκων κύντατ᾽ ὄψεσθαι κακά. He understood: '(having) one sorrow in thy hands (viz., Haemon's corpse), and *giving charge concerning* another [viz., concerning Antigone's body, which Creon had consigned to the guards], thou art likely, on arrival, to see most cruel woes in thy house.' He compared Eur. *Suppl.* 807 τὰ κύντατ᾽ ἄλγη κακῶν (the idea of 'cruel,' or 'ruthless,' coming from that of 'shameless,' as in ἀναιδής, *improbus*).—(2) Brunck: φέρεις for φέρων, and ἥκων for ἥκειν, so that καὶ τάχ᾽ = '*full* soon.'—(3) Semitelos adopts Brunck's changes and makes some others,—thus: τὰ μὲν πρὸ χειρῶν τάδε φέρεις, ἃ δ᾽ ἐν δόμοις | εἴακας, ἥκων καὶ τάχ᾽ εἰσόψει κακά. [He does not explain εἴακας, but perh. intended it to mean, 'hast permitted to happen.']—(4) Hartung : φέρειν for φέρων. He understands : 'thou seemest to bear some woes in thy hands, and to have come (in order) full soon (καὶ τάχ') to see the woes in the house.'—(5) Blaydes adopts φέρειν, and also changes ἥκειν καὶ into εἰσήκων.—(6) Wieseler (*Lectionskatal.*, Götting. 1875—6) proposes ἐοικόθ' ἥκεις for ἔοικας ἥκειν : meaning by ἐοικότα woes that have naturally resulted from Creon's acts.—(7) Wex rejects v. 1280, ἔοικας ἥκειν καὶ τάχ' ὄψεσθαι κακά. He supposes that the Messenger's speech was interrupted, after the word δόμοις (1279), by Creon's hurried question, τί δ' ἔστιν etc. The forged verse was designed to complete the unfinished sentence.—It is obvious that the easiest mode of smoothing the construction would be simply to transpose vv. 1279 f. Then τὰ μὲν πρὸ χειρῶν τάδε φέρων, τὰ δ' ἐν δόμοις would be a case of parataxis (like that in 1112), = ὥσπερ τὰ πρὸ χειρῶν, οὕτω καὶ τὰ ἐν δόμοις. But neither this nor any other change is necessary.

1301 With regard to the traditional reading, ἥδ' ὀξύθηκτος ἥδε βωμία πέριξ, it is generally admitted that the first of the two epithets will not bear the figurative sense, 'with keen resolve.' Hence the conjectures have followed one of three courses.

(1) To read ὀξυθήκτῳ instead of ὀξύθηκτος, and introduce a subst. in the dat., meaning 'knife' or 'sword.' The readings of Arndt and Blaydes have been noticed in the commentary. Gleditsch, with much less probability, suggests ἡ δ' ὀξυθήκτῳ φασγάνῳ περιπτυχής.

(2) To retain ὀξύθηκτος, making the knife the subject of the sentence. Thus Hermann: ἥδ' ὀξύθηκτος οἶδε βωμία πτέρυξ: 'yonder keenly-whetted altar-knife knows (how she perished)':—the Messenger points to the knife, lying near the body. For πτέρυξ, 'blade,' cp. Plut. *Alex.* 16 ὥστε τῶν πρώτων ψαῦσαι τριχῶν τὴν πτέρυγα τῆς κοπίδος.— Hermann further supposes that, after v. 1301, something has been lost. He infers this from the scholium,—ὡς ἱερεῖον περὶ τὸν βωμὸν ἐσφάγη, παρὰ τὸν βωμὸν προπετής,—because it has the appearance of an attempt to explain a defective text.—Donaldson, adopting πτέρυξ, places the lacuna after βλέφαρα,—not, as Hermann does, after 1301. He also differs from Hermann in supposing that the Scholiast read something now lost. Hence, with the scholium for guide, he conjectures:—ἡ δ' ὀξύθηκτος ἥδε βωμία πτέρυξ | λύει κελαινὰ βλέφαρα [προσπίπτει δ' ἐκεῖ | σφάγιον ὅπως βωμοῖσι,] κωκύσασα μέν, etc.

(3) To substitute ὀξύπληκτος for ὀξύθηκτος.—Thus Seyffert : ἴδ', ὀξύπληκτος ἥδε φοινίαν ἀπρὶξ | λύει etc.: 'lo, this woman, sharply smitten with a deadly blow (φοιν., *sc.* πληγήν), from a tightly-clutched weapon (ἀπρίξ),' etc.—Wecklein (*Ars Soph. em.* p. 74) : ἥδ' ὀξύπληκτος βῆμα βώμιον πέριξ ('at the altar steps').—Hartung : ἡ δ' ὀξύπληκτος βωμία περιπτυχής, 'crouching at the altar' ('um den Hauseheerd geschmiegt'), —to represent the Schol.'s προπετής.—Pallis: ἥδ' ὀξύπληκτος ἧμιν οἰκείᾳ χερί.

1342 f. The traditional reading is ὅπα πρὸς πότερον [πρότερον L] ἴδω, πᾷ καὶ θῶ· πάντα γὰρ | λέχρια τάδ᾽ [or τά τ᾽] ἐν χεροῖν.

Verse 1342 is a dochmiac dimeter. But we cannot assume that the dochmiacs answered, syllable by syllable, to those in the strophic verse, 1320. Here, as often in dochmiacs, conjecture is rendered more uncertain by the fact that a dochmiac dimeter admitted of so many different forms. [A clear and accurate synopsis of all the forms in use is given by Schmidt, *Rhythmic and Metric*, p. 77.] It will simplify a study of the various treatments applied to this passage, if we note that they represent three different ideas, viz.:—

(1) πάντα γάρ is to be kept, but without ejecting anything else from v. 1342. Therefore the strophic v., 1320, must be enlarged. Brunck and Boeckh take this view. So, in 1320, Brunck doubles πρόσπολοι, while Boeckh there writes (provisionally), προσπολοῦντες ἄγετέ μ᾽ ὅ τι τάχος, ἄγετέ μ᾽ ἐκποδών. This view is metrically unsound, since it breaks the series of dochmiac dimeters.

(2) πάντα γάρ is to be kept, but something else is to be omitted, in order that v. 1342 may be a dochmiac dimeter.—Seidler first proposed to omit ὅπα, which seems to me the right course. The strong argument for it is that, while the omission of ὅπα makes the metre right, we can also show how ὅπᾳ first came in: it had been a gloss on πᾷ (see comment.). Bellermann is of the same opinion.—Others, keeping ὅπᾳ, preserve πάντα γάρ by some different expedient. Thus Wunder: ὅπᾳ πρὸς πότερον ἴδω· πάντα γάρ.—Kayser: ὅπᾳ πρὸς πότερα κλιθῶ· πάντα γάρ. This is approved by a writer in the *Athenaeum* (May 5, 1888), who thinks that ἴδω πᾷ may have arisen from ΡΑ ΟΠΑΙ, and that the MS. reading is due to the blending of ὅπα πρὸς πότερα κλιθῶ with a v. l., πρὸς ὁπότερον ὅπα κλιθῶ.—Bergk: ὅπα πρότερ᾽ ἴδω καὶ θῶ· πάντα γάρ.— Blaydes: πρὸς πότερον πρότερον ἴδω· πάντα γάρ.—Hermann: πᾷ θῶ, ὅπα πρότερον ἴδω. πάντα γάρ.—Gleditsch: ὅπᾳ πρόστροπος κλιθῶ· πάντα γάρ.

(3) πάντα γάρ is to be omitted. This was first recommended by Nauck. Wecklein writes, ὅπα πρὸς πότερον ἴδω, πᾷ κλιθῶ· and brackets πάντα γάρ.—Pallis: ὅποι πρῶτον ἴδω, ὅπα καὶ κλιθῶ.—G. H. Müller: ὅπα προσπέσω· ἰώ, πᾷ κλιθῶ;—Semitelos: ὅπᾳ πρὸς πότερον ἴδω καὶ κλιθῶ· | λέχρια πάντα γὰρ τάδ᾽· ἐπὶ κρατί μοι etc.,—omitting ἐν χεροῖν, and assuming that πάντα γάρ has been wrongly transposed.

INDICES.

I. GREEK.

The number denotes the verse, in the note on which the word or matter is illustrated. When the reference is to a *page*, p. is prefixed to the number.)(means, 'as distinguished from.'

B

ἐπίνοια as = after-thought, 389
ἐπινύμφειος, 814
ἐπίρροθος, 413
ἐπισκήπτομαι, pass., 1313
ἐπισπᾶν θύραν, 1186
ἐπίσταμαι with infin., 293
ἐπίσταμαι with inf. = to be capable of doing, 686
ἐπιστρέφεσθαι, to turn round, 1111
ἐπισυναλοιφή, 350
ἐπιτάσσειν, 664
ἐπίχειρα ξιφέων, 820
ἐπιχωρεῖν τινι, to side with, 219
ἐπεί with subjunct., 1025
ἐπεί γε δή, 923
ἔπειτα, τό,)(τὸ μέλλον, 611
ἐπέρχεσθαι, of rumour, 700
ἐπέχειν τινί, to assail one, 986
ἐπήβολος, 492
ἐπόψιος, pass., 1110
ἔπτην, 113
ἔργα, τά, a man's merits, 729
ἔργμα and ἔρμα, 848
ἔργον, pregnant sense of, 730
ἐρέσσω, *animo volutare*, 159
ἐρι and ἀρι, compounds with, 348
ἐρινύς, an infatuated impulse, 603
Ἑρκεῖος Ζεύς, 487, 1301
-εσκον, forms in, 949
-εσσι, dat. ending in, 116, 1297
ἑστάναι ὄπισθέν τινος, 640
ἐστί understood, 834
ἑστιοῦχος, 1083
ἐσχάρα, 1016
ἔσχον, came to have, 1229
ἔτι = 'at some future time,' 69
,, with ζῆν, 3
ἕτοιμος, of a doom, 878
ἔτος εἰς ἔτος, 340
εὐ-, temporal aug. of verbs in, 1164
εὐαγής, 521
εὐθύνειν, absol., 'to rule,' 1164
εὔιον πῦρ, 964, cp. 1135
εὐκρότητος, 430
εὐνή, a bride, 1224
εὐνῆς λέχος, 425
ἐφαγνίζειν)(ἀφαγνίζειν, 196
ἐφέξομαι with acc., 351

ἔχειν βάρος = βαρὺς εἶναι, 1273
,, αἰτίαν, two senses of, 1312
,, ὕβριν, etc., 300
ἐχθές and χθές, 456
ἔχω = *cognitum habeo*, 9
,, = 'know how,' constr. of, 270
,, prefixed to aor. part., 1058, 1068, 1272

Z

ζεύγνυσθαι, fig. sense of, 955
Ζεὺς Ἑρκεῖος, 487
ζῆ and ζῆθι, 1169
ζῶν with another participle, 309

H

ἦ interrog., first in its clause, 1281
-η or -ην, in acc. of proper names, 198
ἦ γάρ...; 44
ἦ καί...; 403: where καί belongs to the following word, 752
ἠδέ in tragic dialogue, 673
ἡδέως, use of, 70
ᾔδησθα, not ᾔδης, 447
ἡδονή, sensuous impulse, 648
ἤλεκτρον, 1038
ἡμεροσκόπος, 253
ἦν understood, 948
ἠνσχόμην, an unexampled form, 467
ἤνυον and ἤνυτον, 231
ἦσθα in Attic drama, 447
ἡσυχώτερος and -αίτερος, 1089
Ἥφαιστος = πῦρ, 123

Θ

θάλαμος, fig., of the grave, 804
θανὼν νέκυς, 26, 515
θεήλατος, 278
θεογεννής, 834
θεοὶ ἐγγενεῖς, 199: προγενεῖς, 938
θερμός and ψυχρός, how contrasted, 88
θιγγάνω, alleged use with acc., 546
θίς, masc. or fem.; senses of, 590
θραύειν)(ῥηγνύναι, 476
Θυῖαι = Θυιάδες, 1152

I

ῑ before βρ, 336
-ια for -εια in εὐσεβία, etc., 943, 1028

-ιδά, how added to stems in -ευ, 941

ἰδέ, epic, = ἠδέ, 968

ἰδεῖν, epexegetical, 206

ἴλλω, 340

„ or εἴλλω, p. 250

ἵμερος, 796

ἵππειον γένος, sense of, 341

ἴσθ᾽ ὅτι in adverb. parenthesis, 758

ἰσόθεος with ῑ, 837

ἴσον, subst., = 'an equal part,' 489

ἴσος doubled, 142

ἴσου, ἐξ, = 'no more than,' 516

ἵστασθαι πρός τι, 299

ἰών added to a verb of doing, 768

K

καί = 'and now,' with an imperative, 491

„ emphasising a verb, 280, 1062: where the verb asks a question, 726, 772, 1314

„ gives a modest tone, 719

„ ('indeed') influencing a whole phrase (as κατακτεῖναι νοεῖς), 770, 1253

„ = 'on their part,' 928

καὶ δή, 245

καὶ δῆτα in question, 449

καὶ εἰ, = 'and if,' 234

καὶ μήν, = 'and yet,' 1054

„ in reply, 221

„ introduces a new person, 526

καὶ ταῦτα with partic. or adj., 322

καὶ φημί...κοὐκ ἀπαρνοῦμαι, 443

καθαγνίζειν τινά, of burial-rites, 1081

καθαιρεῖ, 'condemns,' 275

καθάρσιος, of Dionysus, 1143

κακός, 'ill-omened,' 1001

καλύνω, fig., 496

καλυπτός, said of the covering, 1011

καλχαίνω, 20

καλῶς, = 'speciously' (but untruly), 1047

καπνοῦ σκιά, 1170

κάρᾳ, dat., 1272

καρδία, the heart's wish, 1105

κᾆτα as = 'and so' (not, 'and yet'), 1019

κατ᾽ ἄκρας, 201

καταζεύγνυσθαι, of strict imprisonment, 946

καταμᾶν, 601

καταρρηγνύναι τροπάς, 675

καταρρυής, 1010

καταρτύω, to make docile, 477

κατάσχετος, 1253

καταυδᾶν, 86

κατήναρον, 871

κατηργυρωμένος, 1077

κάτωθεν = κάτω, 521

κατῶρυξ as subst., 774

κεῖνοι, the dead, 525

κεῖσθαι, to stand on record, 485

κεκτῆσθαι)(ἔχειν, 1277

κέλευσμα and κέλευμα, 1219

κεντεῖν, fig., 'to stab,' 1030

κέρδη, plur., not of money, 1326

κερκίς, 976

κερτόμιος, 956

κηδεμών, 549

κινεῖν, of sacrilege, 1061

κινεῖν τινα, to keep one alert, 413

κλαύματα, meaning punishment, 932

κλέπτειν τινα, to delude him, 681, 1218

κλῇθρα, of doors, 1186

κλίνομαι, to lean (for support), 1343

κλύειν τινός = κλ. περί τινος, 1182

κνώδοντες, of a sword, 1233

κοινός, of kinship, 1

κοιρανίδαι, princes or nobles, 940

κόλποι, of Eleusis, 1121

κομψεύω, 324

κοπίς, 602

κοσμεῖσθαι, midd. and pass. senses of, 677

κοσμέω, of burial-rites, 396

κουφόνους, epith. of birds, 343

κράτη, a king's powers, 60, 166: = victory, 485

κράτιστος εἶ ζῶν = κράτιστόν ἐστί σε ζῆν, 1327

κρεμαστός, in punishment, 309

κρίνω, = ἀνάκρινω, 'to question,' 399

κρύπτω as = 'bury,' 285

κτερίζειν, 204, 1071

κτῆμα, of a mental quality, 684

κτίζειν, of rites, festivals, etc., 1101

Κυάνεαι, the, 966

κωτίλλειν, 756

Λ

λαβεῖν, epexegetic, 439
λακπάτητος or λαξπάτητος, 1275
λάλημα, 320
λέγειν τι, to say something strong, 757
λέγειν καὶ ἀκούειν, 757
λέγω κἀμέ (instead of κἀμοί), 32
λείπεσθαί τινος, to be deprived of, 548
λεύκασπις, 106
λέχριος, fig., 1344
λιθόστρωτον, epith. of νυμφεῖον, 1204
λιμήν, fig. sense of, 1000; of Hades, 1284
λόγοις, in word only, 543
λόφος, rarely of the human neck, 292
λύειν opposed to ἐφάπτειν, 40
λύειν βλέφαρα, sense of, 1302
λυσσαίνω, 633

M

M and ΛΛ confused in MSS., 436
μα omitted after οὐ, in oath, 758
μάλιστα, marking the better of two alternatives, 327
μᾶλλον added to a comparative, 1210
μάντεων ὑπέρτερον, proverbial, 631
μάταιος, of rash folly, 1339
μέγας = 'presumptuous' (λόγος, etc.), 127
μεῖζον ἢ κατ' ἄνδρα, 768
μέλει, of rulers, 873; of gods, 1335
μελλόγαμος, 628
μέλλω, fut. inf. or pres. inf. after, 460
   ,,   with infin. understood, 939
μέν, emphasising one word (where no δέ follows), 11, 65, 78, 498, 634, 681, 1336
   ,,   omitted before δέ in epanaphora, 806 ff.
   ,,   without an answering δέ (the construction changing), 1199
μὲν οὖν, with distributed force, 65
μέσσος in iambics, 1223
μετάστασις, 718
μή, generic, 179, 494, 685, 691, 697 f., 716, 1325
   ,,   where μὴ οὐ could stand, 443
   ,,   with inf., after verb of denying, 263

μή with inf. after ἀρνοῦμαι, 'deny,' 442
   ,,   with inf. after ἐπίσταμαι, 1094
   ,,   with indic. after verb implying fear (εἴσομαι μὴ καλύπτει), 1253
   ,,   with partic. after an imperat., 1063 ff.
μή 'μοῦ, 83
μὴ οὐ, with inf., 97, 936
μὴ τριβάς (sc. ποιεῖσθε), 577
μηδέν, τό, 234
μηδένα, τόν, etc., 1325
μῆκος = amplitudo, 393
   ,,   adverb., 'at length,' 446
μήν = καὶ μήν (introducing a new comer), 626
μῆνες θεῶν, sense of, 607
μηρός and μηρία, 1011
μήτε misplaced, 204
   ,,   (or οὔτε) understood, 267
μηχανή, rarely μαχανά in trag. lyrics, 349
μία without subst., 'one mother,' 513
μίασμα, religious, idea of, 1044
μῖσος, said of a person, 760
μιτώδης σινδών, 1222
μόλις μέν, with verb understood, 1105
μόνος with genit. of the cases excluded (as, τῶν ἄλλων), 508
μόροι, 1313, cp. 1329
μύδρος, 264
μύω, 421, 1302

N

ναυκληρεῖν πόλιν, 994
νεαρός, senses of, 857
νέατος, sense of, 627
νεῖσθαι, 33
νέκυς redundant with θανών, etc., 26, 515
νέος as = 'novel,' 1266
νεφέλη, a cloud on the brow, 528
νιν = αὐτάς, 577
νομίζεσθαι with genit., 738
νόμισμα, senses of, 296
νόμοι)(νόμιμα, 455; as = 'rules of conduct,' 191
νόσος, fig., in moral sense, 732
νοῦς, ὁ, τῶν φρενῶν, 1090
νυμφεῖα = νύμφη, 568
νυμφεύειν = γαμεῖσθαι, 654
νῦν and νύν, 324

πάνδημος πόλις, 7
πανουργία and πᾶν ἔργον, 300
πανσαγίᾳ, 107
πάντα, adv., 640, 721
πάντ' ἐπίστασαι, closing a speech, 402
πανταχῇ δρῶν, however one may act, 634
παντελεῖς = σύμπασαι, 1016
παντός, ἐκ, from *any* source, 312
παπταίνειν with acc., sense of, 1231
παρά with genit., an inadmissible use of, 966, 1123
παρ' οὐδέν (with ὡς), 35; how used, 466
παραγκάλισμα, 650
παραλλάσσω with infin., 298
παρασπᾶν, fig., 792
παραστάτης, in military sense, 670
πάρεδρος, fig., 797
παρεικαθεῖν, 1102
παρείρω, proper use of, 368
παρήχησις, 103, 470, 974, 1263
πᾶς without art., as = 'the whole,' 178
παστάς, 1207, p. 264
πάταγος)(βοή, 126
πέλας αὐτὸν ὁρῶ, without ὄντα, 580
πέμπω, absol., as = 'to send word,' 162
πέραν)(πέρα, 334
περί after ὁπόσοι ζῶμεν (sc. ἡμῶν), 214
περὶ ξίφει (πίπτειν), 1301
περιβαίνειν with dat., 1209
περιβρύχιος, 336
περιπετής, act., 1223
περιπτύσσειν, of imprisoning, 886
περισκελής, 475
περισσὰ πράσσειν, 68
περιστέλλειν, of funeral rites, 903
πηγαὶ δακρύων, 803
πικρός = in bitter grief, 423
πιμελή, 1011
πίμπρημι rarer in prose than ἐμπίμπρημι, 201
πλέον τι, something advantageous, 40, 268
πλήρης = defiled, 1017
πνείω in tragic lyrics, 1146
πόδα ἔχειν ἔξω κακῶν, etc., 619
ποδαγός, 1196
πόδες, the, of a sail, 715
ποιεῖν understood, 497
ποιεῖσθαι ἑαυτοῦ, 547

πόλεος in iambics, 162
-πολις, sense of adjs. compounded with, 370
πολλά, adv., with adj., 1046
πολλόν in iambics, 86
πολυκτήμων, 843
πολύπλαγκτος, epith. of hope, 615
πολυώνυμος, of Dionysus, 1115
ποσί, τὰ ἐν, 1327
πόσις, the genit. not in Attic use, 909
ποταίνιος as = 'novel,' 849
ποτέ = *tandem aliquando*, 244, 622
  „ with exclamatory οἷος, 866
ποῦ γνώμης ἐστί;)(ποῖ γνώμης εἶσι; 41
πράξεις, plur., = τύχαι, 1305
πράσσειν, 'to fare,' with adverb. phrase (ἐκτὸς ἄτας), 625
πρεσβεύειν = to be best, 720
πρίν, without ἄν, with subjunct., 619
πρὶν καί, 280
πρὸ χειρῶν, 1279
προγενεῖς θεοί, 938
προδιδόναι ἡδονάς, 1166
πρόδρομος, 107
προέχω with dat. (τιμῇ), 208
προπέμπειν, said of a messenger, 1287
πρός with gen. of cause, 51, 170
  „ with dat., after verb of falling, 1189
πρός τι, 'compared with' it, 1171
πρὸς φίλων, on their part, 919
πρὸς χάριν, senses of, 30
προσαύω, 619
προσεῖναι, of circumstances, etc., 1252
προσεύχεσθαι, absol., 1337
προσήγορος, act. or pass., 1185
προσκεῖσθαι, sense of, 94
προσκοπεῖν with genit., 688
προσπίπτειν εἴς τι, 855
προστάσσεσθαι, of soldiers, 670
προστίθεσθαι, to contribute help, 40
προταρβεῖν τινος, 83
προτιθέναι γνώμας, 161
πρόχους, ewer, 430
πτέρυξ, blade of a knife, p. 266
πτόλις not used by Soph., 733
πτύειν with dat., 1232
πτύσας, with loathing, 653
πύργος, city-walls, 953

P

ρ for ρρ (χρυσόρυτος), 950
ῥίζα, of a family, 600
ῥέθος = πρόσωπον, 529
ῥοθέω, 259
ῥυθμίζω, 318

Σ

σαίνειν, of a sight or sound, 1214
σέ τε…σέ τε, 724
σεβίζειν, to respect a law, 943
σείειν κάρα, in defiance, 291
-σθα, term. of 2nd pers. sing., 447
σινδών, 1222
σκαιός, force of, 1028
σκηπτός, senses of, 418
σπαράγματα, mangled corpses, 1081
σπεῦδε βραδέως, 231
σπλάγχνων ἐκ τῶν σῶν τις, 1066
στεγανός, 114
στέλλω)(στέλλομαι, 165
στέργω τινα, = to tolerate, 292
στερεός, stubborn, 1262
στῆναι, to remain constant, 1156
στοχάζομαι, a peculiar sense of, 241
στρατός as = δῆμος, 8
στρέφειν κάτω, absl. (*sc.* ναῦν), 717
στυγερός, 144
συγγιγνώσκω, to become conscious, 926
συγκαταίθειν, 1202
συγκατεύχομαι, 1336
συγκέκραμαι, 1311
σύγκλητος, technical sense of, 160
σύμμετρος τύχῃ, opportune for, 387
σύμπλους, fig., 541
συμφιλεῖν, 523
σύν as adv., 85
  „ of what one wears or carries, 116
συνέχθειν, 523
σύνοικος with genit. instead of dat., 451
σφε, sing. or plur., 44
σχεδόν τι, ironical, 470
σχέτλιος, 47
σχῆμα, outward show, 1169
σχολῇ, 231
  „ ironical, 390
σῴζω, said of a ship, 189

T

τὰ δέ, adverb., 'on the other hand,' 1345
ταγός, 1057
ταλαίφρων, said pityingly, 39
τᾶλις, 628
ταμίας, said of Dionysus, 1154
τἄν (τοι ἄν), corrupted in MSS., 747
ταντάλόω, 134
ταράσσειν νεῖκος, to stir it up, 794
ταύτῃ (adv.) with τοῦτο, etc., 722
τάφον χεῖν, 80
τάφος as = ταφή, 306
τε, instead of δέ, after μέν, 1162
  „ irregularly placed, 121, 1123
  „ …δέ, 1096
  „ …καί, in temporal parataxis, 1186
τείνειν, of strife, or sound, 124
  „ perf. pass. of, said of light, etc., 600
τείνειν ἄγαν, absol., 711
τελευτῶν, adverbial use of, 261
τέλη νυμφικά, nuptial rites, 1241
τέλη πάγχαλκα, 143
τέλος, sense of, in οἱ ἐν τέλει, etc., 67
τεός, 604
τέρπειν, its aor. midd. not Attic, 691
τήκεσθαι, 'to be decomposed,' 906; 'to exude,' 1008
τηλέπορος, distant, 983
τι omitted (καλῶς ἔχον, something good), 687
  „ with genit., in exhortations (τῶν προκειμένων τι χρὴ πράσσειν), 1334
τί δ' ἔστι; 20, 1281; with νέον, 991
τί δ' οὔ…; 460
τί οὐ μέλλω, with inf. understood, 448
τί συμφορᾶς = ποία συμφορά, 1229
τί χρῆμα, 1049
τίθεσθαί (τινα φίλον) = 'to deem,' 187
τιθέναι, 'to deem,' with infin., 1166
τίθημι)(τίθεμαι νόμον, 8
τιμαί, esp. offerings to a god, 745
τιμᾶν χάριν, to render it duly, 514
τις added to predicate, where subject has art., 252, 365
  „ in a sinister hint, 751
  „ in ἁ μοιριδία τις δύνασις, 951

τις omitted after partitive genit., 1068

„ omitted (θνητὸς ὢν δυστυχεῖ), 455

„ repeated (λέγει τις ἢ πράσσει τις), 689

„ with 2nd of two clauses, where it affects both, 257

τις εἶς instead of εἶς τις, 269

τὸ ἐπὶ τήνδε, *quod ad eam attinet*, 889

τὸ μή with inf., instead of simple μή, 27, 535, 544

τὸ σὸν μέρος, adv., senses of, 1062

τοῖος introducing a reason, 124

τοιοῦτος, adverb., 'in such wise,' 1012

τοῖς, τοῖς δέ, the one side,...the other, 557

τοτέ...ἄλλοτε, 367

τοῦτο μέν, followed by ἔπειτα δέ, 61: by τοῦτ' αὖθις, 167

τρέφω with predicative adj. (ἄκοσμα), 660

τριπόλιστος, 858

τροπαῖος Ζεύς, 143

τρόχος)(τροχός, 1065

τυγχάνω with acc., 778

τυμβεύειν, intrans., 888

τυμβήρης, 255

τύπτω, how far in Attic use, 171

τυραννίς, allusions to, 506

τύραννος with a bad sense, 1056

τυφλῷ ἕλκος, 971 ff.

Υ

ῡ before βρ, 1116

ὑγρός, epith. of water, 1123

ὑγρός, 'nerveless,' 1237

υἱέσι, the Att. dat. pl. of υἱός, 571

ὑμέναιος)(ἐπιθαλάμιος, 813

ὔμμε, 846

ὔν and ὖν in κλιτύν, 1143

ὑπαί, in iambics, 1035

ὕπατος, class. use of, 1332

ὑπέρ = ἕνεκα, 932

ὑπερβάς, absol., 663

ὑπεροπλία, with ῑ, 130

ὑπερπόντιος φοιτᾷς, 785

ὑπέρτερον = πλέον, 16

ὑπερτρέχω, fig., to prevail over, 455

ὑπήνεμος, 411

ὑπίλλω, 509

ὑπό with acc. (ὑφ' ἧπαρ), 1315

„ with dat. of instrument, 975

ὑπό with dat., rare in Attic prose, 65

„ „ gen. (οἱ ὑπὸ χθονός), 65

ὑπὸ σκότου, 692; cp. 1248

ὑπόρχημα, substituted for a stasimon, 1115

ὕστερός τινος,)(ἥσσων τινός, 746

ὑστεροφθόρος, 1074

ὑφειμένη, 'lurking,' 531

ὑψίπολις, 370

Φ

φαίνεσθαι, pass., of old sayings, 621

φαίνομαι with adj., without ὤν, 177

φάος, fig. use of, 599

φάρξαι, spelling of, 241, cp. 957

φέρειν with partitive gen., 537

„ = φέρεσθαι, 464

φέρεσθαι, epexegetic of μείζων, 638

Φερσέφασσα, 894

φεύγω = to plead in defence, 263

φημί, accentuation of, 561

φίλος (masc.), said of a wife, 652

φοναῖς, ἐν, 696

φονάω, 117

φορεῖν ἦθος, 705

φρενοῦν, 754

φρονήσας, how used, 1031

φυγαί, means of escape, 363

φύξιμος, governing acc., 786

φύσις, one's age, 727

Χ

χαίρειν, τό, joy, 1170

χαλκόδετοι αὐλαί, 945

χάριν, πρός, 30

χάριν τόλμης, 'on account of' it, 371

χείμαρρος, as adj., 712

χείρεσσι, in iambics, 1297

χελιδονίζειν = βαρβαρίζειν, 1001

χιών, as = 'snow-water,' doubtful, 829

χθές and ἐχθές, 456

χοαί to the dead, 431, 901: when poured by Antigone, 429

χολή and χολαί, 1010

χοραγὸς ἄστρων, of Dionysus, 1147

χορεύω θεόν, in his honour, 1153

χρή with dat., no certain Attic example of, 736

II. MATTERS.

A

abstract for concrete (ἐπανάστασις, a rebel), 533

acc. after phrase equiv. to transitive verb, 211, 857

accus. in appos. with sentence, 44
,, internal, with ἄχνυμαι, 627
,, of part affected, after another acc., 319
,, of place, after ἄγω, 811; καταβαίνω, 822; παραστείχω, 1255
,, of respect (σπέρμα, by race), 981
,, of that by which one swears, 265
,, with inf., where dative could stand, 838
,, with χορεύω, etc., 1153
,, σέ, without verb, in abrupt address, 441
,, agreeing with pers., instead of subst. with prep. (ὑπερπόντιος = ὑπὲρ πόν-τον), 785
,, as epithet of a compound phrase (νεῖκος ἀνδρῶν ξύναιμον, instead of ξυναίμων), 794, 863, 879, 980, 1164

Acheron personified, 816

adj. compounded with noun of like sense as the subst. (σπεῖραι δικτυόκλωσ-τοι), 7, 346, 431, 1210, 1283
,, compounded with the same noun which it qualifies (δύσπνοοι πνοαί), 502
,, compound, = two distinct epithets, 146, 1126, 1286
,, compound, equiv. to adj. and subst. in genit. (αἷμα ἀνδροφθόρον), 1022

adj. doubled (νέος νέῳ), 156, 929, 978
,, to mark reciprocity (φίλη μετὰ φίλου), 73, 142
,, neut. plur., as adv., 546
,, of two terms., poetically of three, 134, 339
,, of three terms., poetically of two, 867
,, proleptic (ὀπτὸς περισκελής), 475
,, used adverbially (ὅρκιος), 305, 1215, 1230, 1301
,, verbal, with act. sense, 582, 875
,, verbal in -τέος, impers. neut. plur. (ἀμυντέα), 677
,, ,, answers to pass. sense of verb, 678
,, ,, governing a case (σὲ φύξιμος), 786

adv. following noun with art. (τῶν λεγόν-των εὖ), 659, 723, 1060

adverbs in -η, 138

Aeschylus, his *Seven against Thebes*,— how related to the *Antigone*, p. x

Alfieri's *Antigone*, p. xxxix

altar of Zeus Herkeios, 487

altars, public and private, 1016

ambiguity, a grammatical, obviated by a natural stress or pause in speaking, 288, 467

Anaea, p. xlii, n. 3

anapaest in 5th place (proper name), 11, 1180

anapaests, use of in the Parodos, 100
,, Doric forms in, 110 f., 804 f., p. 248
,, use of in this play, p. xlviii

Androtion, *Atthis* of, p. xliv